SIX WAYS OF BEING RELIGIOUS

A FRAMEWORK FOR COMPARATIVE STUDIES OF RELIGION

Dale Cannon

Western Oregon State College

Wadsworth Publishing Company
I(T)P™ An International Thomson Publish

Belmont • Albany • Bonn • Boston • Cincinnati • Detroit • London
Mexico City • New York • Paris • San Francisco • Singapore • Tokyo

D1416674

Religion Editor: *Katherine Hartlove*
Editorial Assistant: *Jessica Monday*
Production Services Coordinator: *Debby Kramer*
Production: *Merrill Peterson/Matrix Productions Inc.*
Print Buyer: *Barbara Britton*
Permissions Editor: *Robert Kauser*
Copy Editor: *Lauren Root*
Cover Designer: *Janet Wood*
Cover Photograph: *Winthrop, Massachusetts 1965, by Paul Caponigro. All rights reserved.*
Compositor: *Bay View Publishing Services*
Signing Representative: *Tamy Stenquist*
Printer: *Malloy Lithographing, Inc.*

For more information, contact Wadsworth Publishing Company:

Wadsworth Publishing Company
10 Davis Drive
Belmont, California 94002, USA

International Thomson Publishing Europe
Berkshire House 168-173
High Holborn
London, WC1V 7AA, England

Thomas Nelson Australia
102 Dodds Street
South Melbourne 3205
Victoria, Australia

Nelson Canada
1120 Birchmount Road
Scarborough, Ontario
Canada M1K 5G4

International Thomson Editores
Campos Eliseos 385, Piso 7
Col. Polanco
11560 México D.F. México

International Thomson Publishing GmbH
Königswinterer Strasse 418
53227 Bonn, Germany

International Thomson Publishing Asia
221 Henderson Road
#05-10 Henderson Building
Singapore 0315

International Thomson Publishing Japan
Hirakawacho Kyowa Building, 3F
2-2-1 Hirakawacho
Chiyoda-ku, Tokyo 102, Japan

Library of Congress Cataloging-in-Publication Data

Cannon, Dale S.
 Six ways of being religious: a framework for comparative studies of religion/by Dale Cannon.
   p. cm.
 Includes bibliographical references and index.
 ISBN 0-534-25332-6
 1. Religion—Studying and teaching. 2. Religions—Study and teaching.
3. Religions—Relations. I. Title.
BL41.C35 1996   95-16047
291'.07—dc20

Dedicated to the memory of
Darline and Wayne Cannon,
who taught me to withhold judgment,
not that I might abandon it altogether
but that I might discover what is good
in what initially seems to lack it.

CONTENTS

PREFACE

[J]ust as the natural river systems of this earth and the landscapes shaped by them are extremely different, but all the rivers and streams of the different continents display similar profiles and patterns of flow, obey similar regularities, cut clefts in the hills, wind over the plains, and inexorably seek a way to the sea, so it is with the religious systems of this earth. Although they are extremely different, in many respects they display similar profiles, regularities and effects. Confusingly different though all the religions are, they all respond to similar basic questions. Where does the world and its order come from? Why are we born and why must we die? What determines the destiny of the individual and humankind? What is the foundation for moral awareness and the presence of ethical norms? And they all offer similar ways to salvation over and above their interpretation of the world: ways out of the distress, suffering and guilt of existence—through meaningful and responsible action in this life—to a permanent, abiding, eternal salvation.

    . . . [E]ven those who repudiate the religions . . . have to take them seriously as a fundamental social and existential reality; after all, they have to do with the meaning and meaninglessness of life, with human freedom and slavery, with justice and the suppression of the peoples, with war and peace in history and the present. A historical and systematic analysis of their convergences and divergences, their points of conflict and efforts at dialogue . . . , is clearly called for.[1]

Hans Küng*

Among the many readers of this book, some are on a religious quest of their own, searching for a spiritual home. Some seek a way to understand and better relate to their religious neighbors—whether down the street or on the other side of the globe. Some are motivated to understand their own faith, where they stand, their specific location amid the diversity of human religious phenomena. Some are simply trying to understand better the puzzling, mad, and wonderful world of religion in human life. All have to face and make some sense of the bewildering diversity of the ways people carry on religious life. The diversity to which I refer is not only between religions but also is found within any one religion. The main purpose of this book is to assist its readers' efforts to make sense of this diversity and to understand it from within. The book takes the diversity seriously. It presents a kind of map for sorting it out and it offers a rationale for why religious life should have the diversity it has.

    The book proposes the hypothesis that six generic ways of being religious may be found in any large-scale religious tradition such as Christianity or Buddhism

---

**Excerpts throughout the book reprinted by permission of the publisher from Hans Küng, *Global Responsibility: In Search of a New World Ethic*, trans. John Bowden (New York: Crossroad, 1991), pp. 46, 53–54, 60, 97–98, 125, 128–129, and 132.*

or Islam or Hinduism: sacred rite, right action, devotion, shamanic mediation, mystical quest, and reasoned inquiry. These are recurrent ways in which, socially and individually, devout members of these traditions take up and appropriate their stories and symbols in order to draw near to, and come into right relationship with, what the traditions attest to be the ultimate reality.

Understanding these six ways provides a basis for making sense of the variety of expressions that emerge in any one tradition. While the primary focus of the framework of ways of being religious will be upon comprehending the diversity found in commonly recognized religious traditions, some attention will also be given to accounting for nontraditional religious phenomena. In any case, once grouped together on the basis of the six ways, commonalities between otherwise apparently disparate and opposed traditions become evident, mutual recognition becomes possible, and dialogue is facilitated.

This book is not meant to be a first introduction to the study of the religions of the world. There are many books that serve well in that capacity and this book is not meant to compete with them. An introductory acquaintance with the great religious traditions and with the academic study of religion would be helpful as a background. In any case, the book takes for granted the fact of religious plurality and the value of seeking to understand this plurality as well as one can in a nonpresumptive way.

The framework of ways of being religious is constructed with the intention that justice must be done to the perspectives of insiders—not just insiders to specific (major) religious traditions, but insiders to specific ways of being religious within each religious tradition. But insiders' perspectives often do not acknowledge the diversity within the larger religious tradition of which they are a part or recognize the legitimacy of other ways of practicing it, let alone grant the legitimacy of other religions. Doing justice to these perspectives therefore cannot mean simply taking insiders at their word, especially not their word about other religious views and practices. Both objectivity and empathy are needed at every point, each keeping the other in check.

The book is written for persons who seek to learn about and understand the multiple forms of religious life in a manner as free as possible from the ulterior motives, distorting prejudices, and misleading preconceptions that often characterize reflection on them and the sources of our information about them. At times such motives, prejudices, and preconceptions emerge within a religious perspective, but no less are they the offspring of perspectives unsympathetic to religion in general or to some religion in particular. The book assumes that the reader is aware to some extent how easily distortions in understanding religious life arise, how easy it is to presume mistakenly that our ideas about forms of religion different from our own are fully adequate, and how easy it is to be mistaken in supposing that the ideas we have about our own form of religion are fully adequate as well. It assumes the reader is interested in having his or her understanding grow beyond these distortions and take account of possibilities that he or she cannot now imagine.

More than simply promoting understanding for its own sake, the book aims to foster mutual understanding, communication, and dialogue between persons having different religious orientations and different ways of being religious. As well, it aims to foster understanding, communication, and dialogue between persons of religious orientation and persons of little or no religious orientation in any conventional sense. We live in a world where we cannot avoid dealing with persons whose religious views and practices differ from our own—differences that, because they loom so large, blind us from seeing the interests and concerns we share in common, some of which have to do with our deepest religious concerns. My hope is that this book will help us see beyond those looming apparent differences, both to what we have in common and to the significance of what differences remain. This is not to say that religious differences are unimportant. It is rather to say that the really significant differences do not lie on the surface, no more than do significant commonalities, and that those differences cannot be honestly appreciated without also seeing the commonalities. The book, then, is not written simply for those who wish better to understand religious life from an essentially disengaged and detached perspective. It is written to improve the climate of inter-religious relationships, of how in practice we understand and relate to one another in the religiously plural world we now live within. That is why the academic study of religion, as understood and practiced here, shades imperceptibly into inter-religious dialogue.

It may help to know that the greater part of my professional training and teaching experience has been in philosophy. This makes me more ready to explore the possibility of generic or universal features in the study of religious phenomena than are, say, scholars trained primarily in a historical approach. I deeply respect the historian's sensibility for particularity and unique nuances of meaning due to language and cultural difference, and I must say that virtually all of the data on which I rely are the product of historical research. Traditionally, the historian's sensibility tends to be excessively suspicious of proposals to recognize cross-cultural patterns or abstract conceptual frameworks. If it were left to historians of such a persuasion, all we would have of religious studies would be historical narratives of the different traditions and their interactions, if any. So, to make sense of this multifaceted diversity, some ventures in cross-cultural generalization and theoretical construction must be possible. They will be appropriate, it seems to me, so long as they are required to do justice to the particularities of historical phenomena. In agreement with historians, then, I too hold that the particular phenomena in all of their concreteness must be the final testing ground of any set of abstract categories including the ones I am proposing. Such categories must never be allowed to blind us to aspects of the phenomena they fail to fit.

Trained as a philosopher, I am disposed to be interested in normative questions of truth and value. Yet I have also been trained as a phenomenologist of religion, which disposes me first to understand as fully as possible from within what I am to judge. In an important respect, this book is designed to help provide persons who seek to pursue philosophical reflection on religious life a much sounder basis for reflection than they otherwise are likely to have—an acquaintance in considerable depth with the full spectrum of human religiousness. To presume to reflect philosophically upon a religious practice or belief without that basis of acquaintance is to reflect as a barbarian. The ideal is to reflect with the discrimination of a native. To do that requires that one understand with care and empathetic insight the quite different sorts of things the natives happen to be involved in doing and how good they are at what they do.

I have no intention by means of this book to persuade the reader into believing the superiority of one religious tradition over others, that all religions are equivalent, that all are true and good and rational, that all are false or evil or irrational, that some are true and some false, that one is true and the others are false, or any other such position. Whether any one of these positions is true is an important question. These are questions, however, that can be satisfactorily addressed only after the kind of comparative study of religion that this book is designed to facilitate. I happen to be a believing and practicing Christian, but that circumstance by itself gives no one a privileged position to render judgments about such matters. So, this book will not attempt to answer these questions. It will, however, provide some of the essential groundwork for coming to answers of one's own.

I wish to stress that the framework of ways of being religious aims to facilitate the reader's inquiry rather than provide information. The framework provides a set of tools for carrying out comparative investigations in the study of religion and for structuring dialogue between persons of different faiths. I do not wish to present the reader with my predigested interpretations. By helping readers develop a sensibility for the variety of ways of being religious that can be found in any major tradition, I hope to leave them with a sense for the lay of the land rather than a detailed topographic map. Rather than leaving them with my finished understanding, my hope is that they will be better equipped to understand the diversity of religious practice for themselves.

Finally, I wish to acknowledge that the original idea behind the framework of generic ways of being religious developed here is due to the pioneering work of the late Frederick J. Streng, a fellow philosopher devoted to laying a sound foundation for comparative study of religion and inter-religious dialogue. He conceived of that task and labored away at it on many fronts, not as a lone scholar jealously protecting his own ideas, but as a member of the community of scholars concerned to build upon and draw forth the contributions of others in the common task. Anyone acquainted with Professor Streng's work[2] will immediately see how I have drawn on his work and also how I have departed from it. For both of us, I believe, the idea of generic ways of being religious is less an invention than a discovery—indeed, in some sense a gift. It was not his private possession, nor is it mine. And we hope others will find ways of helping it further grow and mature and bring forth fruit neither of us were capable of foreseeing.

I wish to acknowledge here several persons who have showed keen interest in this project and have been willing to discuss different aspects of the whole at different stages of its maturation. First among these is Fred Streng himself. Others among those I clearly recall include John Carman; William Graham; William Cantwell Smith; Wei-ming Tu; Mark Juergensmeyer; Jack Hawley; Michael Swartz; David Bradford; Aaron Raverty, OSB; Katherine Howard, OSB; Mary Anthony Wagner, OSB; Alan Bouley, OSB; and Patrick Henry. Personal friends and colleagues who have graciously read portions of the manuscript and offered constructive suggestions to improve it include Mike Fargo; John Ritter; Robert Tompkins; Michael Vertin; Shawn Madigan, CSJ; and Joseph Soldati (who generously read the whole with a fine-toothed comb). Reviewers of the manuscript in its three stages of evolution whose critical comments have been invaluable include David W. Chappell, University of Hawaii at Manoa; Eugene Webb, University of Washington, The Henry M. Jackson School of International Studies; John B. Carman, Harvard University, The Divinity School; Roger Corless, Duke University; Ninian Smart, University of California Santa Barbara; Karen McCarthy Brown, Drew University; Paul O. Ingram, Pacific Lutheran University; and Steve Heine, Pennsylvania State University, University Park. I acknowledge with deep gratitude the thoughtfulness, insight, and generosity of each of these persons. To Tracy Bergin I owe considerable gratitude for her helpful assistance on numerous occasions from typing and copying to meeting mail deadlines. I acknowledge with thanks the assistance of Western Oregon State College for several Faculty Development Grants, travel assistance, and a paid sabbatical. A five-month tenure as a Fellow at the Institute for Ecumenical and Cultural Research at St. John's University was indispensible and much appreciated to get the manuscript launched. The greatest debt of gratitude for support, patience, and confidence through the whole process I owe to my lovely wife, Jeanné, and my delightful daughter, Erindale.

1. Hans Küng, *Global Responsibility: In Search of a New World Ethic*, trans. John Bowden (New York: Crossroad, 1991), p. 128f. I quote Küng here because the passage well expresses the theme I wish to set for the book. Although I draw further on this book in what follows and I am broadly sympathetic with much of Küng's work in seriously attempting inter-religious dialogue, I wish to make clear that Küng's own views on religious pluralism should not be confused with mine.
2. For references, see the recommended readings at the end of Chapter 3.

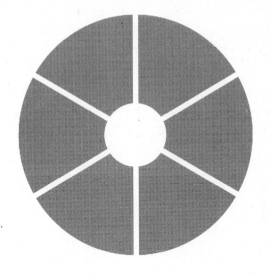

GENERIC WAYS OF BEING RELIGIOUS

The first six chapters of this book (Part I) are devoted to
explaining the basic idea of the framework of six
ways of being religious and establishing its usefulness as a
guide for the comparative study of religion and inter-religious
dialogue. The principal focus will be upon setting out
the theory of a generic way of being religious, clarifying what
role is played by generic ways within specific traditions,
differentiating each of the six ways from each other,

and identifying examples illustrating each way as well as combinations of ways from the religious traditions of the world. Parts II and III are devoted to showing how the framework operates in practice by using it to structure a comparison of two major religious traditions.

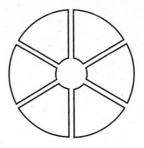

CHAPTER 1

GENERAL
INTRODUCTION

How should we make sense of differences and similarities among religious phenomena? What weight should be given to differences? And what weight should
be given to similarities? How to do justice to both is relevant to the student who
wishes to learn about and relate intelligently to the religious behavior and expressions of her fellow human beings. The question is relevant to the Lutheran
couple who must decide how to relate to the Muslim family that just moved in
next door. Although they may not realize it, it is no less relevant to deciding
how they should relate to the Pentecostal faith of the gentleman their daughter
is dating. It is relevant as well to the young man who desires to find which, if
any, of the religious options he faces has worth in relation to the others.

 The accounts religious traditions give of themselves for the benefit of outsiders usually do not tell you enough. Usually not enough is said to satisfy the
need to understand, and often the desire to seek a new convert or distrust of
outsiders gets in the way. Even less satisfactory are the slanted accounts traditions often give of their relation to other traditions. A source of relatively neutral
information is needed, and so resort is made to the academic accounts of historians and anthropologists who specialize in providing a more or less objective
account.[1] However, simple historical or anthropological descriptions of particular phenomena and particular traditions posed alongside one another are not
enough. Comprehension demands the employment of cross-cultural categories
that are not biased on behalf of the perspective of a particular tradition—for example, categories such as prayer, worship, faith, sacred story, ritual, sacrificial
offering, doctrine, scripture, theological explanation, meditation, or possession

trance. It is difficult to imagine how historical and anthropological descriptions can be developed at all without some resort to cross-cultural categories. The academic study of religion has recognized this for quite some time. A great number of categories have been, and continue to be, variously employed. A number of efforts have been made to bring conceptual clarity and order to them, not least the 1987 publication of *The Encyclopedia of Religion*, edited by Mircea Eliade. Nevertheless, obscurity and disorder remain.

How should we make sense of the differences and similarities among religious phenomena? First, what are we to make of the apparent similarities—at times deep structural parallels—between religious phenomena that have no apparent historical connection? Does that mean that they really amount to the same thing but just in different dress, as it were? For example, is mysticism the same thing in all traditions? Or is shamanism a distinct religion unto itself? Second, what are we to make of the apparent dissimilarities—at times clear contradictions—between the doctrines of one religious tradition and those of another? Does that mean they have nothing of significance in common? For example, must a Muslim deny all validity and worth to Hindus because they do not acknowledge the authority of the *Qur'an* and appear to engage in idolatrous practices? In relation to these two questions, a third question must be addressed: How might these first two questions—about the significance of similarities on the one hand and differences on the other—be sorted out and answered on grounds that do not beg theological and metaphysical questions? Or, how can they be answered without privileging the beliefs of one tradition over another? Any attempt to answer these three questions, especially this last one, raises difficult and controversial issues. Yet that is what this book's exposition of the framework of six generic ways of being religious seeks to do.

To make these abstract questions more concrete, consider the following two situations:

A young Baptist businessman who identifies himself with Evangelical Protestant Christianity (as represented, say, by Billy Graham rather than Jerry Fallwell), for whom the essence of Christianity is to have a "personal saving relationship with Jesus Christ," travels to Sri Lanka. There he has an exposure to Buddhism and an opportunity to learn something about it. He finds that Buddhists who are serious about religion take up a monastic life, sever all ties with this-worldly activities, and devote their entire lives to a rigorous discipline of ascetic practice and meditation for the sake of attaining *nirvāṇa* He thinks, "This is the difference between Christianity and Buddhism: a personal relationship of faith in Jesus Christ involving a surrender to the saving grace of God in Christ, versus a largely solitary pursuit of what appears to be an otherworldly mystical bliss." But is this so? Is this all that Buddhism is and all that Christianity is?

A middle-aged English widow attracted to the writings of the great Western Christian mystics (e.g., John of the Cross, Teresa of Avila, Meister Eckhart), upon reading selections from some of the great Hindu and Sufi mystics from a theosophical publisher, comes to believe that mysticism may be found at the heart of all religions. Impressed by similarities in the writings of these various mystics, she concludes that mysticism is substantially the same thing in all of its many expressions. Indeed, she concludes it is the only authentic and true religion, and that all else is mere external, dispensable trappings. But is this so? Are all forms of religion best understood and assessed by their approximation to the mystical quest? And is mysticism really the same thing beneath its many expressions in different traditions?

Indeed, the situation of these imagined persons is not unlike that of the six blind men in the ancient East Indian parable, who, upon encountering an elephant for the first time, each concluded something very different about what an elephant must be. One, feeling the trunk, concluded the elephant must be like a large snake. The second, feeling the tail, concluded, to the contrary, it was very like a duster. The third, coming up against the side of the elephant, said it must be a kind of curved wall. The fourth felt one of the elephant's legs and concluded it was a species of tree. The fifth caught hold of the elephant's ear and said, "No, it is more like a winnowing basket." And the last, grasping the elephant's tusk, said, "You're all wrong! It is more like a plow."

What is the elephant of human religiousness anyway? Is there a way of comprehending unity in all of the diversity, a unity that recognizes and appreciates significant differences as well? Indeed, what is any one religious tradition? How is it possible to see and comprehend it in the round and not just from one angle only?

Let's consider the parable of the Six Blind Men and the Elephant again, but this time in a different form more analogous to the problem at hand.

Once upon a time there was an elephant and six partially blind elephant handlers, each of whom knew a certain elephant well, very well, or so each thought. But each knew the elephant in a different way and, because of the peculiar nature of his blindness, a lack of peripheral vision, each knew nothing at all of the other ways of knowing the elephant.

The first was the tenth in a long line of ceremonial elephant handlers who, on ceremonial occasions, were placed in charge of this, the King's elephant. He "knew" exactly how this particular elephant should be handled: what words to say, what gestures to use, how appropriately to approach the elephant to get it to do the most impressive things—all in the same way his predecessors had done in the past. Above all, he knew what was right, appropriate, and timely: his handling of the elephant was always and invariably graceful, orderly, and elegant. He "knew" the elephant, or so he was convinced.

The second was a practical, down-to-earth, no-nonsense sort of fellow. He believed that you really didn't know the elephant unless you worked with the elephant as he had in getting practical things accomplished—heavy loads lifted and moved about, jungles cleared, new roads built. From long experience with the elephant in carrying out such tasks, he was confident he "knew" that elephant, or so he was convinced.

The third was a deeply sensitive and passionate person. He believed that you really didn't know an elephant unless you had somehow formed an intimate personal friendship with the elephant as he had, a friendship that shared the joys and sorrows, the accomplishments and frustrations, of daily elephant existence. Moreover, he was convinced that it was a two-way relationship: not only did he know the elephant personally, but from the way the elephant responded sympathetically to his own emotional highs and lows, he was sure that the elephant knew him in the same way too. He "knew" the elephant, or so he was convinced.

The fourth was something of an eccentric. Like those Native American medicine men of the plains who knew how to make contact with the spirit of the bison or the spirit of the antelope to ensure a successful hunt, this man was able, by entering into a trance, to commune so closely with the spirit of that elephant that he was able to bring about an uncanny, cooperative rapport between himself and the elephant. It seemed the elephant would do anything he desired it to without his having to speak aloud or make overt gestures at all. He "knew" the elephant, or so he was convinced.

The fifth was a quiet, contemplative person who believed that you really couldn't get in touch with the elephant unless you let go of all other preoccupations and became very, very quiet, very still, completely receptive to whatever the elephant revealed of its elephant self, as he had been able to do. Above all, the handler was aware. Nothing escaped his notice: the sounds of the elephant's voice, the elephant's digestion, every movement of the elephant; its smells, its moods, its subtle yet meaningful gestures; its eyes; the rhythm of its swaying, its breathing, and the twitching of its tail—subtle revelations that others miss entirely. He "knew" the elephant, or so he was convinced.

The sixth and final man was a very learned person who knew more about this breed of elephant and this specific elephant than most of us can imagine. He had studied all about elephant physiology, elephant metabolism, elephant ethology, elephant psychology, everything ever written about the care and feeding and breeding of elephants, and in particular, the history and genealogy of the particular family of elephants from which this elephant had issued. He knew all there was to know about elephants in general and about this elephant in particular. And it wasn't just abstract, ivory-tower, book knowledge either, for he was so effective at applying this knowledge to the practical care of elephants that the King had wisely appointed him as chief caretaker of all his elephants. He "knew" the elephant, or so he was convinced.

Now, did each of the six men know the elephant? Of course! Indeed, each knew the elephant as well as the elephant could be known—from each man's peculiar angle of approach and in his own way. From the perspective of that way in that place in that time, the elephant could not be known better. But lacking peripheral vision, each knew nothing of what the others knew. And so, each tended to dismiss the others' claim to know the elephant that he knew: "You don't know my 'way' and so you can't possibly know the elephant—at least not as well as I do." Furthermore, each dismissed the idea that he might have something to learn from what the others knew from their different perspectives. Though each supposed he knew the elephant in the round, in fact he did not. What each lacked was an awareness of the limits of his own quite genuine acquaintance. Or, to put the same thing differently, what each man lacked was a sense of the transcendence of the elephant beyond his own limited acquaintance, hence his need (in order to know the elephant in the round) to explore empathetically the other men's knowledge of the elephant. What initially seemed to contradict each man's knowledge and understanding would thereby turn out to complement his own limited perspective.

This parable illustrates how we stand in regard to any religion we think we know well, and how we stand in regard to religion in general. That is to say, each religion is a different elephant, as it were, and there are at least six different ways of being acquainted with it. Or, to put it more precisely, the ultimate reality recognized in a given religion is a different elephant, and a person who identifies with one way of being religious as the primary way to approach that ultimate reality is one of the partially blinded elephant handlers. Given our own first-hand acquaintance with a tradition, we may know fairly well one, two, or maybe (if we've really been involved) three of these ways, but few of us know more. And then, as we begin to extrapolate our limited sense of what a religion is about to unfamiliar traditions, we tend to expect to find the same sort of thing. When we do find the same sort of thing, some of us are inclined to conclude that it must therefore be the same thing, despite the differences. Or, when it turns out that we don't find the same sort of thing, our natural tendency is to conclude that here is something completely different. Of course, this is often true of religions completely different from those with which we have some acquaintance but about which we would like to learn. To rely on certain persons to explain what their tradition is all about is to run the risk that we will receive an account reflective of maybe only one, or perhaps two or three of the ways, in which that tradition is put into practice, but unlikely all of them.

A religion is not at all the sort of thing that lends itself to being fully known from a single perspective. One of the great pioneers in the comparative study of religion toward the end of the nineteenth century, Friedrich Max Müller, regularly asserted that "He who knows only one religion knows none." Although it is somewhat of an exaggeration, it has a certain truth, for the person who has only known and considered her own religious tradition from the perspective of her own practice of it, knows relatively little of it. Just like the six peripherally blinded men, each of us may know a great deal about a given religion—even, in a certain limited way, about religion in general. But how many of us have realized that there may be as many as five other ways of encountering and being acquainted with the fundamental realities that lie at the heart of the religion we think we know, five other ways of getting in touch with it that differ from the way with which we are most familiar? To paraphrase Müller, when you know only one way of being religious in a single tradition, you know none. You don't know that way's specific difference from the others. At best, you know how other ways appear to it. But you know nothing of the limitations and bias of the perspective it embodies. Specifically, you know nothing of the extent to which the appearance of other ways to your perspective are distorted caricatures of what it is really like from within to pursue those ways. And you know nothing of the extent to which the fundamental realities that lie at the heart of your tradition disclose quite different and equally rich facets of those other ways.

The rest of the chapter will present reasons for believing that there are six different generic ways of being religious that, at least in principle, may be realized within a given religious tradition, broadly considered. If indeed these generic possibilities exist, we should be able to find examples of them among the many historical expressions of any major religious tradition. For the most part, this is what we do find. Of course, such examples will be identified for each of the major religions of the world and some outside of those traditions. Some will be described in depth, but most will only be briefly mentioned. That is deliberate, for instead of presenting an in-depth study of the major religions, what this book is proposing is a kind of program for research and comparative study that both students and professional scholars can pursue.

So, what are the six ways? It may help to consider briefly a widely remarked feature of Hinduism (in popular accounts in the West) that indicates a direct recognition, by some adherents within a major religious tradition, of several of the ways.[2]

The religious tradition of Hinduism is an amalgamation of a multitude of diverse forms of religious life—more so, it appears, than any other major religion. It does not have a single founder (if it can be said to have any historically identifiable founders), and its huge body of sacred scriptures seem to have come from widely divergent sources, for they express an incredible diversity of theological concepts and images. Nevertheless, this diversity is from time to time sorted out by persons who presume to represent the tradition at large (though no one really does represent the whole, especially not in a way that could be said to articulate a consensus among all Hindus). Specifically, it has been said that in Hinduism there are four different *yogas* or *margas* (sometimes more than four)—four different sorts of path toward at-onement with what is taken to be the ultimate reality (whether conceived theistically as God—for example, *Kṛṣṇa* or *Śiva*—or as the Godhead beyond personalized conceptions of God, called *Brahman*). Different people with different temperaments, these Hindus say, have different religious needs: each person needs a way of being religious suitable to her or his personality and situation in life.[3]

First is *karmā yoga*, the way to "God"[4] (that is, to what Hinduism variously takes to be the ultimate reality) through selfless performance of duty (including a manifold array of ritual duties, depending on one's caste, one's status in the family and in the local community, and one's stage in life) and righteous action. The point is to carry out one's allotted role in life as a divinely assigned destiny, doing all with the sense that one's role is divinely given and is, as it were, "God" acting *through me,* so that *my* actions originate not in *me* but in the nonpersonally given divine order of the cosmos known as *dharma.* Second is *bhakti yoga,* the way to "God" through adoration and devotional surrender. Here the point is to have one's affections become ablaze with the fire of love for "God" alone, displacing all other affections, in response to his (or her) compassionate grace. Third is *dhyana yogā,* the way to "God" through psychosomatic disciplines (spiritual and ascetic disciplines) designed to shift one's conscious awareness beyond the ego-centered, mundane sphere, to what is said to be the infinite, divine subject within. Finally, there is *jnana yōḡa,* the way to "God" through rational inquiry, argument, and intellectual comprehension, oriented toward the attainment of life-transforming insight into the ultimate basis of all things. The point here is for one's own mind to gain the perspective and wisdom of "Absolute Mind," not for the sake of some egoistic motive but in order to break free of ego-centered understanding altogether.

WAYS OF BEING HINDU

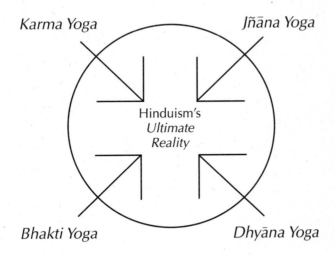

Karma Yoga   Jñāna Yoga

Hinduism's
Ultimate
Reality

Bhakti Yoga   Dhyāna Yoga

Each of these four kinds of paths is widely recognized and respected within the Hindu tradition as a well-established, reliable means to the ultimate goal of union with "God." The four are acknowledged in no less an authoritative scripture than the *Bhagavad Gītā,* which many have called the "New Testament" of popular Hinduism. It must be said, however, that in the *Gītā* the different yogas are not given equal rank, and *dhyāna yoga*, while mentioned, is not clearly distinguished as a path separate from the others. Interpretations of the *Gītā* differ widely. Nevertheless, it is clear that a variety of expressions for each of the yogas exist. What makes up each path in concrete practice and the relative ranking of any one in relation to the others varies considerably from one Hindu subtradition to another.

Many Hindu spokespersons have tried to generalize this idea of "many paths to one ultimate goal" as a model for thinking about the relations between religions. However, these attempts have been quite misleading. Such a model is better understood as an expression of a specific religious faith (in this case a theological conviction about religions), for the evidence in support of it is seriously deficient. But as a basic means of comprehending relations among different ways of organizing and carrying on religious life within a single religious tradition broadly conceived, the idea of "many paths to an ultimate goal" is very promising. In fact, the four yogas sketched above correspond directly to four of the six ways of being religious. *Karma yoga* corresponds (primarily) to what we shall call the **way of right action**; *bhakti yoga* corresponds to the **way of devotion**; *dhyāna yoga* to the **way of mystical quest**; and *jñāna yoga* to the **way of reasoned inquiry**.

In addition to this set of four are the **way of sacred rite** and the **way of shamanic mediation**. The **way of sacred rite** is the way to whatever is taken to be God through participation in divinely authorized rituals, rituals that promise to restore meaningful order and vitality to life by ushering one anew into the sacramental presence of the original divine patterns (archetypes) of meaningful life. The **way of shamanic mediation** is the way to whatever is taken to be God through tapping *supernatural*⁵ resources of imagination and power, by such means as divine possession (trance), ecstatic vision, oracular utterance, and spirit journeying. Hindu accounts do not identify these two as distinct yogas. However, it does not take much field investigation in India to find a plenitude of these two ways of being religious in evidence among Hindus. Upon closer inspection, it turns out that practices that could be differentiated as exhibiting the way of sacred rite are combined, according to traditional Hindu reckoning, with *karma yoga*. That is to say, Hindus do not distinguish practices that could be grouped under the way of right action from those that could be grouped under the way of sacred rite as separate paths to "God." Hindus treat them as a single path.⁶

This points to an important fact: the concepts used in a given religious tradition to describe and comprehend the practices they follow will not necessarily coincide directly with the neat distinctions drawn by the framework of ways of being religious. The latter, it is important to remember, is a product of abstraction from the comparative study of actual religious phenomena. The language and vocabulary of that framework will of necessity be somewhat different—the language of the framework being generic, more abstract, and ideally neutral (i.e., nonjudgmental). (More will be said about this in the next chapter.) On the contrary, the language for describing and talking about different ways within a tradition, though it will be more specific, more concrete, and more familiar to persons who are acquainted with the tradition, will often have been shaped by polemical controversy. To the extent this is so, that language will be quite judgmental and not at all neutral. It may help to be aware of this in adjusting to the unfamiliarity of the terms describing the different ways of being religious.

The six ways of being religious can be put in a visual diagram, shown here.

WAYS OF BEING RELIGIOUS

It may help to think of participants in each of the ways within any one tradition as standing in relation to the fundamental mystery—the ultimate reality—of which their tradition speaks as the six partially blind elephant handlers stood in relation to the elephant that each was convinced he knew so well.

Being equipped with a good sense of the basic variety of ways people happen to be religious puts us in a much better position to make sense of any religious phenomenon we happen to come upon but above all to sort out what religions do and do not have in common. To fail to have a sense for this variety is to be in the situation of the six elephant handlers and to be liable to all sorts of confusions. One frequent confusion is supposing that a particular religion or even all religions are typified by a single way when, with a little investigation, other ways can be found. This is like supposing that the understanding of merely one of the six elephant handlers will suffice for the whole—whether for the one elephant or for all possible elephants. Recall the conclusion of the English widow who decided that mysticism was the common authentic core of all religions. She failed to realize the bias resulting from considering the full range of human religiousness solely from the perspective of one way of being religious.

Another frequent confusion is supposing that the differences between two religious traditions can be reduced to the differences between exemple expressions of each tradition that happen to be instances of two different ways of being religious, both of which can be found in each tradition by looking further. This is like supposing that the difference between two elephants, A and B, is the difference between the understanding of one of the six elephant handlers of elephant A and the understanding of another of the six elephant handlers of elephant B. Recall the Baptist businessman who concluded that the difference between Christianity and Buddhism was the difference between his version of Baptist Evangelical Christianity and Sri Lankan Buddhist monasticism. He failed to realize that the way of devotion with which he identified is also found in Buddhism, though it is evident elsewhere than in Sri Lanka (specifically in East Asia and East Asian immigrant communities). And he failed to realize that the way of mystical quest that seems so prominent in Sri Lankan Buddhism is found as well in Christianity, though it is for the most part limited to Roman Catholic and Eastern Orthodox contexts.

To the contrary, being equipped with an understanding of the six ways of being religious and having some awareness of the range of different ways of being religious that occur within different religious traditions, one will avoid these confusions. More generally, one will be in a much better position to appreciate the many sorts of commonalities and differences that may exist among religious phenomena. A readiness to discover commonality in ways of being religious despite differences in religious belief, and a simultaneous readiness to explore the significance of these differences in view of recognized commonality in ways of being religious, open up possibilities of constructive dialogue between religious traditions. People from different faiths can thereby explore what each other's religious life is like, what they do and do not have in common, without fear of compromising the distinctiveness of their own faith and without worry over violating the faith of the other person. No less true, people of the same faith but of different ways of being religious can discover what they have in common once they have been freed from the misconception that difference in ways of being religious must mean *nonidentity* of religious faith. The framework of ways of being religious thus promotes *within the same religious tradition* constructive dialogue between subtraditions exemplifying the different ways.

Thus presented in a nutshell is the framework of ways of being religious. Much remains to be explained and explored: what is involved in each of the six ways, how they relate to each other, how different religious traditions relate to them in terms of emphasis, stratification, combination, and exclusion, and how to go about using the framework to make sense of particular religious phenomena and religious traditions. In the process, the framework and the description of each of the ways will be progressively elaborated and refined in a kind of spiraling development.

The characterizations of the six ways given thus far are very rudimentary and are far from adequate. For most readers, a firm grasp of each of the six ways—firm enough to be able to apply the categories consistently and with understanding—will be slow in coming. On the one hand, one should not assume that one has understood too quickly, for conventional associations of the names of the six ways and of the terms used in brief definitions, such as those given above, can very easily mislead. On the other hand, as will be repeatedly mentioned later on, a firm understanding of the framework should not be allowed to blind one to the respects in which a given religious phenomenon fails to fit clearly into any one of the six ways. Mastery of the framework will require deliberate care and patient attention to nuance and detail.

Chapter 2 introduces the fundamental assumptions and orientation governing the framework of ways of being religious and the conception of religion on which it relies. In it the generic idea of a way of being religious is explained. Chapter 3 elaborates each of the six ways of being religious and begins to explore some of the relations among them. Chapter 4 is devoted to a description of examples of each of the ways from all of the major religious traditions, examples demonstrating single ways and examples combining more than one. The chapter describes how different traditions and subtraditions have historically emphasized, prioritized, combined, and/or excluded different ways. Chapter 5 introduces the idea of qualitative variation of practice within each way and a commonsense basis for recognizing generic virtue and vice in the practice of each way. Chapter 6 concludes Part I with a discussion of the advantages and liabilities of the framework. Parts II and III of the book, encompassing Chapters 7 through 15, are devoted to showing how the framework makes possible an insightful comparison of religious traditions by applying it in depth to the comparison of Buddhism and Christianity. At the end of the book there is a glossary of the key terms used, with page references to their fullest explanation; when they are introduced in the text, the terms will be highlighted in boldface type.

CHAPTER SUMMARY

This chapter introduces the framework of six generic ways of being religious as a solution to the problem of how to make sense of the similarities and differences that may be found among religious phenomena: how to give due weight both to similarities and to differences without compromising either, and how to do so without privileging the beliefs of one tradition over another. It explains the problem and the proposed solution by means of a parable of six partially blind elephant handlers, each of whom is well acquainted with the same elephant but in an entirely different way. The blindness of each is that of having no peripheral vision: each can make no sense of the possibility that the elephant can be known any better or more fully than his own way of knowing it. But to know the elephant in the round, one needs, nevertheless, to take into account what can be known of the elephant from the perspective of each handler. The elephant stands for any particular religion or, more precisely, the ultimate reality recognized within a particular religion. The six partially blinded men stand for persons identifying with a specific way of being religious as the primary way to approach that ultimate reality. Likewise, the parable teaches that to compare one religion with another and avoid confusion (whether realized or not) one needs to be aware of the many different ways there are of being acquainted with that religion and the ultimate reality to which it purports to bear witness. An awareness of this potential plurality of ways within any given religion is found in the Hindu conception of different *yogas*, different paths to what it takes to be the ultimate reality. This book proposes recognition, therefore, of six different generic patterns of human religiousness, six different ways of approaching whatever a religion takes to be the ultimate reality, or God: sacred rite, right action, devotion, shamanic mediation, mystical quest, and wisdom.

STUDY QUESTIONS

1. Discuss the problem posed at the beginning of the chapter—namely, how to give due weight to the similarities and the differences to be found among religious phenomena. What other examples can you think of that illustrate this problem?

2. Discuss the parable of the six partially blind elephant handlers and explore its relevance to the problem of understanding the religions traditions of which you have some acquaintance. To what extent does it help to explain some of the misunderstandings and confusions that characterize relations between persons of different religious persuasion?

3. Do some library research to find more about the Hindu conception of the four different yogas. (Make use of the references in note 3, starting with the book by Huston Smith.)

NOTES

1. See the discussion of the idea of objectivity as it applies to the study of religion at the beginning of Chapter 2.

2. There is a similar recognition of different paths in certain subtraditions of Buddhism. See Richard Gard, ed., *Buddhism*, Great Religions of Modern Man Series (New York: Washington Square Press, 1962), Ch. 1, p. 3.

3. See Elliot Deutsch, *The Bhagavad Gītā* (New York: Holt, Rinehart and Winston, 1968); A. L. Herman, *A Brief Introduction to Hinduism: Religion, Philosophy, and Ways of Liberation* (Boulder, CO: Westview Press, 1992), Ch. 3; and Huston Smith, *The World's Religions*, 2nd ed. (San Francisco, CA: HarperSanFrancisco, 1991), Ch. 2.

4. In the present case, it should *not* be assumed that what most American readers conventionally mean by God—namely, the Christian or Jewish conception of God—is meant, though in English the closest equivalent happens to be the word *God*.

5. That is to say, supernatural to us in the modern West, who are accustomed to identifying nature with the mundane, material order of things. It is likely that most traditions exemplifying the way of shamanic mediation regard the spirit realm of supramundane power to be a part of the natural order of things and would regard our understanding of nature to be much too narrowly circumscribed.

6. This peculiar fact, I believe, is a result of the peculiar evolution of Hinduism from the the religion of the ancient Aryan peoples expressed in the sacred Hindu scriptures called the *Vedas*. The Vedic religion centered on elaborate sacrificial rituals, many of which remain a part of an orthodox Hindu's duty to the present day but which have little directly to do with the divinities of popular Hinduism that came to the fore (as far as scriptural documentation is concerned) well after the Vedic era. Moreover, the later Vedic scriptures called the *Upanishads* distinguish as penultimate the goals of Vedic sacrificial ritual from the supreme religious goal of at-onement with the absolute Brahman.

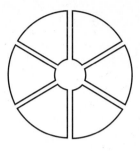

C H A P T E R 2

THINKING GENERICALLY ABOUT RELIGION

FUSING EMPATHY AND OBJECTIVITY

This book assumes the context of the modern academic study of religions. Generally, this contemporary enterprise aims to promote the *objective* study of religious phenomena in the round, that is, study that attempts to take into account and do justice to all relevant perspectives on the phenomena in question, those of insiders as well as outsiders. To take into account perspectives other than one's own, especially insiders' perspectives, *empathy* is required. Thus, the study of religious phenomena in the round requires a fusion of objectivity and empathy.

A great deal depends on what is understood by **objectivity**. It is well worth noting that the word has more than one meaning. One meaning pertains to *a preoccupation with a method of distancing*—of separating the subjectivity of the investigator from influencing conclusions reached about the object of investigation, of submitting all relations with and representations of the object to a rigorous discipline of impersonalization, explicitness, and strict intellectual control. To be objective in this sense, one's knowledge and understanding of the object must be developed wholly from a single external perspective that has had all that can be done to it to make *it* (the perspective) objective. Such a perspective is detached, uninvolved, and impersonal toward what is being studied and requires that the results of one's study be presented in a way that could (ideally) be achieved or agreed to by any other, similarly objective scholar. This first meaning of objectivity is widely supposed to be the ideal of modern physical science and consequently the preferred ideal for all other academic disciplines. Nevertheless, it is a gross misconception of the practice of modern physical science and is disastrous when applied to such subject matters as religious phenomena.[1] Given this meaning of objectivity, objectivity and empathy are incompatible. Unfortunately, a good many studies of religion are carried out in the conviction that there is no other legitimate notion of objectivity.

Another meaning (a more commonsense meaning) of objectivity pertains to *a preoccupation with drawing near to the object of investigation in its transcendence beyond any one perspective.* Where is that? Precisely at the place where multiple perspectives upon it intersect, where all perspectives relevant to grasping and understanding the object in the round come together. Reaching that point is no easy matter, and one can never take for granted that one has achieved it. But it is possible to approach. The process involves no simple, linear application of a single method. Rather, it involves shifts in viewpoint that are only learned about as one strives progressively to draw near to the object, not away from it, and near to it in a manner appropriate to what it is thereby determined to be. Objective nearness to the object is measured by the extent to which one's developing understanding elicits recognition (recognition that one has indeed drawn near to the object, if not fully grasped it) from those who dwell within the intersecting perspectives upon the object and know them well. Significantly, so far as these intersecting perspectives involve discriminations of quality and worth, the pursuit of objectivity in this second sense itself will involve progressively more discerning value judgments—the judgment, for example, whether a ritual is being performed well or poorly, or whether a religious healer is genuinely interested in a patient's well-being or is a charlatan. Objectivity in this second sense, then, is fundamentally a matter of doing justice to the object itself (the object as it exists between our several perspectives onto it, or at the point where our several perspectives intersect). It is this latter sense of objectivity that the modern academic study of religion is about and what this book is about. So, contrary to the charge that objectivity is impossible in the study of religion, when understood in the second sense just described it is a meaningful goal toward which we can make significant progress.

The modern academic study of religion with which this book identifies itself incorporates, on the one hand, the approaches of the many modern disciplines of study that bear upon religious phenomena. These approaches are for the most part perspectives of outsiders: for example, those of history, sociology, cultural anthropology, psychology, philosophy, literary interpretation, and art history and criticism. On the other hand, the modern academic study of religion also incorporates a complementary approach that takes seriously and gives a certain priority to the perspective(s) of religious insiders. This approach centrally involves a disciplined **empathy**, seeking to make accessible to the outsider what is understood and experienced by persons on the inside and thereby to bring about an empathetic understanding that aims to be (for the moment, in an act of imaginative suspension of disbelief) neutral and nonjudgmental, set apart from our own reactions and judgments. This is an approach that seeks to understand a religious phenomenon as much as possible on its own terms, independently of the alien ones we might bring to it—that is, in the terms of those on the inside, or at least in terms roughly convertible with insiders' terms by means of which the phenomenon may be justly compared with phenomena in other traditions. It is an approach that seeks to avoid as much as possible any theological or metaphysical prejudgments that are likely to distort or fail to grasp what is to be found and appreciated on its own terms. This approach of disciplined empathy is sometimes called the **phenomenology of religion**.

Not all who characterize their work as phenomenology of religion follow the approach just sketched.[2] Sometimes phenomenology of religion is identified with the enterprise of developing a catalogue of recurrent, universal patterns of religious phenomena that become evident through comparative study (as in the work of W. Brede Kristensen or Mircea Eliade[3]). The problem with this sort of approach is that the meaning of these patterns (or, rather, the account developed by the person coming up with them) often owes little to the concrete context of their alleged occurrence in particular traditions (despite expressed intentions to the contrary) and is therefore likely to be unknown and unrecognizable to insiders. Although there is a good deal to be learned from such "phenomenologies of religion," their approach relies on uncritical metaphysical and theological assumptions and is at times insufficiently responsible to the phenomena that are to be understood.

The overall approach taken in this book to the study of religion is broadly phenomenological in the sense first described above—or, more precisely, **empathetically objective** in a manner that highlights both similarities and differences. It seeks to do justice to the experience and understanding of participants within a specific cultural and historical context and to counter the presumption that the comparativist must necessarily know and understand the meaning of religious phenomena better than knowledgeable and reflective participants.

This is not to say that empathy is the last word in understanding religion, but it certainly is one of the first and is a fundamental condition apart from which any serious study of religion fails to merit respect. At the very least, religion is a certain orientation toward or view of the world: one among others, and one not necessarily shared by the person who wishes to learn about and understand this view. Accordingly, understanding it requires the effort of imaginatively stepping into the other person's perspective and considering how things look from "over there," *as if one were an insider*, though one is not one in fact. It requires basically the same sort of imaginative stretching that is involved in an actor's learning the part of a character different from himself and bringing that part credibly to life in a drama on stage.[4] What do I mean by a "credible" portrayal? What is success in empathetic understanding? Principally, it is a matter of having (temporarily, in an act of imagi-nation) entered the perspective of the other person sufficiently well to be able to represent it credibly to others, especially and above all in a way that is recognizable and credible to those persons who themselves occupy that perspective.

The point of the book, however, is not just empathy but comparative ex-ploration and study, and for that a common or neutral framework is needed. A century of comparative empathetic study of religion has turned up sufficiently similar structures between historically unrelated traditions to warrant the identifi-cation of a wide range of generic features of religious life, and in large measure this book is an attempt to summarize and consolidate these findings in a way that makes them usable by students in their own studies. As does phenomenolo-gy of religion generally, the framework proposed by this book draws on these findings in establishing a kind of temporary neutral zone for empathetic under-standing and comparative exploration. It does this by employing a *generic* vo-cabulary and taxonomy as free as possible of theological commitments and by relying on generally reliable accounts (widely respected and the least contested) of participants' experiences and understandings.

Is it possible to be truly neutral in this regard? Is it possible to forge a lan-guage that does not favor some religious orientations and offend others? We can-not fully answer all aspects of these questions here. But we must at least be honest and forthright in addressing them. It is important to recognize, first of all, that there are different degrees and types of neutrality. Not all are relevant to the tasks of empathetic understanding and a nonjudgmental comparison of religious phenomena. Moreover, to pursue these tasks is, in certain fundamental respects, not to be neutral; it is to be opposed to presuppositions and points of view that would block or deny them. Nor is it to forsake evaluative judgments altogether, which may not even be possible, let alone desirable. To pursue the tasks of em-pathetic understanding and nonjudgmental comparison is to adopt *temporarily* a posture of neutrality for the sake of understanding from within the different points of view involved, in a manner that is undistorted (or as undistorted as possible) by one's own point of view. It is to attempt to have our understanding *do justice* to them, so that whatever consequent evaluative judgments we reach will be more likely to do justice to them as well. This, of course, assumes that we are not simply occupants of a single point of view but that we are able, in favor-able circumstances, to enter momentarily into points of view other than our own and find opportunity genuinely to explore them in some depth without serious threat to our own well-being, our moral integrity, or our mental grasp of the world. It assumes, as well, that we can be self-critical to a greater or lesser extent about our understanding and articulation of other people's experiences and points of view and that we can make progress in revising our judgments in the interest of doing more justice to those experiences and points of view.[5]

There have been many sorts of categories employed in the comparative study of religion in the attempt to comprehend similarities and remark differences among phenomena of different traditions. From the perspective of the phenomenology of religion not all are equally legitimate or justified. Sometimes certain categories bring with them presuppositions that reflect a specific philosophical or theological orientation and a certain ulterior interest in having the data construed in a certain way, so that a predetermined conclusion results. This occurs when an insider in one religious tradition attempts to comprehend, and reach a judgment about the validity of, a phenomenon in another religious tradition simply in the terms his own tradition provides. It also occurs when a person from a secular perspective unsympathetic to religion attempts to do the same. These are obvious cases. Yet it can sometimes also occur when a person genuinely attempts to be unbiased and empathetic toward the tradition she seeks to understand, for it is terribly easy to be unconscious of the bias that given categories carry.

As the author of this text, I have tried to become conscious of and to eliminate such bias from the categories I employ. The language of the descriptions and formulations I offer may nevertheless, despite my best intention, fall short of the neutrality, empathy, and objectivity at which I am aiming. It may at times reflect a more Christian, or a more modern Western bias than I realize. To the extent that that is so in a way that does injustice to the phenomena I am seeking to represent, then those descriptions and formulations should be criticized and accordingly revised. None of them are final; all are revisable. The reader is hereby advised to make use of them with care, being prepared to modify or reformulate them as needed.

WHAT IS RELIGION?

Religious phenomena include an incredible diversity of objects (e.g., a Native American "medicine bundle," a Roman Catholic priest's stole [an essential part of his attire as a priest], an image of the Hindu goddess Durga); places (e.g., a Japanese Shinto shrine, the location of the Budda's enlightenment, a traditional Chinese family gravesite); practices (e.g., a group of Evangelical Christians singing a devotional song, the giving of *tzedekah* [a charitable contribution] by an Orthodox Jew to a needy person, a Hindu making an offering of clarified butter into the home fire [referred to in Hinduism as "the mouth of the gods"]); experiences (e.g., the insight of a student of Muslim theology into the absolute sovereignty of Allah, being "slain in the Spirit" by a Pentecostal Christian, a Hindu yogi's attainment of *ekagrata* [one-pointed concentration] in which the distinction between subject and object is overcome); beliefs (e.g., that Christ will come again to judge the living and the dead, that Ali was the rightful successor to Muhammad and true heir of Muhammad's *wilaya* [spiritual discernment], that the true *Dao* [or *Tao*][6] is nameless, ageless, and the womb of all things); and, of course, stories, among many other sorts of things. Being religious, being characterized by the quality that distinguishes what people readily identify as religious—namely, the sacred—such phenomena have something to do with what is felt by participants (at least moderately sincere participants) to lie beyond the perspectives of ordinary human awareness and the mundane sphere of everyday life. These phenomena somehow refer participants to, and orient them with respect to, something that to their imagination lies beyond appearances, beyond what meets the eye and ear. For participants a religious phenomenon bears upon *the ultimate conditions of life*, upon the really real, upon that beyond which no further or higher appeal can be imagined, upon ultimate authority or cosmic bedrock, as it were, upon the Alpha and Omega, the beginning and the end of things, and, as well, upon what is of ultimate importance—that is, the source of meaningful order, purpose, and value in life, and, in consequence, direction as to how life ought to be lived.

For such a phenomenon to have a **religious function** and not merely be something associated with religion, it must, as far as participants' understanding is concerned, serve to put them in touch with the dimension of ultimacy, to connect and bring them into some kind of rapport with it—some phenomena doing so in a more central way, some less so. The result will be to change or transform the participants' lives insofar as they will have been (re)connected with and brought (back) into rapport with what gives life meaning, purpose, and direction, with what gives it an ultimate basis or grounding.[7] The transformation will be all the more relevant, powerful, and compelling when participants come to it (the experience of transformation) in the midst of experiences that otherwise leave them with a sense of disconnection from that dimension of ultimacy, unsure about the purpose of life, and uncertain how they should respond. This promise of change or transformation is nicely illustrated by a quotation that the author once found on the back of a package of herbal tea:

> In Japan, a simple open gateway acts as a symbol to mark off the precincts of the shrine. In passing through it, one leaves behind psychologically and symbolically the humdrum ordinary world, and enters the sacred space of the temple. After worship, one again moves through the gate to re-enter the realm of everyday life—but as a renewed person. All peoples have set aside some place to serve as a sacred place, whether it be a mountain top, a garden, or a church [possibly an interior place found in meditation, or a sacred time, such as the Jewish Sabbath], so that it may represent and activate within them a Great Power—another dimension of reality. So, one is allowed time when truth, significance and worth are recognized and cultivated to be carried back into the ordinary world.[8]

In each religious tradition, not only outward forms differ, but what is deemed to be ultimately real is differently understood and imagined: the God of Abraham, Isaac, and Jacob, the Holy Trinity, *Allah*, the Buddha Nature, *Kṛṣṇa*, the *Dao* of Heaven and Earth, the *Kami*, *Wakan-tanka*, or what have you. That there is some conception of an ultimate reality and some conception as to how one should relate to it is generic to all **religion**.[9] In what follows, when *ultimate reality* appears in italics, followed by a small circle (°) the phrase is meant to serve as a variable, to be filled in by the specific religious tradition in question. More specifically, **ultimate reality** ° (capitalized or not, but always highlighted by ital-ics and the small circle) will refer to whatever the people of a given tradition take to be the ultimate ground of meaning and purpose in life. Also is left open (to be filled in by the specific tradition) the question whether and to what extent the means of being put in touch with *ultimate reality*° is divinely given, awak-ened to by the founder of a tradition, or humanly contrived.

The fact that each religion is oriented by a conception of *ultimate reality*° does not itself imply that each such notion refers to or characterizes the same thing or even the same kind of thing, let alone characterizes it equally well—contrary to the claims of some scholars writing as phenomenologists of religion. The theoretical framework of six ways of being religious does not assume that there is a single *Ultimate Reality*° referred to by the different conceptions of *ulti-mate reality*° in all traditions, that there is a single sort of thing (a set of features in common) constituting what the different traditions respectively take to be *ulti-mate reality*°, or even that there exists anything outside the metaphysical func-tion of *ultimate reality*° within specific religious traditions. The framework is deliberately articulated in such a way as to avoid begging all such metaphysical and theological questions. These are legitimate questions, worthy of serious in-vestigation. The theory does not attempt to answer them, however. What it does assume is that any given religion possesses a system of symbols, beliefs, and practices through which access to *ultimate reality*° (i.e., to what the tradition takes to be ultimately real) is alleged to be granted. By itself, the phenomeno-logical study of religion is not competent to answer whether there really is an ul-timate reality or what its nature happens to be. Where the discipline presumes to resolve this question, it has overstepped its role and has implicitly, if not covert-ly, engaged in theologizing—namely, given expression to a position of faith in an ultimate reality (or faith that ultimately there is no such thing). Theology is a respectable activity in its place, but it should not pass itself off as having reached its conclusions on phenomenological grounds.

The claim that each religion is oriented by some conception of *ultimate re-ality*° implies that within the world view of each religion there is a conception (or a set of concepts) that performs the same generic function of ultimacy, serv-ing a foundational role within that religion's world view. The role of this func-tion (or at least one of its roles) is to connect reality and meaning, how things are, and how life therefore ought to be lived. Cultural anthropologist Clifford Geertz had it right when he wrote that the heart of a religious perspective is

> the conviction that the values one holds are grounded in the inherent structure of re-ality, that between the way one ought to live and the way things really are there is an unbreakable inner connection. What sacred symbols do for those to whom they are sacred is to formulate an image of the world's construction [an image encom-passing all that lies beyond the perspective of everyday experience, a more or less comprehensive world view] and a program for human conduct that are . . . reflexes of one another.[10]

We can summarize what has been said so far in terms of some definitions.

A *religious phenomenon* may be defined generically as whatever (e.g., practice, symbol, object, person, encounter, experience, place, intention, doctrine, story, etc.) serves for a person or group of persons in some way to refer to, or connect them with, what they take to be ultimately real.

A thing may be said to *function religiously* in the respect in which it serves for a participant as a means of drawing near to, and coming into right or appropriate relationship with, what is taken to be ultimate reality.

A *religion* may be generically defined as a system of symbols (e.g., words and gestures, stories and practices, objects and places) that function religiously, namely, an ongoing system of symbols that participants use to draw near to, and come into right or appropriate relationship with, what they deem to be ultimate reality.

A few comments on these definitions are in order before proceeding. (The phrase *system of symbols*, introduced in the definition of *religion*, will be taken up and clarified later on in the current chapter.)

As definitions, these three are intended more to focus and explain the functional essence of religion as religion than to delimit the boundaries of what will and what will not count as religion. These definitions have been constructed on the basis of cultural phenomena conventionally recognized to be religious. Such cultural phenomena serve here as paradigm cases of what is religious. The point of the definitions is principally to draw out and comprehend what makes certain phenomena religious. Being phenomena of human culture, religions and religious phenomena will typically have many functions—psychological, social, political, educational, aesthetic, and economic. But in addition to these functions, for participants who are at least moderately serious about their involvement in religion, the set of symbols, beliefs, and practices that make up a religion specifically have a religious function, the one identified above. The definitions, of course, may be used to delimit what will and what will not count as religion beyond conventionally recognized religions, and many nontraditional phenomena of human religiousness (i.e., phenomena that would not conventionally or traditionally be recognized as religious) can be identified and illuminated by means of them. However, again, it is not the so-called boundary problem that concerns us here. It is rather the articulation of what it is about the *functioning of religion as religion* that allows for different ways of being religious.

A related question often raised in connection with definitions of religion is whether all people are in some sense religious, whether they realize it or not. On the basis of the definitions offered above, strictly speaking, the answer would have to be no. Indeed, even sincerely religious people are frequently not particularly wholehearted or sincere in their involvement in religious practices—sometimes despite their best intentions. It is quite apparent that not all people, and certainly not all modern Westernized people, are convinced of the existence beyond the perspectives of ordinary human awareness of an *ultimate reality*^{p} that is a ground of worth, meaning, and purpose, or deliberately seek to orient their lives in relation to an *ultimate reality*^{p}. And even in so-called "primitive" cultures, anthropologists occasionally point out how there often appear to be a few skeptics and relatively nonserious participants in relation to the religious practices of the culture who, to the extent they are involved, are involved more for the sake of nonreligious functions, or solely for their sake, than specifically for drawing near to, and coming into right relationship to, the *ultimate reality*^{p}. Nonetheless, the intent here is to clarify what is involved in the religious function of religious phenomena and the generic varieties of that function.

At times in what follows phrases will be used other than those given in the definitions that mean substantially the same thing but focus attention in a certain way. Thus, on occasion, religion will be referred to as "a means of getting in touch with *ultimate reality*^{p}," and religious practices as "means of seeking at-onement with *ultimate reality*^{p}"; the word **at-onement** (drawing on the English roots of the Christian theological concept of *atonement*) is meant to refer to "the state of being 'at one with' *ultimate reality*^{p}," however it is understood.[11] Used here, it is meant to encompass in its range of meaning "reconciled with," "in right or appropriate relation with," "in rapport with," "in agreement with," "in harmony with," "in conformity to," and "in union with"—with the understanding that the precise characterization of this state of at-onement will differ from one tradition to another.

Among scholars in religious studies and among phenomenologists in particular many different definitions of religion are now in use.[12] All substantially overlap in their reference, so much so that most amount to different phrasings referring to the same things, differing only in the peculiar emphases their author wishes to make. Each, including the ones just offered, has a little arbitrariness about it—other phrasing could probably do as well. But the particular phrasing the definition has reflects nuances that its author wishes to highlight. The phrasings of this book's definitions, of course, reflect particular nuances. Their justification rests solely upon their usefulness in guiding comparative study and illuminating what is to be understood—in the current case, ways of being religious.

Some scholarship in the comparative study of religion gives a much greater stress to the role of social and cultural context in determining the meaning and function(s) of particular religious expressions than this book is prepared to give. For example, some would argue on the basis of that stress that what is common to the many sociocultural subtraditions of Christianity, say, is insignificant in comparison to the differences between them. Thus, given its unique role within Croatian Roman Catholic life, devotion to the Blessed Virgin Mary among women in violence-torn former Yugoslavia could be construed to be a very different thing from devotion to the Blessed Virgin Mary among socially and economically secure adult women Roman Catholics in St. Cloud, Minnesota. And the former of these two may be construed to have significant commonality with devotion to *Kannon* (the female expression of the *Bodhisattva Avalokiteśvara*, often associated with the *Buddha Amida*) among unemployed Pure Land women Buddhists in pre-World War II Nagasaki, Japan, that the latter does not. Though this kind of research is eminently worthwhile, it should be seen as representing one among several possible emphases—one that focuses on the immediate social and cultural context to the relative neglect of more abstract matters, such as the generic functions and patterns of religious life being explored in this text.

THE PROBLEM OF MEANING
AND ITS DIFFERENT ASPECTS

The definitions offered in the preceding section imply that people involve themselves in religious practices as such because they want to draw near (again) to *ultimate reality*°, get (re)connected with it, come (again) into right or appropriate relationship to it. This presupposes that people so involve themselves because, for whatever reasons, they somehow feel that they are not near it (or not near enough), may not be connected with it (or not fully enough connected), may not be in right or appropriate relationship to it. Different religions conceive of this distance from or disrelationship to *ultimate reality*° in very different ways, as being of greater or lesser extent, and as involving all, some, or only certain persons. Some conceive of the disrelationship as radical and objective—for example, a disorder in the nature of things stemming from an original Fall from what was an original perfection; others as an objective but rectifiable condition (e.g., one of impurity from which one can be "cleansed" by means of appropriate purification rites); still others conceive of it as psychological and subjective—a condition of ignorance and distraction that can be corrected through appropriate psychological discipline and philosophical insight. In any case, all religious life seems to presuppose it as a kind of generalized existential predicament for which religious practices promise some resolution.

As will be explained more fully below, this idea does not imply that the resulting motivation for involvement in religious practices is therefore predominantly a negative one—that is, to get out of this predicament. Religious motivation may also be positive, as much to draw near what is deemed to be the source of meaning, vitality, power, virtue, and so forth, as it is to leave behind a condition of experienced lack of meaning, vitality, power, virtue, and so on.

Even so, one might say then that one of the fundamental reasons of religions for being is the apparently universal sense that human life in certain respects is out of joint or on the brink of being so; that it is not at-one with the way things ultimately are and the powers on which life in its fullness seems to depend; and that it (or specifically one's idea of it) is consequently liable, if something is not done about it, to lose its meaning and point, or worse. The varying but fundamental, if somewhat vague, sense of alienation human beings often feel between their everyday selves and a numinous reality felt to lie beyond life's surface appearance is the mystery symbolized in the diverse stories of a primordial Fall from perfection at the beginning of human history that we find in many traditions (or of an original perfect One that disintegrated first into two and then many). Correlatively, the intention of religion is to mark out a way of relating to life in a manner appropriate to the mystery and, so far as possible, in some respect to close or lessen the felt breach of alienation. Hence religion is preoccupied with whatever is believed to restore human rapport with what is understood to be the ultimate ground of life's meaning and vital order.

Following up an idea of the sociologist of religion Max Weber, Clifford Geertz has described this rationale of religion, a felt disrelationship to *ultimate reality*°, as "**the problem of meaning**."[13] This phrase is meant to be an extension and generalization of what in Western philosophical theology has been known as the Problem of Evil—namely, how can the fact of evil and suffering in the world be reconciled with belief in an ultimate good (i.e., an ultimate ground to life's meaning and purpose). There are more aspects to the problematic character of human life than are covered in traditional, intellectual discussions of the problem of evil and, in practice at least, religion has dealt with them in a variety of ways other than through theological inquiry and explanation. For the point of the problem of meaning is that events in human experience from time to time in a variety of different ways pose a threat to the meaningfulness of life. The question is, *how to cope with that threat and, in the face of it, attain to an affirmation of the meaning and worth of life*[14] *despite it*. In large measure, religions are designed to offer practical answers to this question.

According to Geertz's analysis, religion—at least at its most authentic—is not a way of avoiding life's absurdities, pain, and injustice. Rather, in relation to the problem of meaning, religion is a way—for adherents, the most sensible way—of facing them, of taking them on. Generically speaking, religion doesn't deny the undeniable: that life at times seems (1) incomprehensible, (2) overwhelmingly painful, and (3) apparently pointless. These characteristics of life Geertz identifies as three aspects of the problem of meaning—as three existential predicaments (which may, of course, be compounded). Instead of denying them, religion denies the ultimacy of such experiences. Religion characteristically affirms that in the ultimate perspective or in the widest horizon of meaning (to which perspective or horizon the forms of religious practice claim to offer some access) these experiences are not cause for despair, for giving up on human life. Religion affirms that they do not cut one off from the possibility of a meaningful life. More specifically, religion offers means of coping with each aspect of the problem of meaning: (a) resources for investigating and reflecting upon the ultimate reasons why some things are not understandable to us (at least in our present condition), (b) the emotional wherewithal (in terms, for example, of emotional reorientation and focus, pastoral guidance, and community support) to bear up under what seems unbearable, and (c) insight, motivation, and guidance with regard to the *ultimate moral order*° [15] in responding to the inequities and injustices with which life presents us.

In basic agreement with Geertz, Hans Küng puts much the same the point more concretely:

> . . . [A]ll religions offer an answer to the question of the meaning of everything, of life, of history, in the light of an ultimate reality which already has an effect here and now—whether this is described with classical Judaism as "resurrection," with Christianity as "eternal life," with Islam as "paradise," with Hinduism as "moksha," with Buddhism as "nirvana" or with Taoism as "immortality." Precisely in the face of many frustrations and many experiences of suffering and failure, religions can help to lead people on by offering meaning beyond death and giving meaning here and now, not least where moral action has remained unsuccessful.

Küng goes on to say:

> Religions speak with absolute authority, and they express this authority not only with words and concepts, teachings and dogmas, but also with symbols and prayers, rites and festivals—i.e., rationally and emotionally. For religions have means of shaping the whole of human existence, not just for an intellectual elite but also for broad strata of the population—means that have been tested by history, adapted to cultures and made specific for the individual. Religion certainly cannot do everything, but it can disclose a certain "more" in human life and bestow it.
>
> - Religion can communicate a specific depth-dimension, an all-embracing horizon of meaning, even in the face of suffering, injustice, guilt and meaninglessness, and also a last meaning of life even in the face of death: the whither and whence of our being.
> - Religion can guarantee supreme values, unconditional norms, the deepest motivations and the highest ideals: the why and wherefore of our responsibility.
> - Through common symbols, rituals, experiences and goals, religion can create a sense of feeling at home, a sense of trust, faith, certainty, strength for the self, security and hope: a spiritual community and allegiance.
> - Religion can give grounds for protest and resistance against unjust conditions: the longing for the "wholly Other" which is already now at work and which cannot be stilled.[16]

For their participants, religions provide ways in which problematic life experiences are relativized and divested of their threat to meaningful life. Typically, they do so by situating the problematic experience within a larger, encompassing, cosmic context where its problematic aspects are accounted for and resources for coping with them, if not for surmounting them, are provided—resources that (re)establish the lives of these followers in rapport with *ultimate reality*°. As Geertz puts it,

> Having ritually "lept" [sic] (. . . "slipped" might be more accurate) into the framework of meaning which religious conceptions define and, the ritual ended, returned again to the common-sense world, a man is—unless as sometimes happens, the experience

fails to register—changed. And as he is changed so also is the common-sense world, for it is now seen as but the partial form of a wider reality which corrects and completes it.

But this correction and completion is not, as some students of "comparative religion" would have it, everywhere the same in content. The nature of the bias religion gives to ordinary life varies with the religion involved, with the particular dispositions induced in the believer by the specific conceptions of cosmic order he has come to accept.[17]

Geertz identified three aspects of the problem of meaning. It is remarkable that these three aspects directly correlate with three of the six ways of being religious: wisdom, devotion, and right action. This is an interesting confirmation of the hypothesis of six generic ways of being religious, especially insofar as it does not take much reflection to discover three other general types of problematic life experiences that correlate with the remaining three ways: sacred rite, shamanic mediation, and mystical quest. For example, the prospect of facing momentous events (such as birth, puberty, marriage, and death, but also other just as great but less predictable challenges of life) with no sense of propriety that is grounded in anything other than mundane utilitarian considerations—that is, with no sense of propriety that is grounded in some *ultimate archetypal pattern*°—can unhinge the mind (for some people at least) and result in social chaos. A second sort of threat is posed by confrontation with overwhelming practical problems—such as serious illness or injury, great danger, or loss of food supply—whose solutions, if any, lie beyond the resources of power and imagination possessed by mere mortals. A third kind of threat is of an inward nature: an inner discontent with the unreality and insubstantial worth of ordinary life on its surface and unease with the limitations and unconsciousness (of the way things are suspected ultimately to be) that characterize ordinary experience. To these three further aspects of the problem of meaning, religion offers (1) sacred rituals in which participants' lives can be (re)grounded in *divine archetypal patterns*°, (2) shamanic practices through which *supernatural resources*° of power and imagination can be tapped, and (3) meditative disciplines and spiritual direction for developing an extra-ordinary conscious awareness of *ultimate reality*°.

Each of these aspects of the problem of meaning, the latter three combined with the three Geertz identifies, are among the primal motivations to religious practice. (This is not to say they are the only motivations—more on this in the next two paragraphs.) Not only do they motivate people to be religious; they motivate them in a certain direction with a certain interest. They dispose them to involvement more in some sorts of religious practice than in others: specifically toward practices that address and help them deal with that aspect of the problem of meaning that they have to confront. As will be explained further in what follows, where the relevant options are available they tend to motivate a person to become involved more in one way of being religious than in other ways. This is because each of the generic ways of being religious is addressed more to one aspect of the problem of meaning than the other aspects. In this respect, each way of being religious amounts to a generically different way of drawing near to *ultimate reality°* from a different sort of existential predicament, a different way of being not-at-one with it.

As formulated here, the different motivations identified above are construed in negative terms, as problems to be faced, borne, and perhaps overcome. They could equally well be formulated positively in terms of confidence in the specific religious practices—or, rather, confidence in the *ultimate reality°* accessed through those practices—that promise resolution to the problems. For example, people involve themselves in devotional religious practice because of the sustaining grace and solace that they expect and hope to receive through them. This is a more positive way of explaining why they so involve themselves than by saying that they do so because of the burden of suffering they have to carry in their lives.

ASPECTS OF THE PROBLEM OF MEANING

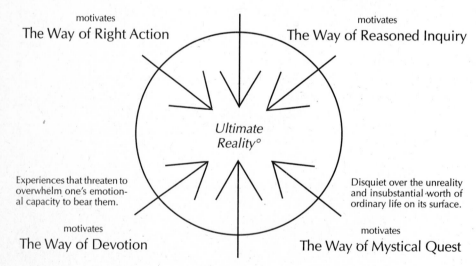

The prospect of living through momentous events with no archetypal pattern to follow, no ultimately grounded sense of propriety.

motivates
The Way of Sacred Rite

The prospect [or actuality] of behavior patterns that contradict a cosmic sense of normative order or justice.

Things that don't make sense that, if they can't be explained, threaten to undermine the sense of things as a whole.

motivates
The Way of Right Action

motivates
The Way of Reasoned Inquiry

Ultimate Reality°

Experiences that threaten to overwhelm one's emotional capacity to bear them.

Disquiet over the unreality and insubstantial worth of ordinary life on its surface.

motivates
The Way of Devotion

motivates
The Way of Mystical Quest

Helplessness in the face of practical crises whose solutions transcend mundane resources.

motivates
The Way of Shamanic Mediation

That these six aspects of the problem of meaning provide basic motivations for people to be involved in religious practice does not exclude other motivations. Often several motivations are coincident and intertwined. Sometimes there may be no alternative ways of being religious open for a person to choose among, forcing their involvement in a single way by constraint. There are a host of possible motivations, many of which are not particularly worthy or notable or religious, for that matter. For example, many people are involved in specific religious practices because they have been raised to do so and identify with their parents' tradition. Others, in the modern world anyway, may do so because they identify more with their peers' beliefs and practices than with those of their parents. Others are involved to get ahead economically or to make a better impression politically. And some motivations—for example, the motive of sheer delight in wonder and awe or of profound gratitude—may seem wholly unconnected with the problem of meaning as just construed. The value of pointing out the different motivating aspects of the problem of meaning lies in their power to explain how and why any one way of being religious appeals to one person and not to another. Accordingly, they can be called **existential motivations**, and the aspect of the problem of meaning that gives rise to any one of them its specific **problematic situation** or **existential predicament**.

In sum, people involve themselves in religion out of a desire to draw near to, and come into rapport with, what they take to be *ultimate reality*^{p}. They do so because they sense at some level of their being that their lives are not at-one with it, or not as fully at-one with it, as they might be. Accordingly, when the opportunity is present, different people involve themselves in a certain way of being religious out of a desire to (re)connect with *ultimate reality*^{p} a dimension of their lives that is otherwise felt in some respect to be out of touch or at odds with it. The different ways of being religious thus correspond to different dimensions of human life.

SYSTEMS OF SYMBOLS THAT ALLOW FOR VARYING INTERPRETATIONS

The different ways of being religious are not to be confused with what makes one religion different from another. Broadly conceived, each of the major religious traditions encompasses several of them, and some encompass all. What differentiates one religion from another involves many things, including factors connected directly with historical, cultural, and geographic circumstance, specific personalities, and of course beliefs—not least a distinctive conception of *ultimate reality*^{p}. But perhaps the most important set of factors, incorporating indirectly much of what has just been mentioned, is the distinctive **system of symbols**,[18] especially certain primary or central **symbols**, that taken together characterize *ultimate reality*^{p}, orchestrate the participants' imagination in a distinctive way, and give rise for participants to "an other world to live in"—in the manner suggested in the following statement by George Santayana:

> Any attempt to speak without speaking any particular language is not more hopeless than the attempt to have a religion that shall be no religion in particular. . . . Thus every living and healthy religion has a marked idiosyncrasy. Its power consists in its special and surprising message and in the bias which that revelation gives to life. The vistas it opens and the mysteries it propounds are *another world to live in*; and another world to live in—whether we expect ever to pass wholly over into it or no—is what we mean by having a religion.[19]

The phrase *system of symbols* designates the complex of stories, scriptures (if the tradition is literate), rituals, symbolic forms, and particular vocabulary for referring to *ultimate reality*° that as an interconnected whole constitute the core of a given religion. This system may include as well such things as fundamental ritual gestures, elementary credal affirmations, distinctive clothing, sacred images (or absence of images), special objects, special times, certain proprieties to be observed, key elements of a distinctive moral code, and so forth, but such things may be more peripheral than central in some traditions and it is often difficult to tell which is core and which is periphery. Though not originally taken from him, this idea of a core system of symbols constituting the heart of a religion is nicely captured in the words of Charles Davis:

> . . . [T]he objective content of faith is embodied in the first place, not in propositions, to which degrees of certainty can be attached, but in a set of symbols. At the center of every religious tradition is a symbolic complex as the primary, indispensable, normative expression of the constitutive content of the tradition. . . . The reason why the objective core of a religious tradition is a set of symbols rather than a body of concepts and propositions, is the nature of religious faith. Faith is not a detached intellectual assent, but the adoption of a fundamental stance in life. It is the choice of a basic attitude to reality, with a corresponding way of life; in other words, it is a fundamental option embracing one's total being and personality. That kind of commitment is not mediated through conceptual analysis or detached argumentation, but through symbols as dynamic images evoking a personal response. . . .
>
> I said . . . that at the center of every religious tradition was a set of symbols. I could have said a series of stories, because the symbols in question are not static representations like statues, but dramatic images, grouping and deploying themselves in narratives. The complex of symbols at the heart of every religion takes the form of sacred stories or myths.[20]

As such, therefore, religion or religious practice involves a system of symbols and symbolic actions for drawing near to and coming into right relationship to *ultimate reality*°. This implies that, at least as far as the approach here taken is concerned, all religions and religious experiences are in some essential sense symbolically mediated or symbolically conditioned.[21]

A given system of symbols (including narratives) constituting the core of a religion usually allows for a considerable variety of possible articulations of its meaning (even though a given representative of the tradition may not recognize more than one). Indeed, it is precisely of the nature of symbol, as distinct from a concept, that it allows for, and even invites, multiple readings.[22] Thus it is possible within any one religion—given large numbers of participants, endurance over time, and geographic spread—to find different (at times even incompatible) systems of conceptual elaboration of doctrine (theological or philosophical) and different systems of practice within a single religion, appealing to the same core system of symbols to establish their *orthodoxy* (rightness of belief) and *orthopraxy* (rightness of practice). However, the interpretation of the core system of symbols is not as such generally a preoccupation of the average member of a religion. Indeed, he is very often quite inarticulate about the meaning of given symbols when asked by outsiders to explain them. His attention for the most part is focused on interpreting not the symbols themselves but rather his own experience by means of those symbols, though usually in line with the shared interpretation and elaboration of them among members of the subtradition to which he belongs.

No religious tradition or subtradition is static or unchanging. Each is an evolving thing, open to all sorts of developments. Nevertheless, it maintains continuity with itself over time and unity amidst its diverse expressions by means of a relatively unchanging primary system of symbols. But more important than maintaining continuity with itself and unity amidst diversity, the primary function of the core system of symbols is to afford access to, and right relationship with, *ultimate reality*ᵖ—which, being ultimate, must in some sense (in the judgment of insiders at least) transcend time and change. Among that primary system of symbols will be a central story or cycle of stories. If the tradition is a literate one, there will be an authoritative scripture or set of authoritative scriptures—a **canon**—that establishes the boundaries of acceptable belief and practice. Any canonical scripture calls for interpretation—especially as time goes by and the linguistic, social, and cultural context of its readers evolves. And every religious community is concerned to exercise some control over the interpretation of its scriptures, to get their meaning right so that rapport with *ultimate reality*ᵖ will be assured. Nevertheless, any canonical scripture necessarily permits a range of varying interpretation (depending on the scripture, some more and some less), at least considered apart from whatever may be the official interpretation of the community at a given time and sometimes even with that interpretation. In this way a variety of different ways of being religious emerge in its terms, if they are not explicitly directed and encouraged to be taken up in its terms and by its leading interpreters. On the other hand, one or more ways may be more or less explicitly rejected or discouraged by what the scripture says and how it is interpreted.

Sometimes there are not sufficient numbers of participants, sufficient endurance over time, or sufficient geographic spread, among other factors, to allow for significant diversity in interpretation and practice to emerge. This is the case with small and close-knit religious groups, new religions, and nontraditional religious phenomena. In these cases it is often not easy to distinguish the core system of symbols from the interpretation of them or to imagine what other interpretations or different forms of practice would look like or how they might emerge.

Hans Küng confirms this distinction between a core system of symbols and specific interpretations of them in terms of a distinction he draws between "the abiding substance of the faith of a religion: the message, the decisive event of revelation, the distinguishing feature," on the one hand—called here its core system of symbols—and "the changing paradigm (macromodel of society, religion and theology): . . . an entire constellation of beliefs, values, techniques, and so on" that constitutes a comprehensive interpretation of the former that happens to be shared by members of a religious tradition or subtradition for a given epoch of its history, on the other.[23] The principal defining characteristic of the religion as a whole, therefore, is less its doctrines or beliefs, particularly as they are elaborated by a given thinker or subtradition, than its primary language: the core system of concrete symbols—above all, the central or foundational stories—that the varieties of the religion share in common.

The core system of symbols is what determines the overall perspective shared in common by the variety of followers of a religion; depending on how they relate to the core system, it is what makes an insider an insider. That is to say, what makes an insider an insider and different from all outsiders is his having come to interpret the world and his experience in terms of a specific system of symbols—words, images, stories, institutions, behaviors—constituting a quite specific and elaborate language. The system of symbols becomes in certain fundamental respects the insider's mental home—certainly her spiritual home. It lies not at the forefront of her mind, as it does for outsiders looking on, but at the back or foundation of her mind. She dwells within that system of symbols. From within it, she attends to the realities it symbolizes while she is involved in specifically religious activities such as worship. Also, from within it, she relates to the things, events, and persons of her everyday life. She *attends from* the system of symbols *subsidiarily* while she *focally attends to* their meaning, on the one hand, and her mundane activities, on the other.[24] Thereby it colors her world, gives life a sense of purpose and place, and shapes her sense of what is possible and appropriate. As Clifford Geertz puts it,

> The major characteristic of religious beliefs as opposed to other sorts of beliefs, ideological, philosophical, scientific, or commonsensical, is that they are regarded as being not conclusions from experience—from deepened social awareness, from reflective speculation and logical analysis, from empirical observation and hypothesis testing, or from matriculation in the school of hard knocks—but as being prior to it. For those who hold them, religious beliefs are not inductive, they are paradigmatic; the world, to paraphrase a formulation of Alisdair MacIntyre's, provides not evidences for their truth but illustrations of it. They are a light cast upon human life from somewhere outside it.[25]

Keeping this in mind, one could equally well say that what makes the insider an insider is her having come to interpret the world and her experience in light of certain mysteries into which she has been initiated by means of the symbolic forms making up the core of her religious tradition. These mysteries constitute the **_other world_**° into which she enters while engaging in religious practice, a symbolically mediated world.

In the context of religious practice, the focus is shifted away from mundane matters, and participants thereby cross a certain **threshold** constituted by the system of symbols (perhaps by way of crossing the physical threshold of a house of worship or the temporal threshold of a holy day or of an auspicious time of prayer). In doing so, they leave mundane life behind and enter into the mysteries to which the symbols of their tradition refer—enter in a manner substantially akin to one's imaginative entry into a work of narrative or dramatic art. Here, too, participants do not directly attend to the symbols in the way that outsiders attend to the symbols, seeing only their surface, seeing only the mere sounds and shapes of some unknown language to which an interpreter may have provided them with some associated meanings. No, insiders instead rely on those symbols to usher them into what to them is the very presence of the _realities_° to which they point.

To an outsider it may appear that, in the context of religious practice, the insiders are attending to the symbols. This is not quite so, for experientially the symbols have in a certain respect changed: they have become transparent (or at least translucent) to their meaning. The insiders are thus attending not to the symbols as such but through them or beyond them to what they mediate. In this respect, the meaning of the symbols becomes for participants not just a conventional linguistic association passed on to them by the elders of their tradition (unless the tradition has for some reason become dead); rather, it comes to be experienced by them as an awesome _reality_° to be encountered and participated in—akin to the way we encounter and become directly acquainted with the characters in a theatrical drama in which we allow ourselves to be caught up. This change in the very appearance and experienced texture of the symbols as one crosses the threshold may be called the **threshold effect**.

Among a tradition's symbols are what an outsider finds strange, even alien about the tradition. They are the things on which the outsider's attention usually remains fixed and which he finds fascinating and/or repulsive, like the hieroglyphs of an unknown language. His awareness of the symbols is of a _focal_ nature. But the insider's attention, to the contrary, is not directed focally _at_ these symbols at all; often she is oblivious of them and their apparent strangeness to the outsider because they are for her so familiar, so much a part of her being. Her awareness of them is primarily of a _subsidiary nature_, for she is attending _from_ them to the horizons of meaning and living they open up as she comes to dwell in them.

The threshold effect is in large measure this very difference between attending to religious symbols and attending from them. The threshold effect is *the change that comes to be experienced as one crosses the threshold, as one comes to attend from the symbols and dwell within them.* To cross this threshold is to be granted entry into the other world made accessible by the system of symbols in question. Although the threshold effect is experienced quite consciously by an adult convert to a tradition, the effect is often taken completely for granted by persons who grow up in the tradition, causing them to find it strange that outsiders do not recognize the meanings that seem so obvious to them. For the outsider the meaning of the symbols is puzzling and alien; they appear opaque; one cannot get past their surface appearance, as it were. But for the insider they become (at least from time to time) more or less transparent; they become **presentative**, ushering insiders into an experience of what is believed and felt to be the very *presence* of what they signify. Instead of being mere representations of something absent and elsewhere, they become presentations of it, or at least intimations of its presence.[26]

Thus far we have spoken as if all the varieties of a single tradition shared a single perspective. Strictly speaking, that is far from true, although there is a sense in which it is true. That it is true is more something evident to outsiders who are free from preoccupation with the nuances that distinguish one variety from another that often seem so important to insiders. But insofar as there are significant varieties of the tradition, there will of course be further differentiation of perspectives. How shall we understand and be prepared to empathize with these differences? Some of the differentiation may be due to variations in the primary language between varieties—that is, when a sectarian branch recognizes as scripture (or as something almost as important as scripture) writings that other subtraditions do not, or when scriptures are translated into an entirely new language, opening up novel interpretations that would have previously seemed implausible. A good deal of the variation, however, will be *due to different readings of the same scriptures*, different interpretations or different employments of the same system of symbols. The range and sorts of interpretation that emerge will be due to a host of factors: in part to the specific ambiguities of the symbols and the possibility of emphasizing certain passages of a common scripture more than others—which emphasis lends a certain orientation to the resulting interpretation, but not simply that. They will in part also be *due to the different specific ways of being religious being pursued by those doing the interpreting and emphasis*, for each way leads its participants to take up and interpret the system of symbols in a manner characteristic of that generic way. In that sense, each generic way tends to have (or be) a distinctive **hermeneutic**, a distinctive approach to interpretation. In principle, each begins with the same text—that is, same stories, same scripture, same core set of symbols—shared by the other ways but approaches it in terms of its ability to "speak" to the specific existential needs that motivate that way. As a result, each finds the text "saying" somewhat different things; each finds different portions of the text more powerfully addressing its peculiar needs; and each finds highlighted different aspects of the *ultimate reality* disclosed through the text. The specific hermeneutical orientation of each of the six ways will be taken up in Chapter 3.

Depending on the particular nature of a given system of symbols (and its development at any given stage), the hermeneutical approach of one way of being religious may find that system of symbols much more open to and directly addressing the kinds of concerns that that way has, whereas the hermeneutical approach of other ways may find the system less open and less directly addressed to their concerns. The precedent of previous interpretations will play an important role in how open or closed these approaches may find the system of symbols—for example, how definitive the previous interpretations are recognized to be as well as how open they are to other possible readings of the same texts. Nevertheless, what any one interpreter finds will be influenced by the specific existential needs she brings to the text, which will have oriented her more toward one way of being religious than another.

Persons long occupied with a single way of being religious within a given tradition will often not be cognizant of, or open to, other ways of interpreting its system of symbols than the way to which they are accustomed. The simple suggestion that there might be other legitimate ways of interpreting them may be met with suspicion, if not hostility. In other words, the respect in which a system of symbols allows for this diversity in interpretation is not necessarily obvious to insiders, for they may regard alternative interpretations with little tolerance and simply dismiss them as wrong. Here is where the politics of empathetic comparative study become difficult, for it is important to retain the confidence and trust of one's informants. One useful guide is to take (and subsequently represent) the informant's views as being no less closed and no more open to other interpretations than in fact it is. This will in the end, of course, require learning the extent and prevalence of other interpretations and, along the way, how closed or open the informant is toward them. A further, important factor to notice is the way one's own perhaps unconscious tendency to identify with one way of being religious more readily than another may bias one's empathetic investigation of a tradition so as to favor one interpretation of that tradition's scripture over another. In other words, one should beware of the influence of one's own unconscious bias toward one or another way at the expense of others.

In addition to the "host of other factors" alluded to above that influence the interpretation of a system of religious symbols, one other factor or sort of factors that bears mentioning at this point is what might be called *the quality of motivation and practice characterizing the pursuit of any given way of being religious.* There are thoughtless religious people as well as thoughtful religious people, mean-spirited as well as generous-spirited, arrogant religious people as well as those with a certain caring humility, et cetera.

On reflection, it seems obvious that *any* religious tradition and any religious practice (whether traditional or nontraditional) can be taken up in thoughtful ways and in thoughtless ways, in wisdom and in superstition, in compassionate ways and in spiteful ways, with humanity and with inhumanity, in psychological health and in psychological pathology, in generosity of spirit and in insistent legalism, in a sincere quest for personal growth and in outward compliance for ulterior motives, with authenticity or inauthenticity. As Hans Küng has written,

> Certainly religions can be authoritarian, tyrannical and reactionary and all too often were so in the past: they can produce anxiety, narrow-mindedness, intolerance, injustice, frustration and social isolation; they can legitimate and inspire immorality, social abuses and wars in a people or between peoples. But religions can also have liberating effects, oriented on the future and beneficial to human beings, and indeed often have had. They can disseminate trust in life, generosity, tolerance, solidarity, creativity and social commitment, and can encourage spiritual renewal, social reforms and world peace.[27]

Consequently, a good working assumption to make in this respect is that, as far as common sense is concerned,[28] no specific religious practice *as such* (e.g., a Roman Catholic Mass, Buddhist *vipassana* meditation, Tlingit shaman soul journeying, or an Orthodox Jewish session of Talmud study) is altogether worthy either of respect or of disrespect. The quality of a particular given instance of that practice may be either virtuous or not or some of both. Whether it is virtuous or not depends not upon the practice as such—or at least not ordinarily upon the practice or upon its origin—*but upon the way it is taken up by people and lived.* Criteria of the merit of a practice can usually be found within the tradition itself—which interestingly often parallel criteria that may be found for similar phenomena within other traditions. Accordingly, in seeking to comprehend the meaning of specific religious practices, one should try to find a way of understanding them that gives the tradition and the practice in question the benefit of doubt, a way that might subsequently be confirmed by thoughtful insiders' recognition. Thus one should always try to make sense of them in a way that allows for them being taken up in thoughtful, authentic ways—without ignoring or failing to note inauthentic, unhealthy, and morally disreputable expressions.

Ideally a religious tradition will cultivate in its followers specific virtues and excellences in its practices, but this is by no means a necessity. Some virtues may be specific, if not unique, to the tradition. As well, some vices may be specifically, if not uniquely, identified by a tradition. However, as Chapter 5 will show, certain virtues and vices correlate with the generic ways of being religious, and they do so in a way that remains remarkably constant from one tradition to another. The extent to which any given representative of a tradition exhibits virtues and/or vices therefore hinges less on the specific tradition he follows than on how the tradition is taken up and interpreted by that representative. More specifically, it hinges on the attitude, or quality of motivation, with which he has taken it up and interpreted it. This attitude may very well be influenced by the precedent of previous interpretations, but again there is no necessity. Moral paragons can show up in almost any tradition, as can moral monsters, and everything in between. The point is that the attitude depends crucially upon the person. There is potential virtue to be realized in each tradition and in each way of being religious, as well as potential vice. Any one of the six ways of being religious in any tradition may be taken up thoughtfully or thoughtlessly, mean-spiritedly or generously, arrogantly or with a spirit of caring humility.

A WAY OF BEING RELIGIOUS GENERICALLY CONSIDERED

It is appropriate now to sum up what a generic way of being religious is.

As far as this book is concerned, a **way of being religious** is one characteristic manner and pattern among others of drawing near to and coming into right or appropriate relationship with *ultimate reality°*. Differently put, it is one way among others of going about entering into a religion's *other world°*—in the light of which the mundane world is believed to be put in proper perspective— and of participating in its *central mysteries°*.

A way of being religious is a generic type: it does not itself fully characterize any actual religious phenomenon or practice. In this respect it is like the generic category "mammal." If you go to the zoo to see a mammal, you will never find one as such. Of course you will see many mammals, but not apart from being differentiated according to a certain species and geographic location. So also, you will never find an example of the way of sacred rite as such. Rather, you will only find particular expressions of Christianity's sacred rituals, Hinduism's sacred rituals, and so forth (each differentiated to some extent by geography, culture, and historical circumstance)—yet which, generically considered, will have certain features in common.

A way of being religious is thus an abstraction, an abstract category, derived from certain recurrent patterns that show up in the comparative study of religious traditions. A way does not correspond to what makes a religion the specific religion it happens to be (though indirectly a particular religion might favor and place primary emphasis on one way of being religious more than others). Hence the differences between the six ways are not to be confused with differences between specific religions or differences between different conceptions of *ultimate reality°*. Instead, each way appears to correspond to certain universal, generic possibilities for carrying on religious life in any religious tradition (unless circumstances discourage or prevent the way's emergence within that tradition).

The ways are not mutually exclusive. More or less pure examples of each way unmixed with characteristic features of other ways can often be found (though not in just any religious tradition). At times sectarian expressions of a tradition will exemplify what appears to be an exclusive emphasis on a single way, in such a manner that other ways are rejected as inferior, inauthentic, or

even heretical. Contrariwise, what might be called a **catholic** expression of a tradition is one that encompasses or generously tolerates, within the boundaries of
acceptability, manifestations of most all of them. Not infrequently, individuals
within a single tradition may pursue more than one way of being religious within that tradition. And sometimes religious practices will incorporate features of
more than one way so that the features of one way shade imperceptibly into the
features of another, so much so that the two ways in such instances are virtually
indistinguishable. It may help to remember that clarity of distinction between the
categories is a product of abstraction from comparative study, which is always to
some extent selective and artificial. In the actual expressions of particular religious traditions, the relevant ways of being religious will not often be found to
be so distinct.

Considered unto themselves, the ways may be distinguished in terms of five
factors. First, they each employ a characteristic mode of approach to the *ultimate
reality^p*: sacred rites, right action, fervent devotion, shamanic mediation, ascetic
and meditative disciplines, and rational dialectical inquiry. However, though one
way thus concentrates on ritual, another on deeds, and a third on reasoning, the
pursuit of any way may involve each of these elements. Where they differ is in
the peculiar way in which they place emphasis upon this element as the central
or primary way of drawing near the *ultimate reality^p* and coming into right relationship to it. Second, each way addresses itself more directly than the others to a
certain aspect of the problem of meaning: namely, characteristic problematic situations in life that in one way or another seem to distance or alienate one from *ultimate reality^p*, which is taken to be the ground and source of life's meaning and
purpose. Differently put, each way most directly addresses certain existential
needs or motivations, which result in their attracting some people and not others.
Third, each gives rise to a characteristic hermeneutic (or type of hermeneutic), a
certain way of taking up and interpreting the symbol system (especially the stories and scriptures) that constitutes the core of a particular religion. As a result,
each tends to highlight and emphasize certain characteristic features more than
others of the *ultimate reality^p* to which those symbols purport to give access.
Fourth, something not mentioned before, each way gives rise to certain characteristic social structures supporting its distinctive approach to *ultimate reality^p*. This
will be discussed more fully in what follows, but to anticipate a little, the way of
sacred rite gives rise to the social roles of priest and acolyte; right action to the
roles of moral teacher, moral reformer, and moral exemplar; devotion to the roles
of pastor, charismatic preacher, and devotee; shamanic mediation to the roles of
shaman, prophet-oracle, wonder worker, and visionary; mystical quest to the roles
of mystic, spiritual master, spiritual hermit, and monk; and reasoned inquiry to
the roles of sage, theologian, philosopher, and student. So also, characteristic social institutions are generated: the way of sacred rite gives rise to temples, sacramental churches, and related sacerdotal institutions; right action to legal and
judicial institutions, alternative communities, and movements of moral and social

reform; devotion to intimate and informal communal gatherings that provide emotional support and fellowship for its members; shamanic mediation to shamanic guilds and informal charismatic gatherings; mystical quest to monastic-like institutions, and reasoned inquiry to seminaries and academies. Fifth, each way appears to have certain characteristic virtues and vices associated with it. More specifically, each way has a certain liability to degenerate in characteristic ways. It is these characteristic vices that representatives of other ways of being religious are usually quickest to point out and occasionally use as stereotypical caricatures in criticism of those ways. Thus the way of sacred rite can degenerate, for example, into empty formalism and the way of right action into legalism; the way of devotion can degenerate into sentimentalism and the way of shamanic mediation into black magic or charlatanism; the way of mystical quest can degenerate into quietism and the way of reasoned inquiry into pedantry. There is no necessity that any of the ways degenerates in these respects, for within each there is the possibility for renewal and for characteristic noble and virtuous expressions. The potential for virtue and for vice in each way will be explored at length in Chapter 5.

COMMON SENSE IN RELIGION

The framework of generic ways of being religious is a hypothesis, an interpretive hypothesis. It holds that there exist different ways of taking up and embodying (almost) any given religious tradition, different ways of interpreting the stories and symbols that constitute the primary language of that tradition. Differently put, the hypothesis is that within any major tradition there are a plurality of possible ways participants go about (or might go about) getting in touch with, and attaining at-onement with, what that tradition takes to be *ultimate reality*[P]. It maintains that these ways are recognizably similar across different cultures and traditions. So much are they evident that they appear to manifest generic possibilities for carrying on religious life—indeed, a finite set of generic possibilities built into the human condition.

If this is so, then the framework of generic ways of being religious provides a basis for recognizing what might be called **religious common sense**. This is to say, it points to a basis of common sense considerations, relatively independent of the *theological*[P] considerations (considerations relating to the core system of symbols) that divide one tradition from another, a basis on which many of the differences between religious viewpoints and practices can be mutually understood, allowed for, handled amicably, and in some cases reconciled. Common sense here does not mean commonplace ideas and truisms that a given group of religious people happen to hold about religion. Rather, the term refers to aspects of the common human condition with regard to religious belief and practice that are fairly readily discoverable by almost anyone in any tradition who has a modicum of thoughtful sensitivity, curiosity, open-mindedness, and empathy. Being generic, these commonsense considerations have a certain independence from the specifics of any given religious tradition.

Yet they are not the sort of things that outsiders to any religious practice are likely to notice, for they pertain to forms of religious practice that recur from one religious tradition to the next and only infrequently outside those traditions. Recognition of these considerations is the fruit of thinking generically about religion.

The framework thus calls attention to a basis for making religious sense in common among persons who differ religiously from each other. It points out how religious people have a lot more in common than it may at first appear. With the framework, insiders who identify primarily with one way of being religious should be able to understand and appreciate why other insiders from the same religion might identify with a quite different way of being religious and still be worshiping the same *ultimate reality*[p]. With the framework as well, insiders who identify primarily with one way of being religious should be able to understand and appreciate much of the religious life of insiders from another religious tradition who identify primarily with the same generic way of being religious, even though they hold quite different fundamental beliefs about *ultimate reality*[p].

Chapter 5 will explain at some length how the framework implies a commonsense basis for evaluating the quality of practice within each of the ways of being religious. Much of what insiders judge regarding noble expression and degeneration, virtue and vice, in the practice of any one way can be sorted out on this basis. It accounts for why assessments of quality for one way should be kept distinct from assessments of quality for other ways. In other words, what is good for sacred rite is not necessarily something good for devotion or mystical quest, and what is bad for shamanic mediation is not necessarily something bad for right action or wisdom. An understanding of these matters is directly relevant not only to helping people relate to others who differ from themselves religiously but also to helping people grow and mature in their own religious life. As well, by clarifying the conditions under which a practice within a given way of being religious moves between excellence and degeneration, such understanding is directly relevant to maintaining the health and well-being of a religious tradition. Thinking generically about ways of being religious in this respect contributes directly to the achievement of a commonsense practical wisdom.

The six generic ways point to a common basis of appeal in handling religious differences, criticizing and reforming religious practice, and generally helping people find meaning and maturity in their religious lives, a commonsense basis alongside and complementary to the specific norms of a religion embodied in authoritative scripture and tradition. The framework of the six ways predicts that in every tradition it is possible to find religious common sense more or less operative.

CHAPTER SUMMARY

This chapter is devoted to the assumptions and theoretical considerations that lie behind the framework of ways of being religious. The framework assumes the context of the modern academic study of religion and, within that context, phenomenology of religion in particular. That context, as far as this book is concerned, aims to promote and carry on an *objective* study of religious phenomena in the round, a study that fuses objectivity (a meaning of objectivity appropriate to the study of religion) and empathy. The point is to do justice to religious phenomena in the round, taking seriously all relevant perspectives onto them, above all, the perspective(s) of insiders. To accomplish this task, a relatively neutral framework of generic categories must be devised and employed, in which comparative studies can proceed without privileging the ultimate convictions of one tradition over another.

A working definition of religion is given as a system of symbols (e.g., words and gestures, stories and practices, objects and places) that participants use to draw near to, and come into right or appropriate relationship with, what they deem to be ultimate reality. The phrase *ultimate reality^p* thus becomes a placeholder or variable standing for whatever the people of a given tradition take to be the ultimate ground of meaning and purpose in life. Insofar as the distinctive function of religion is to draw near to *ultimate reality^p*, religion in general presupposes a certain distance from or disrelationship with *ultimate reality^p*. That disrelationship is identified as the problem of meaning. Each of the ways of being religious in effect address a different aspect of the problem of meaning—which helps account for why some people (when they have the option) are drawn to one way rather than another.

What primarily distinguishes religious traditions from each other are their core systems of symbols, each of which includes a set of sacred stories and, if the tradition is a literate one, a canonical scripture (or set of scriptures). Systems of religious symbols inherently have multiple meanings and layers of meaning, allowing for multiple interpretations—within certain limits. Different meanings disclose themselves to different hermeneutical orientations. One subtradition differs from another often on the basis of a different hermeneutical orientation that is connected with a specific aspect of the problem of meaning and its correlative way of being religious. Further variations in interpretation and practice are due to a host of factors, but among them special note is taken of variations in quality of practice. In this respect, the worthiness of respect due a particular example of religious practice stems primarily not from the symbol system in which it resides and not from the way of being religious it exemplifies but from the way both are taken up by participants and lived out.

A generic way of being religious is one characteristic manner and pattern among others of drawing near to and coming into right or appropriate relationship with *ultimate reality^p*. It is distinguished from the other ways by its mode of approach to *ultimate reality^p*, the aspect of the problem of meaning it most directly addresses, the orientation it takes to the interpretation of the stories and scriptures of a tradition, typical forms of social structure and organization, and specific sorts of virtue and vice to which it is subject. The framework of generic ways of being religious thus identifies certain commonalities shared between religious traditions that otherwise might be profoundly opposed, especially commonalities between participants in the same generic way of being religious. These commonalities constitute a basis of religious common sense, which in turn is a basis for making sense in common between persons of differing faiths.

STUDY QUESTIONS

1. Discuss the need for objectivity, empathy, and neutrality in the study of religion. Clarify what sense of objectivity is appropriate and what is not. Similarly, clarify what sense of neutrality is appropriate and what is not. To what extent are objectivity, empathy, and neutrality each realistically possible or approachable? Specifically, what does empathy consist of?

2. In connection with question 1, explore in discussion what it means to think generically about religion—that is, about the generic features of religious life as distinct from features specific to individual traditions.

3. Explore in discussion the author's definition of the nature of religion. How does it align or fail to align with other definitions you may be familiar with? To what extent does it illuminate what goes on in actual religious practice and activity? Explore how it applies to specific examples.

4. Discuss the idea of the problem of meaning as the problem religion is specifically designed to address. Explore the different aspects of the problem of meaning and how each correlates with a different way of being religious. How do they differ from each other? Do the different aspects help explain why some people are drawn to one sort of religious tradition rather than another?

5. Explore in discussion the author's idea of the *threshold effect*—the respect in which symbols change in their appearance and texture as one shifts from attending to them focally from the outside to attending from them subsidiarily on the inside. To what extent does this describe what you are familiar with in this kind of experience? Why is it important to recognize the threshold effect in the effort to empathize with a religious practice very different from what you may be familiar with?

6. Explore in discussion the idea that religions are systems of symbols open to multiple interpretations—not as a liability giving rise to disagreement but as an asset giving rise to a richness of many complementary meanings. Can you think of examples that illustrate the idea?

7. Explore in discussion the implications of the idea of religious common sense that is posed in this chapter—namely, that there is a basis for mutual recognition of commonality between persons of divergent religious faith (especially between participants in the same generic way of being religious). Insofar as there is such a thing, what possibilities does it open up for interreligious dialogue and cooperation?

FOR FURTHER READING

Recommended articles in the *Encyclopedia of Religion,* edited by Mircea Eliade (New York: Macmillan, 1987) include: *Phenomenology of Religion; Religion; Religion, Study of; Problem of Evil; Suffering; Scripture;* and *Symbolism.*

Two good general discussions of generic features of religious life are William Calloley Tremmel, *Religion: What Is It?,* 2nd ed. (New York: Holt, Rinehart and Winston, 1984), and Roger Schmidt, *Exploring Religion,* 2nd ed. (Belmont, CA: Wadsworth, 1988). A good, brief overview of the different academic approaches to the study of religion is found in Frederick J. Streng, *Understanding Religious Life,* 3rd ed. (Belmont, CA: Wadsworth, 1985), Part 3. Much more thorough coverage is found in E. J. Sharpe, *Comparative Religion: A History* (London: Duckworth, 1975). An excellent anthology of representative examples of different orientations in phenomenology of religion can be found in Sumner B. Twiss and Walter H. Conser, Jr., eds., *Experience of the Sacred: Readings in the Phenomenology of Religion* (Hanover, NH: Brown University Press/University Press of New England, 1992).

Readers interested in reflecting on the problem of meaning are encouraged to read Clifford Geertz's classic essay, "Religion as a Cultural System," in his *The Interpretation of Cultures* (New York: Basic Books, 1973). It is also discussed in the books by Tremmel and Schmidt above. Geertz's essay on the task of empathy is also very good: "'From the Native's Point of View': On the Nature of Anthropological Understanding," in his *Local Knowledge: Further Essays in Interpretive Anthropology* (New York: Basic Books, 1983). For further clarification on the nature of phenomenological understanding and the possibility of neutrality, see Dale Cannon, "Having Faith, Being Neutral, and Doing Justice: Toward a Paradigm of Responsibility in the Comparative Study of Religion," *Method and Theory in the Study of Religion* 5:2 (1993), 155–176.

NOTES

1. For a fuller critique of this motion of objectivity see Dale W. Cannon, "The 'Primitive'/'Civilized' Opposition and the Modern Notion of Objectivity: A Linkage," *PRE/TEXT: An Interdisciplinary Journal of Rhetoric* 2 (Spring-Fall, 1981), pp. 151–171.

2. See the article "Phenomenology of Religion" in the *Encyclopedia of Religion,* ed. Mircea Eliade (New York: Macmillan, 1987); and *The Experience of the Sacred: Readings in the Phenomenology of Religion,* ed. Sumner B. Twiss and William H. Conser, Jr. (Hanover, NH: Brown University Press/University Press of New England, 1992). The approach taken here falls into the second of the three schools of phenomenology of religion discussed by Twiss and Conser: essentialist, historico-typological, and existential-hermeneutical. It has important affinities with the third, however, especially in its assumption that all human experience is mediated by language and symbolic systems.

3. See W. Brede Kristensen, *The Meaning of Religion: Lectures in the Phenomenology of Religion,* trans. John B. Carman (The Hague: Nijhoff, 1960); and Mircea Eliade, *Patterns in Comparative Religion,* trans. Rosemary Sheed (New York: Sheed and Ward, 1958; first published 1949). It should be said that Eliade (at least in his later work) refrained from identifying his own work as phenomenology of religion in favor of "history of religions."

4. For more on the process involved in empathy, see note 26 below.

5. The need for neutrality and empathy to enable us to learn and develop our thinking through conversation with persons with whom we disagree is brought out well by Donald Shriver in the following words: "Mind changing has about it a quality of moral discipline

and moral humility. It is hard for all parties to any human conflict, because in conflict intellectual positions tend to harden, unless one brings to the conflict a steady, stubborn *humility* that expects to learn from people of different persuasions from one's own." Donald W. Shriver, Jr., "From Island to Continent: Is There Room in American Politics for Both Fundamentalists and Their Enemies?" *The Fundamentalist Phenomenon*, ed. Norman J. Cohen (Grand Rapids, MI: Eerdmans, 1990), p. 207.

A fuller justification and elaboration of the specific sense of neutrality here alluded to is found in my essay "Having Faith, Being Neutral, and Doing Justice: toward a Paradigm of Responsibility in the Comparative Study of Religion," *Method and Theory in the Study of Religion* 5:2 (1993), 155–176.

6. I am here following the Pin-Yin system of transliteration, rather than the Wade-Giles system.

7. See Frederick J. Steng, *Understanding Religious Life*, 3rd ed. (Belmont, CA: Wadsworth, 1985), pp. 2–3. There Streng defines religion as "a means to ultimate transformation."

8. Celestial Seasonings Sleepytime Herb Tea, © 1975.

9. Beware of assuming that the phrasing of these generic features of religion can be straightforwardly translated into the language of specific traditions. Some traditions would object. For example, certain philosophical expressions of Mahayana Buddhism contend that what is conventionally taken to be the "meaning" of something (as in the phrase "the meaning of life") in the ultimate perspective makes no sense and does not exist. They say very similar things about the notion of "reality" as if "ultimate reality" referred to some special cosmic "being" or "thing" lying beyond appearances. I do not wish to dispute these contentions. Nor do I wish to concede simply that Buddhists of this persuasion have no notion of ultimate reality, that Buddhism isn't concerned with drawing near to and coming into right relationship with *ultimate reality* as they conceive of it, or that they do not seek an ultimate ground for meaning and purpose in life. Rather, I wish first of all to place Mahayana Buddhist rhetoric alongside the theological and philosophical rhetoric of other religious traditions and attempt to make some generalizations about them all in a kind of neutral, generic metalanguage. Mahayana Buddhist rhetoric is hardly ever what it appears to be on the surface. It is designed to usher a person into an intuitive grasp of what Mahayana Buddhists take to be the ultimate and true perspective onto things. Articulating what is evident to that perspective in ordinary, mundane language (no matter how carefully nuanced philosophically) is notoriously difficult, and perhaps finally impossible. In that perspective, for example, it is said that things have no self-being, no autonomous being whatsoever; that all things are characterized by "emptiness," which as far as I am able to understand it is not the absence of meaning but a meaningfulness that transcends every conventional and statable sense of meaningfulness. My point in laboring this example is that, properly qualified, these Mahayana Buddhists have a conception of *ultimate reality* no less than do persons in other religious traditions, but it is not to be identified with some conventional notion of reality, let alone what some other traditions take "ultimate reality" to be. The same holds true for what they have to say about "meaning" and "meaningfulness."

10. Clifford Geertz, *Islam Observed* (Chicago, IL: University of Chicago Press, 1968), p. 97.

11. Robert S. Paul, *The Atonement and the Sacraments* (London: Hodder and Stoughton, 1961), pp. 17–32.

12. For an overview of the problem of definition and some of the varieties, see Ronald R. Cavanagh, "The Term *Religion*" and "Religion as a Field of Study" in *Introduction to the Study of Religion*, ed. T. William Hall (New York: Harper and Row, 1978), pp. 4–29. See also Winston L. King, "Religion," *Encyclopedia of Religion*, Vol. 12, ed. Mircea Eliade (New York: Macmillan, 1987), pp. 282–293. For a fuller and more carefully nuanced critical discussion, see Robert D. Baird, *Category Formation and the History of Religions* (The Hague: Mouton, 1971), especially pp. 1–27.

13. See Clifford Geertz, "Religion as a Cultural System," in his *The Interpretation of Cultures* (New York: Basic Books, 1973), pp. 100–108.

14. See note 9 above.

15. Here and elsewhere in what follows, words and phrases that are italicized and followed by a small circle are meant, like "*ultimate reality°*," to be variables standing in for concepts specific to religious traditions.

16. Hans Küng, *Global Responsibility: In Search of a New World Ethic*, trans. John Bowden (New York: Crossroad, 1991), pp. 60, 53f. Reprinted by permission of the publisher.

17. Geertz, "Religion as a Cultural System," *op. cit.*, p. 122.

18. Ibid., pp. 91–94.

19. Quoted by Clifford Geertz *ibid.*, p. 87, my emphasis. The original is in George Santayana, *Reason in Religion*, The Life of Reason, Vol. 3 (New York: Dover Publications, 1982/1905), pp. 5–6.

20. Charles Davis, *Temptations of Religion* (New York: Harper and Row, 1973), pp. 22, 29.

21. There is a major controversy going on in certain academic circles as to whether "true" mystical experience transcends all symbolic mediation and conditioning or not. One of the best overviews of the controversy is Bernard McGinn, "Theoretical Foundations: The Modern Study of Mysticism," an appendix to his *The Foundations of Mysticism,* Vol. 1 of *The Presence of God: A History of Christian Mysticism* (New York: Crossroad, 1991), pp. 265–343. See especially pp. 314–326. I take the position that all mystical experience insofar as it is religious is in some sense necessarily so mediated or conditioned. Among the most important arguments to the contrary of the position I take here are found in Robert K. Forman, ed., *The Problem of Pure Consciousness* (New York: Oxford University Press, 1990).

   In this matter I follow Clifford Geertz's reasoning ("Religion as a Cultural System," *op. cit.*, p. 98): "For what else do we mean by saying that a particular mood of awe is religious and not secular, except that it springs from entertaining a conception of all-pervading vitality like mana and not from a visit to the Grand Canyon? Or that a particular case of asceticism is an example of a religious motivation, except that it is directed toward the achievement of an unconditioned end like nirvana and not a conditioned one like weight-reduction? . . . A man can indeed be said to be 'religious' about golf, but not merely if he pursues it with passion and plays it on Sundays: he must also see it as symbolic of some transcendent truths. And the pubescent boy gazing soulfully into the eyes of the pubescent girl in a William Steig cartoon and murmuring, 'There is something about you, Ethel, which gives me a sort of religious feeling,' is, like most adolescents, confused." In any case, it is because religious experience is symbolically mediated that empathetic investigation is called for in religious studies. Symbolic mediation constitutes the difference in points of view that calls for empathy to be comprehended.

22. In this I follow the hermeneutical reflections of Paul Ricoeur. For a summary discussion of Ricoeur's views on this subject, see David E. Klemm, *The Hermeneutical Theory of Paul Ricoeur: A Constructive Analysis* (Lewisburg, PA: Bucknell University Press; distributed by Associated University Presses of East Brunswick, NJ, 1983), pp. 62–66.

23. Hans Küng, *Global Responsibility, op. cit.*, p. 125. Küng here draws upon the ideas of historian of science Thomas Kuhn in developing this distinction from the "abiding substance" and the "changing paradigms" to illuminate the history of Christianity.

24. This distinction between *attending from* and *attending to* and between *subsidiary* and *focal* is developed by the philosopher Michael Polanyi in a number of his writings. See especially Michael Polanyi, *The Tacit Dimension* (Garden City, NY: Anchor Doubleday, 1966), pp. 9–25.

25. Geertz, "Religion as a Cultural System," *op. cit.,* p. 98.

26. Anyone who wishes to enter a tradition empathetically in order to understand it needs to be aware of the crucial role of the threshold effect. Because a tradition's system of

symbols is what determines the overall perspective shared by the insiders of a given tradition, it is precisely what an outsider who may wish to empathize with them must also temporarily in an act of imagination come to dwell in and subsidiarily attend from. We too must begin to experience in our imagination the threshold effect if we are to become acquainted with the insiders' perspective and the things to which they testify. In Samuel Taylor Coleridge's apt phrase, we must "willingly suspend our disbelief" and imaginatively project ourselves into that other world *as if* we were insiders. (The phrase, "willingly suspend one's disbelief" is from Samuel Taylor Coleridge, *Biographia Literaria*, ch. XIV, reproduced in *Romantic Poetry and Prose*, edited by Harold Bloom and Lionel Trilling [New York: Oxford University Press, 1973], p. 645.) The task of empathy here is not a matter of putting ourselves into the other persons' skins, achieving some inner correspondence of spirit with them, or swimming in the stream of their experience; rather is it a matter of "figur[ing] out what the devil they think they are up to" as they involve themselves with these symbolic forms. (See Clifford Geertz, "From the Native's Point of View: On the Nature of Anthropological Understanding," in his *Local Knowledge: Essays in Interpretive Anthropology* [New York: Basic Books, 1974], pp. 55–70.) Phenomenological empathy is a matter of learning the symbolic forms within their specific native context well enough to "try them on for size"—as an actor might find his way into a new character role—with the goal of finding a fit well enough to make coherent sense and merit the recognition of accredited insiders. It is very much like learning a foreign language. Recall that foreign words for whom the foreign language is an unknown tongue are sounds and shapes only; one's attention is focused on the surface, and one is only aware of patterned sounds or visual shapes. But as one comes to understand them a bit more, the words intimate more and more meaning; they become translucent as it were. Then as one advances to fluency, the words become completely transparent, so much so that one may be entirely unaware in a focal sense of the sounds and shapes, which have come to figure wholly subsidiarily in one's understanding. The same holds true in learning the "language" of a system of religious symbols.

27. Hans Küng, *Global Responsibility, op. cit.*, p. 46.

28. Members of the specific religious tradition in which these practices are found may have reasons specific to their tradition to respect certain traditional practices regardless of the quality with which they are carried out. But these reasons would not in that respect constitute commonsense considerations.

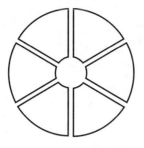

CHAPTER 3

DIFFERENT WAYS
OF BEING
RELIGIOUS

MAKING SENSE OF THE
DIFFERENT GENERIC WAYS

Each of the six ways of being religious is a different, generic way of drawing near to *ultimate reality*ᴾ. Considered within a single religious tradition, they are different angles of approach to the same *ultimate reality*ᴾ. What the ways amount to concretely, however, is given only in terms of the system of symbols making up a particular religious tradition. By itself, each is an abstract sketch, a skeletal structure, apart from the flesh and blood of actual practice within a living tradition of religious life.

The formulations offered herein are the product of a systematic effort to discover generic structures and differentiate them from what is specific to particular religious traditions and their systems of symbols. More specifically, these formulations are focused on generic structures in things people *do* in carrying on religious life rather than in what they believe. It is not that what they believe is unimportant, not at all. And what people believe about *ultimate reality*ᴾ will certainly influence and structure what they do. But what they believe is clearly connected with and a part of a specific system of symbols, which in turn is usually linked in a historical way with certain other specific systems of symbols, and is for that reason less likely to be something generic to human religiousness. So features have been systematically factored out of the formulations of each way of being religious that are specific to particular religious traditions and especially features deriving from specific convictions as to the nature of *ultimate reality°*. Such beliefs or convictions shall be called **theological°** convictions, whether they refer to *ultimate reality°* in a theistic manner as God or Gods, or in a non-theistic manner as in the Buddhist concept of *nirvāṇa* or the conceptions of the *Dao* in Confucianism and Daoism. At a later point we will discuss how specific theological convictions combine with any one way of being religious to produce quite different, distinctive expressions of that way of being religious in the different traditions. But in order to grasp the generic ways themselves, the categories employed need to be separated from *theological°* considerations.[1] To fail to keep these two things distinct is to commit a variety of what Alfred North Whitehead called "the fallacy of misplaced concreteness."[2]

In seeking to comprehend what follows, readers should take care to give more weight to the description given than to associations that the name of the way may already seem to have. Not just any religious ritual amounts to the way of sacred rite; nor is any instance of religious devotion the way of devotion, nor any intellectual study of scripture and tradition the way of reasoned inquiry, and so forth. Elements of ritual, devotion, and study, for instance, may be found in connection with *each* of the six ways. So also some concern with right behavior, apparent "supernatural" phenomena, and meditation can occur with *any* of the ways. The simple presence of one of these elements or concerns does not distinguish one of the ways from the others. *Only when they become a major focus and preoccupation of religious life—that is, a primary way of getting in touch with* ultimate reality°—*do they constitute an instance of a way of being religious.* So also, readers should endeavor not to confuse with the descriptions offered here notions of religious ritual, shamanism, mysticism, and so forth, derived from theoretical discussions of them by other scholars. Such notions may helpfully complement what is said here or they may simply confuse matters. Try using this occasion to attempt to think about the nature of these phenomena afresh from the perspective of their being generic patterns of religious life.

To readers relatively unacquainted with the diversity of religious phenomena, the general descriptions that follow may be difficult to understand without consideration of a variety of examples of each. One should not worry too much if the general sketches fail to make complete sense at this stage. A variety of examples of each way will be discussed in Chapters 4, 7, and 8. Descriptions in depth of examples from the traditions of Buddhism and Christianity may be found in Chapters 9 through 14.

Finally, to readers relatively inexperienced in empathizing with different sorts of religious orientations, some of the general descriptions may be difficult to make sense of because of a natural tendency to sympathize with certain ways and not others. That toward which we are naturally sympathetic we tend to find more intelligible and obvious. But a practice toward which we are not naturally sympathetic we will tend to find less intelligible and not obvious at all. Being well acquainted with one way of being religious within a certain tradition will not suffice to acquaint a reader with other ways within that same tradition, let alone other ways within other traditions. It will, however, make much easier the process of understanding that same way in another tradition. So, as readers gradually come to an understanding of a way they hadn't known before in a specific tradition, they will find the process of empathizing with that way in different traditions that much easier. Empathetic understanding is not simply a matter of stepping into the moccasins of a religious tradition one wishes to understand (i.e., entering its system of symbols), for each way of being religious within that tradition has, so to speak, a different style of moccasins—or, to change the metaphor, a different way of putting on and wearing the moccasins of the tradition. Empathetic understanding of ways of being religious other than those with which one naturally sympathizes—whether in one's own tradition or in another—presents a different sort of challenge than empathizing with the same way of being religious in another tradition. Some ways may be more difficult for a given reader to understand than others and they may take more time. Understanding will come, however, with patience and effort. Readers should keep this in mind as they work at stretching their empathetic capacity.

THE SIX DIFFERENT
WAYS DESCRIBED

The **way of sacred rite** centers on the use of sacred **ritual** or **rite**, as its name suggests. Yet students unacquainted with the diverse forms of sacred ritual may need to have their imagination stretched to include in their notion of ritual not only the repetition of carefully prescribed words and gestures but many other things as well, including objects specifically used in ritual: sacred images, objects, sounds (music, silence, rhythms), incense, vestments, architecture, and ornamentation; priestly roles and clerical institutions; sacred places, centers, routes, and zones of pilgrimage; sacred and auspicious times of the day, the month, the year and multiyear cycles; life cycle passages (birth, naming, puberty, adulthood, marriage, elderhood, and death); establishment and disestablishment of agreements (marriage, divorce, adoption, contracts, treaties), relationships, identities, institutions, communities, and nations; rituals of purification that acknowledge what is sacred and keep it separate from what is profane; and so forth.

Rituals can be found in every religious tradition and in virtually every subtradition, though clearly some subtraditions emphasize them more centrally and strictly than others. But just because a ritual is involved does not mean that the way of sacred rite is present. Religious ritual serves many functions: it gives a certain decorum and order to religious activities; it enables many people cooperatively to carry out complex activities that would otherwise be impossible to do in an orderly way; it provides a context of meaningful symbols that focus and orient the mind in accordance with tradition; it satisfies the need for habitual pattern so that appropriate behavior becomes second nature and the mind is free to attend to deeper meanings; and so forth. All religious rituals symbolically make reference to the *realities°* found within the *other world°* of the religion and represent some kind of acknowledgment of, interaction with, or participation in those *realities°*. But not all such rituals themselves actually constitute for participants entry into that *other world°* or direct involvement with those *realities°*. Many merely symbolize an entry or involvement—made, say, at another time, inwardly in independence of the ritual, or perhaps never seriously undertaken at all. The way of sacred rite is specifically present only when ritual itself is serving as a means, a primary means, of drawing near to and coming into right relationship to *ultimate reality°*, where symbols do not merely represent *ultimate realities°* but are *presentations* of them. That is what makes them **sacred**.

A ritual exemplifying the way of sacred rite, which we shall call a **sacramental ritual**, is not an ordinary action in the mundane course of events (though it may be similar to such actions and for its meaning draw analogically upon them). It is a symbolic or sacramental action. Strictly speaking, it is not an action in the mundane ordinary world at all. Rather, it is an action set within a religious tradition's *other world°*. The "time" of the rite is a sacred time that is not of this world: it partakes of the eternal. It is the timeless time of the central story (or stories) of the tradition. Typically, the symbols of a sacramental rite, though apparently simple, allude implicitly to whole constellations of meaning, layer upon layer. That is to say, though the rite may seem to have considerable meaning by itself, the rite has the meaning it has not abstractly but concretely in virtue of its being placed within that specific *other world°*. In this connection, recall again the quotation cited in Chapter 2, which is especially appropriate to the way of sacred rite:

> In Japan, a simple open gateway acts as a symbol to mark off the precincts of the shrine. In passing through it, one leaves behind psychologically and symbolically the humdrum, ordinary world, and enters the sacred space of the temple. After worship, one again moves through the gate to re-enter the realm of everyday life—but as a renewed person. All peoples have set aside some place to serve as a sacred place, whether it be a mountain top, a garden, or a church, so that it may represent and activate within them a Great Power—another dimension of reality. So, one is allowed time when truth, significance and worth are recognized and cultivated to be carried back into the ordinary world.[3]

Identifying which rituals exemplify the way of sacred rite and which do not may be difficult without opportunity to explore in depth how the rituals function for their participants and how they are being taken by them. A difficulty here also is that there may be a difference between theory and practice, between the official account of a ritual and what participants, perhaps inarticulately, experience. For example, Baptists, among Protestant Christians, have traditionally played down or denied the sacramental significance of their observance of Baptism.

According to official pronouncements, although Baptism is an "ordinance" required of all Christians, it is "merely an outward symbol" referring to an "inward spiritual change" that otherwise is to have taken place. Nevertheless, individual Baptists occasionally report their own Baptism and being present at the Baptism of others to be "deeply meaningful" and definitively renewing of their identity as Baptists. A somewhat similar official denial of the sacramental significance of religious ritual is found among Theravada Buddhists and Sunni Muslims, though members of these traditions too may speak of their rites in a way that suggests a sacramental significance. Nevertheless, in what follows, examples of the way of sacred rite will be drawn for the most part from traditions that recognize the sacramental significance of rituals.

More than any of the other ways, the way of sacred rite involves participants' bodies and typically makes use of symbols that address the senses holistically, invite bodily participation, and constitute an experience of perceptible beauty—lifting participants out of the ordinary and imperfect and into the extraordinary and ideal. This way calls upon great artistic talents to collaborate in the design and construction of symbolic and ritual patterns that are capable of disclosing (or at least intimating) the sublime and timeless, archetypal forms of *ultimate reality*ᵖ. More than disclosure, its purpose is to enable participants to enter holistically into the presence of these numinous forms and enable those forms to become a living presence in the lives of participants.

People who pursue the way of sacred rite seek at-onement with sacred **archetypal form**. The word *archetype* in its root meaning refers to an original model or type after which other similar things are patterned. In religion, and specifically in the way of sacred rite, an archetype or archetypal form is an ideal divine model or pattern for some aspect of human life found in the *other world*ᵖ articulated in a tradition's system of symbols.[4] It is experienced as not of this world (i.e., not of this ordinary, mundane world), but as partaking of *ultimate reality*ᵖ. That is to say, it is experienced as grounded in *ultimate reality*ᵖ, or itself an expression or manifestation of *ultimate reality*ᵖ. While it may be manifest through a particular concrete symbolization (say, a temple statue of the Buddha or the Jewish ritual of Passover), it is not itself particular and concrete but may be manifest repeatedly in different ways and settings. It presents itself as a universal ideal form or pattern that is nevertheless specific to a tradition.

In any case, the sacred archetype experienced in living sacramental ritual is not inert; it is a source of energy, vitality, and meaningful order. For participants, it is the source of their sense of propriety, a sense indistinguishably aesthetic and sacred of what is appropriate to do and what attitudes are appropriate to assume in facing the momentous and unsettling events of life. When having to take on such challenges, especially to communal life, participants seek restoration of that sense of propriety and of the rightful order and orientation to life that renewed participation in the sacred archetype brings. This is the characteristic existential need to which the way of sacred rite is addressed.

The core symbol systems of each religion conceive *ultimate reality*° in different ways, and accordingly present different sacred archetypes in the foundational stories that they tell. Indeed, the characteristic interpretive orientation or hermeneutic of the way of sacred rite is to highlight archetypes of meaningful order and vitality within a tradition's symbol system, archetypes that might be accessed through sacred ritual. The Native American Sioux tell of how White Buffalo Cow Woman in the time of yore brought the sacred pipe and the seven sacred ceremonies of their religion, through which the Sioux find access to the vital and energizing archetypes of their life as it is meant to be. Buddhists never tire of retelling the story of Siddartha Gautama's Enlightenment, and in it they find the original archetypes of their sacred ceremonies and way of life: the awakening of faith; the sight of old age, sickness, death, and the seriousness of a monk's quest; the great renunciation, the finding of a middle way between indulgence and asceticism, the classic form of meditation, the conquering of temptation, the breakthrough to *nirvāṇa*, the Buddha's compassion, the fundamentals of *Dharma* (the Buddha's teaching), and the form of showing homage to the Buddha. Christians who pursue the way of sacred rite (Eastern Orthodox, Roman Catholic, Lutheran, and Anglican) find in the Gospel accounts of Jesus (in his Life, Death, and Resurrection, and in his Second Coming, when the Kingdom of God will be fully realized) the archetypes of their life and worship, above all what is disclosed through what they call the sacraments: Baptism, Holy Communion, Confirmation (or Chrismation), Reconciliation of a Penitent, Anointing of the Sick, Marriage, and Ordination. In the sacred rituals of these traditions, the vital and energizing divine archetypes become present anew, temporal and spatial distance from them is overcome, and participants newly find themselves at-one with them.

Essentially, the way of sacred rite involves a symbolic **anamnesis** and **mimesis** of the archetypal forms: a remembering or memorializing that makes present and an imitation, reenactment, or embodiment. Specifically, it involves bodily participation in a mimesis of the sacred archetype(s) in the confidence that thereby representation will become re-*presentation*, symbol will become sacrament, and alienation from the sacred archetype will be overcome. Participants enter anew into its presence and are transformed, touched by its power to renew life and reestablish identity within the *original divine order of things*°.

The way of sacred rite is typically a communal enterprise rather than an individual one—more so than the other ways of being religious. The identities, relationships, and order it serves to establish (and renew) are typically interpersonal and social. Complex and especially hierarchical social order calls for elaborate ritual to authorize, establish, and maintain. There must be some who know well the proper rites—not only know how to perform them but are also capable of orchestrating and performing them. Even more, they must be divinely authorized to do so. This is what a **priest** or **priestess** is: a master of sacred ritual, a keeper of the rites, who is duly authorized to perform them. Acolytes are his (or her) assistants. Typical of sacred rite are well-defined religious roles and functions.

Typical as well are sacred edifices to house and provide an appropriate place for the rites to take place: temples, altars, pilgrimage sites, and shrines.

Each of the features of the way of sacred rite that have been mentioned can go awry, can fail to realize its characteristic purpose, can be misused for ulterior and egoistic motives, and so forth. When they fall short of ideal realization—in different respects and to varying degrees—we find characteristic vices to which the way of sacred rite is subject, such as meaningless ritualism, idolatry of ritual form, and clerical corruption. But the opposite potential is there too for ideal realization, and there we find virtues specific to the way of sacred rite. (Specific virtues and vices of the way of sacred rite and the other ways will be taken up in greater detail in Chapter 5.)

> Putting these different features together in a compact definition, the way of sacred rite consists of participation in the *sacred archetypal patterns*° through which *ultimate reality*° is manifest, by means of symbolic ritual enactments or presentations that enable participants repeatedly to enter their presence, attain at-onement for the moment with them, and thereby establish and renew their sense of meaningful order, identity, and propriety. It is typically communal rather than individual.

The **way of right action**, as its name suggests, is concerned with right action or behavior, both individual and communal. All religious life involves some concern for appropriate conduct, whether it be a matter of rules of discipline freely taken on, advice from a spiritual mentor, institutional regulations, basic moral principles, special obligations, or absolute imperatives. But just because concern for appropriate conduct is involved doesn't mean that the way of right action is present. The way of right action comes into play only when a certain sort of conduct in the world (which sort of conduct will depend on the tradition or subtradition) comes to be a primary way of drawing near and coming into right relationship to *ultimate reality*°—that is to say, when it becomes inwardly or spiritually imperative.

Such conduct may encompass prescribed rituals, but here the principal focus is not participation in the *sacred other world of ultimate reality*°, as is the case with the way of sacred rite, but action and behavior in the ordinary, mundane world—that is, on doing one's proper task, on playing one's role, on fulfilling one's ultimate responsibilities. Indeed, where the way of right action has primary emphasis, the focus is upon the whole of human activity—or at least all activity over which one has some control or influence—as opposed to some separate sacred sector of life. It is a matter of bringing the secular and mundane sphere of life into alignment with the sacred, of extending the dominion of the sacred, as it were, over the secular and mundane.

The way of right action thus involves a concerted effort to bring life, both individual and communal, into agreement with *the way things are ultimately supposed to be°*. What the latter is, is conceived differently in different traditions. (The interpretive orientation, or hermeneutic, of the way of right action is to pick out and emphasize those features of a tradition's symbol system that convey a sense of *how things are ultimately supposed to be°*.) It may be conceived as a transcendent, absolute imperative in opposition to the present social order, as in the divine call for justice in the prophets of ancient Israel or in the denunciation of idolatry found in the Muslim *Qur'an*. Contrariwise, it might be conceived to be immanent in the very grain of things, as is the intuitively apprehended *Dao* of heaven and earth in Daoism or the rationally apprehended *Dao* of heaven and earth in Confucianism, which in either case tends to take existing social structures for granted or works within them. Then again it may be conceived as the eternal, natural order of the universe and society, as in the *Dharma* of Hinduism with its correlative law of moral cause and effect (*karma*). It may be focused in a few abstract directives for action such as Jesus' summary of the *Torah* in the two commandments to love God and love neighbor. It might be focused in a single principle of ego-less compassion (*karuna*) for all sentient beings, as in Mahayana Buddhism. At the opposite extreme, it may be expressed in innumerable concrete expectations tied to social status, relationship, and stage of life, as in Hinduism, Confucianism, or traditional Rabbinic Judaism. Although these several visions of *the way things are ultimately supposed to be°* hardly coincide, they nonetheless significantly overlap in many areas. They all seek to bring to realize and bring to fulfillment *the intended divine order of things°* in the midst of mundane, this-worldly existence—to *be* it.

Primarily, the way of right action seeks to realize this *intended divine order°* not for the sake of attaining some ulterior good, whether in present life or in some life to come, though many will seek to do so for the sake of that good. Nor does it do so to avoid some evil consequence or threat of punishment, though again many will do so to avoid such consequences. Persons who pursue the way of right action do so primarily for the sake of that *intended divine order°*; simply because this is the way life is supposed to be lived; because this is (partly, at least) what life is for; because this fulfills (partly, at least) one's own inherent nature. They do so because not to do so is to be for this time and place not-at-one with what is believed to be *ultimate reality°* and to do so is to be for this time and place at-one with what is believed to be *ultimate reality°*. In the final analysis, then, "God's will" is to be done because it is "God's will," but also because true fulfillment for self and community is believed to be solely realized thereby. Accordingly, worse than mistaken or inappropriate involvement is indifference or no involvement at all.

The key existential motivation for the way of right action is the awareness (or anticipation) of a contradiction between the way things are and *the way things ought to be°*: perceived inequities and injustices but also legitimate needs and necessities that, if unmet, keep life (individual and communal) from realizing its inherent purpose. The motivating imperative to right action is an inwardly felt summons (whether outwardly proclaimed or not) to move from being part of the problem to being part of the solution, to help bridge the gap between the way things are and the way they ought to be, to help make things right. People who pursue the way of right action then seek to bring life, ultimately all of life, into conformity to what is deemed to be *the way things are ultimately supposed to be*ᵖ in the conviction that that realization itself will be at-onement with *ultimate reality*ᵖ and the greatest joy. Thereby mundane life will be made sacred, and earth and heaven, this world and the *other world*ᵖ, will be made one.

The way of right action operates out of the conviction that the content of *the way things are ultimately supposed to be*ᵖ is in some sense already known or has been revealed and that it is possible of realization. Consequently, it requires spokespersons to declare that divine order and provide directives for action. The kind of spokesperson will depend in large part on how that content is conceived: **moral prophet**, **moral sage**, or **moral teacher**. So also, moral leadership in implementing or embodying *the intended divine order*ᵖ is needed: charismatic moral leader, moral reformer, moral sage, moral saint, and possibly martyr. Then, of course, the humble follower, disciple, or moral soldier is needed. The way of right action gives rise to characteristic social forms as well: legal and judicial institutions, alternative model communities, movements of moral and social reform, and so on.

Ideal realizations of these many features will exhibit characteristic virtues of the way of right action. Failures, degenerations, and egoistic manipulation exhibit its characteristic vices—as in legalism, perfectionism, and moral hypocrisy.

> Putting the various features together into a compact definition, the way of right action consists in the concerted effort to bring all of life, individual and communal, into conformity with *the way things are ultimately supposed to be*ᵖ (however understood)—that is, to realize and fulfill *the sacred intendedness of life*ᵖ—that promises individual fulfillment, social justice, and the embodiment of *divine ideality*ᵖ in the midst of mundane, this-worldly life.

The **way of devotion** is centered on devotion, as one might expect, but not just any devotion. In a certain respect, all sincere religion involves devotion, whatever the way of being religious. What is commonly taken to be religious devotion, however, is considerably broader than what is here identified with the way of devotion. In consequence, not everything readers may be accustomed to identify as instances of religious devotion will be an example of the way of devotion. The way of devotion only occurs where personal affection as such becomes a principal way of drawing near to and coming into right relationship with *ultimate reality*ᵖ. Even so, there may be aspects of the way of devotion to be found in connection with examples that are chiefly instances of other ways of being religious.

In the way of devotion, unlike the other ways, one's capacity for devotion is the avenue to at-onement with *ultimate reality*ᵖ. Persons who pursue this way are preoccupied with expressing certain feelings and cultivating certain attitudes toward what they take to be a personal manifestation of *ultimate reality*ᴾ. Usually they do so in common with other persons, but devotional worship in common is not essential. In any case, they tend to withdraw from activities that interfere with or inhibit those feelings and attitudes. The way of devotion specifically involves cultivation of a personal relationship to *ultimate reality*ᴾ of whole-hearted adoration, devotional surrender to its transforming grace, and trust in its providential care. Accordingly, the way of devotion tends to arise or emerge only when *ultimate reality*ᴾ is conceived to have some sort of personal manifestation or "face" oriented toward potential devotees, along with a capacity for grace and a power to arrange events for the well-being of devotees. The hermeneutical orientation of the way of devotion, accordingly, highlights and identifies with those aspects of a tradition's system of symbols (e.g., its scripture) that manifest or at least intimate the personal side or "face" of *ultimate reality*ᴾ and its interest in the welfare of potential devotees.

The point of the way of devotion is to have *ultimate reality*ᴾ (or rather its personal "face") come to be the center of one's personal life, the central focus of one's primary affections. The expectation is that this devotional centering will result in the influx of sustaining energy, hope, and a sense of nearness to it. Typically, attainment of such a devotional centering (or recentering) of life will involve some kind of conversion experience (from a life not affectively centered on *ultimate reality*ᴾ to one that is so centered) and passage through an emotional catharsis (a purifying or figurative cleansing of the emotions). Repeated passage through some sort of emotional catharsis, for many who follow the way of devotion, appears to be widely practiced and encouraged. Thus, at-onement with *ultimate reality*ᴾ is principally sought by way of inward, personal devotion—not primarily by way of outward "acts of devotion," however, but by a sustained commitment to cultivate an inner attitude of adoration toward *ultimate reality*ᴾ in every circumstance of one's life, whatever one may be doing outwardly. It is characteristic of persons who pursue this way to place little emphasis on outward actions (whether of a ritual or a moral nature) as a means of establishing rapport with *ultimate reality*ᴾ—especially not when such actions are undertaken in the absence of the right devotional attitude.

Persons who freely choose the way of devotion often do so with the existential motivation that in no other way can one find the emotional wherewithal to bear up under the pain, loneliness, and emotional traumas of everyday life, the guilt at having betrayed what is highest and best, the profound sense of one's own inadequacy, or the despair at not being able to cope on one's own or in one's own strength. These persons seek a focus for their otherwise disparate affections—an "object" worthy of worship, yet also one that affirms who they are in their weakness, a compassionate source of grace and coping power. It is through giving themselves in devotional surrender to *ultimate reality*ᴾ in its compassionate, grace-full aspect, letting go entirely the attempt to "make it" in their own strength, that they find their lives brought back into meaningful shape and the grace to bear what otherwise would be unbearable—and more. Theirs is the faith that through such a devotional surrender they will find as well an ongoing, personally affirming intimacy with *ultimate reality*^{p}, with other devotees, and with all other things. It is, ideally at least, not for oneself alone that this personally transforming intimacy is sought, but just as much for the sake of others—extending the reach of joyful intimacy with *ultimate reality*^{p} to the larger community of devotees and beyond, including, in some traditions, even the nonhuman realm of nature.

Different religious traditions portray *ultimate reality*^{p} in very different ways, yet remarkable parallels can be found in the way of devotion at work in Protestant Evangelical Christianity, which focuses on being "born again" through giving one's heart in devotional surrender to God in response to His gift of salvation in Jesus Christ; in Jodo-shin-shu Buddhism, which focuses on cultivating a relationship of complete reliance on, and faith in, the grace of Amida Buddha to meet the trials of this life and be reborn in the Pure Land in which true enlightenment is found; and in Śri Vaishnavite Bhakti Hinduism, which focuses on cultivating a relationship of passionate intimacy with the compassionate, most personally accessible form of the divine among human beings, *Kṛṣṇa*. Expressions of the way of devotion can be found in other traditions as well, but perhaps no more distinctly than in these three.

The way of devotion tends to generate social forms that facilitate cultivation of the appropriate feelings and attitudes and dealing with emotional problems and crises. Characteristic leadership roles include the charismatic **preacher** or **storyteller** who is a master at bringing people to the point of conversion, devotional surrender, and catharsis, and the **pastor** who is a master in counseling and helping devotees cope with the ups and downs of their devotional lives. Social institutions tend to be quite informal and more subject to local congregational control than not. Indeed, little more is necessary than informal gatherings of devotees joining in devotional praise to *ultimate reality*^{p}, sharing stories of *its*^{o} (whether "his" or "her") compassion and grace toward devotees, and offering fellowship and support for one another.

Each of these features of the way of devotion has the potential for ideal realization and for corruption. When participants find meaning, the wherewithal to cope with physical and emotional suffering, a sense of fulfilling intimacy with *ultimate reality*^{p}, and lives changed for the better, the way's characteristic virtues may be found. Where devotional life becomes nothing but indulgence in sentiment on the one hand or an otherworldly passion that eclipses all mundane concerns on the other, or where emotions are manipulated for self-serving motives, there may be found the characteristic vices.

Putting these several features together into a compact definition, the way of devotion consists in cultivation of a personal relationship to *ultimate reality*^{p} of whole-hearted adoration, devotional surrender to *its*^{o} transforming grace, and trust in *its*^{o} providential care, anticipating in return an influx of sustaining energy, hope, and a sense of affirming presence or at-onement. It typically involves a conversion experience and emotional purgation.

The **way of shamanic mediation** is existentially concerned with meeting the overwhelming challenges that life offers, such as serious illness or injury, great danger, or loss of food supply. It is not simply a concern with great challenges; it is rather a concern with challenges that overwhelm the resources of power and imagination available in the mundane, ordinary world. It operates out of a confidence that "supernatural"[5] or spiritual resources for meeting these challenges really do exist. Even more: it boldly assumes that there is a whole other dimension of existence, an autonomous realm of spiritual realities (at least part of the tradition's *other world*°) on which mundane life depends for good and ill. Persons who pursue this way of being religious are convinced that the "supernatural" resources of the spirit world can be tapped and brought to bear on present needs through certain practices that mediate between the spirit world and the mundane world. A master of these practices or a person who is able to play such a mediating role is a **shaman**, whether male or female.

Among the six ways of being religious, shamanic mediation is the least compatible with the so-called modern scientific world view. The modern scientific world view presumes to explain all phenomena in terms of natural, material causes—that is, resolutely nonsupernatural causes. As well, it stresses human autonomy vis-à-vis all allegedly higher powers. For Buddhists and Christians who identify with the modern world view, for example, shamanic phenomena in their respective traditions are viewed as archaic holdovers from an earlier credulous age, contaminations of "high religion" by animistic folk religion, and in no sense essential to true Buddhism or true Christianity. We shall not enter into this controversy here except to note that the evidence is fairly clear that shamanic phenomena have occupied a place in each of these traditions all along, at least on the fringes of institutionalized orthodoxy. The same is true in most other religions. Readers are encouraged for the sake of understanding to suspend this modern prejudice and approach shamanic expressions of religion with no less empathy than is due toward examples of other ways of being religious.

From what has been said so far, the impression may have been conveyed that the way of shamanic mediation is a kind of spiritual technology—that is, simply a matter of harnessing "supernatural" resources for the solution of mundane problems. This is a misleading impression. Recall that a way of being religious is a way of drawing near to and coming in right relationship with *ultimate reality*°. Thus considered, the way of shamanic mediation is a way of becoming united with *ultimate reality*° in *its*° purpose to bring about healing, well-being, and fulfillment for the world. This points to the hermeneutical orientation of the way of shamanic mediation—always looking for clues in the tradition's symbol system to the availability of "supernatural" resources, to the readiness and disposition of *ultimate reality*° to make available those resources, and how to come into alignment with that disposition. In other words, the "supernatural" spirit resources that shamanic mediation would tap are not just there for exploitation. It is rather that they are ultimately and comprehensively disposed ("intended" may not be too strong a word) for the welfare of the world. They may also be misused for ill effect—but at the prospect of dire consequences for the person who misuses them, so say knowledgeable shamans of almost every tradition. The way of shamanic mediation therefore seeks to mediate or be a channel for, and thus be an intimate ally of, the beneficent power of *ultimate reality*[P] to meet the needs of the individual and the community.

In the way of shamanic mediation, a person gains access to the spirit world through what might be called the deep imagination, which is largely unconscious in most persons, in an altered state of consciousness. Typically it involves entering a state of trance in which, at least in initial stages, one loses consciousness of the mundane, ordinary world but gains consciousness of the spirit world and is thereby enabled to move about in it. Fully developed shamanic mediation, however, involves bridging or mediating between both worlds, enabling the resources of the spirit world to be received by, or transmitted to, persons and circumstances in the ordinary world. Typical shamanic phenomena include being "filled," "taken over," or "empowered" by a "supernatural" divine spirit to do what is otherwise beyond human capacities; seeking and receiving ecstatic visions that give direction, purpose, and personal identity; oracular utterances that bestow divine instruction, guidance, and otherworldly knowledge; and going on "spirit journeys" into the other world for the sake of divine instruction, spiritual maturation, or solving some problem in the mundane sphere such as "soul loss" (in which a person has lost the spark of life).

Accordingly, this way of being religious gives rise, depending to some extent on the religious tradition in which it occurs, to more specialized shamanic roles, such as oracle, prophet, visionary, medium, wonder worker, spiritual healer, geomancer (one who discerns auspicious and inauspicious sites for human activity in terms of the alleged flow of spiritual energies in the landscape), necromancer (one who communicates with the spirits of persons who have died), and so forth. Being more attuned to the unpredictable movements of the spirit(s) than to mundane considerations, shamanic mediation tends not to establish enduring social institutions other than those directly associated with the largely individualized, charismatic role of the shaman, whether as generalist or as specialist. In some traditions, the role of shaman may nevertheless be more social than individual, however, and thus an institution—meaning that, as one holder of the role either dies or loses her (or his) charisma (spiritual connection and power), another is found to take her (or his) place. More or less informal shamanic guilds can often be found that maintain what can be a considerable body of shamanic lore and a regimen of apprenticeship for would-be shamans.

It is important to recognize that according to every tradition of shamanic mediation not all spiritual powers are identical, not all are compatible, not all are necessarily good; and many are downright dangerous. All traditions attest to the need to cultivate some form of "spiritual discernment." Some traditions accredit the activities of shamans in other traditions, while some do not. Few if any traditions engage in or accredit all shamanic practices. Most traditions explicitly warn against, if they do not forbid, involvement in certain practices.

Expressions of the way of shamanic mediation are found throughout the world in almost all long-standing religious tradition, unless for some reason the tradition discourages or condemns shamanic practices. They are particularly evident in indigenous, nonliterate, small-scale cultures. They may be found as well in major religious traditions, particularly where people find themselves confronted with overwhelming, life-threatening problems and grossly insufficient mundane resources with which to solve them. In Christianity, shamanic practices are found in Pentecostal Protestantism and the more recent, interdenominational Charismatic Movement. Outside the bounds of Christian orthodoxy, the Spiritualist Church in England and North America puts the way of shamanic mediation at the center of religious life. In Arabic Muslim countries, although shamanic-type practices tend to be censored as non-Muslim by mainstream authorities, the wonder-working shamanic figure of the *wali* ("friend of God") can often be found among poor and nonliterate folk. Aspects of shamanism may be seen in Hasidic Judaism, especially in its formative years in eighteenth- and nineteenth-century Eastern Europe. Shamanic practices can be found throughout Asia and are often regarded as a holdover from "primitive" indigenous religions. Nevertheless, in places they have found a relatively stable home within Buddhism (e.g., Tibetan Vajrayana Buddhism), Hinduism, and Daoism. In addition, they are a major phenomenon in Korean religious life and have had a long-standing place within rural Japanese Shintoism, as well as in the New Religions of Japan

Because of its involvement in unusual and sometimes apparently bizarre parapsychological phenomena, the way of shamanic mediation is sometimes the object of intense curiosity. This alone makes it ripe for unscrupulous exploitation and charlatanism. And because of its promise of supernatural resources for the solving of mundane problems, it has the potential for degenerating into occult magic (where *ultimate reality*ᴾ is treated as a mere means for mundane, egoistic ends). In any case, it would be a great mistake to suppose that the way of shamanic mediation is adequately represented by its most degenerate forms. That is to say, these expressions are examples of the characteristic vices to which the way of shamanic mediation is subject. At the opposite end of the spectrum, though, are the virtues exemplifying shamanic mediation is at its best—namely, practices whereby beneficent power of *ultimate reality*ᴾ is channeled with genuine effectiveness to meet the real needs of individuals and the community.

Putting these various features together into a compact definition, the way of shamanic mediation consists in entry into altered states of consciousness in which persons become mediators or channels for *the intervention of spiritual reality*ᴾ, in the expectation that "supernatural" (transmundane) resources of imagination, power, and guidance will be released for solving or dealing with otherwise intractable problems of life. Expressed through phenomena such as "possession trance", "oracular utterance," "ecstatic vision," and/or "spirit journeying," it seeks at-onement with *ultimate reality*° in what is taken to be *its*° readiness to bring about healing, well-being, and fulfillment for the world.

The **way of mystical quest** is a deliberate endeavor, using ascetic and meditative disciplines, to transcend the limitations of ordinary conscious experience—specifically, its unconsciousness of *ultimate reality*°—for the sake of conscious union with *ultimate reality*°. Several elements in this statement need to be highlighted in order to distinguish the way of mystical quest from the confusion surrounding common usage of the words "mysticism," "mystical experience," and "mystic." Notice the emphasis on "deliberate endeavor" and "use of ascetic and meditative disciplines" and not on supernatural visions, psychic phenomena, or mysterious happenings. According to the classification given here, the latter, so far as there are such things, are to be associated more with the category of shamanic mediation than mystical quest. Notice also that the emphasis is not on seeking after "mystical experiences," whatever they might be—which, being *experiences* of something (even if they be of "no-thing") could only be *appearances* of *ultimate reality*° and not that *ultimate reality*° itself. The emphasis is rather on seeking *ultimate reality*° itself (as opposed to experiences of it) and being immediately united with it. Notice too that the focus of the definition phrased here is not on the end result (e.g., on the culmination of the quest, or on those "mystics" who have attained that culmination, whether by deliberate endeavor, unbidden miraculous grace, or however) but on the path, on the deliberate, long-term endeavor—on the lived meaning of the quest. Hence it includes all those who trod the path and not merely those who arrive at the end. In short, it is about the path itself and the practices that constitute the path.

Persons who pursue the way of mystical quest are discontent with merely accepting what others say about *ultimate reality*°; they want nothing less than to experience it directly for themselves. Not merely *ultimate reality*°, they seek to become aware of all things, both within and without, *as they ultimately are*°—which is to say, as they have been testified to by the tradition to which they belong. In an important respect they distrust appearances and what is on the surface. This disposition characterizes as well the hermeneutical orientation of the way of mystical quest toward the scriptures and symbols of traditions: the meaning sought is always the deeper meaning and not the literal meaning on the surface, and the passages it highlights are those that intimate a way forward to a deeper realization of *ultimate truth*°.

Those who pursue the mystical quest have a passion to reach out and taste *what is ultimately real*° with their very being. In that respect they are discontent with ordinary awareness as a species of unconsciousness, conditioned and fettered by ignorance, lust, and egoism. Persons who pursue the way of mystical quest passionately seek an extra-ordinary, contemplative consciousness of *ultimate* *reality*^{p} that is free of the distortions and distractions of ordinary experience and the distractions of extra-ordinary experience too (including experiences associated with shamanic mediation). Additionally, they are discontent with any lack of integration between awareness on the one hand, however true that awareness may be, and how life is lived on the other; they seek to be integrally united with *ultimate reality*^{p} in their whole being. The way of mystical quest thus pursues not only a transformation of one's conscious awareness but also a transformation of one's entire self, so that nothing of oneself might be in conflict with or out of touch with *ultimate reality*^{p}.

The would-be **mystic** pursues her goal by way of meditative and ascetic disciplines designed to uncondition and unfetter her experience of things, to free it of distortions and distractions. Such disciplines serve to interrupt, slow down, focus, and/or otherwise break through the obscuring impulses and patterns of ordinary experience to enable her to become more and more directly aware of, receptive to, and grounded in the *ultimate reality*^{p} she seeks. In well-established traditions of mystical quest, she will trod a relatively well-groomed path under the guidance of a **spiritual master** or **spiritual director** who has already trodden it before or who has at least progressed farther along it. Because it is often such an all-consuming, solitary preoccupation, persons who pursue the way of mystical quest are drawn to a way of living that facilitates and supports it, free of the distractions and busyness of ordinary life. Some, accordingly, choose to live with others in a monastic setting, where life is pared down to its essentials and they are free to devote time and energy to the quest in a mutually supportive way. Others choose the life of a hermit or, as in India, the life of a wandering mendicant. Although it may appear so, in most traditions of the way of mystical quest it is not for herself only that a person pursues the mystical quest, but typically she pursues it for the sake of improving and intensifying others' awareness of, and connection with, *ultimate reality*^{p} as well.

As is fairly well known, the way of mystical quest can be found in all of the major religious traditions, though not always in their mainstream expressions. Buddhism places it front and center, as it were, in most of its principal subtraditions for the sake of achieving *nirvāṇa* via some adaptation of the Eightfold Path, at least for those who are ready to undertake the quest. Islam has several varieties of *Sufism*; Judaism has *Kabbala*; Roman Catholic and Eastern Orthodox Christianity, since the fourth century at least, have had a revered place for contemplative monasticism; Hinduism has multiple varieties of what in Chapter 1 was called *dhyāna yoga*, Daoism has its revered forms of the mystical quest, and even Confucianism and Shintoism have given expression to it.

Some writers, impressed with the striking and profound similarities between the way of mystical quest in each of these traditions, are only too ready to draw the conclusion that the mystical quest is the same in each tradition. But this, on the basis of the author's investigations, is a premature judgment, to say the least; it conveniently ignores the differences that remain to be explored by confusing generic structure with specific form. For example, in virtually all Christian examples of the way of mystical quest, ascetic and mystical techniques by themselves are said to accomplish little of significance. Much more important than techniques or anything one can do is to wait upon (that is, make oneself available to) the intervention of divine grace, upon God's freely electing to reveal himself to the seeker. Indeed, some would emphasize that the Christian mystical quest presupposes having already become a member of "the Body of Christ" through Baptism and regular participation in the sacramental life of the Church. To the contrary, virtually all Buddhist examples of the way of mystical quest make no reference whatsoever to divine intervention or to the necessity (as distinct from the usefulness) of formally joining the Buddhist *Saṃgha* (monastic community), and place primary responsibility on the efforts of the individual pursuing Enlightenment. Although there may be unacknowledged aspects of something akin to the experience of grace in the Buddhist quest and unacknowledged greater dependency on technique than most Christian mystics explicitly allow, a clear difference seems evident.

Finally, the way of mystical quest, too, has a potential for characteristic vices as well as virtues. Its vices include mystical dilettantism (e.g., seeking after extraordinary "mystical experiences"), using the mystical path as a means of escape from things one cannot face in the mundane world, spiritual elitism, and extreme self-mortification, among others. Virtue in the way of mystical quest is found not only in attainment in the mystical quest itself, but also (if not more so) in such things as thoughtful consideration for fellow pursuers of the quest, good humor in coping with human foibles and limitations, and the humility that abhors self-inflation at having attained some goal on the path.

> Putting these various features together into a compact definition, the way of mystical quest consists in employment of ascetic and meditative disciplines in a deliberate quest to interrupt, slow down, or otherwise become free of, the obscuring limitations and distracting compulsions of ordinary life in order to attain a direct awareness of *ultimate reality°*, come to be wholly at-one with *it°*, and have life and one's relations with all things become transparently grounded in *it°*.

The **way of reasoned inquiry** is concerned with *understanding* things, grasping how things fit together and why things are the way they are, first of all for oneself, but for the sake of others' understanding too. Hence the existential need that motivates this way is lack of understanding and discontent with the ignorance, unreasoned opinions, and secondhand answers with which others rest content.

The way of reasoned inquiry involves investigation into, and a pondering of, the nature of things. It begins with the study of scripture and past attempts to articulate *how things ultimately are°*—which for the way of reasoned inquiry contain not a set of pre-established answers but the starting point, basis, and set of clues for moving to an understanding of *ultimate reality*° and how it relates to the matters of immediate concern. This indicates something of its characteristic hermeneutical orientation: it looks for clues that will lead to a comprehension of the problems and perplexities of life (especially ones that suggest reasons for why things are they way they are), clues to a reasoned view of the world as a whole within *the ultimate perspective*°, and rationales for (and promise of) reasoned inquiry as a means to at-onement with *ultimate reality*°. Hence, it can be simply called **theology**°. Characteristically, though, the way of reasoned inquiry does not involve just any sort of study. It is where study takes on the dimensions of a passionate quest, a way of drawing near to and coming into right relationship with *ultimate reality*°, a way of worship. What is sought is an understanding of *reality as it ultimately is*°, as it is for *ultimate reality*° or "God." Hence, implicit in its pursuit of understanding of any given thing is a pursuit of a progressive at-onement with *ultimate reality*°: the ground and source of truth, the ultimate reason for being of all things, *the Absolute itself*°. Truly to seek truth is to seek *Truth*°, which in most traditions is one of the names of *ultimate reality*°.

The truth and understanding thus sought are ultimately, then, not a matter of "right" or "correct answers" but an at-onement of mind with *Mind*°, a life-transforming insight into *the ultimate nature of reality as a whole*° and the place of the part with which one may be concerned within that whole. The goal is not so much knowledge as it is wisdom, divine wisdom, the ultimate basis of sound judgment—a wisdom just as practical as it is theoretical, a wisdom that clarifies how life therefore is to be lived. Nevertheless, it should be said here that some traditions, whose core symbol systems emphasize the normative, action-guiding features of *ultimate reality*°, dispose the way of reasoned inquiry more in a practical than a theoretical direction. Other traditions, whose symbol systems do not emphasize the normative, action-guiding features of *ultimate reality*°, or that stress *ultimate reality*° as being beyond good and evil, dispose the way of reasoned inquiry, to the contrary, in a more theoretical direction. Nevertheless, the way of reasoned inquiry seeks not truth for one's own sake, but truth for truth's sake, and, as an attendant responsibility, participation in the making known of truth to, and the appropriation of truth by, the community of faith and beyond it to humankind at large.

The process of coming to an understanding of fundamental things and drawing near to *Truth*° is almost never straightforward—at least not for those who seek to understand things freshly for themselves. It is almost always a dialectical struggle to move beyond the mistaken, distorted, and partial apprehensions characteristic of conventional, this-worldly understanding to draw progressively nearer to the *Truth*° that lies beyond them. Depending on the particular religious tradition, the struggle is sometimes laced with paradox because what it is one seeks to understand is fundamentally incompatible with a conventional, this-worldly frame of reference (in Buddhist terms, a "samsaric" point of view). In such a case, the conventional frame of reference must at some point be challenged, broken through, and displaced for *true insight°* to occur. For example, in the *Prajñā-pāramitā "theology°"* of Mahayana Buddhism, the shift is so radical that conventional categories for speaking of what is real are said to have no application to *ultimate reality°*, which is characterized as "emptiness" (*śūnyatā*), as having no "self-being" in the conventional sense at all.

Despite the involvement of intuitive leaps of insight (more so in some traditions, little or none in others), the characteristic mark of the way of reasoned inquiry is the use of reason. Persons authentically drawn to the way of reasoned inquiry never rest content with things that don't make sense or are not reasoned through. Reason here, though, is not to be understood as necessarily discursive or explicit in form. Some reasons may make sense only upon a shift in one's perspective. Some reasons may be grasped intuitively but not be statable in plain language at all. According to certain traditions, as in Mahayana Buddhist *Prajñā-pāramitā*, crucial steps in understanding require leaps of intuitive comprehension that cannot be mapped as explicit inferences. They will be leaps that make perfect sense within their own frame of reference but from the perspective of other traditions and mundane ways of making sense they may appear irrational. To the contrary, other traditions, such as traditional Jewish Talmudic study, are bastions of systematic, discursive reasoning that have no tolerance for intuitive leaps of insight at all.

The way of reasoned inquiry finds expression in most of the great religious traditions, some more centrally than others. In some it is stands by itself, but in others (at least in some subtraditions) it is closely allied with the way of right action or with the way of mystical quest. In traditional Rabbinic Judaism, participation in serious dialectical study of the *Torah* and *Talmud* has been expected of all males, to the extent of their ability, and has been counted as worthy as prayer, and by some as even more worthy. Here the focus is primarily upon practical or prudential wisdom, on the many implications of the Divine Commandments for the living of life. Islam, too, although it has traditionally been wary of liberal theological tendencies, has given special honor to the serious study of theology and religious law. Confucianism's elevation of the ideal of sagehood above all other ideals made the way of reasoned inquiry and role of the scholar, focused on study of the Confucian Classics, central to its tradition. Here too the goal stressed is primarily prudential wisdom pertaining to human relationships, yet it is concerned more with cultivation of virtue than with rule and law as in Judaism and Islam. Buddhism has placed a central emphasis upon the pursuit of wisdom combined or balanced with contemplative meditation. In a somewhat similar way, Hinduism recognizes and honors the path of *jñāna yoga*, the path of knowledge and insight that has about it some elements of mystical quest. Christianity in its different subtraditions has variously emphasized serious theological and scriptural inquiry—some more discursive, some more intuitive. Although some pietistic Protestant sects have gone so far as to explicitly discourage theological inquiry, most major Christian denominations have stressed serious study of scripture and theological tradition (at least for clergy) as a help for drawing near to God, if not actually a way to God.

Characteristically, the way of reasoned inquiry involves study of sacred texts and commentaries on them. But just as important is apprenticeship (formal or informal) to the greatest interpreters (living and dead) of those texts and working collaboratively with others who agree to hold each other's reasoning responsible. Current reflection and inquiry thereby become part of an ongoing conversation and argument concerning *ultimate reality°* that includes sages of the past and appeals to generations yet to come. In its social manifestation, the way of wisdom naturally spawns teachers and students, ***theologians°*** (persons who have attained competence in a given tradition's expression of the way of wisdom and mastery of its classic texts), master teachers and **sages**; schools, academies, and seminaries; critical editions of scripture, scriptural commentaries, responses to commentaries, treatises on *theology°*, and *theological°* textbooks; and, of course, libraries.

And, just as the other ways have a potential for characteristic virtues and for characteristic vices, the same is true for the way of reasoned inquiry. Each of the features mentioned above is capable of ideal realization and failure in one respect or another. Characteristic vices include pedantry, nitpicking, intellectual pretentiousness, and losing sight of the partiality of one's own understanding and perspective. Characteristic virtues, on the other hand, include a commitment to reason things through thoroughly and articulate them freshly, a clear sense of the heart of the matter to be understood and communicated, a thoughtful sensitivity toward the ability of others to understand and follow an argument, and a keen awareness of the limitations of one's own understanding and perspective.

> Putting these various features together into a compact definition, the way of reasoned inquiry consists in the rational, dialectical struggle to transcend conventional patterns of thinking in the effort attain understanding of, and consciousness-transforming insight into, *the ultimate what, how, and why of things°*—that is, to bring together and unite, so far as possible, mind with *the ultimate Mind°* and thereby acquire a portion of *divine wisdom°*. It typically involves systematic study of a tradition's scripture and previous attempts to articulate *what is ultimately the case°*.

SIX HERMENEUTICAL ORIENTATIONS

In Chapter 2, the concept of different orientations to the interpretation of the same system of religious symbols was introduced, and specifically orientations determined in large measure by each of the generic ways of being religious. The claim was made that an essential aspect of each of the ways was a distinctive **hermeneutic** (interpretive orientation) toward a tradition's system of symbols governed in large measure by the specific existential needs to which each way is addressed. In the previous section, some allusion was made to the hermeneutic characteristic of each of the ways. The following chart sketches in greater detail the six hermeneutical orientations, the existential needs with which each is correlated, and some typical characteristics of *ultimate reality°* that are highlighted as a result of each orientation.

A more concrete sense of what is involved in these different orientations may be obtained by thinking of a single passage of scripture—say, the Jewish and Christian story of the Creation and Fall of Humankind in Genesis 2:4 to 3:24—being read and interpreted simultaneously from the perspective of each hermeneutic with its peculiar existential need. Notice how the story differently speaks to each need, how it invites multiple simultaneous interpretations, and how each way of being religious has, as it were, different eyes with which to see and different ears with which to hear.

EXISTENTIAL NEED THAT MOTIVATES	HERMENEUTICAL ORIENTATION	ASPECTS OF *ULTIMATE REALITY°* HIGHLIGHTED
	Sacred Rite	
The prospect of facing momentous events with no archetypal pattern to follow, no ultimately grounded sense of propriety.	Looks for *divine archetypes°* to reenact ritually and re-present in ritual art, symbols and phrases to incorporate directly into awe-inspiring ritual, patterns of sacred rite, aesthetic and proprietary considerations, and persons who model the way of sacred rite—as well as rationales for sacred ritual as a means to at-onement with *ultimate reality°*.	Awe-inspiring, sublime characteristics; *primordial archetype(s) of meaningful order and vitality°*, source of all that is sacred and pure; the ground and basis of all propriety; source and goal of all things; well-spring of beauty, wholeness, and perfection.
	Right Action	
The sense that the way things happen to be is not *the way they are ultimately supposed to be°*, or that they would certainly not be what ultimately they should be if *the divine order* now being followed were not followed.	Looks for disclosure of *the way things are supposed to be°*, patterns of right action and behavior (both social and individual), criteria for assessing current practice, directives for action in current circumstances, clues for overcoming one's own failures, and persons who model the way of right action—as well as rationales for right action as a means to at-onement with *ultimate reality°*.	*The normative order of all things°* (whether immanent or transcendent); *the cosmic imperative°*, source of the summons to do what is right and just; *the ordered whole°* in which each thing finds its rightful place and its just due.
	Devotion	
Experiences that threaten to overwhelm one's emotional capacity to bear them and a sense of personal inadequacy to attain anything of substantial worth on one's own.	Looks for a focus of devotional worship, summons to emotional reorientation, surrender and catharsis, words of pastoral guidance, promises of personal comfort and reassurance, confidence builders in providence, and persons who model true devotion—as well as rationales for devotional surrender to divine grace as a means to at-onement with *ultimate reality°*.	*Providential grace°*, compassion, love, beneficence, personal interest and care, responsiveness to pure devotion and trust, capacity to become intimately (personally) present and to enter into personal relationships with devotees.

EXISTENTIAL NEED THAT MOTIVATES	HERMENEUTICAL ORIENTATION	ASPECTS OF *ULTIMATE REALITY*° HIGHLIGHTED
Shamanic Mediation		
Helplessness in the face of practical crises whose solutions transcend mundane resources.	Looks for promise of, and directives for, receiving spiritual power and vision to bring down, mediate, or channel *"supernatural" power*° to meet mundane problems, models of shamanic mediation, insights into constructing a "map" of *the spirit world*°—as well as rationales for shamanic mediation as a means to at-onement with *ultimate reality*°.	*"Supernatural" (trans-mundane) power*°; source of ecstatic visions, dreams, and prophetic messages; ground of creativity and charismatic gifts; *ultimate agent behind "supernatural" intervention*°; source of spiritual guidance, *Lord and master of the realm of spirits*°; victor over demonic forces.
Mystical Quest		
Disquiet over the unreality and insubstantial worth of ordinary life on its surface.	Looks for anagogic or "inward" meanings, spiritual direction, truths to be "verified" in one's own meditative experience, methods or techniques to break through mundane "unconsciousness," and persons who model the mystical quest—as well as rationales for mystical quest as a means to at-onement with *ultimate reality*°.	*The absolute subject*°, *the beyond within*°, the still center of the turning world, *utterly uncon-ditioned reality*°, beyond all appearances, beneath egoistic consciousness, the unitive contemplation of which is utter bliss, *the Beatific Vision*°.
Reasoned Inquiry		
Things that don't make sense, lack explanation, and, if unanswered, threaten to undermine the ultimate sense of things.	Looks for clues to comprehension of the cognitive problems of life, adumbrations of rational argumen-tation and of a comprehensive and systematic world view, and persons who model the way of wisdom—as well as rationales for (and promise of) reasoned inquiry as a means to at-onement with *ultimate reality*°.	*Reality*°, *Truth*°, *Wisdom*°, *Omniscience*° (knowing of all things), *Logos*° or *Reason*° (ground of intelligibility and rationality), the source and ground of *the rational order of the cosmos*°.

RELATING THE WAYS TO EACH OTHER AND TO PERSONALITY TYPES

The positioning of each of the six ways in relation to each other in the following diagram is not random and is meant to reflect several considerations.

WAYS OF BEING RELIGIOUS

First, the three ways in the upper half of the diagram have a certain affinity in opposition, to some extent, with the affinity shared with the three ways in the lower half of the diagram. Practices in the ways of right action, sacred rite, and reasoned inquiry tend to be relatively more well defined, focused, and ordered—objectified, as it were—than are practices in the ways of devotion, shamanic mediation, and mystical quest. The latter are relatively more informal, spontaneous, and open-ended. In addition, the focus of attention in their practices seems to have more to do with things outside the self than inside the self, whereas the focus of attention for the ways in the lower half of the diagram seems more turned inward.

Second, the pair on the vertical axis, sacred rite and shamanic mediation, tend more to employ concrete symbols (though not in the same way). Both address, fascinate, and occupy the senses. To the contrary, those away from the vertical axis have less use for concrete symbols and are, relatively speaking, more abstract. Interestingly, the two ways on the vertical axis predominate in small-scale, nonliterate, relatively undifferentiated societies; it is hard to find clear indications of the other ways in such contexts—especially not as ways unto themselves. Contrariwise, distinct expressions of ways away from the vertical axis tend to emerge only in larger-scale, differentiated societies in which individual religious predilections are given opportunity to develop and express themselves. In this connection, it is noteworthy that those to the right of the vertical axis are some-what more reflectively governed, those to the left somewhat less so.

Third, notice the oppositional pairings: sacred rite with shamanic mediation, right action with mystical quest, and reasoned inquiry with devotion. An alternative way of construing the diagram would be in terms of a set of three coordinates or axes in three dimensions, with each opposing pair in the current diagram serving as one of the three axes. Thus construed, it would be possible to speak of the relationship between any two ways independently of their relationships to others. Also it would be possible to plot within that three-dimensional space the location of a given religious phenomenon that combined more than one way of being religious. Nonetheless, within each pair is a tensed opposition or oppositional tension, with each way serving, or capable of serving, as a kind of balance or complement to the other.

The practices associated with the way of sacred rite are, as they must be, clearly ordered and well defined in advance; relatively little is left to spontaneity, improvisation, and intuition—except for the private thoughts, feelings, and associations of the participants. By way of contrast, practices associated with the way of shamanic mediation, while often involving certain rituals, are for the most part quite informal, spontaneous, and intuitive, always leaving room for "the movement of (the) spirit." Indeed, they involve giving up mundane human control in order to allow the spirit(s) to take over—a prospect directly at odds with the typical sensibility associated with the way of sacred rite. Whereas sacred rite centers essentially on a symbolic recovery and presentation of timeless archetypes—which is an essentially conservative enterprise—shamanic mediation very often centers on the emergence of new (previously unknown) archetypes of the sacred, or fresh, unconventional, and unpredictable expressions of old (previously known) ones. Accordingly, priests are usually linked to and serve the established social order (within which they often hold a privileged place), whereas shamans, being never wholly domesticated and representing sacred power uncontrolled by any human agenda, are always a potential threat to vested mundane interests. Accordingly, shamans are specialists in dealing with the *liminal* regions of life—those areas that are unstructured, unknown, and radically other—dealing with them as liminal, rather than attempting to impose on them some structure. In the history of Western religions (including primarily Judaism, Christianity, and Islam), rarely if ever do priest and shaman-prophet coincide in the same person. Sometimes, however, they are found in a kind of creative tension alongside one another in a given religious tradition. Each would seem to need some aspect of the other to keep its balance, for sacred rite (left to itself?) can degenerate in spiritless ritualism, and shamanic mediation (left to itself?) can degenerate into a kind of spiritual autism or chaos. In Eastern Asian religions and indigenous African religions priest and shaman frequently coincide. Why that should be so is an interesting question. At least in China, this may be due in part to the differentiation in social roles between the Confucian and Daoist traditions, for there the opposition between priest and prophet characteristic of Western religion is more closely paralleled by the opposition between Confucian scholar and Daoist shaman-priest.

Right action is the quintessential journey outward, into the world. It is above all concerned with doing something, undertaking tasks, and making a difference. Mystical quest, to the contrary, is the quintessential journey inward, a withdrawal from the world (even though it may ultimately involve a return to the world and be for the sake of the world). It is above all concerned with quieting down, letting go, and finding "the still center of the turning world." Both seek *ultimate reality*^ᵖ but in apparently opposite directions. Yet each seems to require something of the other to keep on track and be at its best, for right action (left to itself?) can degenerate into hyperactivism (frenzied activity without grace or center), and mystical quest (left to itself?) can degenerate into quietism (uncaring indifference and shirking of responsibility).

The way of reasoned inquiry is the way of the intellect. It is above all concerned with gaining reasoned comprehension of the highest and most comprehensive truths. Devotion is the way of the heart and the affections. It is above all concerned with cultivating purity of heart in whole-hearted worship of, and devotional surrender to, the all-sufficient grace of *ultimate reality*^ᵖ. By way of contrast with the careful differentiations of the way of reasoned inquiry, the way of devotion groups things together in terms of how they feel (how they relate to the heart) and how they participate in praise of *ultimate reality*^ᵖ. The intellectually gifted and educated person is often drawn to one way, the simple and uneducated person more often to the other. This correlation has many exceptions and is by no means meant to imply a value judgment. In any case, no two ways could seem more opposed. Yet, again, each seems to require something of the other to keep it balanced and authentic, for the way of wisdom (left to itself?) can degenerate into insensitive, heartless intellectualism, and the way of devotion (left to itself?) can degenerate into mindless sentimentality.

The basic conception of generic ways of being religious suggests a possible correlation between ways of being religious and types of personality. This has certainly been recognized in Hinduism, as mentioned in Chapter 1, where it has been taught that the different "paths to God," or yogas, are suited to different personalities and that it would be inappropriate, or at least frustrating, for a person of a personality type suited to one yoga to attempt to seek at-onement with "God" through another. A similar teaching can be found in certain traditions of Mahayana Buddhism (e.g., Tibetan *Gelukpa* and Chinese *T'ien-t'ai* or Japanese *Tendai*), which assigns a different path of Buddhist practice to different personality types, some of which correlate with the six ways. Both in terms of what were called their existential motivations in Chapter 2 and in terms of their characteristic practices, it seems plausible that, where choice among alternatives is available, certain persons are more likely to be drawn to, or be reasonably satisfied with, one way (or certain ways) of being religious over others. Inversely, when choice among alternatives is available, these same persons are more likely to avoid, or be unsatisfied with, certain other ways of being religious. A person usually does not choose the religious subtradition in which she is raised or that is most immediately available in her culture. That subtradition may very well emphasize one way of being religious over others, perhaps at the exclusion of others. It is plausible that, in the event of a poor "fit" between her own personality and existential needs on the one hand and the immediately available way of being religious on the other, she would be motivated to seek satisfaction of her own religious needs elsewhere, outside that subtradition, or at least withhold her full participation in it. Thus, the framework of ways of being religious may offer some insight into what leads people to move from one subtradition to another, if not from one religion to another. Contrariwise, it would explain how a subtradition that generously included within itself multiple ways of being religious addressed to different peoples' religious needs would more likely satisfy the full range of its members' needs.

The correlation of personality types with ways of being religious makes up a whole field yet to be seriously explored.[6] However, despite the rich possibility that this seems to represent, it must not be forgotten that a stronger, natural motivation for involvement in a certain way of being religious exists than affinity with a certain personality type—namely, the existential predicament that raises the problem of meaning in one of its specific aspects. For example, even though persons may by personality be drawn, say, to the way of devotion, they may be compelled by dint of circumstance to confront momentous events requiring an archetypally grounded sense of propriety (e.g., a wedding or a death) that sacred ritual provides. Or they may find themselves forced to confront a situation of radically unjust behavior that calls for rectification through right action. Thus personality type, though it is no doubt a factor in determining an individual's way of being religious, is hardly a determining factor unto itself.

APPLYING THE FRAMEWORK TO SPECIFIC TRADITIONS

It is important to realize that the framework of ways of being religious is not by itself a source of information about actual religions or religious phenomena. It is designed to be a tool for guiding research and investigation. Primary attention, therefore, needs to be given to the actual phenomena to be investigated, and use of the the tool should be determined by the degree to which it helps empathy and understanding move forward. Chapter 6 will return to this topic and so too will Parts II and III, which will illustrate use of the framework in depth by means of a comparative study of Buddhism and Christianity. At this stage, however, a few practical considerations in the use of the framework ought to be placed firmly in mind.

Readers should beware of taking any of the capsule descriptions of ways of being religious that have been offered as an adequate description of any actual religious phenomenon. In reality, a way of being religious does not stand by itself; it is always embodied within a specific religious tradition. The descriptions given above are only sketches of skeletal generic structures, not accounts of any actual, flesh-and-blood religious practice. They must be applied, and applied in a way that does justice both to the phenomenon in all its context-embedded concreteness and to the perspectives of the participants.[7]

The process of application should always be tentative·and exploratory. One should first look to see what indications of any of the ways might be present. One should not expect that in any one religious tradition all ways or any given way must be present. Initial indications of the presence of a certain way of being religious may well turn out to be apparent only, or involved in some kind of combination of ways, with a different way predominant than the one that first was suspected.

It helps to keep in mind that any secondary account one may read about a tradition is always selective to some extent and will probably never represent the full range of phenomena within that tradition. Also, the account may be colored (and therefore somewhat distorted) by the tendency of the interpreter to be sympathetic or antipathetic to one way of being religious over other ways, leading him unintentionally to neglect or overlook aspects that are significant to the practices he is representing.

As one begins exploration, it is more likely that one will first encounter a few particular phenomena of a tradition or a single one, rather than the full range of phenomena to be found within that tradition. The question will then be, of which of the six ways of being religious is this phenomenon illustrative? Sometimes one will have to search hard to learn about the context and setting of a particular phenomenon in order to make a firm identification. One should take care to focus on actual phenomena as embodied and lived, and not just on abstract elements such as certain beliefs or symbols. In other words, into what larger pattern of carrying on religious life within the tradition does it fit? How do participants relate to it and what do they do with it? In what circumstances—physical, temporal, social—do they do these things? What sort of people are involved with it? What is their place within the society in which they are located? What are their reasons, motivations, and attitudes (the ones they would tell if you asked)? What sort of problem (if any) motivates their involvement at this time? What other religious practices are they involved in that go along with this particular practice? What do they say about, and what are their attitudes toward, other practices (exemplifying other ways of being religious) within the same tradition? It may be that more than one way of being religious is involved in the phenomenon under consideration, or it may become clear that only one is involved. Alternatively, it may be that the participant or participants are successively involved in more than one way of being religious, first in this phenomenon and then in another. Often much latent, background information needs to be learned before one can determine with confidence that this or that way of being religious is present and operative.

As has been mentioned already, one should take care not to confuse just any religious ritual with the way of sacred rite, or any instance of religious devotion with the way of devotion, or any study of scripture and tradition with the way of reasoned inquiry, and so forth. There are many minor religious phenomena that do not fall clearly into any one of the ways, especially when abstracted from a larger pattern of religious life. It is only when they become a primary way of drawing near to *ultimate reality*° that they constitute an instance of a way of being religious.

The general idea of generic ways of being religious, the description of each way, and the differentiation of each way from the others presented in this book are all products of a very human enterprise of making sense of similarities and differences among religious phenomena. As one reads about the ways, it is tempting simply to take them as necessary and universal structures of the reality of human religiousness, as more real than the particular phenomena they are designed to help one understand. It may well be that they do point to some such underlying structures. *But they are not themselves those structures.* In other words, it is very easy to lose sight of their nature as tentative human constructions, imperfect and partial attempts to grasp what appears to be a skeletal structure beneath the living flesh of religion.

Do the six ways exhaust all ways of being religious? The framework of the six ways certainly was not constructed with the intent of presenting an exhaustive account. The framework is intended primarily to sort out ways as they may be found in existing traditions. As for nontraditional occurrences, most tend to fall into one or a combination of two or more of the six generic ways delineated in this book. Nothing seems to indicate that further generic ways are likely to emerge from the study of traditional or nontraditional religious practice.

CHAPTER SUMMARY

This chapter describes in some detail the basic features of each of the six ways of being religious. It begins by pointing out how the descriptions of the ways are the result of factoring out features of actual religious phenomena (grouped together on the basis of similarities) that are due to the specific symbol system and *theological*° beliefs of the traditions in which they occur in order to isolate the underlying generic pattern. In effect, the descriptions result from removing the flesh and blood of the phenomena in order to get at the underlying skeletal structure. Readers are warned not to confuse associations they are likely to attach to the names of the ways with the ways themselves. For example, not every instance of religious ritual is a case of the way of sacred rite, and not all ideas about religious ritual drawn from the work of other scholars (having been developed with other purposes in mind) are likely to be congruent with the descriptions offered here. The descriptions are the result of an attempt to apprehend and articulate generic structural commonalities shared by religious phenomena, not the particular phenomena themselves. They are abstractions derived from those phenomena and so they should not be taken as more real than those phenomena. Their value and justification depend on how well they promote empathetic understanding of, and do justice to, the actual phenomena of human religiousness as we find them.

The way of sacred rite focuses on participating anew in archetypal manifestations of *ultimate reality*° that are rendered present through sacramental symbol and ritual. Right action centers on conforming individual and social behavior to the *ultimate normative order of things*°. The way of devotion is preoccupied with centering one's affections in devotional surrender to *ultimate reality*° as compassionate and grace bestowing. Shamanic mediation seeks to be united with *ultimate reality*° as mediator or channel of *its*° "supernatural" intervention in mundane affairs through entering altered states of consciousness. Mystical quest pursues a direct, conscious union of one's entire self with *ultimate reality*° by using ascetic and meditative techniques designed to overcome the obscuring limitations and distracting compulsions of ordinary experience that, as it were, have gotten in the way. The way of reasoned inquiry aims for a union of mind with *the ultimate mind*° in seeking a reasoned understanding of things in *the ultimate perspective*°.

The distinctive hermeneutic each way employs in its interpretation of a tradition's scripture and symbol system is briefly described. Abstract relations of tension and balance between each of the ways are explored and possible correlations with personality types are suggested. Finally, practical suggestions in making use of the categories to classify and interpret phenomena of actual religious traditions are offered.

STUDY QUESTIONS

1. From the descriptions offered in this chapter, with which of the ways do you find yourself most sympathetic and with which are you least sympathetic? Which do you think you best have a sense of at this stage and which do you think you understand least? For those you understand least, identify those features that seem most puzzling or off-putting to you and try to find out more about them by asking your instructor or doing some library research. You may find helpful reading whichever chapter of Part III that presents at length an example from Buddhism and Christianity of the way you seek to understand more.

2. In the interest of building a good, working understanding of each of the ways, put in your own words what you understand each way to be about

and share your interpretation with others who are trying to do the same thing. Allow your interpretation to be revised through the process of discussion. See if you can come up with a couple of good examples illustrating the main features of each way and then find out to what extent others working on the same project agree with your examples.

3. Discuss the relations between the ways as they are arranged on the diagram at the beginning of the section Relating the Ways to Each Other and to Personality Types. Do you notice any interesting relations between the ways that were not identified in this section? Explore the suggestion that the ways opposite each other on the circle complement each other and perhaps may be capable of helping to keep each other in some kind of healthy balance.

4. Are there problems, misgivings, or disagreements you have with the descriptions of the ways and the distinctions drawn between them? Identify what they are and discuss them with your instructor. Could it be that what seems a real disagreement may be only apparent? For example, some phenomena placed in the same category may not seem to you to belong together. Could the difference you note be due not to a difference in the generic way of being religious but to a difference in the specific symbol system in which the phenomenon is found (which may be a feature of more than one religious tradition)?

5. Try out differing hermeneutical orientations on a given passage of scripture from any religious tradition. The passage suggested in the chapter was the Jewish and Christian story of the Creation and Fall of Humankind in Genesis 2:4 to 3:24. Whatever you choose, choose a passage that seems rich with meaning. Not all passages lend themselves well to multiple interpretations, nor are all equally relevant (in any obvious way) to each of the orientations. Some passages of scripture (e.g., a genealogical list of names) may bear little relevance to any of the orientations. Once you have chosen a rich passage, read and carefully attempt to interpret it from each perspective, one at a time. Note down how the story differently speaks to each need. Compare and contrast the different results.

FOR FURTHER READING

In what follows are a few references on each generic way of being religious that should be particularly helpful in building up a fuller understanding of each way and begin to launch a student on a comparative study of that way in two or more religious traditions. Students should be aware, however, that the purposes of, and approach taken by, the authors may not be congruent in all respects with the framework of ways of being religious.

On the Way of Sacred Rite

Recommended articles in the *Encyclopedia of Religion* edited by Mircea Eliade (New York: Macmillan, 1987) include: *Ritual; Ritual Studies; Ceremony; The Sacred and the Profane; Sacred Space; Sacred Time; Symbolic Time; Anamnesis; Archetype; Worship and Cultic Life; Sacraments; Liturgy; Li; Pūjā; Rites of Passage; Domestic Observances; Drama; Dance; Masks; Music; Priesthood; Ordination; Initiation; Consecration; Sacrifice; Purification; Pilgrimage; Stupa Worship; Relics; Circumambulation; Procession; Symbolism; Images; Icons; Iconography; Sacrifice, Architecture, Temple; Biblical Temple; Synagogue; Mosque; Basilica, Cathedral, Church; Shrines;* and articles on specific religious traditions exemplifying the way of sacred rite.

One of the most helpful studies of sacred rite as one way of being religious among others (although his approach is not entirely congruent with the approach taken here) is Frederick J. Streng, *Understanding Religious Life*, 3rd ed. Ch. 3, "Creation of Community Through Sacred Symbols" (Belmont, CA: Wadsworth, 1985). His bibliographical suggestions are very helpful. See also Frederick J. Streng, Charles L. Lloyd, Jr., and Jay T. Allen, eds., *Ways of Being Religious: Readings for a New Approach to Religion* Part 2: "Creation of Community through Myth and Ritual" (Englewood Cliffs, NJ: Prentice-Hall, 1973). Although Streng treats them as a different category altogether, some nontraditional religious phenomena akin to sacred rite are covered in Ch. 9 of *Understanding Religious Life*, "The Power of Artistic Creativity," and Part 7, selections 1 and 7, of *Ways of Being Religious*.

Other particularly helpful studies include: Ronald L. Grimes, *Beginnings in Ritual Studies*, rev. ed. (Columbia, SC: University of South Carolina Press, 1995) (Grimes's book is helpful in giving readers the developing state of ritual studies and in developing a comprehensive understanding of ritual, within which the way of sacred rite is a specific type); Catherine Bell, *Ritual Theory, Ritual Practice* (New York: Oxford University Press, 1992) (helpful in the manner of Grimes's study, especially in its survey of theories of ritual, but more concerned with developing a theory of "ritualization" in general and not as helpful on getting clear sacred rite as one distinctive way of being religious among others); Caroline Humphrey and James Laidlaw, *The Archetypal Actions of Ritual: A Theory of Ritual Illustrated by the Jain Rite of Worship* (New York: Oxford University Press, 1994) (similar to Bell, though significantly differing with regard to their theory of "ritualization"); Mircea Eliade, *The Myth of the Eternal Return, or Cosmos and History*, trans. Willard R. Trask (Bollingen Series 46; Princeton, NJ: Princeton University Press, 1954) (overgeneralizing all of religion, in this and the following entry, but particularly insightful regarding the way of sacred rite); Mircea Eliade, *The Sacred and the Profane*, trans. Willard R. Trask (New York: Harcourt Brace Jovanovich, 1959); J. S. LaFontaine, ed., *The Interpretation of Ritual* (London: Tavistock, 1972) (a collection of essay studies of the nature of ritual and different types of ritual); Gerald A. Pottebaum, *The Rites of People: Exploring the Ritual Character of the Human Experience*, rev. ed. (Washington, DC: Pastoral Press, 1992) (written within a Roman Catholic orientation but illuminates the nature and role of sacred ritual in human experience generally); and Victor Turner, *The Ritual Process: Structure and Anti-Structure* (Chicago, IL: Aldine, 1968) (discusses different types of ritual, ritual symbolism, and a theory of the ritual process from the perspective of cultural anthropology).

For good examples of the way of sacred rite in Buddhism and in Christianity, see Chapter 14, below.

On the Way of Right Action

Recommended articles in the *Encyclopedia of Religion,* edited by Mircea Eliade (New York: Macmillan, 1987) include: *Morality and Religion; Orthopraxy; Community; Politics and Religion; Law and Religion; Legalism; Merit; Religious Communities; Conscience; Cosmic Law; Dharma; Ahimsā; Buddhist Ethics; Christian Ethics; Hindu Dharma; Islamic Law; Israelite Law; Halakhah;* and articles on specific religious traditions exemplifying the way of right action..

Though many studies of religious ethics in various traditions exist, not many explore the pursuit of right action as a way of being religious, that is, the spirituality of right action as a way of approach to "ultimate reality." One of the best attempts in this direction is Frederick J. Streng, *Understanding Religious Life*, 3rd ed., Ch. 4, "Living in Harmony with Cosmic Law" (Belmont, CA: Wadsworth, 1985). His bibliographical suggestions are very helpful. See also Frederick J. Streng, Charles L. Lloyd, Jr., and Jay T. Allen, eds., *Ways of Being Religious: Readings for a New Approach to Religion.* part 3: "Living Harmoniously through Conformity to the Cosmic Law" (Englewood Cliffs, NJ: Prentice-Hall, 1973). Although Streng treats them as a different category altogether, some nontraditional religious phenomena akin to the way of right action are covered in Ch. 7 of *Understanding Religious Life*, "The Religious Significance of Social Responsibility," and Parts 6 and 7 of *Ways of Being Religious*; "Achievement of Human Rights through Political and Economic Action" and "The New Life through Technocracy."

A useful survey of manifestations of certain aspects of the way of right action in the religious traditions of the world is Denise L. Carmody and John T. Carmody, *Shamans, Prophets, and Sages: A Concise Introduction to World Religions*, Part 2: "Prophets." (Belmont, CA: Wadsworth, 1985). The categories of "prophet" and "prophecy" these authors use, tend to be slanted by taking their model from the role of prophet and prophecy from the Bible.

Other helpful studies include David Chidester, *Patterns of Action: Religion and Ethics in a Comparative Perspective* (Belmont, CA: Wadsworth, 1987); David Little and Sumner B. Twiss, *Comparative Religious Ethics* (New York: Harper & Row, 1978); Ronald M. Green, *Religion and Moral Reason: A New Method for Comparative Study* (New York: Oxford University Press, 1988); and Meredith B. McGuire, *Religion: The Social Context*, 2nd ed. (Belmont, CA: Wadsworth, 1987).

For examples of the way of right action in Buddhism and in Christianity, see Chapter 11, below.

On the Way of Devotion

Recommended articles in the *Encyclopedia of Religion,* edited by Mircea Eliade (New York: Macmillan, 1987), include *Devotion; Popular Religion; Bhakti; Grace; Faith; Pietism; Evangelical and Fundamental Christianity; Vaiṣṇavism; Kṛṣṇaism; Śaivism; Jōdoshū; Jōdo Shinshū; Hasidism;* and articles on specific religious traditions exemplifying the way of devotion.

Not many good studies of devotion as one way of being religious among others, exist. One of the best attempts in this direction is Frederick J. Streng, *Understanding Religious Life*, 3rd ed., Ch. 2, "Personal Apprehension of a Holy Presence" (Belmont, CA: Wadsworth, 1985). Streng groups some phenomena under this category that I would classify differently under mystical quest and shamanic mediation. Nevertheless, many of his remarks are helpful, especially his bibliographical suggestions. See also Frederick J. Streng, Charles L. Lloyd, Jr., and Jay T. Allen, eds., *Ways of Being Religious: Readings for a New Approach to Religion*, Part 1: "Rebirth through Personal Encounter with the Holy" (Englewood Cliffs, NJ: Prentice-Hall, 1973). Although Streng treats them as a different category altogether, some nontraditional religious phenomena akin to the way of devotion are covered in Ch. 6 of *Understanding Religious Life*, "The Religious

Significance of Fulfilling Human Relationships," and Part 5 of *Ways of Being Religious*, "Attaining an Integrated Self through Creative Interaction."

For examples of the way of devotion in Buddhism and in Christianity, see Chapter 12, below.

On the Way of Shamanic Mediation

Recommended articles in the *Encyclopedia of Religion*, edited by Mircea Eliade (New York: Macmillan, 1987), include *Shamanism; Power; Miracles; Visions; Healing; Prophecy; Oracles; Divination; Glossolalia; Ecstasy; Spirit Possession; Demons; Exorcism; Necromancy; Geomancy; Theurgy; Witchcraft; Magic; Spells; Occultism;* and articles on specific religious traditions exemplifying the way of shamanic mediation.

A useful survey of manifestations of the way of shamanic mediation in the religious traditions of the world is Denise L. Carmody and John T. Carmody, *Shamans, Prophets, and Sages: A Concise Introduction to World Religions*, Part 1: "Shamans" (Belmont, CA: Wadsworth, 1985).

A good introduction to the variety of shamanic phenomena and shamanic traditions can be found in I. M. Lewis, *Ecstatic Religion: An Anthropological Study of Spirit Possession and Shamanism* (Middlesex, England: Penguin Books, 1971); Gary Doore, ed., *Shaman's Path* (Boston, MA: Shambhala Books, 1988); Shirley Nicholson, ed., *Shamanism: An Expanded View of Reality* (Wheaton, IL: Quest, 1987); and Joan Halifax, ed., *Shamanic Voices: A Survey of Visionary Narratives* (New York: E. P. Dutton, 1979). One of the most respected of the classic studies of shamanism (which stresses common themes over the differences made by the particular traditions in which it is found) is Mircea Eliade, *Shamanism: Archaic Techniques of Ecstasy* (Princeton, NJ: Princeton University Press, 1964).

For examples of the way of shamanic mediation in Buddhism and in Christianity, see Chapter 13, below.

On the Way of Mystical Quest

Recommended articles in the *Encyclopedia of Religion*, edited by Mircea Eliade (New York: Macmillan, 1987), include: *Mysticism; Mystical Union; Meditation; Consciousness, States of; Attention; Spiritual Discipline; Asceticism; Yoga; Samādhi; Prāṇa; Monasticism; Monastery; Eremiticsm; Mendicancy;* and other articles on specific religious traditions exemplifying the way of mystical quest.

Though many studies of mysticism exist, not many approach it from the specific perspective outlined in this book. One of the best attempts in this direction is Frederick J. Streng, *Understanding Religious Life*, 3rd ed., Ch. 5, "Attaining Freedom Through Spiritual Discipline" (Belmont, CA: Wadsworth, 1985). Streng's account is hampered, somewhat, from his assignment of all expressions of personalistic mystical traditions to what I classify as the way of devotion. Nevertheless, his remarks are very helpful, as are his bibliographical suggestions. See also Frederick J. Streng, Charles L. Lloyd, Jr., and Jay T. Allen, eds., *Ways of Being Religious: Readings for a New Approach to Religion*, Part 4: "Spiritual Freedom through Discipline (Mysticism)" (Englewood Cliffs, NJ: Prentice-Hall, 1973). Although Streng treats them as a different category altogether, some nontraditional religious phenomena akin to the way of mystical quest are covered in Part 8, selections 2 and 6.

An excellent critical overview of the controversies and major theories of the nature and study of mysticism is given in Bernard McGinn, "Theoretical Foundations: The Modern

Study of Mysticism," an appendix to his "The Foundations of Mysticism," Vol. I of *The Presence of God: A History of Western Christian Mysticism* (New York: Crossroad, 1992), pp. 265–343. McGinn's book itself, the first of a four-part series, is an excellent source on Christian mystical quest. Another good survey of the field, but with somewhat more specific content is Ninian Smart, "Mysticism, History of," *The Encyclopedia of Philosophy*, ed. Paul Edwards (New York: Macmillan, 1972), Vol. 5, pp. 419–429. One of the better collections of essays on the meaning, methodology, interpretation, and evaluation of mysticism in various traditions is Richard T. Woods, ed., *Understanding Mysticism* (Garden City, NY: Doubleday Image Books, 1980). A basic overview of the mystical quest in world religions is Sidney Spencer, *Mysticism in World Religion* (Baltimore, MD: Penguin, 1963). A comprehensive, cross-cultural and cross-tradition survey of ascetic practices is found in Vincent L. Wimbush and Richard Valantasis, eds., *Aceticism* (New York: Oxford University Press, 1995).

For examples of the way of mystical quest in Buddhism and in Christianity, see Chapter 9, below.

On the Way of Reasoned Inquiry

Recommended articles in the *Encyclopedia of Religion*, edited by Mircea Eliade (New York: Macmillan, 1987) include *Wisdom; Truth; Reason; Knowledge and Ignorance; Doctrine; Philosophy; Theology; Theodicy; Law and Religion; Cosmology; Scholasticism; Jñāna; Prajñā; Avidyā; Kalām; Jewish Thought and Philosophy;* and other articles on specific traditions exemplifying the way of reasoned inquiry.

Though many studies of philosophy and theology in the different religious traditions of the world exist, not many approach them from the specific perspective outlined in this book for the way of reasoned inquiry—i.e., intellectual inquiry as itself a means of approach to *ultimate reality*. And, specifically, very few explore the process of inquiry itself as religious practice. One of the best attempts in this direction is Frederick J. Streng, *Understanding Religious Life*, 3rd ed., Ch. 8, "The Power of Rationality," and Ch. 10, "The Religious Response to Physical Existence" (Belmont, CA: Wadsworth, 1985).

A useful survey of manifestations of the way of reasoned inquiry in the religious traditions of the world is Denise L. Carmody and John T. Carmody, *Shamans, Prophets, and Sages: A Concise Introduction to World Religions,* Part 3: "Sages" (Belmont, CA: Wadsworth, 1985). The categories of "sage" and "sagacious tradition" these authors use, encompass not only the way of reasoned inquiry but aspects as well of the way of mystical quest.

A completely different study of the way of wisdom, well worth the effort, is Seyyed Hossein Nasr, *Knowledge and the Sacred,* Gifford Lectures, 1981 (New York: Crossroad, 1981). Nasr's book is not written from a putatively neutral academic perspective but aims to give voice to, and advocate, the way of reasoned inquiry in all traditions over against the modern secular world view. It minimizes differences between wisdom traditions, and is rooted in a way of wisdom in Shi'ite Islamic Sufism.

Other studies of value include Jacob Needleman, "Why Philosophy Is Easy," in his *Consciousness and Tradition* (New York: Crossroad, 1982), pp. 12–22; several of the essays in *Sacred Tradition and Present Need*, ed. Jacob Needleman and Dennis Lewis (New York: Viking Press, 1975), especially those by Lhalungpa, Reymond, Nasr, and Lavastine.

For examples of the way of reasoned inquiry in Buddhism and in Christianity, see Chapter 10, below.

NOTES

1. When they are not kept separate, confusion results. Some examples will help to make clear my point.

Until relatively recently, shamanism as a religious phenomenon has almost solely been the object of anthropological study. Anthropology has focused its research primarily upon nonliterate, small-scale, tribal cultures—where shamanic phenomena are remarkably widespread. Although shamanic phenomena may be found in virtually all of the great religions too, their occurrence in local, unsophisticated, non-text-oriented, "folk practice" contexts has frequently led scholars to exclude them from "mainstream" accounts of the great religions and to suppose them to be the result of the infusion of indigenous and "primitive" religious elements. Some scholars, impressed with the deep similarities between shamanic phenomena around the world, have as a result proposed that shamanism be identified as a religion unto itself. Drawing on these anthropological accounts, popularized accounts of shamanism found in New Age Religion literature portray shamanism as a phenomenon more or less independent of its specific cultural-religious, *theological*? context and thus as a practice that can be appropriated by persons outside that context. (See for example, *Shaman's Drum: A Journal of Experiential Shamanism* [P.O. Box 430, Willits, CA 95490]. See also the fall 1990 [Vol. 13, No. 2] issue of *ReVision: The Journal of Consciousness and Change* [4000 Albemarle Street, NW, Washington, DC 20016], which was dedicated to the topic, "Shamanism: The Transpersonal Dimension.") Some New Age "shamans" and "gurus" now presume to teach and initiate followers into this "religion"—an eclectic hodgepodge of elements from diverse shamanic traditions, taking as authoritative texts the works of anthropologists! Sometimes they are anthropologists themselves—e.g., Michael Harner, *The Way of the Shaman: A Guide to Power and Healing* (New York: Harper and Row, 1982). What all of this amounts to, I suggest, is taking a generic structure, abstracted from any specific symbol system, and treating it as if it were a specific practice—sort of like taking the category "mammal" and treating it as if it were a species, and then creating a new species modeled on the generic category. For another angle on this phenomenon, see Ronald L. Grimes, "Parashamanism," in his *Beginnings in Ritual Studies*, rev. ed. (Columbia, SC: University of South Carolina Press, 1995), pp. 253–268.

Another example of the same sort of confusion is the recurrent idea that mysticism is not many things but more or less a single thing in all of its instances in the many religious traditions of the world, and a further development of the idea that takes mysticism to be the true and authentic core of all religions, once one peels away all of their outward and largely inauthentic trappings. A third example is the proclivity of several Enlightenment thinkers to identify morality (or the approximation to a universal morality) as the true and authentic core of all religions—along with a pared-down, minimalist philosophical theism—and the correlative presumption to call it "natural religion" (as distinct from presumably unnatural "revealed religions") and attempt to practice and teach it as Deism. Still a fourth example is an aspect of the work of the great scholar of the comparative study of religions, Mircea Eliade. Among his many accomplishments, he is certainly to be credited with opening up and making generally accessible a basic understanding of what I call the way of sacred rite as that can be found in virtually every religious tradition in human history, but especially in so-called "archaic" traditions. No other single scholar that I am aware of has done so much to clarify in a comparative way the kind of sensibility that accompanies this way of being religious. However, not invariably but at times in his writings, the way of sacred rite—or, as he puts it, the effort to participate anew in original, archetypal forms of the sacred—comes across as the inner core of all religion and as virtually the same theme with endless variations from one religious tradition to the next. As a result, one gains little sense from his work of the integrity and distinctive "other world to live in" of any specific tradition, and one is left with the implication that it is ultimately only the comparativist (belonging to no one tradition) who can know the meaning of religious phenomena.

The inverse category mistake, treating the specific as if it were generic or constructing generic categories out of specific traits, is just as widespread though perhaps less encountered outside of academic study. One example is found in the academic discipline of the philosophy of religion. The basic categories, themes, and questions dealt with in this discipline have related almost exclusively to Western theism—at least until very recently—yet the discipline has presumed to draw conclusions that are supposed to hold for religion universally. A similar confusion—taking forms specific to one or two traditions to be characteristic of religion as such—flaws most major modern critical theories of religion, such as those of Feuerbach, Marx, and Freud. Many early efforts in the comparative study of religion similarly defined religion as involving some sort of belief in and worship of a god or gods, which generated unnecessary controversy as to whether Theravada Buddhism, Confucianism, and so-called Philosophical Daoism—which involve no such belief or practice—qualify as religions. Another less problematic example is the effort to classify religions according to the nature of their specific conceptions of *ultimate reality*[p] as, e.g., monotheism, polytheism, pantheism, and atheism (possibly including, in addition, henotism, panentheism, and other more refined categories); or traditions that take *ultimate reality*[p] to be transcendent to the natural order versus traditions that take *ultimate reality*[p] to be immanent within the natural order. I say these classifications are less problematic because they are useful for certain limited purposes and need not lead to significant misunderstandings. However, if they are taken to imply that a religious tradition has little or nothing (or nothing significant) in common with religions not in the grouping into which it has been placed, they serve as blinders to comparative study.

There are some very good surveys available of the diversity of generic forms of religious life that may be met with. (One of the very best is Roger Schmidt, Exploring Religion, 2nd ed. [Belmont, CA: Wadsworth, 1988]. A few have attempted to identify generic ways of being religious. But only one writer, Frederick Streng, has previously attempted in a sustained way to clarify just what such ways involve in practice. (See the recommended readings for this chapter.) It was some of his early work that originally inspired the conception of the framework presented in this book.

My own account owes a great deal to Streng's account, yet our two accounts differ in many respects. The major differences between our two accounts stem from my interest in identifying truly generic ways of being religious that are effectively differentiated from the specific religious traditions in which they are exemplified and particularly from *theological*[p] convictions as to the nature of *ultimate reality*[p]. Streng's categories, on my reading, do not completely differentiate generic ways from specific *theological*[p] convictions.

2. Alfred North Whitehead, *Science and the Modern World* (New York: Macmillan, 1925), Ch. 3.

3. See Chapter 2, note 8.

4. Although the theory of archetypes of Jungian psychology may seem to be suggested here, I do not wish to invoke it. Carl Jung's theory of archetypes no doubt draws profoundly on the experience of archetypal forms in the way of sacred rite. (Plato's theory of forms, for that matter, does too.) However, Jung's conception of psychological archetypes as truly universal and not specific to the symbol systems of particular traditions (let alone his theory of the collective unconscious to account for them) goes far beyond what the description here offered presupposes. Though I do not rule out the possibility of truly universal (or generic) archetypes, I refer here specifically to archetypal forms specific to particular religious traditions.

5. "Supernatural" is placed in quotation marks here in respect for those traditions that re-gard the spirit world and the extraordinary powers that may be found there as part of the natural order of things. For such traditions, shamanic powers are *super*-natural only in re-lation to the narrow conception of a purely material nature in the modern world view.

6. This possibility will be discussed further in Chapter 6.

7. As readers become more familiar with actual examples of each way, it is possible to gain a feeling for the similar skeletal structure underlying each. Thereby a reader may come to a slightly different formulation that is more useful and does more justice than the one I offer. Should that happen, I will have achieved more of my goal than had the read-er simply accepted and appropriated my formulations without question.

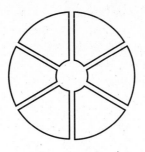

C H A P T E R 4

THE WAYS OF
BEING RELIGIOUS
· EXEMPLIFIED

The present chapter is devoted to conveying a more concrete sense of ways o
being religious. Examples of each way of being religious will be cited in a variety of traditions as well as in some nontraditional forms. Then various possible
relationships between the ways will be discussed. Typically, religious traditions
prioritize or super-ordinate certain ways in relation to others and in some cases
may suppress the emergence of one or more ways. These prioritizations occasionally change. When religions are not confined to a relatively small-scale tribal group, they typically evolve over time and through geographic and demographic
dispersion. When such change happens, it usually is from a more compact, less
differentiated state to a less compact, more differentiated state, from one way or
a few ways of being religious to many ways. When a religion moves into a new
cultural context, circumstances may stimulate the emergence of new ways of
being religious that may appear as a kind of syncretism. Whereas some expressions of a religion exemplify a single way and little else, other expressions integrate several ways at once. And whereas some subtraditions take an exclusive
attitude toward the practice of a single way, other subtraditions take an inclusive
attitude that generously tolerates the practice of several different ways of being
religious, and perhaps all six. Examples of each of these kinds of relationships
between the ways will be cited.

A precaution: the examples cited and the interpretive descriptions of them should not be regarded as final. Depending on their acquaintance with the traditions and religious phenomena cited, some readers may be inclined to classify and describe them somewhat differently. That is to be expected. In other words, the reader must exercise her or his own judgment in making use of the framework, trying to see further, perhaps, and with keener sensitivity.

WAYS OF BEING RELIGIOUS IN AMERICAN CHRISTIANITY

So far the discussion of ways of being religious has dealt in rather abstract generalities. What do the ways look like exemplified in the largely Christian but nevertheless pluralist sort of religious life found in the United States?

Mention "sacred ritual" in connection with Christianity, and most Americans will think "Roman Catholic." To a large extent, the way of sacred rite is central to the religious life of Roman Catholics, though their pattern of worship has become much less formal than it used to be prior to the change from the Latin Mass to vernacular worship in the late 1960s. What is not often recognized is that sacred rite is also central to the religious life of Lutherans, Episcopalians (or Anglicans), and Eastern Orthodox as well. It is not what distinguishes Roman Catholic worship from Protestant worship, despite what is commonly supposed. (Yet, because most American Protestants have a fairly informal, nonsacramental structure of worship and suppose that they represent all Protestants in this respect, it is easy to see how the idea is so widespread.)

What is it about worship in these traditions that makes it a manifestation of the way of sacred rite? Typically, the primary form of worship in each includes the sacrament of Holy Communion, the Mass, the Divine Liturgy, the Eucharist (all different names for the same thing)—a highly structured, symbolic transaction, a sacred ritual meal, in which the whole congregation participates simultaneously on many levels: bodily, emotionally, aesthetically, and intellectually. Behind the scenes, a comprehensive array of liturgical arts (architecture, choreography, visual art, vestment making, poetry, and music) work together to facilitate holistic, communal participation. All of these elements are premised on a crucial assumption, that the sacred ritual is itself a way of directly connecting with God in Jesus Christ, and above all with the Sacrificial Redemption of Christ through which all things are renewed and find their meaning. Thus, Holy Communion isn't just about Jesus Christ and the message of salvation. It isn't just a matter of calling to mind the events of salvation and an acknowledgment of his lordship over their lives. It isn't just an offering of praise and thanksgiving. It is all of these things and more: for the symbols central to the worship are not mere symbols; they are not simply representative. To wholehearted participants, they are presentative of God in Christ; they are means by which God in Christ becomes present to the congregation and to the individual participants. Inversely expressed, they are means by which participants enter holistically into the presence of God in Christ, receive his[1] grace, and renew their sense of what life is all about.

Although these subtraditions centrally emphasize the way of sacred rite, they may also strongly but subordinately emphasize other ways, such as right action. Even so, a number of Christian traditions in America do give primary emphasis to the way of right action. Among the oldest of these traditions is the Mennonite tradition, the most conservative branch of which is called Old Order Amish. Characteristic of Mennonites (and several other traditions like them) is a stress on simply living the teachings of Jesus in a practical, day-to-day, communal lifestyle distinct from the culture and society at large. To be Christian for them is to live a life of discipleship to Jesus, a life patterned after him in self-denial. Belief in Jesus, while important, is no substitute for personal conduct, and participation in sacramental ritual has no meaning apart from practicing the example of Christ. Accordingly, worship is simple and ministers are virtually indistinguishable from laypersons. Evidence of one's "conversion to Christ" is shown in living as Christ himself lived, doing the will of God, loving one's enemies, and suffering as Christ did. Notable is the historic stand of Mennonites against coercive violence of any kind (especially war), their active efforts on behalf of peace and reconciliation, and their national and international humanitarian relief activities. They do not understand these actions as means of earning one's salvation, as other Protestants may suppose. It is rather that these things are themselves evidence of salvation; they are part of what salvation is all about. To support and participate in them is for Mennonites to experience in some measure at-onement with God in Christ; to participate in them is to be about God's business, carrying out his redemptive work in the world.

Except for a few aspects of other ways of being religious that directly support and contribute to right action (e.g., theological study and some forms of meditative prayer), about the only other way of being religious evident among traditional Mennonites is the way of devotion as expressed in the cultivation of an intimate, devotional relationship to Christ in one's personal life. However, even here, the way of devotion is clearly subordinate to right action.

Other traditions that give an especially strong or central emphasis to right action—though not necessarily in a way that would be in agreement with Mennonites—include Swiss Brethren, Hutterites, the Quaker or Friends tradition, Liberal Protestantism (which is not a denomination, but a modern movement of persons and congregations within mainstream Protestant denominations), the so-called Liberation Theology movement in Third World Roman Catholic cultures, Seventh-Day Adventists, the Church of Jesus Christ of Latter Day Saints (Mormons), and Jehovah's Witnesses.

Among American Christians, the way of devotion is given central emphasis in traditions that identify with the label "evangelical." As used here, the label does not represent a specific denomination or even a group of denominations (though some denominations as a whole are clearly evangelical). Rather, is it a religious movement within preexisting Protestant denominations, outside denominations (e.g., in community churches and nondenominational revival meetings and crusades), and sometimes spawning denominations, that goes back through a series of national revivalist movements to the so-called Great Awakening in the British colonies prior to the American Revolution. The distinguishing mark of Evangelical Protestant identity is first priority placed upon an experience of "personal salvation," a being "born again," a "conversion experience," in which one prayerfully surrenders to a process of emotional purgation whereby Jesus Christ (understood as an inward spiritual presence) becomes the central focus of one's affective life, one's "personal Lord and Savior." A close second priority is the Evangelical activity of bringing other people to the threshold of this experience: "introducing other people to Jesus" and "winning souls for Christ." All other things, by comparison, for most Evangelicals tend to fall into insignificance (although some find room for aspects of other ways of being religious). Accordingly, religious activity for them consists primarily in cultivating and renewing this sense of the presence of Christ through corporate worship and individual devotional practices, and creating occasions for persons to make a "decision for Christ." Evangelical worship is typically simple and informal, focusing on congregational singing, prayer, and "Gospel preaching"—which traditionally culminates in an "invitation" to open one's heart to Jesus (whether for the first time or for renewal). Protestant denominations that may be characterized as Evangelical include Baptist, Nazarene, Free Methodist, Wesleyan Methodist, Church of the Brethren, Christian Church, Disciples of Christ, and all Pentecostal denominations (although Pentecostals are more than simply Evangelical, as will be explained below).

Although they prefer to identify themselves with Evangelical Protestantism (even as the true or most genuine of Evangelical Protestants), Fundamentalist Protestants, in their comprehensive opposition to secular humanistic orientations in society, culture, and "liberal religion," tend to emphasize the way of right action over the way of devotion, contrary to the predominant greater stress on the way of devotion among Evangelicals generally. This emphasis on right action is evident in their insistence that true Christians (1) adhere to "the fundamentals" of correct Christian belief over and against non-Fundamentalist Christians, (2) "come out from among" those deemed going to Hell and publically declare their faith in Christ (i.e., affirm "the Fundamentals") by joining "the righteous remnant" who are going to Heaven, (3) be committed to "win new souls for Christ," (4) obey "the absolute standards of Christian conduct," and (5) uphold and enforce "biblical values" and "biblical teachings" in American society and American public institutions that are being undermined by secular humanistic patterns of thought.

The way of shamanic mediation in American Christianity generally is not very evident and in some places it has been actively discouraged or suppressed—with the exception of two significant movements: (1) the Pentecostal Movement, which began as a nondenominational, revivalist movement at the turn of the twentieth century and produced a number of different Pentecostal denominations (e.g., Assembly of God, Church of God, Pentecostal Holiness, etc.), and (2) the Charismatic Movement, which began around 1960 as a non- or inter-denominational, lay movement within existing Protestant and Roman Catholic churches. In both movements, shamanic mediation remains closely fused with and largely subordinated to the Evangelical pattern of the way of devotion described above. What makes them instances of the way of shamanic mediation and not simply the way of devotion is a deliberate invocation of what they take to be the supernatural agency of the Holy Spirit, intervening in the lives of persons (in service of the purposes of God) to accomplish things beyond their natural human capacity: to enthuse, inspire, give vision, provide guidance, exhort, predict events, provide knowledge and understanding, reveal truth, change lives, console, encourage, heal physically, heal psychologically, heal spiritually, and exorcise demonic powers. Access to the agency of the Holy Spirit is not direct, but depends on the willingness of persons, as believers in Christ, to give themselves over to the inward control of the Holy Spirit, becoming channels or mediators of its power on behalf of the ongoing purposes of Christ in the world. This experience is known among Pentecostals and Charismatics as "Baptism in the Holy Spirit." It is typically, but not always, manifested through "speaking in tongues" or glossolalia. The latter manifestation is said to be the Holy Spirit speaking through one's own voice in a language beyond one's direct comprehension.

Pentecostal worship especially, but also informal worship of Charismatic Christians that takes place outside of any non-Charismatic worship in which they may be involved, is typically a dynamic, highly expressive, (predictably) unpredictable, body-involving event, characterized by spontaneous release of joy and of personal suffering faced, purged, and surmounted. Though an evangelical "invitation" to accept Christ as Lord and Savior may occur in the midst of Pentecostal worship, the focus is more often on what is taken to be some supernatural manifestation of the Holy Spirit. It may be speaking in tongues, prophecy, a "word of wisdom," or healing prayer. Music, both vocal and instrumental, is an important contributor to the whole, as are rhythmic movement and dynamic, audience-involving preaching.

It is worthwhile noting that Afro-American Christians have had a significantly influential effect upon the emergence and development of Pentecostalism in America and on the style of its music and worship. From its emergence among black slaves, with their roots in aboriginal African culture and religion, Afro-American Christianity has always been more expressive, more dynamic, and more spontaneous in its worship than mainstream white American religion. Many features of Pentecostal worship can be directly traced to antecedents in Afro-American Christianity.

Outside the Pentecostal and Charismatic movements, the occasional recurrence of visionary phenomena within Roman Catholic popular piety (e.g., visions of the Virgin Mary) and attendant alleged miracles are clear evidence of the way of shamanic mediation in that tradition.

Before leaving shamanic mediation, mention should be made of various spiritualist groups that have been on the fringes of American Christianity, when not actively excluded, from early times. They became especially strong in a number of nineteenth-century religious movements, which resulted in the founding of the American Spiritualist Church and, in a considerably attenuated form (in fusion with the way of reasoned inquiry), in the Christian Science Church.

The way of mystical quest has not generally been encouraged in American Christianity until recently, even in the historic traditions that have been known to encourage it in other cultural contexts—namely, Eastern Orthodox Christianity and Roman Catholicism. This may have something to do with the pragmatic disposition of Americans to prefer doing over being and activity over contemplation. Nevertheless, the way of mystical quest has had a continuing place in American Christianity, though a relatively small and somewhat hidden one, among Roman Catholic contemplative monastic communities and in small numbers of lay contemplatives in the Episcopal and Quaker traditions, among others. Recently, however, the picture has changed considerably, along with the flood of interest in Oriental and alternative spiritualities that took hold in the 1960s and the "rediscovery" of long-standing traditions of mystical quest in Christianity by Christians who had never realized that such a thing existed. One result has been a phenomenal growth in a market for publications on contemplative spirituality, both Eastern and Western, a blossoming of interest in spiritual direction and retreat experiences at contemplative centers, and something of a (re)birth of interest in contemplative monasticism: Roman Catholic (e.g., Cistercian or Trappist, Carthusian, Carmelite, Contemplative Benedictine), Eastern Orthodox, Episcopal, and some interdenominational Protestant attempts).

What is involved in pursuit of the way of mystical quest in a Christian contemplative tradition such as Trappist monasticism (which, despite the recent growth of interest, has been going on in this form for a very long time)? First, it involves living in a quiet place apart from the distractions and interferences of conventional life. In important respects it represents a renunciation of conventional life. It is to live a life stripped down to its bare essentials in order to grapple in a deliberate and focused way with the obstacles within oneself to at-onement with God in Christ. Trappist monks voluntarily take upon themselves a set of spiritual disciplines in common and, in addition, certain disciplines specific to themselves in their own spiritual quest. Among the common disciplines are commitment to live apart, in charity with others, in a single place, under obedience to the community and its abbot, as together the community seeks to discern and follow the will of God, to labor manually each day in support of the community, to participate each day in the cycle of corporate monastic prayer, to maintain an atmosphere of recollection and silence, to restrain one's appetites, and in all to seek a progressively fuller and more complete conversion of one's life, in all of its aspects, to God. Individual disciplines vary, but generally they include some form of meditative prayer: a solitary, quiet centering and a deepened attentiveness to God in scripture, in liturgy and sacrament, in nature, in one's fellow monks, and in oneself. The idea is to break through the illusions, distortions, and distractions of ordinary conscious experience in order to become directly aware of God and of all things in God and become wholly grounded in him and responsive to him. It is a form of religious life unfamiliar, it seems, to most American Christians, yet one of increasing attraction for many.

American Christian expressions of the way of reasoned inquiry are many and varied, ranging from individual study of the Bible to the composition of systematic expositions of Christian belief by seminary theologians. Because Protestants generally emphasize scriptural literacy and have done so since the Protestant Reformation, encouragement of individual study of scripture is a part of virtually all Protestant traditions. Roman Catholicism has given a central, strong emphasis to theological study in all of its educational institutions in America. Moreover, it has consistently required extensive theological study by all of its priests and bishops. However, Roman Catholicism has not emphasized the individual study of scripture as much as Protestants have, but it is not uncommon nowadays to find Roman Catholic laypersons who seriously study scripture to build up their knowledge and understanding of the Christian revelation—though usually this is done with the guidance of their church's traditional interpretation.

Although much of scriptural study among Christians is simply to learn what scripture says and to comprehend the content of Christian revelation, the prime motive of scriptural and theological study is to make sense of the world, of the times through which one is living, of puzzling aspects of one's own experience, and of choices one is facing in light of the revelation of God as disclosed in scripture (and mediated by tradition). The aim is to attain clear understanding of something initially not understood through the illumination of "God's ultimate truth," as that discloses itself through diligent examination of scripture and tradition. Among professional theologians, such inquiry is less focused on individual puzzlements than that of laypersons; is more systematically concerned to take into account the interpretations and arguments of other theologians, present and past; and on the whole is more rigorously and comprehensively thought through in every detail. Nevertheless, it remains essentially the same sort of enterprise as that of a layperson's serious study of scripture.

For example, a theologian of my acquaintance in a midwestern Methodist seminary recently completed and published a profound, critical study of modern economic theory in light of an understanding of economy implicit in the Bible.[2] Its primary motivation lay in wrestling with the crises of human livelihood in today's global economy and discovering something that hardly anyone had realized before—namely, that the ultimate, theoretical assumptions that govern contemporary economic decision making call for serious examination and challenge in the light of the Christian revelation. Another, very different example is the work of feminist theologian Elisabeth Schüssler Fiorenza, who is seeking a renewed understanding of Christian revelation as found in scripture that is free of traditional, male-dominated patterns of thought, and therewith a more theologically grounded basis for assessing contemporary gender bias.[3]

The work of professional theologians like these two typically takes place in church seminaries and church-related colleges and universities. Traditions of rigorous theological reflection are particularly associated with Lutheran, Presbyterian, Congregational, and Roman Catholic academic institutions, and currently with such interdenominational seminaries as Union Theological Seminary in New York, Yale Divinity School, Harvard Divinity School, the University of Chicago Divinity School, Claremont School of Theology in Los Angeles, and the Graduate Theological Union in Berkeley, California.

Thus, we have six patterns of religious life, each exemplified by more than one American Christian tradition that gives it special emphasis and priority. However, do not suppose that any of these Christian traditions are primarily identified with a single way of being religious. Hardly any exclusively focus on a single way. And even when they seem to do so, individual members of such traditions can often be found whose religious life involves aspects of other ways. The so-called sacramental Christian traditions, for example, do not exclusively identify with sacred rite. While sacred rite is central for them, other ways are often evident in the lives of individual participants and sometimes in congregational activities as well.

Thus, some members of a larger Episcopalian congregation will be involved in the Charismatic Movement, an interdenominational Christian movement that believes in, and actively solicits, the supernatural intervention of the Holy Spirit in the lives of Christians, exemplifying the way of shamanic mediation. Overlapping with the Charismatic group, but not identical to it, are a number of congregants whose personal devotion to Jesus is for them as vital as participation in Sunday Eucharist, exemplifying the way of devotion. For these Evangelical Episcopalians, Jesus is a living spiritual presence at the center of their lives that they deliberately cultivate through personal prayer, devotional reading of scripture, informal gatherings with other like-minded Christians for singing, sharing, and prayer, and evangelical efforts to introduce others to their divine Friend. A scattering of others in the congregation spend several weekend retreats a year at a nearby (Roman Catholic) Trappist Monastery open to non-Roman Catholic retreatants. There, guided by a spiritual director, they practice a discipline of "Centering Prayer," a Christian instance of the way of mystical quest. The assistant priest, presiding at the worship service, has a Ph.D. in philosophical theology, participates regularly in professional conferences such as those of the Society of Christian Philosophers, and teaches extension courses in theology for a regional Episcopal seminary. On the intellectual side of his Christian life at least, he pursues a Christian variety of the way of reasoned inquiry, fitting together into a coherent whole the sometimes conflicting conclusions of modern thought, contemporary science, and traditional Christian faith. Still another group within the Church are members of the

Episcopal Fellowship of Reconciliation, an organization that works actively on behalf of peace movements around the world. Many members of this group, oriented strongly in the way of right action to make a difference in the world on behalf of Christian values, are also involved in activities such as Habitat for Humanity (building affordable housing for low-income families), a soup kitchen for the homeless, and political lobbying for minority rights. In addition to Episcopalians, Roman Catholics, Lutherans, and Eastern Orthodox occasionally practice these other five ways of being religious as well, although not necessarily in the same manner as here expressed.

Protestant denominations other than Lutherans and Episcopalians do not encompass as many of the different ways of being religious. With some important exceptions, already mentioned, what one finds in these denominations is the way of devotion pursued almost exclusively or in some combination or fusion with one or two of the other ways (or aspects of them)—mainly reasoned inquiry and right action—but rarely more than two. The fact that Eastern Orthodox, Roman Catholic, and Episcopal traditions generally acknowledge and give some place to all six ways of being religious (though not all in the same respects) seems to be an important aspect of the meaning of the name "catholic" with which they take special interest in identifying themselves. The root meaning of "**catholic**" is usually given as "universal," "comprehensive" or "inclusive of all parts." But here it would seem to connote wholeness, completion, and perhaps balance, too. In those Protestant churches where there is not the same readiness to affirm all of the ways, there is a corresponding reticence to identify with being "catholic," even though most claim to identify with "the universal Church." (Largely, of course, they shun use of the term in order to distinguish and distance themselves from the Roman Catholic Church.) The point is that at least some Christian traditions consciously embrace all six ways.

From this quick survey, we see that all six ways of being religious can be found in various forms with different relative emphases within American Christianity. By extrapolation, one can easily imagine how they can be found in Christian communities in other parts of the world. This feature is not unique to Christianity, for the same is largely true for the other great religious traditions of the world.

SOME NONTRADITIONAL WAYS OF BEING RELIGIOUS IN NORTH AMERICA

One of the principal theses of this book is that there are certain generic patterns of human religiousness that are universal human possibilities, dormant potentials answering to existential needs of human beings that require only the right circumstances to emerge. Being to a large degree independent of the specific symbol system within which they occur, the tendency of people inclined to one of the ways is to make use of whatever symbol system is at hand that for them articulates and makes accessible *ultimate reality°* in order to draw near to and come into right relationship with that *ultimate reality°*. In a modern, largely secularized, pluralistic culture such as that found in the United States—especially with the encouragement American culture gives to individual experimentation and expression in independence of institutional constraints—it should not be surprising to find these generic patterns of religious life cropping up in contexts wholly outside conventional religious life. The fact that some symbol systems happen to be not in any conventional sense religious and perhaps even atheistic and antireligious (i.e., opposed to traditional religions) is no particular barrier to their functioning in a religious manner (in the sense assumed by this book), so long as people take them to represent *how things ultimately are°*.

What follows is not intended to be a survey or even a representative sampling of all that might be called nontraditional religious phenomena. There are good surveys available that attempt just that.[4] Instead, as the preceding section sought simply to illustrate ways of being religious in the context of American Christianity, this section will cite and briefly discuss examples of nontraditional religious phenomena for each of the different ways. They are drawn from two areas: American civil religion and secular American culture (both popular and elite).

For the last several decades, scholars in the study of religion have come to identify something they call "civil religion" in America, alongside and largely independent of conventional religious institutions and practice.[5] It does not identify itself as a religion, nor is it regarded by the public as a religion. Civil religion consists of the set of symbols, sacred stories, rituals, expectations of conduct, and *theology°* (actually, competing *theologies°*) by means of which the people of the United States maintain their national and civic identity and collectively renew their vision of what their collective life is *ultimately°* all about. Within the range of activities that American civil religion includes, three ways of being religious are clearly manifest: sacred rite, right action, and reasoned inquiry. The way of sacred rite is manifest in the rituals associated with national holidays such as the Fourth of July, Memorial Day, and the birthdays of Washington and Lincoln; in pilgrimage to national shrines (among them, the National Archives Building to see the Declaration of Independence and the Constitution, the Nation's Capitol, the Presidential Memorials, the War Memorials, Mt. Vernon, Independence Hall in Philadelphia, and major battlefields in America's wars); and in the elaborate ceremonies at presidential inaugurals and presidential funerals, and so forth. The point of such ritual activity is to return sacramentally to those sacred times and places in which the archetypal, identity-bestowing patterns of American life were originally given or were made specially evident. The way of right action is manifest in the urgent sense of calling many feel to transcend private interests and contribute to the realization of an ultimate public good by becoming involved in public-spirited, local, regional, and national civic activities; in the political process of electing public leaders and establishing political policy; in contributing to civic deliberation and debate of public issues; in political lobbying; in assuming public office through election or appointment; and in serving the country in the armed forces. The way of reasoned inquiry is manifest in efforts among political theorists, members of the judicial system (especially as it relates to constitutional law), political advisors, and political analysts to discern what is ultimately wise and just and appropriate to maintain America upon its allotted course and fulfill its destiny—for example, in reconciling liberty and justice in human rights controversies.[6]

Ways of being religious can be detected as well in other places within secular American culture, both elite culture and popular culture.[7]

For some persons the arts—especially drama, dance, classical music, and opera, but sometimes literary and visual arts as well—put them in touch with the deepest truths and, at times, convey a sublimity beyond articulation. For such serious, passionate participants in the arts, participation is as much an experience of sacred, sacramental rite as any conventionally religious ritual. This can be as true for the serious viewer/listener/reader as for the serious performer, composer, or writer. It is, of course, not always true for any one person, at any given time, in any circumstance, at any performance, or with any composition. But often it is. This kind of secular religious experience through the arts first came into its own in Western culture during the Renaissance, with the idea that through the liberal arts we connect with the grandeur and pathos of human existence, and it has remained for many an option ever since. In a diminished mode (and doubtless to the consternation of most who identify with elite culture), much the same can be said at a level of unsophisticated, popular culture for avid watchers of popular films, followers of television serials, and participants in rock concerts.

Secular activists of one sort or another often go at their work with a seriousness and passion that reflects a kind of religious idealism that often goes unavowed, though sometimes it may be. They thus express a secular version of the way of right action. Social organizers, leaders in the Labor Movement, civil rights leaders, feminist spokespersons, radical environmentalists, and so forth, all pursue their visions of *what is ultimately right and just*° no less passionately than religious activists, with no less of a sense that this cause is *cosmically imperative*°, and with no less a sense of ultimacy than Martin Luther had in declaring, "Here I stand. I can do no other!" For them, to work at their cause is to be lifted out of mundane, ordinary life and to be connected with what at some deep level they are convinced is of *ultimate value*°. At times, even an ordinary, lower-middle-class, apparently wholly secularized couple who give their all to living honestly, morally, and cleanly, putting their very best into their jobs, raising good and healthy children, volunteering time in civic projects for the local community, and so forth, can experience a sense of direct participation in *what is ultimately supposed to be*° and connecting in some hard-to-articulate sense with *ultimate value*°.

Adulation of television stars, movie stars, and vocal music stars can at times take on the dimensions of the way of devotion. Witness the intensity and "purity" of the devotion focused on Elvis Presley in his lifetime and afterward. The way of devotion can as well show up in the form of passionate romantic love as presented in what for lovers are the sacred stories of Tristan and Isolde, Romeo and Juliet, and Tony and Maria—reflected *ad infinitum* in films, novels, soap operas, and supermarket romances. In classical romantic love—which is to be clearly distinguished from erotica of all sorts—the beloved functions as a kind of angel, bestowing the grace to transcend ordinary mortal existence and experience that to lovers is a kind of divine union of souls.

Much in the recent growth of interest in alternative medicine and healing practices is suggestive of the way of shamanic mediation: a conviction that somehow sickness involves being out of touch with *the encompassing spiritual context of life°* (especially that of nature conceived as having a spiritual dimension), the belief that healing involves tapping a reservoir of *cosmic energy°* beyond oneself, the use of the active imagination (and dreams) in visualizing wholeness and well-being, and having other persons "channel healing energy" to the patient. Not a little of what is going into the general mix known as "alternative medicine" comes directly or indirectly from traditional shamanic healers in indigenous tribal cultures. There are even persons offering and receiving training in shamanic practice outside any conventional religious context (outside even native religious traditions and sometimes opposed by native traditions from which practices and symbols have been "borrowed"). A kind of vision quest among certain users of psychotropic drugs seems to involve aspects of shamanic mediation. Quite apart from these examples, elements of shamanic mediation appear to be involved in the kind of altered states of consciousness sought by some participants in jazz and rock music.[8]

Suggestions of the kind of meditative and ascetic practices—even life as a hermit—associated with the way of mystical quest show up from time to time in what is called by some scholars American "nature religion."[9] For example, the diaries of persons such as Henry David Thoreau, John Muir, and Loren Eiseley manifest persons in quest of a transcendent or spiritual dimension of nature, beyond our ordinary awareness and understanding, a dimension of meaning beyond and other than that of the human. Meditation and yoga practices, as almost everyone knows, have sprung up all over the country—often wholly unconnected with any conventional religious trappings, whether Eastern or Western. By themselves these practices do not constitute the mystical quest as such, but here and there one can find persons pursuing them in serious search of *what is ultimately real°*.

Finally, secular participants in the way of reasoned inquiry are not so hard to find, for whom pursuit of *the ultimate truth about things°* is a controlling passion. The most serious scientists and philosophers of our culture appear at times to have something religious about them. Many have been consciously aware of it. But even intellectuals who have been avowedly atheistic—for example, Freud, Marx, and Nietzsche—did the work they did in the conviction that they were bringing to light *the ultimate truth of things°* and *the deepest wisdom°*—however disillusioning (especially disillusioning to conventional religious ideas) that that *truth°* was conceived to be. For some scientists, modern science functions as "a kind of religion," and the same has always been true of philosophy for some philosophers (as they have conceived it).[10] The same, surely, is true (in however diminished a mode) for amateur scientists and philosophers of our day, who in turn devour semipopular accounts of scientific discovery and/or philosophical insight in pursuit of *ultimate wisdom°*.

So, even outside of conventional religious life, the ways of being religious can be found, functioning in the lives of people in a manner quite analogous to the way they function in the lives of conventionally religious people.

PRIORITIZING OF THE WAYS IN DIFFERENT TRADITIONS

Within any actual religious tradition—such as Buddhism, Islam, or Christianity—one is likely to find all six ways of being religious. In any one of a tradition's subtraditions that will not be as likely. Some ways in a religious tradition (even more so in a subtradition) will receive greater emphasis and prestige than others, depending on several factors. Three factors are especially determinative.

First of all, there is the factor of the symbol system of the religion itself: how flexible it is, how open it is to differing interpretations and further development, and to what extent it (e.g., a passage of canonical scripture) directly emphasizes or discourages a certain way or ways of being religious. Depending on the nature of a particular system of symbols, one way of being religious may be especially encouraged relative to others, with the result that it becomes dominant within that tradition, while another way may be discouraged, with the result that it never receives official endorsement by elders of the tradition and may even be suppressed.

For example, the Muslim's holy book, the *Qur'an*, uncompromisingly rejects any practice that amounts to "associating" something that is not God with God in his singular transcendence. This has tended as a matter of course to make Sunni Islam (the broad mainstream of the Islamic religion) uneasy with, if not wholly intolerant of, (a) shamanic phenomena (the way of shamanic mediation), (b) tendencies in popular piety to presume to cultivate a "personal relationship" with Allah (the way of devotion), (c) sacramental interpretations of Muslim ritual (the way of sacred rite), and (d) pretensions to mystical union with God among Sufi mystics (the way of mystical quest). Indeed, even (e) pursuit of the way of reasoned inquiry in Islam has been subject to censorship when it has ventured to question the literal truth of what the *Qur'an* straightforwardly states. Thus, principally because of the express nature of the *Qur'an* as understood in classical Sunni Islam, the way of right action largely dominates all other ways in mainstream Islam—so much so that frequently spokespersons for Sunni Islam deny that these other phenomena are expressions of authentic Islam. Nevertheless, expressions of all six can be found within Sunni Islam, though not in all locales.[11]

Other examples of the same sort of prioritizing of the specific ways of being religious by the canonical symbol system can be found in Buddhism, Hinduism, and the relatively new religion of Baha'i. The historical Buddha, according to what is supposed to be the earliest (Pali) scriptures, placed central emphasis upon a coordinated cultivation of the ways of reasoned inquiry, right action, and mystical quest as the means to achieve *nirvāṇa*. He explicitly rejected reliance upon acts of worship and ritual practice as in any way helpful to achieving that goal. For similar reasons he discouraged engagement in "supernatural" (shamanic) practices—while nevertheless acknowledging shamanic powers as a byproduct of advanced attainment on the path to *nirvāṇa*. As a result of these strictures in the primary system of symbols, there has continued to this day in Buddhism a bias against expressions of sacred rite and shamanic mediation. Although there are Buddhist expressions of sacred rite and shamanic mediation, they are subordinated to other ways, except perhaps in so-called Vajrayana Buddhism, which found a home in Tibet, China, and Japan. It is interesting how the Sanskrit canon (officially recognized and delimited collection of authoritative texts) of scripture in Mahayana Buddhism (the Buddhism of Central and East Asia) was for many centuries left relatively undefined, allowing "new" scriptures to appear that have given justification to further ways of being Buddhist.[12] In Hinduism, the oldest and most authoritative scriptures, the *Vedas* and their commentaries, primarily center on sacred rite, though later parts of them emphasized reasoned inquiry, mystical quest, and right action. They make no mention of devotional religion and give no encouragement to it at all. It was not until the composition, several centuries later, of the *Bhagavad Gītā* and its popular reception as scripture (along with subsequent sectarian scriptures, the *Puāṇas*) that today's most prevalent form of Hindu religious life, *Bhakti*, or Devotional Hinduism, came to flower. In this case it took a significant new development in the primary system of symbols for this way of being religious to become established.[13] Finally, the Baha'i religion, which emerged in nineteenth-century Iran, is an unusual combination of the ways of reasoned inquiry and right action almost exclusively, as far as the present stage of its development is concerned. This is due in large part to the specific character of its scriptures (primarily the writings of its prophet, Baha'u'llah, and other early leaders), which prescribe a minimum of ritual and meditational practice (no sacramental ritual and no path of meditation aimed at altering conscious awareness that this author is aware of), and give no encouragement to devotional religion or shamanic mediation. Should Baha'i last, and it appears that it will, new ways of being Baha'i may well emerge by way of further developments of those scriptures or novel interpretations of the existing scriptures.[14]

Second, there is the factor of precedent set at any given stage by persuasive interpretations and specific institutionalizations of a tradition's system of symbols. Say that only three ways of being religious become well established in the formative years of a tradition; the result will be increased difficulty for other ways to emerge and become established within the tradition, at least until new social, cultural, or geographic contexts give them opportunity. Take Buddhism, for example. The famous Eightfold Path, taught by the historical Buddha, Siddartha Gautama, was embodied in the institution of early monastic Buddhism. It emphasized moral conduct, wisdom, and contemplation, with special emphasis on contemplation. The consequence was that it has given dominant precedent to the ways of right action, wisdom, and mystical quest in monastic Buddhism to the present day. When Buddhism moved into the new geographic and cultural contexts of Tibet, China, and Japan, other ways of being religious and new variations of already established ways of being religious became established and institutionalized, including forms of nonmonastic, devotional Buddhism and the esoteric Vajrayana subtradition already mentioned. The latter two developments, however, were anticipated by the emergence, still within the Indian Buddhist context, of Pure Land and Tantric Sanskrit scriptures. How much they reflected significant expressions of Indian Buddhist religious life at the time is unknown.[15]

A different case of the same sort of influence from precedent occurred in traditional Rabbinic Judaism. After the destruction of Jerusalem and the Second Jewish Temple in 70 C.E. (Common Era, 70 C.E. = 70 A.D.) by the Romans, the traditional religion of the Jewish people, which had been centered in the sacrificial ritual of the Temple, was forced to change drastically to survive. Among the several religious orientations competing to determine the future of the Jewish people, it was the teaching of the leaders of the so-called Pharisee party that devised a Judaism that was able to survive without the Temple. That teaching became the core of the *Talmud*, an exposition of the implications of the *Torah* (the "Revelation from God"[16] that they believe to have been given through Moses at Mt. Sinai). For the ensuing Jewish tradition, the *Talmud* came to have an authority almost equal to scripture until modern times. With the *Talmud*'s central emphasis on participation in serious *Torah* study (for all males) and a life sanctified by the many commandments of God, it gave central primacy to the way of reasoned inquiry and the way of right action over all other ways. Nevertheless, the way of sacred rite was given considerable room for expression in traditional, post-Biblical Judaism (more than in Islam, perhaps partly because of the background of the ancient Temple rites in Jerusalem). For example, the weekly Sabbath observances and the annual festivals such as Passover clearly involve presentational symbols and sacramental actions. The Rabbis advise that each generation is to understand itself through the ritual of Passover as being rescued by God from slavery in Egypt. Also, to be present at the ritual reading of a portion of the *Torah* in the synagogue, pious Jews understand themselves to be present again at Mt. Sinai when God first presented the *Torah* to Israel. Nevertheless, here sacred rite remains relatively subordinate to right action as something done because it is commanded by God rather than a direct means of approach to God. Even so, to participate in such rites is sacramentally to return to and become a part of the events of Jewish sacred history. *Kabbala*, the way of mystical quest in Judaism, has long had a revered though subordinate and somewhat restricted place. It involves deciphering and meditating upon esoteric meanings of virtually every passage of the *Torah*, meanings that pertain to one's inner, spiritual life and are believed to link the latter to the redemptive activity of God in the world at large. Where *Kabbala* did emerge, it remained a largely hidden, esoteric underside to the outward observances of Jewish religious life for the relative few who became involved in it, rather than expressing itself in some independent institutional form. There are suggestions here and there in the Jewish tradition of aspects of the way of devotion—for example, in the optional prayers of the *Siddur* (traditional Jewish book of worship). However, significant expressions of the way of devotion and the very possibility of any expression of way of shamanic mediation (after the end of Biblical prophecy, which manifests aspects of shamanic mediation), seem to have required the emergence of a novel form of Judaism known as Hasidism (see later discussion) in the eighteenth century, which also marked a new stage in the evolution of *Kabbala.* In early Hasidism, individual piety and religious fervor took precedence over study of *Torah*, and the Hasidic leaders, or *Rebbes*, became charismatic mediators of divine presence and power for their followers. (A case could be made that the way of devotion, somewhat like *Kabbala*, was always a kind of hidden underside to outward observance among unsophisticated, ordinary Jews—especially for those for whom the intellectually demanding practice of traditional *Torah* study was not a serious option.)[17]

A third factor influencing whether and to what extent a given way of being religious emerges is the particular existential motivation(s) of the major historical interpreters of the tradition in any given epoch and the need(s) of the people they serve. For example, Rabbinical Judaism through its postbiblical history more or less systematically discouraged, if it did not suppress, the emergence of a vigorous individual devotional life as well as interest in shamanic phenomena and practice (including the idea that there might be some new prophetic word from God). But violent persecution, severe poverty, and a moribund state of Talmudic scholarship in Eastern Europe in the late eighteenth century set conditions ripe for the emergence of a radically new form of Judaism, Hasidism, which gave significant place to both. Interestingly, the emergence of Hasidism in East European Jewry roughly coincided with the Pietist movement in European Christianity and its American counterpart, the First Great Awakening (the first great revivalist movement) in the American colonies. Some of the same reasons historians have cited for the emergence of Hasidism have been cited by other historians to account for the emergence of Pietism. In any case, the birth of what has since come to be known as Evangelical Christianity originated at this time—largely, it appears, in response to a deep hunger of ordinary people for a vibrant Christianity of the heart that was relevant to their individual lives, in contrast to the nonrelevance and moribund state they felt (whether rightly or not) had come to characterize traditional Protestantism. Much the same could be said of the rise of the fifteenth-century Pietist Movement in Europe known as the *Devotio Moderna*, which profoundly influenced the leaders of the Protestant Reformation.

This influence of people's existential needs upon the emergence of a way of being religious is not unique to the way of devotion. A very similar account with different motivations could be given for flourishing of the mystical quest in the history of Christianity from time to time—for example, the rise of Christian monasticism with the Desert Fathers in the fourth and fifth centuries, the Carthusians in the eleventh, the Cistercians in the twelfth, Rhineland and English Mysticism in the fourteenth, and Spanish Mysticism in the sixteenth—although it has never attracted the large numbers of people that the way of devotion has. Similarly, the flourishing of philosophical theology in Islam (one expression of the way of reasoned inquiry in Islam)—especially that known as *Mu'tazilite* Theology in the ninth century— was in large measure a response to the need of reflective Muslims to come to terms with the more intellectually sophisticated philosophical ideas and challenges it encountered in the writings of Plato and Aristotle. Substantially the same problem was faced by medieval European Christians in the twelfth and thirteenth centuries, resulting in the emergence of scholastic philosophical theology.[18]

COMPACTNESS, DIFFERENTIATION, AND SYNCRETISM

As noted in Chapter 3, in small-scale, nonliterate, tribal societies—so-called "primitive" or native cultures—only the ways of sacred rite and shamanic mediation are distinctly evident. Virtually all Native American traditions, for example, have both. The same is true for native African traditions, native Asian traditions, the native peoples of the Pacific, and Australian Aborigines. Most (secular) historians of religion hold that this is probably true as well for the earliest forms of religious life reflected in archaeological evidence around the world. We do occasionally see indications of the other ways in compact, relatively undifferentiated cultures but in such instances never as distinct ways of carrying on religious life that stand on their own apart from sacred rite and shamanic mediation. In any case, it seems clear that ways of being religious other than the ones a tradition starts with are able to emerge only as the tradition extends over time, geographic area, and population diversity, as those populations become literate (especially insofar as they develop a religious literature to any extent), and as the traditions are elaborated sufficiently to allow for diversity of expression and a more individualized form of religious life to develop. This suggests that sacred rite and shamanic mediation may be a kind of matrix or womb out of which other ways differentiate themselves. Historically this is certainly not true of all religions, taking each of them on their own. However, it appears that religions that did not begin with sacred rite and shamanic mediation emerged as the errant offspring of preexisting religions that did so begin and whose precedents in ways of being religious appear to have played an important role in influencing the shape of the daughter religions, at least by way of reaction.

An interesting case in which just such a "primitive" religious tradition has become differentiated in this way over time is Shinto, Japan's native religious tradition. It has by no means remained "untainted" by other religious influences—notably Buddhism, Confucianism, Daoism, and, to a lesser extent, Christianity, but it has retained much of its distinctive character despite this syncretism. Most of its sacred rituals (especially those associated with Shrine worship) are traceable to pre-Buddhist contact, and its shamanic elements remain vital in many rural areas (and in some suburban areas) to this day. Yet, partly through the stimulus and precedent of these other influences, there have emerged Shintoist expressions of each of the other ways (especially when some of the so-called New Religions of Japan are included as subtraditions or offshoots of Shinto): right action, devotion, mystical quest, and reasoned inquiry.[19]

This raises the question of how to sort out religious expressions that are the result of a kind of **syncretism** between preexisting religious elements and elements that are imported from the outside. Are all such expressions "genuine" or "true" expressions of the original tradition? The very phrasing of the question may beg the question. In virtually every religion that has moved across cultural (or even subcultural) borders, so-called syncretic phenomena can be found. How does one decide whether such phenomena are authentic or not? This author does not pretend to resolve this question here but would like to suggest something that he does not believe has been proposed before. Sometimes (and this is far from including all cases of syncretism) the imported religion and the preexisting religion exemplify different ways of being religious. On the one hand, converts to the new religion from the old will bring with them some existential motivations addressed by the old religion but unaddressed by the new. They will also likely bring with them elements of a religious sensibility (such as expectations, dispositions, or a sense of what is appropriate and not appropriate) linked with the way of being religious found in the old religion. As a result, so far as the new religion is flexible enough to adapt itself, new religious forms will more than likely result, bringing expression to the old way of being religious within the new system of religious symbols. Significantly, at times this is not so much syncretism—least of all a syncretism that compromises essentials in the new tradition—but rather an occasion for the emergence of one more way of being religious within the new tradition, one that might very well have already found emergence in another time and place. Alongside this development, persons who remain adherents of the old religion, seeing how the way of being religious in the new religion addresses existential needs that the old religion never addressed well, if at all, may attempt to adapt the old religion's symbol system to incorporate the new way of being religious. And of course, a new religious movement might begin with a symbol system resulting from a merger of both prior traditions—in which case it would be unquestionably syncretic.

Examples of both kinds of appropriation and adaptation can be found throughout the history of religions wherever different religions have encountered and competed with one another, especially in the history of missionary religions like Buddhism, Christianity, and Islam in each of the countries they entered. Buddhism's introduction into Tibet, for example, resulted in new forms of Buddhism and specifically the emergence and institutionalization of a form of Buddhism, Tibetan Vajrayana, that incorporates elements of the ways of shamanic mediation and sacred rite.[20] Some Western interpreters have argued that this represented a compromise to original Buddhism by taking into itself the alien forms of the indigenous religion of Tibet, known as *Bon*. Though some of this may be at work, what happened can also be interpreted as an occasion where two generic ways of being religious emerged within the Buddhist tradition that for a variety of reasons had not had opportunity or as much opportunity to develop freely before. In any case, they clearly seemed to address the existential needs of the people of Tibet.

A similar thing can be said for shamanic practices in rural, so-called folk religious practice within Islam, Christianity, and Buddhism in other parts of the world. As already mentioned, African Americans, with a religious sensibility rooted in native African religion, influenced the rise of Pentecostalism in America. Also, it is interesting to note the emergence of uniquely African forms of Christianity, in South Africa for instance, that place a central emphasis on shamanic mediation and have only a tenuous resemblance to the Protestant Christianity first introduced there by European missionaries.[21] In such cases, it is not so much a religious practice alien to these traditions as it is a generic way of being religious that might just as well have emerged in these traditions as in any other, though it seems to have taken exposure to this way within another indigenous tradition for it to come to birth in these traditions too. To say this is not to endorse such phenomena as fully authentic to, say, Islam or Christianity, for there may be aspects of the core system of symbols that some spokespersons would say denies them legitimacy. But it implies that it is only natural that such a thing does occur and perhaps that one should be more tolerant of it and open-minded toward it when it does occur than one otherwise might be.

Another interesting case is the way that *Zen* Buddhism (the Japanese name for what is called *Ch'an* in China and *dhyāna* in Indian Sanskrit) came to be the major patron of traditional Japanese art forms (including the martial arts) as ideal contexts for realizing and expressing the enlightened "Buddha-mind" that is supposed to be there, beneath the superficial mind, in each person.[22] These highly ritualized art forms called *dō*—including calligraphy, flower arranging, painting, landscape gardening, cooking, carpentry, archery, swordmaking, swordfighting—are unlike anything in Buddhism found elsewhere, except to some extent in Chinese Ch'an. Though some of their roots lie in pre-Buddhist Shinto culture, they have in this case become thoroughly Zen Buddhist expressions of both the way of right action and the way of sacred rite. They are particularly well epitomized in *Cha-dō* or *Cha-no-yu*, the Tea Ceremony—which, if anything, is a sacramental rite comparable to the Mass for Roman Catholic Christians.[23] Has Buddhism here become something alien to itself? Hardly.

Combinations of
Different Ways

Cha-dō, the "way of tea," is an interesting case in which two ways, the way of right action and the way of sacred rite, are simultaneously expressed. For Zen Buddhists, when rightly entered into, it is both a practical realization of "the Buddha-mind" (the Buddhist *ultimate reality*, which is immanent within the cosmos, not transcendent to it as in Western religions) in one's actual life and a sacramental ritual participation in "the Buddha-mind."

This illustrates how the ways of being religious may not only coexist along- side each other but at times may be so intertwined with each other in a given re- ligious practice as to be indistinguishable. The ways are not necessarily opposed to each other at all, though at times they can be. What is called *halakhic* piety in an observant Orthodox Jewish community—namely, the sanctification of virtual- ly every aspect of life through the performance of the many "Commandments of God," such as those pertaining to the preparation and eating of food, the obser- vance of the Sabbath restrictions, and the Morning, Noon, and Evening Prayers— also combines elements of sacred rite and right action. A very similar phenomenon is found in the effort by pious Muslims to bring all of life into submission to the will of God as revealed in "the holy *Shari'a* [Law] of Allah as revealed in the *Qur'an*," in the ritually circumscribed everyday life of a pious Hindu following the *Dharma* appropriate to his caste and stage of life, and in the life of a sincere Confucian whose studied social interactions are meant to be a sacred ritual grace- fully embodying "the *Dao* of Heaven and Earth."

Other combinations of ways can readily be found. In the writings of sixteenth- century Spanish Christian mystic Teresa of Avila, the ways of mystical quest and devotion are inseparably joined. So also, Francis of Assisi in twelfth-century Italy, who combined with these ways the way of right action as well. St. Augustine's writings in the fourth to fifth century embodied mystical quest, devotion, and reasoned inquiry. As all of these persons were good Catholic Christians, sacred rite was an important part of their lives as well. Mother Teresa of Calcutta com- bines the way of right action with sacred rite quite differently from the examples mentioned above, as is shown in her declaration that she would not be able to see and serve Christ in the poorest of the poor if she did not first meet him at the altar in Holy Communion.[24]

Similar combinations in individual figures as well as particular local practices in almost every religious tradition can be found.

Almost all monastic Buddhists, by virtue of their monastic practice, combine mystical quest, reasoned inquiry, and right action, although, depending on the subtradition to which they belong and the particular orientation of their individual practice, one or another of these will be more emphasized. In a Japanese Rinzai Zen Monastery, though primacy there is given to the way of mystical quest, almost equal emphasis is placed upon the way of reasoned inquiry in its preoccupation with solving *koāns* (intellectual riddles that help occasion enlightenment) and question-and-answer sessions (*sanzen*) with the *roshi* (spiritual master). So also the involvement of members of the community in all aspects of mundane work in and around the monastery and their pursuit of traditional, highly ritualized arts like calligraphy, archery, and swordsmanship, all in a manner manifesting "the Buddha heart of emptiness," exemplifies the way of action. Further, much of their time is taken up with ritual ceremonial, which betokens the way of sacred rite—though clearly not the elaborate kind of sacramental rites found in *Shingon* (Japanese Vajrayana) Buddhism. So here is an example that combines four of the ways.[25]

ATTITUDES OF INCLUSION AND EXCLUSION

As should now be clear, the ways are not necessarily opposed to each other at all. It is possible to find more or less pure examples of each within many of the major religious traditions. Among these examples, one can find occasional instances of a **sectarian** insistence upon a single way or specific few ways of being religious that eclipses or at least prejudges the authenticity and legitimacy of other ways within the same religious tradition. The insistence is usually less an exclusion of other ways than an assertion of the superiority and self-sufficiency of a certain way or ways. But mostly one finds subtraditions that tolerate (if they do not actually endorse) other ways for other persons in other subtraditions. In other words, a sectarian insistence (upon a single way or set of ways as the only authentic expression of a tradition) is not inevitable. Where there is no such insistence, one may find a given individual involved in a single way for her whole life, while her neighbor in the same religion, with whom she is on good terms, will be involved in other ways (possibly two or more at once) and, over the course of his life, in still other ways.

Examples of a sectarian insistence upon a single way of being religious may be found from time to time in the history of American Evangelical Protestantism. Among Evangelicals, the focus tends to be concentrated upon the salvation of souls and the cultivation of a simple devotional faith—with other ways (to the extent that they tend toward autonomy from, or compromise in any way to, that primary focus) coming under suspicion as failing to "keep Christ first in one's heart."[26] Some twentieth-century Christians, who identify with the Liberation Theology Movement, focus efforts solely on the cause of social justice and castigate persons involved in other ways of being Christian as betrayers of genuine Christianity insofar as their lives either support the (unjust) social status quo or ignore it.[27] We have already alluded to the priority placed upon the way of right action in mainstream Sunni Islam. At times within certain Islamic reform movements this priority is so stressed that all other ways of being religious in

Islam are condemned as non-Islamic or heretical movements.[28] In Japanese Buddhism, a recent subtradition called *Sokka Gakkai*, whose roots go back to a thirteenth-century Buddhist *prophet* by the name of Nichiren, pursues a Buddhist form of the way of right action and condemns other forms of Buddhism for failing to rectify the social ills of the age.[29] Some expressions of Pure Land Buddhism, a family of East Asian Buddhist subtraditions that pursue the way of devotion, have at times regarded the state of the world with respect to Buddhist ideals and teaching to be so degenerate that no other Buddhist path can hope to move one toward the goal of *nirvāṇa*; reliance in pure faith upon the grace of the Buddha Amitabha alone can hope to bring about salvation.[30] Similar examples can be found in Hinduism and in other religions. There are, of course, examples of subtraditions that place an exclusive stress upon, say, two ways of being religious and condemn others.

At the opposite extreme, subtraditions can be found that not only tolerate but give welcome recognition to several or all of the ways of being religious within the same religion. (It should be clear that we are not talking here about welcome recognition of other religions, but only welcome recognition of other ways within the same religion.) However, it is rare when you can find all six ways of being religious exemplified in a given locale or subtradition. What one more often finds are subtraditions that emphasize one, two, or three of the ways, while they acknowledge and show respect to other expressions of the same religion that exemplify other ways. Even though exclusivistic attitudes are not present, tensions can still arise between persons identifying with different ways. Such tensions may or may not be accommodated. One of the complications that can arise is when the predominant quality of practice of one of the ways becomes degenerate or fails to be true to its own sources of authority. Negative attitudes toward the quality of practice easily become indistinguishable from negative attitudes toward the practice itself. When accommodation cannot be realized, such tensions can lead to condemnations, schisms, and even persecutions. Although there were many other things involved besides tensions between ways of being religious, the Protestant Reformation in important respects was a shift from central (but not exclusive) emphasis upon the way of sacred rite to a central (but not exclusive) emphasis upon the way of devotion with its insistence upon "faith alone, apart from works." In the so-called "left-wing" of the Reformation (also called "Radical Reformation Protestants," encompassing the Anabaptist traditions and the Quakers) the shift was to a central emphasis on the way of right action, accompanied by a subordinate emphasis upon devotion, with its insistence that Christians live differently from the habitual life patterns of "the world."[31]

One would expect that spokespersons for an inclusive or **catholic** religious tradition that happens to embrace all of the six ways of being religious would explicitly acknowledge the legitimacy of each as well as provide justification for them from within the system of symbols characterizing the tradition (i.e., provide a *theological* explanation and justification for them). Interestingly, that is exactly what we find in the Hinduism of the *Bhagavad Gītā* (and elsewhere) which acknowledges the different yogas as different approaches to "God" designed for different types of personality.[32] We also find something similar in certain Chinese Mahayana (e.g., *T'ien-T'ai*) and Tibetan Vajrayana attempts to acknowledge, incorporate, and assign a place to each of the many Buddhist schools of thought and practice. In these two Buddhist cases, the different schools are assigned a kind of hierarchical ranking from introductory to more advanced and from exoteric (understandable and implementable to almost anyone) to esoteric (understandable and implementable only to a highly developed initiate). In this regard, some ways of being Buddhist are interpreted to be "better" or "higher" than others. Nevertheless, any one way will be identified as most right or appropriate for particular persons, depending on their stage of spiritual development.[33] A final example is the Roman Catholic Christian tradition, wherein no major theological justification has ever been developed that would accommodate and justify the six ways of being religious, whatever they might be named. Yet there has for the most part been an inclusive tolerance of and respect for Roman Catholics being involved in this or that way of carrying on their Christian lives, so long as they did not in any major way challenge central doctrines or displace the central emphasis placed on the way of sacred rite (and the institution of the clerical hierarchy that implements that emphasis).[34]

What would it take for such an inclusive, catholic attitude to become more widespread? Is it possible that the framework of ways of being religious—once understood and used to orient an empathetic exploration of the different ways—will encourage religious leaders and laypersons to show more understanding and acceptance of other ways of being religious within their own religion? It would seem that it could, especially when combined with an understanding of how different persons have different religious needs, not all of which are met by any one way of being religious.

CHAPTER SUMMARY

Through presentation of numerous concrete examples, the present chapter has sought to communicate a more concrete sense of the different ways of being religious as they can be found among actual religious phenomena throughout the world, starting with Christianity in the United States. A sampling was given of examples of the ways within religious phenomena falling outside what would conventionally be recognized as religious. Beyond straightforward examples of each way, examples were cited and discussed of how traditions differently emphasize, prioritize, subordinate, tolerate on the fringe of acceptability, exclude, and suppress specific ways. It helps to differentiate in this respect between religious traditions taken as a whole, such as Christianity or Hinduism, and subtraditions within them. One subtradition can often be differentiated from another in terms of what way or ways of being religious it chooses to emphasize relative to the emphases of other subtraditions. Within a given tradition or subtradition, the relationships between the ways sometimes change as the tradition evolves and differentiates itself over time, especially insofar as it moves from one culture to another. This is especially evident in the great missionary religions of Buddhism, Christianity, and Islam, but it is not limited to them. The course of change is typically from a less differentiated to a more differentiated state, from one way or a few ways of being religious to many ways. Finally, at any given stage in their development, both traditions and subtraditions may be characterized by the manner in which they tend to identify exclusively with one, two, or three ways and little else, or inclusively encourage and accept all ways within their symbol systems.

STUDY QUESTIONS

1. Drawing upon your own experience and knowledge of different sorts of religious practice, identify what way or combination of ways of being religious they exemplify. Don't just label them, but think about them carefully and justify why you are inclined to classify them the way that you do.

2. On the basis of a well-rounded acquaintance with a specific religious subtradition (e.g., a Christian denomination), identify what way or ways of being religious the subtradition especially emphasizes. What other ways (or aspects of ways) seem to be present and what relationship do they have to those that are especially emphasized? Does the subtradition relate exclusively, indifferently, or inclusively toward other ways than those it especially emphasizes? Again, don't just label, but think about the tradition carefully and justify your conclusions.

3. Read a good survey text in religious studies on a specific religious tradition that offers concrete descriptions of the variety of practices found in that tradition (such as one of the survey texts listed below). As you read, identify which way or ways of being religious each of the described practices exemplifies, and justify your answer. What ways are especially emphasized in each subtradition that is discussed? And how does each subtradition relate to ways other than those it emphasizes? So far as the text does not provide enough information to answer one of these questions, do further focused research to find the answer.

4. For each of the ways, group together two or more instances of traditional religious practice that exemplify them. Starting with the groups representing two of the ways and making use of some good survey texts (and other sources of knowledge, if available), compare and contrast the groups for the sake of identifying for yourself what characteristics tend to distinguish each group from the others. Look especially for distinctive religious practices and distinctive patterns of social organization.

5. Select an instance of a major or significant change in a religious tradition or subtradition—for example, a renewal, a reformation, a schism, the birth of a new subtradition or daughter religion, and so forth. Explore to what extent tensions and conflicts between different ways of being religious can account for what happened (including not just different religious practices but also the different existential needs, different orientations to interpreting the authoritative sources of the tradition, and different patterns of social organization that correspond to the different ways).

6. Read a good survey of elements of civil and/or cultural religion in America. For example, Chapters 13 and 14 of Catherine Albanese's text cited below discuss multiple concrete examples of nontraditional religious phenomena. Identify what way or ways of being religious are exemplified in each case and justify your answers. Can you think of still other examples that are not mentioned in the text? Describe them and justify how you are inclined to classify them.

FOR FURTHER READING

Follow up references cited in the chapter notes on specific topics. Not all survey texts offer sufficiently concrete descriptions of different practices to enable clear identification of what way or ways of being religious are being discussed. The following are suitable for this task.

Catherine L. Albanese, *America: Religions and Religion*, 2nd ed. (Belmont, CA: Wadsworth, 1992).
Theodore M. Ludwig, *The Sacred Paths: Understanding the Religions of the World*, 2nd ed. (New York: Macmillan, 1994).
David S. Noss and John B. Noss, *A History of the World's Religions*, 8th ed. (New York: Macmillan, 1990).
Ninian Smart, *The Religious Experience of Mankind*, 3rd ed. (New York: Charles Scribner's Sons, 1984).

On specific religions, the Prentice-Hall series on World Religions, edited by Robert S. Ellwood, and the HarperSanFrancisco Religious Traditions of the World series, edited by H. Byron Earhart, are quite useful for the task as well.

NOTES

1. Here and in what follows I refrain from entering into Christian and Jewish theological controversy over inclusive gender pronominal reference to God. The justification for my usage here is simply that it reflects traditional usage.
2. M. Douglas Meeks, *God the Economist: the Doctrine of God and Political Economy* (Minneapolis, MN: Fortress Press, 1989).
3. Elisabeth Schüssler Fiorenza, *In Memory of Her: A Feminist Theological Reconstruction of Christian Origins*, 10th anniversary edition (New York: Crossroads, 1994); and *Jesus: Miriam's Child, Sophia's Prophet* (New York: Continuum, 1995)

4. See, for example, Catherine L. Albanese, *America: Religion and Religions*, 2nd ed. (Belmont, CA: Wadsworth, 1992), Chs. 13 and 14.

5. See *ibid.*, ch. 13; and Russell E. Richey and Donald G. Jones, eds., *American Civil Religion* (New York: Harper and Row, 1974).

6. It should be more than obvious to most readers that virtue as well as vice may be found in each of these ways of civil religious practice. Generic virtues and vices specific to each way will be taken up in Chapter 5.

7. See John Wiley Nelson, *Your God is Alive and Well and Appearing in Popular Culture* (Philadelphia, PA: Westminster Press 1976); Russel Nye, *The Unembarrassed Muse: The Popular Arts in America* (Two Centuries of American Life Bicentennial Series; New York: Dial Press, 1970); and Catherine L. Albanese, *America: Religions and Religion, op. cit.*, Ch. 14.

8. See Neil Leonard, *Jazz: Myth and Religion* (New York: Oxford University Press, 1987). See also Gilbert Rouget, *Music and Trance: A Theory of the Relations between Music and Possession*, trans. Brunhilde Biebuyck (Chicago, IL: University of Chicago Press, 1985).

9. See Catherine Albanese, *Nature Religion in America: From the Algonkian Indians to the New Age* (Chicago, IL: University of Chicago Press, 1990).

10. See Huston Smith, "Western Philosophy as a Great Religion," in his *Essays on World Religion*, ed. M. Darroll Bryant (New York: Paragon House, 1992), pp. 205–223.

11. See Fazlur Rahman, *Islam*, 2nd ed. (Chicago, IL: University of Chicago Press, 1979); John L. Esposito, *Islam: The Straight Path* (New York: Oxford University Press, 1988); and Frederick Mathewson Denny, *An Introduction to Islam* (New York: Macmillan, 1985).

12. See Richard H. Robinson and Willard L Johnson, *The Buddhist Religion: A Historical Introduction*, 3rd ed. (Belmont, CA: Wadsworth, 1982).

13. See Thomas J. Hopkins, *The Hindu Religious Tradition* (Belmont, CA: Dickenson/ Wadsworth, 1971).

14. See Jessyca Russell Gaver, *The Baha'i Faith: Dawn of a New Day* (New York: Hawthorn Books, 1967).

15. See Robinson and Johnson, *The Buddhist Religion, op. cit.*

16. Traditionally Jews regard the name of God as so holy and powerful that it must not be pronounced, except under the most careful and appropriate of circumstances. The text of the holy *Torah* scrolls are written in consonants only, with vowels supplied by a knowledgeable reader. In a passage in which the name of God would occur, the phrase "the LORD" would be substituted. In continuation of this custom, Orthodox Jews, when writing in English, write "G–d," instead of "God."

17. See Jacob Neusner, *The Way of Torah: An Introduction of Judaism*, 4th ed. (Belmont, CA: Wadsworth, 1988); Leo Trepp, *Judaism: Development and Life*, 3rd ed. (Belmont, CA: Wadsworth, 1982); and Michael A. Fishbane, *Judaism* (San Francisco, CA: Harper and Row, 1987). For a fuller introduction to Kabbala as mystical quest, see Aryeh Kaplan, *Meditation and Kabbalah* (Northvale, NJ; Jason Aronson, 1995). On aspects of shamanic mediation in Judaism, see Gedalyah Nigal, *Magic, Mysticism, and Hasidism: The Supernatural in Jewish Thought* (Northvale, NJ: Jason Aronson, 1994)

18. See F. E. Peters, *Children of Abraham: Judaism, Christianity, Islam* (Princeton, NJ: Princeton University Press, 1982).

19. See Yamamoto Yukitaka, *Way of the Kami* (Stockton, CA: Tsubaki American Publications, 1987); Stuart D. B. Picken, *Shinto: Japan's Spiritual Roots* (Tokyo: Kodansha International, 1980); and H. Byron Earhart, *Japanese Religion: Unity and Diversity*, 3rd ed. (Belmont, CA: Wadsworth, 1982).

20. See Robinson and Johnson, *The Buddhist Religion, op. cit.*, Ch. 9; Giuseppe Tucci, *The Religions of Tibet* (Berkeley, CA: University of California Press, 1980).

21. See Gerhardus C. Oosthuizen, *The Healer Prophet in African Churches*, Studies in Christian Mission (New York: E. J. Brill, 1992).

22. See Richard B. Pilgrim, *Buddhism and the Arts of Japan* (Chambersburg, PA: Anima Books, 1981); Horst Hammitzsch, *Zen in the Art of the Tea Ceremony* (New York: St. Martin's Press, 1980); Trevor Legett, *Zen and the Ways* (Boulder, CO: Shambhala, 1978); William La Fleur, *The Karma of Words: Buddhism and the Literary Arts in Medieval Japan* (Berkeley, CA: University of California Press, 1983); and Daisetz T. Suzuki, *Zen and Japanese Culture*, Bollingen Series, 64 (Princeton University Press, 1959).

23. For a fuller discussion of Tea Ceremony as an expression of Zen Buddhism in juxtaposition to Holy Communion in Eastern Orthodox sacramental Christianity, see Chapter 14 below.

24. Malcolm Muggeridge, *Something Beautiful for God* (San Francisco: Harper and Row, 1971).

25. See Phillip Kapleau, *The Three Pillars of Zen: Teaching, Practice, and Enlightenment*, rev. ed. (Garden City, NJ: Anchor Doubleday, 1980); Isshu Miura and Ruth Fuller Sasaki, *The Zen Koan: Its History and Use in Rinzai Zen* (New York: Harcourt, Brace and World, 1965); Peter N. Gregory, ed., *Sudden and Gradual: Approaches to Enlightenment in Chinese Thought*, Studies in East Asian Buddhism, 5 (Honolulu, HI: University of Hawaii Press, 1988); and Conrad Hyers, *Once-Born, Twice-Born Zen: The Soto and Rinzai Schools of Japanese Zen* (Wolfeboro, NH: Longwood Academic, 1989). See also Ronald L. Grimes, "Modes of Zen Ritual," in his *Beginnings in Ritual Studies*, rev. ed. (Columbia, SC: University of South Carolina Press, 1995), pp. 104–118.

26. See F. Ernest Stoeffler, *The Rise of Evangelical Pietism*, Studies in the History of Religions—Supplements to Numen, 9 (Leiden: Brill, 1965); and Mark A. Noll, David Bebbington, and George A. Rawlyk, eds., *Evangelicalism: The Popular Protestantism of North America and the British Isles, 1700–1990* (New York: Oxford University Press, 1993).

27. See David Hollenbach, *Claims in Conflict* (New York: Paulist Press, 1979); Leonardo Boff and Clodovis Boff, *Introducing Liberation Theology*, trans. Paul Burns (Maryknoll, NY: Orbis Books, 1987); and Philip Berryman, *Liberation Theology: Essential Facts about the Revolutionary Religious Movement in Latin America and Beyond* (New York: Crossroad, 1987).

28. See John L. Esposito, *Islam: The Straight Path* (New York: Oxford University Press, 1988), Ch. 5; and John L. Esposito, ed., *Voices of Resurgent Islam* (New York: Oxford University Press, 1983).

29. See Daniel Alfred Metraux, *The History and Theology of Soka Gakkai: A Japanese New Religion*, Studies in Asian Thought and Religion, Vol. 9 (Lewiston, NY: Edwin Mellen Press, 1988).

30. See James C. Dobbins, *Jodo Shinshu: Shin Buddhism in Medieval Japan* (Bloomington, IN: Indiana University Press, 1989).

31. See Steven Ozment, *The Age of Reform, 1250–1550: An Intellectual and Religious History of Late Medieval and Reformation Europe* (New Haven, CT: Yale University Press, 1980).

32. See Eliot Deutsch, *The Bhagavad Gītā*, (New York: Holt, Rinehart and Winston, 1968); A. L. Herman, *A Brief Introduction to Hinduism* (Boulder, CO: Westview Press, 1991), Ch. 3; and Krisha Sivaraman, ed., *Hindu Spirituality: Vedas through Vedanta* (New York: Crossroads, 1989). See also Huston Smith, *The World's Religions*, rev. ed. (San Francisco, CA: HarperSanFrancisco, 1991), Ch. 2.

33. See David J. Kalupahana, *A History of Buddhist Philosophy: Continuities and Discontinuities* (Honolulu: University of Hawaii Press, 1992).

34. See Lawrence Cunningham, *The Catholic Experience* (New York: Crossroad, 1985); Stephen Happel and David Tracy, *A Catholic Vision* (Philadelphia, PA: Fortress, 1984); and Thomas E. Helm, *The Christian Religion: An Introduction* (Englewood Cliffs, NJ: Prentice-Hall, 1991), Ch. 10.

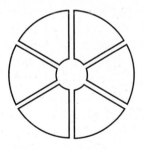

C H A P T E R   5

Variations in Quality of Practice of The Ways

This chapter departs somewhat from the orientation of the preceding chapters. It takes up the theme of variation in quality of practice of the different ways of being religious. "Quality of practice" refers to the merit or worth of a given expression of religious practice, how deserving it is of respect or disrespect, considered in terms of the traditional pursuit of that way of being religious in which it occurs. Although variation in quality of practice has been alluded to before, virtually all discussion of the ways of being religious up to this point has been generally neutral and judgments of worth or merit have been deliberately suspended.

The suspension of evaluative judgment characteristic of a phenomenological approach to the study of religion is for a certain, well-defined purpose: to enable a truly empathetic understanding of religious phenomena undistorted by evaluative preconceptions. As will be explained further below, that approach is not meant to rule out evaluative judgment. It is rather meant to enable more discriminating judgment, judgment that does fuller justice to the phenomena and to the persons involved in them by excluding judgment based on presuppositions alien to the phenomena. The purpose of this chapter is to indicate how the transition from empathetic understanding to a more discriminating judgment can be made (in certain limited respects) and how it is aided by the framework of ways of being religious.

In effect, as the author of this text, I am asking readers to develop their own powers of discriminating judgment, to make up their own minds about given instances of different kinds of religious practice *on the basis of an empathetic acquaintance of them from within.* One may or may not fully agree with some of the characterizations, but I offer them on the basis of generic criteria that I believe are recognizable by insiders and can be shown to be so—that is to say, I offer them on the basis of what I have earlier called religious common sense. When it comes to these matters, we are not just left with separate traditions of faith and individual value systems. These are commonsense criteria that are out there between us, as it were, that are not simply a function of specific faith commitments. Accordingly, insofar as readers may be inclined to disagree with some of the judgments I tentatively offer, I invite them to determine whether their judgment is as empathetically discriminating as I have sought to have mine be and as grounded in a mutually recognizable, religious common sense. I claim no finality to my own judgments in this respect, and each of them is open to criticism, correction, and revision. The point is to come to conclusions for what we can establish to be good reasons independently of personal preference and specific *theological* assumptions.

Beginning with a discussion of widespread undiscriminating judgments of a stereotypical nature, I introduce the concept of evaluative judgments made from within a tradition of variations in quality or merit of religious practice. I shall distinguish between criteria of judgments that are specific to a tradition (being uniquely specified by its authoritative sources) and criteria of a generic commonsense nature that in principle can be shared by persons of other traditions. I then offer a justification of the shift from description to evaluation that this involves. Following this I give a characterization of virtues or excellences of practice and vices or degenerations of practice for each generic way of being religious.

SPECIAL PROBLEMS IN EMPATHIZING WITH DIFFERENT WAYS

Efforts to acquire an empathetic understanding of actual expressions of any one of the different ways of being religious often have to wrestle with stereotypes and caricatures of them. These biased preconceptions are often prevalent in the subculture where we find ourselves. They are views we naturally tend to take for granted. They may even express our personal prejudices, which we may not be aware of as prejudices. For example, in our own largely Christian but dominantly Protestant North American culture, the Roman Catholic tradition is often thought to be dominated by clericalism (the power and prestige of priests, bishops, and Pope) and filled with largely meaningless rituals and symbols suggestive of idolatry and standing in the way of a personal relation to God. Many view the kind of serious theological study found among Roman Catholics and some mainstream Protestants (especially Lutherans and Presbyterians) as religious intellectualizing and liable to interfere with a vital religious faith. Others tend to think of Evangelical Protestants as dominated by a kind of emotional piety that has no intellectual coherence or theological depth. Pentecostal and Charismatic

Christians are frequently castigated as having opted out of rationality and proper order of worship altogether and regressed to primitive superstition. Social-activist Christians are branded as preoccupied with other people's lives, as trying to earn their own salvation by doing good works, and as having lost any sense of personal religion. And Christians into contemplative spirituality (especially monks and nuns) are tarred as navel-gazers who cannot face the real world. Another widely held but less specific caricature is a dichotomy between "personal religion" and "institutional religion," as if the two were inherently opposed to one another. "Personal religion" is usually portrayed as better—for example, more genuine, fresh, spontaneous, individual, and experiential—while "institutional religion," is portrayed as worse—for example, conforming, stale (secondhand religion), legalistic, socially homogeneous, and formal.[1] There are, of course, many other such caricatures of the same traditions and of others; this is meant only as a brief sampling.

These preconceptions may be held quite innocently and unconsciously, but they are no less misconceptions for being so held. As a result, they are that much more difficult to identify, effectively criticize, and overcome. Implicit in them is usually a value judgment, a negative value judgment, that the religious practice in question is unworthy of respect. The problem is not that value judgments are being made where we should not be making them, but that the value judgments in question, being based on misleading preconceptions, are premature, insufficiently discriminating, and of a sweeping nature. They fail to do justice. Some expressions of a given way of being religious are worthy of respect and some are not. The solution is not to cease making value judgments but to develop a capacity to discriminate between the sort of thing that is worthy of respect and the sort of thing that is not within each way, based on a fuller understanding of what is involved in each way and the range of variations in practice possible within each way. That requires getting past the preconception to see what it fails to represent.

It is interesting to observe how, when confronted with exceptions to a preconception they happen to hold of a certain way of being religious, persons often are unready to recognize the exceptions as contradicting their preconception. The unreadiness indicates that they have a greater psychological investment in maintaining the preconception than they may suppose. In that case the preconception reveals more about themselves than it does about the way of being religious it purports to represent. The investment may be due to a host of different factors, from the weight of indoctrinated attitudes to the pain of victimization (whether these persons' own or their sympathy with others' pain). Sometimes it is rooted in a genuine disappointment of a person's existential motivations: somehow her own religious needs (or those of persons with whom she sympathizes) on some occasion were not met, and were deemed unlikely ever to be met, by a certain religious practice, a particular religious group, or a particular religious leader. In defensive rationalization, the object of the disappointment is caricatured in an unattractive or repulsive fashion and generalized to represent all instances of that form of religious practice, all expressions of that way of being religious: for example, "Religious ritual is empty, meaningless show, and priests only want to control your lives." Persons drawn primarily to one way of being religious, especially upon finding that other ways fail to address their concerns with any effectiveness, often develop an antipathy toward other ways. They are usually the carriers of the most negative, sweeping misconceptions one can find of other ways of being religious.

Suppose a person has come to recognize that she holds stereotypical preconceptions of certain ways of being religious herself; what then?

First, it is important to recognize the partial truth of such stereotypes. They are distortions, but they also have enough of a grain of truth in them to make them credible to persons who would like an excuse to differentiate themselves from, if not stand against, the practice or tradition being caricatured. That is to say, one can usually find more than one actual expression of the tradition or practice in question that comes pretty close to matching the stereotype. For example, religious ritual occasionally happens to be an empty, meaningless show and priests are sometimes preoccupied with manipulating others to their own egoistical ends. The problem is that these expressions are not generally representative—except in one sense. They may represent fairly well the worst cases of the specific practice or tradition in question; such are usually cases that even knowledgeable insiders (in their best and least defensive frame of mind) would not hesitate to refer to as degenerate, or at least seriously deficient. Second, in order to understand and appreciate the tradition in a less distorted way, such insiders would say, look instead at other, more representative expressions; indeed, look first at cases of the tradition at its best (i.e., cases that reflective and dispassionate insiders of that specific tradition or subtradition would regard as among its best expressions), and then the deficient and degenerate cases can be fairly seen and understood and criticized for what they are.

For any one way of being religious within a given religion, these best expressions may unproblematically be regarded as embodying virtue of a certain sort: the virtue or virtues for that way of being religious in that religious tradition, at least in the judgment of reflective and dispassionate insiders. Those identifiable as its worst expressions can unproblematically be regarded as embodying a kind of vice: the vice or vices for that way in that tradition. Within each way of being religious in a tradition where it is found, then, there is a spectrum of possible variations in quality of practice. It is not a case of either/or, either virtue or vice. There is a whole range of possibilities in between, as anyone well acquainted with the tradition can attest. Any tradition or practice has its better expressions, its worse expressions, and its middling expressions. To be responsible, empathetic outsiders, no less than insiders, need to learn how to discriminate one from the other, what constitutes virtue and what constitutes vice, what constitutes better expressions and what constitutes worse expressions, for any given way. To this end, negative stereotypes are sometimes a useful starting place for identifying what are more than likely characteristic vices. In any case, the point is to realize that any given way in any tradition can be taken up and practiced in qualitatively more excellent, more virtuous ways, in qualitatively degenerate, virtueless ways, and everything in between.

DIFFERENTIATING SPECIFIC CRITERIA AND GENERIC CRITERIA WITHIN A TRADITION

In any religious tradition in which a given way of being religious is allowed to emerge and persist over time, practice of that way by different individuals and groups in different times and places will never be the same in all respects. Not only will there be variation in style, emphasis, and detail of practice—occasionally with considerable creativity, sometimes with none at all—but also there will be **qualitative variation in practice**.

There will of course be a question of rightness, correctness, or authenticity of practice, setting roughly the boundaries of permissible variation. Rightness, correctness, and authenticity are normally a question of fidelity to the tradition's authoritative sources and to models or paradigms of practice specified within those sources. Faithfulness to the sources requires establishing, in the face of any question as to its faithfulness, that the practice in question is at least fully consistent with, if not dictated by, the core system of authoritative symbols—for example, establishing that it agrees with scripture. A **sectarian tradition**, by definition, is a subtradition that rejects the rightness of the practice and/or beliefs of an earlier tradition or traditions from which it has differentiated itself in terms of a different conception of what constitutes fidelity to its sources; it draws the boundaries of permissible variation differently and usually more narrowly. **Heresies** or **heretical practices**, by definition, are variations in teaching or practice that a tradition has established (for itself) to be unfaithful to the core system of authoritative symbols, to be beyond permissible boundaries. At times these matters are a source of considerable controversy within a tradition.

Within the bounds of permissible variation, there remains room for considerable variation in quality of practice for any way of being religious—variation that is deemed acceptable if not always respectable. Consider, for example, the performance of an elaborate ritual—say, the Zen Buddhist Tea Ceremony or the Muslim *Hajj* (pilgrimage) to Mecca. There are, for each, certain boundaries of permissible variation established in part by authoritative texts and in part by the word of respected, more or less authoritative elders who are regarded as embodying the tradition in question and specifically a practical knowledge of how things should and should not be done.

In the Tea Ceremony, for instance, one does not do anything that would embarrass one's guests; nor can the ceremony take place in a busy, crowded, noisy location; nor are matters of heated controversy allowed to be the subject of conversation. On pilgrimage, the Muslim is forbidden to engage in sexual relations, to wear any but the proper garments, not to be "standing" on the plain of Arafat on the proper day, etc. But within these limits, persons carry out these rituals more and less well. Sometimes mistakes are made; sometimes the performance is flawless. Sometimes the ritual is done awkwardly, sometimes with grace. Sometimes it is performed mechanically, sticking strictly to the rubrics (guidelines for ritual practice); sometimes it is performed with appropriate improvisation and style. Sometimes participation is sincere and meaningful; sometimes it is simply a matter of going through the motions. Sometimes it is done with generous and hospitable concern for others, sometimes in an inhospitable and uncaring manner. To an outsider observing an instance of any one of these rituals, it is unlikely that any of these variations would be observed at all, let alone discriminated as to how well or how badly the ritual would be judged to have been performed in the manner of a knowledgeable insider. Qualitative discriminations are nevertheless made by insiders and can be made thoughtfully and consistently on the basis of sensible and appropriate criteria, though the criteria be quite informal.

What is interesting in this connection is the respect in which many of the criteria employed, though not all, are remarkably similar as one moves from one tradition to the next but stays with instances of the same way of being religious, whereas they are importantly different as one moves from instances of one way of being religious to those of another, even within the same religious tradition. These criteria have to do with what in Chapter 2 were called commonsense considerations. Why call them "commonsense"? One reason is that they involve considerations that involve little or no specific reference to the central core of authoritative symbols, little if anything to do with being specifically Zen Buddhist or Muslim, and little if anything to do with a specific conception of *ultimate reality*. They are for that reason not *theological* considerations. Indeed, they tend to translate well from one tradition to another without threat of challenging the boundaries of permissible practice. They involve considerations having to do with common aspects of being human involved in this sort of religious practice, this generic way of being religious. In that sense they are not common sense for all ways of being religious (though perhaps some considerations are), but common sense among persons at home with any one way of being religious, whatever be their tradition. Each way, as it were, has its own commonsense considerations.

Among such commonsense considerations, some may be directly found in or implied by the central core of authoritative symbols. Thus, guidelines for an ideal pilgrimage, available in the form of a handbook to Muslim pilgrims, are drawn from the advice and example of Muhammad and other saintly figures of Muslim history. That they are so found does not necessarily mean that they are any less matters of common sense that could not be reached on one's own; it merely means that the authoritative sources of the tradition add their imprimatur or blessing to them. Others are simply reached on the basis of reflection on practical experience and refined on the basis of further experience, the pooling of shared practical judgment, and the process of "natural selection" as they are passed on from one generation to another. This is another reason why they can appropriately be called "matters of common sense." They are in principle discoverable by anyone who takes the trouble to get to know well on a practical basis what is involved in an ongoing practice of this way of being religious in concert with other persons and what it takes to realize well (and what is likely to derail or block) the distinctive satisfactions it promises. Above all, they concern what it takes for this way of being religious to serve reliably to draw one (along with others) near to, and into right relationship with, *ultimate reality°*. They are community-based considerations and they will ordinarily be considerations of a community that seeks to persist in these practices over time, from one generation to another, and to benefit from them.

Consequently, variations of practice that do not contribute to, or are likely to interfere with, the distinctive religious satisfactions promised by a way of being religious, friendly relations between members of the immediate community involved, and the passing on intact of the practice (with the values to be realized through it) to subsequent generations will tend to be regarded as degenerations or **vices**. Variations that do contribute to these goals will accordingly tend to be regarded as **virtues**. Taken together, such commonsense considerations constitute, in any one tradition, a fund of pooled practical wisdom for the communal practice of a distinctive way of carrying on religious life. To the extent they are substantially the same from one tradition to the next, becoming familiar with them is requisite to understanding well any one generic way of being religious.

To what extent are they and are they not the same? That is a worthy subject of comparative study. Indeed, it is a worthy subject of dialogue between religious traditions, for these sorts of things are the very things that insiders of one tradition are most ready to recognize in common or learn from other traditions—namely, how to pursue better and more effectively the practice of the way of being religious they are now pursuing. One remarkable example of this is a dialogue between Buddhist monks and Christian monks pursuing the way of mystical quest, preserved in published form as the book *Speaking of Silence: Christians and Buddhists on the Contemplative Way.*[2] In principle, the same sort of dialogue could be pursued with similar results in regard to any of the other ways of being religious. Much remains unexplored or insufficiently explored.

Most of what is available second-hand in the best studies of different traditions does not treat the subject of quality of practice, at least not directly in any depth. Nevertheless, enough has been turned up to suggest that commonsense considerations regarding virtues and vices in the practice of each way of being religious in different traditions are not just a hodgepodge of maxims and rules of thumb. Many of them, perhaps most, can be grouped around *three basic parameters of assessment* (sliding scales of qualitative variation) without overmuch distortion: competence/incompetence, balance/imbalance of divergent forces, and selflessness/egoism. Each of the three might be said to constitute a generic virtue/vice spectrum.

Thinking about them abstractly, it is easy to lose sight of the fact that the three parameters are abstract constructions devised in the attempt to bring order to a myriad of unsystematic, concrete evaluative considerations. In other words, my hypothesis is that something very much like these parameters lies behind the concrete evaluative considerations regarding quality of practice for a given way of being religious that can be found in any tradition.

The first of the parameters—**competence/incompetence**—is fairly straightforward and easy to understand. The practice of any given way in a specific tradition requires a practical know-how, an experiential familiarity, a certain lore, that is acquired to different degrees and is quite different for each way of being religious. This is true not just for the leader or expert in a tradition. It is also true, though to a lesser extent, for the lay participant so far as she is to get anything out of participating and find her existential needs met. Each way calls for a distinctive kind of "spiritual formation," as it is sometimes called. The lore of a priest (and even of a lay participant in an elaborate ritual) is quite different from that of a shaman (and the lay participant in shamanic practices); and each of these is quite different from that of a devotional pastor (and devotee), that of a philosopher-*theologian*° (and student), that of a master of a path of contemplative meditation (and novice), and that of a moral teacher-reformer (and disciple).

Some practitioners of a given way of being religious devote their lives to that way and, among them, a few (sometimes even unlettered lay persons) come to be respected as master sources of authoritative guidance for others, even though they may hold no formal office and receive no remuneration for it. Some acquire sufficient competence to qualify for positions of leadership—for example, as priest, pastor, teacher, or spiritual director. Once in positions of leadership, these individuals may or may not seek to develop further their competence. Of them, some are barely competent, some are extraordinarily skilled and competent at the practice and serve as models for others to emulate, while the rest are spread out in between with varying degrees of competence in carrying out their special roles. Many people pursuing a given way of being religious learn only enough for minimal participation, have no aspiration to learn more, and could not begin to explain what is going on, even if they had to. Accordingly, along the parameter of competence/incompetence, vice is practice that fails to be competent—for example, awkward, uncertain, fumbling, and characterized by mistakes and improprieties—whereas virtue is competent, knowledgeable practice—for example, confident, appropriate, and characterized by minimal flaws and mastery of relevant details.

The second parameter—**balance/imbalance of divergent forces**—is the most difficult to understand of the three but is in some ways the most important. As this author has come to understand it, religious practice, in every case, involves an effort to bring together, reconcile, and hold in some sort of vital tension divergent forces or polarities:[3] what is tangible and intangible, what is static and dynamic, what is old and fresh, what is active and receptive, what is temporal and eternal, and what is ordered and spontaneous, what is formed and formless letter and spirit, body and soul, extrinsic motivation and intrinsic motivation, this world and the *other world*°, ordinary reality and *ultimate reality*°. As a kind of shorthand for these polar oppositions but not meant to reduce them all to a single type, we shall speak of reconciling and integrating matters finite with matters infinite, the finite aspects of the practice with the nonfinite aspects. Actual religious practice inherently involves working out and living out some kind of balance between these polarities in the lives of real persons.[4] Many religious traditions place explicit emphasis (though not all in the same respects) on cultivating a virtue of balance, moderation, a middle way between extremes. Buddhism speaks of the Middle Way, Confucianism of the Great Mean, Daoism of balance in all things (especially of *yin* and *yang*), Hinduism of balance among the four aims of life (pleasure, material prosperity, duty, and liberation), Judaism and Islam of combining enjoyment of the good and struggle against evil (avoiding both self-denial and selfish indulgence), and Christianity of temperance, sobriety, moderation, and "being in the world but not of it."

Although not all religious conceptions of balance are identical, there does exist between them sufficient overlap to conclude that they recognize in common the good of finding and living a balanced life that avoids certain inappropriate extremes, and conversely that they recognize in common certain tendencies to imbalance in life that result in, or are, a kind of evil and that must therefore be deliberately counteracted. I am not saying that any of these religions teaches that all good is a matter of balance or all evil is a matter of imbalance (though so-called philosophical Daoism seems to come close to this). Even less am I saying that religions generally teach that balance is the supreme good outweighing all other goods so that no other consideration could ever take precedence. Nor am I implying that any two religious traditions would strike a balance in precisely the same way, or even that any two ways of being religious in the same tradition would strike a balance in precisely the same way. Rather, I wish to claim that the different religions teach (or tend on the whole to teach, or at least are prepared on the whole to recognize) (1) that cultivation of balance between the divergent forces identified above is normally one of the primary tasks to be pursued in order to realize excellence in the practice of any way of being religious, and (2) that loss of balance between these divergent forces tends toward evil and is, for the most part, a vice to be avoided. However, even were it the case that a religion did not explicitly authorize the pursuit of balance in this respect, a good case could be made for it strictly on commonsense grounds, as Aristotle has so influentially done (though not specifically in regard to religious practice) for the Western world and for the ethical traditions of Judaism, Christianity, and Islam in particular.[5]

What are regarded by reflective insiders as healthy, vital, and virtuous expressions of a tradition, whatever the way of being religious involved, in addition to their agreement with the tradition's authoritative norms, will ordinarily involve some kind of balance between the polarities mentioned above. What are regarded as unhealthy, moribund, and degenerate expressions, even though they outwardly agree with the norms of the tradition, will often be so because they lack this balance. Imbalance will generally result in, or be a mark of, what is seen to be degeneration and vice. Balance and equipoise will in general result in, or be a mark of, what is seen to be health and virtue. Any such synthesis reconciling divergent forces has a tendency or liability—which is to say, a temptation—to instability that must be continually counteracted to maintain excellence and well-being. It is easy, terribly easy at times, to lose balance rather than keep it. To strike an appropriate balance, to find a healthy tension between finitude and infinitude, no precise rule, no "answer" in any ordinary sense, will suffice, for such a rule is itself a finite form that would have to be interpreted and applied. And any rule for interpreting and applying that rule would in turn have to be interpreted and applied. The finding of balance requires something in the participant herself, something akin to what Aristotle identified as *prudential common sense*:[6] the crucial capacity for finding appropriate balance between extremes, the integration of polar opposites, that constitutes moral virtue. Whether or not prudential common sense is all that is required to find the requisite balance in religion (note: I don't think it is all and many religions would disagree that it is all), it seems to play a major role. As said before, it all depends on how a tradition is taken up and lived out. Of course, there are no guarantees that a tradition will be taken up in healthy, thoughtful, and "common-sensible ways."

All this will become clearer as we examine more closely what imbalance in the direction of finitude (**vice of finitude**) or imbalance in the direction of infinitude (**vice of infinitude**) consists of. *The vice of finitude, or loss of infinitude*, is expressed in a variety of ways, varying to a great extent with the way of being religious that is being pursued. It happens when the animating spark of inspiration of a tradition is lost, and one is left with only outward form, the finite aspects of a religion. All the words, gestures, and actions may be right and correct, but somehow the spirit is absent. The resulting practice is dull, wooden, or perfunctory, with no sense of freshness or life to it, nothing to inspire awe or passion, no depth or sublimity, nothing ultimate or transcendent about it. If it has anything of strong feeling about it, it is marked by obsession with matters of insignificance, sentimentalism (e.g., nostalgia for "old time religion"), or simply satisfaction of the baser human appetites. It is entirely too down-to-earth, too reflective of human failing and finitude; it has no challenge to it, no invitation to change or to transformation. At the opposite extreme, *the vice of infinitude, or loss of finitude*, is also expressed in a variety of ways depending on what way of being religious is being pursued. It occurs when the animating spark of inspiration is allowed to overwhelm one's respect for the finite, this-worldly, human aspects of oneself, one's practice, and one's community, and the result is a kind of denial, rejection, or repression of finitude. One of its signs is loss of a sense of humor. This is where one may find idolatry—where finite form (e.g., symbol, form of worship, method of meditation, moral rule, interpretation, judgment, type of shamanic expression) is invested with the esteem and passion that is due the infinite, and the absolute is misidentified with the relative—and, in consequence, probably most of the evil done in the name of religion.

With this imbalance one comes subtly and perhaps unconsciously, for all intents and purposes, to equate one's own judgment with the judgment of God and one's own will with God's will. With no sense left of one's own finitude, one becomes immune to the appeal of common sense. At that point, criticism of oneself can provoke the passion of divine retribution. The problem lies not in having a conception of what is absolute (i.e., of what is infinite in value or importance) but in supposing that one's conception of it, one's handle on it, can be something more than finite. Other expressions of the loss of finitude would seem to include such things as (a) extreme ascetic practices that harm the physical body with no significant compensating benefit to the spirit; (b) extreme otherworldly emphases that refuse to ameliorate (either in the short term or the long term) pressing needs of those closest to oneself, of the community to which one belongs, or of the common lot of humanity at large, or that treat others without compunction, merely as means for one's own otherworldly ends; and (c) overemphasis upon change, spontaneity, and dynamism at the expense of continuity, the integrity of communal order, and passing on the wisdom of past experience. Thus, imbalance—especially serious imbalance—either in the direction of finitude or in the direction of infinitude is a degeneration of healthy and vital religion.[7]

Mention should be made in this connection of the oppositional pairing of the six ways of being religious that was discussed in Chapter 3: sacred rite with shamanic mediation, right action with mystical quest, and devotion with wisdom. It may be that a key to health and well-being in religion lies in keeping these oppositional pairs in balance (and perhaps more than any two pairs), such that pursuit of one way combined with some involvement in its opposite tends to counteract the specific degenerations characteristic of that way. Although it is somewhat speculative, it seems plausible that this could be the case. It is possible to find significant and respected writers in different traditions who testify in agreement. For example, the great Muslim theologian al-Ghazzali models and argues for a kind of four-way balance between Muslim theological and legal learning (reasoned inquiry), Sufi devotionalism (devotion), implementation of the divine law in all aspects of life (right action), and the Sufi quest to mystical union with God (mystical quest).[8] Another example in very recent times is the remarkable convergence—mainly among Christians—between many social activists, on the one hand, and many contemplatives, on the other, each coming to see the need for the other's practice (namely, right action and mystical quest) to fill out and balance its own practice.[9]

The third parameter of assessment of practice in ways of being religious—**selflessness/egoism**—is fairly easy to grasp. It overlaps to some extent with conventional notions of ethics and morality and has generally to do with one's relations with others (including nonhuman realities). Virtually all religious traditions reject egoism or self-centeredness, although they understand it in somewhat different ways. Yet all basically agree that the ego or self that insistently asserts the centrality and priority of its immediate interests at the expense of the interests of others—especially the interests of others within the group—ought not be as it is: its centrality is a false centrality and the priority of its interests is a false priority. The different religious traditions generally take egoism to be the locus of most (if not all) of what is wrong with the world, and systematically set out strategies to overcome it—whether to transform and redirect the ego, to dissolve the ego, to harmonize the ego with otherwise competing interests in the encompassing social and natural order of things, or to merge the ego with a larger, cosmic self. To pursue one of these strategies, of course, is no guarantee that members or even leaders of these traditions succeed in overcoming egoism. Virtue, in this connection, is said to be an ideal state of "selflessness."

While some traditions speak of the ideal of selflessness as a state of having dissolved altogether the ordinary human ego, some as a state of having merged one's identity with a larger, social or cosmic self, others as a state of harmonization of the individual self with other selves, and still others as a state of having become a different, reoriented self, the ideal in each case embodies (and thus persons actively pursuing the ideal aspire to embody) certain very similar traits. These traits include the humility that is ready to grow and be changed by being brought into closer relationship with *ultimate reality*[p], sincerity in the sense of being free of hypocrisy and duplicitous motivation, openness to take in and appreciate what is other than oneself as no less and no more than what it is, presuming no special importance or status of oneself in relation to others (or to the finite whole of which one is a part), not being anxious or (overly) defensive about oneself or one's reputation, not seeking unfair advantage for oneself over others, never treating others as mere means to one's own ends, readiness to see and take in how things are from the other's perspective, respect for other persons' need to see and understand and make up their minds about things for themselves, willingness to hear and respond to criticism honestly and nondefensively, and identification with the welfare of all (indeed, of all life). (Note that selflessness here described should not be confused with disesteem for oneself in preference for esteem for others.[10]) At the opposite end of the scale is the generic vice of egoism that would presume to set the immediate interests and concerns of the unreformed self above those of others and above the welfare of all. Here we find such traits as unreadiness to be changed or transformed by coming in relation to *ultimate reality*[p], insincerity as in hypocrisy and duplicitous motivation, being excessively defensive about oneself and one's reputation; readiness to use sacred and holy things for profane purposes, readiness to manipulate the good faith of others to personal and material advantage, treating others as mere means for one's own ends, and closed-mindedness to things and other persons outside one's own frame of reference.

Though egoism may be condemned and selflessness praised in regard to individuals, not as often do we find egoism criticized and selflessness praised in regard to groups in the great religions. This pertains to the relations between insiders to a group and outsiders, or between a group as a whole and other groups. Egoism in regard to groups is characterized by the immediate interests and concerns of a group being set above the interests and concerns of outsiders and other groups. And selflessness is characterized by the members of the group transcending or setting aside those interests and concerns for the sake of the welfare of all concerned and hospitality to the outsider. Criticism and praise do not often develop at this level. Happily sometimes they do, but there are often powerful social forces ranged against it. It is not easy for commonsense reasoning to be effective at this level, for the respective parties unfortunately may all too easily avoid listening to and having to get along with each other. Even so, selflessness here too remains a virtue and egoism a vice, and they may be considered an extension of the parameter of assessment as it applies to individuals.

These three parameters of assessment—competence/incompetence, balance/imbalance of divergent forces, and selflessness/egoism—are not proposed as covering every possible commonsense consideration regarding virtue and vice in the practice of different ways of being religious. Perhaps other parameters can be found. In any case, what they involve in a more concrete way becomes clear only when they are applied to each different way of being religious. Thus, competence in the way of sacred rite is a very different thing from competence in the way of wisdom, and both are very different from competence in the way of shamanic mediation, and so forth. So also, the balance of divergent forces involved in the way of devotion is a different thing from the balance of the divergent forces involved in mystical quest, while both are very different from the balance of divergent forces involved in right action. Although selflessness would seem to be quite similar from one way of being religious to another, what it means in practice will vary in its expression. In this respect we can speak of generic virtues or traits of excellence specific to each of the ways of being religious. Similarly, the vices correlative with these generic virtues vary with each way of being religious—so much so that we can speak of generic vices or degenerations specific to each way of being religious that recur from one tradition to the next.

From "Is" to "Ought," from Description to Judgment

Readers may have misgivings about the account of qualitative variation in practice of the different ways of being religious here offered. One source of misgiving is that it appears to conflict with conventional ideas about the phenomenological approach to the study of religion. A second is that it appears to conflict with the scholarly obligation to be strictly objective. A third is that it appears suspiciously to derive normative conclusions from factual premises. This section addresses these misgivings and offers justification for the apparent shift in this chapter from description to evaluative judgment.

Being essentially a descriptive enterprise, the phenomenological approach to the comparative study of religion presumably should avoid drawing normative conclusions. The phenomenology of religion can report the nature of experience, practice, and understanding found in different religious traditions, can state what evaluative judgments are made about these matters by members of these traditions, and can explain the basis on which such evaluative judgments are made. All this is a matter of description. But to make judgments of value, to offer claims to the effect that some variations of practice are virtues and other variations are vices or degenerations, is to go beyond mere description, beyond reportage. It is to agree or disagree with the judgments made by others; it is not merely to report on the judgments of other persons. It is to step beyond the posture of an onlooking spectator. It is, so to speak, to take up residence in the same world as the persons whose religious life is being phenomenologically described. Consequently, an analysis of qualitative variation in practice of ways of being religious that claims to be phenomenologically based seems problematic on its face. Some would charge that this constitutes a transgression of the boundary of responsible phenomenological practice.

The phenomenology of religion adopts a suspension of judgment (called the *epoché*) as an essential aspect of its method. It does so not as an end in itself, but as a means to accomplish certain purposes. Specifically, its purpose is to circumvent and counteract *judgmental preconceptions* so as to enable apprehension and representation of the phenomena being studied on their own terms, instead of force-fitting or reducing them to alien preconceptions. Thus phenomenological neutrality is not meant to be a permanent orientation to take toward religious phenomena, as if it were the only just or responsible posture to take. On the contrary, it is meant to be a temporary strategy to facilitate arriving at an undistorted, genuinely empathetic understanding of the phenomena in question. Once that understanding is reached, the need for the suspension of judgment is past. Indeed, to remain permanently in a posture of suspended judgment is to merit the charge of irresponsibility, of refusing to take a stand on matters that call for a stand to be taken. It is to pretend that one lives outside the common world all of us share, religious and nonreligious. Rightly understood, then, the phenomenology of religion does not reject normative evaluation and judgment as such, but only premature and insufficiently discriminating judgment.[11] As stated at the beginning of this chapter, the solution to the problem of stereotypical judgments is not to cease making value judgments but to develop one's capacity for more discriminating judgment.

A second source of misgiving about entering into value judgments is the widely held view that objectivity, whether in the study of religion or in any other subject, requires one to refrain from being subjective in any way, as is necessary in making value judgments, and to draw only those conclusions that would in principle be drawn by any other similarly objective scholar. Thus considered, value judgments can never be objective; they are only the expression of human subjectivity, which varies from culture to culture and person to person. Consequently, the analysis presented here of qualitative variation of practice in ways of being religious cannot possibly claim to be objective, unless it be construed merely as an objective report of the (subjective) evaluative judgments of insiders of religious traditions and how they happen to arrive at them.

An adequate response to this misgiving requires challenging the preconception of objectivity on which it rests. As already discussed at the beginning of Chapter 2, it is very important to recognize that there is a second, no less legitimate notion of **objectivity**. That notion is fundamentally a matter of doing justice to the object itself, which lies at the point where the several perspectives relevant to determining the nature and meaning of the object intersect. Objectivity in this sense is a matter not of drawing away from but rather drawing nearer to the object, specifically in a manner appropriate to what it is thereby determined to be. Insofar as those perspectives involve discriminations of quality and worth, then drawing near to that to which they give access will necessarily involve some assessment of those discriminations and making them oneself. Thus conceived, the pursuit of objectivity in this second sense is inescapably an enterprise of discerning value judgment.

A third source of misgivings is a long-standing controversy in philosophy, which can be traced back to David Hume and possibly even as far back as Aristotle's account of the practical syllogism, concerning the alleged impossibility of deriving a statement involving a normative claim (e.g., that something *ought* to be done or valued) from statements involving only factual claims (e.g., that something *happens to be the case*). The predominant (but by no means universal) philosophical opinion is that it cannot be done and that to presume to do so is to commit a logical fallacy. Applying it to the present case, the conclusion that certain variations of practice should be esteemed as virtues and others disesteemed as vices because this or that religious tradition happens to so esteem and disesteem them, would appear to be an inference of an "ought" from an "is" and thus a commission of the same fallacy.

In response, I wish to stress that the analysis of qualitative variation in religious practice being offered is not presented as a conclusion derived simply from reports of the value judgments that religious insiders happen to make. It is based on an attempt to empathize sensitively with their struggles to realize excellence and virtue and avoid degeneration and vice in ongoing religious practice. It is the result of an attempt to see for myself (and to help readers see for themselves) what religious insiders see, to see what inspires and awes them, on the one hand, and to see what disappoints, frustrates, and discourages them, on the other. It is an attempt at a "meeting of our minds" over matters of practical importance, at making sense in common despite our differences. If so, then there is no fallacious inference of value statements from strictly factual statements involved.

A strictly neutral empathetic phenomenology treats the insiders of any given tradition in a separate religious (or cultural) world from every other. In an important sense that is true, but only in a sense. Strictly speaking, the supposition that they live and think in a world apart is a methodological fiction—useful in its place and within certain limits, but misleading if taken literally in an ongoing sense. Religious insiders live and carry on their religious practices in the same commonsense world that other human beings live in. Moreover, to the extent that they appeal to common sense (as they very often do) in sorting out what is qualitatively more or less virtuous in religious practice, it is to a common sense that is in principle shared with persons who are not simply (or necessarily) insiders to their tradition but who are in a position to discriminate among the same sorts of things. Indeed, the very idea that there are generic ways of being religious that cross traditional lines is such a commonsense notion. It presupposes the possibility of mutual recognition by (thoughtful, reflective, knowledgeable) people of different religious traditions of practices, concerns, and values they share in common despite their many differences. It presupposes that commonsense virtues and vices in religious practice are matters that can be discovered and recognized between us. This of course does not mean that everyone will be able or ready to recognize them in just any circumstance, especially if recognition involves a readiness to undergo self-criticism. Nevertheless, in principle, on commonsense grounds, and if they have not closed their minds to it, people in *any* tradition are able to recognize, and commonly do recognize, for example, how pernicious religious practice can be that combines egoism with imbalance in the direction of infinitude (i.e., losing awareness of one's own finitude, say, by presuming one's own egoistic will to be "the will of God" or its counterpart in the tradition in question).

If this is so, then, in addition to the norms of practice that are specific to a religious tradition, there are commonsense norms for assessing qualitative variation in religious practice as well—norms recognizable by both insiders and empathetic outsiders. There are likely other such norms as well, sufficient to constitute at least a minimal commonsense morality. On the basis of such a commonsense morality, representatives from different religious traditions (as well as nonreligious cultural traditions) can meet and find much in common, once they sort through the often greatly different ways they have for thinking and speaking about these things. Happily, that is largely what we find when people from different traditions come together in open dialogue and honestly seek what they might recognize in common.

In his recent book, *Global Responsibility: In Search of a New World Ethic,* Christian theologian Hans Küng has called for a concerted effort on the part of leaders of the major religions of the world to undertake a joint search for a new ethic of global responsibility. Significantly, his argument addresses, head on, both bystanders, who are skeptical that religions having been the source of so much conflict and ill will could possibly come together, and partisans of religion, who believe they have the answers. Here Küng appeals to the general sort of common-sense considerations I have offered (though not the specific formulations).

Küng's argument would not have as much persuasive power had it not grown out of a major effort on his own part to enter into dialogue with other religious traditions and participate in international interfaith dialogues that have come to remarkable agreement on such matters as basic human rights. The sort of dialogue he envisions and attempts to practice aims to avoid the defects of both absolutist-exclusivist and relativist-inclusivist positions: "The aim can only be a critical or self-critical differentiation which measures any religion critically by its own origin and by a humane ethic, without claiming it [i.e., without claiming to possess or embody that ethic] for itself. We do not arrive at peace through syncretism but through reform of ourselves; we arrive at renewal through harmony, and at self-criticism through toleration."[12] For this self-critical differentiation in and through interfaith dialogue, Küng postulates three different criteria:[13] (1) "According to the general ethical criterion a religion is true and good if and insofar as it is human, does not suppress and destroy humanity, but protects and furthers it." (2) "According to the general religious criterion a religion is true and good if and insofar as it remains true to its own origin or canon, to its authentic 'nature,' its normative scripture or figure, and constantly refers to it." (3) Each religion has its own specific criterion that directly applies to itself, its central criterion of value, and that indirectly, without any arrogance, may also be applied to the other religions, "to the critical illumination of the question whether and to what degree in other religions, too . . . there is something of that spirit which we describe as [uniquely Christian, Jewish, Muslim, Confucian, Hindu, or Buddhist]."

Quite apart from embracing these specific formulations, I consider Küng's book and the ongoing efforts at inter-religious dialogue of which it is a part as independent confirmation of the existence of a religious common sense of the sort I have been presenting (as opposed to the specific formulations I have offered) and of the possibility of mutual recognition between religions of generic virtues and vices in the practice of religion. I do not cite his book and argument as the ideal model for achieving a commonsense religious ethic. Nor do I embrace his position as a whole on inter-religious dialogue. I cite it as a significant, independent effort to achieve religious common sense in regard to ethics.

Now that the misgivings have been answered, let us take up again the basic thesis of the chapter. On the basis of a kind of religious common sense, each generic way of being religious has a potential for characteristic noble and praiseworthy expressions and a potential for characteristic ignoble and blameworthy expressions. Within actual traditions where a given way is found, we should expect to find these potentials recognized and guidance given with respect to them—as largely in fact we do. Furthermore, such expressions of virtue and vice in the practice of a given way of being religious should be recognizable as such to persons well acquainted with that way in other traditions, so far as these other persons are able empathetically to grasp what is going on. And this too we find largely to be the case. (Of course, they may in addition also praise or fault the expressions in the respect to which those expressions conform to the distinctive criteria of their own traditions.)

GENERIC VIRTUES AND VICES OF EACH WAY

It is now time to become more specific. To what extent is it possible to identify traits of religious practice within each of the six ways of being religious that characterize that way at its best and traits that characterize that way at its worst? What follows is my attempt to answer this question, making use of the three parameters identified above: competence/incompetence, balance of finitude and infinitude, and selflessness/egoism. I list as well a characteristic weakness in the competent practice of each way—the shadow side of its strength, as it were—from which develop its characteristic vices. It is important to keep in mind that these are virtues and vices in the practice of *generic* ways of being religious; hence they are generic, commonsense virtues and vices of religious practice that are not specifically formulated in terms of any one religious tradition. In addition to them there may be, specific to each religious tradition, further virtues and vices or further nuances of these generic virtues and vices. It is also important to keep in mind that they are not meant to cover the field of religious ethics, nor even the field of commonsense generic religious ethics (so far as there is such a thing). Here they pertain strictly to qualitative variation in the practice of different ways of being religious.

THE WAY OF SACRED RITE

Basic description: Participation in the *sacred archetypal patterns°* through which *ultimate reality°* is manifest, by means of symbolic ritual enactments or presentations that enable participants repeatedly to enter their presence, attain at-onement for the moment with them, and thereby establish and renew their sense of meaningful order, identity, and propriety. It is typically communal rather than individual.

CHARACTERISTIC VIRTUES OR EXCELLENCES OF PRACTICE	CHARACTERISTIC VICES OR DEGENERATIONS OF PRACTICE

CHARACTERISTIC VIRTUES
OR EXCELLENCES OF PRACTICE

1. **Competence:** Sensible to archetypal form; possesses a developed aesthetic sense; graceful and decorous; keenly sensible to timing; master of the art of participating in sacred ritual; master of ritual detail and the art of choreographing ritual action; thoroughly acquainted with and possesses a lively sense of and an ability to enter into and interpret the basic stories and symbols of the tradition.

2. **Balance of finitude and infinitude:** Possessed of profound awe and reverence in the presence of the *sacred°* as archetypal form while realistically appreciating the finite conditions of its lively mediation; freshly sensible to *archetypal patterns°* as transcendent to, though disclosed through, finite and familiar symbolic forms; reappropriates time-worn forms with freshness and creative imagination; sensible to what is important and what is not; composed in the face of small crises that occasionally occur in the midst of sacred ritual.

3. **Selflessness:** Sincerely involved in sacred worship for its own sake; ready to enter fully into collective ritual activity for the sake of the group; open to being challenged and changed by participation in sacred ritual; humbly regards ritual status as service and as meriting no special recognition or advantage over others; ready to help the least participant enter fully into sacred worship.

CHARACTERISTIC VICES
OR DEGENERATIONS OF PRACTICE

1. **Shadow side of competence:** Ready to treat all problems as calling for resolution through participation in sacred ritual; tends to overstructure activities and events; overly conservative.

2. **Incompetence:** Insensible to archetypal form; lacking a developed aesthetic sense; uncognizant of religious kitsch (religious art that manifests no genuine aesthetic sensibility); ignorant of basic stories and symbols of the tradition, lacking a lively sense of them, or unable to enter into and interpret them to others; ignorant of ritual proprieties; awkward, uncertain, or fumbling in ritual performance; prone to ritual mistakes and improprieties.

3. **Imbalance: Loss of finitude:** Idolatrous toward ritual form and symbol, where secondary symbols and ritual details are identified with sacred meaning as opposed to being its vehicle and mediator; absolutely closedminded to consideration of creative variations or alternative ritual forms.

4. **Imbalance: Loss of infinitude:** Merely perfunctory or wooden in the execution of ritual; preoccupied with ritual detail, or variation of ritual form, at expense of enabling participants' access to the *sacred archetypes°*; uncreative in repeating time-worn symbolic forms; insensible to the *sacred°* in and through the symbols; lacking awe and reverence for the transcendent dimension of the *sacred archetypal patterns°*; discomposed in the face of small crises of ritual detail.

5. **Egoism:** Making use of sacred rite, sacred symbols, or the prerogatives of ritual status to promote profane mundane interests, material advantage, or other egoistic interests whether at the individual or community level; unwilling to enter fully and sincerely into the collective ritual activity of the group and be challenged and changed by it.

THE WAY OF RIGHT ACTION

> **Basic description:** The concerted effort to bring all of life, individual and communal, into conformity with *the way things are ultimately supposed to be*° (however understood)—that is, to realize and fulfill *the sacred intendedness of life*°—that promises individual fulfillment, social justice, and the embodiment of *divine ideality*° in the midst of mundane, this-worldly life.

<table>
<tr><td align="center">CHARACTERISTIC VIRTUES
OR EXCELLENCES OF PRACTICE</td><td align="center">CHARACTERISTIC VICES
OR DEGENERATIONS OF PRACTICE</td></tr>
</table>

CHARACTERISTIC VIRTUES OR EXCELLENCES OF PRACTICE	CHARACTERISTIC VICES OR DEGENERATIONS OF PRACTICE
1. **Competence:** Master of the art of implementing and living out the *ideal divine pattern of life*°; decisive; courageous; steadfast; a clear sense of what is right and fitting; undeterred by social opposition; proactive versus reactive; realistically in touch with concrete obstacles and opportunities; effectively critical of the status quo; master of the arts of teaching morality and exercising moral leadership.	1. **Shadow side of competence:** Ready to treat all problems as solvable by bringing individual and communal life into conformity with the *divine ideal*°; frenetic activity, doing things with little or no inward centering or reflection.
2. **Balance of finitude and infinitude:** Passionately committed to the implementation of the *divine ideal*° but not overly serious (maintains a sense of humor); ready to recognize and admit mistakes but confident of the possibility to change and start anew; committed to justice but with a generosity of spirit that can show mercy and forgive; courageous and composed in doing what is appropriate and sensing what is important in the face of major obstacles and otherwise discouraging prospects.	2. **Incompetence:** Indecisive; lacking courage; of wavering or mixed motivation; ignorant or unclear as to what is right and fitting; overly concerned about what others will think; reactive versus proactive; insufficiently realistic as to the circumstances in which one must act; uncognizant of the moral shortcomings of the status quo; unable to convey to others a sense for what is right and fitting.
3. **Selflessness:** Selfless action; identified with the welfare of all; sincere in doing what is right for its own sake and free of ulterior motivation (especially egoistic motivation); committed to ongoing moral growth and improvement; never treats others as mere means to one's ends; free from resentment and not (overly) defensive about oneself or one's reputation; open to criticism of oneself and one's project (and group openness to criticism of itself and its projects); concerned to help others see for themselves what is right.	3. **Imbalance: Loss of finitude:** Perfectionist; over serious; radically utopian with little or no sense of the concrete obstacles to implementation; failing to distinguish one's finite will and plan (or that of one's group) from *divine ideality*° itself; unready to recognize one's own mistakes, to change, or to start anew; uncognizant of what lies outside one's frame of reference.
	4. **Imbalance: Loss of infinitude:** Legalistic; preoccupied with detail at expense of moral substance; obsessed with the letter of obligation at the expense of the right spirit; uncritically repetitious of the precepts of the tradition without thought or fresh reappropriation.
	5. **Egoism:** Morally hypocritical or pretentious; doing what on the surface is right and appropriate but primarily (or strictly) for the sake of some ulterior egoistic motive or material advantage; identified with the welfare of some at the expense of others; ready to treat others as mere means for one's ends; overly defensive about oneself or one's reputation; nursing of resentment or of desire for revenge; unconcern for others' need to see for themselves what is right.

THE WAY OF DEVOTION

> **Basic description:** Cultivation of a personal relationship to *ultimate reality*° of wholehearted adoration, devotional surrender to *its*° transforming grace, and trust in *its*° providential care, anticipating in return an influx of sustaining energy, hope, and a sense of affirming presence or at-onement. It typically involves a conversion experience and emotional purgation.

CHARACTERISTIC VIRTUES OR EXCELLENCES OF PRACTICE	CHARACTERISTIC VICES OR DEGENERATIONS OF PRACTICE
1. **Competence:** In touch with deeper feelings (one's own as well as others'); discerning of feelings; fully acquainted with the processes of personal conversion and devotional surrender, what occasions them, and how they should be guided; master of the art of pastoral counseling;	1. **Shadow side of competence:** Ready to treat all problems as solvable through devotional surrender to the providential grace of *ultimate reality*°; unreflectively trustful of feeling; passive.
2. **Balance of finitude and infinitude:** Love of *ultimate reality*° coupled with appropriate, penultimate care for finite realities and finite duties; simply trustful of providence (readiness to "Let go and let God") coupled with a readiness to do what one is in one's power; inwardly devotionally surrendered coupled with outward autonomy; at ease with the whole range of feelings and able to help others be at ease with feelings, yet not wholly subject to the sway of feelings; sensible to what is important and what is not, what is deep and what is only on the surface.	2. **Incompetence:** Out of touch with one's own feelings (or "having no feelings"); fickle (inconstant, changeable, capricious); caught up with superficial feelings of devotion but not yet given over to deep surrender; distrustful of feeling or of devotional surrender; of the supposition that one can pursue this way on one's own or in one's own strength; pastorally responsible for others but insensitive to others' feelings (unempathetic); lacking understanding of the processes of personal conversion and devotional surrender.
3. **Selflessness:** Sincere of heart; committed to ongoing personal transformation through surrender to the providential grace of *ultimate reality*°; possessed of a "generosity of soul" that includes and welcomes others within its circle of friendship; compassionate and sympathetic toward others; appropriately responsive to others' feelings; a good listener; able to let others have their own feelings.	3. **Imbalance: Loss of finitude:** Passionate in an intense, otherworldly way that eclipses into insignificance or disvalues all mundane concerns and the importance of others' feelings; failing to distinguish powerful feelings of *ultimate reality*° from *ultimate reality*° itself; wholly subject to the sway of powerful religious emotions.
	4. **Imbalance: Loss of infinitude:** Overly sentimental and emotional; enamored with cultivating feelings for their own sake (at the expense of theological depth or breadth), with little or no connection with *ultimate reality*°; imitating secondhand feelings and the appearance of devotional surrender, without genuineness or substance.
	5. **Egoism:** Insincere of heart; self-centered; insensitive to the feelings and emotional struggles of others; manipulative of religious affections (whether one's own or others') to promote egoistic motives or material advantage.

THE WAY OF SHAMANIC MEDIATION

> **Basic description:** Entry into altered states of consciousness in which persons become mediators or channels for the *intervention of spiritual reality°*, in the expectation that *"supernatural" (trans-mundane) resources°* of imagination, power, and guidance will be released for solving or dealing with otherwise intractable problems of life. Expressed through phenomena such as "possession trance," "oracular utterance," "ecstatic vision," and/or "spirit journeying," it seeks at-one-ment with *ultimate reality°* in what is taken to be *its°* readiness to bring about healing, well-being, and fulfillment for the world.

CHARACTERISTIC VIRTUES OR EXCELLENCES OF PRACTICE	CHARACTERISTIC VICES OR DEGENERATIONS OF PRACTICE
1. **Competence:** Mastery of *the spirit realm°*; mastery over oneself vis-à-vis the spirit realm; discernment of spirits (distinguishing good from bad or evil spirits); highly developed imagination; direct, sustained acquaintance with the spirit realm and not just second-hand knowledge that has been acquired from others; acquired charisma that evokes and keeps other persons' trust; developed trust in the processes of shamanic mediation.	1. **Shadow side of competence:** Readiness to treat all problems as solvable through shamanic mediation; spiritual impulsiveness and lack of structure.
2. **Balance of finitude and infinitude:** Awesome sense of *the mysteries of the spirit world°* coupled with deep appreciation for the fragile beauty and good of the mundane world; openness to and trust in the deep imagination but not indiscriminate trust; composure and confidence with respect to *spiritual powers°* (yet not overconfident), coupled with appreciation of the arts and crafts of mundane practice (e.g. mundane healing arts); knowledge of one's own limitations coupled with a sense of a shaman's high calling.	2. **Incompetence:** Lack of basic, sustained acquaintance with *the spirit world°*; lack of spiritual discernment; uncognizance of danger, recklessness and foolhardiness (flirting with danger) in relation to *the spirit world°*; overconfidence in one's mastery of *the spirit world°* and of oneself; distrust and skepticism toward *the spirit world°* and the processes of shamanic mediation.

3. **Imbalance: Loss of finitude:** Inordinate preoccupation with *the spirit world°* and shamanic mediation in a way that eclipses mundane concerns and appreciation of mundane practice (e.g. mundane healing arts and technology) and ordinary common sense; indiscriminate trust in "supernatural" powers and spirit guidance (occultism). |
| 3. **Selflessness:** Sincerity of commitment to spiritual guidance, healing, and empowerment for the sake of the greater good of the person, the group, and the larger living community (i.e., commitment to so-called "white magic" spiritual power for good); radical honesty and sincerity (freedom from duplicitous motivation); open commitment to spiritual growth and transformation; always treating other persons as spiritual ends in themselves, never as mere means. | 4. **Imbalance: Loss of infinitude:** Charlatanism and fakery; spiritual adventurism and "power tripping"; shamanic dilettantism; preoccupation with the outer forms and rituals of shamanism with no genuine involvement or personal transformation; loss (or lack) of the sense of the awesome mystery of the *the spirit realm°*.

5. **Egoism:** So-called "black magic" or "black sorcery," where supernatural and occult forces, or the appearance thereof, are employed to promote egoistic motives, material advantage, or the detriment of some person or group. |

THE WAY OF MYSTICAL QUEST

Basic description: Employment of ascetic and meditative disciplines in a deliberate quest to interrupt, slow down, or otherwise break through and become free of, the obscuring limitations of distracting compulsions of ordinary life in order to attain a direct awareness of *ultimate reality°*, come to be wholly at-one with *it°*, and have life and one's relations with all things become transparently grounded in *it°*.

CHARACTERISTIC VIRTUES OR EXCELLENCES OF PRACTICE	CHARACTERISTIC VICES OR DEGENERATIONS OF PRACTICE
1. ***Competence:*** Inwardly self-mastered, at-one with oneself; profoundly acquainted with the deeper truths of which one's tradition testifies on the basis of personal contemplative experience; master of a path that leads to their personal realization; skillful in the practice of its ascetic and meditative disciplines; master in guiding others along the path.	1. ***Shadow side of competence:*** Ready to treat all problems as solvable through mystical spiritual disciplines; quietistic; apathetic toward what lies beyond or outside the mystical quest.
2. ***Balance of finitude and infinitude:*** Passionately in pursuit of *enlightenment°* (a direct seeing into, and union with, *ultimate reality°* that will enable all things to be seen for what they really are and related to in their integrity) by way of practices that anticipate it; diligent in the practice of the relevant disciplines but never confusing the means with the goal; possessed of quiet centeredness and inner simplicity coupled with practical realism; attentive to what is going on both within and without; dispassionate and detached (i.e., free from this-worldly passions and attachments) while still appreciating finite goods in their place; living a life centered upon what is essential, with all else held lightly.	2. ***Incompetence:*** Not inwardly in touch with oneself; inexperienced; reckless and naively venturesome in tackling ascetic disciplines and meditative practices that are inappropriate for one's present stage of development; offering spiritual advice at second or third hand; lacking in empathy toward others' spiritual growth and ignorant of what is appropriate for them.
	3. ***Imbalance: Loss of finitude:*** Wholly other-worldly in outlook; disposed to extreme self-mortification; disdainful of mundane concerns and the welfare of others; tending to confuse the means, or a certain stage of development, with the goal; overserious (possessing no sense of humor); impatient with things beyond one's control.
3. ***Selflessness:*** Free of self-preoccupation, pretentiousness, and the distortions of consciousness that arise from the unenlightened self; committed to ongoing spiritual transformation and willing to take on spiritual discipline for its sake when appropriate (i.e., freedom from the presumption to "having arrived"); boundless and compassionate in hospitality of spirit; affirming of each person's need to find and follow his own path at his own pace.	4. ***Imbalance: Loss of infinitude:*** Characterized by spiritual adventurism and mystical dilettantism—seeking "Mystical Experiences"—with little if any commitment to personal transformation or sincere pursuit of at-onement with *ultimate reality°*; preoccupied with correct method (the outer forms) of mystical quest at the expense of its substance; characterized by acedia (spiritual boredom, loss of passion for what is higher).
	5. **Egoism:** Spiritually elitist (disdain for persons who lack spiritual enlightenment); escapist (pursuit of mystical quest as a way of escape from outward problems); exploitative of mystical experiences, lore, or status in service of egoistic motives or material advantage.

THE WAY OF REASONED INQUIRY

> **Basic description:** The rational, dialectical struggle to transcend conventional patterns of thinking in the effort to attain understanding of, and consciousness-transforming insight into, *the ultimate what, how, and why of things°*—that is, to bring together and unite, so far as possible, mind with *the ultimate Mind°* and thereby acquire a portion of *divine wisdom°*. It typically involves systematic study of a tradition's scripture and previous attempts to articulate *what is ultimately the case°*.

CHARACTERISTIC VIRTUES OR EXCELLENCES OF PRACTICE	CHARACTERISTIC VICES OR DEGENERATIONS OF PRACTICE

CHARACTERISTIC VIRTUES
OR EXCELLENCES OF PRACTICE

1. **Competence:** Knowledgeable and learned; master of *authoritative scripture and traditional commentary°*; accomplished in intellectual concentration and analysis; patient and skillful in reasoning; adroit in intellectual debate; able to explain things well and simply to others.

2. **Balance of finitude and infinitude:** Wise; both theoretically and practically thoughtful; keenly sensitive to the larger picture (comprehensiveness of vision) coupled with appreciation for detailed structure; appreciative of depth, importance, and mystery as well as of breadth, detail, and rigor; sensitive to one's own limitations and ignorance coupled with a passion to seek out understanding of *the greatest truths°*; sensible that *the deepest truths°* may transcend straightforward articulation and call for personal transformation to be apprehended and understood rightly.

3. **Selflessness:** Intellectually sincere; ready to change and develop one's own thinking further when reason indicates; committed to the pursuit of truth and to making it known for its own sake, even at risk and cost to oneself; self-critical and open to taking in the sound criticism of others; committed to thinking things through for oneself and respectful of the need of others to think things through for themselves; hospitable to others' ideas; patient with the pace of others' understanding.

CHARACTERISTIC VICES
OR DEGENERATIONS OF PRACTICE

1. **Shadow side of competence:** Ready to treat all problems as calling for an intellectual resolution; intellectualizing without heart.

2. **Incompetence:** Ignorant and ready to speak out of ignorance; reliant upon second-hand teachings (that have not been reasoned out and comprehended for oneself); possessed of unreasoned understandings (lacking in mental discipline, inconsistent, prone to logical mistakes, and sloppy in reasoning); inadequately acquainted with the *authoritative sources°* and insufficiently learned in *traditional commentary°*.

3. **Imbalance: Loss of finitude:** Passionately preoccupied with the present focus of one's intellectual quest, one's own ideas, or one's own perspective in a way that eclipses all other concerns, ideas, and perspectives (e.g., in intense intellectual debate); unable to distinguish one's own ideas about *ultimate reality°* from *ultimate reality°* itself; unaware and out of touch with one's own limitations and ignorance.

4. **Imbalance: Loss of infinitude:** Lacking in passion for *ultimate truth°*; unready for personal transformation in the quest for wisdom; unable to distinguish the heart of the matter from insignificant details; unable to distinguish genuine explanation from rationalization; intellectually heartless; pedantic; characterized by intellectual nit-picking and hair-splitting; tending to repeat and rehash existing ideas.

5. **Egoism:** Intellectually pretentious, intellectually hypocritical, or intellectually dishonest —i.e., using intellectual talent and understanding, or the appearance thereof, to conceal egoistic motivation or pursuit of material advantage; unready to own up to one's own ignorance; overly defensive about one's own ideas and thinking (or those of one's group), or unnecessarily aggressive toward those of other persons or groups.

CHAPTER SUMMARY

This chapter introduces the concept of evaluative judgment made from within a tradition in regard to quality of religious practice. The point is to gain a sense of the basis on which insiders discriminate between virtue and vice in religious practice, between practice that is worthy of esteem and respect, on the one hand, and practice that is not worthy and merits criticism or condemnation, on the other. Some judgments of this nature are based on criteria that are specific to a tradition (being uniquely specified by its authoritative sources) or to the general criterion of fidelity to those authoritative sources. Others are based on criteria of a commonsense nature that may or may not be specified by the tradition but in principle can be shared by members of other traditions. Interestingly, the latter criteria vary depending on the way of being religious under consideration. In other words, for each generic way of being religious, there appear to be commonsense generic virtues and generic vices that are recognizable within any tradition in which that way can be found (although they may not in fact be recognized by any given person).

Commonsense considerations regarding virtues and vices in the practice of each way of being religious in different traditions are not just a hodge-podge of maxims and rules of thumb. Many can be grouped around three basic parameters of assessment (sliding scales of qualitative variation): competence/incompetence; balance/imbalance of infinite, intangible, other-worldly aspects of the practice with finite, tangible, this-worldly aspects; and selflessness/egoism. Each of the three might be said to constitute a generic virtue/vice spectrum. What each of these parameters involves in a more concrete way becomes clear only when they are applied to each different way of being religious.

The second section of the chapter offers justification for the apparent shift from phenomenological description to evaluative judgment in this chapter. First, the suspension of judgment involved in a phenomenological approach to the study of religion is not an absolute; it is not incompatible with evaluative judgment. It is only a means for acquiring understandings that will be more just because they are empathetic. Second, objectivity, properly understood, does not forbid judgment; it may in fact call for it. Third, the criteria for the normative judgments here proposed are drawn not from mere factual, "objective" data, but from traditions of religious practice explored in an empathetic, dialogical way that seeks a meeting of minds across the boundaries of tradition.

In the third section, tables list specific qualities that characterize virtue and vice along each of the three parameters for each generic way of being religious. A growing familiarity with these qualities and how they differ from one way of being religious to the next will do much to fill out one's developing understanding of each of the ways. The point is to develop a sense for the capacity to discriminate quality of practice in each of these ways.

STUDY QUESTIONS

1. What negative stereotypes and caricatures of the different ways are you aware of? Suppose that there are a few individual instances of which these stereotypes capture some truth. But now imagine variations of these same practices without the negative traits. In other words, imagine the practices ideally carried out in ways that inspire others and merit respect.

2. In regard to the thought experiment in question 1, do a research project to determine whether there have been actual examples of such ideal practice and learn about them.

3. Do a field research project in which you build empathetic rapport with insiders to a specific religious practice sufficient to learn from them what sorts of things constitute virtue in that practice and what sorts of things constitute vice. Don't limit yourself to a single informant. Use the three parameters of assessment identified in this chapter to prompt questions, but avoid using jargon. (For example: what are some of the things that would indicate competence in the performance of this role and what are some that would indicate incompetence? Can self-centeredness sometimes be a problem? Is it possible to be so caught up in the details that the spirit is lost or missed altogether? On the other hand, is it possible to be so enthused about the overall goal that one fails to take care of the necessary details?)

4. Do the research project in question 3 on another tradition for the purpose of eventually comparing the results with the first project. Pick a practice representing the same way of being religious but in another subtradition of the same religion. Or, pick a practice representing the same way but in a completely different religion. Or, pick a practice representing another way in the same religion.

5. Take one of the tables of virtues and vices of one way of being religious at a time, and see if you can identify particular examples from your own observation, reading, or secondhand knowledge of the traits listed. For any one example of a virtue, imagine, if you can, what a corresponding vice in that practice would be like. For any one example of a vice, imagine, if you can, what a corresponding virtue in that practice would be like. In a similar way, work through each of the other five tables.

6. Are there other virtues or vices of a commonsense nature in religious practice than the principal ones identified in this chapter? Are there positive or negative traits specific to the quality of practice of one of the ways of being religious other than those listed in the six tables?

7. What problems do you see, if any, with the approach to evaluative judgment in quality of religious practice advocated in this chapter?

FOR FURTHER READING

Sensitive, empathetic, systematic assessments of quality of religious practice in published form are largely nonexistent, especially from a commonsense or inter-religious basis. Or rather, the field is in its infancy. The following books are a good place to begin further study, though most are written within a largely Christian context.

Margaret P. Battin, *Ethics in the Sanctuary* (New Haven, CT: Yale University Press, 1990).

Charles Davis, *Temptations of Religion* (New York: Harper & Row, 1973).

Ronald L. Grimes, *Ritual Criticism: Case Studies in Its Practice, Essays on Its Theory* (Columbia, SC: University of South Carolina Press, 1990). (Grimes here attempts to establish an academic field of ritual criticism, not only of religious ritual but also of ritual in drama and other areas of life. He is concerned with identifying what makes ritual come off well or badly, what makes it succeed, and what makes it fail.)

Hans Küng, in his *Global Responsibility: In Search of a New World Ethic*, trans. John Bowden (New York: Crossroad, 1991). (Küng develops his argument within an explicitly inter-religious context and does not hesitate to raise critical questions about practice within each religious tradition. His argument, however, remains at the level of generalizations and does not get down to many specifics.)

Julius H. Rubin, *Religious Melancholy and Protestant Experience in America* (New York: Oxford University Press, 1994).

Gregory Max Vogt, *Pathological Christianity: The Dangers and Cures of Extremist Fundamentalism* (Notre Dame, IN: Cross Roads Books, 1994).

Conrad W. Weiser, *Healers—Harmed and Harmful* (Philadelphia, PA: Fortress Press, 1994).

Richard Wentz, *Why People Do Bad Things in the Name of Religion*, rev. ed. (Macon, GA: Mercer University Press, 1993).

NOTES

1. This dichotomy is sometimes uncritically assumed even by serious scholars, not least Max Weber and many of those he has directly influenced. See, for example, A. James Reichley, "Pietist Politics," in *The Fundamentalist Phenomenon*, ed. Norman J. Cohen (Grand Rapids, MI: Eerdmans, 1990), pp. 73–98. For a critique of this antithesis as it applies to the religion of ancient Israel, one of the first subjects to which Weber applied it, see Rodney R. Hutton, *Charisma and Authority in Israelite Society* (Philadelphia, PA: Fortress Press, 1994).

2. Susan Walker, ed., *Speaking of Silence: Christians and Buddhists on the Contemplative Way* (New York: Paulist Press, 1987). This book contains a brief annotated bibliography on the contemplative way in each tradition and on Buddhist-Christian dialogue. See also the informative *Bulletin of the North American Board for East-West Dialogue* (focused on monastic inter-religious dialogue) published by the Abbey of Gethsemani, 3642 Monks Road, Trappist, KY 40051-6102. The bulletin contains reports, announcements, articles, and reviews of books and other resources. Another, more academic, resource is the *Society for Buddhist-Christian Studies Newsletter* published by the Society for Buddhist-Christian Studies, Graduate Theological Union, 2400 Ridge Road, Berkeley, CA 94709. Gilbert G. Hardy, *Monastic Quest and Interreligious Dialogue* (New York: Peter Lang, 1990) develops a theoretical and theological justification for intermonastic dialogue.

3. On the concept of reconciling divergent forces, see E. F. Schumacher, "The Greatest Resource—Education," in his collection of essays, *Small is Beautiful: Economics As If People Mattered* (New York: Harper and Row, 1973), pp. 72–94. There he attributes the idea to G. N. M. Tyrell. Schumacher gives a fuller treatment of the concept in his book, *A Guide for the Perplexed* (New York: Harper and Row, 1977), Ch. 10: "Two Types of Problems," pp. 121–136.

4. For this conception I am relying, to some extent, on the ontology of human existence developed by Søren Kierkegaard in his book, *The Sickness Unto Death*, trans. Walter Lowrie (Princeton, NJ: Princeton University Press 1941).

5. See his *Nichomachean Ethics*, Book 2, Secs. vi–ix. There are aspects of Aristotle's catalogue of virtues that directly reflect the culture of ancient Greece, lending force to the charge that virtue ethics generally is culturally relative. However, despite this, it can be argued that Aristotle provides an approach to the identification of nonculturally relative virtues. See Martha Nussbaum, "Non-Relative Virtues: An Aristotelian Approach," *The Quality of Life*, ed. Martha Nussbaum and Amartya Sen (a study prepared for the World Institute for Development Economics Research of the United Nations University; Oxford: Clarendon Press, 1993), pp. 242–269.

6. Aristotle simply called it prudence (*phronesis*). See *ibid.*, Book 6, Secs. v, viii, and xiii.

7. Charles Davis has identified and insightfully analyzed four problematic "temptations of religion"—namely, lust for certitude, cosmic vanity, pride of history, and anger of morality—each of which falls into my classification of the vice of infinitude, or loss of finitude. Although he primarily refers to Christianity, most of his observations can be readily generalized to other religious traditions, and thus are substantially in agreement with the conception of qualitative variation in religious practice being developed here. See Charles Davis, *Temptations of Religion* (New York: Harper and Row, 1973).

8. See W. Montgomery Watt, "Ghazali, Abu Hamid al-," *Encyclopedia of Religion*, Vol. 5, ed. Mircea Eliade (New York: Macmillan, 1987), pp. 541–544, and the bibliographical references at the end of Watt's article.

9. See Thomas Merton, *Contemplation in a World of Action* (Garden City, NJ: Doubleday, 1971); Rebecca S. Chopp, "Praxis," *The New Dictionary of Catholic Spirituality*, ed. Michael Downey (Collegeville, MN: Michael Glazier/Liturgical Press, 1993), pp 756–764; and Kenneth Leech, "Spirituality and Social Justice," *The Study of Spirituality*, ed. Cheslyn Jones, Geoffrey Wainwright, and Edward Yarnold (New York: Oxford University Press, 1986), pp. 582–584. For discussions of the uniting of contemplation and action in other traditions, see Yusuf Ibish and Ileana Marculescu, eds., *Contemplation and Action in World Religions* (Seattle, WA: University of Washington Press; a Rothko Chapel Book, 1978).

10. There is a growing body of literature (often allied with the feminist critique of gender bias in Western culture) that is critical of the ideal of selflessness that has been maintained at times in certain moral and religious traditions within American culture. (See Carol Gilligan, *In a Different Voice: Psychological Theory and Women's Development* [Cambridge, MA: Harvard University Press, 1982], and Eva Feder Kittay and Diana T. Meyers, eds., *Women and Moral Theory* [Totowa, NJ: Rowman and Littlefield, 1987].) In part, the force of the criticism is that the ideal of selflessness is used to legitimate servitude, reinforce unhealthy relations of codependency, and discourage healthy patterns of self-development. In Carol Gilligan's scheme of moral development, a selfless placing of the interests of others before one's own interests, while better than sheer egoism, is nevertheless a penultimate stage. Psychological health requires that it be surmounted by the higher stage of balanced caring for the interests of oneself along with the interests of others.

I think there may be something to what Gilligan is getting at beyond its reference to American culture in particular that has genuine relevance to the matter currently at issue.

However, it needs much more careful working out in relation to living traditions of religious common sense than I am presently prepared to accomplish. At first thought, it suggests that the parameter of qualitative variation here identified as selflessness/egoism might better be conceived as a matter of balance/imbalance, like the second parameter discussed above. In that case, moving more and more in the direction of selflessness would not necessarily be a good thing. Rather, it suggests the parameter should be reconceived as a matter of finding an appropriate balance between the opposite extremes of pro-ego interests and anti-ego interests. Though it has a certain plausibility, I am not at all sure whether this conception is compatible with Buddhist, certain Hindu, and Sufi Muslim traditions that speak of the dissolution of the separate ego. I suspect it may not be compatible. If not, then it clearly will not do as a component of religious common sense.

11. For a fuller discussion of these issues, see my article, "Having Faith, Being Neutral, and Doing Justice: Toward a Paradigm of Responsibility in the Comparative Study of Religion," *Method and Theory in the Study of Religion* 6:1 (1993), pp. 155–176. In the introduction to their anthology, *The Experience of the Sacred: Readings in the Phenomenology of Religion* (Hanover, NH: Brown University Press/University Press of New England, 1992), Sumner B. Twiss and Walter H. Conser, Jr., discuss how the existential-hermeneutical approach to the phenomenology of religion is oriented not to detachment and neutrality as such but to these techniques as serving certain normative existential aims, insights, and hunches about what is most important in the human condition.

In a transcribed panel discussion of "Neutrality and Responsibility in the Comparative Study of Religion" at the 1992 Annual Meeting of the American Academy of Religion, Judith Berling, scholar of Chinese religions and dean of the Graduate Theological Union at Berkeley, advocated a very similar approach: "I have a responsibility to use the knowledge that I have of Chinese culture to sophisticate, to nuance, to enrich perceptions that people in the field of Chinese religion—that students of Chinese religion, whether they're freshmen in the classroom or graduate students or in the culture at large—have about the religious dimensions of life, to sharpen my own and my audience's perception, their focus, their ability to discern aspects of religious life with both appreciation and critical discernment. Here I want to add a theme to the notion that our task is to interpret, which it certainly is. Recently I have come to think about 'discernment language' as a useful addition to the theory of interpretation. An interesting metaphor for this would be the kind of discernment, the kind of discrimination, that we try to cultivate when we are trying to understand and appreciate dance or the visual arts. That is, training the eye, the mind—dare I say even the soul—to appreciate what is there to see, to discern, to notice, to be aware of, what is there. And also to discern both excellence and the variations: to be able to see subtleties, to see variations, to see excellences and make judgments, critical judgments, that perhaps we could not have seen before."

12. Hans Küng, *Global Responsibility: In Search of a New World Ethic*, trans. John Bowden (New York: Crossroad, 1991), p. 132.

13. *Ibid.*, p. 97f.

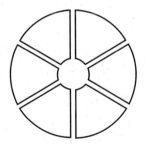

C H A P T E R 6

USING THE FRAMEWORK

The first five chapters have presented a basic introduction to the framework of generic ways of being religious, to its application to the study of religious traditions, and secondarily to its relevance to inter-religious dialogue. The time has come to step back and reflect on the framework as a whole in terms of its use in religious studies: What are the advantages of making use of it as opposed to some other framework or none at all? What are the disadvantages or liabilities of making use of the framework?

ADVANTAGES OF USING THE FRAMEWORK

As a framework for the comparative study of religion, the hypothesis of six generic ways of being religious offers several practical advantages, especially to the beginning student in the comparative study of religions. Some advantages of using the framework may be obvious and some have already been pointed out. It may help to have them summarized in a single place. First, some advantages of personal relevance will be identified; second, some advantages relevant to the health and well-being of religious traditions will be mentioned; and, finally, six advantages relating to acquiring better understandings of religions and religious phenomena will be discussed.

First, what personal advantages does it hold? *The framework is an aid to the process of self-knowledge and personal fulfillment.* It helps a person locate herself and her own subtradition on the landscape of traditional religions and religious practices. Should she be personally searching for a tradition to call her own, the framework can help her locate a subtradition that is more likely to satisfy her specific religious needs than are others. That is to say, it helps one understand why certain subtraditions of a given religion are likely to be personally more satisfying, whereas others (for the present at least) likely will not, and why some people—perhaps even one's close friends and relatives—will be drawn to subtraditions (i.e., ways of being religious) other than those one will personally be drawn to. It shows how there can be considerable religious differences between members of a single religious tradition while each nevertheless remains loyal to the central convictions, stories, and symbols that define the larger tradition. Moreover, it offers a basis for recognizing a range of nontraditional religious practices, para-religious practices, and surrogate religious practices—for it is possible to find a variety of examples of each way, or something very much akin to each way, in contemporary culture in which no system of symbols identifiable with conventional religion is operative. Thus, it provides a rationale for many of the religious differences that occur between persons, helping to minimize misunderstanding, reduce tension, and build mutual respect between them. In addition, it enriches one's sense of a tradition—one's own as well as any other tradition. It poses the possibility that there are other authentic expressions of a tradition and more ways of interpreting the central stories of the tradition than one may have previously encountered or may have imagined, whether already in existence or yet to be developed.

Second, *the framework provides a commonsense basis for differentiating healthy from degenerate expressions of a tradition.* In addition, it provides a basis for assessing the potential for renewal of that tradition beyond what may be its present degenerate forms. As initially proposed in Chapter 2 and developed further in Chapter 5, an understanding of the framework of ways of being religious indicates the existence of religious common sense—something directly relevant to maintaining the health and well-being of a religious tradition. What the framework does is to highlight and call attention to matters that are—or that should in principle be—recognizable by insiders from within any tradition. For example, under certain conditions and within certain limits set by the authoritative norms of the tradition, it is common sense that there should be expressions of both the way of sacred rite and the way of right action, respectively motivated by different sorts of existential needs, as well as expressions of the other ways. And it is common sense that certain sorts of expression of each of these ways are degenerate, whereas others are worthy of great respect. Recognition that the framework articulates part, at least, of what makes for religious common sense would go a long way to help persons who differ religiously to make religious sense in common as well as be more sensitive to the potential for both degeneration and excellence in their own (and each other's) traditions.

Third, turning to somewhat more objective considerations—namely, those respects in which the framework leads to improved and more just understandings of religions and religious phenomena in general—six advantages bear mentioning.

1. The framework helps avoid false or reductive generalizations by helping one understand that religion is not simply one thing but is many things—not just one generic thing but several different generic things. Particularly at the introductory level, students need to have their oversimplifying preconceptions broken down—for example, their tendency to assume that any expression of a religious tradition to which they have been exposed (whether as insider or outsider) is representative of the whole tradition or is somehow a normative standard in relation to which other expressions are deviations. An introduction to the framework of the six generic ways—but more so an exposure to authentic, representative examples of each of the six ways—effectively counteracts this tendency, nipping it in the bud. Specifically, the framework keeps one from supposing an entire religion is simply the one or two ways of being religious discovered on becoming acquainted with one of its subtraditions, however major that subtradition happens to be or however close to the origin of the religion that subtradition is able to trace itself back. It prompts one to look for other ways than those yet found and does not assume that a way need be inauthentic to a religion just because it was not separately identifiable in the earliest years of the religion. So also, it counteracts the supposition that all religions can be reduced at their core to a single way, whether it be taken to be mysticism, as the theosophists would have it, sacred rite, as certain cultural anthropologists would have it, or right action, as certain liberal Protestant theologians would have it. Indeed, by fostering appreciation for the complexity of religious traditions and the different priorities and motivations that members of a tradition have in virtue of their identification with one or another way of being religious, it brings to light how such reductionist views may themselves be motivated by their authors' identification with (or antipathy toward) a single way of being religious.

2. The framework helps one understand better the examples of any one way of being religious. It is directly intended to facilitate empathetic understanding of religious practices different from those with which one happens to be familiar. The difficulty of empathetically understanding a different way of being religious from one with which one is already familiar in the same tradition may be greater than that of coming to understand an example of the same way in a completely different tradition. For example, a student familiar with Theravada Buddhist monasticism will likely find it more difficult to empathetically understand *Jodo-shin-shu* Buddhism (a form of Japanese devotional Buddhism) than to empathetically make sense of Cistercian Christian monasticism, even when he has had little prior acquaintance with Christianity. A solid grasp of the framework of ways of being religious thus goes a long way to prepare the student in advance for understanding the variety of religious expressions of any tradition she is likely to encounter. One specific way it does this is by prompting the student who seeks to understand a puzzling religious phenomenon (e.g., a religious rite, a theological explanation, or an account of a mystical experience) to investigate what is the ongoing way of carrying on religious life to which it belongs. Thus, an intellectual expression of a tradition encountered as a literary text (whether theological or philosophical) is often best understood by placing it in the living context of an ongoing pursuit of the way of reasoned inquiry within that tradition, in juxtaposition to other ways of being religious in the same tradition. Otherwise puzzling aspects of the intellectual expressions of a tradition may become comprehensible and clear when so considered. For example, the early medieval Christian philosopher-theologian Anselm's famous ontological proof of the existence of God, when viewed in this manner, discloses itself to be a Platonic, intellectual "ascent out of the cave" to a direct, mystical encounter with God (uniting, as is typical of so much of Christian Platonism, the ways of reasoned inquiry and mystical quest).[1] In a similar way, the framework prompts the study of mysticism to focus not on "mystical experiences" or "mystical literature" in the abstract but instead on the ongoing practice of people who are pursuing the way of mystical quest in particular traditions. Thus, the Islamic mystic Djalâl-od-Dîn Rûmî's copious writings, in which are found accounts of his own mystical experiences, are best understood within the context of the ongoing practice of *Mawlawi* Sufism, of which all agree he is its greatest master and reformer.[2]

3. The framework sorts out different sorts of religious differences, instead of treating them only as historical-cultural variations upon single, unique traditions. It distinguishes differences due to generic ways of being religious from differences due to the specific content of religious traditions (deriving from its central stories and beliefs, its core symbol system) and, for each way within a single tradition, from variations in practice of that way. Failure to keep these differences distinct results in all sorts of confusion and misunderstanding—from identifying Buddhism simply with the monastic pursuit of *nirvāṇa* to setting up a romantic opposition between personal religion (individual, spontaneous, experiential) and institutional religion (social, formal, legalistic). Similarly, failure to keep these differences distinct has resulted in a blindness to the emergence in contemporary Western culture (perhaps as well as in other cultures and previous cultural epochs) of ways of being religious outside of systems conventionally regarded as religions. The framework allows for—indeed, it prompts—recognition of generic or universal options of human religiousness built into the human condition while nevertheless granting due recognition to the historical and cultural conditionedness of the religious phenomena in which those features are manifest. Thereby it opens up a range of additional causal factors relevant to historical explanation that otherwise remain obscure. For example, many of the historical disagreements between Christian traditions become much more intelligible when viewed in its light. Specifically, the Protestant Reformation at its heart is revealed to involve a shift of central emphasis from the way of sacred rite to the way of devotion. This latter emphasis comes to be even more clearly expressed in subsequent Pietist movements. Similar applications of the framework can be readily made in explaining the origin and rise of different Buddhist traditions in Eastern Asia. Yet despite its employment of generic categories, establishing profound similarities between different religious traditions, the framework does not prejudice appreciation of differences as insignificant; it leaves the question of their significance completely open.

4. The framework suggests fruitful comparative studies in depth. Specifically, it suggests that in-depth similarities between traditions will be found when examples of the same way (or even the same or roughly the same combinations of ways) of being religious are compared. It is not just that the same things are likely to be done in similar circumstances in each case, but that the same sorts of problems are being faced (referred to earlier as existential motivations) with the same general strategy (the same generic way of being religious, the same generic way for coming into right relationship with *ultimate reality*) for solving or dealing with them. So close will these "solutions" be at times that the store of practical wisdom (often largely oral) built up over time in one tradition will have profound resonances with that of others that have little or no historical relationship to it. So much so that members of each may have much of personally relevant value to learn from and share with the others—insofar as they are able to get together in some kind of nonhostile, open, and empathetic dialogue. This author has himself witnessed such an encounter between a female representative of the Roman Catholic Charismatic movement, deeply involved in the ministry of "inner healing prayer," and a female practitioner of "healing shamanism," initiated in a North African and at least one Native American shamanic tradition. A similar sort of thing is seen in the several encounters and dialogues that have taken place between Christian and Buddhist monastics;[3] participants and observers alike have often remarked at how much participants in these dialogues discover they have in common and how much they have to learn from each other. In each of these separate cases, while many profound similarities have surfaced, like the proverbial iceberg, many more promise to come to light as empathetic research is pursued further. Some obvious comparisons suggested by the framework include a joint study of Evangelical Protestantism and *Jodo-shin-shu* Buddhism as subtraditions of Christianity and of Buddhism exemplifying the way of devotion,[4] and a joint study of Martin Luther (founder of the Protestant Reformation and of Lutheran Protestantism in particular) and Shinran Shonin (founder of *Jodo-shin-shu*), both of whom underwent a profound conversion experience early in their careers and came to stress in their teaching the primacy of "grace" and "faith" over "works" to attain "salvation."[5] A more general and inclusive study might be of the role of priest in different traditions exemplifying the way of sacred rite, or of the roles of shaman, moral prophet, devotional pastor, and so forth. A specific promising joint study would be that of classical rabbinic Judaism with its stress upon the way of right action (performance of the divine commandments in all areas of life, many of them of a ritual nature) and the way of reasoned inquiry (through traditional study of the *Torah* and *Talmud*) and classical Confucianism with its stress upon the way of right action (realizing true humanity through the maintenance of right social relationships and proprieties) and the way of reasoned inquiry (through traditional study of the Chinese Classics and the ideal of the scholar-sage). Still another fruitful study would be a comparison of subtraditions of different religions that are known for their inclusive attitude toward several if not all of the ways of being religious—for example, Roman Catholic Christianity and *T'ien-t'ai* Chinese Buddhism (*Tendai* in Japan).

5. The framework helps one recognize and appreciate genuine differences between religions and avoid false or misleading contrasts. Specifically, it can help students avoid attributing differences between expressions of one tradition and expressions of another to differences between the two traditions when those differences happen to be largely due to differences between two ways of being religious, both of which can be found in each tradition. For example, Christianity and Buddhism are not very fruitfully contrasted by juxtaposing North American Evangelical Protestant Christianity with Sri Lankan Theravada Buddhist Monasticism—especially not when much more interesting comparisons and contrasts can be found between Protestant Evangelicalism and the various forms of Pure Land Buddhism on the one hand (such as the *Jodo-shin-shu* tradition mentioned above) and between Theravada Monasticism and Roman Catholic Cistercian Monasticism on the other. It may be obvious at this stage, but the framework of the six ways of being religious implies that the best and most effective way to explore what the differences between two religious traditions in living practice amount to is to explore how pursuit of the same ways of being religious differs in each tradition and what priority, if any, is assigned to certain ways in relation to others. An attempt to draw contrasts between Buddhism and Islam on the basis, say, of an abstract juxtaposition of ideas, doctrines, and/or scriptures, without attending to how differently those ideas, doctrines, and scriptures are taken up and interpreted in the lived practice of different ways of being religious pursued in each tradition—especially given (most of) Islam's priority of right action and (most of) Buddhism's priority of mystical quest—is likely to result in misleading oversimplifications that correspond to no reality at all. The advantage of the framework of the six ways, as said before, is that it establishes a basis for recognizing similarities without prejudicing in the least the significance of differences. By its means generic differences between ways of being religious can be factored out, as it were, so that differences between traditions can be most fully appreciated.

6. The framework opens up several promising lines of inquiry. Some promising lines of inquiry have been indicated already. Beyond these relatively straightforward comparative studies, several other possibilities suggest themselves under several headings.

The Study of Nontraditional Ways of Being Religious   Chapter 4 made reference to ways of being religious outside conventional religious traditions (i.e., outside what conventionally in our culture we regard as religion or religious). There have been a number of studies[6] of these sorts of phenomena, from Robert Bellah's work on civil religion[7] and various scholars' analyses of Marxism and Maoism as religions[8] to Michael Novak's study of the religion of sport in America.[9] The framework of ways of being religious not only confirms and provides a kind of further rationale of such findings, but also points to still other cultural practices that might fruitfully be explored as ways of being religious. Thus, some practices in psychotherapy seem clearly to verge on being religious in ways suggestive of the way of devotion;[10] some practices involving jazz and rock music seem to involve the way of shamanic mediation;[11] some people aggressively pursuing certain philosophies of how businesses should be run seem to exemplify the way of right action; and some persons within the scientific community clearly pursue their work in ways that seem definitely to involve the way of reasoned inquiry. Many—perhaps most—of these persons would not identify themselves as religious in any conventional sense in doing what they do, yet the framework promises considerable insight into aspects of their practice, sufficient it would seem to identify them at least as parareligious practices, if not outrightly religious altogether.

Philosophy of Religion and Religious Philosophy   The framework of ways of being religious assumes a much broader and more complex notion of religion (as practice) than has been used in philosophy of religion as traditionally pursued. So one line of inquiry would be, What difference would the framework make for the philosophy of religion; what new and different questions would it be asking as a result? Less attention should be focused on belief than on practice—specifically, practice of the different ways—and on the presuppositions involved in these different practices.[12] Another line of inquiry would involve explorations based on the idea that *theological*[o] and philosophical inquiry as practice can become itself a way of drawing near to and coming into right relationship to *ultimate reality*[o]—that is, can be itself a way of being religious (the way of reasoned inquiry).[13] Clearly, as one looks over the history of Western philosophy and theological reflection, some philosophers stand out not only as significant thinkers but also as religious in the passionate way they went about their inquiries. Their inquiries were for them part of (if not entirely) a path of salvation: Plato and Plotinus certainly, but also Augustine, Anselm, Bonaventure, Aquinas, Spinoza, Hegel, Kierkegaard, Marx, and Wittgenstein.[14] To clarify how, in what respects, and under what circumstances philosophy comes in such thinkers to be religious, to be transformative in the sense of the way of reasoned inquiry, would be most worthwhile. In connection with this, a third line of inquiry might look at the place of theological-philosophical study (and jurisprudential study), particularly in the traditions of Judaism, Christianity, and Islam as practice and not merely in terms of its products as an expression of the way of reasoned inquiry. A fourth would be to investigate the role of commonsense, nonprofessional, philosophical reflection as a reforming and moderating agent within religious traditions, whatever way of being religious may happen to be involved, in helping to counteract their inherent tendencies to degeneration.

Religious Ethics and the Ethics of Religion   In Chapter 5 the concept of generic variations in quality of practice within each way was introduced—that is, characteristic potentials for degeneration and for excellence that recur from one tradition to the next that appear to be recognized within each tradition. The extent to which this is indeed the case is a considerable field of promising research. It suggests that there is a mutually recognizable, cross-tradition basis (common at least to those traditions that pursue the same ways of being religious) for evaluation and assessment of religious practice of generic ways of being religious, at least along certain parameters. This would be in large part religious common sense. How complete or adequate this basis would be for practical purposes is a question that further research and interfaith dialogue should be able to answer. In effect, it would be a basis for an internally relevant, yet cross-tradition critique of religion, and a challenge to excellence in practice as well.[15] Another line of inquiry would be to investigate to what extent and under what circumstances the ethical teachings of a religious tradition come to function as the focus of the way of right action pursued in that tradition—that is, as a principal means of drawing near to and coming into right relationship with *ultimate reality*—and when they do not.

Psychology of Religion and Religious Formation   In Chapter 3, the different ways were correlated with a variety of personality traits. There are many promising lines of inquiry in psychological research that these correlations suggest that seem to develop further the notion of a religious common sense.[16] To what extent are people with certain personality traits more likely to identify with and pursue the way of being religious that appears to correlate with those traits?[17] In this regard it would be worthwhile to compare taxonomies of personality types that have been developed in some traditions (e.g., Hindu, Buddhist, Daoist, Islamic [in Sufism]) for the purpose of directing persons to practices geared to their particular needs, and to see to what extent they correlate with the six ways. To what extent are people whose personality does not correlate with a given way likely to experience alienation and be motivated to noninvolvement or leave it for another? Within any one way, what helps a person attain psychological balance and maturity and avoid the degenerations to which that way is subject?[18] To what extent does involvement in other ways (e.g., its polar opposite) contribute to this end? Do the results of these inquiries vary significantly from tradition to tradition, or are they pretty much the same?

A quite distinct line of inquiry would be to study what sorts of formation process are used for each way of being religious in different traditions.[19] In other words, in what ways are persons prepared for full-fledged participation in a given way of being religious within a tradition? What practical "know-how" and sensibility is expected of them to function well? To what extent are there similarities in this regard as one moves from one tradition to the next? To what extent is this practical "know-how" and sensibility transferable from one subtradition to another within a single religious tradition? To what extent is it transferable between religious traditions without compromise to either tradition?

Interfaith Dialogue   To what extent would an understanding of the framework contribute to and facilitate dialogue between religious traditions? Anything that facilitates empathetic understanding in this connection would seem to be of direct help in sorting through misunderstandings, finding points of commonality, and pinning down actual (and not merely apparent) differences. What the framework suggests, however, is bringing together people pursuing the same way of being religious within the different traditions, rather than trying to get, say, a Roman Catholic sacramentalist to dialogue with a Muslim Sufi mystic. Too often, it seems to me, dialogue has foundered, or come close to foundering, because attention has not been given to avoiding crossing generic ways, and thus avoiding an unnecessary clash of religious sensibilities. By bringing together representatives of the same way of being religious, there is much more likelihood that commonalities will be found and appreciated, providing a much more amicable basis for determining and appreciating each other's differences.[20]

Intrafaith Dialogue   For dialogue between representatives of subtraditions within a single religious tradition (assuming they can come together openly, empathetically, and seriously committed to discovering an authentic unity among them), the framework of ways of being religious offers a natural basis for ecumenism in which many, though not all, differences might be understood, appreciated, and perhaps even recognized as a needed part of the whole without compromising theological integrity. In this context (though probably not in the context of interfaith dialogue), each way may be seen as a different path to the same goal of at-onement with *ultimate reality*^{p}. Moreover, the framework points to ways that persons from separate subtraditions pursuing (or interested in pursuing) the same way of being religious might have much to learn from each other.

LIABILITIES OF USING THE FRAMEWORK (HOW NOT TO APPLY IT)

The framework of ways of being religious is one of many possible conceptual frameworks for sorting out religious phenomena. It is not meant to be the only or even the primary framework for use in understanding religious phenomena. Some frameworks are better than others, depending to some extent on the purposes they are employed to serve. No one framework is suitable for all purposes, and some clearly do more justice to the phenomena than others. So, in addition to advantages or assets, the framework of ways of being religious has certain disadvantages or liabilities if used uncritically or by itself without supplementation.

These liabilities group themselves under four headings: (1) taking the abstract categories of the framework to be more real than the concrete phenomena they are used to describe; (2) presuming, with the help of the framework, to occupy a better position to understand a religious phenomenon than does a participant-insider;

(3) losing sight of what doesn't fit into the categories of the framework; and (4) theologizing with the framework. These liabilities are not unique to the framework, however; they are common to any phenomenological study of religion making use of generic categories. Responsible use of the framework requires that these liabilities be kept in check.

First, it is easy to lose sight of the derivative nature of alleged generic features of religious life and take those descriptions to be more real than the particular phenomena from which they have been derived and which they purport to represent and explain. This is especially a problem for those who have no first-hand knowledge of the phenomena in question and who have to rely on the accounts of others—accounts that, however well intentioned, are invariably filtered and skewed by the language, culture, interest, and biases of the reporter.

For example, it is easy to suppose upon hearing a phenomenologist say that all religious traditions recognize something called "the sacred" that all of them must be referring unambiguously to the same thing (or same kind of thing). However, when examined more closely, it becomes clear that these traditions (especially traditions other than those articulated in European languages) do not use this precise category, "the sacred." Instead, they employ terms and phrases in very different languages—for example, *Mana* in Polynesian, *Wakan* in Native American Sioux, *Kodesh* in Hebrew, *Dao* in Chinese—each of which has quite different connotations of meaning and different things to which it is used to refer. The respective usages of these terms and phrases are far from parallel, though many similarities can be found. Now it may possibly be that they do ultimately refer (some if not all) to the same thing, but then again they may not. How are we to tell? It so happens that the traditional philosophical problem of universals is at stake in this question: Are there indeed discoverable universal *kinds* or *types* of things built into the nature of reality that our words more or less approximate (the realist answer), or are such kinds and types merely human and cultural constructs (the nominalist answer)? Does the phenomenological category of "the sacred" represent something really there, underlying the many different names with their different connotations? Or is it merely a derivative abstract summary of *Mana*, *Wakan*, *Kodesh*, *Dao*, and so forth, that nevertheless trades to some extent on the distinctive, preexisting connotations and etymological roots of "*sacra*" in European languages and Latin in particular? If this philosophical uncertainty is true for the category of "the sacred," it must hold true also for the categories of "sacred rite," "right action," "devotion," "shamanic mediation," "mystical quest," and "reasoned inquiry." It must also hold for the specific descriptions given for each. Do these descriptions really refer to underlying universal religious options built into the human condition or are they merely derived, abstract summaries of the patterns we just happen to find in the varieties of religious life we find in the world?

There is no simple answer to this problem. The phenomenologist's temptation is to be the realist here. His temptation is to take the generic category that he has forged so carefully to be more real than the phenomena that he supposes to be its manifestations and to overlook aspects of those phenomena that don't fit the category. The nominalist position is usually championed by the historian, particularly the specialist historian, and occasionally the anthropologist. Her temptation is to take the phenomena to be more real than any generic category and to question whether they really have anything in common beyond what has demonstrable historical connection. For her, concrete context is the locus of meaning: what a given symbol or practice means depends entirely on the specific function and usage it has in the lives of the particular parties involved. There is no easy resolution of the disagreement between these viewpoints. There is an inherent presumptiveness in each orientation that should be counteracted.

Leaving aside the historian's responsibility here, a responsibility rests upon the phenomenologist and anyone making use of his categories to avoid taking generic categories (and, specifically, his differentiation and formulation of them) to be more real than the phenomena they purport to describe and explain. The phenomenologist has in the first place derived his formulations of them from careful comparative observation of the phenomena (or taken them over from someone who has done so). In that regard they are never absolutely final or definitive; they are in principle always revisable. Are they useful (in their current form) for making sense of the phenomena? Do they indeed adequately capture and comprehend the alleged underlying reality? Confirmation that they do depends entirely upon how well they fit the phenomena when the phenomena are left free to call them into question—that is, when they are free to show that the formulations don't quite fit, that they need further revision, and that another formulation would do better. That is why responsible employment of generic categories demands an awareness and appreciation of the particular phenomena to which they are to be applied that are independent of the categories, so that the question of "fit" is always posed and reflected upon. It demands as well, of course, an awareness that the categories are always revisable.

It would therefore be a great mistake to take the formulations proposed for any of the ways of being religious, or even the distinctions made between them, as final or definitive. They are subject to revision and further qualification, and that should always be the case. Accordingly, they should be handled lightly and flexibly and never as an *a priori* straitjacket into which religious phenomena must necessarily fit. What justification they have lies in their ability to structure comparative study and dialogue so as to help us more effectively enter into, and empathetically comprehend, the religious meaning of actual phenomena. So far as they do so, they will have their justification. To the extent they fall short of that goal, they should either be revised or set aside.

The second liability is related to the first. It is easy, terribly easy, when one is pursuing comparative phenomenological research, to presume that one is in a better position to know and comprehend the meaning of a particular religious phenomenon (i.e., to know and comprehend the proper category in which the phenomenon should be classified) than is the reflective and competent insider.

In one respect, the comparative scholar surely is in a better position to know and understand the similarities and differences between this phenomenon and phenomena in other traditions and to be able to articulate and explain its meaning in a cross-cultural way. But whatever superiority that amounts to is a matter of degree—a degree of difference that is always able to be reduced and possibly overcome insofar as the insider becomes acquainted with other traditions and how his own stands in relation to them.

More important, however, is the fact that the comparative scholar remains necessarily reliant upon his own and other persons' firsthand empathetic acquaintance with, and account of, the phenomena in their own historical-cultural context, the best test for the success of which is a confirmation by knowledgeable and reflective insiders that an empathizer has gotten it right. In that sense, the knowledgeable and reflective insider's understanding remains in a certain fundamental sense primary and authoritative. The point is that, although we may occasionally be in a better position to comprehend the meaning of a religious phenomenon in a tradition to which we do not belong than some insiders may be, we should never presume that we occupy that position. Our supposition that we have interpreted the phenomenon well remains contingent in certain respects (if not all respects) upon the confirmation of insiders. There are of course all sorts of ways in which this confirmation can go awry: the insider may mistake or misunderstand the phenomenological account; the insider may not be interested at all in helping outsiders come to understand the tradition with empathetic objectivity; the insider may be committed to presenting a certain preconceived image of her tradition, or have some other agenda that competes with the phenomenologist's interest. In principle, however, confirmation by knowledgeable, reflective insiders who are open-minded and free of ulterior agendas remains requisite to determine whether justice has been done.

Third, in relying on the framework of ways of being religious, it is easy to lose sight of things that do not fit, of whatever the framework leaves out of consideration. It does not include everything about human religiousness. Consequently, it is important to be aware of the kinds of things that fall outside the net of the framework or that are liable to slip through it unnoticed.

The framework does not suffice for full studies of any tradition or even any subtradition—not even for basic introductory studies—primarily because it deliberately chooses to focus upon generic features of religious practice at the expense of focusing upon features specific to the tradition (or subtradition) deriving from its core system of symbols (including scriptures, stories, and *theological* beliefs), but also because it does not pay direct attention to the particulars of history and culture and individuality. Insiders (at least when they are seriously religious) are primarily concerned with features specific to a tradition and to thinking within a context and frame of reference constituted by that core system of symbols. So, if we are concerned empathetically to get fully in touch with the insider's perspective, familiarity with that core system of symbols and how it is interpreted in practice is absolutely requisite. The framework of ways of being religious offers little direct help here. Moreover, a historian specializing in a religious tradition is interested primarily in understanding the features of that tradition within their full historical, cultural, and geographic contexts as they develop over time. Generally she isn't much interested in cross-tradition comparisons (particularly those involving nonhistorical relationships) and is usually suspicious of generic, cross-tradition categories. (I would hope that she might find the framework of some help to her work, nevertheless.) That is as it should be, for her task is to ensure that justice is done to the tradition so far as possible in the full specificity of its particulars. So, if one is concerned to understand a tradition or any part of it as it evolves and changes over time, one needs to pay attention to the best historical scholarship on the tradition. The framework of ways of being religious will be of limited use here as well.

However, the inverse is not true. A critical and responsible use of the framework needs the sensitivity to nuances and particulars that the perspective of the insider and the perspective of the specialist historian bring to the study of religious phenomena. It is precisely a familiarity with what these perspectives put one in touch with that can keep the user of the framework from doing injustice to the phenomena to which he would apply it and enable him progressively to improve it. In other words, the framework is not designed to be used independently of these perspectives but in close association with them.

It is well to ask at this point, Are there more ways of being religious than the six here identified and explained? As I have said many times before, I make no claims about the definitive status of the framework as a whole or to any of its parts. It is not intended to be exhaustive. However, virtually all means of approach to *ultimate reality* in the various traditions fall readily into one of these categories or into some fusion of two or more of them. If more than these six are to be recognized, it is likely they will come about through further differentiation of the existing categories. The important thing to keep in mind here is that the categories are meant to be modified and refined as the religious phenomena under investigation call for and justify that modification and refinement.

The framework by itself is not likely to be of much help in carrying out comparative studies of the substantive, *theological* features of two or more traditions—say, of their scriptures, their central stories, or their convictions of the nature of *ultimate reality*. It will of course help in factoring out apparent but insubstantial differences, namely, in ways of being religious, and it will help to identify some of the underlying rationales of differing *theological* perspectives within a given tradition. But it will directly contribute little in the way of helping understand the *theological* ideas and *theological* viewpoints involved.[21]

Finally, there is a good deal about any religious tradition and most any religious phenomenon that tends to fall outside strictly empathetic and historical studies, aspects that are the subject of sociological studies, political studies, economic studies, art studies, literary-critical studies, psychological studies, comparative philosophical studies, and cultural anthropological studies, among others. These too have their place and importance and for the most part will not be picked up by limiting oneself to studying religion simply in terms of the framework of ways of being religious.[22] However, the framework would have valuable insights to contribute to them and they to persons using the framework. For example, religious people are not just religious, of course, but are always simultaneously caught up in a tangle of social, economic, familial, and interpersonal relationships with others. Why different people become engaged in the particular religious practice at a given time and place, with the specific persons, and with the specific motivations they do is due to a host of factors, many of them factors of power, which one can get at and understand only if one approaches them with some psychological, sociological, and probably anthropological sophistication. The framework of ways of being religious may be of help here, but used by itself will not go far. So also, what influence or role that religious involvement has in people's lives outside of their specifically religious practices requires the same sorts of study. Here the framework will be of even less help. In short, the social embeddedness of religious life is something that requires far more than the framework of ways of being religious to comprehend.

A fourth liability to counteract in using the framework is the temptation to use it directly as a basis from which to *theologize*°—that is, for drawing *theological*° conclusions independent of the canonical (e.g., scriptural) warrants of a tradition. For example, some may wish to argue on the basis of the framework alone that each of the six ways within a tradition (say, Christianity) has equal merit, dignity, and authenticity, and that all Christians should so acknowledge them. Strictly speaking, that would be inappropriate *theologizing*°, for merit, dignity, and authenticity within a specific tradition must be argued out on the basis of the existing authoritative warrants of that tradition—for example, on the basis of scripture—which may or may not justify such a conclusion. The framework may be of help to insiders of a tradition in finding new interpretations of old familiar texts or new options of warranted religious practice that would otherwise be overlooked. It provides what for many will be a wider yet not alien perspective, offering new angles to consider and occasion for rethinking old assumptions. What it does bring to light is the matter of religious common sense. This includes a grasp of the different sorts of things involved in each of the generic ways of being religious, the conditions that make for excellence in each, and the liabilities in each for degeneration. Just as commonsense considerations play a significant role in virtually every tradition (usually successfully, but by no means always), so also considerations brought to light by the framework could rightly have a role to play in insider discussion, argumentation, and modification of current practice—but not on their own in independence of the existing authoritative warrants of the tradition.

In short, the framework is limited. It is not designed to provide a complete understanding of religion or religious phenomena. It is not intended to be used by itself. And it carries with it no authority for making evaluative judgments beyond a kind of religious common sense. There are many things that fall outside its scope and there are a host of nuances and details that can slip unnoticed through its categories. For certain purposes it can be of considerable help. But its limits must be respected and its use, to be responsible, must be grounded in terms of an acquaintance with the traditions to which it is applied.

CHAPTER SUMMARY

The framework of ways of being religious offers several practical advantages, particularly for the beginning student in the comparative study of religion but also for the seasoned veteran. It can be an aid to the process of self-knowledge in placing oneself and one's own religious predelictions in relation to others both familiar and strange, and it can help to sort out one's options, as it were. Moreover, it provides a commonsense basis for beginning to distinguish healthy from degenerate expressions of a given practice, and perhaps for seeing more positive potential in a tradition than first meets the eye. In terms of a more objective study and understanding of religious phenomena, the framework has several assets: (1) it helps avoid false or oversimplifying generalizations about religion; (2) it helps one understand better and empathetically examples of any one way of being religious in their difference from examples of other ways, especially ones that at first seem strange; (3) it helps disentangle different sorts of religious differences, instead of supposing all are unique to each tradition; (4) it suggests fruitful comparative studies in depth; (5) it helps one identify and appreciate genuine differences between religions and avoid being misled by surface contrasts; and (6) it opens up several promising lines of further inquiry. Areas of inquiry on which the framework offers new and interesting perspectives include: nontraditional religious phenomena, philosophy of religion and religious philosophy, religious ethics and the ethics of religion, psychology of religion and religious psychology, dialogue between religions, and dialogue between different subtraditions of the same religion.

In addition to assets and advantages, the framework of ways of being religious has certain liabilities or disadvantages, especially if used uncritically or by itself without supplementation. (1) It is easy to take the abstract categories of the framework to be more real than the concrete phenomena they are used to describe, when it is the phenomena that are the testing ground of the categories. The six ways and their formulations as proposed here remain tentative, revisable, human constructions that call for further refining in light of the phenomena. (2) It is easy to presume, with the help of the framework, that one understands a religious phenomenon better than participant-insiders, whereas it is their understandings to which the comparativist is obliged to do justice. (3) It is easy to lose sight of what doesn't fit into the categories of the framework, and how the framework focuses only on a part of the whole picture. Finally, (4) it is tempting to use the framework to warrant *theological*[1] conclusions—for example, about the legitimacy of a certain religious practice—whereas such conclusions may appropriately be drawn only in terms of the existing authoritative warrants of the tradition in question.

STUDY QUESTIONS

1. Making use of the framework, reflect on your own involvement in and/or encounter with religion. What ways of being religious have you been involved in? Are there one or two ways to which you are more drawn, and others you have no desire to be involved with? Are there ways you think you would like to learn more about?

2. By means of the framework and the discussion of virtues and vices of the generic ways of being religious in Chapter 5, try to identify from your own observations and experiences instances of generic virtue and generic vice within as many of the ways as you can.

3. What advantages do you see in use of the framework as a guide in the comparative study of religion? Can you identify advantages other than those listed? Identify and explain an example illustrating each of the advantages.

4. Among the promising lines of inquiry listed, is there one or more that particularly strikes your interest? Sketch out how you might go about researching it. What do you foresee to be the contribution of the framework to that area of inquiry?

5. What liabilities or disadvantages do you see in use of the framework as a guide in the comparative study of religion? Can you identify problems other than those listed?

FOR FURTHER READING

Follow up references cited in chapter notes on specific topics.

NOTES

1. See the Christian Example in Chapter 9, below.
2. See Eva de Vitray-Meyerovitch, *Rûmî and Sufism*, trans. Simone Fattal (Sausalito, CA: The Post-Apollo Press, 1987); and Jalal al-Din Rumi, *The Sufi Path of Love: The Spiritual Teachings of Rumi*, trans. William C. Chittick (Albany, NY: State University of New York Press, 1983).
3. See Chapter 5, note 2.
4. See Masatoshi Doi, "Dynamics of Faith: A Dialogical Study of Pure Land Buddhism and Evangelical Christianity," *Japanese Religions* 7:2–3 (September 1980), pp. 56–73; D. T.

Adamo, "Soteriological Dialogue Between Wesleyan Christians and Pure Land Sect Buddhism," *Journal of Dharma: An International Quarterly of World Religions* 14 (October-December 1989), pp. 311–406; and Alfred Bloom, "A Spiritual Odyssey: My Encounter with Pure Land Buddhism," *Buddhist-Christian Studies* 10 (1990), pp. 173–175.

5. See Paul O. Ingram, "Faith as Knowledge in the Teaching of Shinran Shonin and Martin Luther," *Buddhist-Christian Studies* 8 (1988), pp. 23–35; John Ishihara, "Luther and Shinran: *simul iustus et peccator* and *nishu jinshin*," *Japanese Religions*, 14:4 (1987), pp. 31–54; and Gregory Alles, "'When Men Revile You and Persecute You': Advice, Conflict, and Grace in Shinran and Luther," *History of Religions* 25 (1985), pp. 148–162.

6. Frederick J. Streng has been one of the few scholars to attempt a systematic study of nontraditional modes of religious expression but he does not seek to correlate them with what he calls traditional ways of being religious. He does, however, draw some connections with certain traditional practices. See his *Understanding Religious Life*, 3rd ed. (Belmont, CA: Wadsworth, 1985), Part 2. See also Frederick J. Streng, Charles L. Lloyd, Jr., and Jay T. Allen, eds., *Ways of Being Religious: Readings for a New Approach to Religion* (Englewood Cliffs, NJ: Prentice-Hall, 1973), pp. 333–612. See also Catherine L. Albanese, *America: Religions and Religion*, 2nd ed. (Belmont, CA: Wadsworth, 1992), Ch. 14: "Cultural Religion: Explorations in Millennial Dominance and Innocence."

7. Robert N. Bellah, *The Broken Covenant: American Civil Religion in Time of Trial* (New York: Seabury Press, 1975); and Robert N. Bellah and Phillip E. Hammond, *Varieties of Civil Religion* (San Francisco, CA: Harper and Row, 1980). See also Catherine L. Albanese, *America: Religions and Religion*, 2nd ed. (Belmont, CA: Wadsworth, 1992), Ch. 13, "Civil Religion: Millennial Politics and History."

8. See R. C. Zaehner, "A New Buddha and a New Tao," *Concise Encyclopedia of Living Faiths*, ed. R. C. Zaehner (New York: Hawthorn Books, 1959), pp. 402–412; Ninian Smart, *Beyond Ideology: Religion and the Future of Western Civilization* (San Francisco, CA: Harper and Row, 1981), Ch. 7: "Secular Ideologies: A First Anatomy," and Ch. 8: "The Chinese Experience in the Modern World"; Ninian Smart, *The Religious Experience*, 4th ed. (New York: Macmillan, 1991), Ch. 12: "The Humanist Experience;" Frederick J. Streng, *Understanding Religious Life*, 3rd ed. (Belmont, CA: Wadsworth, 1985), Ch. 8: "The Religious Significance of Social Responsibility"; and Frederick J. Streng, Charles L. Lloyd, Jr., and Jay T. Allen, eds., *Ways of Being Religious: Readings for a New Approach to Religion* (Englewood Cliffs, NJ: Prentice-Hall, 1973), Ch. 6: "Achievement of Human Rights through Political and Economic Action."

9. Michael Novak, *The Joy of Sports: End Zones, Bases, Baskets, Balls, and the Consecration of the American Spirit* (New York: Basic Books, 1976).

10. See Paul C. Vitz, *Psychology as Religion: The Cult of Self Worship* (Grand Rapids, MI: Eerdmans, 1977). Vitz's account is developed from a conservative Protestant perspective, yet it has a number of insights of significance beyond his own perspective. A more neutral, phenomenological perspective is found in Frederick J. Streng, *Understanding Religious Life,* 3rd ed. (Belmont, CA: Wadsworth, 1985), Ch. 6: "The Religious Significance of Fulfilling Human Relationships;" and Frederick J. Streng, Charles L. Lloyd, Jr., and Jay T. Allen, eds., *Ways of Being Religious: Readings for a New Approach to Religion* (Englewood Cliffs, NJ: Prentice-Hall, 1973), Ch. 5: "Attaining an Integrated Self through Creative Interaction."

11. Neil Leonard, *Jazz: Myth and Religion* (New York: Oxford University Press, 1987). See also Gilbert Rouget, *Music and Trance: A Theory of the Relations between Music and Possession*, trans. Brunhilde Biebuyck (Chicago, IL: University of Chicago Press, 1985).

12. One venture in this direction is Ninian Smart, *Philosophy of Religion* (New York: Oxford University Press, 1979). Another is Stephen R. L. Clark, *The Mysteries of Religion: An Introduction to Philosophy through Religion* (New York: Basil Blackwell, 1986). See also

Thomas Dean, ed., *Religious Pluralism and Truth: Essays on Cross-Cultural Philosophy of Religion* (Albany, NY: State University of New York Press, 1994); and the series of books published by the State University of New York Press, "Toward a Comparative Philosophy of Religions," ed. Paul J. Griffiths and Laurie L. Patton.

13. An example of this kind of exploration is adumbrated by John A. Taber, *Transformative Philosophy: A Study of Sankara, Fichte, and Heidegger* (Honolulu, HI: University of Hawaii Press, 1983). An important retrospective view of theology as a monastic *practice* distinct from scholasticism in the medieval period is given in Jean Leclerq, *The Love of Learning and the Desire for God: A Study of Monastic Culture*, trans. Catherine Misrahi (New York: Fordham University Press, 1974). Still a different view identified with what has been called inter-religious perennialism or primordialism is found in Seyyed Hossein Nasr, *Knowledge and the Sacred: The Gifford Lectures 1981* (New York: Crossroad, 1981); in Jacob Needleman, *Consciousness and Tradition* (New York: Crossroad, 1982), especially the leading essay, "Why Philosophy Is Easy," pp. 12–22; and in Jacob Needleman, ed., *The Sword of Gnosis: Metaphysics, Cosmology, Tradition, Symbolism*, 2nd ed. (Boston, MA: Arkana, 1986).

14. See Huston Smith, "Western Philosophy as a Great Religion," in his *Essays on World Religion*, ed. M. Darrol Bryant (New York: Paragon House, 1992), pp. 205–223.

15. Hans Küng, in his *Global Responsibility: In Search of a New World Ethic*, trans. John Bowden (New York: Crossroad, 1991), has sought to advance this project particularly as it relates to the way of right action. Other important forays into what might be called the ethics of religion are listed under the references in For Further Study at the end of Chapter 5.

16. A useful overview of the psychology of religion as it relates to most of the ways of being religious as here presented is Wayne E. Oates, *The Psychology of Religion* (Waco, TX: Word Books, 1973). Although Oates writes from a conservative Protestant perspective, his commitment to a phenomenological approach makes his insights and observations useful and relevant for other traditions.

17. Three attempts to correlate personality types with different forms of Christian spirituality are Charles J. Keating, *Who We Are Is How We Pray: Matching Personality and Spirituality* (Mystic, CT: Twenty-Third Publications, 1987), and Chester P. Michael and Marie C. Norrisey, *Prayer and Temperament: Different Prayer Forms for Different Personality Types* (Charlottesville, VA: The Open Door, 1984), and Allan H. Sager, *Gospel-Centered Spirituality: An Introduction to Our Spiritual Journey* (Minneapolis, MN: Augsburg Fortress, 1990). None of these three fully correlates with the six ways of being religious. The first two make use of the Myers-Briggs Type Indicator (which identifies sixteen personality types) and (primarily) the main historical forms of contemplative spirituality (primarily oriented to mystical quest and devotion) in Roman Catholicism. None of the Myers-Briggs types correlate directly with the ways of being religious. An advantage of the *Prayer and Temperament* book is that it discusses the the liability for imbalance and the need for balance in each type. The third book makes use of a fourfold typology first developed by Urban T. Holmes that correlates directly with the ways of right action, wisdom, mystical quest, and devotion in both personality type and type of spirituality. It too addresses the liability for imbalance and the need for balance in each type. A quite different scheme for connecting personality types with different patterns of spiritual growth is the use of the Enneagram. Like the Myers-Briggs types, however, none of the nine Enneagram types correlate directly with the six ways of being religious, although in both cases certain types clearly seem likely to associate more with one way of being religious than with another. However, Barbara Metz and John Burchill's, *The Enneagram and Prayer: Discovering Our True Selves Before God* (Denville, NJ: Dimension Books, 1987) organizes the nine types in three groups of three—head-centered, gut-centered, and heart-centered persons—and correlates with each group a most appropriate pattern of prayer: focused meditation, quiet

prayer, and expressive prayer, respectively. These three suggest a loose correlation with reasoned inquiry, mystical quest, and devotion. A fuller overview of the nine personality types of the Enneagram in terms of their potential for maturation and for degeneration is Don Richard Riso, *Understanding the Enneagram: The Practical Guide to Personality Types* (Boston, MA: Houghton Mifflin, 1990), and Andreas Ebert and Marion Küstenmacher, eds., *Experiencing the Enneagram*, trans. Peter Heinegg (New York: Crossroad, 1992).

18. An important attempt to address this problem in the way of mystical quest is *Spiritual Choices: The Problem of Recognizing Authentic Paths to Inner Transformation*, ed. Dick Anthony, Bruce Ecker, and Ken Wilber (New York: Paragon House, 1987). See also the previous note.

19. A number of studies have begun to make forays in this field, many of them the fruits of inter-religious dialogue. See *Spirituality in Interfaith Dialogue*, ed. Tosh Arai and Wesley Ariarajah (Maryknoll, NY: Orbis Books, 1989); Susan Rakoezy, *Common Journey, Different Paths: Spiritual Direction in Cross-Cultural Perspective* (Maryknoll, NY: Orbis Books, 1992); and *Ultimate Reality and Spiritual Discipline*, ed. James Duerlinger (God: The Contemporarary Discussion Series; New York: New Era Books, 1984). Another source of insight into these matters is recent studies of attempts to "indigenize" Christianity—e.g., *Asian Christian Spirituality: Reclaiming Traditions*, ed. Virginia Fabella, Peter K. H. Lee, and David Kwang-sun Suh (Maryknoll, NY: Orbis Books, 1992). A quite different approach is taken by philosopher Robert C. Neville in his study of the quest for spiritual liberation or perfection through the models of the spiritual soldier, the sage, and the saint, *Soldier, Sage, Saint* (New York: Fordham University Press, 1978).

20. See Chapter 5, note 2, and the suggestions in For Further Study at the end of Chapter 15.

21. One of the best places for a novice to begin any such study is with the *Encyclopedia of Religion*, ed. Mircea Eliade (New York: Macmillan, 1987), reading articles both on specific religious tradition and on cross-tradition categories. Another good place is with a good textbook survey of the religions of the world. One of the current best of these is Theodore M. Ludwig, *The Sacred Paths: Understanding the Religions of the World* (New York: Macmillan, 1989).

22. A good brief overview of the different approaches to an objective study of religion is given in Frederick J. Streng, *Understanding Religious Life*, 3rd ed. (Belmont, CA: Wadsworth, 1985), Part 3. The most thorough and comprehensive overview available is Frank Whaling, ed., *Contemporary Approaches to the Study of Religion*, 2 vols. (New York: Mouton, 1985).

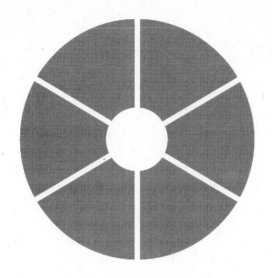

APPLYING THE
FRAMEWORK TO A
COMPARISON OF
WHOLE TRADITIONS

The intention of Parts II and III is to illustrate the power of the
framework of the six ways of being religious to guide the
comparative study of any two religious traditions. Buddhism and
Christianity have been chosen for this comparison, though any two
major traditions would do. In Part II (Chapters 7 and 8) the
framework is used to interpret and compare Buddhism
and Christianity comprehensively as whole traditions, encompassing

their many subtraditions. Part III is devoted to in-depth comparison of examples of each of the six ways of being religious from the two traditions. The primary intent is not to present the results of one scholar's investigation but to show how comparative study can proceed, using the framework as a guide.

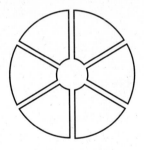

CHAPTER 7

APPLYING THE FRAMEWORK TO THE WHOLE OF BUDDHISM

INTERPRETING A WHOLE TRADITION AND SUBTRADITIONS

Several considerations should be kept in mind when setting out to apply the framework of ways of being religious to an entire tradition or even to a major subtradition.

First, one should expect diversity and avoid reductionism. Entertain simplifications skeptically. In applying the framework of ways of being religious to a major tradition as a whole, it makes a great deal of difference how well acquainted one is with the concrete diversity of practices the tradition happens to hold. The more one becomes acquainted with that diversity, the less likely one will be tempted to take one practice (exemplifying a single way or a certain combination of ways of being religious) as representative of the whole, even when a presumably authoritative spokesperson for the tradition, an apparently authoritative passage of scripture, or a seemingly reliable secondary account asserts (or seems to assert) it to be representative of the whole. An informant may be quite reliable with regard to her own local subtradition, but she may be quite unreliable with regard to her readiness to hold forth about the tradition or subtradition as a whole, especially in regard to variations from the specific practices with which she particularly identifies. A subtradition that has long exemplified a single way—given changed circumstances, a new generation of adherents, and new leadership—may come to develop aspects of other ways. That is one of the reasons why an older version of a tradition or subtradition is not necessarily more authentic, although our Western and largely Protestant bias is to suppose it must be. Insiders who presume to speak for a tradition or major subtradition and sympathetic outsider interpreters very often, and frequently without realizing it, commit a kind of reductionism in this respect, if for no other reason than that they are naturally inclined toward one way of being religious over others or they are preoccupied with the specific aspect of the problem of meaning (i.e., the existential need) that corresponds to that way. To avoid reductionism, there is no shortcut to learning what ways of being religious are and are not exemplified in a tradition apart from getting to know that tradition fairly well at close hand and to be wary of generalizing about the tradition beyond the extent of one's acquaintance. To that end a good historical and geographic survey of the tradition is indispensable. (It is important to keep in mind, however, that an historical orientation toward a tradition may bring with it elements of a worldview at odds with insiders' understandings of that tradition.[1])

Second, although one may find clear examples of a single way of being religious, it is best not to expect that "pure" instances of a single way are what one is most likely to find and not to insist that a given religious phenomenon must be classified as wholly of one way rather than some other. More likely what will be found are phenomena exemplifying predominantly a single way or a fusion of two or three ways, while aspects of other ways may be present in a subordinate fashion. For example, concern with right action is present to a varying extent in Evangelical Protestant Christianity, as is serious study of scripture (i.e., reasoned inquiry), but both are comparatively minor and definitely subordinate aspects relative to a predominant emphasis upon the way of devotion.

Third, one should be prepared for the possibility that dominant expressions of a given way in a given subtradition within a given epoch might well be degenerate and corrupted in various respects (i.e., exhibiting more vices than virtues of the sort described in Chapter 5). In the event one finds that to be true, one should avoid directly drawing the conclusion that the way of being religious is well represented in such an instance, that the subtradition in question has always been so practiced, that this instance represents what the subtradition is like in other locales, or even that it is corrupt for all followers within the circumstances in question—let alone for times and circumstances yet to come. In other words, it is important to distinguish between the way within the tradition (or subtradition) in question and the (level of) quality of practice of that way in any other given instance.

What is high-quality and authentic practice in a given tradition and what is not is not just a matter of the generic criteria discussed in Chapter 5. Just as important—for insiders, clearly more important—is how well it accords with the authoritative norms of the tradition: its primary system of symbols, its central story or stories, its scriptures. It is important in this respect to discover how the ways of being religious within a tradition relate to, and are ultimately an expression of, how the primary system of symbols, the central stories, and the scriptures are interpreted.

When we speak here of Buddhism and Christianity we mean to speak of them holistically, in a way that encompasses their many different subtraditions. Not all of their subtraditions agree with or recognize the authenticity of the others. Some differences between their subtraditions run so deep that a few serious scholars have questioned whether it makes sense to speak of Christianity as a whole or of Buddhism as a whole. Nevertheless, the account given here proceeds on the assumptions that, with proper qualifications, it does make good sense to speak of them as wholes and that there are unifying traits and sibling resemblances in each tradition that connect its subtraditions together within a single family, however recalcitrant some of its members may be. The same might be said of the other great religious traditions such as Hinduism, Judaism, Confucianism, Daoism, and Islam—indeed, of any religious tradition large enough to permit a variety of subtraditions to emerge.

Conceived holistically, both Buddhism and Christianity in particular give expression to several varieties of all six ways of being religious. What is true for a whole tradition, however, is not necessarily true for its subtraditions. Many subtraditions of both Buddhism and Christianity have differentiated themselves in large measure by their insistent identification with a specific way or combination of ways of being religious—in some cases exclusively so but in other cases nonexclusively by prioritizing a certain way or set of ways in relation to other ways. In other words, many (perhaps most) subtraditions do not exemplify all six ways and certainly not with equal emphasis. Some subtraditions have differentiated themselves in some respects by their insistent rejection or repudiation of a specific way (or ways) of being religious. But taken as a whole, these two major traditions encompass all of the ways.

A SURVEY OF THE
DIFFERENT WAYS IN BUDDHISM

Buddhism as we find it today is divided into two main branches or lineages, *Theravāda* (the "way of the elders")[2] and *Mahāyāna* (the "greater vehicle"). From Mahayana many other branches or lineages have grown, some considerably different from others, whereas Theravada has remained fairly constant in its essentials where it has taken root in one culture and another, though it varies in style and nuance of practice. Sometimes a third branch, *Vajrayāna* (the "diamond vehicle"— also called *Mantrayāna*, the "mantra vehicle," and *Tantrayāna*, the "vehicle of esoteric ritual-meditations and shamanic powers"), is distinguished, but its teachings overlap substantially with those of Mahayana and it is often conceived as a subtradition of Mahayana. There is no commonly accepted collection of authoritative texts (or canon) of scripture between them, though a large fund of texts is common to all versions. All three branches originated in India over several centuries of evolution of Buddhism from its historical founder, Siddhartha Gautama (563–483 B.C.E.), although there remain relatively few Buddhists in India today. (During the first centuries of Buddhism there is evidence that some eighteen different schools existed, but either they did not last or they were absorbed into these three.) The history of Buddhism's spread and evolution to the present day is an involved and interesting story that won't be rehearsed here. Good accounts are readily available.[3]

The central story of Buddhism is the story of Siddhartha Gautama's life or, more specifically, the story of his search for Enlightenment (*Buddha* means "enlightened one"), his breakthrough to Enlightenment, and his teaching designed practically to help others attain it. The state of Enlightenment (*nirvāṇa* in Sanskrit or *nibbāna* in Pali) is variously characterized, but mostly by saying what it is not or by what it transcends. It is alleged to be a deliverance beyond all of the suffering, dis-ease, and ego-centeredness that plagues human life—an attainment of the pure bliss of at-onement with an ultimate, unconditioned *reality*[p] transcending all definite reference and finite description (hence not *a* reality among realities in any usual sense at all[4]). All ways of being religious in Buddhism are ways of drawing near to, of participating in, and of being grounded in this state. It is the Buddhist *ultimate reality*[p]. All forms of Buddhism in different ways revolve around the story of Siddhartha Gautama and its elaborations—some of which concern other Buddhas and Bodhisattvas ("Buddhas-to-be"), for the Buddha Gautama is not regarded as unique. While there is little doubt there was a historical founder of Buddhism named Siddartha Gautama, the central story is thus *not essentially historical*, for in its essentials it could have happened at any time and place and, according to Buddhists, it has happened in innumerable times and places in the infinite reaches of time and space. The life of a Buddhist monk or nun in its most important aspects reenacts and emulates the key features of the story in pursuit of Enlightenment. Lay Buddhists too, to the extent that they are able, seek to follow the path and implement the teachings. And they, along with nuns and monks, in worship give honor and respect (in varying degrees) to the Buddha's attainment, the principles embodied in his person, his compassion, and his teaching.

Theravada Buddhism

Theravada Buddhism now predominates in Southeast Asia, with the exception of Vietnam. It makes the claim (which is contested by Mahayanists) to be the oldest, original, and most authentic form of Buddhism. Its scriptures in the ancient Pali language—a nonliterary, vernacular dialect derived from the Sanskrit language and featuring devices facilitating several centuries of oral transmission—portray a master teacher in touch with common folk and addressing eminently practical problems.

By comparison with Mahayana teachings, Theravada teachings are simple, direct, down to earth, and wholly practical—in the manner of an old-fashioned medical doctor who is concerned to have his patient focus solely on recovering from his disease. They give little encouragement to the speculative intellect, and so disinterested are they in whether gods exist and how they should be worshiped that Theravada seems atheistic. (The worship of conventional gods and goddesses, especially of the variety found in Hinduism where Buddhism first arose, is deemed by all forms of Buddhism to be irrelevant to the attainment of Enlightenment and a serious distraction from the kind of effort necessary to its attainment. Such beings are deemed subject to conditioned existence and the round of rebirth. Accordingly, they do not share in the unconditioned *reality*^{p} of *nirvāṇa/nibbāna.*)

Theravada Buddhism is marked by the prominence and esteem it gives to the monastic pursuit of Enlightenment, and thus to a distinction between monastic followers and lay followers of the Buddha.[5] Actually, there are two options of monastic life: life in a community (usually in or near a larger population area) under the rule of an abbot or abbess, the most popular form, and the more rigorous life of a homeless mendicant (usually in uninhabited or sparsely inhabited regions). In Theravada at least, lay and monastic Buddhists are not regarded as on a common level spiritually; monastics are conceived as being on a distinct, more advanced level on a path beginning not in the current life but, in terms of the doctrine of "reincarnation" (*saṃsāra*), in an unfathomable past and continuing, one life following another, up to the present. In other words, only some are considered ready in this life to undertake the advanced rigors of monastic discipline and even fewer to attain Enlightenment thereby. One's destiny (*kamma*), as far as one's present life is concerned, is deemed to have been set by the choices one has made and the merit one has accumulated in previous lives. The ultimate goal, however, is not a better rebirth but Enlightenment, which is supposed to be a deliverance from having to continue in the cycle of rebirth.

In any case, the teaching of the Buddha and the rules of monastic discipline ideally keep monks and nuns focused on cultivating *paññā* ("wisdom"), through the analysis and comprehension of suffering, its arising, and its overcoming—involving the study and assimilation of the Buddhist scriptures; *sīla* ("ethical virtue"), the practice of moral and ascetic disciplines as stipulated in the rules of monastic life; and *samādhi* ("mental concentration"), a step-by-step progressive development of inward calmness and intensified awareness. As the three legs of a three-legged stool are each indispensable to the others, these three are the mutually indispensable parts of the Buddha's Eightfold Path to Enlightenment: *paññā* encompasses right understanding and right thought; *sīla* encompasses right speech, right action, and right livelihood; and *samādhi* encompasses right effort, right awareness, and right concentration. The goal is a mystical realization for oneself of Enlightenment, attained through a systematic uprooting of egoistic desire (attachment to pleasure), egoistic aversion (antipathy to pain), and confused or ignorant states of mind that fuel the condition of suffering that is the transmigrating "ego." In practice, this amounts to a balanced synthesis of the ways of reasoned inquiry, right action, and mystical quest, with primacy of emphasis, as this author understands it, given to mystical quest in terms of what in Theravada is called *vipassanā* ("insight") meditation.[6] *Vipassanā* involves the development of an utterly calm and detached intense awareness of the most mundane of ordinary activities.[7] Within the religious life of monastic Theravada Buddhism, the only other way of being religious that is apparent is a diminished and subordinate expression of the way of sacred rite supporting the monastic pursuit of Enlightenment. This is exemplified in the daily and monthly cycle of monastic activities (i.e., meditation, study, begging for food, eating, chanting, sleeping—actually, even seated meditation has an archetypal ritual aspect to it), ritualized relationships between members of the monastic community, seasonal rituals of the monastic community, pilgrimage to sacred Buddhist sites, and ordination ceremonies (initiation for novices and higher ordination for full-fledged monastics).

The religious life of lay followers and their relations with the monastic community in Theravada Buddhism has given rise to other ways of being religious as well as other expressions of the ways already mentioned.[8] For example, because laypersons are deemed unable to make much direct progress on the rigorous path to which monks and nuns devote themselves[9]—though they sometimes do practice scaled-down versions of *paññā*, *sīla*, and *samādhi* in a distant or short-term emulation of monastic life—they are reliant upon the compassionate aid ("grace"?) of *ultimate reality* embodied in the Buddha and the monastic community in terms of Buddhist teaching, spiritual guidance, conduct of seasonal and life cycle rituals, and bestowal of spiritual power for well-being. In this respect, the devotion they express toward the Buddha (as focused in shrines, temples, relics, and images), toward the *Sangha* (the monastic community), and toward individual monks and nuns (by way of homage, gifts of food and other necessities, reliance for advice and instruction, and solicitation of spiritual blessings) exemplifies many typical features of the way of devotion.[10] Aspects of sacred rite within Theravada lay religious life are more prevalent and significant—more sacramental it appears—than those associated with monastic life. Within the Hindu context of its origins, Buddhist laypersons would have relied upon Hindu Brahman priests to administer domestic and community rituals. But when Buddhism moved into cultural contexts where there was no developed ritual system or where Buddhism may have displaced such indigenous systems, Buddhist monastics more and more came to assume these priestly functions. The symbolic structure of relationships between lay and monastic Buddhists is largely governed by sacred ritual. For auspicious occasions, Buddhist monks are called upon regularly to chant specially selected words of the Buddha (called the performance of *paritta* and thought to hold great sacred power), for the purpose of ensuring that things go well. In some respects, participation in sacred rite is shared between lay and monastic Buddhists—in pilgrimage, for example, and in visits to the sacred symbolic spaces such as those of a temple or relic shrine (*stupa*).

Some aspects of the way of shamanic mediation sometimes show up in relations between Buddhist monastics and laypersons.[11] Reference to the extraordinary spiritual powers of the Buddha and monks of high attainment can be found throughout Buddhist literature, and, although these are not to be sought for their own sake or manipulated for egoistic motives, they may be used in compassion to benefit others.[12] Also, according to scripture, magical spells were explicitly allowed by the Buddha to ensure protection against evils such as snakebite, and talismans are frequently used among Theravada Buddhists.[13] In rural areas of Southeast Asia the boundary between indigenous healing shamanic practices and Buddhist practice appears to be often difficult to discern.

Finally, the way of right action among lay Theravada Buddhism has at times taken on a life of its own, particularly in relation to civic life and social welfare.[14] The precedent for this development is due to the legacy of the mid-third-century B.C.E. monarch Ashoka, who is sometimes called the second founder of Buddhism. Largely because of his initiative and vision, there developed a lay tradition parallel to the Theravada *sangha* dedicated to achieving Buddhist ideals within the political and social order. A very recent development that has placed first priority on the way of right action is the movement founded by Bhimrao Ramji Ambedkar (1891–1956) and called Ambedkar Buddhism. It has concentrated on improving the lot of the untouchable castes in India.[15]

Mahayana Buddhism

Mahayana expressions of Buddhism either predominate or have a strong presence in Central and Far East Asia and in Vietnam. Although they no longer are a significant presence in India, the seeds (if not the actual manifestation) of almost all forms of Mahayana sprouted there. The scriptures of Mahayana were originally in Sanskrit, a highly developed literary language. They include not only the bulk of the works found in the Theravada Pali collection but many others as well, which are often more elaborate, more developed philosophically, more systematic, and more polished as literature. There are two different canonical collections of the Mahayana scriptures, one in Chinese and one in Tibetan. Some Mahayana scriptures present themselves as the teaching of the Buddha reserved for his more advanced followers. In any case, their content goes far beyond that found in the Pali collection. A characteristic feature of many of the sectarian developments within Mahayana (at least within China and points further East) has been an identification with one (or a select few) of the Mahayana scriptural texts, allowing those texts to determine their version of Buddhist doctrine at the expense of drawing upon other scriptural texts. (This was due, in part, to the unsystematic way scriptural texts reached China over a period of several centuries and attained Chinese translation, distribution, and reception.)

As mentioned earlier, there have been many branches of Mahayana. Despite their many differences, they generally hold or take for granted certain common understandings. Mahayana teaching differs from Theravada teaching in several respects. Its traditional view of itself as the "greater vehicle" (*mahāyāna*), that is, the "more inclusive vehicle," in contrast to "the lesser vehicle" (*hīnayāna*) underscores its conviction that all people, laypersons and monastics alike, are equally on the path toward Enlightenment. Not only those who have turned away from the world to the monastic life have hope of reaching the goal. Mahayana has thus tended to minimize or erase the boundary between lay and monastic life and not to place the latter on a qualitatively higher spiritual level. In many Mahayana sects monks have been permitted to marry and have families. Second, Mahayana differs in terms of what it takes to be the ultimate goal. For Theravada the goal is Enlightenment, or *nibbāna,* as embodied in the *arahat* ("one who is worthy" from having attained Enlightenment), as distinct from a Buddha who not only attains Enlightenment but blazes the trail and enables others to find the way. Mahayana construes the goal of the *arahat* as an individualistic or selfish pursuit—"Enlightenment for oneself"—whereas to Mahayanist thinking the worthier goal is "Enlightenment for all living beings" as embodied in the *bodhisattva* ("a buddha in the making"). In contrast with the *arahat*, the *bodhisattva* compassionately places the welfare and salvation of all living beings ahead of his own ultimate bliss. Indeed, for Mahayana, compassion is at the heart of the *ultimate reality*[°] to which Enlightenment is an awakening.

A third important difference is Mahayana's rejection of the idea that *nirvāṇa* is an elsewhere, as if it were temporally, spatially, and conceptually distinct from, and in opposition to, the world of ordinary human life, the realm of suffering and rebirth (*saṃsāra*). For it to be so conceived would, so they believe, make it conditional and finite. So also, our own *ultimate nature*[°] (our ultimate potentiality), being at one with Enlightenment, should not be conceived as distinct from and in opposition to our present true nature (which is not to be identified with our unenlightened sense of ourselves and our experience). In other words, there is no real distance between the one and the other, our present true nature and our *ultimate nature*[°]. On the contrary, to be Enlightened is to see and experience *reality*[°], both finite and infinite, *as it ultimately is*[°], no longer from the perspective of the finite, self-centered ego but from the perspective of our *original true nature*[°] at one with all things and indistinct from the *ultimate nature*[°] that is manifest in the Buddha. Correlatively, a fourth difference is a proliferation in Mahayana of Buddhas and Bodhisattvas compassionately ready to aid and help living beings along the path to Enlightenment. Yet what seems to Western eyes to be a polytheism, on closer investigation discloses itself to be something else. For the whole Mahayana pantheon of Buddhas and Bodhisattvas, being metaphysically selfless or empty (*śūnya*) of finite being, is conceived ultimately to be the cosmic manifestation of "the one ultimate, unconditioned, infinite reality" at the root of all things: the Dharma Body (*Dharmakāya*) of the Buddha, of all Buddhas, of the universe itself.

As far as practice is concerned, what the difference between Mahayana and Theravada amounted to was a loosening up of the tight pragmatic (means–end) synthesis of *paññā*, *sīla*, and *samādhi* that in the Theravada monastic tradition is so strongly oriented to making steady progress on the Eightfold Path to Enlightenment. Together these same principles of practice (*prajñā*, *sīla*, and *samādhi* in Sanskrit) are also present and central in Mahayana, but they each find a variety of creative expressions in different syntheses that constitute independent paths of drawing near to and coming into right relationship to *ultimate reality*[p] as Buddhism understands it.

Two sectarian developments in Mahayana appear to have given first priority to *Sīla* or the way of right action as the way to at-onement with *ultimate reality*[p]: the Chinese Sect of the Three Stages (*San-chieh-chiao*) founded by Hsin-hsing (540–593), which did not survive the great persecution of 845,[16] and those forms of Japanese sectarian Buddhism spawned by Nichiren (1222–1282), including *Nichiren Shu*, *Nichiren Shoshu*, *Sokka Gakkai*, *Rissho Koseikai*, and *Reiyukai*.[17] Nevertheless, the distinctive Mahayana teachings mentioned above—in particular, the idea of compassion as a spontaneous outgrowth or manifestation of persons being grounded in *ultimate reality*[p] here and now in the world of *samsāra*—have given a certain proactive quality to Mahayana Buddhism with regard to human welfare and charitable works. In Far East Asia, for example, Mahayana Buddhists have been very much involved in public-spirited projects such as caring for the aged and sick, helping the poor, distributing food in times of shortage, and establishing public facilities such as bath houses and rest houses for travelers. It is important to realize, however, that Mahayana Buddhist right action is not merely a spiritual discipline for the sake of attaining Enlightenment. Mahayanists would understand it as an expression of our original (or ultimate) "Buddha nature" and thus as an expression (if only in anticipation) of Enlightenment.[18]

The way of reasoned inquiry in Mahayana found a number of significant expressions constituting different schools of Buddhist philosophy (or *theology*[p], to refer to it according to the generic term introduced earlier).[19] In contrast to Theravada, Mahayana has taken a more liberal attitude toward philosophical speculation and the idea of doctrinal development. The different philosophical schools in Mahayana have been especially associated with the so called *Prajñā-paramitā* ("the wisdom that has gone beyond") scriptures and their commentaries. To belong to one of these "schools" of Buddhist philosophy is not just a matter of studying the relevant scriptures and commentary and subscribing to its basic assumptions and worldview. It is a matter of developing philosophical acumen, reasoning, and debating ability, and above all dialectical insight into one's own nature and the nature of other things, so that through deepening insight and liberation from false views one will come to realize experientially an at-onement with *ultimate reality*[p]. Pursuing these paths in practice necessarily involved aspects of meditation (mystical quest) and ethical conduct (right action) as well. It is important to note that they have been associated with major study centers, often what amounted to Buddhist universities. Two of the most important philosophical schools are *Mādhyamika* (*San-lun* in China, *Sanron* in Japan), of which the greatest representative and founder was Nāgārjuna (circa 150–250 C.E.),[20] and *Yogācāra* or *Vijñānavāda* (*Fa-hsiang* in China, *Hosso* in Japan), of which the greatest representative was Vasubandhu (circa fourth century C.E.).[21] *Mādhyamika* is noted for its teaching of the emptiness (*śūnyatā*) of all things, that no things have substantial being—including the secular world of *saṃsāra*. Indeed, for *Mādhyamika*, one of the principal characteristics of *ultimate reality* (i.e., the Buddha nature and *nirvāṇa*) is *śūnyatā,* or emptiness—which is interpreted to mean without "ownness," egoless, nonsubstantial, not existing as a thing over against other existing things. *Yogācāra* is noted for its assertion that all things are fundamentally a kind of mental projection from within us, and that progress toward Enlightenment involves the progressive purification and refinement of the "storehouse-" or "womb-consciousness" within, which is supposed ultimately to be none other than the *Dharmakāya* from which all Buddhas are born and of which they are all manifestations. Later in China still more schools of Buddhist philosophy developed. Remarkable are the *Hua-yen* school (*Kegon* in Japan),[22] whose greatest representative was Fa-tsang (643–712), and the *T'ien-t'ai* school (*Tendai* in Japan),[23] whose greatest representatives were Chih-i (538–597) and Saicho (767–822). Both were all-inclusive schools that sought to comprehend the place of each of the many apparently contradictory Buddhist schools of thought within an encompassing systematic understanding. Tendai's emphasis upon study is the most thorough in Japanese Buddhism; the basic course now lasting twelve years at one time lasted twenty-one. The same comprehensive philosophical orientation is found in some Vajrayana schools. In Tibet, the *Gelukpa* sect, with which the Dalai Lama is associated and which was founded by Tsong-kha-pa (1357–1419), is known for the strong emphasis it has placed on systematic doctrinal studies as an essential aspect of the path to Enlightenment.[24] Study in both Tendai and Gelukpa revolves around public examinations and rigorous debate. Although these several philosophically oriented schools of Buddhism place central emphasis on the way of wisdom, it would be a mistake to suppose that any emphasized it to the exclusion of meditative practice (mystical quest) or conduct in accord with *Dharma* (right action), or other ways of being religious for that matter.

The way of mystical quest also found a diversity of expressions in Mahayana unlike those found in Theravada.[25] Partly this was due to the philosophical developments unique to Mahayana and to its more liberal attitude toward new methods of achieving the same ultimate goals. Partly it appears to have been due to the quite different cultural sensibilities of China, Japan, and Tibet, for example, into which Mahayana Buddhist teaching was received. An emphasis on progressive inner calmness and penetrating insight for the sake of liberation from ego-centered motivations and delusions is shared with Theravada, but the specific techniques of meditation that occur in Mahayana vary remarkably from one subtradition to another. A full grasp of the extent of this diversity and reliable accounts of the differing techniques involved has yet to be achieved, for much is still relatively unknown to Western scholarship. And some subtraditions that we know were once strong and influential now have no current living masters from

whom the meditation practice at its best can be learned. At present the most accessible (both in terms of living masters and good written accounts in English)
are the different forms of *Zen* meditation (*Ch'an* in China, *Sŏn* in Korea, *Thien*
in Vietnam) and Vajrayana meditation.

Meditation and the quest for Enlightenment came to have less priority than
other factors in most of Chinese Buddhism. In opposition to this development,
Ch'an Buddhism (*Zen* in Japanese, both of which translate the Sanskrit *dhyāna*,
"meditative trance") gained the reputation in China of being *the* meditation sect.
It probably arose in the early eighth century, although legend traces it back to
the arrival in China from India of the monk Bodhidharma in 470 C.E. The prime
focus of Ch'an (and that of its progeny in Japan, Korea, Vietnam, and elsewhere) is
upon the way of mystical quest. Although conceiving itself as a return to the original authentic teaching of the Buddha in India, it seems to owe much to a distinctly
Chinese Daoist sensibility and in its specific Japanese forms to an indigenous
Japanese aesthetic sensibility.[26] In any case, the objective is to realize *nirvāṇa* in
the midst of *saṃsāra* by intuitively awakening to a deep spontaneous body-
mind-world unity in the present moment (the "Buddha-mind," "one's original nature"). This appears to be substantially the sort of thing that philosophical Daoists
speak of as becoming one with the cosmic *Dao* that courses through all things.
The experience has a markedly aesthetic dimension. First, because it expresses
itself in a variety of artistic media. Second and more important, because the spontaneous body-mind-world unity is itself an experience of aesthetic sublimity—
"enlightenment with the eyes open" rather than with them closed,[27] or, in different
words, "a perfect fusion of aesthetic perception and noumenal awareness, of
stillness and motion, utility and grace, conformity and spontaneity."[28] Above all,
Ch'an Buddhists pursue this objective through seated meditation and the direct
personal guidance of a master within a monastic setting.

Although some five differing schools of Ch'an existed at one time, primarily
two have survived: the so-called Northern or "Sudden Enlightenment" School
(*Lin-chi* in China, *Rinzai* in Japan) and the so-called Southern or "Gradual
Enlightenment" School (*Ts'ao-tung* in China, *Sōtō* in Japan).[29] Though these remain distinct in Japan, the two have become much less distinct in China in recent
centuries, and in Korea and Vietnam as well. In any case, the former specialized in
the use of *kung-an* (*kōan* in Japan) meditation, riddles designed to tease, frustrate,
and ultimately bring about a complete breakdown of the process of ordinary intellectualizing and a breakthrough to Enlightenment. This and other practices in effect amounted to a reintegration of the way of reasoned inquiry in balance with
that of mystical quest. The latter school—and its most important Japanese spokesperson, Dōgen (1200–1253), in particular—generally opposed the seeking of "breakthrough" experiences and the expectation of "sudden" Enlightenment. Indeed, it
has opposed any notion of seeking Enlightenment as a "thing-to-be-acquired." It
has concentrated instead on simply carrying out everyday activities—"chop wood,
carry water," but above all just sitting in the meditation posture—in which the

Buddha-mind is already said to be realized. This would seem to amount to a balanced integration or fusion of the way of right action with that of mystical quest.

Despite the emphasis on intuitive spontaneity, communal monastic activity in Ch'an Buddhism is a comprehensively organized ritual pattern, stripped down to its essentials and heightened aesthetically by both its choreographed style and its architectural setting. Thus aspects of sacred rite subtly figure within its pursuit of the way of mystical quest. Ch'an's commitment early on to manual labor to support itself and be less dependent on lay support resulted in a concern to integrate meditation with physical work—*nirvāna* in *samsāra* again—and thus aspects of right action figure generally within its way of mystical quest as well, and not just in the Southern School. Indeed, these two dimensions found further elaboration and development in Japanese Rinzai Zen, where a number of traditional arts (*dō*) have been adapted to become meditative disciplines integrating mystical quest, sacred rite, and right action and expressing the "Buddha-mind": calligraphy, dry-brush ink painting, poetry, *Noh* drama, pottery; flower arranging, gardening, swordsmanship, archery, and Tea Ceremony, among others.[30]

A separate sect of Japanese monastic Buddhism, *Tendai*, which has been already mentioned, makes use of a form of marathon running as a meditative discipline, among several other forms of strenuous ascetic practices.[31] Tendai is noted for its inclusive orientation toward, and encouragement of, a great diversity of meditative practices.

Many of the same sorts of expression of sacred rite found in Theravada are also in evidence within Mahayana, with some exceptions. The monastic way of life within Mahayana Buddhism has for the most part never had quite the elevated sacred status relative to that of laypersons that it has had in Theravada. The result is that relations between lay and monastic Buddhists in Mahayana are not structured and governed so strongly by sacred rituals. Also, at least in China and Japan, as in India, many forms of Mahayana Buddhism came to exist alongside, and to respect, pre-Buddhist ritual systems relating to domestic and communal life (e.g., Confucian and Taoist in China, Shinto in Japan). Consequently, for the most part Mahayana monastics have not assumed the priestly functions that Theravada monastics have in Southeast Asia. (Tibetan Buddhism is an exception to this generalization.) Nevertheless, one area of life where they often did come to assume that role was in relation to rituals of death and burial. This was largely because of the much more highly developed conception of life after death in Buddhism than that possessed by pre-Buddhist religions. At times there developed elaborate ceremonial worship in connection with Buddhist temples. Sacred rite clearly came to have a primary role within Vajrayana Buddhism, which will be discussed below. And especially in connection with the highly developed Japanese aesthetic sensibility, as was mentioned above, sacred rite plays a fairly significant role in the different traditions of Japanese Buddhism, especially Zen.

By far the most popular forms of Mahayana Buddhism, especially throughout Far East Asia, have been expressions of the way of devotion.[32] It is inconceivable that these traditions could have arisen in a Theravada as opposed to a Mahayana context, for they center upon the *theology*° of the compassionate *bodhisattva* and Mahayana scriptural texts that tell of the great Bodhisattvas and Buddhas, their marvelous works, and their vows to help those who call upon their aid. Especially prominent among them are the Bodhisattva *Avalokiteśvara* (known also in China and Japan as the female Bodhisattva *Kuan-yin* or *Kannon*), the Buddha *Amitābha* (*Ami-to-fo* in China, *Amida* in Japan), and the coming Buddha *Maitreya*. These devotional forms of Mahayana address directly many of the existential concerns of, and circumstantial constraints upon, the layperson householder: hope in the midst of oppressive circumstances, promise of divine assistance in progressing toward Enlightenment, and divine mercy for coping with the heavy responsibilities of ordinary life. Mahayana expressions of the way of devotion have neither led to nor centered upon a monastic institution, as most other forms of Buddhism have done. Some monastic expressions of Mahayana, however, have gone beyond mere tolerance to support and encourage them. They appeal to simple folk who know their own limitations and who (at least in their own thinking) lack the talent and opportunity to take up the rigors of monastic discipline.[33]

Many of these devotional Buddhist traditions appeal to the Buddhist teaching that between the coming of one Buddha and another the understanding and practice of the *Dharma* (the teachings of the Buddhas) inevitably degenerates so that fewer and fewer people are able to reach Enlightenment on their own with the resources left behind by the previous Buddha. They find convincing the thought that we are now well into the third and most degenerate stage of development, meaning that there is little anyone can do to make significant progress toward Enlightenment despite her or his best intentions and that our only resort is the supernatural "other power" of the Bodhisattvas and Buddhas who have promised to help those who call upon their aid. Above all, appeal is made to the Buddha *Amitābha* (*Ami-to-fo* in Chinese, *Amida* in Japanese), who, out of his infinite store of merit built up from eons of practice, has created a Pure Land where there is no evil, a supremely happy place enabling straightforward realization of Enlightenment for whoever is reborn there by aid of his grace. According to certain Mahayana scriptures, long before becoming the Buddha *Amitābha*, the Bodhisattva *Dharmākara* made certain vows to the effect that, upon becoming a Buddha, whoever hears his name—even though the person may have done evil—calls upon his help, repents, and reforms will be assured of rebirth in the Pure Land. Worship for Pure Land Buddhism (in China *Ching-t'u-tsung* founded by T'an-luan [476–542], and in Japan *Jodo-shu* founded by Honen [1133–1212] and *Jodo-shin-shu* founded by Shinran [1173–1262]) is often congregational as well as individual, focusing on praise and gratitude to Amita, stories of his saving help, and chanting his name.[34] Even though all this may appear (especially to Western eyes) to be a strange departure from other forms of Buddhism, Pure Land Buddhism has had some articulate and sophisticated apologists from time to time who show how it fits into the larger Buddhist frame of reference and how the distinctive Pure Land concepts correspond to traditional Buddhist notions (e.g., how the Pure Land is a state of mind one can experientially enter here and now in devotional meditation or how the Pure Land is itself something to be magically visualized in a complex meditation).[35] While Pure Land Buddhism has given first priority to the way of devotion, it has nevertheless at times incorporated in a subordinate way aspects of right action, mystical quest, sacred rite, and reasoned inquiry.

Concerning expressions of shamanic mediation in Mahayana Buddhism, not much is covered in most accounts, except for the Vajrayana traditions that will be shortly taken up. As in Theravada, in those places where shamanic phenomena seem to be present there is a certain tendency, at least among Western interpreters, to regard them as a contamination of authentic Buddhism from contact with indigenous, non-Buddhist traditions. Here too much remains unknown, and much of the knowledge we do have is colored by assumptions that may have biased inquiry. In any case there is evidence of widespread vision quests, especially in connection with mountain pilgrimages, and other practices suggestive of shamanism: magical spells, fire rituals, visionary experiences, divination, and so forth.[36] As mentioned in connection with Theravada, there are references from time to time to the extraordinary powers that Mahayana Buddhists of allegedly great attainment have employed on behalf of others.[37] One specific tradition that should be mentioned here is that of the colorful mountain ascetics (*yamabushi*) of Japan called *Shugendō* ("the way [*dō*] of mastering [*shu*] extraordinary religious power [*gen*]").[38] In this case we clearly have a full-fledged case of the way of shamanic mediation whose frame of reference is explicitly Buddhist. They go into the mountain wilderness in Japan to practice rigorous shamanic austerities to acquire power for combating evil spirits, for healing, and for divination on behalf of others.

Vajrayana Buddhism

Vajrayana Buddhism has predominated, until very recently, in numerous subsects within Tibet (and, since the Chinese Communist takeover in 1959, in the Tibetan diaspora in India, Europe, and the United States).[39] It is also a major sect of Buddhism in Japan called *Shingon*, founded by Kukai (774–835).[40] Significant aspects of Vajrayana have also been incorporated into Japanese *Tendai* Buddhism, founded by Saichō (767–822),[41] and, by way of Shingon and Tendai, into Japanese *Shugendō* mentioned above. In early Medieval times it had a strong presence throughout Southeast Asia and in China (called *Chen-yen* in Chinese), though no longer. Along with Theravada and Mahayana, it too originated in India and its original scriptures are in Sanskrit. Those scriptures basically consist of the Mahayana scriptures plus an additional group of scriptures called *Tantras* and their commentaries. Vajrayana is an outgrowth, if not a subtradition, of Mahayana. It has a certain inclusive orientation about it that seeks to include and assign some place— if only a subordinate or preliminary place—for the teaching and practice of other

forms of Buddhism. However, what it regards as the supreme teaching and practice of Buddhism, associated with the Tantric scriptures, is esoteric: it is not, it
contends, for the insufficiently developed mind to understand or apply. The
Tantras purport to come directly from teachings the Buddha passed on secretly
to his most advanced disciples, and they are so written that their true meaning is
obscure or unintelligible to the uninitiated. Among the subsects or subtraditions
making use of the *Tantras* in Tibet, these teachings have been given somewhat
different emphases and interpretations.

In their pursuit of Enlightenment Vajrayana Buddhists, in addition to conventional Buddhist practices, may make use of esoteric rituals, sacred implements,
gestures (*mudras*), sacred word-sounds (*mantras*), elaborate visualizations aided
by visual diagrams (*mandalas*), magical spells, rigorous physical ordeals, and extraordinary psychic powers under the strict guidance of a spiritual guide (*guru or
lama*) who is himself a master of these techniques. All are said to be designed to
lead directly to the realization of Buddhahood.[42] In effect, they endeavor to enlist
the whole panoply of the powers of the lived body, the imagination, and the unconscious—including one's deepest fears and highest ideals—into the struggle for
liberation from desire and suffering. As in many esoteric mystical traditions, there
is assumed to be a correspondence between this microcosm of the inwardly felt
lived body (a mystical physiology) and the macrocosm of the universe. The
Vajrayana pantheon of Buddhas, Bodhisattvas, gods, and demons (going far beyond the Mahayana pantheon), each with their feminine consorts and taken together with them to represent the whole array of cosmic powers at large in the
universe, is believed to correspond to a corresponding array of psychic powers
within oneself. By the aid of appropriate esoteric techniques typically inolving visualization these powers are harnessed, as it were, to carry one along the path to
Enlightenment—yet ultimately in a way that one realizes that they too are empty
(*śūnya*), they too lack separate being.

The Tantric adept aims to transcend the passions not by destroying them or
leaving them behind but by experiencing them from a pure perspective, entirely
liberated from their control. Because different personalities have different dominant passions, a specific course of practice for each person is prescribed.
Presupposing the *Prajñā-pāramitā* teaching that *Saṃsāra* and *Nirvāṇa* are not
separate and therefore that all things are pure to the pure of mind, things that to
non-Tantric Buddhists seem impure or taboo might be engaged in by some Tantric
Buddhists under specific conditions and with a specific frame of mind in the process of overcoming a dominant passion. For example, under carefully controlled
conditions, at an appropriate stage of development, and under the direction of a
spiritual guide, a form of ritual sexual intercourse is practiced in some Vajrayana traditions to overcome the dominant tendency in persons of a hostile temperament.

Vajrayana Buddhism in this way brings into full play the ways of sacred
rite and shamanic mediation in connection with that of mystical quest.[43] Certain
subtraditions of Tibetan Vajrayana uphold the paradigm of a freely wandering

wonder-working practitioner not bound to celibacy—e.g., in Tibet, the *Nying-ma-pa* sect, allegedly founded by Padmasambhava in the latter eighth century, and the *Kargyüpa* sect, founded by Mar-pa (1012–1097), whose most popular saint is its Second Patriarch, Milarepa (1040–1123). Typical among the adepts of these subtraditions is a readiness to utilize the shamanic powers developed by means of the practices discussed as well as others to help, heal, and assist others who face otherwise unmanageable difficulties in their lives. (On the surface, at least, this seems to be much the sort of thing going on in Japanese *Shugendō*.) For example, some Tibetan monks regularly work with people at the point of death to help them meet death with equanimity and to conduct the "transmigrating ego" during the transition time to avoid dangerous traps for the unwary and to attain a better rebirth. So also, due to their knowledge of ritual and competence in its performance, Vajrayana monks—certainly in Tibet and to a lesser extent in Japan—often assume priestly ritual and ceremonial functions on behalf of communities, families, and individuals.

Despite this strong integrated emphasis upon mystical quest, sacred rite, and shamanic mediation in Vajrayana Buddhism, at least aspects of the ways of reasoned inquiry, right action, and devotion have their place as well, depending somewhat upon the specific subtradition of Vajrayana. Some subtraditions, notably Tibetan *Gelukpa*, as mentioned above, have placed a high priority upon conventional learning and study and their monasteries have served as universities, teaching secular subjects as well as religion.

CHAPTER SUMMARY

This chapter introduces the application of the framework to whole traditions and then to Buddhism in particular.

Buddhism divides into two main branches, Theravada and Mahayana, which differ principally in geographic location, doctrinal teaching, specific practices, and what is taken to be authoritative scripture. Whereas Theravada tends to be relatively uniform from culture to culture, Mahayana tolerates within its range a host of divergent subtraditions. What is sometimes identified as a third branch, Vajrayana, may also be construed as a further branching of Mahayana. Aspects of all six ways may be found in each of these three branches. All ways of being religious in Buddhism are conceived as a way of drawing near to, participating in, and being grounded in what it was that Gautama Buddha realized in his Enlightenment: a state of deliverance from all the suffering to which conditioned human existence is subject, called *nirvāṇa/nibbāna*. Dominant in Theravada are the ways of mystical quest, reasoned inquiry, and right action in a close synthesis articulated by the Eightfold Path, but emphasizing a monastic pursuit of of mystical quest. The many Mahayana subtraditions have tended to emphasize a single way, though usually the emphasized way is fused with aspects of other ways. In Mahayana little emphasis is laid on the distinction between laypersons and monastics. Particularly remarkable examples are the Pure Land subtraditions, which focus on the way of devotion, the Vajrayana (and Vajrayana-influenced) subtraditions that employ esoteric ritual forms and shamanic practices, the flowering of a number of wisdom subtraditions, and the uniquely aesthetic synthesis of ways found in Zen. Finally, mention is made of certain Mahayana traditions, notably certain Vajrayana and (Vajrayana-influenced) traditions, which have developed a grand and inclusive vision that grants legitimacy and place to virtually all varieties of Buddhist teaching and practice.

STUDY QUESTIONS

1. What obstacles are likely to arise in applying the framework of ways of being religious to whole traditions? Are there problems other than those mentioned in the first section of this chapter that might arise?

2. Are you aware of traditions other than Buddhism to which the application of the framework is likely to pose problems that do not arise in applying the framework to Buddhism?

See also the study questions for Chapter 8.

FOR FURTHER READING

Follow up references cited in chapter notes on specific topics in Buddhism. Also recommended are articles on Buddhism and Buddhist topics in the *Encyclopedia of Religion*, edited by Mircea Eliade.

NOTES

1. Roger J. Corless, in *The Vision of Buddhism: The Space Under the Tree* (New York: Paragon House, 1989), explicitly seeks to counter the usual *historical* approach to Buddhism taken by Western scholarship by utilizing an ahistorical orientation drawn from Buddhism itself.
2. The Mahayanist typology of Buddhist schools of thought usually characterizes what is here called *Theravāda* as *Hīnayāna* (the "lesser vehicle"), but when they speak of it in this way they do not have a living lineage in mind. Many popular accounts of Buddhism in the West have unfortunately adopted this somewhat pejorative name.
3. See, for example, Richard H. Robinson and Willard L. Johnson, *The Buddhist Religion: A Historical Introduction*, 3rd ed. (Belmont, CA: Wadsworth, 1982) and their excellent annotated bibliography, pp. 243-269. A much briefer but useful overview is William R. LaFleur, *Buddhism: A Cultural Perspective* (Englewood Cliffs, NJ: Prentice-Hall, 1988). Other excellent sources are Charles S. Prebish, ed., *Buddhism: A Modern Perspective* (University Park, PA: Pennsylvania State University Press, 1975); and P. V. Bapat, ed., *2500 Years of Buddhism* (New Delhi: Government of India, Publications Division, 1956). On

Chinese Buddhism see Kenneth Ch'en, *Buddhism in China: A Historical Survey* (Princeton, NJ: Princeton University Press, 1964).

4. See above Chapter 2, note 9.

5. See, for example, Donald K. Swearer, *Buddhism and Society in Southeast Asia* (Chambersburg, PA: Anima Books, 1981).

6. See Winston King, *Theravada Meditation* (University Park, PA: Pennsylvania State University Press, 1980); Jack Kornfeld, *Living Buddhist Masters* (Santa Cruz, CA: Unity Press, 1977); and Takeuchi Yoshinori, ed., *Buddhist Spirituality: Indian, Southeast Asian, Tibetan, and Early Chinese*, World Spirituality, Vol. 9 (New York: Crossroad, 1993). A course in *vipassanā* is described at some length in the Buddhist Example in Chapter 9, below. For Theravada teachings, see K. N. Jayatilleke, *Early Buddhist Theory of Knowledge* (London: Allen and Unwin, 1963); and Herbert V. Guenther, *Philosophy and Psychology in the Abhidharma* (Berkeley, CA: Shambhala, 1976).

7. Strictly speaking, *vipassanā* meditation is founded on a preliminary mental stabilization or calming of the mind called *samatha*.

8. See Jane Bunnag, *Buddhist Monk, Buddhist Layman* (London: Cambridge University Press, 1973); Hans-Dieter-Evers, *Monks, Priests and Peasants: A Study of Buddhism and Social Structure in Central Ceylon* (Leiden, Netherlands: Brill, 1972); and B. J. Terwiel, *Monks and Magic, An Analysis of Religious Ceremonies in Central Thailand* (London: Curzon Press, 1975).

9. There is clear reference in the early Pali scriptures to the attainment of Enlightenment by laypersons. But this is not deemed to be a realistic expectation among Theravada Buddhists today.

10. See Pe Maung Tin, *Buddhist Devotion and Meditation: An Objective Description and Study* (London: SPCK, 1964).

11. See Ruth-Inge Heinze, *Trance and Healing in Southeast Asia Today* (Berkeley, CA: Independent Scholars of Asia, 1988); Melford E. Spiro, *Burmese Supernaturalism* (Englewood Cliffs, NJ: Prentice-Hall, 1967); S. J. Tambiah, *Buddhism and the Spirit Cults in Northeast Thailand* (Cambridge, England: Cambridge University Press, 1970); and Terence P. Day, *Great Tradition and Little Tradition in Theravada Buddhist Studies*, Studies in Asian Thought and Religion, Vol. 7 (Lewiston, NY: Edwin Mellen Press, 1988) [contains a critical review of and response to Spiro and Tambiah's accounts].

12. See Corless, *The Vision of Buddhism, op. cit.*, pp. 188–191. Corless refers to Buddhaghosa, *The Path of Purity*, 3 vols., trans. Pe Maung Tin (London: Pali Text Society, 1923–1931), Ch 12.

13. See Corless, *The Vision of Buddhism, op. cit.*, pp. 194–196; Stanley Jeyaraja Tambiah, *The Other Side of Theravada Buddhism: The Buddhist Saints of the Forest and the Cult of Amulets* (Cambridge, England: Cambridge University Press, 1984).

14. See Winston L. King, *In the Hope of Nibbana: An Essay on Theravada Buddhist Ethics* (LaSalle, IL: Open Court, 1964); Ken Jones, *The Social Face of Buddhism: An Approach to Political and Social Activism* (London: Wisdom Publications, 1989), especially Ch. 24; Joanna Macy, *Dharma and Development: Religion as Resource in the Sarvodaya Self-Help Movement* (West Hartford, CT: Kumarian Press, 1983); Sulak Sivaraksa, *Seeds of Peace: A Buddhist Vision for Renewing Society* (Berkeley, CA: Parallax Press, 1992); and Reginald A. Ray, *Buddhist Saints in India: A Study of Buddhist Values and Orientations* (New York: Oxford University Press, 1993). On Ashoka see N. A. Nikam and Richard McKeon, *The Edicts of Asoka* (Chicago, IL: University of Chicago Press, 1959). On the role of Buddhism and political life in Southeast Asia, see Bardwell L. Smith, ed., *Religion and Legitimation of Power in Sri Lanka, Thailand, Laos, and Burma* (Chambersburg, PA: Anima Books, 1978); Trevor O. Ling, *Buddhism, Imperialism and War: Burma and Thailand in Modern History* (London: Allen and Unwin, 1979); and E. Sarkisyanz, *Buddhist Backgrounds of the Burmese Revolution* (The Hague, Netherlands: Nijhoff, 1965).

15. See Corless, *The Vision of Buddhism*, *op. cit.*, pp. 62–63. A similar expression of the way of right action in Sri Lankan Buddhism is described at length in Chapter 11, below.

16. See Robinson and Johnson, *The Buddhist Religion*, *op. cit.*, p. 175f.

17. See Robert S. Ellwood and Richard Pilgrim, *Japanese Religion* (Englewood Cliffs, NJ: Prentice-Hall, 1985); Masaharu Anesaki, *Nichiren, the Buddhist Prophet* (Cambridge, MA: Harvard University Press, 1916); Richard Causton, *Nichiren Shoshu Buddhism* (San Francisco, CA: Harper and Row, 1989); Daniel Alfred Metraux, *The History and Theology of Soka Gakkai: A Japanese New Religion* (Studies in Asian Thought and Religion, Vol. 9; Lewiston, NY: Edwin Mellen Press, 1988); and Kiyoaki Murata, *Japan's New Buddhism* (New York: Walker/Weatherhill, 1969).

18. See Charles Wei-hsun Fu and Sandra A. Wawrytko, eds., *Buddhist Ethics and Modern Society* (New York: Greenwood Press, 1991); Gunapala Dharmasiri, *Fundamentals of Buddhist Ethics* (Antioch, CA: Golden Leaves, 1989); Fred Eppsteiner, ed., *The Path of Compassion: Writings of Socially Engaged Buddhism*, rev. ed. (Berkeley, CA: Parallax Press, 1988); Jones, *The Social Face of Buddhism*, *op. cit.*; Christopher Ives, *Zen Awakening and Society* (Honolulu, HI: University of Hawaii Press, 1992); Tson-khu-pa Blo-bzan-grags-pa, *Ethics of Tibet*, trans. Alex Wayman (Albany, NY: State University of New York Press, 1991); and Reginald A. Ray, *Buddhist Saints in India: A Study of Buddhist Values and Orientations*, *op. cit.*

19. See David J. Kalupahana, *A History of Buddhist Philosophy: Continuities and Discontinuities* (Honolulu, HI: University of Hawaii Press, 1992); and Hirakawa Akira, *A History of Indian Buddhism: From Śākyamuni to Nāgārjuna*, trans. Paul Groner (Honolulu, HI: University of Hawaii Press, 1990).

20. See Frederick J. Streng, *Emptiness: A Study in Religious Meaning* (Nashville, TN: Abingdon Press, 1967); Richard H. Robinson, *Early Mādhyamika in India and China* (Madison, WI: University of Wisconsin Press, 1967); and C. W. Huntington, Jr., with Geshé Namgyal Wangchen, *The Emptiness of Emptiness* (Honolulu, HI: University of Hawaii Press, 1989).

21. See Ashok Kumar Chatterjee, *The Yogācāra Idealism* (Banaras, India: Hindu University Press, 1962); Chhote Lal Tripathi, *The Problem of Knowledge in Yogācāra Buddhism* (Varanasi, India: Bharat-Bharati, 1972); Jeffrey Hopkins, *Meditation on Emptiness* (London: Wisdom, 1983), pp. 365–397; and Corless, *The Vision of Buddhism*, *op. cit.*, pp. 174–184.

22. See Garma Chen-chi Chang, *The Buddhist Teaching of Totality: The Philosophy of Hua-yen Buddhism* (University Park, PA: Pennsylvania State University Press, 1971); Francis H. Cook, *Hua-yen Buddhism, The Jewel Net of Indra* (University Park, PA: Pennsylvania State University Press, 1977); and Thomas Cleary, *Entry into the Inconceivable: An Introduction to Hua-yen Buddhism* (Honolulu, HI: University of Hawaii Press, 1992).

23. See Paul L. Swanson, *Foundations of T'ien T'ai Philosophy: The Flowering of the Two Truths Theory in Chinese Buddhism* (Berkeley, CA: Asian Humanities Press, 1989); and Ng Yu-kwan, *T'ien-t'ai Buddhism and Early Madhyamika* (Honolulu, HI: University of Hawaii Press, 1993).

24. See Herbert V. Guenther, *Tibetan Buddhism without Mystification* (Leiden, Netherlands: Brill, 1966). For an understanding of what pursuit of Tibetan Buddhist philosophical understanding is like in practice, see Guy Newland, *Compassion: A Tibetan Analysis* (London: Wisdom, 1984); Daniel Perdue, *Introductory Debate in Tibetan Buddhism* (Dharmshala, India: Library of Tibetan Works and Archives, 1976); Geshe Lobsang Tharchin, et al., *The Logic and Debate Tradition of India, Tibet, and Mongolia: History, Reader, Resources* (Ithaca, NY: Snow Lion, 1979); and José Ignacio Cabezón, *Buddhism and Language: A Study of Indo-Tibetan Scholasticism* (Albany, NY: State University of New York Press, 1994).

25. See Shinzen Young, "Buddhist Meditation," in Robinson and Johnson, *The Buddhist Religion*, pp. 226–235; Minoru Kiyota, ed., *Mahayana Buddhist Meditation: Theory and Practice* (Honolulu, HI: University of Hawaii Press, 1978); Peter N. Gregory, ed., *Traditions*

of Meditation in Chinese Buddhism, Studies in East Asian Buddhism 4 (Honolulu, HI: University of Hawaii Press, 1987); Charles Luk (K'uan-Yü Lu), *The Secrets of Chinese Meditation* (London: Rider and Co., 1964); and Takeuchi Yoshinori, ed., *Buddhist Spirituality: Indian, Southeast Asian, Tibetan, and Early Chinese*, World Spirituality, Vol. 9 (New York: Crossroad, 1993). See also Holmes Welch, *The Practice of Chinese Buddhism* (New York: Atheneum, 1968); and *Lives of the Nuns: Biographies of Chinese Buddhist Nuns from the Fourth to Sixth Centuries*, trans. Kathryn Ann Tsai (Honolulu, HI: University of Hawaii Press, 1994).

26. See Heinrich Dumoulin, *Zen Buddhism: A History*, 2 vols. (New York: Macmillan, 1990). See also Thien-An Thich, *Buddhism and Zen in Vietnam, in Relation to the Development of Buddhism in Asia* (Rutland, VT: Charles E. Tuttle, 1975); Mu Soeng Sunim, *Thousand Peaks: Korean Zen—Tradition and Teachers* (Cumberland, RI: Primary Point Press, 1991); and Robert E. Buswell, Jr., *The Zen Monastic Experience in Contemporary Korea* (Princeton, NJ: Princeton University Press, 1994).

27. Campbell, *The Masks of God: Oriental Mythology* (New York: Viking Press, 1962), p. 29f.

28. Robinson and Johnson, *The Buddhist Religion, op. cit.*, p. 206. This quotation was originally intended to refer to the goal of the traditional arts nurtured by Japanese Rinzai Zen. My use of it here is based on the conviction that the goal in question has long been an aim of Ch'an meditation.

29. Peter N. Gregory, ed., *Sudden and Gradual: Approaches to Enlightenment in Chinese Thought*, Studies in East Asian Buddhism 5 (Honolulu, HI: University of Hawaii Press, 1988); T. P. Kasulis, *Zen Action, Zen Person* (Honolulu, HI: University of Hawaii Press, 1981); and Conrad Hyers, *Once-Born, Twice-Born Zen: The Soto and Rinzai Schools of Japanese Zen* (Wolfeboro, NH: Longwood Academic, 1989). Also especially recommended are Kenneth Kraft, ed., *Zen: Tradition and Transition* [a sourcebook by Contemporary Zen Masters and Scholars] (New York: Grove Press, 1988); Jiyu Kennett, *Selling Water by the River: A Manual of [Sōtō] Zen Training* (New York: Vintage Books/Random House, 1972) [later published as *Zen is Eternal Life* (Emeryville, CA: Dharma Publications, 1976)]; Phillip Kapleau, *The Three Pillars of Zen: Teaching, Practice, and Enlightenment*, rev. ed. (Garden City, NJ: Anchor Doubleday, 1980); and Isshu Miura and Ruth Fuller Sasaki, *The Zen Koan: Its History and Use in Rinzai Zen* (New York: Harcourt, Brace and World, 1965).

30. See Richard B. Pilgrim, *Buddhism and the Arts of Japan* (Chambersburg, PA: Anima Books, 1981); Masaharu Anesaki, *Buddhist Art in Its Relation to Buddhist Ideals: With Special Reference to Buddhism in Japan* (Boston: Houghton Mifflin, 1915); Horst Hammitzsch, *Zen in the Art of the Tea Ceremony* (New York: St. Martin's Press, 1980); Trevor Legett, *Zen and the Ways* (Boulder, CO: Shambhala, 1978); William La Fleur, *The Karma of Words: Buddhism and the Literary Arts in Medieval Japan* (Berkeley, CA: University of California Press, 1983); and Daisetz T. Suzuki, *Zen and Japanese Culture*, Bollingen Series 64 (Princeton University Press, 1959). An extended account of *Cha-no-yu* as an expression of the way of sacred rite in Rinzai Zen is given in Chapter 14, below.

31. John Stevens, *The Marathon Monks of Mount Hiei* (Boston, MA: Shambhala, 1988).

32. See the comprehensive histories of Buddhism mentioned above in note 1, under the topics of "Pure Land Buddhism" and worship of *Amitābha/Ami-to-fo/Amida, Avalokitesvara/Kuan-yin/Kannon*, and *Maitreya*. See also articles in the *Encyclopedia of Religion*, ed. Mircea Eliade (New York: Macmillan, 1987), under "Pure Land Buddhism" and related topics. A helpful interpretive reconciliation of devotional and mystical Buddism in a Chinese context may be found in John Blofeld, "The Path of Faith and Compassion," in his *Beyond the Gods: Taoist and Buddhist Mysticism* (London: Allen and Unwin, 1974), pp. 69-88.

33. I should acknowledge here that my account of devotional forms of Buddhism here and in what follows reflects something of a bias toward their Japanese forms. Partly this is a result of the lack of readily available scholarship on other forms. The reader should keep this in mind.

34. See Kenneth K. Tanaka, *The Dawn of Chinese Pure Land Buddhist Doctrine: Ching-ying Hui-yuan's Commentary on the Visualization Sutra* (Albany, NY: State University of New York Press, 1990); James C. Dobbins, *Jodo Shinshu: Shin Buddhism in Medieval Japan* (Bloomington, IN: Indiana University Press, 1989); Alfred Bloom, *Shinran's Gospel of Pure Grace*, Association for Asian Studies: Monographs and Papers, No. XX: (Tucson, AZ: University of Arizona Press, 1965); *Shin Buddhist Handbook*, (Los Angeles, CA: Buddhist Sangha of America, 1973); Daisetz Teitaro Suzuki, *Collected Writings on Shin Buddhism*, ed. Eastern Buddhist Society (Kyoto, Japan: Shinshu Otaniha, 1973); Lloyd Arthur, *The Creed of Half Japan* (New York: E. P. Dutton, 1912); Gendo Nakai, *Shinran and His Religion of Pure Faith* (Kyoto, Japan: Kanao Bunendo, 1946); and Nishu Utsuki, *The Shin Sect* (Kyoto, Japan: Pub. Bureau of Buddhist Books, 1937). An account of the basic teachings of Jodo-shin-shu in Shinran's own words is given in Chapter 12, below.

35. E.g., Taitetsu Unno, "The Nature of Religious Experience in Shin Buddhism," in *The Other Side of God: A Polarity in World Religions*, ed. Peter L. Berger (Garden City, NY: Anchor Books/Doubleday, 1981), pp. 252–271. See also Stephen Beyer, *The Buddhist Experience: Sources and Interpretations* (Belmont, CA: Wadsworth, 1974), pp. 117–124.

36. See, for example, Beyer, *The Buddhist Experience: Sources and Interpretations, op. cit.*, Ch. 6.

37. See Corless, *The Vision of Buddhism, op. cit.*, pp. 191–194; and James B. Robinson, *Buddha's Lions: The Lives of the Eighty-four Siddhas* (Berkeley, CA: Dharma Publishing, 1979).

38. See H. Byron Earhart, *A Religious Study of the Mount Haguro Sect of Sugendo* (Tokyo: Sophia University, 1970); Ichiro Hori, *Folk Religion in Japan: Continuity and Change*, ed. Joseph M. Kitagawa and Alan L. Miller, Haskell Lectures on History of Religions, new series, no. 1 (Chicago, IL: University of Chicago Press, 1968), Ch. 5; and Carmen Blacker, *The Catalpa Bow: A Study of Shamanistic Practices in Japan* (London: Allen and Unwin, 1975). An account of certain practices by Buddhist women shamans is given in Chapter 13, below.

39. See John Powers, *Introduction to Tibetan Buddhism* (Ithaca, NY: Snow Lion Press, 1995); Shashibhusan Dasgupta, *An Introduction to Tantric Buddhism* (Berkeley, CA: Shambhala, 1974); Giuseppe Tucci, *The Religions of Tibet* (Berkeley, CA: University of California Press, 1980); Geshe Lhundrup Sopa and Jeffrey Hopkins, *Practice and Theory of Tibetan Buddhism* (New York: Grove Press, 1976); and Takeuchi Yoshinori, ed., *Buddhist Spirituality: Indian, Southeast Asian, Tibetan, and Early Chinese*, World Spirituality, Vol. 9 (New York: Crossroad, 1993).

40. See Minoru Kiyota, *Shingon Buddhism: Theory and Practice* (Los Angeles, CA: Buddhist Books International, 1978); and Taiko Yamasaki, *Shingon: Japanese Esoteric Buddhism*, trans. Richard and Cynthia Peterson, ed. Yasuoshi Morimoto and David Kidd (Boston: Shambhala, 1988).

41. See Hakuju Ui, "A Study of Japanese Tendai Buddhism," in *Philosophical Studies of Japan*, Vol. 1, compiled by Japanese Commission for UNESCO (Tokyo: Japan Society for the Promotion of Science, 1959); Bruno Petzold, *Tendai Buddhism* (Tokyo: International Buddhist Exchange Center, 1979); and Michael Saso, *Tantric Art and Meditation: The Tendai Tradition* (Honolulu, HI: Tendai Educational Foundation, 1990).

42. See Stephen V. Beyer, *The Cult of Tara* (Berkeley, CA: University of California Press, 1973); Jamgon Kongtrul, *The Torch of Certainty* (Boulder, CO: Shambhala, 1976); Rinbochay Khetsun Sangpo, *Tantric Practice in Nying-ma*, trans. Jeffrey Hopkins and Anne Klein (London: Rider, 1982); John Blofeld, *The Way of Power: A Practical Guide to the Tantric Mysticism of Tibet* (London: Allen and Unwin, 1970; reprint Boulder, CO: Prajna Press, 1982); and Janice Dean Willis, *The Diamond Light* (New York: Simon and Schuster, 1972).

43. See Thubten Legshay Gyatsho, *Gateway to the Temple: Manual of Tibetan Monastic Customs, Art, Buildings, and Celebrations,* trans. David Paul Jackson (Kathmandu, Nepal: Ratne Pustak Bhandar, 1979); Robert B. Ekvall, *Religious Observances in Tibet: Patterns and Function* (Chicago, IL: University of Chicago Press, 1964); Detlef Ingo Lauf, *Secret Doctrines of the Tibetan Book of the Dead* (Boulder, CO: Shambhala, 1977); and Sherry B. Ortner, *Sherpas through Their Rituals* (Cambridge, England: Cambridge University Press, 1978).

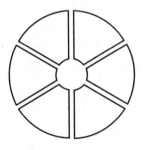

C H A P T E R 8

APPLYING THE FRAMEWORK TO THE WHOLE OF CHRISTIANITY

A SURVEY OF THE DIFFERENT WAYS IN CHRISTIANITY

Christianity as we find it today is divided into three major branches, Eastern Orthodoxy, Roman Catholicism, and Protestantism.[1] From Protestantism many other branches have grown, most out of a desire to recover anew an authentic original Christianity disclosed in scripture. Eastern Orthodoxy and Roman Catholicism have always sought to keep reform movements from disrupting continuity with the past and unity in the present. That is in large measure what both of the latter mean in identifying themselves as versions of "Catholic" Christianity, though their emphasis upon unity and continuity allows for considerable variation from personality, culture, geographic circumstance, and historical situation. The history of the development of these traditions from the earliest Apostles of Jesus to the present day is a long, involved, and interesting story that we will not begin to go into here. There are many good and readable accounts readily available.[2]

Unlike the lack of a commonly agreed canon of scripture among Buddhist traditions, Protestants, Eastern Orthodox, and Roman Catholics all agree to the canonical status of the twenty-seven books of the (Greek) New Testament as the primary scripture of the Christian revelation, and they basically agree over the constitution of the canonical Old Testament. The Old Testament is the Christian name for the scriptures of Judaism, the religious tradition in which Christianity first emerged. The so-called apocryphal books of the Old Testament over which the three branches of Christianity have historically disagreed have not significantly contributed to differences in doctrine or practice. The Old Testament for the three traditions has always been subject to interpretation in terms of what they hold to be the clearer light of the New Testament. All three hold that therein is proclaimed the ultimate revelation of God come to restore his fallen creation to himself[3] in the historical person of Jesus the Christ (3 B.C.E.-30 C.E.). In other words, at the core of the Christian conception of salvation (its conception of the means of at-onement with *ultimate reality*[p]) is a twofold conviction. The first is that, in Jesus, God (the *ultimate reality*[p] as Christians understand it) has decisively acted to overcome the breach of alienation between humankind and God. The second is that in and through that "cosmic event" God has decisively communicated himself, made known his innermost character and intention for humankind. In consequence of this twofold conviction, it is believed that at-onement with God is not attainable, and essential knowledge about God is not had, apart from access to that event. All ways of being religious in Christianity are different ways of drawing near to, of participating in, and of being grounded in, the event of God's reconciliation of the world with himself in Jesus Christ.

The three branches of Christianity agree that the heart of Christianity is the receiving and communication of the revelation of God in Christ. How each conceives of the relation of revelation to scripture, though, differs. For Protestants (traditionally at least) scripture, especially New Testament scripture, has been *the* document of the Christian revelation; it contains the first and last word concerning the essentials of Christianity to those who read it and hear it in faith, seeking the guidance of the Spirit of God.[4] Protestant traditions differ among themselves as to how these matters are explained in scripture—for example, whether scripture is to be regarded as an integral part of the revelation itself or as the primary witness to the revelation. Eastern Orthodoxy conceives the revelation of God in Christ to be an unchanging divine mystery passed down, starting with Jesus' original apostles, from one generation to another in the church at large. They understand the revelation to be embodied in a living practice and implicit understanding—called Holy Tradition—partially made explicit in scripture, doctrine, and liturgy, but never wholly made explicit in any one. Revelation is not for them—at least not first of all—an explicit intellectual content.[5] Scripture for Eastern Orthodox Christians is an authentic expression of this Holy Tradition and is to be read and interpreted accordingly. Roman Catholicism conceives the revelation of God in Christ (or rather, the Church's *understanding* of that revelation) to be a largely explicit legacy from Jesus' original apostles that has developed and unfolded to the present day in the teaching of the hierarchy of the Church under the guidance of the Spirit of God.[6] Scripture for Roman Catholic Christians is the expression of this legacy closest to its very source and is to be interpreted accordingly.

The central story of Christianity, the story central to Protestantism, Eastern Orthodoxy, and Roman Catholicism, centers on the person of Jesus, the Christ (from *christos*, the Greek word for Messiah, the inaugurator of the Kingdom of God to come, foretold by the Old Testament prophets)—his life, teachings, suffering, crucifixion, and resurrection. Contrary to widespread supposition, however, the central character of the story is not Jesus simply as an historical person. The central character is, rather, "the person of God"—*ultimate reality*, the singular transcendent ground of all that is, the infinite measure of all that is good, right, just, and beautiful, but here conceived as "person"—become present to humanity in the person of Jesus. The story is the story of God-incarnate. The story tells of the redemption God has accomplished and made available for fallen humanity in and through Jesus' life, death, and resurrection: "In him [Jesus, the Christ]," writes the Apostle Paul in Colossians 1:19–20 [RSV], "all the fullness of God was pleased to dwell, and through him God was pleased to reconcile to himself all things, whether on earth or in heaven, by making peace through the blood of his cross." Many different images and theological conceptions have been employed in the attempt to explain the mystery of how this is to have taken place and the manner in which it is to be appropriated. Nevertheless, all Christian traditions affirm that personal appropriation of the gift of salvation in Christ brings about at-onement with God, both now and for all eternity.

The story is called the Gospel (*evangelion* in Greek, meaning "good news"). Elaborated in the way we find it in the New Testament, this story encompasses Jesus' moral teachings, how he related to persons in need, how he dealt with this or that challenge, how he met suffering and death, the promise embodied in his resurrection, and so forth. Its overall message, though, is the "Good News" of God's reconciliation with fallen humanity in Jesus Christ. The proclamation (*kerygma* in Greek) of that message "in word and sacrament" (many Protestants dispute the phrase "and sacrament") is the principal means the Christian revelation is communicated, and its "power unto salvation" (Romans 1:16) transmitted, to those who receive it in faith. It (the *kerygma*) is understood to be the paradigm case, the ideal place, in which the Word of God (which is identified with Christ) "speaks" to the hearer. There the hearer is offered a new or deepened relationship of at-onement with God. Thus, above all else, it is the *kerygma* that awakens and deepens faith. For the Christian who is intent on having her life brought into right relationship and at-onement with God, whether formally undertaken as a religious vocation or not, the Gospel presentation of Jesus' life makes up the supreme model to follow. For other Christians unready for that intense of a commitment, the story gives a focus for their honor, praise, and worship, a touchstone of divine authorization and blessing for all that is good, worthy, and right, sustaining grace in the midst of suffering, and the hope of resurrection.

Earlier it was said that the central story of the Buddha's Enlightenment in Buddhism is not essentially historical, for in essential respects it could have happened in any time or place and that Buddhists believe that, in essence, it has happened many times before and that it will happen again. On the contrary, the central story of the Gospel for Christians is not a "once upon a time" story abstractable from its having historically happened. For them it is essentially connected with an utterly unique, once-and-for-all-time set of (allegedly) historical events, yet it is simultaneously full of significance for all times and places. The Christian claim is that in these events God has in fact, in historical time, reconciled the world to himself. As a result, there is in Christianity a preoccupation with the historicity of those events. Christians often busy themselves with efforts to verify them, learn all they can about the historical and cultural circumstances of Jesus' life and teachings, revisit the places and scenes of these events, and endeavor to find out things about them that are unknown or incompletely known. More important than all these efforts, though, is the Christian preoccupation with *returning* to them in a sacramental way and to their life transforming power— whether in biblical preaching and teaching, the sacrament of Holy Communion, or a devotional reading and contemplation of the biblical story.[7]

This preoccupation with historicity makes Christians vulnerable to the critical investigations of modern (and so-called postmodern) *secular* historical scholarship into the events of Jesus' life and the rise of Christianity (meaning not at all an investigation of faith and very possibly an investigation that could undermine or refute faith). Christians are all the more vulnerable because most liberal Protestant and liberal Roman Catholic biblical scholarship nowadays is indistinguishable from secular scholarship in this sense.[8] The supposedly objective results of such scholarship are at times confusing and disorienting for Christians but also for non-Christians who would like to learn something about Christianity. Some textbooks that attempt a survey of Christianity in a context of comparison with other religions and in a presumably empathetically objective manner, rely uncritically on this scholarship and distinguish between the Jesus of history and the Christ of Christian faith, attributing the latter (i.e., the Gospel) to the "creative theologizing" of the Apostle Paul and other early Christian theologians, as if this distinction were perfectly innocent and noncontroversial. But the distinction itself, as usually developed (i.e., uprooting the Gospel and the Christ of faith from any historicity), is highly controversial as far as theology is concerned, though the unsuspecting reader would be the last to know. The point is not that the story of the Gospel is historically true, but that all traditional Christians have been and are convinced that it is historically true and *consider its historicity to be of its very essence*. In the remarks that follow about Christianity I shall not presume to differentiate the Jesus of history from the Christ of faith.

Eastern Orthodox Christianity

Eastern Orthodox Christianity now predominates among Christians in the Eastern Mediterranean, in Greece, in most of Eastern Europe, and in the former USSR. Significant, growing numbers of Orthodox Christians may be found throughout the world, especially in North America. From an outsider's point of view, closely allied with Eastern Orthodox and highly similar in many practices are a group of much smaller, ancient but distinct Christian traditions, often called Oriental Orthodox (encompassing Nestorian, Monophysite—including the Coptic Church in Egypt and the Ethiopian Church—and Jacobite traditions).[9] Oriental Orthodox Christians are found in many places throughout the Middle East, in parts of India, in Northeast Africa (especially Egypt and Ethiopia), and at one time they penetrated Asia as far as China. Mention should also be made here of Uniate churches (e.g., Ukranian Catholics and Lebanese Maronites), that have an Eastern Orthodox or Oriental Orthodox orientation but that have recently entered into association with the Roman Catholic Church while maintaining their traditional liturgies and practices. Orthodox Christians, however, clearly distinguish themselves from so-called Oriental Orthodox Christians, referring to them as non-Orthodox—indeed, as heterodox—principally because of the historic nonagreement of these groups with certain Orthodox doctrinal formulations. For most Orthodox Christians, their Christianity is deeply entwined with their cultural and ethnic identity. Their language and music of worship and the style of their religious art and architecture are in many respects as much an expression of the latter as of the former. Thus, to be Greek, for many at least, is to be Greek Orthodox Christian. To some extent the opposite is true also, though the Greek Orthodox Church includes non-Greek ethnic groups as well. For only a few is being an Orthodox Christian the result of an individual act of free affiliation independent of cultural identity, though this is coming to be true for more and more in religiously pluralistic cultures such as that of the United States. (This phenomenon is not at all unique to Christianity. The same is true, for example, for cultural groups that are traditionally linked with one or another Buddhist subtradition.) Of course, Orthodox Christians may freely elect to take their Christianity more seriously and pursue the promise of life transformation that it offers.

Despite the diversity that results from its linkage with ethnic identity and national or regional structures of church governance (there is no central authority), Eastern Orthodox Christianity is strongly united on the essentials of faith and worship.[10] Eastern Orthodox Christianity conceives itself not as a denomination but as the ancient, original, and authentic form of Christianity, passed down unaltered from the original Apostles and explicated in New Testament scripture, in the teachings of the Apostolic Fathers (in the early centuries of the Church), and in the rulings of the Seven Ecumenical Councils of the undivided Church (the first in the fourth and the last in the eighth century), which laid down essential doctrines and teachings of the Christian faith. (Oriental Orthodox groups split off in rejecting one or another of these Ecumenical Council rulings.) Accordingly, there is a sense of timelessness and a pervasive presence of the past about Orthodox life and worship, which they take to symbolize the presence of eternity. Orthodox Christianity has never identified with the dynamism of change and development that in many respects have characterized Roman Catholic and Protestant Christianity, especially in their modern forms. To Orthodox thinking, that would be to exchange the kernel for the shell, reality for appearance, eternity for mere time. On the contrary, Orthodoxy is convinced that what really matters is the nontemporal, transcendent mystery of the redemption of the world in Christ and the life in God into which that mystery ushers the Orthodox Christian. Every aspect of Orthodox life and worship is oriented to reinforcing this conviction. The schism of 1054, between itself and the Western Church centered in Rome, Orthodox Christianity believes to have been the result of a departure by the Roman Catholic hierarchy from the original Holy Tradition that Eastern Orthodoxy believes it alone has preserved inviolate.[11]

The central and foremost mode of approach to God in Christ for Eastern Orthodoxy is the Divine Liturgy—especially as set within the context of the annual liturgical cycle of holy days, holy seasons, and days of special observance; the daily liturgical cycle of Vespers (Evening Prayer) and Matins (Morning Prayer), at least on the evening and morning preceding the Divine Liturgy; and the life cycle of the sacraments, of Baptism, Chrismation, regular Confession, Unction (when ill), Matrimony (if married), and Holy Orders (if ordained), and other sacramentals, such as the rituals relating to birth and to death. This of course requires ritual specialization and sacramental authority, an ordained status, made up of bishops, priests, and deacons. Whereas Orthodox Bishops are often drawn from monastic life and are therefore celibate, Orthodox priests and deacons usually are married (although priests may not change marital status after ordination). Among Christians, Orthodox Christians are the most formal and sacramental in their mode of worship and the most involving of all the bodily senses, through beautiful poetry; vocal music and chant (no instrumental music); dramatic ritual; visual icons; elaborate vestments; sacred ritual implements; a powerfully structured sense of sacred architectural space; candles; incense; bread and wine to eat; fasting and feasting; and manifold gestures, including kissing and prostration. Though worship language, liturgical style, vocal music, and particular anthems vary from one area of one Orthodox subtradition to another, the fundamental structure of the Divine Liturgy is the same, having been basically finalized in what is now its current form in the late sixth century. To participate fully and faithfully in Orthodox worship is to be transported into another, heavenly dimension and sacramentally ushered into the presence of the Holy Trinity (Father, Son, and Holy Spirit), the holy angels, and the saints of heaven, there to be progressively transformed into fuller and fuller at-onement with the Holy Trinity.[12] This gives the way of sacred rite absolute primacy in an Orthodox Christian's life, with other ways being given a subordinate place (to a greater or lesser degree) in relation to it.

Next in importance to sacred rite for Orthodox Christianity and sometimes conjoined with it is the way of mystical quest. Basic Christian doctrines, according to Orthodoxy, are not only things to be accepted on faith; they are realities to be experienced through liturgy and mystical prayer. The aim of Christian life, Orthodoxy insists, is to be taken up into God—to be transfigured, made holy, changed in one's very nature from mortality to immortality, divinized (*theosis*), to "become participants in the divine nature" (II Peter 1:4 [RSV])—by his mystically transforming grace in Christ. God did not become human in Christ primarily to satisfy divine justice (as much Roman Catholic and Protestant theology has put it), but to enable people to come to share intimately in the very life of the Holy Trinity.[13] Those who have dedicated themselves most fully to this end have largely taken up the monastic life. In this respect, both eremitic (i.e., in the manner of a hermit) and communal monasticism in Orthodox Christianity have long had a revered place. However, the goal of deification, according to Orthodox Christianity, is for all Christians, not just monastics; so (nonmonastic) laypersons are encouraged to make themselves available to, and to cooperate synergistically with, the mystically transforming grace of God no less than monastics. Contrary to what is found in much of Buddhism, the monastic vocation is not held up in Orthodoxy (or in Roman Catholicism for that matter) as the preferred or better way for all. Specific methods of meditation and spiritual guidance are provided (ideally, at least) for both monastics and laypersons.

The most comprehensive written compilation of spiritual guidance in Orthodoxy is called the *Philokalia* (meaning, in Greek, "the love of [spiritual] beauty"). It was assembled and published by Macarius of Corinth and Nicodemus of Naxos in 1782 and includes texts that go back many centuries before.[14] The path of meditation there most strongly endorsed has come to be known as hesychasm (from the Greek *hesychia*, meaning "quietness, rest, inner peace" and specifically referring to the path of solitary inner prayer). It centers on what is called "the Prayer of the Heart," the most classic form of which makes use of the ceaseless repetition of Jesus' name ("the Jesus Prayer") in coordination with breathing. In essence, the path involves centering in solitude and silence, vigilantly guarding the heart by the mind from distraction—"standing with the mind in the heart before God"—while continually invoking the name and merciful grace of Jesus.[15] There are many stories told of how persons who diligently pursue this path have had profound and overwhelming experiences of God, transforming them and bestowing on them a godlike radiance in their very being. Mention should be made in this connection of perhaps the greatest mystic to exemplify and poetically celebrate hesychasm, Symeon the New Theologian (949–1022), and the most articulate apologist for its theory and practice, Gregory Palamas (1296–1359).

Aspects of the ways of devotion and right action receive emphasis in Eastern Orthodoxy, sometimes and in some places more so than at others, but never to my knowledge have they attained the status of ways independent of sacred rite or mystical quest. Both lay and monastic Orthodox Christians are often involved in (and encouraged to be involved in) charitable actions beyond basic moral obligations.[16] And private Orthodox piety is typically of a devotional nature, sometimes intensely so, and may involve a vital personal relationship with Jesus, Mary (*Theotokos*, "bearer of God"), and various saints. Shamanic mediation is certainly no independent way in Orthodox Christianity, yet stories abound of Orthodox saints and holy persons (as well as icons and relics of the same) exercising miraculous powers on behalf of persons in special need. The Orthodox tradition has always taught that in Baptism and Chrismation (which in Eastern Orthodox Christianity occur together) the Orthodox Christian receives "the [supernatural] gifts of the Holy Spirit,"[17] though few appear to develop their alleged full potential. In recent years, the so-called Charismatic Movement (to be described below) has had some impact on Orthodox Christians in America, motivating participants to seek out and exercise these "supernatural gifts."

Only rarely does there occur in the Eastern Orthodox tradition full-fledged expressions of the way of reasoned inquiry, where serious intellectual inquiry is taken to be a way or even an important aspect of a way to at-onement with God. There are occasionally remarkable Eastern Orthodox philosophers and theologians, but there has been no special ongoing tradition of Orthodox philosophical or theological inquiry, as distinct from exposition of traditionally held theological views. It is clear, however, that philosophically and theologically sophisticated thinking has contributed significantly to the formulation of key points of Orthodox theology and hesychastic theory. Virtually all important aspects of Orthodox theology have become aspects of Orthodox liturgy—for example, as special hymns or prayers—rather than classic texts to be studied and interpreted. Moreover, Orthodox writers often emphasize that "theology" for the Orthodox tradition refers first not to an intellectual study of matters of explicit belief but to the experiential (mystical) knowledge of God. Thus, to the extent that a tradition of theologizing is present in Orthodoxy, it is made to serve worship and mystical prayer. After all, as is frequently pointed out, *ortho-doxa* means just as much right worship (one of the meanings of *doxa* is "glory") as it does right teaching or right belief, and for Orthodox Christians even more so.

Roman Catholic Christianity

Roman Catholic Christianity now predominates in parts of Europe (especially Italy, Spain, Portugal, France, Belgium, Ireland, Austria, Southern Germany, and Poland—though prior to the Protestant Reformation in the sixteenth century, it was the church of all of Western Europe, being, in short, Western Christianity), Latin America, other countries colonized by Italy, Spain, Portugal, and France, and may be found in significant numbers in North America and in still other countries throughout the world. By every measure, the Roman Catholic Church has more members by far than any other Christian tradition. It is known to its members as *the* Catholic Church (*catholic* meaning "universal, comprehensive, inclusive of all parts"), or simply "the Church." Giving credence to this conception is its supranational hierarchical structure, centered in the Pope (no other religious body of near comparable size is so centrally controlled) and, until the mid-1960s, its common use of Latin in worship, theological study, and formal Church business. Nevertheless, it has traditionally given considerable scope for variations in general practice and additional practices to develop in specific cultural locales and, therewith, a strong linkage between faith and ethnic identity. The supranational, centralized, and (until recently) linguistically homogeneous structure of the Roman Catholic Church, of course, keeps these vernacular tendencies in check. As has been the case for most Eastern Orthodox Christians, for most Roman Catholics being Roman Catholic has not been the result of an individual act of free affiliation. Thus, to be Irish or Italian, for many at least, is to be Catholic—though of course how seriously one takes one's Roman Catholic identity has always been a personal choice. Nevertheless, whether one is a member of the Roman Catholic Church or not is becoming more a matter of individual affiliation as societies become increasingly pluralistic.

Like Eastern Orthodox Christianity, Roman Catholicism considers itself to be carrying on original and authentic Christianity passed down in an unbroken line from the first Apostles. But for Roman Catholics this connection with its origin is conceived more as a continuous line of development than as an unchanging, timeless legacy. It considers the Eastern Church to have departed from itself, not the other way around. Several matters led to the split in 1054 and these matters remain controversial to the present. The relation between the two traditions in recent decades, however, is much more amicable than it has been at any time in the last nine and a half centuries, but major differences still divide them. The most important of these issues has been and remains the institution of the papacy. Orthodox dispute the whole idea that the Bishop of Rome (the Pope) has greater authority of an administrative or judicial nature than the other ancient patriarchates (Constantinople, Antioch, Jerusalem, and Alexandria), and they reject altogether that he has legislative authority to make declarations of doctrine or on any other matter of Christian essentials. Such authority for them belongs solely to an Ecumenical Church Council representing the whole Church everywhere. To the contrary, Roman Catholics have traditionally held that the primacy of the Bishop of Rome in these respects was authorized by Jesus, having made Peter (who ended up in Rome) chief among the Apostles. The Eastern Church declared itself separate from Roman Catholicism in 1054 because it refused to accept the Pope's administrative authority over them and his alleged legislative authority to make innovations in essential matters such as the Nicene Creed. For Roman Catholics, though, the hierarchy of the Church, represented by the Pope, is "the possessor, the guarantor and the interpreter of the tradition of Christ, including the scriptures."[18] Somewhat like the U.S. judicial system culminating in the Supreme Court, Roman Catholics have traditionally believed that its hierarchy culminating in the Pope has by Christ been given the authority to interpret what is divine law for Christians. In that sense, judicially (though probably most Roman Catholic theologians would not say legislatively) the Pope has the last word in declaring the limits of faith and morals. However, though the First Vatican Council (1869–1870) acknowledged the "infallibility" of the Pope in Council and when pronouncing on dogma, it is rare that such authority is ever invoked. In any case, the meaning, reference, and limits of papal "infallibility" are at present highly controversial issues among Roman Catholic theologians.

This emphasis upon law, legal authority, and obedience to Christ's representative on earth that became characteristic of the Western Church may be traced as far back as the late fourth century when the Church fatefully entered into a marriage of convenience, so to speak, with the Roman state, with its sophisticated, hierarchical understanding of the rule of law and its highly developed legal and political institutions. Thereby Christianity (Eastern as well as Western) left behind its status as the religion of a persecuted minority (a church of martyrs) and became favored by the state (and thus by the wealthy and powerful). Not only embracing favored status, it took on the role of a legitimating ideology for the state and, with the state's power of enforcing uniformity, it assumed jurisdiction over the whole of society and all of its members (no longer just those who were Christian by voluntary association). It has taken a long time for the Church, Protestant, Catholic, and Eastern Orthodox, to come to realize that a society can function reasonably well without sameness of religious faith—not until the so-called radical wing of the Protestant Reformation that repudiated this "marriage" of church and state had come to leave its mark on subsequent Western culture.[19] There are signs that significant parts of the Roman Catholic Church (e.g., in post-Communist Poland) and the Eastern Orthodox Church (e.g., in post-Communist Russia) are still reluctant to embrace the idea of church-state separation.

The central and foremost approach to God in Christ for Roman Catholics is the Liturgy of the Eucharist (formerly called the Mass), especially as set within the annual liturgical cycle of holy days and seasons. The life cycle of Catholics is celebrated in the sacraments of Baptism, Confirmation, personal and communal Confession (now called Reconciliation), Anointing for healing (formerly Extreme Unction), Marriage (if married), and Ordination (if ordained). Other rites pertaining to life changes, celebrations, and death are also an important part of religious life for all Roman Catholics.[20] For those who join a religious order, an initiating ritual of Profession is celebrated within the Eucharistic liturgy. A ritual structuring of life is especially marked for those who are members of Roman Catholic religious communities, for their lives are lived out in a context set by a daily cycle of liturgical prayer, the Divine Office, which normally includes a celebration of the Eucharist.

The way of sacred rite thus has primacy for all Roman Catholics, though more so for some than for others. Some participate daily in the Mass as well as perform other ritual observances. Pilgrimage to shrines and sacred places is a highly developed practice among Catholics. The Mass itself, in comparison with the Divine Liturgy of the Eastern Orthodox Church, has traditionally been simpler, less elaborate, less mysterious (or at least more effort has gone into explaining it), and for the most part more solemn. The traditional solemnity of the Latin Mass, however, has been significantly transformed through changes wrought by the Second Vatican Council (1962–1965) into a much more joyful and communally participative liturgy. In any case, to participate fully and faithfully in the

Mass is sacramentally to return to and enter into Christ's redemptive love, and come to be at-one with his sacrifice of himself, his death and resurrection, for the redemption of the world. So to participate is quite tangibly to receive his body and his blood in order that the community will be enabled to live in the contemporary world as the manifestation of the Body of Christ. Those who thus receive the Body affirm its power as they live the life God intends humans to live in relationship with God and all people, both now and in the world to come. The primary aim here is not an experiential (mystical) participation in God, though that is not at all ruled out. The primary aim is upon righteousness, on coming to be right with God in one's life in the world and conforming to his divine intention (integrating the ways of sacred rite with right action). Nowadays Catholics speak of this aim as the unity of a community whose love affirms what all human communities are intended to be, one in love. .

Roman Catholics have ministers specially ordained to transmit the sacramental grace of Christ. These are consecrated ritual specialists understood to be called by Christ and consecrated through Ordination to serve the people. Bishops, priests, and deacons are believed to be links of an unbroken chain of "apostolic succession" back to the original Apostles and therewith to Christ. Since the early Middle Ages priests and bishops have had to be celibate.

Beyond common participation in sacred rite, there has been in the Roman Catholic tradition a broad acceptance of members being involved, and encouragement to become involved, in further aspects of religious life—specifically, in one or more of the different ways of being religious, with no expectation that participation in any, let alone all, is required. All that need be present is the deep motivation, the inner personal "calling," to do so, so long as it does not interfere with one's basic duties as a good Catholic. From time to time significant expressions of each of the ways of being religious has emerged and blossomed in the Roman Catholic Church. Though many persist over centuries to this day, many also have diminished and died. Often they have been associated with the formation of "a religious order." Traditionally, Roman Catholics have distinguished between "religious vocations" and "secular vocations." (One should bear in mind that the significance of this distinction has recently been undergoing considerable change and will likely turn out to be something very different from what it has been in the past. One general tendency of this largely secularizing development has been to minimize the difference between the two, especially as to the traditionally elevated, "sacred" or "holy" status of religious vocations. Protestantism rejected the distinction altogether.)

The distinction between secular and religious vocations is complicated by the fact that it does not coincide with the distinction between ordained and nonordained Christians. There are, for example, "secular priests" and "women religious." "Religious vocations" are formally distinguished by virtue of persons undertaking religious vows (usually vows of poverty, chastity, and obedience, though not always, and not always understood by all in the same sense) upon entering one of many "religious orders" of the Church (which are characterized by following a specific set of spiritual disciplines), and thereby taking upon themselves to live by Jesus' teachings in the New Testament Gospels ("the evangelical counsels"). "Secular" Christians have not·been understood to be subject to such demanding expectations; they have only been expected to abide by basic moral guidelines such as the Ten Commandments—except for "secular clergy," who of course have special expectations relating to their liturgical responsibilities. In effect, to be "religious" in this sense is to become a monastic of a sort, yet most "religious" (in modern times at least) have not been connected with a monastery, least of all an enclosed ("cloistered") one. ("Women religious" are called "nuns" or "sisters." Nuns are cloistered, and engage in lives set apart from other people. Sisters engage in varieties of ministries, and live among the people in their communities. "Male religious" are called "brothers" or [upon ordination] "priests." "Monks" are brothers [and ordained brothers called priests] who live in monasteries with other monks.)

Traditionally at least, a Roman Catholic who was *really* serious about her or his faith—that is, who passionately sought at-onement with God and felt called by God to follow a more disciplined way of life—would be called "a religious" and could be recognized as such by the official Church through an act of Profession. Most of these would be encouraged to join with others in an already established community and "rule of life." It has always been possible for new religious orders to come into being, however, which typically first began with the "calling" of a single person who then came to gather others around him or her.[21] There are also persons who might become lay associates of some order, as in Third Order Franciscans or Benedictine Oblates.

Roman Catholics who are drawn to the way of right action have found support and have been encouraged from earliest times in the Church.[22] Above all, this has happened by way of attempts to put directly into practice Jesus' teachings (which summon one to go far beyond the call of common moral duty) and especially to feed, clothe, and otherwise care for the poor, the sick, and the destitute. Such actions are typically engaged in out of the conviction that as it is done to the least of these persons it is done (simultaneously) to Jesus (Matthew 25:40) *and* that such actions, done in the right frame of mind, are a way that Jesus carries on his redemptive work in the world in and through the lives of his followers. Traditionally, this has been especially true of Roman Catholics who, upon entering a "religious order," thereby place themselves under the "evangelical counsels" (i.e., Jesus' Gospel admonitions), in comparison to those who, remaining in "secular life," were only expected to follow general ethical guidelines. Because the distinction between "religious" and "secular" vocations has been blurred somewhat in recent years, many contemporary Roman Catholics not under formal vows are seeking to live out their lives with this vision. In any case, within every generation such efforts have been carried on, sometimes in a more organized way, sometimes in a quiet, individualized way. Many (in terms of sheer numbers, probably most) Catholic religious orders have been oriented to one or another form of active service. In addition to charitable work, education, social work, pastoral work, and missionary work should be counted here as well. Furthermore, most communal Catholic religious orders from the beginning have sought to realize a countercultural form of life, characterized by mutual love, absence of competition, life pared down to simple essentials, and communal property.

Since the middle of the twentieth century, there has developed an especially strong sensibility toward matters of social justice among most Roman Catholics.[23] In the Third World, this has found expression in the movement known as Liberation Theology, which interprets the Gospel in terms of its implications for social change and rectification of social inequities. Most of the persons who have been identified as saints in the history of the Church are persons whose lives have been occupied with extraordinary charitable work. (This is true in the Eastern Orthodox tradition as well.) Among the best contemporary examples of this way of being religious in the Roman Catholic tradition are Mother Teresa of Calcutta and her Sisters and Brothers of Charity, Dorothy Day and the Catholic Worker movement, Edwina Gately, and the pastoral martyrs of El Salvador, male and female.[24]

Those who are motivated in the direction of the way of reasoned inquiry have likewise almost always found strong encouragement and support in the Roman Catholic tradition.[25] This is in large measure due to the Roman Catholic conception of their own understanding of the revelation of God in Christ. They conceive that understanding to be something that gradually unfolds and develops over time as Church theologians rethink its nature and implications within each new generation under the guidance of the Spirit of God. Theological reflection, then, within the Roman Catholic tradition is supposed to be a way that the Spirit of God guides and maintains the faithful in the unfolding truth of the Gospel. The work of the theologian is regarded as a very high calling among Roman Catholics, placing the way of reasoned inquiry, perhaps, as a close second to sacred rite—traditionally even higher in priority of emphasis than right action. Consequently, theological literacy has as high if not a higher priority among Roman Catholics as any other Christian tradition. A very strong theological and philosophical component to Catholic education in the liberal arts and to seminary curricula for Catholic priests remains characteristic to this day, much stronger than that found in non-Roman Catholic Christian institutions of higher education.

The Christian pursuit of at-onement with God through serious and sustained theological (and philosophical) inquiry received early on a powerful model in the life and writings of Augustine of Hippo (354–430).[26] Augustine set the precedent for one of two major strands of theological-philosophical inquiry in the Western Church—one that is suffused with a passionate love of truth, where inquiry is a personal quest to come more deeply into rapport with it, and which seeks to culminate in a mystical union with it. In that sense it is a path that combines or fuses the way of reasoned inquiry with that of mystical quest. For

Augustine and this strand of theological thinking, all intellectual inquiry at its profoundest is a dialogue with God, who is the ultimate truth and the light of all understanding. Salvation in Christ serves to transform the heart of a person, reorienting it from self-gratification to love of truth for its own sake—a reorientation requisite for full knowledge of truth in any field, according to Augustinian thinking. This strand came to be particularly linked with the Benedictine monastic tradition in the West, founded by Benedict of Nursia (480–550), which placed a high priority on education and theological study yet encouraged them as aspects of a spiritual quest.[27] It has sometimes been called "monastic theology."

The other major strand came to fullest expression in the twelfth and thirteenth centuries with the rise of the *secular* universities (secular in the sense that enrollment did not entail religious vows or obedience to a religious rule of life)—namely, "scholastic theology."[28] The most famous exemplar of this second strand is Thomas Aquinas (1225–1274). Scholastic theology, in contrast to monastic theology, has sought, through strictly rational argumentation, to develop a comprehensive system of theological truths that harmonizes apparent divergences among the voices that convey divine revelation (including scripture) and the conclusions of natural reason and extends their implications to issues of vital contemporary concern. Here, too, participants in the tradition of scholastic theological inquiry understand and experience the elaboration of systematic theology as an awesome drawing near to the omniscient wisdom of God. For Aquinas, *every* act of comprehension, every valid and true judgment, exercises the "nobler" element of the mind (*lumen intellectus agentis*, the "light of the active intellect") by which human beings participate in God's knowledge of things and fulfill their true end of exercising likeness to God. Every such act and judgment thus is not only an expansion of the knower's own being but also an expanding participation in God's nature and, by virtue of the analogy of being between creation and Creator, a distant and imperfect but nonetheless genuine and positive knowledge of God.

Catholics who feel called to pursue the way of mystical quest, at least since the beginnings of communal monasticism in the fourth-century deserts of Egypt and Syria, have generally found acceptance if not always encouragement in the Roman Catholic tradition[29]: "If you feel the call, then go right ahead and God be with you!—as long as it doesn't lead you into conflict with Church authority." The Church fairly early on encouraged the organization and regularization of those called to a monastic mode of life. Once monasticism became an accepted social institution, by no means all of those who entered monastic life could be supposed to be committed to the mystical quest. Nevertheless, the setting was of a contemplative nature that largely supported the would-be mystic, some monastic institutions more so than others.[30] Though there are many well known individual mystics within the Western Church up to the time of the Protestant Reformation—for example, Bernard of Clairvaux (1090–1153), Hildegard of Bingen (1098–1179), Meister Eckhart (c. 1260–1327), John Ruysbroeck (1293–1381), Julian of Norwich (c. 1342–c.1413)—and a good many within the Roman Catholic Church since—for example, Teresa of Avila (1515–1582), John of the Cross (1542–1591), Jeanne-Marie Guyon (1648–1717), and Charles de Foucauld (1858–1916)—for the most part they have not been regarded as exemplifying a way of being religious for all Christians.

A mystical experience of God has rarely been regarded as the birthright, so to speak, of the Christian in Western Christianity that it has been in Eastern Christianity. Instead, mystics and mystical experiences have tended to be regarded (officially at least) as unique products of the miraculous and unpredictable sovereign intervention of God, not on a continuum with other ordinary folk and ordinary experiences. In consequence, although there have been many books written by major Western Christian mystics in the attempt to provide guidelines for persons called to the mystical quest, several traditions of meditational prayer (e.g., Franciscan, Ignatian, Sulpician), several monastic religious orders explicitly identified as contemplative (e.g., Cistercian, Carmelite), and long-standing traditions of spiritual direction,[31] the Roman Catholic tradition by and large has shied away from identifying (or encouraging the idea of) a definite path at the end of which is to be found, in this life at least, a mystical union with God. Theologically, it has seemed that this prospect would threaten the idea of the sovereignty of divine grace that has been strongly emphasized in the Western Church. The practical implication, according to Roman Catholic teaching, is that deep mystical experience is regarded as the culmination of a path for which one has been individually called and gifted by God and not a result of following some general prescription or recipe. More contemporary Catholic approaches to mysticism stress the variety of forms that may beckon any serious believer to quest for the mystery of God's presence within oneself and in all things.[32] Persons drawn to this quest are encouraged to study the great mystics, engage a trustworthy spiritual advisor, and become aware of stages through which mystics typically have passed and of the dangers they have encountered.

Though somewhat different accounts are given by different mystics, the development undergone by Christian mystics is generally held to involve a comprehensive inward transformation prompted and governed by divine grace (purgation), a bestowal of mystical knowledge and insight (illumination), and ultimately a mystical at-onement with God in Christ (union), particularly in terms of an identification with Christ's passion and sufferings.[33] The process generally is spoken of in language that intimates more passivity or surrender to the mystical graces of God than activity or cooperation on the part of the mystic, in contrast to the language of synergistic cooperation that characterizes Eastern Orthodox spirituality.[34]

Those motivated toward the way of devotion in Roman Catholicism have generally found much encouragement over the centuries, particularly in terms of private or at least more personal devotional practices that supplement or complement participation in the sacramental life of the Church (as opposed to ones that might compete with sacramental participation).[35] Some of these practices were directly related to sacramental life, such as Adoration of the Blessed Sacrament. Others stemmed from pastoral guidance and advice given in connection with the sacrament of Confession. Some blended with other ways of being religious such as shamanic mediation and sacred rite—as in devotional practices oriented to one or another of the saints, especially the Virgin Mary, pilgrimage to shrines, or veneration of relics; some in relation to mystical quest—as in the prayer of the Rosary; and some in connection with right action. Private devotional prayer has always been encouraged, even when it is done in connection with the more formal liturgy of worship.

Devotional practice and a personalized devotion to Jesus or Mary, then, is pervasive in Roman Catholicism, but, as with ways of being religious other than sacred rite, it is deemed by most to be more an option than an essential. Until recently, it was rare to find in Roman Catholicism the conviction (a sense that is pervasive in traditional Protestantism) that a vital devotional life and a personal, devotional relationship to Jesus are the heart of what it means to be Christian—with at least one important and major exception. In the late Middle Ages, prior to, but laying an important precedent for, the Protestant Reformation, a movement called the *Devotio Moderna* became widespread throughout Europe.[36] The most well known of its lasting legacies is the classic devotional work, the *Imitation of Christ* by Thomas à Kempis (c. 1380–1471). It is interesting to find this stress on a vital devotional relationship to Jesus very strong among contemporary Charismatic Catholics, which movement will be explained later.

Persons who are attracted to the way of shamanic mediation in Catholicism have generally been accorded a place but not always a welcome reception and hardly ever an active encouragement. The Church's hierarchy has for the most part been wary of spontaneous, charismatic phenomena of a shamanic sort (as have most established churches in Protestantism), especially anything that might prove recalcitrant to clerical authority, and has sought to ascertain its genuineness before according its endorsement. By their very nature, such phenomena are not subject to external mundane control. Moreover, the Church has always held that not all shamanic phenomena are the work of the Spirit of God, that some are due to evil forces that must be carefully guarded against and counteracted. Nevertheless, at the level of popular piety, there has always been widespread belief in the possibility of divine intervention on behalf of ordinary people's pressing needs and that people who are deemed close to God are likely able to bring about or influence such intervention. This is certainly a large part of what lies behind the so-called cult of the saints in Roman Catholicism.[37] It also lies behind the widespread belief in visionary experiences, such as apparitions of the Virgin Mary at Lourdes, Guadalupe, and Medjugorje, around which so many miracles are alleged to happen.[38]

Since medieval times it has been commonly assumed in Roman Catholicism that, to be genuine, a saint must actually perform publicly attestable miracles either during her lifetime or after her death for those who call upon her aid. The stories of saints throughout the ages are filled with accounts of miraculous cures, rescues, and supernatural interventions of one sort or another.[39] This is particularly true of the earliest years of Christianity as recorded in the Acts of the Apostles in the New Testament. And according to the New Testament Gospels, Jesus himself demonstrated shamanic powers throughout his public career. But since the early centuries of the Church, the Christian way of shamanic mediation has played no central role. Like mystical experience, the Western Church has largely considered the *miraculous* "gifts of the Holy Spirit" to be not the "birthright" of each Christian but the result of the unpredictable sovereign intervention of God: when it occurs, handle it as best you can, but don't expect it, least of all in yourself.

Nevertheless, in the middle of the twentieth century a remarkable phenomenon known as the Charismatic Movement took hold among a group of Catholics in the United States, partly through the influence of certain Pentecostal Protestant groups, which has since become a major movement throughout the world, largely ignoring Christian denominational lines.[40] Though it clearly includes significant aspects of the way of devotion (akin to those of Evangelical Protestantism), it centers upon the experience of supernatural empowerment by the Holy Spirit ("Baptism in the Holy Spirit") believed available for each Christian, to live the Christian life and carry on the *supernatural* ministry of Christ in the world—that is, upon a peculiarly Christian form of the way of shamanic mediation. Despite continuing suspicions by many Catholics, it has had a largely positive, renewing effect upon Catholic parishes throughout the world and has even received the blessing of the Pope.

Protestant Christianity

Protestant Christianity now predominates (though not exclusively) in Northern Europe, North America, Australia, in some African nations, and may be found in significant numbers in every continent and, except for predominantly Muslim areas, in almost every nation—yet in total number of members it is considerably smaller than Roman Catholicism but considerably larger than Eastern Orthodoxy. Protestantism is not a single institution, as are Roman Catholicism and to a large extent, though more loosely united, Eastern Orthodoxy (not including Oriental Orthodox Churches). Looked at as a whole, it would seem to be anti-institutional on a large or universal scale, for there are actually more than 20,000 different Protestant traditions, each with its own institutional structure and in some cases different doctrine, many of which (at least at some time in their history) have fiercely prized their independence from the others.[41] A better understanding of Protestant Christianity may be had by conceiving it as a *vernacular reformulation* of Western Christianity,[42] begun in sixteenth century Northern Europe, that chose to abandon what seemed to have become an opaque medium through which divine revelation was supposed to be transmitted. That medium—namely, the Roman Catholic Church—had come to be for them a foreign language and culture (Latin)

in which worship and divine revelation were formulated; a kind of spiritual bu-
reaucracy (of saints, "religious," and priests) that stood between the lay believer
and God; a centralized, hierarchical, and distant structure of Church authority un-
responsive to local concerns; and, not least, an institution infected by human corruption throughout.

The dominant way of being religious in the Western European Church, as
already explained, had been sacred rite, but on the eve of the Protestant
Reformation (even Roman Catholic historians now concede) sacred rite was suffering from widespread degeneration. Among the characteristic vices to which
practice of the way of sacred rite is subject (covered in Chapter 5), widespread
examples of the following could be found: idolatry of ritual form and symbol on
the one hand, perfunctory and wooden execution of ritual on the other; ritual incompetence; sacramental insensibility; and use of sacred rite, symbol, and status
to serve and promote profane interests. The sacred forms had for many ceased
to afford transparent access to "ultimate reality." Simultaneously, among many of
the reformers at least, there was a hunger for personal assurance of salvation—
the very kind of existential need to which the way of devotion is addressed. At
the heart of the Protestant Reformation, then, we discover a comprehensive shift
in spiritual sensibility taking place, *from first priority upon the way of sacred rite
to first priority upon the way of devotion.* The alternative to which the reformers
turned was what seemed to be direct access to divine revelation in the voice of a
vernacular scripture that they could read for themselves, biblical expository
preaching, communal worship in their own language and cultural forms, and an
immediate, personal, devotional relationship to Jesus Christ. Everything else, especially claims made by the Catholic Church to sacred tradition outside what
seemed to them to be the plain sense of scripture, appeared to the reformers to
be a presumptuous, even idolatrous, identification of the traditions of men (i.e.,
human culture) with divine revelation, and so it was subject to rejection. The
point was to simplify and eliminate everything that stood between the simple lay
believer and God as revealed in Christ.[43] Especially repugnant in this connection
was the Catholic distinction between religious and lay vocations, apparently placing the former on a higher level of respect and closeness to God because of
something that they outwardly did (i.e., join a religious order and conform to its
rule of life) quite apart from whether they did or did not have inward faith. In
throwing out the distinction, most Protestants threw out monasticism as an option altogether and most of the spiritual and ascetic disciplines that went with it.

The option against what was (Roman) Catholic was, for perhaps most
Protestants, an option for what was vernacular. This was not entirely true, however, for it was sacred scripture read in the vernacular, not the vernacular itself,
that became the single criterion for judging what was of God in local (vernacular) culture and what was not. Nevertheless, because the Protestant Reformation
was a vernacular reformulation of Christianity, each local culture and social group
where it took place came to shape the peculiar form of Protestantism that rose

within it differently than the forms that rose elsewhere. The same has happened in every subsequent vernacular reformulation in which another Protestant denomination has come to birth to the present day.

Because of Protestantism's emphasis upon the Bible as *the* channel of divine revelation and upon each Christian's need to become biblically literate—"to read, mark, and inwardly digest" the Word of God, indeed, spiritually "to feed upon it"—it was natural that certain aspects of the way of reasoned inquiry became pervasive in Protestantism. For the most part (until recent times) such study has often not been historically oriented, as generally theological literacy was more or less historically oriented within Roman Catholicism. Nor has it been as philosophically oriented or as speculative, being intent on recovering the full, divine Biblical revelation liberated from what it conceived to be accretions of human traditions and philosophies. Serious theological reflection in Protestantism, thus, primarily functions to interpret scripture, and on that basis aims to develop a comprehensive understanding of the revelation of God in Christ among the faithful in meeting the challenges of the current day. Until the employment of modern historical scholarship, Protestants have generally approached scripture with the assumption that it was possible to ignore pretty much entirely and dispense with the intervening history of interpretation, and gain direct access to the meaning of the text as something transhistorical, equally accessible in every age and context. Nowadays, however, that assumption is no longer generally shared, except in very conservative Protestant circles. Nevertheless Protestant biblical scholarship, and theological reflection growing out of it, early became a serious quest, both personal and systematic, to come to know and understand the saving revelation of God in Christ, especially in Lutheran and Reformed traditions; and it remains so to this day[44]—though more so in conservative circles and Fundamentalist circles, with laypersons as well as clergy, than is generally true in liberal circles.

Of the several Protestant traditions that emerged in the sixteenth century, viewed from the perspective of historical distance and seeing what subsequently came of the precedents that were then set, different groupings stand out. First is the division between sacramental and nonsacramental Protestants. There is a widespread but mistaken notion that Protestantism as such is nonsacramental. While the way of devotion has historically played a major and at times central role in the Lutheran and Anglican/Episcopal traditions, nevertheless they are markedly sacramental, meaning that they both embody and place significant priority on the way of sacred rite and consider the sacraments as "sure and certain" means by which the divine grace of God in Christ is communicated to the participant.[45] Nevertheless, some Lutherans and some American Episcopalians (commonly identified by the phrase "low church" as opposed to "high church") appear to be almost nonsacramental in practice. Virtually all other Protestants are nonsacramental, though clearly some are more so than others. In other words, they place no central priority upon, though some certainly do retain aspects of, the way of sacred rite. Some of these Protestant traditions, depending on the social class with which they are associated, retain a moderately formal and aesthetically pleasing order of worship (e.g., Reformed/Presbyterian churches and, among churches of more recent vintage, some Methodist and some Congregational churches). But no Protestant tradition other than Lutheran and Episcopal, to my knowledge, retains the idea that the sacraments are "sure and certain means of grace." While all view the sacraments as symbolically representing the realities of the Gospel, none (officially at least) view them as actually *presenting* those realities. Accordingly, none identify their ministers as priests (i.e., specialists in sacramental ritual). (As a matter of fact, most Lutherans prefer not to use the title "priest" in reference to their pastors, though Anglicans/Episcopalians don't hesitate to do so.)[46]

A second major division among the Protestant traditions that emerged in the sixteenth century was between those who sought a radical separation between church and state (and between church and culture) and those who wanted to keep them together. The roots of the idea of a church-state "marriage" go back to the fourth century when Christianity became the official religion of the Roman state. It is the idea that the church should be the church of an entire community, not just of a group within it, and that to belong to a particular ethnic or national group means that one also belongs to a particular church. Those Protestant traditions constituting the mainstream of the Protestant Reformation initially kept this idea. They sought to reform the whole of the Church within the particular state in which they resided and drew upon the power of the state to assist their efforts. Those who rejected the idea constitute what is often called the "radical wing" of the Reformation (in England they were called "dissenters" as opposed to "consenters"). They sought to have the Church be made up only of those persons who had faith, who believed in and personally appropriated the salvation of God in Christ, and who voluntarily were ready to stand apart, be different, and live a life that bore witness to God and his will for humankind. Accordingly, they rejected the validity of infant baptism, which had become for many a perfunctory cultural practice, and early on came to be known as Anabaptists (re-baptizers). This was to place central priority upon the way of right action along with the way of devotion among the churches of the radical reformation—for example, Mennonite, Swiss Brethren, Hutterite, and Quaker—and to a somewhat lesser extent among their later offspring—including Puritan, Baptist, Congregational, and other Free Church traditions. Not all of these traditions emphasized the way of right action to the same extent or in the same manner.[47] Those that go back the farthest generally have emphasized it more strongly, usually undertaking a radically nonviolent and pacifist stance, a vigorous involvement in social welfare activities, and a strong commitment to an alternative communal lifestyle.

The more recent offspring have typically been concerned more narrowly with personal conduct and inner attitudes, though they have strongly emphasized local, congregational control at the expense of granting authority to larger denominational bodies. In any case, the most influential legacy of the Radical Reformation has been the ideas of church-state separation, freedom of conscience and free association in religion as fundamental human rights, and freedom from governmental interference in matters of religion. The influence of this legacy has been so pervasive—allied as it has been with the secular Enlightenment concern to keep government free from interference by religious ideas and religious groups—that most Protestants and probably most Roman Catholics in modern Western nations take it for granted.[48]

It should be mentioned here that a concern for the way of right action has never been absent from the mainstream Protestant churches, both in terms of personal conduct and broader concerns with social issues, though it has clearly waxed and waned over time.[49] The reformers' elimination of the hierarchical division between religious and laypersons served to endow the activities and relationships of ordinary life with a new depth of meaning; it became a field of religious endeavor. Now occupational work of all kinds could be experienced as a sacred calling. Every aspect of life, individual, social, institutional, came to seem open to question and change in order to be brought into line with God's will and purpose. This orientation became even more emphasized in traditions influenced by John Calvin (1509–1564), giving rise to what has come to be known as the Protestant work ethic. There, success in disciplined application of oneself to one's worldly calling, social duties, and personal responsibilities came to be interpreted as one of the signs of at-onement with God.

Nevertheless, right action for mainstream Protestantism has for the most part been subordinated to a primary emphasis on the way of devotion (or on the ways of devotion and sacred rite together in sacramental Protestant traditions) until the emergence of what is called Liberal Protestantism and the Social Gospel Movement in the late nineteenth century. Liberal Protestantism, which has been a movement within mainstream Protestant churches and never a denomination in itself, is an attempt to reformulate Christianity on the basis of modern thinking, modern learning, and modern scientific understandings (i.e., on the basis of the secular humanistic ideas of the European Enlightenment)—to make Christianity credible to modern men and women and to modify or jettison all that cannot be so modified. Virtually the only ways of being religious straightforwardly compatible with the ideas of the Enlightenment are the way of right action and, to some extent, a largely secularized version of the way of reasoned inquiry. Indeed, many Enlightenment figures—foremost among them Immanuel Kant—held that the essential, rational function of religion was to serve as a foundation for the practice of universal morality and social justice. The implication was that, were religion to be involved in anything else, especially anything at odds with that function, it would be a corruption of that essential function and would in that measure merit criticism and reform. Though there was much more involved in the rise of Liberal Protestantism (and its near cousin, Roman Catholic Modernism, which appeared briefly in the late nineteenth century, then was crushed, only to be revived in altered guise in the latter twentieth century), its practical thrust has been to follow out these Enlightenment ideas in prioritizing the way of right action in relation to, and largely at the expense of, all other ways of being religious.[50] One of the specific results of this development in the late nineteenth century was a deepening concern with matters of social justice, exemplified in the Social Gospel Movement founded by Walter Rauschenbusch (1861–1918), which sought not just change in an individual's heart and action but change in the structures of society that condition an individual's thinking and conduct.[51] The Social Gospel Movement as originally conceived did not last, but its priority of concern with matters of social justice has lasted among Liberal Protestants and it continues strongly to the present day, now linking up with the movement known as Liberation Theology (primarily based in Roman Catholic and Third World cultures).

What now identifies itself as Evangelical Protestantism came to birth in the eighteenth century with what is called the Pietist Movement in Europe and the First Great Awakening in North America. This development was in part a reaction to degeneration in the then existing forms of mainstream Protestantism.[52] While it renewed many of the classic themes of the Reformation, it exemplified even more completely (and at times almost exclusively) the way of devotion, in its insistence upon the need for a person to have a definite conversion experience—surrendering one's life wholly to God in Christ so one might come to know personally his love and forgiveness (i.e., to "invite Jesus to come into your heart to become your personal lord and savior"), to cultivate a simple devotional reliance upon the providential grace of God, and to join in fellowship with others in a pilgrimage through life that eventually will lead, at death, to a "heavenly home" with Jesus and dear ones among the faithful who have died before. It was a simple version of the Christian faith, easily communicated, met a number of profound (especially emotional) religious needs of people, and especially appealed to persons of scant education, meager economic status, and little cultural sophistication. This is not to say that it had no appeal to the better educated, the economically privileged, or patrons of high culture. It has, however, put little stock in refined theological and biblical learning, differences between the major Protestant denominations in creed and form of worship, and institutional structures. All those things may have some value and place, depending on different persons' needs but, above all such considerations, what really mattered in their judgment was a simple, childlike faith in Christ. The true Church, it held, was made up of persons with this kind of faith wherever they might be; it was not made up of outward differences. In effect, the movement of Evangelical Protestantism lent support to the Radical Reformation legacy of freedom of religion and a privatization and individualization of religion that is in large measure the corollary of separation of church and state (at least as it came to be understood in the United States). Evangelical Protestantism has become immensely popular and, at times, with the help of evangelists and revivalists, the effort to "win souls for Christ" has spread like wildfire. Though the movement has waxed and waned over the years, it remains strong and vital to the current time, directly giving rise in the last two centuries to missionary efforts around the globe and in virtually every living language.[53] An interesting recent development in Evangelical Protestantism is the remarkable growth of large, so-called "nondenominational" community churches (sometimes several thousand members strong), completely independent of established Protestant denominations, which then spawn daughter congregations.

This picture of Evangelical Protestantism suggests that it is exclusively identified with the way of devotion. At times, it has been just that. But any religious movement as large and diverse as it is, over time, must begin to address those existential needs of its members not directly served by the way of devotion, as well as deal with those passages of scripture that seem directly to encourage other ways of being religious. And so, aspects of each of the other ways have emerged from time to time in given Evangelical congregations and in the lives of individual members, though these usually remain strictly subordinated to a central emphasis on the way of devotion. It should be said also that Evangelical Protestanism has generally emphasized aspects of the way of right action: living a changed personal life in accordance with one's inner change of heart and communicating the Gospel of personal salvation to others. Charitable activities, involvement in social reform frequently characterize Evangelical Christians, while a commitment to high standards of moral character in all relationships is generally characteristic of all Evangelicals (despite occasional notorious lapses in individual cases). Also, they manifest at times what appear to be aspects of the way of reasoned inquiry in their study of scripture to discern the fullness of God's revelation. Scriptural study and biblical theology at times become quite sophisticated in Evangelical circles. And at times aspects of mystical quest, shamanic mediation, and sacred rite are evident. Interestingly, some of the pressure to meet demand for other ways of being religious is handled in yet another way, at least in religiously pluralistic cultures like the United States: considerable numbers of individuals move between one Evangelical church and another, and between Evangelical churches and other Protestant churches (and between them and Roman Catholic and Eastern Orthodox churches), depending on personal need and available supply.

Not all of Evangelical Protestantism has been so strongly focused on the way of devotion. One of the most well known of evangelists during the early years was John Wesley (1703–1791), founder of Methodism—which became, despite Wesley's intention, a "dissenting" church independent of the state supported, "consenting" Church of England.[54] Interestingly, one of Wesley's impacts on the Evangelical Movement was to stress that a personal relationship with Jesus Christ needed to be expressed in a *life of personal and social holiness* empowered and directed by the Holy Spirit. In consequence, at least in the Methodist tradition and its many offshoots, there has been a particularly strong alliance between the way of devotion and the way of right action (more so at some times than others). A similar alliance (if not a complete shift to a variety of the way of right action) is evident in some of the nineteenth-century Millennialist movements in the United States, which focused on the expectation of the imminence of Christ's Second Coming.[55] For example, it clearly can be seen in different ways in the communitarian Shaker and Oneida Perfectionist movements, in the Mormon Church founded by Joseph Smith (1805–1844), in the Seventh Day Adventist Church founded by Ellen G. White (1827–1915), and in the Jehovah's Witness organization founded by Charles Taze Russell (1852–1916). And finally, an alliance between devotion and right action—and probably a subordination of devotion to right action—must be recognized as well in the rise and growth (primarily in the present century) of the Fundamentalist movement within largely Evangelical circles (but by no means identical with it). Fundamentalism has sought to check the tide of "liberalism" in the Church and "secular humanism" in society on the basis of non-negotiable fundamentals—above all the fundamental principle that sacred scripture in its "literal meaning" is the infallible word of God that is absolutely normative for individual and social conduct.[56] Its stress upon conformity to absolute biblical norms of belief and conduct, despite its avowal of the Evangelical emphasis upon devotional surrender to Christ, indicates a priority on a certain kind of right action as the means of at-onement with God. Fundamentalist Protestants have become increasingly politically active in recent years, though less in hopes of reforming society on biblical principles than in stopping the state from contributing to what they see to be the further erosion of biblically based values in society and culture.

The way of shamanic mediation has had little if any place in Protestantism until around the beginning of this century with the rise of the Pentecostal Movement and the more recent Charismatic Movement, both of which began in the United States but have spread throughout many parts of the world. In the middle of the nineteenth century a movement called the Holiness Movement began, primarily in Methodist circles. Its followers were dedicated to reviving John Wesley's teaching concerning the life of "Christian perfection" in personal and social holiness to which each Christian was called, but which could become a present reality only as a person gave herself over to the direction and enabling power of the Holy Spirit—a process called the experience of "entire sanctification" that was supposed to be subsequent to and distinct from Christian conversion (called the experience of "justification").[57] From the Holiness Movement, a number of Protestant denominations have grown: among them, the Free Methodist Church, the Church of the Nazarene, the Salvation Army, and the Church of God of Anderson, Indiana. Around the beginning of the twentieth century, a confluence of the Holiness Movement and Protestant Evangelicals of African-American heritage—who were freer in their expression of worship and freer in their trust in the Holy Spirit to direct worship—gave birth to Pentecostalism.[58] Pentecostals are Evangelical Protestants who believe that the supernatural empowerment by the Holy Spirit of Jesus' Apostles that is recounted in the second chapter of the book of the Acts of the Apostles in the New Testament (the event known as Pentecost) is something intended for all Christians and is available for the asking, so to speak, in an experience called "the Baptism of the [Holy] Spirit." Though Pentecostals have tended to focus on "the gift of tongues" (glossolalia), the point of Spirit Baptism is to be supernaturally gifted and empowered to carry out Christ's ministry today with miraculous healing and other extraordinary signs. A few have taken this to the extreme by handling poisonous snakes and drinking poison, relying upon New Testament promises (Mark 16:17–18 and Luke 10:19) that believers in Christ should be able to do this without harm. Pentecostalism tended to generate many new churches (the largest of which is the Assembly of God Church) rather than revive existing ones, not least because of the strong op- position it encountered in the established churches.

The more recent Charismatic Movement, which began in the late 1950s, has spread ecumenically throughout existing major denominations (including the Roman Catholic Church, as has been already mentioned, and, to a very limited extent, Eastern Orthodox Christianity). It has continued many of the Pentecostal themes and practices, for the most part without the schismatic tendencies of the older Pentecostal movement.[59] Interestingly, Pentecostal churches and Charismatic- tending congregations of other churches are growing rapidly in Latin American and other Third World countries. Moreover, independent Christian churches in Africa—some from Pentecostal or Charismatic influence, some it seems from in- digenous African influences—appear to give a similar, strong place to the way of shamanic mediation in their religious life.[60]

The only remaining way of being religious yet to be discussed in relation to Protestantism is mystical quest. For the most part, mystical quest has not had a welcome home in Protestant traditions, partly from the early reformers' opposi- tion to monasticism and in part from their insistence upon the helplessness of human beings to approach God by their own efforts. It is worthwhile noting that a few small monastic, even some eremitic, expressions can be found among Anglicans and Lutherans, though many Anglicans and Lutherans (let alone other Protestants) remain ignorant of them. The new quasi-monastic, ecumenical (Protestant and Catholic) communities of Iona in the Scottish Hebrides and Taizé in France, founded just before the Second World War, are certainly worth men- tioning in this connection. Moreover, here and there aspects of mystical quest, such as voluntary meditative disciplines, can be found in the history of Protestantism within every major Protestant tradition,[61] especially the Anglican, Methodist, Quaker, and Holiness traditions where there has been special emphasis on expe- rientially realizing the presence of God in one's life. Currently, there appears to have emerged an unprecedented, widespread interest among modern Western Christians, both Protestant and Roman Catholic, in matters relating to the way of mystical quest within the Christian tradition. This is evidenced by a plethora of books on the subject being sold in North America, by Protestants undertaking contemplative retreats (often in ecumenically minded Roman Catholic monasteries and retreat centers), and by seminars and talks being given by acknowledged experts on the subject.[62]

COMPARING BUDDHISM AND CHRISTIANITY AS WHOLE TRADITIONS, WITH SPECIAL REGARD TO COMBINATIONS AND THE PRIORITIZING OF WAYS OF BEING RELIGIOUS

Reflecting on the surveys of ways of being religious in Buddhism and Christianity just completed, we find that several initial or preliminary observations can be made. First, because each tradition taken as a whole is so complex and diverse, it is clear that few simple generalizations for the purpose of comparison will fairly characterize either tradition as a whole and may very well seriously misrepresent one or more of its parts. The framework of ways of being religious makes clear how each tradition is a highly complex combination of diverse subtraditions having different priorities with respect to ways of being religious. Buddhism is not just one thing, nor is Christianity. It is clear, for example, that not all of Buddhism can be characterized as centrally concerned with the monastic, mystical quest for *nirvāṇa/nibbāna*, and that not all of Christianity can be characterized as focused on sacramentally participating in the sacrifice of Jesus Christ for the sins of the world, or on cultivating a devotional relationship with him as one's personal lord and savior—at least not without taking up the partisan judgments of specific subtraditions of each. So also, it is clear that, for a comparison to be fair, care must be taken to compare the best expressions of any ways found in one tradition with the best expressions of whatever ways are found in the other tradition, along with the tendencies *in each* for degeneration in actual practice. The point is that it would be unfair to juxtapose, say, sophisticated and articulate *lamas* (spiritual masters) of Vajrayana Buddhism with unsophisticated but devout laypersons from the Evangelical Holiness tradition (say, a Church of the Nazarene congregation), or to place examples of the best expressions of, say, Roman Catholic sacramental worship in Ireland alongside examples of the worst expressions of Theravada monasticism in Thailand. In other words, one should respect the complexity of each tradition, recognize the strengths and weaknesses of its subtraditions, avoid presumptive generalizations, and practice the principle of charitable tentative interpretations concerning what one does not yet know well.

Second, although the surveys above have not made this point very evident, the meanings of central concepts in each tradition are in certain fundamental respects impossible to pin down with exactness in a manner that permits straightforward comparison of concepts from one tradition with those of another. The central concepts in each tradition are in significant ways ambiguous, at times revealing significantly different meanings (or dimensions of meaning) depending on the way of being religious and historical tradition of interpretation in which they are taken up. They often do not mean what they first appear to mean, especially to an outsider unfamiliar with their implications in lived practice. Another way of putting the same point is to say that the meaning of key concepts in significant respects is given in terms of the implicit, lived practice of the tradition (including ideal practice, degenerate practice, and everything in between), and also in terms of the way that lived practice varies according to each specific subtradition and the way or ways of being religious that are centrally emphasized in that subtradition. Thus, for example, Buddhists talk of an impersonal law of *karma/kamma* that governs all sentient existence, an irrelevance of whatever gods there may be to salvation, and a necessary extinction of self to attain *nirvāṇa/nibbāna*—concepts which at first glance seem alien to a Christian frame of reference. So also Christians talk of the destiny of all life being ordered by a personal God, salvation as available only by the grace of God in Jesus Christ, and an eternal life of fellowship with God for those who are made new in Christ—concepts which at first glance appear alien to a Buddhist frame of reference, indeed, concepts apparently directly at odds with the Buddhist concepts just mentioned.

But are these concepts what we initially and with seeming confidence take them to be? To what extent do our understandings of them reflect (or fail to reflect) their function in lived practice among members of their respective traditions and subtraditions, and (insofar as our understandings of them do reflect lived practice) not just the practice that we, consciously or unconsciously, happen to favor personally? My point is that abstract comparison of doctrines of Buddhism and Christianity is liable to be seriously misleading apart from a sensitivity to how doctrinal concepts function in lived practice. What first looks like a fundamental difference and disagreement in doctrine—for example, the respective understandings of the self in Buddhism and Christianity—may turn out to be not such a difference after all (at least not the significant difference it was first thought to be). The self that is to be extinguished in Buddhism is ultimately not identifiable metaphysically with the self that experiences transformation in Christ in Christianity; however, the latter conception of self must undergo what St. Paul calls the death of "the old Adam."[63] And what first looks like a fundamental similarity or agreement in doctrine—for example, the respective ethical teachings of Buddhism and Christianity, an apparent common subscription to the Golden Rule, and a common esteem for the virtue of compassion—may turn out to be a significant divergence (or at least not the commonality it was first thought to be): Christianity aims to align itself with God's intention as Good over against Evil while Buddhism aims to transcend the opposition of good and evil.[64] Important qualifications need to be made on both sides of this issue, however, that make the divergence not as great as these words suggest.

Furthermore, these concepts (but even more so, other fundamental concepts in each tradition) shift in meaning as one moves from one subtradition to another: "Buddha" as one shifts from Theravada lay devotion to Rinzai Zen *kōan* meditation, and from the latter to Pure Land Buddhism or the marathon running meditation of Tendai monks; or "Christ" as one shifts from Orthodox hesychastic practice to participation in a Roman Catholic high Mass, or from the latter to Mennonite social action or a Charismatic "prayer and praise" gathering. The point again is that with basic theological and philosophical concepts, too, there is a complexity that is easily overlooked, making straightforward comparison problematic and fraught with tripstones to the unwary.

Nevertheless, despite these reasons for hesitation, a few comparative observations are worth venturing. These will be deliberately focused on relative weightings and combinations of ways of being religious in each tradition. Many other sorts of comparison are possible and, given the above cautions, doctrinal comparisons are certainly to be commended. Please note that these remarks are only a beginning to the worthwhile observations that can be made. I am only attempting to exemplify what can be done.

Most of the principal differences between Buddhism and Christianity, whether superficial or profound, are rooted in differences between their respective central stories. Certainly the peculiarly different prioritizing of ways of being religious in each is rooted here.

Buddhism, with a few exceptions, has all along given central priority to the way of mystical quest, usually in close conjunction with the ways of reasoned inquiry and right action and paradigmatically embodied in a monastic expression of some sort. The life of a Buddhist monk, pursuing Enlightenment through meditation, study, and the moral discipline of a monastic community whose structure is supposed to be based on merit alone, straightforwardly recapitulates the quest of Gautama for Enlightenment. Even the usually present but very much subordinated aspects of the way of shamanic mediation in Buddhism (with the exception of that found in Vajrayana, where they are not so subordinated) recapitulate features of shamanic mediation that may be found in the central story. Aspects of the way of devotion in the story are pretty much limited to laypersons in their relations to the Buddha, which is to say persons who are unable or are not ready to undertake the full rigors of monastic life, which merely formalize the Buddha's own quest for *nirvāṇa/nibbāna*. Explicit discouragement of the expectation of divine assistance found in the story and in Gautama's teaching—in large measure a reaction to degenerate versions of such expectation in the Hinduism of Gautama's day (late Vedic religion)—certainly militated against a fuller emergence of the way of devotion.

For the way of devotion to find full expression in Buddhism, as in East Asian Pure Land Buddhism, an initially peripheral story had to be brought into central or near central place—namely, the story of the Buddha Amitabha, his previous life as Bodhisattva Dharmakara, and the total dedication of his infinite powers to assist all sentient beings to attain Enlightenment. Basically the same sort of thing was required for the fuller flowering of the way of reasoned inquiry in Mahayana than in Theravada and for the new and different forms of meditation that emerged in Mahayana and Vajrayana.

The severely subordinated status of the way of sacred rite in most of Buddhism appears to be due to the repudiation of a degenerate sacramentalism and high caste status of priests (based not at all on merit) that characterized the Hinduism (Vedic religion) of Gautama's day, a repudiation clearly expressed in the central story. Except for the emergence of the Tantric scriptures and Vajrayana, sacred rite would have been mostly limited to a formalization of Buddhist behavioral practices (e.g., sitting meditation, begging for food, initiation into the monastic community), of Buddhist devotion (e.g., paying homage to the Buddha, his teaching, and the monastic community), and of recognition and transference of merit (i.e., achievement of Enlightenment-oriented values as a kind of spiritual capital usable for good). Except perhaps in connection with the last of these, such ritual activities have generally been regarded as nonsacramental, not themselves efficacious in drawing near to and coming into right relationship to *ultimate reality*^{p}. (I suspect that the use of sacred traditional arts in Japanese Zen may constitute an exception to this generalization.) With Tantric extensions of the central story, however, sacred rite (plus some elements of shamanic mediation) was taken into direct relationship with mystical quest and fused with it, such that the central way of being religious in Vajrayana became focused on participation in a set of esoteric sacred ritual meditations manipulating supernatural powers in pursuit of *nirvāṇa*.

In Christianity, the central Gospel story establishes a very different set of precedents. Which precedent is set depends very much on what version of the story one happens to concentrate on. There are four different entire books that present themselves as "Gospels" in the New Testament, each with a somewhat different content and a different slant. Moreover, there are many much shorter versions of the Gospel story, some more concrete, some more abstract, found throughout the other writings of the New Testament—yet all versions purport to be authentic re-tellings of the same set of sacred-historical happenings while making different emphases and drawing out different meanings. So, at the level of the New Testament, we already have different tellings of the Gospel story involving different ways of interpreting its significance and calling for different ways of being religious.[65] It seems to me that the New Testament Gospel tellings, taken together, rather than assigning one greater weight relative to the others, give no clear and unambiguous prioritizing among ways of being religious in Christianity. For that very reason, it should be no surprise that there are such different prioritizing of ways in different Christian subtraditions.

All six ways find precedent and encouragement from different parts of the New Testament. In the Gospels of Matthew, Mark, and Luke, a strong precedent is set for a Christian way of right action, perhaps coupled with shamanic mediation: the emphasis there is upon action, following Christ, doing what he did to usher in the Kingdom of God by the power of the Spirit. In early Christianity, they seem to have given strong encouragement to the way of right action in so-called Jewish Christianity and Ebionite Christianity, but these subtraditions did not survive for long. Persons drawn to the way of right action in different Christian subtraditions in every age have found authorization and encouragement from these three Gospels (plus the Letter of James). Similarly persons drawn to the way of shamanic mediation have looked to these Gospels, the Book of Acts, and Paul's First Letter to the Corinthians, where Jesus' and his Apostles' miraculous healings, exorcisms, and other supernatural empowerments by the Holy Spirit are clearly presented and discussed. The three Gospels by themselves contain little that directly encourages the other ways of being religious. Except for references to John the Baptist, Jesus facing temptation alone in the wilderness, and his spending time alone in prayer, for example, there is little to encourage mystical quest. With the writings of John (the Gospel, his three Letters, and the Book of Revelation), however, there is a strong encouragement given to the way of mystical quest and the way of sacred rite, especially when combined with the Letter to the Hebrews. The way of reasoned inquiry also gets some encouragement from the Gospel of John (especially in the prologue) and in some of the writings of Paul.

But what Paul most strongly encourages and gives extended theological rationale for is the way of devotion. It is no accident that it was Luther's renewed reading of Paul's Letter to the Romans that launched the Protestant Reformation. Mainstream Protestant Reformers were strongly impressed with Paul's condemnation of perfectionist degenerations in Pharisaic Judaism, combined with Jesus' criticisms of spiritless and egoistic degenerations in Pharisaic Judaism, and the relevance of each to degenerations perceived in sixteenth-century Roman Catholicism. As a result, those Reformation leaders set the precedent of suspicion toward, and subordination of, the way of right action to devotion in most of Protestantism until modern times—indeed, toward anything one might presume to do to earn God's favor, hence also toward the spiritual disciplines of mystical quest and the activities of sacred rite (even at times for sacramental Protestants).

What we find, then, in the different subtraditions of Christianity are different prioritizings of ways of being religious on the basis of a certain overall reading and interpretation of the New Testament, giving certain texts within the New Testament canon a weightier interpretive authority over others.

Buddhism's subtraditions also differ from a selective prioritizing of scriptural texts, except that Buddhism has had a much less clearly defined canon of scripture than has Christianity. The distinctively Mahayana scriptural texts are not accepted as authentic or authoritative by Theravada Buddhists, and the distinctively Vajrayana scriptural texts are accepted neither by other Mahayana subtraditions nor by Theravada.

The somewhat more lax attitude in Buddhism toward defining the limits of scripture reflects another deeper difference. As earlier noted, Christianity shares with Judaism and Islam the fundamental conviction that God has decisively acted in history and *revealed* himself and his redemptive purposes for humankind; he has made himself known—has communicated himself—in and through certain particular people in particular historical, cultural, and geographical circumstances. One implication of this is that, for Christianity, God and his redeeming message would not in certain essential respects be known apart from his having revealed himself. In other words, *ultimate reality*[p] is not, as a result, just there, in itself, inert and impersonal, waiting to be discovered; it has made itself known and knowable in Jesus Christ. Thereby, *ultimate reality*[p] has revealed itself as self-disclosing, as intentional, and as self-relating (i.e., relating itself in covenant relationship to those who hear and respond in confident trust)—in short, as *personal*. And evil is thereby disclosed as resulting from a breakdown of relationship with God, requiring and motivating his venture in Christ to restore that relationship with his creatures. This makes Christianity not only in an essential respect historical but also an emissary religion. Christianity purports to carry a saving message of divine revelation to all who will hear—and more: a saving relationship to God himself.

Buddhism, by way of contrast, speaks of Gautama as *discovering* (actually, "waking up" to) the eternal saving truth that he taught (the *Dharma/Dhamma*). So also, it regards that truth as more or less *impersonal* (perhaps better phrased as nonpersonal or transpersonal), a matter of natural law, always there, waiting to be discovered by a Buddha, taught by him to others, and, in turn, personally verified by his followers. Though most persons in this era happen to hear of the saving truth of the *Dharma/Dhamma* only because it was passed on to them from the Buddha's teaching, it is inessential that it came from Gautama. The teaching is not unique. Indeed, in principle if not in practicality, it is something they could discover for themselves. Evil and suffering are explained as the product of ignorance, attachment to the pleasant, and antipathy toward the unpleasant—a problem, in short, between yourself and yourself, a failure to realize what you ultimately are, not a failure to measure up to the expectation of a transcendent God or a breakdown in a relationship with him. The central story teaches these things. Nevertheless, Mahayana scriptures and teachings qualify them somewhat and speak of Gautama and all other Buddhas as compassionate manifestations of the *dharmakāya* ("dharma body" or "essence of buddhahood") at the heart of the entire universe, and in the Pure Land scriptures of Amitabha as compassionately reaching out to the lost and fallen so that they too can attain salvation. (Even Theravada speaks of the Buddha as being himself the manifestation of *Dhamma*.) In these respects, some Buddhist teachings at least begin to *sound* a little *like* revelation, to speak of *ultimate reality*[p] as having personlike characteristics, and to be a kind of message to carry to the unsaved. So also, evil begins to *appear as if* it were a movement against the compassionate grain of the universe, such that it requires the compassionate heart of the universe to take initiative to be rectified.[66]

Given the overall orientation established by these differences, it is no surprise that Buddhism should give such high priority to a philosophical pursuit of the way of reasoned inquiry (combined, to be sure, with the way of mystical quest), whereas Christianity should in general eye it with suspicion lest it depart from the content of divine revelation or downplay the sovereign and paradoxical personlike qualities of divine reality. Nevertheless the way of reasoned inquiry pursued as the systematic, expository study of scriptures has an esteemed place in most of the subtraditions of each religion, though in some clearly more so than in others. It is only to be expected, as well, that the way of mystical quest should be so confidently recommended and systematically pursued in Buddhism, not being dependent, as it is claimed to be in Christianity, upon the sovereign intervention of divine grace to be fulfilled. Characteristically, mystical quest in Christianity is more dynamic, more uncertain, more an adventure than in Buddhism, and tends to culminate in an intimate uniting of the mystic with the "person" God is (i.e., one of the persons of the Holy Trinity or the abyssal essence of God that discloses itself in the persons of the Trinity) rather than what is said to be an utter loss of individuality and distinctness in *nirvāṇa*. The high priority placed on wisdom and mystical quest in Buddhism naturally encouraged the development of a class of highly trained intellectuals and highly sophisticated experts in religious psychology and spirituality—a kind of hierarchy of spiritual merit and wisdom (as open, to be sure, to corruption as any other religious hierarchy). Partly for the reasons just mentioned, this specific sort of hierarchy in Christianity never did develop to the same extent. One can find it somewhat in the Roman Catholic tradition as far as theological study and recognition among members of religious orders are concerned, and one can find it as well to a limited extent in Eastern Orthodoxy in the esteem shown to monks and nuns of profound spiritual achievement, but hardly ever in Protestantism (though it can be found somewhat in Lutheran and Reformed [e.g., Presbyterian] theological study).

Given the differences between Christianity, as focused on the saving revelation of a personal God, and Buddhism, as focused on the discovery of saving truth concerning the impersonal laws governing human suffering, it is natural that the way of devotion should find prominent expression in Christianity and little room to emerge in Buddhism apart from the legitimation offered through the Pure Land scriptures. And given the utter uniqueness yet universal significance of the events of which the Gospel speaks, it is a matter of course that a sacramental return to them (or sacramental re-presentation of them) in the sacred rite of Holy Communion (known also as the Divine Liturgy, the Mass, the Eucharist) should prove to be central to most of Christianity, whereas in Buddhism it is not the unique events of Gautama's life itself that are seen as saving but only the appropriation and implementation of the universal truths that he made known. Consequently, there is in Buddhism less need for sacred rite to establish access to the means of salvation.

In the case of Vajrayana, with its peculiar esoteric fusion of mystical quest, sacred rite, and shamanic mediation (supported by reasoned inquiry and right action), there seems little that corresponds to it in Christianity. At first consideration, anyway, it is hard to find anything that comes close, especially anything that might correspond to the private ritual meditations found in Vajrayana. On the other hand, a Tibetan Vajrayana *sadhāna* (corporate ritual meditation) or the Japanese Shingon *goma* (fire ritual for purification), both elaborate, semipublic, sacred rites, appear akin (despite their esoteric meditative and shamanic significance) to high sacramental ritual in Roman Catholic, Eastern Orthodox, and Anglican Christian traditions. And occasionally one can find shamanic-like interpretations of Christian sacramental ritual (e.g., as mediating supernatural power), and there exists a considerable body of literature on what is called sacramental mysticism in these traditions—but these are never the primary focus.

On further thought there is another possible correspondence. It is important to see that some (by no means all) Tantric practices involved apparent violations of some of the basic rules of Buddhist monastic life. The same was true of Tantric practices within the context of classical Hinduism. In consequence, they were as a rule not looked on with favor by non-Tantric Buddhists and, in some cases, with hostility. This was one of the reasons for their esoteric or secretive status. So, if we are to try to find something comparable in the Christian tradition, we should look for expressions within the tradition that have been subject to serious question, persecution, and possible suppression. Among the variety of expressions of Christianity officially judged heretical (i.e., to be distortions of Christian truth) and which have been subject to persecution over the centuries, there are a few that have involved esoteric rituals and shamanic practices in connection with primary emphasis upon a mystical quest—namely, Christian Gnosticism and Christian Hermeticism. Nothing comparable to what is publicly available about Buddhist Vajrayana is known about them, but increasingly thorough studies are becoming available.[67] Comparative study here is simply waiting to be carried out.

CHAPTER SUMMARY

This chapter has continued the comparative survey begun in Chapter 7 with a survey of ways of being religious in Christianity. Christianity divides into three main branches, Eastern Orthodox Christianity, Roman Catholicism, and Protestantism, which differ somewhat in terms of geographic location and culture but mostly in terms of doctrinal emphasis (shading into doctrinal disagreement at times), conception of authority, organizational structure, and prioritization of ways of being religious. All ways of being religious in Christianity are conceived as ways of drawing near to, participating in, and being grounded in the reconciliation of the world with himself that God has brought about in the life, death, and resurrection of Jesus Christ. Eastern Orthodox Christianity places central emphasis on the way of sacred rite in terms of participation in the Divine Liturgy and other sacraments. Orthodoxy's second emphasis is on mystical quest, whereby a person comes to participate in the very life of God, followed by subordinate expressions of the ways of devotion, right action, and shamanic mediation. Little encouragement is given to the way of reasoned inquiry. Roman Catholicism, too, places central emphasis on the way of sacred rite in terms of participation in the Mass and other sacraments. From there on, *all* other ways of being religious find encouragement and legitimation within the inclusive ambience of the Church (though not all in all places within it), with strong encouragement especially given to the way of reasoned inquiry in terms of systematic theology and other intellectual inquiry (in seminaries and educational institutions), right action in active religious orders, mystical quest in contemplative religious orders, devotion in voluntary practices supplementing participation in formal liturgy, and shamanic mediation in the Charismatic movement.

Being so diverse, Protestantism is more difficult to characterize easily. Virtually all Protestants (with the exception of Liberal Protestanism) emphasize the way of devotion—either foremost, in conjunction with one other way, or as a close second—in terms of coming to experience and cultivate a devotional relationship to Jesus as Savior and Lord. Evangelical Protestantism has sought to elevate and renew this central emphasis until the present day. Because of Protestantism's emphasis on the Bible, the way of reasoned inquiry in the form of scriptural and theological study has a significant place among all Protestants, though not for all in the same respects. Similarly, there has been at least a subordinate emphasis on right action in terms of living a changed life. Beyond these points of comparison, Protestants differ among themselves. Sacramental Protestants centrally emphasize sacred rite along with devotion. Churches of the left, or radical, wing of the Reformation and those they have strongly influenced give central emphasis to right action along with devotion. Pentecostal and Charismatic Protestants centrally emphasize shamanic mediation along with devotion. Liberal Protestantism, however, has shifted central emphasis from the way of devotion to the way of right action.

Because Buddhism and Christianity are so complex and diverse, it is clear that few simple generalizations for the purpose of comparison fairly characterize either tradition as a whole and may very well seriously misrepresent one or more of its parts. Also, because the meanings of the central concepts in each tradition sometimes shift as one moves from one subtradition to another and from one way of being religious to another, any straightforward comparison of concepts from one tradition with those of another is fraught with dangers. Nevertheless, a few comparative observations are ventured.

Most of the main differences between Buddhism and Christianity are rooted in differences between their respective central stories. The peculiarly different prioritizing of ways of being religious, for example, seem to be rooted here. The difference between the Buddha's *discovery* of saving truth concerning the impersonal laws governing human suffering and the saving *revelation* of a personal God in Jesus Christ directly gives stimulus to different ways of being religious. Thus, Buddhism gives high priority to the ways of mystical quest and reasoned inquiry, in which great emphasis is placed on individual initiative, rational inquiry, and verification for oneself. Accordingly, these ways are not so freely encouraged in Christianity lest one lose hold of the content of divine revelation, downplay the sovereignty of God, or take for granted divine grace. Conversely, the ways of sacred rite and devotion find strong stimulus in Christianity, whereby sacramental return to the "saving event" of the Gospel is made possible and devotional appropriation of its relationship to oneself is realized. These ways find less direct encouragement in Buddhism, because there is no special need to gain access to a unique "saving event" and relatively little sense of "a saving personal relationship" with *ultimate reality* apart from the Pure Land scriptures.

STUDY QUESTIONS

1. Look back over the survey of Buddhist ways of being religious and Christian ways of being religious in the last two chapters. What similarities stand out and seem especially remarkable? What differences?

2. Overall, what ways or combination of ways are given greater emphasis and priority in Buddhism overall? Which in Christianity? To what are these emphases and priorities due?

3. To what extent do the emphases and priorities identified in question 2 reflect the respective central sacred story in each?

4. Identify a specific subtradition in Buddhism that seems akin to a specific subtradition in Christianity. In what respects are they similar and in what respects are they dissimilar? What accounts for the similarity? What accounts for the difference?

5. Given the complex diversity of Buddhism and of Christianity presented in Chapters 7 and 8, what are some generalizations you have heard or read (or perhaps have at one time made yourself) that now seem misrepresentations or distortions? Be specific as to why they are misrepresentations.

6. Identify at least one important concept from Buddhism that is interpreted differently in different subtraditions of Buddhism. Explain how its meaning shifts from one subtradition to the next. Do the same for an important concept in Christianity.

FOR FURTHER READING

Follow up references cited in chapter footnotes on specific topics in Christianity. Also recommended are articles on Christianity and topics in Christianity in the *Encyclopedia of Religion,* ed. Mircea Eliade. For references to other works comparing Buddhism and Christianity, see the recommended readings at the end of Chapter 15.

NOTES

1. See D. B. Barrett, ed., *World Christian Encyclopedia: A Comparative Study of Churches and Religions in the Modern World, A.D. 1900–2000* (Oxford, England: Oxford University Press, 1982). For an introductory overview of the different traditions of Christianity today, see Ninian Smart, *In Search of Christianity* (New York: Harper and Row, 1979).

2. See Stephen Reynolds, *The Christian Religious Tradition* (Encino, CA: Dickenson, 1977); James B. Wiggins and Robert S. Ellwood, *Christianity: A Cultural Perspective* (Englewood Cliffs, NJ: Prentice-Hall, 1988); Mary Jo Weaver, *Introduction to Christianity*, 2nd ed. (Belmont, CA: Wadsworth, 1991); or Denise Lardner Carmody and John Tully Carmody, *Christianity: An Introduction*, 2nd ed. (Belmont, CA: Wadsworth, 1989). For a much fuller treatment see W. O. Chadwick, gen. ed., *Pelican History of the Church*, 6 vols. (Baltimore, MD: Pelican Books, 1960–71); and Jaroslav Pelikan, *The Christian Tradition: A History of the Development of Christian Doctrine*, 5 vols. (Chicago, IL: University of Chicago Press, 1971).

3. See Chapter 4, note 1.

4. See Robert McAfee Brown, *The Spirit of Protestantism* (New York: Oxford University Press, 1965), Chapters 6, 14, and 17.

5. See Lazarus Moore, *Sacred Tradition in the Orthodox Church* (Minneapolis, MN: Light and Life Publishing, 1984); and Timothy Ware, *The Orthodox Church*, rev. ed. (New York: Pelican, 1980), Chapter 10.

6. See Karl F. Morrison, *Tradition and Authority in the Western Church 300–1400* (Princeton, NJ: Princeton University Press, 1969); and Richard P. McBrien, *Catholicism*, rev. ed. (San Francisco, CA: HarperSan Francisco, 1994).

7. See Mircea Eliade, *The Myth of the Eternal Return or, Cosmos and History* (Bollingen Series 46; Princeton, NJ: Princeton University Press, 1954), Chapters 3 and 4; and Charles D. Barrett, *Understanding the Christian Faith* (Englewood Cliffs, NJ: Prentice-Hall, 1980), Ch. 3.

8. See Robert Wilken, *The Myth of Christian Beginnings: History's Impact on Belief* (New York: Doubleday, 1972). For a more recent account, see Marcus J. Borg, *Meeting Jesus Again for the First Time: The Historical Jesus and the Heart of Contemporary Faith* (San Francisco, CA: HarperSanFrancisco, 1994).

9. See Andrew Walls, "Christianity," in *A Handbook of Living Religions*, ed. John R. Hinnells (New York: Viking Penguin, 1984), pp. 96–102. See also Robert M. Haddad, *Syrian Christians in a Muslim Society* (Princeton, NJ: Princeton University Press, 1970); John Joseph, *The Nestorians and Their Muslim Neighbors*, Princeton Oriental Studies, Vol. 20 (Princeton, NJ: Princeton University Press, 1961); Edward Wakin, *A Lonely Minority: The Modern Story of Egypt's Copts* (New York: Morrow, 1963); and Malachia Ormanian, *The Church of Armenia*, 2nd ed. (London: Mowbray, 1955).

10. See John Meyendorf, *The Orthodox Church: Its Past and Its Role in the World Today*, 3rd ed. (Crestwood, NY: St. Vladimir's Seminary Press, 1981); Alexander Schmemann, *The Historical Road of Eastern Orthodoxy* (Crestwood, NY: St. Vladimir's Seminary Press, 1963); Timothy Ware, *The Orthodox Church*, op. cit.

11. On these issues see G. Every, *Misunderstandings Betwen East and West*, Ecumenical Studies in History, 4 (Richmond, KY: John Knox, 1966).

12. See Benjamin D. Williams and Harold B. Anstall, *Orthodox Worship: A Living Continuity with the Synagogue, the Temple, and the Early Church* (Minneapolis, MN: Light and Life, 1990); Archimandrite Vasilios, *Hymn of Entry*, trans. Elizabeth Briere (Crestwood, NY: St. Vladimir's Seminary Press, 1984); and Alexander Schmemann, *Introduction to Liturgical Theology* (Crestwood, NY: St. Vladimir's Seminary Press, 1966). A much revered, classic exposition of the meaning of the Divine Liturgy is Nicholas Cabasilas, *The Life in Christ*, trans. Carmino J. de Catanzaro (Crestwood, NY: St. Vladimir's Seminary Press, 1974). An extended description of the Orthodox Divine Liturgy is given in Chapter 14, below.

13. See John Meyendorf, *St. Gregory Palamas and Orthodox Spirituality* (Crestwood, NY: St. Vladimir's Seminary Press, 1974); Vladimir Lossky, *The Mystical Theology of the Eastern Church* (Crestwood, NY: St. Vladimir's Seminary Press, 1976); and Georgios I. Mantzaridis, *The Deification of Man: St. Gregory Palamas and the Orthodox Tradition*, trans. Liadain Sherrard (Crestwood, NY: St. Vladimir's Seminary Press, 1964); and Archimandrite Cherubim, *Contemporary Ascetics of Mt. Athos*, 2 vols. (Crestwood, NY: St. Vladimir's Seminary Press, 1994). See also Sergius Bolshakoff and M. Basil Pennington, *In Search of True Wisdom* (Garden City, NY: Doubleday, 1979) [documented interviews with Orthodox masters of the spiritual life].

14. *The Philokalia: The Complete Text*, 5 vols., compiled by St. Nikodimos of the Holy Mountain and St. Makarios of Corinth, trans. G. E. H. Palmer, Philip Sherrard, and Kallistos Ware (London: Faber and Faber, 1979–1984).

15. See Elisabeth Behr-Sigel, *The Place of the Heart: An Introduction to Orthodox Spirituality*, trans. Stephen Bigham (Torrance, CA: Oakwood Publications, 1992). See also *The Way of a Pilgrim*, trans. R. M. French (New York: Seabury, 1965). An extended account of the Prayer of the Heart in pursuit of *hesychia* is given in Chapter 9, below

16. See Demetrios Constantelos, *Byzantine Philanthropy and Social Welfare* (New Brunswick, NJ: Rutgers University Press, 1968); and Stanley S. Harakas, *Living the Faith: The Praxis of Eastern Orthodox Ethics* (Crestwood, NY: St. Vladimir's Seminary Press, 1994).

17. See George Nicozisin, *"Born Again Christians," "Charismatics," "Gifts of the Holy Spirit": An Orthodox Perspective* (New York: Greek Orthodox Archdiocese of North and South America, Dept. of Communications, n.d.).

18. Andrew Walls, "Christianity," *op. cit.*, p. 105.

19. See T. M. Parker, *Christianity and the State in the Light of History* (London: A. and C. Black, 1955).

20. See Lucien Deiss, *The Mass*, trans. Lucien Deiss and Michael S. Driscoll (Collegeville, MN: Liturgical Press, 1989); Mary Anthony Wagner, *The Sacred World of the Christian, Sensed in Faith* (Collegeville, MN: Liturgical Press, 1993); Marion J. Hatchett, *Sanctifying Life, Time and Space: An Introduction to Liturgial Study* (New York: Seabury Press, 1982); and Raymond Vaillancourt, *Toward a Renewal of Sacramental Theology*, trans. Matthew J. O'Connell (Collegeville, MN: Liturgical Press, 1979).

21. See Patricia Wittberg, *The Rise and Fall of Catholic Religious Orders: A Social Movement Perspective* (Albany, NY: State University of New York Press, 1994).

22. See John Mahoney, *The Making of Moral Theology: A Study of the Roman Catholic Tradition* (Oxford, England: Clarendon Press, 1987); Charles E. Curran, *The Living Tradition of Catholic Moral Theology* (Notre Dame, IN: University of Notre Dame Press, 1992); and James F. Childress and John Macquarrie, eds., *The Westminster Dictionary of Christian Ethics* (Philadelphia, PA: Westminster, 1986).

23. See Alec Vidler, *A Century of Social Catholicism* (London: SPCK, 1964); Joseph H. Fichter, *Sociology of Good Works: Research in Catholic America* (Chicago, IL: Loyola University Press, 1993); David Hollenbach, *Claims in Conflict* (New York: Paulist Press, 1979); Deane William Ferm, ed., *Third World Liberation Theologies: A Primer* (Maryknoll, NY: Orbis Books, 1986); Philip Berryman, *Liberation Theology: Essential Facts about the Revolutionary Religious Movement in Latin America and Beyond* (New York: Crossroad, 1987); and Sharon D. Welch, *Communities of Resistance and Solidarity: A Feminist Theology of Liberation* (Maryknoll, NY: Orbis Books, 1985).

24. See Malcolm Muggeridge, *Something Beautiful for God* (San Francisco: Harper and Row, 1971); Dorothy Day, *The Long Loneliness* (New York: Image Books, 1968); Edwina Gately, *I Hear a Seed Growing* (Trabuco Canyon, CA: Source Books, 1992); and Ana Carrigan, "Roses in December" (film), and Ilan Ziv, "A Question of Conscience: The Murder of the Six Jesuit Priests in El Salvador" (film), both available from Virgina Beach, VA:

Palisades Home Video, circa 1990. An account of Dorothy Day and the Catholic Worker Movement is given in Chapter 11, below.

25. See Pelikan, *The Christian Tradition, op. cit.* For a major theological statement by a contemporary Roman Catholic theologian, see Karl Rahner, *Foundations of Christian Faith* (New York: Seabury, 1978). A different example by another important contemporary Roman Catholic theologian is Avery Dulles, *The Craft of Theology: From Symbol to System* (New York: Crossroad, 1993).

26. See Peter Brown, *Augustine of Hippo: A Biography* (Berkeley, CA: University of California Press, 1969); and Charles Norris Cochrane, *Christianity and Classical Culture: A Study of Thought and Action from Augustus to Augustine* (New York: Oxford University Press, 1957). An extended account of a later medieval expression of the Augustinian model or paradigm of the way of reasoned inquiry—namely, Anselm's conception of "faith seeking understanding"—is given in Chapter 10, below.

27. See Jean Leclerq, *The Love of Learning and the Desire for God: A Study of Monastic Culture*, trans. Catherine Misrahi (New York: Fordham University Press, 1961), and Steven Ozment, *The Age of Reform, 1250–1550: An Intellectual and Religious History of Late Medieval and Reformation Europe* (New Haven, CT: Yale University Press, 1980).

28. See Josef Pieper, *Scholasticism* (London: Faber and Faber, 1961); Maurice De Wulf, *An Introduction to Scholastic Philosophy: Medieval and Modern* (first published as *Scholasticism Old and New*, New York: Dover 1956); Simon Tugwell, *Albert and Thomas: Selected Writings*, The Classics of Western Spirituality Series (New York: Paulist Press, 1988); and Josef Pieper, *Guide to Thomas Aquinas* (New York: Mentor-Omega, 1962).

29. See Louis Bouyer, Jean Leclercq, and François Vandenbroucke, *A History of Christian Spirituality*, 3 vols. (New York: Seabury 1982); Don Saliers and Louis Dupré, eds., *Christian Spirituality: Post-Reformation and Modern* (New York: Crossroad, 1991); Harvey Egan, *An Anthology of Christian Mysticism* (Collegeville, MN: A Pueblo Book/Liturgical Press, 1991); and Louis Dupré and James A. Wiseman, eds., *Light from Light: An Anthology of Christian Mysticism* (New York: Paulist Press, 1988).

30. See C. H. Lawrence, *Medieval Monasticism: Forms of Religious Life in Western Europe in the Middle Ages*, 2nd ed. (New York: Longman, 1989). For a commentary on the Rule of St. Benedict that brings out the mystical quest at its heart, see Emmanuel Heufelder, *The Way to God According to the Rule of St. Benedict*, trans. Luke Eberle (Kalamazoo, MI: Cistercian Publications, 1983).

31. See Kenneth Leech, *Soul Friend: An Invitation to Spiritual Direction* (San Francisco, CA: HarperSanFrancisco, 1977).

32. See Harvey Egan, *What Are They Saying About Mysticism?* (New York: Paulist Press, 1982), pp. 117–119; and the summary in "Mysticism," *The New Dictionary of Catholic Spirituality*, ed. Michael Downey (Collegeville, MN: Liturgical Press, 1993), pp. 681–93.

33. A fine attempt to synthesize different accounts of the stages of the mystical quest in Western Christianity is given in Francis Kelly Nemeck and Marie Theresa Coombs, *The Spiritual Journey: Critical Thresholds and Stages of Adult Spiritual Genesis* (Collegeville, MN: Michael Glazier/Liturgical Press, 1987).

34. On these matters, see Andrew Louth, *The Origins of the Christian Mystical Tradition: From Plato to Denys* (Oxford, England: Clarendon Press, 1981).

35. See Richard Kiekhefer, "Major Currents in Late Medieval Devotion," in *Christian Spirituality II: High Middle Ages and Reformation*, ed. Jill Raitt (New York: Crossroad, 1987), pp. 75–108; Elizabeth A. Johnson, "Marian Devotion in the Western Church," *ibid.*, pp. 392–414; Keith P. Luria, "The Counter-Reformation and Popular Spirituality," in *Christian Spirituality III: Post-Reformation and Modern*, eds. Louis Dupré and Don Saliers (New York: Crossroad, 1989), pp. 93–120; and Carl Dehne, "Roman Catholic Popular Devotions," in *Christians at Prayer*, ed. John Gallen (Notre Dame, IN: University of Notre Dame Press, 1977), pp. 83–99.

36. See Ozment, *The Age of Reform*, *op. cit.*; Otto Gründler, "Devotio Moderna," in Raitt, *Christian Spirituality II*, *op. cit.*, pp. 176–193; and Regnerus R. Post, *The Modern Devotion* (Leiden, Netherlands: Brill, 1968).

37. Peter Brown, *The Cult of the Saints: Its Rise and Function in Latin Christianity* (Chicago: University of Chicago Press, 1983).

38. See Sandra L. Zimdars-Swartz, *Encountering Mary: From La Salette to Medjugorje* (Princeton, NJ: Princeton University Press, 1991); Ruth Cranston, *The Miracle of Lourdes*, rev. ed. (New York: Image Books, 1988); and Jonathan Sumption, *Pilgrimage: An Image of Medieval Religion* (London: Faber and Faber, 1975). For a fine overview of Christian visionary literature, see Carol Zaleski, *Otherworld Journeys: Accounts of Near-Death Experience in Medieval and Modern Times* (New York: Oxford University Press, 1987); also see her bibliography.

39. See Patricia Treece, *Nothing Short of a Miracle: The Healing Power of the Saints* (New York: Image Books, 1988); Patricia Treece, *The Sanctified Body* (New York: Doubleday, 1989); Herbert Thurston and J. H. Crehan, eds., *The Physical Phenomena of Mysticism* (Chicago, IL: Henry Regnery, 1952); Morton Kelsey, *The Christian and the Supernatural* (Minneapolis, MI: Augsburg, 1976); Ronald A. N. Kydd, *Charismatic Gifts in the Early Church: An Exploration Into the Gifts of the Holy Spirit During the First Three Centuries of the Christian Church* (Peabody, MA: Hendrickson, 1984); and Gabor Klaniczay, *The Uses of Supernatural Power: The Transformation of Popular Religion in Medieval and Early Modern Europe*, trans. Susan Singerman, ed., Karen Margolis (Princeton, NJ: Princeton University Press, 1994).

40. On the Roman Catholic Charismatic movement, see Killian McDonnell, *Charismatic Renewal and the Churches* (New York: Seabury Press, 1976); Richard Quebedaux, *The New Charismatics* (San Francisco, CA: Harper and Row, 1983); and Francis MacNutt, *Healing* (Notre Dame, IN: Ave Maria Press, 1974). An example of Roman Catholic Charismatic Christianity is described in Chapter 13, below.

41. Robert McAfee Brown, *The Spirit of Protestantism* (New York: Oxford University Press, 1965); and John Dillenberger and Claude Welch, *Protestant Christianity: Interpreted Through Its Development* (New York: Charles Scribner's Sons, 1954). The figure of 20,000-plus denominations is from the *World Christian Encyclopedia*, *op. cit.* pp. 792–793. It includes marginal Protestant and nonwhite indigenous Christian traditions as well as conventional Protestant traditions.

42. This phrase and concept comes from Andew Walls, "Christianity," *op. cit.*, p. 105ff.

43. See Owen Chadwick, *The Reformation* (Baltimore, MD: Penguin, 1967); Ozment, *The Age of Reform, 1250–1550*, *op. cit.*; and Wilhelm Pauck, *The Heritage of the Reformation* (Glencoe, IL: Free Press, 1961). See also Karl Holl, *The Cultural Significance of the Reformation* (Cleveland, OH: World, 1959).

44. See Pelikan, *The Christian Tradition*, *op. cit.*; Heinrich Schmid, *The Doctrinal Theology of the Evangelical Lutheran Church* (Philadelphia, PA: Lutheran Publication Society, 1889); Heinrich Heppe, *Reformed Dogmatics* (London: Allen and Unwin, 1950); and William Hordern, *A Layman's Guide to Protestant Theology*, rev. ed. (New York: Macmillan, 1968).

45. See Charles Price and Louis Weil, *Liturgy for Living*, The Church's Teaching Series 5 (New York: Seabury, 1979); Leonel L. Mitchell, *Praying Shapes Believing: A Theological Commentary on* The Book of Common Prayer (Harrisburg, PA: Morehouse, 1991); M. H. Shepherd, Jr., *Worship of the Church*, The Church's Teaching Series 4 (Greenwich, CT: Seabury Press, 1952); Eric W. Gritsch, *Fortress Introduction to Lutheranism* (Minneapolis, MN: Augsburg Fortress, 1993); and Luther Reed, *The Lutheran Liturgy*, 2nd ed. (Philadelphia, PA: Fortress, 1954).

46. See James F. White, *Protestant Worship: Tradition in Transition* (Louisville, TN: Westminster/John Knox, 1989); Richard Paquier, *Dynamics of Worship*, trans. Donald Macleod (Philadelphia, PA: Fortress, 1967); and Frederick W. Schroeder, *Worship in the Reformed Tradition* (Boston, MA: United Church Press, 1966). See also Cheslyn Jones,

Geoffrey Wainwright, and Edward Yarnold, eds., *The Study of Liturgy* (New York: Sheed and Ward, 1935).

47. See George Williams, *The Radical Reformation* (Philadelphia, PA: Westminster, 1962); Donald F. Durnbaugh, *The Believers' Church: The History and Character of Radical Protestantism* (New York: Macmillan, 1968); J. Howard Kaufmann and Leland Harder, *Anabaptists Four Centuries Later: A Profile of Five Mennonite and Brethren Denominations* (Scottsdale, PA: Herald Press, 1975); W. C. Braithwaite, *The Beginnings of Quakerism*, rev. ed. by Henry J. Cadbury (Cambridge, England: Cambridge University Press, 1970); and Gerald Jonas, *On Doing Good: The Quaker Experiment* (New York: Charles Scribner's Sons, 1971).

48. See Denise Lardner Carmody and John Tully Carmody, *The Republic of Many Mansions: Foundations of American Religious Thought* (New York: Paragon House, 1990); and George C. Bedell, Leo Sandon, Jr., and Charles T. Wellborn, *Religion in America*, 2nd ed., (New York: Macmillan, 1982), Ch. 2.

49. See Carter Lindberg, *Beyond Charity: Reformation Initiatives for the Poor* (Minneapolis, MN: Augsburg Fortress, 1992).

50. See Shailer Matthews, *The Faith of Modernism* (New York: AMS Press, 1924); Bedell, Sandon, and Wellborn, *Religion in America*, op. cit., Ch. 6; Winthrop S. Hudson and John Corrigan, *Religion in America*, 5th ed. (New York: Macmillan, 1992), Chs. 11 and 12; Claude Welch, *Protestant Thought in the Nineteenth Century*, 2 vols. (New Haven, CT: Yale University Press, 1972, 1985); and George F. Forell, ed., *Christian Social Teachings: A Reader in Christian Social Ethics from the Bible to the Present* (Minneapolis, MN: Augsburg, 1966).

51. See Walter A. Rauschenbusch, *A Theology for the Social Gospel* (Nashville, TN: Abingdon Press, 1945); and Ernst Troeltsch, *The Social Teachings of the Christian Churches* (New York: Harper and Brothers, 1960).

52. See F. Ernest Stoeffler, *The Rise of Evangelical Pietism* (Studies in the History of Religions—Supplements to Numen, 9; Leiden: Brill, 1965); Mark A. Noll, David Bebbington, and George A. Rawlyk, eds., *Evangelicalism: The Popular Protestantism of North America and the British Isles, 1700–1990* (New York: Oxford University Press, 1993); Leonard I. Sweet, *The Evangelical Tradition in America* (Macon, GA: Mercer University Press, 1984); and David F. Wells and John D. Woodbridge, *The Evangelicals: What They Believe, Who They Are, Where they are Changing* (Nashville, TN: Abingdon, 1975). An extended account of the Evangelical Christian experience of being "born again" by Billy Graham is given in Chapter 12, below.

53. See Stephen Neill, *A History of Christian Missions* (Baltimore, MD: Penguin, 1964).

54. See Henry Bett, *The Spirit of Methodism* (London: Epworth, 1945); and R. F. Wearmouth, *Methodism and the Struggle of the Working Classes, 1850–1900* (Leicester, England: Backus, 1954). See also Donald W. Dayton, *Discovering an Evangelical Heritage* (New York: Harper and Row, 1976).

55. See Sidney E. Ahlstrom, *A Religious History of the American People* (New Haven, CT: Yale University Press, 1972); and Catherine L. Albanese, *America: Religions and Religion* (Belmont, CA: Wadsworth, 1981). See also Edward Di Andrews, *The People Called Shakers: A Search for the Perfect Society* (New York: Oxford University Press, 1953); Thomas F. O'Dea, *The Mormons* (Chicago, IL: University of Chicago Press, 1957); David Mitchell, *Seventh-Day Adventists: Faith in Action* (New York: Vantage, 1956); Barbara Grizzuti Harrison, *Visions of Glory: A History and a Memory of Jehovah's Witnesses* (New York: Simon and Shuster, 1978); and James A. Beckford, *The Trumpet of Prophecy: A Sociological Study of Jehovah's Witnesses* (Oxford, England: Basil Blackwell, 1975).

56. See George F. Marsden, *Fundamentalism and American Culture, 1875–1925* (New York: Oxford University Press, 1980). See also Jerry Falwell, *Listen America!* (Garden City, NY: Doubleday, 1980) and Joe Edward Barnhart, *The Southern Baptist Holy War* (Austin, TX: Texas Monthly Press, 1986).

57. Vinson Synan, *The Holiness-Pentecostal Movement in the United States* (Grand Rapids, MI: Eerdmans, 1972); Melvin E. Dieter, *The Holiness Revival of the Nineteenth Century* (Metuchen, NJ: Scarecrow Press, 1980); and John L. Peters, *Christian Perfection and American Methodism* (Nashville, TN: Abingdon, 1956).

58. See Synan, *The Holiness-Pentecostal Movement, op. cit.;* Vinson Synan, *The Twentieth Century Pentecostal Explosion* (Plainfield, NJ: Logos 1975); J. Rodman Williams, *The Pentecostal Reality* (Plainfeld, NJ: Logos, 1972); Robert Mapes Anderson, *Vision of the Disinherited: The Making of American Pentecostalism* (New York: Oxford University Press, 1979); and Irwin Winehouse, *The Assemblies of God* (New York: Vantage, 1959).

59. See W. J. Hollenweger, *The Pentecostals: The Charismatic Movement in the Churches,* trans. R. A. Wilson (Minneapolis, MN: Augsburg, 1972); Michael P. Hamilton, ed., *The Charismatic Movement* (Grand Rapids, MI: Eerdmans, 1974); Steven J. Land, "Pentecostal Spirituality: Living in the Spirit," in Dupré and Saliers, *Christian Spirituality III, op. cit.,* pp. 479-499; Marcus Bach, *The Inner Ecstasy: The Power and the Glory of Speaking in Tongues* (Nashville, TN: Abingdon Press, 1969).

60. See Gerhardus C. Oosthuizen, *The Healer Prophet in African Churches,* Studies in Christian Mission (New York: E. J. Brill, 1992); A. Hastings, *A History of African Christianity, 1950–1975* (Cambridge, England: Cambridge University Press, 1979); E. W. Fasholé-Luke, A. Hastings, and G. Tasie, eds., *Christianity in Independent Africa* (Bloomington, IN: Indiana University Press, 1978); and W. R. Read, V. M. Monterroso, and H. A. Johnson, *Latin American Church Growth* (Grand Rapids, MI: Eerdmans, 1969).

61. See Raitt, *Christian Spirituality II, op. cit.;* Dupré and Saliers, *Christian Spirituality III, op. cit.;* Jones, Wainwright, and Yarnold, *The Study of Spirituality, op. cit.,* Chs. 8 and 10; Frank C. Senn, ed., *Protestant Spiritual Traditions* (New York: Paulist Press, 1986); Louis Bouyer, Jean Leclercq, and François Vandenbroucke, *A History of Christian Spirituality,* Vol. 3: *Orthodox Spirituality and Protestant and Anglican Spirituality* (New York: Seabury 1982); Bengt R. Hoffman, *Luther and the Mystics* (Minneapolis: Augsburg, 1976); Robert G. Tuttle, Jr., *Mysticism in the Wesleyan Tradition* (Grand Rapids, MI: Frances Asbury Press/Zondervan, 1989); Ann Freemantle, *The Protestant Mystics* (Boston: Little, Brown, 1967); Daniel Liechty, ed., *Early Anabaptist Spirituality: Selected Writings,* Classics of Western Spirituality, No. 81 (New York: Paulist Press, 1994); and Steven Ozment, *Mysticism and Dissent* (New Haven, CT: Yale University Press, 1973).

62. See one of the earliest of such books, Elizabeth O'Connor's *Search for Silence* (Waco, TX: Word Books, 1972).

63. This theme is developed and documented by Winston L. King in his essay "No-Self, No-Mind, and Emptiness Revisited," in *Buddhist-Christian Dialogue: Mutual Renewal and Transformation,* ed. Paul O. Ingram and Frederick J. Streng (Honolulu, HI: University of Hawaii Press, 1986), pp. 155-176. See also Frederick Streng, "Selfhood Without Selfishness: Buddhist and Christian Approaches to Authentic Living," *ibid.,* pp. 177–194.

64. This theme is developed and documented by Masao Abe in his essay, "The Problem of Evil in Christianity and Buddhism," in *Buddhist-Christian Dialogue,* edited by Ingram and Streng, *op. cit.,* pp. 139–154.

65. See Norman Perrin and Dennis Duling, *The New Testament, An Introduction: Proclamation and Parenesis, Myth and History,* 2nd ed. (New York: Harcourt Brace Jovanovich, 1982). See also John Driver, *Understanding the Atonement for the Mission of the Church* (Scottsdale, PA: Herald Press, 1986).

66. Inversely, it seems possible to construe some of the truth of the Christian revelation as more nonpersonal than personal, as a kind of natural law obscured by human degradation, sin as action oblivious to that natural moral order, heaven and hell as natural consequences of action in relation to it, and the "event" of salvation as a transhistorical (not essentially historical) revelation of that order and how to overcome sin. But such a

construal would certainly approach heresy (i.e., an officially declared distortion of Christian truth), if it would not be so in fact.

67. The available literature is not as helpful as one might like for comparative purposes. A good place to start is the *Encyclopedia of Religion*, ed. Mircea Eliade (New York: Macmillan, 1987): Antoine Faivre, "Esotericism"; Gilles Quispel, "Gnosticism from Its Origins to the Middle Ages"; Ioan Petru Culianu, "Gnosticism from the Middle Ages to the Present"; Pheme Perkins, "Gnosticism as a Christian Heresy"; and Antoine Favre, "Hermetism." Also see Antoine Faivre, *Access to Western Esotericism* (Albany, NY: State University of New York Press, 1994); Peter Roche de Coppens, *Divine Light and Fire: Experiencing Esoteric Christianity* (New York: Continuum, 1994); Walter Nigg, *The Heretics* (New York: Knopf, 1962); Pheme Perkins, *The Gnostic Dialogue* (New York: Dialogue, 1980); and Kurt Rudolpf, *Gnosis* (San Francisco, CA: Harper and Row, 1983). For contemporary manifestations, see Antoine Faivre, Jacob Needleman, and Karen Voss, eds., *Modern Esoteric Spirituality* (World Spirituality: An Encyclopedic History of the Religious Quest Series, Vol. 21; New York: Crossroad, 1992); and Jacob Needleman, ed., *The Sword of Gnosis: Metaphysics, Cosmology, Tradition, Symbolism*, 2nd ed. (Boston, MA: Arkana, 1986).

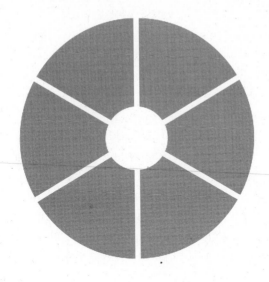

APPLYING THE FRAMEWORK TO A COMPARISON OF PARALLEL WAYS IN DIFFERENT TRADITIONS

Part III continues the application of the framework of the six
ways of being religious to a comparative study of
Buddhism and Christianity, but in a more concrete and
in-depth way. For each of the six ways, Chapters 9 through 14
compare an example from Buddhism with an example
from Christianity. Chapter 15 is a retrospective

reflection on the entire project of comparing the two traditions by means of the framework.

The examples in these chapters are not fully representative of the whole of either tradition. Given the diversity brought out in the last two chapters, no examples could be. They are not atypical or unrepresentative either. They certainly do represent significant subtraditions of practice within the broader tradition of which they are a part, and each provides a glimpse into what that tradition is like as lived. Each example exemplifies fairly clearly what it is like to pursue a given way of being religious in each tradition.

A few general comments about the background and context preface each example. The reading selections are excerpts from works that were written to present and explain the practices in question, not to exemplify the framework of the ways of being religious. Using these excerpts, readers will be able to apply for themselves the generic categories making up the different ways of being religious and discern for themselves the similarities and differences between Buddhism and Christianity as they are exemplified in each way, instead of simply being invited to take this author's word for it. Following the excerpts are questions designed to assist the reader in exploring these similarities and differences as well as the generic features of each of the six ways of being religious.

It is important to realize that the examples presented in these excerpts do not stand by themselves, nor do they have the meaning that they have for participants, apart from the broader and fuller tradition from which they have been abstracted.

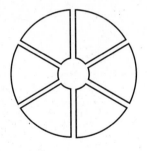

C H A P T E R   9

THE WAY OF MYSTICAL QUEST IN BUDDHISM AND CHRISTIANITY

BUDDHIST EXAMPLE: THERAVADA SATIPAṬṬHĀNA MEDITATION

As we have already seen, the way of mystical quest is given a primary emphasis throughout most of Buddhism's subtraditions but is never found without some sort of balance or fusion with the ways of wisdom and right action. However, the specific ascetic disciplines and meditative practices involved in Buddhist subtraditions vary. The following excerpt is by a revered Buddhist teacher from Sri Lanka, Nyanaponika Thera.[1] It is from the Theravada Buddhist tradition and represents a specific course of meditative practice taught in Rangoon, Burma: the *satipaṭṭhāna* method of "establishing mindfulness," also called *sukkha vipassanā* (the practice of "bare insight"). It is recommended as a useful practice for all people, but only a few are said to have the single-mindedness necessary to follow through to its ultimate result. It is a method more suitable for some personality types than for others. Much more is provided in Nyanaponika Thera's account than is here presented, and the interested reader is encouraged to read the entire account. This teacher specifically recommends that a person who desires to practice this method should do so under the guidance of a meditation master. Moreover, he recommends for most persons that, before practicing *satipaṭṭhāna*, they first develop proficiency in *samatha* (meditation that leads to "tranquillity"), a method whereby the mind attains a very high degree of concentration, purity, and calm, and reaches deep down into the subconscious sources of intuition.

INSTRUCTION FOR THE METHODICAL PRACTICE OF *SATIPAṬṬHĀNA* AS TAUGHT IN BURMA

General Remarks

A course of practice at . . . [the Thathana Yeiktha] meditation centre lasts usually one to two months. After that period the meditators are expected to continue the practice at their own abodes, in adaptation to their individual conditions of life. During the course of strict practice the meditators do not engage themselves in reading and writing, or any other work than that of meditation and the routine activities of the day. Talk is limited to the minimum. The lay meditators, at that institution, observe, for the duration of their stay there, the Eight Precepts (*atthanga-sīla*)[2] which include, e.g. abstinence from taking solid food (and certain liquids, as milk, etc.) after twelve o'clock noon.

A brief written statement on practical meditation, even if limited to the very first steps as is done here, cannot replace personal guidance by an experienced teacher who alone can give due consideration to the requirements and the rate of progress of the individual disciple. The following notes are therefore meant only for those who have no access to an experienced meditation master. The fact that their number will be very great, in the West as well as in the East, has induced the writer to offer these notes, with all their inherent shortcomings, as a practical supplement to the main body of the book.

It is a fundamental principle of the Satipaṭṭhāna method that the disciple should take his very first steps on the firm ground of his own experience. He should learn to see things as they are, and he should see them for himself. He should not be influenced by others giving him suggestions or hints about what he *may* see or is expected to see. Therefore, in the aforementioned course of practice, no theoretical explanations are given, but only the bare instructions about what to do and not to do, at the start of the practice. When, after some initial practice, mindfulness becomes keener, and the meditator becomes aware of features in his object of mindfulness which were hitherto unnoticed, the meditation master may, in individual cases, decide not merely to say (as usual), "Go on!" but indicate briefly the direction to which the disciple's attention may be turned with benefit. It is one of the disadvantages of a written statement that even these indications cannot be given, as they necessarily depend on the progress of the individual meditator at the start of his practice. Yet, if the instructions given here are closely followed, the meditator's own experience will become his teacher and will lead him safely onwards, though it has to be admitted that progress is easier under the direction of an experienced meditation master.

Soberness, self-reliance and an observant, watchful attitude are the characteristics of this meditative practice. A true Satipaṭṭhāna Master will be very reticent in his relationship with those whom he instructs; he will avoid seeking to "impress" them by his personality and making "followers" of them. He will not have recourse to any devices that are likely to induce autosuggestion, hypnotic trance or a mere emotional exultation. Those who employ such means, for themselves or for others, should be known to be on a path averse to the Way of Mindfulness.

In taking up this practice, one should not expect "mystical experiences" or cheap emotional satisfaction. After one has made one's earnest initial aspiration, one should no longer indulge in thoughts of future achievements or hanker after quick results. One should rather attend diligently, soberly and exclusively to those very simple exercises which will be described here. At the outset, one should even regard them just as purposes in themselves, i.e. as a technique for strengthening mindfulness and concentration. Any additional significance of these exercises will naturally unfold itself to the meditator, in the course of his practice. The faint outlines of that significance which appear at the horizon of the meditator's mind, will gradually grow more distinct and finally become like commanding presences to him who moves towards them steadily.

The method outlined here falls into the category of Bare Insight (*sukkha vipassanā*), that is the exclusive and direct practice of penetrative insight, without the previous attainment of the meditative absorptions (*jhāna*).[3] The method aims, in its first stage, at a discernment of bodily and mental processes (*nāma-rūpa-pariccheda*) in one's own personality by one's own experience. An increasingly keen awareness of the nature of these processes, and a strengthened concentration . . . will result in a deepening insight into the Three Characteristics of existence—Impermanence, Suffering and Egolessness—gradually leading to the attainment of the Stages of Sanctity (*magga-phala*), that is to final Liberation. . . .

Preliminaries: Physical

Posture. . . . The best known Yoga posture, with fully crossed legs, the *padmāsana* or lotus posture, is rather difficult for most Westerners. Though it is advantageous for meditations aiming at full mental absorption (*jhāna*), it is of less importance for the Satipaṭṭhāna practice. We shall, therefore, not describe it here, but turn to the description of two easier postures.

In the *vīrāsana* ("hero's posture") the bent left leg is placed on the ground and the right leg upon it, with the right knee resting on the left foot, and the right foot on the left knee. There is no crossing, only a bending of legs in this posture.

In the *sukhāsana* ("the comfortable posture") both bent legs are placed on the ground evenly. The heel of the left foot rests between the legs; the toes are between the knee bend of the right leg which provides, as it were, the outer frame of the left leg. Since there is no pressure on the limbs whatsoever, this posture is the most comfortable one, and is, therefore, recommended in the Burmese meditation centre aforementioned.

For comfort in either of these postures it is essential that the knees rest firmly and without strain on their support (the floor, the seat, or on the other leg). The

advantages of a posture with legs bent are so considerable for an earnest meditator that it will be worth his effort to train himself in any such posture. But if these
postures come not easily to him, . . . one should not delay or disturb one's determined attempt to achieve and sustain a higher degree of mental concentration,
and for that purpose one may use, for the time being, a mode of sitting that is
comfortable, dealing as best as one can with the disadvantages mentioned before. One may, then sit on a straight-backed chair of a height that allows the legs
to be placed on the floor without strain.

When sitting with legs bent, one may place a pillow, a folded cloth or blanket
under the lower back, bringing it level with the legs. The body should be kept
erect but not rigidly stiff or tense. The head should be slightly bent forward and
the gaze should gently (not rigidly) rest where it naturally falls at that position of
the head. One may place at that spot any small and simple object for focusing
one's glance on it; preferably a geometrical shape like a cube or cone, without a
shining or light-reflecting surface, and without anything else that may divert
thoughts. Such a device is, of course, not a necessity.

Female meditators in the East do not sit in either of the postures with legs bent
as described above, nor with legs crossed. They kneel on ample-sized, well-stuffed
cushions, sitting on their heels, the hands resting on the knees.

As to the mode of sitting, the meditator will have to use his own discretion,
and apply to his individual case the "clear comprehension of suitability."

Clothing should be loose, for instance at the waist. Before one starts with the
meditation one should make sure that muscles are relaxed, for instance, neck,
shoulders, face, hands, etc.

Eating. In the countries of Theravāda Buddhism, those who take up a strict
course of full-time practice in a meditation centre, usually observe, among other
rules, the sixth precept of the monk, that is they abstain from solid food and nourishing liquids after mid-day. For those, however, who work all day, this will hardly be practicable though it will be feasible for periods of meditation during a
weekend or holidays. In any case, however, for one who wishes to take up in
earnest regular meditative practice, it will be very desirable that he should be
moderate in eating. It was not without reason that the Buddha recommended repeatedly "moderation in eating" to those devoted to meditation. Experience will
confirm the benefits of it to those who are determined to make actual progress in
meditation and are not satisfied with casual attempts.

Preliminaries: The Mental Attitude

The aim of the meditative practice to be described here, is the highest which the
teaching of the Buddha offers. Therefore, the practice should be taken up in a mental attitude befitting such a high purpose. The Buddhist meditator may begin with
the recitation of the Threefold Refuge, keeping in mind the true significance of that
act.[4] This will instill confidence in him, which is so important for meditative progress:
confidence in the peerless Teacher and Guide, the *Buddha*; confidence in the liberating efficacy of his Teaching (*Dhamma*), and in particular the Way of Mindfulness;
confidence aroused by the fact that there have been those who have realized the
Teaching in its fullness: the Community of Saints (*ariya-sangha*), the Accomplished

Ones (*arahats*). Such conviction will fill him with joyous confidence in his own capacity and will give wings to his endeavour. In such a spirit, the follower of these Three Ideals should start his meditation practice with the quiet but determined aspiration to attain the highest, not in a distant future but in this very life.

"*I shall be going now the Path trodden by the Buddhas and the Great Holy Disciples. But an indolent person cannot follow that Path. May my energy prevail! May I succeed!*"

But also the non-Buddhist will do well to consider that, in following even partly the Way of Mindfulness, he enters ground that is hallowed to the Buddhist, and therefore deserving of respect. Such courteous awareness will help him in his own endeavours on the Way.

It will bring firmness to his steps on the Way if he makes a solemn aspiration like the following ones or any other that he may formulate for himself:

> *For mind's mastery and growth effort must be made*
> *If once you see the need. Why not make it now?*
> *The road is clearly marked.*
> *May what I win bring weal to me and to all beings!*

> *Mind brings all happiness and woe. To conquer woe*
> *I enter now the Path of Mindfulness.*
> *May what I win bring weal to me and to all beings!*

The Programme of Practice

1. *Training in general mindfulness.* During a course of strict training the time of practice is the whole day, from morning to night. This does not mean that the meditator should all that time attend exclusively to a single, that is the primary subject, of meditation with which we shall deal below. Though he should certainly devote to it as much of the day and night as he possibly can, there will of course be pauses between the single spells of the main practice; and for beginners these pauses will be fairly frequent and of longer duration. But also during these intervals, be they long or short, the guiding rope of mindfulness must not be dropped or allowed to slacken. Mindfulness of all activities and perceptions should be maintained throughout the day to the greatest possible extent: beginning with the first thought and perception when awakening, and ending with the last thought and perception when falling asleep. This general mindfulness starts with, and retains as its centre piece, the Awareness of the four Postures (*iriyāpatha-manasikāra*) i.e. going, standing, sitting and lying down. That means, one has to be fully aware of the posture presently assumed, of any change of it (including the preceding intention to change it), of any sensation connected with the posture, e.g. pressure, i.e. touch consciousness (*kāya-viññāna*), and of any noticeable feelings of pain or ease ("Contemplation on Feeling"). For instance, when lying down for the night and waking up in the morning, one should be aware of one's reclining posture and of touch ("lying down, touching").

The meditator may not be able at once to attend mindfully to all or even a greater part of the activities and impressions of the day. He therefore may start with the postures alone and gradually extend the scope of mindfulness to all routine activities, as dressing, washing, eating, etc. This extension will come naturally when, after the first few days of full-time practice, the mind becomes calmer, observation keener and mindfulness more alert.

One example may illustrate how mindfulness may be applied correctly to a series of activities: a wish arises to clean the mouth in the morning, and one is aware of that wish (thought-conscious: "he knows mind and mental objects"); one sees the glass and water jug, at some distance (visual consciousness); one goes towards that place (posture-conscious); stops there (posture-conscious); stretches the hand towards the jug ("acting with clear comprehension when bending and stretching"); one grasps the jug (touch-conscious), etc.

While performing these activities, one should also notice the arising of any pleasant or unpleasant feelings ("Contemplation of Feeling"), of stray thoughts interrupting the flow of mindfulness (Mind Contemplation: "unconcentrated mind"), of lust (e.g. when eating; Mind Contemplation: "mind with lust;" Mind-object Contemplation: Hindrance of Sense Desire, or Fetter arising through tongue and flavours), etc. In brief, one should be aware of all occurrences, bodily and mental, as they present themselves. In that way, one will attend to all four objects, or Contemplations, of Satipaṭṭhāna, during the day of practice.

Such a detailed application of Mindfulness involves a considerable slowing-down of one's movements which can be maintained only in periods of strict practice, and not, or only rarely, during every-day life. The experience, and the effects, of that slowing-down practice will, however, prove wholesome and useful in many ways.

In attending to those routine activities of the day, mindfulness need not be directed to all minute phases of them (as it should be with the principal subjects). By doing so, the slowing-down would be too great. It will be sufficient if mindfulness goes watchfully along with these activities, noticing only those details which present themselves without effort.

The initial purpose of this general application of Mindfulness is the strengthening of awareness and concentration to an extent enabling the meditator to follow the unceasing flow of variegated mental and bodily impressions and activities, for an increasingly long period and without a break of attention or without an *unnoticed* break. It will count as "uninterrupted mindfulness," if the meditator is not carried away by his stray thoughts, but if breaks of attention are noticed at once when they occur, or soon after. For the beginner, the standards of "general mindfulness" will be satisfied by that procedure.

2. The main practice with selected subjects. After one has attended mindfully to the various routine activities of the morning, one sits down on the meditation seat, being aware of one's preceding intention to sit down, the single phases of the act, and then of "touching" and "sitting." Now one turns one's attention to the regular *rising and falling movement of the abdomen*, resulting from the process of breathing. The attention is directed to the slight sensation of pressure caused by that movement, and not so visually observing it. This forms the *primary object (mūl' ārammana)* of mindfulness, in the course of practice described here. It has been introduced into the practice by the Venerable U Sobhana Mahathera (Mahasi Sayadaw) as it was found to be very effective.

It should be well understood that one must not think *about* the movement of the abdomen, but keep to the bare noticing of that physical process, being aware of its regular rise and fall, in all its phases. One should try to retain that awareness without break, or without *unnoticed* break, for as long a period as possible without strain. The insight at which the method aims, will present itself to the mind spontaneously, as the natural result, or the maturing fruit, of growing mindfulness. The Meditation Master said: "The knowledge will arise by itself" (*ñāṇam sayam eva uppajjissati*). It will come in the degree in which, through sharpened awareness, features of the observed process appear which were hitherto unnoticed. Insight arrived at in this way will carry the conviction conveyed by one's own indubitable experience.

Though it is the breathing which causes the abdominal movement, the attention directed to the latter must not be regarded as a variety of the "Mindfulness of Breathing" (*ānāpānasati*). In the practice described here the object of mindfulness is not the breath but just the rise and fall of the abdomen as felt by the slight pressure.

In the case of beginners, the abdominal movement is not always clearly noticeable at once and sometimes may remain distinct only for short recurring periods. This is nothing unusual and will improve in the course of diligent practice. As a help in making the movement of the abdomen perceptible more often and for a longer stretch, one may lie down; by doing so it will become more distinct. One may also place one's hand on the abdomen for tracing the movement first in that way; it will then be easier to keep track of it even when the hand is removed. If one feels it helpful, one may well continue the exercise in a reclining position, provided one can keep off sleepiness and lassitude. But, in between, one may try it repeatedly in the sitting posture.

Whenever the awareness of the abdominal movement ceases or remains unclear, one should not strain to "catch" it, but should turn one's attention to "*touching*" and "*sitting*." This should be done in the following way. From the many points of contact, or better, perceptions of touch, that are present in the apparently uniform act of sitting—e.g. at the knees, thighs, shoulders, etc.—six or seven may be chosen. The attention should turn to them successively, traveling, as it were, on that prescribed route, ending with the awareness of the sitting posture, and starting again with the same series: touching—touching—touching—sitting; touching—touching—touching—sitting. One should dwell on the single perception just for the length of these two-syllable words (spoken internally, and later to be abandoned when one has got into the time rhythm). It should be noted that the object of mindfulness is here the respective sensation, and not the places of contact themselves, nor the words "touching-sitting." One may change, from time to time, the selection of "touches."

This awareness of "touching-sitting" is, as it were, a "stand-by" of the awareness of the abdominal movement, and is one of the secondary objects of the main practice. It has, however, a definite value of its own for achieving results in the domain of Insight.

When, while attending to "touching-sitting," one notices that the abdominal movement has become clearly perceptible again, one should return to it, and continue with that primary object as long as possible.

If one feels tired, or, by sitting long, the legs are paining or benumbed, one should be aware of these feelings and sensations. One should keep to that awareness as long as these feelings and sensations are strong enough to force attention upon them and to disturb the meditation. Just by the act of noticing them quietly and continuously, i.e. with Bare Attention, these feelings and sensations may sometimes disappear, enabling one to continue with the primary object. In the awareness of the disturbing sensations one stops short at the bare statement of their presence without "nursing" these feelings and thus strengthening them by what one adds to the bare facts, i.e. by one's mental attitude of self-reference, excessive sensitivity, self-pity, resentment, etc.

If, however, these unpleasant sensations, or tiredness, persist and disturb the practice, one may change the posture (noticing the intention and the act of changing), and resort to *mindfully walking up and down*. In doing so, one has to be aware of the single phases of each step. The sixfold division of these phases as given, e.g. in the Commentary to the Discourse, will be too elaborate for the beginner. It is sufficient to notice three (A) or two (B) phases. For fitting into a two-syllable rhythm it is suggested to formulate them as follows: A. 1. lifting, 2. pushing, 3. placing; B. 1. lifting, 2. placing, of the foot. Whenever one wishes to walk somewhat quicker, one may use the twofold division; otherwise the threefold one is preferable as affording a closer sequence of mindfulness, without a gap.

This practice of mindful walking is, particularly for certain types of meditators, highly recommendable both as a method of concentration and as a source of Insight. It may therefore be practiced in its own right, and not only as a "change of posture" for relieving fatigue. In the Discourses of the Buddha we meet a frequently recurring passage, saying: "By day, and in the first and third watches of the night, he purifies his mind from obstructing thoughts, while *walking up and down or sitting.*"

If walking up and down is taken up as a practice in its own right, it is desirable to have for that purpose a fairly long stretch of ground, either in the house (a corridor or two adjoining rooms) or outdoors, since turning around too often may cause disturbance in the continuous flow of mindfulness. One should walk for a fairly long time, even until one feels tired.

During the entire day of practice, stray thoughts, or an unmindful "skipping" of steps (in walking), phases or sequences of the abdominal movements, or of parts of any other activities, should be clearly noticed. One should pay attention to the fact whether these breaks in attention have been noticed at once after occurring, or whether, and how long, one was carried away by stray thoughts, etc., before resuming the original object of mindfulness. One should aim at noticing these breaks at once, and then returning immediately to one's original object. This may be taken as a measure of one's growing alertness. The frequency of these breaks will naturally decrease when, in the course of practice, mental quietude and concentration improve. Growing competence in this practice of immediate awareness of breaks of attention will be a valuable help in the strengthening of one's self-control, and in checking mental defilements (*kilesa*) as soon as they arise. Its importance for one's progress on the Path and one's mental development in general is evident.

One should not allow oneself to be irritated, annoyed or discouraged by the occurrence of distracting or undesirable thoughts, but should simply *take these disturbing thoughts themselves as (temporary) objects of one's mindfulness*, making them thus a part of the practice (through the Contemplation of the State of Mind). Should feelings of irritation about one's distracted state of mind arise and persist, one may deal with them in the very same way; that is, take them as an opportunity to the Contemplation of Mind-objects: the Hindrance of aversion, or of restlessness and worry. In this context the Meditation Master said: Since a multiplicity of thought-objects is unavoidable in ordinary life, and such defilements as lust, aversion, etc., are sure to arise in all unliberated minds, it is of vital importance to face these variegated thoughts and defilements squarely, and to learn how to deal with them. This is, in its own way, just as important as acquiring an increased measure of concentration. One should therefore, not regard it as "lost time" when one is dealing with these interruptions of the methodical practice.

The same method should be applied to interruptions from outside. If there is, for instance, a disturbing noise, one may take brief notice of it as "sound;" if it was immediately followed by annoyance about the disturbance, one should register it, too, as "mind with anger." After that, one should return to the interrupted meditation. But if one does not succeed at once in doing so, the same procedure should be repeated. If the noise is loud and persistent and keeps one from attending to the subject of meditation, one may, until the noise ceases, continue to take it as an object of mindfulness, namely as one of the six sense-bases, within the frame of the Contemplation of Mind-objects[5] . . . : "He knows the ear and sound, and knows the fetter (annoyance) arising dependent on both . . ." In the fluctuations of sound one can observe "rise and fall;" in its intermittent occurrence, its origination and disappearance, and its conditioned nature will become clear.

In that way, *disturbances of the meditative practice can be transformed into useful objects of the practice*; and what appeared inimical, can be turned into a friend and teacher.

Nevertheless, when the mind has been quieted or the outer disturbances have disappeared, one should return to the primary subject of meditation, since it is the sustained cultivation of it that will make for quicker progress.

Three to four hours of continuous mindfulness, i.e. without unnoticed breaks, are regarded as the minimum for a beginner undergoing a course of strict practice. This, of course, does not mean that three or four hours are sufficient for the whole day of practice. If one has "lost the thread" of mindfulness, be it after, or before, that minimal period, one should take it up again and again, and continue with the practice of sustained concentration, as long as possible.

Quiet sustained effort, without too much regard to bodily discomfort, is recommended, particularly during a course of strict practice. Often, when disregarding the first appearance of fatigue, one will discover behind it new resources of energy, a "second wind." On the other hand, one should not go to extremes, and should allow oneself rest when effort ceases to be useful. These intervals of rest will also form parts of the practice (with less intense focusing) if one keeps mindful. The more natural and relaxed the flow of one's mindfulness is, or becomes, in following the continual arising and disappearing of its selected or variegated objects, the less fatigue will be caused by it.

When alertness grows one may also give particular attention to one's thoughts or moods of satisfaction or dissatisfaction, even if very subtle. They are the seeds of stronger forms of attraction and aversion, and of feelings of pride or inferiority, elation or depression. It is therefore important to get acquainted with them, to notice them and to stop them early. One should also avoid futile thoughts of the past or the future, as Satipaṭṭhāna is concerned with the present only.

The primary and secondary objects dealt with here (i.e. abdominal movement, touching-sitting, walking) are retained throughout the whole practice, i.e. during a strict course and afterwards, without anything being added in the way of new devices, etc. If there is persistent application to them, these simple exercises are capable of leading gradually to the highest results.

Reprinted with permission of the publisher from Nyanaponika Thera, *The Heart of Buddhist Meditation: A Handbook of Mental Training Based on the Buddha's Way of Mindfulness* (York Beach, ME: Samuel Weiser, 1965; first published in London: Rider and Co., 1962), pp. 87–99.

A CHRISTIAN EXAMPLE: ORTHODOX CHRISTIAN HESYCHASM

The way of mystical quest in Christianity has never had the focused, central emphasis that it has had in Buddhism. In particular, it has not had the precedent of specific and systematic guidelines laid down by Jesus that the Buddhist mystical quest was given by its founder, Siddhartha Gautama. What guidelines it does possess have been laboriously developed, for the most part by trial and error, by many generations of spiritual fathers and mothers over the course of the development of Christian contemplative monasticism. There has been accordingly much less unanimity from one subtradition to another and much less of a systematic character to those guidelines than is characteristic of Buddhism. Moreover, there is another, more important reason why Christian traditions of mystical quest have never become systematic: a virtually unanimous conviction concerning the sovereignty of divine grace that is believed to govern the quest. This means that ultimately God is supposed to be actively involved and in charge of the process and that one's proper role should always be one of attentive discernment and responsive obedience to divine leading. It is believed that human beings cannot by their own power attain to a mystical experience of God, in part because of the transcendence of God and in part because of human sinfulness (humans having turned their backs to divine grace through the Fall). On the contrary, so far as there is such a thing as a genuine mystical experience of God, it is only because of what is understood to be the grace of God in Christ that one is called, equipped, and enabled to participate in such an experience. Western Christian mysticism has tended to emphasize the role of divine grace at the expense of human initiative and activity. Eastern Christian mysticism speaks of a synergy of divine grace and human activity and is more encouraging of things a person can specifically do to prepare for, invite, and expect the infusion of divine grace that is said to culminate in a mystical experience of God. Accordingly, it tends to be somewhat more systematic than its Western Christian counterpart.

The following excerpt is from the Eastern Orthodox tradition of *hesychasm* ("tranquillity") and presents an account of the practice known as "the prayer of the heart," which makes use of the Jesus Prayer. It is by Kallistos Ware, Bishop of Diokleia.[6] It is recommended that persons who undertake this practice do so under the guidance of a spiritual director (*geron* in Greek, *starets* in Russian). Moreover, it is a practice that is not meant at all to compete with participation in the sacramental life of the Church. Rather, it presupposes participation in that life and that the participant is herself a baptized and chrismated member in good standing of the Church, regarded as the Body of Christ. In that sense, the practice is believed to rely on and develop the supernatural gifts consequent to being united with Christ through the sacraments.

It should be said here that the Jesus Prayer is used in a variety of contexts within Christianity and within Eastern Orthodox Christianity in particular. Its use is not exclusive to the way of mystical quest. It is often used as a more spontaneous and less disciplined, personally focused prayer ("free" as opposed to "formal") that is more suggestive of the way of devotion than mystical quest. One might say that its use as described below represents a kind of fusion of some aspects of the way of devotion with the way of mystical quest, which fusion often characterizes the mystical quest within Christianity. (Ware at one point in what follows calls it "a prayer of affection" and at another "an invocation specifically addressed to another person."[7]) While that may be so, the apparent fusion may also be accounted for in terms of the distinctive symbol system of Christianity that conceives of the relationship between the individual person and God in personally intimate terms and explicitly solicits petitionary prayer.

THE POWER OF THE NAME

Prayer and Silence

"When you pray," it has been wisely said by an Orthodox writer in Finland, "you yourself must be silent . . . ; let the prayer speak" [Tito Colliander[8]]. To achieve silence: this is of all things the hardest and the most decisive in the art of prayer. Silence is not merely negative, a pause between words, a temporary cessation of speech—but, properly understood, it is highly positive: an attitude of attentive alertness, of vigilance, and above all of *listening*. The hesychast, the person who has attained *hesychia*, inner stillness or silence, is *par excellence* the one who listens. He listens to the voice of prayer in his own heart, and he understands that this voice is not his own but that of Another speaking within him. . . .

But how are we to start? How, after entering our room and closing the door, are we to begin to pray, not just by repeating words from books, but by offering inner prayer, the living prayer of creative stillness? How can we learn to stop talking and to start listening? Instead of simply speaking to God, how can we make our own prayer in which God speaks to us? How shall we pass from prayer expressed in words to prayer of silence, from "strenuous" to "self acting" prayer (to use Bishop Theophane's terminology), from "my" prayer to the prayer of *Christ in me*?

One way to embark on this journey inwards is through the Invocation of the Name.

"Lord Jesus . . . "

It is not, of course, the only way. No authentic relationship between persons can exist without mutual freedom and spontaneity, and this is true in particular of inner prayer. There are no fixed and unvarying rules, necessarily imposed on all who seek to pray; and equally there is no mechanical technique, whether physical or mental, which can compel God to manifest his presence. His grace is conferred always as a free gift, and cannot be gained automatically by any method or technique. The encounter between God and man in the kingdom of the heart is therefore marked by an inexhaustible variety of patterns. There are spiritual masters in the Orthodox Church who say little or nothing about the Jesus Prayer. But, even if it enjoys no exclusive monopoly in the field of inner prayer, the Jesus Prayer has become for innumerable Eastern Christians over the centuries the standard path, the royal highway. . . . Wherein, we ask, lies the distinctive appeal and effectiveness of the Jesus Prayer? Perhaps in four things above all: first, in its simplicity and flexibility; secondly, in its completeness; thirdly, in the power of the Name; and fourthly, in the spiritual discipline of persistent repetition. Let us take these points in order.

Simplicity and Flexibility

The Invocation of the Name is a prayer of the utmost simplicity, accessible to every Christian, but it leads at the same time to the deepest mysteries of contemplation. Anyone proposing to say the Jesus Prayer for lengthy periods of time each day—and, still more, anyone intending to use the breathing control and other physical exercises in conjunction with the Prayer—undoubtedly stands in need . . . of an experienced spiritual guide. Such guides are extremely rare in our day. But those who have no personal contact with a *starets* may still practise the Prayer without any fear, so long as they do so only for limited periods—initially, for no more than ten or fifteen minutes at a time—and so long as they make no attempt to interfere with the body's natural rhythms.

No specialized knowledge or training is required before commencing the Jesus Prayer. To the beginner it is sufficient to say: Simply begin. "In order to walk one must take a first step; in order to swim one must throw oneself into the water. It is the same with the Invocation of the Name. Begin to pronounce it with adoration and love. Cling to it. Repeat it. Do not think that you are invoking the Name; think only of Jesus himself. Say his Name slowly, softly and quietly" ["A Monk of the Eastern Church," Lev Gillet].

The outward form of the prayer is easily learnt [*sic*]. Basically it consists of the words "Lord Jesus Christ, Son of God, have mercy on me." There is, however, no strict uniformity. We can say " . . . have mercy on us," instead of "on me." the verbal formula can be shortened: "Lord Jesus Christ, have mercy on me," or "Lord Jesus," or even "Jesus" alone, although this last is less common. Alternatively, the form of words may be expanded by adding "a sinner" at the end, thus underlining the penitential aspect. . . . The one essential and unvarying element is the inclusion of the divine Name "Jesus." Each is free to discover through personal experience the particular form of words which answers most closely to his or her needs. The precise formula employed can of course be varied from time to time, so long as this is not done too often: for, as St Gregory of Sinai warns, "Trees which are repeatedly transplanted do not grow roots."

There is a similar flexibility as regards the outward circumstances in which the Prayer is recited. Two ways of using the Prayer can be distinguished, the "free" and the "formal." By the "free" use is meant the recitation of the Prayer as we are engaged in our usual activities throughout the day. It may be said, once or many times, in the scattered moments which otherwise would be spiritually wasted: when occupied with some familiar and semi-automatic task, such as dressing, washing up, mending socks, or digging in the garden; when walking or driving, when waiting in a bus queue or a traffic jam; in a moment of quiet before some especially painful or difficult interview; when unable to sleep, or before we have gained full consciousness on waking, part of the distinctive value of the Jesus Prayer lies precisely in the fact that, because of its radical simplicity, it can be prayed in conditions of distraction when more complex forms of prayer are impossible. It is especially helpful in moments of tension and grave anxiety. . . .

The "free" recitation of the Jesus Prayer is complemented and strengthened by the "formal" use. In this second case we concentrate our whole attention on the saying of the Prayer, to the exclusion of all external activity. The Invocation forms part of the specific "prayer time" that we set aside for God each day. Normally, along with the Jesus Prayer, we shall also use in our "set" time other forms of prayer taken from the liturgical books, together with Psalm and Scripture readings, intercession, and the like. A few may feel called to an almost exclusive concentration upon the Jesus Prayer, but this does not happen with most. Indeed many prefer simply to employ the Prayer in the "free" manner without using it "formally" in their "set" time of prayer; and there is nothing disquieting or incorrect about this. The "free" use may certainly exist without the "formal."

In the "formal" usage, as in the "free," there are no rigid rules, but variety and flexibility. No particular posture is essential. In Orthodox practice the Prayer is most usually recited when seated, but it may also be said standing or kneeling—and even, in cases of bodily weakness and physical exhaustion, when lying down. It is normally recited in more or less complete darkness or with the eyes closed, not with open eyes before an icon illuminated by candles or a votive lamp. . . .

A prayer-rope or rosary (*komvoschoinion, tchotki*), normally with a hundred knots, is often employed in conjunction with the Prayer, not primarily in order to count the number of times it is repeated, but rather as an aid to concentration and the establishment of a regular rhythm. It is a widespread fact of experience that, if we make some use of our hands as we pray, this will help to still our body and to gather us together into the act of prayer. But quantitative measurement, whether with a prayer-rope or in other ways, is on the whole not encouraged. . . .

The Prayer is sometimes recited in groups, but more commonly alone; the words may be said aloud or silently. In Orthodox usage, when recited aloud it is spoken rather than chanted. There should be nothing forced or labored in the recitation. The words should not be formed with excessive emphasis or inner violence, but the Prayer should be allowed to establish its own rhythm and accentuation, so that in time it comes to "sing" within us by virtue of its intrinsic melody. Starets Parfenii of Kiev likened the flowing movement of the Prayer to a gently murmuring stream. . . .

Completeness

Theologically, as the Russian Pilgrim rightly claims, the Jesus Prayer "holds in itself the whole gospel truth;" it is a "summary of the Gospels." In one brief sentence it embodies the two chief mysteries of the Christian faith, the Incarnation and the Trinity. It speaks, first, of the two natures of Christ the God-man (Theanthropos): of his humanity, for he is invoked by the human name, "Jesus," which his Mother Mary gave to him after his birth in Bethlehem; of his eternal Godhead, for he is also styled "Lord" and "Son of God." In the second place, the Prayer speaks by implication, although not explicitly, of the three Persons of the Trinity. While addressed to the second person, Jesus, it points also to the Father, for Jesus is called "Son of God": and the Holy Spirit is equally present in the Prayer, for "no one can say 'Lord Jesus,' except in the Holy Spirit" (I Cor 12:3). So the Jesus Prayer is both Christocentric and Trinitarian.

Devotionally, it is no less comprehensive. It embraces the two chief "moments" of Christian worship: the "moment" of adoration, of looking up to God's glory and reaching out to him in love; and the "moment" of penitence, the sense of unworthiness and sin. There is a circular movement within the Prayer, a sequence of ascent and return. In the first half of the Prayer we rise up to God: "Lord Jesus Christ, Son of God . . . "; and then in the second half we return to ourselves in compunction: ". . . on me a sinner." . . .

These two "moments"—the vision of divine glory and the consciousness of human sin—are united and reconciled in a third "moment" as we pronounce the word "mercy." "Mercy" denotes the bridging of the gulf between God's righteousness and the fallen creation. He who says to God, "Have mercy," laments his own helplessness but voices at the same time a cry of hope. He speaks not only of sin but of its overcoming. He affirms that God in his glory accepts us though we are sinners, asking us in return to accept the fact that we are accepted. So the Jesus Prayer contains not only a call to repentance but an assurance of forgiveness and restoration. . . .

Such are among the riches, both theological and devotional, present in the Jesus Prayer; present, moreover, not merely in the abstract but in a vivifying and dynamic form. The special value of the Jesus Prayer lies in the fact that it makes these truths come alive, so that they are apprehended not just externally and theoretically but with all the fullness of our being. To understand why the Jesus Prayer possess such efficacy, we must turn to two further aspects: the power of the Name and the discipline of repetition.

The Power of the Name

"The Name of the Son of God is great and boundless, and up holds the entire universe." So it is affirmed in *The Shepherd of Hermas*, nor shall we appreciate the role of the Jesus Prayer in Orthodox spirituality unless we feel some sense of the power and virtue of the divine Name. If the Jesus Prayer is more creative than other invocations, this is because it contains the Name of God. . . .

In the Hebrew tradition, to do a thing *in the name* of another, or to *invoke* and *call upon his name*, are acts of weight and potency. To invoke a person's name is to make that person effectively present. "One makes a name alive by mentioning it. The name immediately calls forth the soul it designates; therefore there is such deep significance in the very mention of a name" [Johannes Pederson].

Everything that is true of human names is true to an incomparably higher degree of the divine Name. The power and glory of God are present and active in his Name. The Name of God is *numen praesens*, God with us, *Emmanuel*. Attentively and deliberately to invoke God's Name is to place oneself in his presence, to open oneself to his energy, to offer oneself as an instrument and a living sacrifice in his hands. . . .

This Hebraic understanding of the Name passes from the Old Testament into the New. Devils are cast out and men are healed through the Name of Jesus, for the Name is power. . . .

It is this biblical reverence for the Name that forms the basis and foundation of the Jesus Prayer. God's Name is intimately linked with his Person, and so the Invocation of the divine Name possesses a sacramental character, serving as an efficacious sign of his invisible presence and action. . . .

The Name is power, but a purely mechanical repetition will by itself achieve nothing. The Jesus Prayer is not a magic talisman. As in all sacramental operations, the human person is required to co-operate with God through active faith and ascetic effort. We are called to invoke the Name with recollection and inward vigilance, confining our minds within the words of the Prayer, conscious who it is that we are addressing and that responds to us in our heart. Such strenuous prayer is never easy in the initial stages, and is rightly described by the Fathers as a hidden martyrdom. St Gregory of Sinai speaks repeatedly of the "constraint and labor" undertaken by those who follow the Way of the Name; a "continual effort" is needed; they will be tempted to give up "because of the insistent pain that comes from the inward invocation of the intellect." "Your shoulders will ache and you will often feel pain in your head," he warns, "but persevere persistently and with ardent longing, seeking the Lord in your heart." Only through such patient faithfulness shall we discover the true power of the Name.

This faithful perseverance takes the form, above all, of attentive and frequent repetition. Christ told his disciples not to use "vain repetitions" (Mt 6:7); but the repetition of the Jesus Prayer, when performed with inward sincerity and concentration, is most emphatically not "vain." The act of repeatedly invoking the Name has a double effect: it makes our prayer more unified and at the same time more inward.

Unification

As soon as we make a serious attempt to pray in spirit and in truth, at once we become acutely conscious of our interior disintegration, of our lack of unity and wholeness. In spite of all our efforts to stand before God, thoughts continue to move restlessly and aimlessly through our head, like the buzzing of flies (Bishop Theophane) . . . . To contemplate means, first of all, to be present where one is—to be *here* and *now*. But usually we find ourselves unable to restrain our mind from wandering at random over time and space. We recall the past, we anticipate the future, we plan what to do next; people and places come before us in unending succession. We lack the power to gather ourselves into the one place where we should be—*here*, in the presence of God; we are unable to live fully in the only moment of time that truly exists—*now*, the immediate present. This interior disintegration is one of the tragic consequences of the Fall. The people who get things done, it has been justly observed, are the people who do one thing at a time. But to do one thing at a time is no mean achievement. While difficult enough in external work, it is harder still in the work of inner prayer.

What is to be done? How shall we learn to live in the present, in the eternal Now? How can we seize the *kairos*, the decisive moment, the moment of opportunity? It is precisely at this point that the Jesus Prayer can help. The repeated Invocation of the Name can bring us, by God's grace, from dividedness to unity, from dispersion and multiplicity to singleness. "To stop the continual jostling of your thoughts," says Bishop Theophane, "you must bind the mind with one thought, or the thought of One only."

. . . Rather than gazing downwards into our turbulent imagination and concentrating on how to oppose our thoughts, we should look upwards to the Lord Jesus and entrust ourselves into his hands by invoking his Name; and the grace that acts through his Name will overcome the thoughts which we cannot obliterate by our own strength. Our spiritual strategy should be positive and not negative: instead of trying to empty our mind of what is evil, we should fill it with the thought of what is good. "Do not contradict the thoughts suggested by your enemies," advise [the ascetic Fathers] Barsanuphius and John, "for that is exactly what they want and they will not cease from troubling you. But turn to the Lord for help against them, laying before him your own powerlessness; for he is able to expel them and to reduce them to nothing."

. . . "The rational mind cannot rest idle," says St. Mark the Monk, for thoughts keep filling it with ceaseless chatter. But while it lies beyond our power to make this chatter suddenly disappear, what we can do is to detach ourselves from it by "binding" our ever-active mind "with one thought, or the thought of One only"— the Name of Jesus. We cannot altogether halt the flow of thoughts, but through the Jesus Prayer we can disengage ourselves progressively from it, allowing it to recede into the background so that we become less and less aware of it.

According to Evagrius of Pontus (†399[9]), "Prayer is a laying aside of thoughts." A *laying aside*: not a savage conflict, not a furious repression, but a gentle yet persistent act of detachment. Through the repetition of the Name" we are helped to "lay aside," to "let go," our trivial or pernicious imaginings, and to replace them with the thought of Jesus. But, although the imagination and the discursive reasoning are not to be violently suppressed when saying the Jesus Prayer, they are certainly not to be actively encouraged. The Jesus Prayer is not a form of meditation upon specific incidents in the life of Christ, or upon some saying or parable in the Gospels; still less is it a way of reasoning and inwardly debating about some theological truth . . . . In this regard, the Jesus Prayer is to be distinguished from the methods of discursive meditation popular in the West since the Counter Reformation . . . .

As we invoke the Name, we should not deliberately shape in our minds any visual image of the Saviour. This is one of the reasons why we usually say the Prayer in darkness, rather than with our eyes open in front of an icon. Keep your intellect free from colors, images and forms," urges St Gregory of Sinai; beware of the imagination (*phantasia*) in prayer otherwise you may find that you have become a *phantastes* instead of a *hesychastes*! "So as not to fall into illusion (*prelest*) while practising inner prayer," states St. Nil Sorskii (†1508), "do not permit yourself any concepts, images or visions." "Hold no intermediate image between the intellect and the Lord when practising the Jesus prayer," Bishop Theophane writes. ". . . The essential part is to dwell in God" and this walking before God means that you live with the conviction ever before your consciousness that God is in you, as he is in everything: you live in the firm assurance that he sees all that is within you, knowing you better than you know yourself. This awareness of the eye of God looking at your inner being *must not be accompanied by any visual concept, but must be confined to a simple conviction or feeling.*" Only when we invoke the Name in this way—not forming pictures of the Saviour but simply *feeling* his presence— shall we experience the full power of the Jesus Prayer to integrate and unify.

. The Jesus Prayer is thus a prayer in words, but because the words are so simple, so few and unvarying, the prayer reaches out beyond words into the living silence of the Eternal. It is a way of achieving, with God's assistance, the kind of non-discursive, non-iconic prayer in which we do not simply make statements to or about God, in which we do not just form pictures of Christ in our imagination, but are "oned" with him in an all-embracing, unmediated encounter. Through the Invocation of the Name we feel his nearness with our spiritual senses, much as we feel the warmth with our bodily senses on entering a heated room. We know him, not through a series of successive images and concepts, but the unified sensibility of the heart. So the Jesus Prayer concentrates us into the *here* and *now*, making us single-centered, one-pointed, drawing us from a multiplicity of thoughts to union with the one Christ. "Through the remembrance of Jesus Christ," says St Philotheus of Sinai (?ninth–tenth century), "gather together your scattered intellect," gather it together from the plurality of discursive thinking into the simplicity of love.

Many, on hearing that the Invocation of the Name is to be non-discursive and non-iconic, a means of transcending images and thoughts, may be tempted to conclude that any such manner of praying lies altogether beyond their capacities. To such it should be said: the Way of the Name is *not* reserved for a select few. It is within the reach of all. When you first embark on the Jesus Prayer, do not worry too much about expelling thoughts and mental pictures. As we have said already, let your strategy be positive, not negative. Call to mind, not what is to be excluded, but what is to be included. Do not think about your thoughts and how to shed them; think about Jesus. Concentrate your whole self, all your ardor and devotion, upon the person of the Saviour. Feel his presence. Speak to him with love. If your attention wanders, as undoubtedly it will, do not be discouraged; gently, without exasperation or inner anger, bring it back. If it wanders again and again, then again and yet again bring it back. Return to the center—to the living and personal center, Jesus Christ.

Look on the Invocation, not so much as prayer emptied of thoughts, but as prayer filled with the Beloved. Let it be, in the richest sense of the word, a prayer of *affection*—although not of self-induced emotional excitement. For while the Jesus Prayer is certainly far more than "affective" prayer in the technical Western sense, it is with our loving affection that we do right to begin. . . .

Inwardness

The repeated Invocation of the Name, by making our prayer more unified, makes it at the same time more inward, more a part of ourselves, not something that we *do* at particular moments, but something that we are all the time; not an occasional act but a continuing state. Such praying becomes truly prayer of the *whole person*, in which the words and meaning of the prayer are fully identified with the one who prays. . . .

. . . In Orthodoxy, as in other traditions, prayer is commonly distinguished under three headings, which are to be regarded as interpenetrating levels rather than successive stages: prayer of the lips (oral prayer); prayer of the *nous*, the mind or intellect (mental prayer); prayer of the heart (or of the intellect in the heart). The Invocation of the Name begins, like any other prayer, as an oral prayer, in which words are spoken by the tongue through a deliberate effort of will. At the same time, once more by a deliberate effort, we concentrate our mind upon the meaning of what the tongue says. In course of time and with the help of God our prayer grows more inward. The participation of the mind becomes more intense and spontaneous, while the sounds uttered by the tongue become less important; perhaps for a time they cease altogether and the Name is invoked silently, without any movement of the lips, by the mind alone. When this occurs, we have passed by God's grace from the first level to the second. Not that vocal invocation ceases altogether, for there will be times when even the most "advanced" in inner prayer will wish to call upon the Lord Jesus aloud. (And who, indeed, can claim to be "advanced"? We are all of us "beginners" in the things of the Spirit.)

But the journey inwards is not yet complete. A person is far more than the conscious mind; besides the brain and reasoning faculties there are the emotions and affections, the aesthetic sensitivity, together with the deep instinctive layers of the personality. All these have a function to perform in prayer, for the whole person is called to share in the total act of worship. Like a drop of ink that falls on blotting paper, the act of prayer should spread steadily outwards from the conscious and reasoning center of the brain, until it embraces every part of ourselves.

In more technical terms, this means that we are called to advance from the second level to the third: from "prayer of the intellect" to "prayer of the intellect in the heart." "Heart" in this context is to be understood in the Semitic and biblical rather than the modern Western sense, as signifying not just the emotions and affections but the totality of the human person. The heart is the primary organ of our identity, it is our inner-most being, "the very deepest and truest self, not attained except through sacrifice, through death" [Richard Kehoe]. According to

Boris Vysheslavtsev, it is "the center not only of consciousness but of the unconscious, not only of the soul but of the spirit, not only of the spirit but of the body, not only of the comprehensible but of the incomprehensible; in one word, it is the absolute center." Interpreted in this way, the heart is far more than a material organ in the body; the physical heart is an outward symbol of the boundless spiritual potentialities of the human creature, made in the image of God, called to attain his likeness.

To accomplish the journey inwards and to attain true prayer, it is required of us to enter into this "absolute center," that is, to descend from the intellect into the heart. More exactly, we are called to descend not from but with the intellect. The aim is not just "prayer of the heart" but "prayer of the intellect in the heart," for our varied forms of understanding, including our reason, are a gift from God and are to be used in his service, not rejected. This "union of the intellect with the heart" signifies the reintegration of our fallen and fragmented nature, our restoration to original wholeness. Prayer of the heart is a return to Paradise, a reversal of the Fall, a recovery of the *status ante peccatum*. This means that it is an eschatological reality, a pledge and anticipation of the Age to Come—something which, in this present age, is never fully and entirely realized.

Those who, however imperfectly, have achieved some measure of "prayer of the heart," have begun to make the transition about which we spoke earlier—the transition from "strenuous" to "self-acting" prayer, from the prayer which I say to the prayer which "says itself" or, rather, which Christ says in me. For the heart has a double significance in the spiritual life: it is both the center of the human being and the point of meeting between the human being and God. It is both the place of self-knowledge, where we see ourselves as we truly are, and the place of self-transcendence, where we understand our nature as a temple of the Holy Trinity, where the image comes face to face with the Archetype. In the "inner sanctuary" of our own heart we find the ground of our being and so cross the mysterious frontier between the created and the Uncreated. "There are unfathomable depths within the heart," state the Macarian Homilies. ". . . God is there with the angels, light and life are there, the kingdom and the apostles, the heavenly cities and the treasures of grace: all things are there."

Prayer of the heart, then, designates the point where "my" action, "my" prayer, becomes explicitly identified with the continuous action of Another in me. It is no longer prayer to Jesus but the prayer of Jesus himself. This transition from "strenuous" to "self-acting" prayer is strikingly indicated in The Way of a Pilgrim[10]: "Early one morning the Prayer woke me up as it were." Hitherto the Pilgrim has been "saying the Prayer"; now he finds that the Prayer "says itself," even when he is asleep, for it has become united to the prayer of God within him. Yet even so he does not consider that he has as yet attained prayer of the heart in its fullness.

Readers of The *Way of a Pilgrim* may gain the impression that this passage from oral prayer to prayer of the heart is easily achieved, almost in a mechanical and automatic fashion. The Pilgrim, so it seems, attains self-acting prayer in a matter of weeks. It needs to be emphasized that his experience, while not unique, is altogether exceptional. More usually prayer of the heart comes, if at all, only after a lifetime of ascetic striving. . . .

Prayer of the heart, when and if it is granted, comes as the free gift of God, which he bestows as he wills. It is not the inevitable effect of some technique. St Isaac the Syrian (seventh century) underlines the extreme rarity of the gift when he says that "scarcely one in ten thousand" is counted worthy of the gift of pure prayer, and he adds: "As for the mystery that lies beyond pure prayer, there is scarcely to be found a single person in each generation who has drawn near to this knowledge of God's grace." One in ten thousand, one in a generation: while sobered by this warning, we should not be unduly discouraged. The path to the inner kingdom lies open before all, and all alike may travel some way along it. In the present age, few experience with any fullness the deeper mysteries of the heart, but very many receive in a more humble and intermittent way true glimpses of what is signified by spiritual prayer.

Breathing Exercises

It is time to consider a controversial topic, where the teaching of the Byzantine Hesychasts is often misinterpreted—the role of the body in prayer.

The heart, it has been said, is the primary organ of our being, the point of convergence between mind and matter, the center alike of our physical constitution and our psychic and spiritual structure. Since the heart has this twofold aspect, at once visible and invisible, prayer of the heart is prayer of the body as well as soul: only if it includes the body can it be truly prayer of the whole person. A human being, in the biblical view, is a psychosomatic totality—not a soul imprisoned in a body and seeking to escape, but an integral unity of the two. The body is not just an obstacle to be overcome, a lump of matter to be ignored, but it has a positive part to play in the spiritual life and it is endowed with energies that can be harnessed for the work of prayer. If this is true of prayer in general, it is true in a more specific way of the Jesus Prayer, since this is an invocation addressed precisely to God Incarnate, to the Word made flesh. Christ at his Incarnation took not only a human mind and will but a human body, and so he has made the *flesh* into an inexhaustible source of sanctification. How can this flesh, which the God-man has made Spirit-bearing, participate in the Invocation of the Name and in the prayer of the intellect in the heart?

To assist such participation, and as an aid to concentration, the Hesychasts evolved a "physical technique." Every psychic activity, they realized, has repercussions on the physical and bodily level; depending on our inner state we grow hot or cold, we breathe faster or more slowly, the rhythm of our heart-beats quickens or decelerates, and so on. Conversely, each alteration in our physical condition reacts adversely or positively on our psychic activity. If then, we can learn to control and regulate certain of our physical processes, this can be used to strengthen our inner concentration in prayer. Such is the basic principle underlying the Hesychast "method." In detail, the physical technique has three main aspects:

(i) *External posture.* St Gregory of Sinai advises sitting on a low stool, about nine inches high; the head and shoulders should be bowed, and the eyes fixed on the place of the heart. He recognizes that this will prove exceedingly uncomfortable after a time. Some writers recommend a yet more exacting posture, with the head held between the knees, following the example of Elijah on Mount Carmel [1 Kings 18:42].

(ii) *Control of the breathing.* The breathing is to be made slower and at the same time coordinated with the rhythm of the Prayer. Often the first part, "Lord Jesus Christ, Son of God," is said while drawing in the breath, and the second part "have mercy on me a sinner," while breathing out. Other methods are possible. The recitation of the Prayer may also be synchronized with the beating of the heart.

(iii) *Inward exploration.* Just as the aspirant in Yoga is taught to concentrate his thought in specific parts of his body, so the Hesychast concentrates his thought in the cardiac center. While inhaling through his nose and propelling his breath down into his lungs, he makes his intellect "descend" with the breath and he "searches" inwardly for the place of the heart. Exact instructions concerning this exercise are not committed to writing for fear they should be misunderstood; the details of the process are so delicate that the personal guidance of an experienced master is *indispensable.* The beginner who, in the absence of such guidance, attempts to search for the cardiac center, is in danger of directing his thought unawares into the area which lies immediately below the heart—in the abdomen, that is, and the entrails. The effect on his prayer is disastrous, for this lower region is the source of the carnal thoughts and sensations which pollute the mind and the heart.

For obvious reasons the utmost discretion is necessary when interfering with instinctive bodily activities such as the drawing of breath or the beating of the heart. Misuse of the physical technique can damage someone's health and disturb his mental equilibrium; hence the importance of a reliable master. If no such *starets* is available, it is best for the beginner to restrict himself simply to the actual recitation of the Jesus Prayer, without troubling at all about the rhythm of his breath or his heart-beats. More often than not he will find that, without any conscious effort on his part, the words of the Invocation adapt themselves spontaneously to the movement of his breathing. If this does not in fact happen, there is no cause for alarm; let him continue quietly with the work of mental invocation.

The physical techniques are in any case no more than an accessory, an aid which has proved helpful to some but which is in no sense obligatory upon all. The Jesus Prayer can be practised in its fullness without any physical methods at all. St Gregory Palamas (1296–1359), while regarding the use of physical techniques as theologically defensible, treated such methods as something secondary and suited mainly for beginners. For him, as for all the Hesychast masters, the essential thing is not the external control of the breathing but the inner and secret Invocation of the Lord Jesus.

Orthodox writers in the last 150 years have in general laid little emphasis upon the physical techniques. The counsel given by Bishop Ignatii Brianchaninov (1807–67) is typical:

> We advise our beloved brethren not to try to establish this technique within them, if it does not reveal itself of its own accord. Many, wishing to learn of it by experience, have damaged their lungs and gained nothing. The essence of the matter consists in the union of the mind with the heart during prayer, and this is achieved by the grace of God in its own time, determined by God. The breathing technique is fully replaced by the unhurried enunciation of the Prayer,

by a short rest or pause at the end, each time it is said, by gentle and unhurried breathing, and by the enclosure of the mind in the words of the Prayer. By means of these aids we can easily attain to a certain degree of attention.

As regards the speed of recitation, Bishop Ignatii suggests:

To say the Jesus Prayer a hundred times attentively and without haste, about half an hour is needed, but some ascetics require even longer. Do not say the prayers hurriedly, one immediately after another. Make a short pause after each prayer, and so help the mind to concentrate. Saying the Prayer without pauses distracts the mind. Breathe with care, gently and slowly.

Beginners in the use of the Prayer will probably prefer a somewhat faster pace than is here proposed—perhaps twenty minutes for a hundred prayers. In the Greek tradition there are teachers who recommend a far brisker rhythm; the very rapidity of the Invocation, so they maintain, helps to hold the mind attentive. . . .

The existence of a physical technique in connection with the Jesus Prayer should not blind us to the Prayer's true character. The Jesus Prayer is not just a device to help us concentrate or relax. It is not simply a piece of "Christian Yoga," a type of "Transcendental Meditation," or a "Christian mantra," even though some have tried to interpret it in this way. It is, on the contrary, an invocation specifically *addressed to another person*—to God made man, Jesus Christ, our personal Saviour and Redeemer. The Jesus Prayer, therefore, is far more than an isolated method or technique. It exists within a certain context, and if divorced from that context it loses its proper meaning.

The context of the Jesus Prayer is first of all one of *faith.* The Invocation of the Name presupposes that the one who says the Prayer believes in Jesus Christ as Son of God and Saviour. Behind the repetition of a form of words there must exist a living faith in the Lord Jesus in who he is and in what he has done form me personally. Perhaps the faith in many of us is very uncertain and faltering; perhaps it coexists with doubt; perhaps we often find ourselves compelled to cry out in company with the father of the lunatic child, "Lord, I believe: help my unbelief" (Mk 9:24). But at least there should be some *desire* to believe; at least there should be, amidst all the uncertainty, a spark of love for the Jesus whom as yet we know so imperfectly.

Secondly, the context of the Jesus Prayer is one of *community.* We do not invoke the Name as separate individuals, relying solely upon our own inner resources, but as members of the community of the Church. Writers such as St Barsanuphius, St Gregory of Sinai or Bishop Theophane took it for granted that those to whom he commended the Jesus Prayer were baptized Christians, regularly participating in the Church's sacramental life through Confession and Holy Communion. Not for one moment did they envisage the Invocation of the Name as a substitute for the sacraments, but they assumed that anyone using it would be a practicing and communicant member of the Church. Yet today, in this present epoch of restless curiosity and ecclesiastical disintegration, there are in fact many who use the Jesus Prayer without belonging to any Church, possibly without having a clear faith either in the Lord Jesus or in anything else. Are we to condemn them? Are we to forbid them the use of the Prayer? Surely not, so long as they are sincerely searching for the Fountain of Life. Jesus condemned no one except hypocrites. But, in all humility and acutely aware of our own faithlessness, we are bound to regard the situation of such people as anomalous, and to warn them of this fact.

The Journey's End

The aim of the Jesus Prayer, as of all Christian prayer, is that our praying should become increasingly identified with the prayer offered by Jesus the High Priest within us, that our life should become one with his life, our breathing with the Divine Breath that sustains the universe. The final objective may aptly be described by the Patristic term *theosis*, "deification" or "divinization." In the words of Archpriest Sergei Bulgakov, "The Name of Jesus, present in the human heart, confers upon it the power of deification." "The Logos became man," says St Athanasius, "that we might become god." He who is God by nature took our humanity, that we humans might share by grace in his divinity, becoming "partakers of the divine nature" (2 Pet 1:4). The Jesus Prayer, addressed to the Logos Incarnate, is a means of realizing within ourselves this mystery of *theosis*, whereby human persons attain the true likeness of God.

The Jesus Prayer, by uniting us to Christ, helps us to share in the mutual indwelling or *perichoresis* of the three Persons of the Holy Trinity. The more the Prayer becomes a part of ourselves, the more we enter into the movement of love which passes unceasingly between Father, Son, and Holy Spirit. Of this love St Isaac the Syrian has written with great beauty:

> Love is the kingdom of which our Lord spoke symbolically when he promised his disciples that they would eat in his kingdom: "You shall eat and drink at the table of my kingdom." What should they eat, if not love? . . . When we have reached love, we have reached God and our way is ended: we have passed over to the island that lies beyond the world, where is the Father with the Son and the Holy Spirit: to whom be glory and dominion.

In the Hesychast tradition, the mystery of *theosis* has most often taken the outward form of a vision of light. This light which the saints behold in prayer is neither a symbolical light of the intellect, nor yet a physical and created light of the senses. It is nothing less than the divine and uncreated Light of the Godhead, which shone from Christ at his Transfiguration on Mount Tabor and which will illumine the whole world at his second coming on the Last Day. . . .

The Jesus Prayer causes the brightness of the Transfiguration to penetrate into every corner of our life. Constant repetition has two effects upon the anonymous author of *The Way of the Pilgrim*. First, it transforms his relationship with the material creation around him, making all things transparent, changing them into a sacrament of God's presence. He writes:

> When I prayed with my heart, everything around me seemed delightful and marvelous. The trees, the grass, the birds, the earth, the air, the light seemed to be telling me that they existed for man's sake, that they witnessed to the love of God for man, that everything proved the love of God for man, that all

*things prayed to God and sang his praise. Thus it was that I came to under-
stand what* The Philokalia *calls "the knowledge of the speech of all creatures."
I felt a burning love for Jesus and for all God's creatures.*

In the words of Father Bulgakov, "Shining through the heart, the light of the
Name of Jesus illuminates all the universe."

In the second place, the Prayer transfigures the Pilgrim's relation not only with
the material creation but with other humans:

*Again I started off on my wanderings. But now I did not walk along as before,
filled with care. The Invocation of the Name of Jesus gladdened my way.
Everybody was kind to me, it was as though everyone loved me. . . . If anyone
harms me I have only to think, "How sweet is the Prayer of Jesus!" and the injury and the anger alike pass away and I forget it all.*

. . . The Jesus Prayer helps us to see Christ in each one and each one in Christ.

The Invocation of the Name is in this way joyful rather than penitential, world-
affirming rather than world-denying. To some, hearing about the Jesus Prayer for
the first time, it may appear that to sit alone in the darkness with eyes closed, constantly repeating ". . . have mercy on me," is a gloomy and despondent way of
praying. And they may also be tempted to regard it as self-centered and escapist,
introverted, an evasion of responsibility to the human community at large. But
this would be a grave misunderstanding. For those who have actually made the
way of the name their own, it turns out to be not somber and oppressive but a
source of liberation and healing. . . .

Moreover, so far from turning our backs on others and repudiating God's creation when we say the Jesus Prayer, we are in fact affirming our commitment to
our neighbor and our sense of the value of everyone and everything in God.
"Acquire inner peace," said St. Seraphim of Sarov (1759–1833), "and thousands
around you will find their salvation." By standing in Christ's presence even for no
more than a few moments of each day, invoking his Name, we deepen and transform all the remaining moments of the day, rendering ourselves available to others, effective and creative, in a way that we could not otherwise be. . . .

"Prayer is action; to pray is to be highly effective" [Tito Colliander]. Of no prayer
is this more true than of the Jesus Prayer. While it is singled out for particular mention in the office of monastic profession as a prayer for monks and nuns, it is
equally a prayer for laymen, for married couples, for doctors and psychiatrists, for
social workers and bus conductors. The Invocation of the Name, practised aright,
involves each one more deeply in his or her appointed task, making each more
efficient in his actions, not cutting him off from others but linking him to them,
rendering him sensitive to their fears and anxieties in a way that he never was before. The Jesus Prayer makes each into a "man for others," a living instrument of
God's peace, a dynamic center of reconciliation.

Reprinted by permission of the publisher from Bishop Kallistos, *The Power of the Name* (Oxford: SLG
Press, 1986).

CHAPTER SUMMARY

As a Buddhist example of the way of mystical quest, the excerpt presents a straightforward prescription for a course of *satipaṭṭhāna* meditation as taught in a Theravada meditation center in Rangoon, Burma. Very concrete and specific as it is, it is nevertheless presented as one of the most direct paths to enlightenment: liberation from all that binds one to the suffering of *saṃsāra* and at-one-ment with that transcendent mysterious state known as *nirvāṇa/nibbāna*. Step-by-step it covers attitude, posture, breathing, mindful awareness of all that is going on within oneself, focus of attention, how distractions should be handled, and so forth. Little is said of what one is to experience as a result; mostly the emphasis is on mindful attention of what is concretely going on here and now in one's present psychophysical, samsaric state—namely, the state from which one is supposed ultimately to become liberated.

The Christian example of the way of mystical quest is an account of the Prayer of the Heart from the Eastern Orthodox tradition of spirituality known as *hesychasm*. Much less a step-by-step prescription than the Buddhist example, this account characterizes the course of meditation as an entry into a dynamic rapport of one's heart with God, focused by means of the Jesus Prayer: "Lord Jesus Christ, Son of God, have mercy upon me, a sinner." Here too some attention is given to attitude, posture, breathing, mindful awareness of all that is going on within oneself, focus of attention, how distractions should be handled, and so forth. Little is said of what one is leaving behind, but much is said of what is anticipated to be the transformation (*theosis*) of oneself as the Jesus Prayer by divine grace comes to pray itself, and one is said to be taken up into the very presence and life of God/

STUDY QUESTIONS ON SIMILARITIES AND DIFFERENCES

The two methods of meditation, *satipaṭṭhāna* and *hesychasm*, have a number of remarkable similarities as well as several differences. Spend some time comparing the accounts. Keep in mind the danger of generalizing from these specific forms of meditative practice to all forms of meditative practice in either tradition. Also be mindful of how much may be involved implicitly in the actual practice of these specific forms that may be going unsaid in the two accounts just given. Consider the following questions.

1. What similarities do you find? What similar functions or purposes do the specific features of the practice of each method seem to have (e.g., posture, manner of breathing, self-control, role of guidance, undistracted attentiveness, method of dealing with distractions, effort to enter wholly into the

present moment, avoidance of imagination, the kind of overall goal or objective sought, etc.)?

2. With respect to features they have in common, which of the two emphasizes that feature more than the other? (E.g., *satipaṭṭhāna* emphasizes posture and setting more than *hesychasm*.)

3. Assuming that both of these practices exemplify the same generic way of being religious in two distinct religious traditions, what if anything do the similarities identified in answer to the first question indicate that is essential to that way of being religious (which the framework identifies as mystical quest)?

   a. What, if anything, do these two practices have in common regarding their respective means of approach to *ultimate reality*?

   b. What characteristic existential problems are each concerned with and seeking to address? What do the accounts presume to be motivating their respective readers?

   c. Is there anything that indicates the characteristic way each interprets its broader tradition's scripture and symbol system in a manner distinct from other traditional ways of taking them? What sorts of features of *ultimate reality* does each specifically highlight? That is, what kind of "face" does each envision *ultimate reality* to have?

   d. What sorts of social structures (social organization, group activity, roles and responsibilities, etc.) does each have or recommend?

   e. What specific virtues in the practice of its religious life does each appear to commend, whether explicitly or implicitly, and what specific vices in that practice does each appear to condemn? (Be careful here to distinguish criticisms each may apparently offer of the religious practices of others from critical expectations set for its own members.) That is, what ideal(s) of practice does each uphold? And what sorts of things would fall short of those ideals?

4. What differences do you find (e.g., in respect to specific dos and don'ts, techniques of meditation, role of guidance, focus on *theological* conviction, engagement with *metaphysical realities*, reliance upon *divine assistance*, etc.)? Is one more definite about what to expect when? Is one more open and dynamic, more open to surprising discovery? What specific goals or objectives is each setting out to accomplish?

5. How specifically is the nature of the respective meditative experience (the experience of the meditative practice itself) something different in each case?

6. What among the differences identified in questions 4 and 5 seem to be due to what makes the one Buddhist (or specifically Theravada Buddhist) and the other Christian (or specifically Eastern Orthodox Christian)? (Again beware, here, of concluding that these practices represent all instances of the way of mystical quest in their respective traditions.)

FOR FURTHER READING

Recommended articles in the *Encyclopedia of Religion*, edited by Mircea Eliade (New York: Macmillan, 1987), include *Mysticism; Mystical Union; Meditation; Consciousness, States of; Attention; Monasticism; Monastery; Eremiticism; Mendicancy; Spiritual Discipline; Asceticism; Enlightenment; Eightfold Path; Nirvāṇa; Christian Spirituality; Deification; Via Negativa;* and articles on historical figures in the history of Buddhist Spirituality and Christian Spirituality.

Stephen V. Beyer, *The Cult of Tara* (Berkeley, CA: University of California Press, 1973). One of the finest introductions to the practice of Vajrayana Buddhist meditation.

Philip Kapleau, *Three Pillars of Zen: Teaching, Practice, and Enlightenment,* rev. ed. (Garden City, NY: Anchor Books/Doubleday, 1980). Contains several first-person accounts of both Soto and Rinzai Zen meditation practice and breakthroughs to Enlightenment.

Winston L. King, *Theravada Meditation: The Buddhist Transformation of Yoga* (University Park, PA: Pennsylvania State University Press, 1980). Contains as an appendix a diary account of a person practicing *vipassanā* meditation describing in detail his experiences until reaching the point of breakthrough to Enlightenment.

Minoru Kiyota, ed., *Mahayana Buddhist Meditation: Theory and Practice* (Honolulu, HI: University of Hawaii Press, 1978). A collection of essays on different traditions of Mahayana meditation.

Jack Kornfield, *Living Buddhist Masters* (Santa Cruz, CA: Unity Press, 1977). An excellent introduction to most of the great living Theravada Buddhist masters, with an major selection from the writings of each.

Nyanaponika Thera, T*he Heart of Buddhist Meditation* (New York: Samuel Weiser, 1962). The whole text is strongly recommended in order to understand fully the excerpt reproduced above.

Takeuchi Yoshinori, Jan Van Bragt, James W. Heisig, Joseph S. O'Leary, and Paul L. Swanson, eds., *Buddhist Spirituality I: Indian, Southeast Asian, Tibetan, and Early Chinese* (New York: Crossroad, 1992). A collection of essays by specialists explaining the traditions of spiritual discipline, including techniques of meditation, in most of the major Buddhist traditions prior to the modern era. Does not include Zen.

Shinzen (Steven) Young, "Buddhist Meditation," in *The Buddhist Religion: A Historical Introduction,* by Richard H. Robinson and Willard L. Johnson, 3rd ed., Religious Life of Man Series (Belmont, CA: Wadsworth, 1982), pp. 226–235. A very good, brief introduction to the basic varieties of Buddhist meditation.

Elisabeth Behr-Sigel, *The Place of the Heart: An Introduction to Orthodox Spirituality,* trans. Stephen Bigham (Torrance, CA: Oakwood Publications, 1992). A fine introduction as a whole to the Hesychastic practice of the Prayer of the Heart.

Sergius Bolshakoff and M. Basil Pennington, *In Search of True Wisdom* (Garden City, NY: Doubleday, 1979). Documented interviews with Orthodox masters of the spiritual life.

Louis Dupré and James A. Wiseman, OSB, eds. *Light from Light: An Anthology of Christian Mysticism* (New York: Paulist Press, 1988). One of the very best anthologies available of Christian mystics, with excellent introductions.

Harvey Egan, *An Anthology of Christian Mysticism* (Collegeville, MN: A Pueblo Book/ Liturgical Press, 1991). A superior anthology of mainly Western Christian mystics.

Vladimir Lossky, *The Vision of God* (Crestwood, NY: St. Vladimir's Seminary Press, 1963). One of the better accounts of the ultimate goal of the Eastern Orthodox mystical quest.

George A. Maloney, ed., *Pilgrimage of the Heart: A Treasury of Eastern Christian Spirituality* (San Francisco, CA: Harper and Row, 1983). A wonderful anthology of writings from Eastern Orthodoxy on different aspects of the way of mystical quest.

John Meyendorf, *St. Gregory Palamas and Orthodox Spirituality* (Crestwood, NY: St. Vladimir's Seminary Press, 1974). A good historical overview of Hesychastic spirituality.

Francis Kelly Nemeck and Marie Theresa Coombs, *The Spiritual Journey: Critical Thresholds and Stages of Adult Spiritual Genesis* (Collegeville, MN: Michael Glazier/Liturgical Press, 1987). A first-rate synopsis of the many accounts of the stages of mystical quest in Western Christianity.

Archimandrite Sophrony, *The Monk of Mount Athos: Staretz Silouan 1866–1938*, trans. Rosemary Edmonds (Crestwood, NY: St. Vladmir's Seminary Press, 1973; a revised edition of *The Undistorted Image*, published in 1958). A very readable account of a twentieth-century Russian Orthodox mystic who throughout his life practiced the Prayer of the Heart.

The Way of a Pilgrim, trans. R. M. French (New York: Seabury, 1965). A classic on the use of the Jesus Prayer in Russian Orthodox piety.

NOTES

1. Nyanaponika Thera, *The Heart of Buddhist Meditation: A Handbook of Mental Training Based on the Buddha's way of Mindfulness* (New York: Samuel Weiser, 1962), pp. 97–99.

2. The Eight Precepts are (1) not to harm sentient beings, (2) not to steal, (3) not to engage in sexual misconduct, (4) not to lie, (5) not to drink alcohol, (6) not to eat after midday, (7) not to watch secular entertainments or use perfume or ornaments, and (8) not to use a luxurious bed or to sleep indulgently.

3. I.e., the developmental stages of *samatha*.

4. The Threefold Refuge is a formalized entrustment of oneself to the Buddha, the Dhamma, and the Sangha.

5. The six sense bases include the eye and visible forms, the ear and sounds, the nose and smells, the tongue and flavours, the body and tactile objects, and the mind and mind-objects.

6. Bishop Kallistos, *The Power of the Name: The Jesus Prayer in Orthodox Spirituality* (Oxford, England: Sisters of the Love of God Press, 1976); republished with North American spelling and punctuation in *The Place of the Heart: An Introduction to Orthodox Spirituality* by Elisabeth Behr-Sigel, trans. Stephen Bigham (Torrance, CA: Oakwood Publications, 1992), pp. 135–172. The quotations in the essay are fully referenced in footnotes, which are not reproduced here. The authors of the quotations that are mentioned in the footnotes are here placed in brackets. The main body of the book by Behr-Sigel gives an an analysis and historical overview of the development of "the prayer of the heart" in Orthodox spirituality from the early Church to the present century.

7. See pp. 249 and 254.

8. Instead of reproducing all the footnotes in the original text, the sources cited by Ware will be indicated by the name of the author only.

9. The symbol † refers to date of death.

10. *The Way of a Pilgrim*, trans. R. M French (New York: Seabury, 1965).

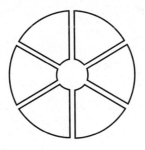

CHAPTER 10

THE WAY OF REASONED INQUIRY IN BUDDHISM AND CHRISTIANITY

A BUDDHIST EXAMPLE: NAGASENA REPLIES TO THE QUESTIONS OF KING MILINDA

The way of reasoned inquiry, like that of mystical quest, has received high priority in most (though not all) subtraditions of Buddhism, at least as a fundamental aspect of the way to Enlightenment. Its speculative tendencies are curbed by a pragmatic insistence (1) that it contribute directly to the goal of Enlightenment and (2) that it does not feed the delusive craving of the ego for autonomous existence by postulating metaphysical entities that might serve to rationalize that craving. Nevertheless, rational philosophical inquiry has for the most part been given free rein in Buddhism (except in cases where the tradition has simply degenerated into unthinking repetition of traditional teachings). Mere quieting of the mind in concentrative absorption is insufficient by itself for Enlightenment; there must also be insight into, and reasoned understanding of, the impermanence, insubstantiality, and turmoil that characterize all things in mundane existence. As much or more than anything else, it is lack of insight into and misunderstanding of these matters that is believed to keep a person trapped in an unenlightened state. In this respect, the example of Buddhist mystical quest already given has an aspect of the way of reasoned inquiry already built into it.

In other subtraditions of Buddhism, especially in Mahayana, this aspect plays a greater role, though a role that varies depending on the subtradition in question. In some subtraditions, notably the *Gelukpa* sect of Tibetan Vajrayana Buddhism and the *Tendai* sect of Japanese Buddhism, a serious systematic study of Buddhist philosophy is a requisite, major part of communal monastic life. To be a Buddhist in these traditions is to have one's understanding of basic Buddhist teaching developed and refined through intense and rigorous debate, as well as through renewed encounter with the great Buddhist philosophers of the past by way of their writings and courses of study with master teachers in the present. The point is not to rethink and imitate what others have thought in a secondhand manner but to make for oneself the mental connections, inferences, and leaps of insight that acquaint one mentally with the thinking that leads to, and is, Enlightenment.

The excerpt that follows is taken from a recent translation of a classic work in Theravada Buddhist *theology*,[1] *The Questions of King Milinda* (*Milindapañha*), which was probably composed in the first century B.C.E. The *Milindapañha* has served over the centuries as a model of *theological* inquiry and debate in Theravada Buddhism and in some Mahayana traditions as well. It is composed as a dialogue between King Milinda, a Greek king (Menander) who ruled the northeast of India (Bactria) in the latter part of the second century B.C.E., and a learned monk called Nagasena. Milinda is portrayed as very bright, knowledgeable about Buddhism, inquisitive, philosophic-minded, skilled in debate, but skeptical—raising a host of serious questions and puzzlements about Buddhism, questions and puzzlements that, according to the story, most monks at the time were incapable of answering. Only the formidable Nagasena—miraculously born for this very purpose—was equal to the task. In the dialogue itself, Nagasena plays a part akin to the Platonic Socrates, overcoming one by one each of King Milinda's misgivings by rational argument and apt simile. In the end King Milinda is converted to Buddhism, establishes a great monastic center, and ultimately attains Enlightenment.

The few selections chosen here[2] focus on the nonexistence of the soul and the nature of *nirvāṇa*, here called by its Pali name, *nibbāna*. One could just as well say that the selections seek to demonstrate the systematically misleading character of ordinary language in attempting to speak of *ultimate reality*. For Buddhism, there is no individual soul or self as a linguistically identifiable, enduring metaphysical entity. The difficulty in saying just what it is that a person ultimately is should not, however, be taken to imply that it does not exist. And similar to the way God in Christianity is said to transcend the categories of human comprehension, here *nirvāṇa/nibbāna* is said to transcend mundane categories of understanding. While full comprehension to the unenlightened mundane intellect lies beyond reach, aspects of *nirvāṇa/nibbāna* may nevertheless be intimated by means of analogy with familiar things. The point is not to rest content with the limited intimations of a mundane understanding but to allow such reasonings provoke a breakthrough of insight to a higher level, intuitive comprehension that will itself be Enlightenment.

THE QUESTIONS OF KING MILINDA

The Soul and Rebirth

King Milinda went to Nagasena and after exchanging polite and friendly greetings, took his seat respectfully to one side. Milinda began by asking:

"How is your reverence known, and what sir, is your name?"

"O king, I am known as Nagasena but that is only a designation in common use, for no permanent individual can be found."

Then Milinda called upon the Bactrian Greeks and the monks to bear witness: "This Nagasena says that no permanent individual is implied in his name. Is it possible to approve of that?" Then he turned to Nagasena and said, "If, most venerable Nagasena, that is true, who is it who gives you robes, food and shelter? Who lives the righteous life? Or again, who kills living beings, steals, commits adultery, tells lies or takes strong drink? If what you say is true then there is neither merit nor demerit, nor is there any doer of good or evil deeds and no result of *kamma* [Pali for the Sanskrit *karma*]. If, venerable sir, a man were to kill you there would be no murder, and it follows that there are no masters or teachers in your Order. You say that you are called Nagasena; now what is that Nagasena? It it the hair?"

"I don't say that, great king."

"Is it then the nails, teeth, skin or other parts of the body?"

"Certainly not."

"Or is it the body, or feelings, or perceptions, or formations, or consciousness [the Five Aggregates of Being, i.e., five kinds of phenomena into which the samsaric life of a human being can be exhaustively analyzed according to Theravada]? Is it all of these combined? Or is it something outside of them that is Nagasena?"

And still Nagasena answered: "It is none of these."

"Then ask as I may, I can discover no Nagasena. Nagasena is an empty sound. Who is it we see before us? It is a falsehood that your reverence has spoken."

"You, sir, have been reared in great luxury as becomes your noble birth. How did you come here, by foot or in a chariot?"

"In a chariot, venerable sir."

"Then, explain sir, what that is. Is it the axle? Or the wheels, or the chassis, or reins, or yoke that is the chariot? Is it all of these combined, or is it something apart from them?"

"It is none of these things, venerable sir."

"Then, sir, this chariot is an empty sound. You spoke falsely when you said that you came here in a chariot. You are a great king of India. Who are you afraid of that you speak an untruth?" And he called upon the Bactrian Greeks and the monks to bear witness: "This King Milinda has said that he came here by a chariot but when asked 'What is it?' he is unable to show it. Is it possible to approve of that?"

Then the five hundred Bactrian Greeks shouted their approval and said to the king, "Get out of that if you can!"

"Venerable sir, I have spoken the truth. It is because it has all these parts that it comes under the term chariot."

"Very good, sir, your majesty has rightly grasped the meaning. Even so it is because of thirty-two kinds of organic matter in a human body [distinct parts of the body specifically identified for the purpose of meditation in Theravada] and the five aggregates of being [see above] that I come under the term Nagasena. As it was said by Sister Vajira in the presence of the Blessed One [Gautama Buddha], 'Just as it is by the existence of the various parts that the word "Chariot" is used, just so is it that when the aggregates of being are there we talk of a being.'"

"Most wonderful, Nagasena, most extraordinary that you have solved this puzzle, difficult though it was. If the Buddha himself were here he would approve of your reply."

Then the king said, "Venerable sir, will you discuss with me again?"

"If your majesty will discuss as a scholar, yes; but if you will discuss as a king, no."

"How is it then that scholars discuss?"

"When scholars discuss there is summing up, unravelling; one or other is shown to be in error and he admits his mistake and yet is not thereby angered."

"And how is it that kings discuss?"

"When a king discusses a matter and he advances a point of view, if anyone differs from him on that point he is apt to punish him."

"Very well then, it is as a scholar that I will discuss. Let your reverence talk without fear."

"It is well your majesty."

. . . Thinking, "This monk is a great scholar, he is quite able to discuss things with me," the king instructed Devamantiya, his minister, to invite him to the palace with a large company of monks and went away muttering, "Nagasena, Nagasena."

. . . [A]fter the monks had arrived at the palace and finished their meal, the king sat down on a low seat and asked, "What shall we discuss?"

"Let our discussion be about the Dhamma [Pali for the Sanskrit *Dharma*, the true nature of reality (according to Buddhism) and the Buddha's teaching of it]."

And the King said, "What is the purpose, your reverence, of your going forth [a reference to the action of taking on the condition of a Buddhist monk, reenacting the great going forth of Gautama Buddha] and what is the final goal at which you aim?"

"Our going forth is for the purpose that this suffering may be extinguished and that no further suffering may arise; the complete extinction of grasping without remainder is our final goal."

"Is it, venerable sir, for such noble reasons that everyone joins the Order?"

"No. Some enter to escape the tyranny of kings, some to be safe from robbers, some to escape from debt and some perhaps to gain a livelihood. But those who enter rightly do so for the complete extinction of grasping."

The king said, "Is there anyone who is not reborn after death?"

"Yes there is. The one who has no defilements is not reborn after death; the one who has defilements is reborn."

"Will you be reborn?"

"If I die with craving in my mind, yes; but if not, no."

"Does one who escapes from rebirth do so by the power of reasoning?"

"He escapes both by reasoning and by wisdom, confidence, virtue, mindfulness, energy, and by concentration."

"Is reasoning the same as wisdom?"

"No. Animals have reasoning but they do not have wisdom."

"What, Nagasena, is the characteristic mark of reasoning; and what the mark of wisdom?"

"Taking hold is the mark of reasoning, cutting off is the mark of wisdom."

"Give me an illustration."

"How do barley reapers reap the barley?"

"They grasp the barley into a bunch with the left hand and, with a sickle in the right hand, they cut the barley."

"Just so, O king, the recluse takes hold of his mind with reasoning and cuts off the defilements with wisdom."

"Is cessation nibbāna?"

"Yes, O king. All foolish worldlings take pleasure in the senses and their objects; they find delight in them and cling to them. Hence they are carried down by that flood [of passion—translator's interpolation] and are not set free from birth and suffering. The wise disciple of the noble ones [i.e., Buddhas] does not delight in those things. And in him craving ceases, clinging ceases, becoming ceases, birth ceases, old age, death, grief, lamentation, pain, sorrow and despair cease to exist. Thus it is that cessation is nibbāna."

The Bliss of Nibbāna

"Is nibbāna entirely blissful or is it partly painful?"

"It is entirely blissful."

"But that I cannot accept. Those who seek it have to practise austerity and exertion of body and mind, abstention from food at the wrong time, suppression of sleep, restraint of the senses, and they have to give up wealth, family and friends. They are blissful who enjoy the pleasures of the senses but you restrain and prevent such pleasures and so experience physical and mental discomfort and pain."

"O king, nibbāna has no pain; what you call pain is not nibbāna. It is true that those who seek nibbāna experience pain and discomfort but afterwards they experience the unalloyed bliss of nibbāna. I will tell you a reason for that. Is there, O king, such a thing as the bliss of the sovereignty of kings?"

"Yes there is."

"Is it mixed with pain?"

"No."

"But why is it then, O king, that when the frontier provinces have revolted kings have to set out from their palaces and march over uneven ground, tormented by mosquitoes and hot winds, and engage in fierce battles at the risk of their lives?"

"That, venerable Nagasena, is not the bliss of sovereignty. It is only the preliminary stage in the pursuit of that bliss. It is after they have won it that they enjoy the bliss of sovereignty. And that bliss, Nagasena, is not mixed with pain."

"Just so, O king, nibbāna is unalloyed bliss and there is no pain mixed in it."

Description of Nibbāna

"Is it possible, Nagasena, to point out the size, shape or duration of *nibbāna* by a simile?"

"No it is not possible; there is no other thing like it."

"Is there then any attribute of *nibbāna* found in other things that can be demonstrated by a simile?"

"Yes that can be done.

"As a lotus is unwetted by water, *nibbāna* is unsullied by the defilements.

"Like water, it cools the fever of defilements and quenches the thirst of craving.

"As the ocean is empty of corpses,[3] *nibbāna* is empty of all defilements; as the ocean is not increased by all the rivers that flow into it, so *nibbāna* is not increased by all the beings who attain it; it is the abode of great beings [those who have attained enlightenment], and it is decorated with the waves of knowledge and freedom.

"Like food which sustains life, *nibbāna* drives away old age and death; it increases the spiritual strength of beings; it gives the beauty of virtue, it removes the distress of the defilements, it drives out the exhaustion of all sufferings.

"Like space, it is not born, does not decay or perish, it does not pass away here and arise elsewhere, it is invincible, thieves cannot steal it, it is not attached to anything, it is the sphere of ariyans who are like birds in space, it is unobstructed and it is infinite.

"Like a wish-fulfilling gem, it fulfills all desires, causes delight and is lustrous.

"Like red sandalwood, it is hard to get, its fragrance is incomparable and it is praised by good men.

"As ghee is recognizable by its special attributes, so *nibbāna* has special attributes; as ghee has a sweet fragrance, *nibbāna* has the sweet fragrance of virtue; as ghee has a delicious taste, *nibbāna* has the delicious taste of freedom.

"Like a mountain peak, it is very high, immoveable, inaccessible to the defilements, it has no place where defilements can grow, and it is without favouritism or prejudice."

The Realisation of Nibbāna

"You say, Nagasena, that *nibbāna* is neither past, nor present nor future, neither arisen, nor not arisen, nor producible. In that case does the man who realises *nibbāna* realise something already produced, or does he himself produce it first and then realise it?"

"Neither of these O king, yet *nibbāna* does exist."

"Do not, Nagasena, answer this question by making it obscure! Make it clear and elucidate it. It is a point on which people are bewildered and lost in doubt. Break this dart of uncertainty."

"The element of *nibbāna* does exist, O king, and he who practises rightly and who rightly comprehends the formations [which give rise to the egoistic self that is bound to *saṃsāra*] according to the teachings of the Conqueror [i.e., the Buddha], he, by his wisdom, realises *nibbāna*.

"And how is *nibbāna* to be shown? By freedom from distress and danger, by purity and by coolness. As a man, afraid and terrified at having fallen among enemies, would be relieved and blissful when he had escaped to a safe place; or as one fallen into a pit of filth would be at ease and glad when he had got out of the pit and cleaned up; or as one trapped in a forest fire would be calm and cool when he had reached a safe spot. As fearful and terrifying should you regard the anxiety which arises again and again on account of birth, old age, disease and death; as filth should you regard gain, honours and fame; as hot and searing should you regard the three-fold fire of lust, hatred and delusion.

"And how does he who is practising rightly realise *nibbāna*? He rightly grasps the cyclic nature of formations and therein he sees only birth, old age, disease and death; he sees nothing pleasant or agreeable in any part of it. Seeing nothing there to be taken hold of, as on a red-hot iron ball, his mind overflows with discontent and a fever takes hold of his body; hopeless and without a refuge he becomes disgusted with repeated lives. And to him who sees the terror of the treadmill of life [i.e., *samsāra*, or the samsaric experience of life] the thought arises, 'On fire and blazing is this wheel of life, full of suffering and despair. If only there could be an end to it, that would be peaceful, that would be excellent; the cessation of all mental formations, the renunciation of grasping, the destruction of craving, dispassion, cessation, *nibbāna*!'

"Therewith his mind leaps forward into the state where there is no becoming. Then has he found peace, then does he exult and rejoice at the thought, 'A refuge has been found at last!' He strives along the path for the cessation of formations, searches it out, develops it, and makes much of it. To that end he stirs up his mindfulness, energy and joy; and from attending again and again to that thought [of disgust with mental formations—*translator's interpolation*], having transcended the treadmill of life, he brings the cycle to a halt. One who stops the treadmill is said to have realized *nibbāna*."

Where is Nibbāna?

"Is there a place, Nagasena, where *nibbāna* is stored up?"

"No there is not, yet it does exist. As there is no place where fire is stored up, yet it may be produced by rubbing two dry sticks together."

"But is there any place on which a man might stand and realise *nibbāna*?"

"Yes there is; virtue is the place;[4] standing on that and with reasoning, wherever he might be, whether in the land of the Scythians or the Bactrians, whether in China or Tibet, in Kashmir or Gandhara, on a mountain top or in the highest heavens; the one who practises rightly realises *nibbāna*."

"Very good, Nagasena, you have taught about *nibbāna*, you have explained about the realisation of *nibbāna*, you have praised the qualities of virtue, shown the right way of practice, raised aloft the banner of the Dhamma, established the Dhamma as a leading principle, not barren nor without fruit are the efforts of those with right aims!"

Reprinted by permission of the publisher from Bhikkhu Pesala, ed., *The Debate of King Milinda: An Abridgement of the Milinda Panha* (Buddhist Traditions, Vol. XIV; Dehli: Motilal Barnarsidass, 1991), pp. 3–6, 19, and 83–86.

A CHRISTIAN EXAMPLE:
ANSELM'S FAITH SEEKING
UNDERSTANDING

The way of reasoned inquiry in Christianity did not receive the kind of early emphasis and direction that it did in Buddhism. It has had to struggle from time to
time against two worries. First, it was feared that too great a latitude given to rational inquiry might threaten appropriate understanding of the truth of Revelation
(what was believed to have been revealed of God in Christ) and culminate in
heretical teaching. Second, the sense of autonomy, pride, and pretentiousness
that are naturally engendered in rational inquiry were seen to be in potential, if
not actual, conflict with the requisite attitude of humble and simple faith. The
Gospel was regarded as more accessible to simple, uneducated folk than to any
educated intellectual elite. For many in Christendom, because the content of
Revelation to their thinking is already clearly and unambiguously explicit, the
only appropriate response is obedience, and not at all to question why, or what
does it mean, or is it really so.

This view, however, did not predominate. Because of the strong precedent
set by early Christian thinkers such as Justin Martyr (100–165), Origin (185–254),
and Augustine (354–430), the way of reasoned inquiry came to have a significant
place, especially in Western Christianity. For them, the Revelation of God in Christ
was an inexhaustible mystery evoking wonder. In their understanding, Christ was
the universal *Logos* or Reason of God, linking all Christians with reason and truth
wherever it might be found. In consequence, rational inquiry for them was not to
be limited simply to the study and interpretation of what had been made explicit
of the Christian Revelation (e.g., in scripture, ecumenical council, or papal pronouncement). For them, rational inquiry was a way of entering more deeply into
the the mystery of that revelation. Moreover, by being joined with the *Logos* of
God, human reason was deemed capable of accessing truth in all realms and motivated to do so.

With the rediscovery of classical learning (and the writings of Aristotle, above
all) and the rise of the medieval universities in twelfth-century Europe, a distinctive
form of *theological* study known as scholasticism emerged. The result was an establishment of the basic parameters for most of subsequent *theological* reflection
in Western Christianity, especially for Roman Catholic theology but also for much of
Protestant thought. It was developed through intensive study of church doctrine, of
the writings of respected earlier Christian thinkers, and of sacred scripture (especially as these bore upon issues of disagreement and controversy), honed through
rigorous debate, and elaborated in a systematic form that sought to account for all
major theological questions. *Theology* in this approach aspired to be a kind of rational science. Systematic theology in this sense is clearly an expression of the way
of reasoned inquiry—though what it amounts to in practice as a distinctive way to

draw near to and come into right relationship with God (i.e., as a distinctive spirituality) has rarely been explicitly reflected upon. Nevertheless, *theologicaP* study in this sense has been a large and respected part of Christian life in the West, especially for priests, ministers, and persons involved in religious vocations in Roman Catholic and mainstream Protestant traditions since the thirteenth century.

Long preceding the rise of scholasticism and continuing as a counterpoint to scholastic theology into modern times, there has been a less systematic and more mystically oriented sort of inquiry, in which the inquiry itself is unmistakably a personal religious quest (fusing some aspects of the way of mystical quest with the way of reasoned inquiry). This alternative pattern of inquiry was given its strongest precedent by Augustine, especially in his early works, and became characteristic of *theologicaP* reflection pursued in a monastic context. It came to be known as monastic theology and distinguished itself from scholastic theology once the latter fully emerged.[5] Illustrated perhaps most clearly in Augustine's *Confessions*, intellectual inquiry in this approach involves, or rather is, a kind of dialogue with God in Christ, and specifically with the divine *Logos* that is believed to illuminate the mind and be the source of creative insight. To inquire *theologically°*, accordingly, is *personally* to draw near to God. After Augustine, the major figure who most clearly exemplifies this orientation is Anselm (1033–1109)—monk, prior, and abbot of a Benedictine monastery at Bec and later Bishop of Canterbury.

The selections that follow are about and by Anselm.[6] They focus upon a little book of meditations, entitled *Proslogion* and subtitled *Fides quaerens intellectum* ("faith seeking understanding"). This small book has come to exercise an extraordinary influence and provocation of thought down to the present day because of a remarkable argument in its second and third chapters, apparently drawing the conclusion of the existence of God from the idea that faith has of God. Most subsequent discussion of this so-called "ontological argument" (which has continued unabated until the present day) fails, however, to take account of its context in the life of monastic spirituality and its explicit intention "to seek to understand what is believed" and thereby raise the mind from "faith in God" to "the contemplation of God"—a contemplative, mystical knowing that transcends explicit representation. That is to say, the argument is designed to shift the reader's attention from the idea of God to the reality of God, from thinking about God to comprehending that one stands mentally in the very presence of God.

ANSELM OF CANTERBURY: A MONASTIC SCHOLAR

For Anselm an essential part of . . . [the] process of conversion was an intellectual one. [Note: all Benedictine monastics are directed to understand monastic life as involving a lifelong *conversion* to God and to his service.] The intellect is an integral part of man's created being and needs, as much as the rest of him, to be brought into contact with God for restoration and cleansing. "To discover the rational basis of the monastic life" [was one of two principal concerns of Anselm upon becoming a monk, according to his biographer and disciple, Eadmer. The other and first was simply to be a true monk.] . . . . "The rational basis"—what did Anselm mean by "*ratio*"? To find out one looks rather at the *Monologion* and the *Proslogion* than at the *Prayers*. The first title Anselm gave to the *Monologion* was "*De ratione fidei*," an ambiguous title which he soon dropped. More appropriate for what he was trying to do was his sub-title, "*Fides quaerens intellectum*," for the *Proslogion*—that treatise in which prayer and intellectual thought are most wonderfully combined. It is here that we can see what Anselm meant by "*ratio*," and how it formed part of his prayer.

The *Proslogion* [explicitly] begins as a meditation . . . . [And it] is clear that the major part of the *Proslogion*—twenty-one chapters out of twenty-five—is a meditation, a prayer reflecting upon the nature of belief in God. But to look only at those is to side-step the issue, for the early chapters contain a philosophic statement about the existence and nature of God more exciting than any produced in a monastery before or since and which has, more than anything else, given to Anselm—mistakenly—the title "Father of Scholasticism." It is a demonstration which has aroused and continues to arouse, lively interest among philosophers and theologians, including Descartes, Kant, Hegel, Leibnitz and Barth. . . .

"God is that than which nothing greater can be thought." It is important to see this [idea of God, the premise on which hinges Anselm's demonstration] in context and not in isolation, and especially in the context of its first expression. At Bec Anselm was exercising all the abilities of his mind to discover "the rationale of the nature of God as the true faith holds it to be," when suddenly "one night during matins [one in the cycle of formal community prayers, sometimes prayed at midnight] the grace of God shone in his heart, the whole matter became clear to his mind, and a great joy and jubilation filled his whole being."[7] It was a matter of illumination about what was already believed, and it is this that provided the starting point for his arguments, not the reverse. It happened in the middle of a monastic service, and the whole setting of it is a prayer of longing and desire for God which is entirely monastic in tone. There is a joy and excitement which is far removed from the logical demonstrations of scholasticism and closer to the mystical experience of prayer. Anselm was not constructing a logical structure and imposing it upon God; nor was he proposing to discover by logical argument the existence of God as the end term of his own propositions. His fundamental way of doing theology was to bring all the powers of his mind to bear upon what he already believed, and this experience at Bec produced the gift of understanding more.

It has often been said that the "proofs" of the *Proslogion* would never convince an unbeliever. For Anselm, theology is only true insofar as it corresponds to the being of God, and "*ratio*" for him is "*ratio dei*," the living word of God which is beyond all systems of human thought. Applying to the utmost all the powers of intellect and reason to "seeking God," the basis is nonetheless a confrontation with God himself and his saving purposes, which will in itself clear the mind of its darkness and restore it to that contact with God in himself which can be described either as true theology or as prayer. To do this Anselm uses every kind of concept: the Scriptures, dogma, and credal statements on the one hand, the secular concepts of philosophy on the other. "God is that than which nothing greater can be thought" affirms the impossibility of proving the unknowable essence of

God by human reasoning. It is a way of knowledge that is apophatic; it is a demonstration rather than a proof. And from it Anselm explores whatever can be said or thought about God, using this first insight as the basis of his prayer and thought. "Thank you, good Lord," he exclaims, "for by your gift I first believed and now by your illumination I understand."

This encounter with God, which he calls "illumination," is the attitude of a monk who having dedicated his entire being to God offers the whole of his mind, as well as his body, to knowing that truth which is beyond concepts, and to receiving it as a transfiguring experience. This is how Anselm understood the rational basis of the monastic life—not by looking for reasons to justify it, but by seeing the truth in God.

The mystics tell us that no experience of God remains static or unused, it must communicate itself. This leads to the third of Eadmer's points about Anselm: "He expounded it to others."

Anselm was not primarily a teacher, a school-man, a pedagogue . . . . He is concerned with his personal search for God and it is significant that he uses the dynamic word "seek." For Anselm prayer is not a static reception of something that can be passed on to others but an ardent and vigorous quest in which others may join him if they wish. . . .

The *Proslogion* was also a prayer, an *"exemplum meditandi"* ["example meditation"], and it was written, Anselm says, to share with others the joy he had felt in his experience of God. His concern is that everyone, even the "fool," should be brought to some experience of God whose nature it is to desire to bring sinners to repentance. Anselm's teaching always has this connotation of enabling others to experience God for themselves. He was not, like Lanfranc [Anselm's teacher who first advised him to become a monk at Bec], a master of the schools, attracting pupils from outside the monastery and teaching them according to a system. Anselm preferred to talk with his friends, with a few intelligent monks [as well as laypersons], with whom he could discuss ideas and communicate by talking rather than by teaching.

Reprinted by permission of the publisher from Benedicta Ward, "Anselm of Canterbury: a Monastic Scholar," in her *Signs and Wonders: Saints, Miracles and Prayers from the 4th Century to the 14th* (Brookfield, VT: Variorum/Ashgate, 1992), pp. 8–12.

PROSLOGION

Chapter I
In which the mind is aroused to the contemplation of God

> Come now, little man,
> turn aside for a while from your daily employment,
> escape for a moment from the tumult of your thoughts.
> Put aside your weighty cares,
> let your burdensome distractions wait,
> free yourself awhile for God
> and rest awhile in him.
> Enter the inner chamber of your soul,

shut out everything except God
and that which can help you in seeking him,
and when you have shut the door, seek him.
Now, my whole heart, say to God,
"I seek your face,
Lord, it is your face I seek."

O Lord my God,
teach my heart where and how to seek you,
where and how to find you.
Lord, if you are not here but absent,
where shall I seek you?
But you are everywhere, so you must be here,
why then do I not seek you?
Surely you dwell in light inaccessible—
where is it? and how can I
have access to light which is inaccessible?
Who will lead me and take me into it
so that I may see you there?
By what signs, under what forms, shall I seek you?
I have never seen you, O lord my God,
I have never seen your face.
Most High Lord,
what shall an exile do
who is as far away from you as this?
What shall your servant do,
eager for your love, cast off far from your face?
He longs to see you,
but your countenance is too far away.
He wants to have access to you,
but your dwelling is inaccessible.
He longs to find you,
but he does not know where you are.
He loves to seek you
but he does not know your face.
Lord, you are my Lord and my God,
and I have never seen you.
You have created and re-created me,
all the good I have comes from you,
and still I do not know you.
I was created to see you,
and I have not yet accomplished that for which I was made. . . .
I confess, Lord, with thanksgiving,
that you have made me in your image,
so that I can remember you, think of you, and love you.
But that image is so worn and blotted out by faults,

so darkened by the smoke of sin,
that it cannot do that for which it was made,
unless you renew and refashion it.
Lord, I am not trying to make my way to your height,
for my understanding is in no way equal to that,
but I do desire to understand a little of your truth
which my heart already believes and loves.
I do not seek to understand so that I may believe,
but I believe so that I may understand;
and what is more,
I believe that unless I do believe I shall not understand.

Chapter 2
That God really exists

Now, Lord, since it is you who gives understanding to faith, grant me to understand as well as you think fit, that you exist as we believe, and that you are what we believe you to be. We believe that you are that thing than which nothing greater can be thought. Or is there nothing of that kind in existence, since "the fool has said in his heart, there is no God"? But when the fool hears me use this phrase, "something than which nothing greater can be thought," he understands what he hears; and what he understands is in his understanding, even if he does not understand that it exists. For it is one thing to have something in the understanding, but quite another to understand that it actually exists. It is like a painter who, when he thinks out beforehand what he is going to create, has it in his understanding, but he does not yet understand it as actually existing because he has not yet painted it. But when he has painted it, he both has it in his understanding and actually has it, because he has created it. So the fool has to agree that the concept of something than which nothing greater can be thought exists in his understanding, since he understood what he heard and whatever is understood is in the understanding. And certainly that than which nothing greater can be thought cannot exist only in the understanding. For if it exists only in the understanding, it is possible to think of it existing also in reality, and that is greater. If that than which nothing greater can be thought exists in the understanding alone, then this thing than which nothing greater can be thought is something than which a greater can be thought. And this is clearly impossible. Therefore there can be no doubt at all that something than which a greater cannot be thought exists both in the understanding and in reality.

In a nutshell, these last four sentences constitute the main body of the demonstration. They pass by so quickly that the suspicion easily arises that some kind of verbal trick is being played. Take care and read them through again.

Note here that the idea of God implicit in faith, according to Anselm, is not "the greatest" or "the most perfect being imaginable." That would put the idea of God at the end of the scale as a definite something. On the contrary, God is "that than which nothing greater can be thought." Whatever you can definitely imagine on the scale of more and less great, God is greater. In effect, the idea of God is the idea of something off the end of the scale. It is thus not an idea of something definite but rather of something infinite. Yet the idea here articulated is nevertheless thinkable. It is the thought of that which transcends thought in the direction of perfection or greatness. Here the mind, as it were, is at its limit and discovers the peculiarity of a thought of something necessarily lying beyond its grasp, the thought of something that of its very nature the mind cannot encompass, and which therefore cannot be merely *in* the mind. In this one instance, at least, the mind encounters an infinitude transcending itself. At this point the idea comes to seem no mere representation of something that may or may not exist outside the mind but rather a token of the actual presence to the mind of that thing. Anselm now goes on to demonstrate the peculiar kind of existence or being that it has.

Chapter 3
That which it is not possible to think of as not existing

This *is* so truly, that it is not possible to think of it not existing. For it is possible to think of something existing which it is not possible to think of as not existing, and that is greater than something that can be thought not to exist. If that than which nothing greater can be thought, can be thought of as not existing, then that than which nothing greater can be thought is not the same as that than which nothing greater can be thought. And that simply will not do. Something than which nothing greater can be thought so truly exists that it is not possible to think of it as not existing.

This being is yourself, our Lord and God. Lord my God, you so truly are, that it is not possible to think of you as not existing. And rightly so. For if someone's mind could think of something better than you, the creature would rise higher than its creator and would judge its creator; which is clearly absurd. For whatever exists except you alone can be thought of as not existing. Therefore you alone of all most truly are, and you exist most fully of all things. For nothing else is as true as that, and therefore it has *less* existence. So why does the fool say in his heart, "there is no God," when it is perfectly clear to the reasoning mind that you exist most fully of all? Why, except that he is indeed stupid and a fool?

Chapter 4
That what the fool said in his heart
is something that it is not possible to think

Now how has he "said in his heart" what it is not possible to think; for how could he avoid thinking that which he "said in his heart," for to say in one's heart is to think. But if he really did, or rather because he really did, both think, because he said in his heart, and not say in his heart, because he was not able to think, then there is not only one way of saying in one's heart and thinking. For in a way one thinks a thing when one thinks the word that signifies the thing; but one thinks it in another way when the thing itself is understood. So in one way it is possible to entertain the concept that God does not exist, but not in the other way. For no one who truly understands that which God is, can think that God does not exist, though he may say those words in his heart, either without any, or with a special, meaning. For God is that than which nothing greater can be thought. Whoever truly understands this, understands that he is of such a kind of existence that he cannot be thought not to exist. So whoever understands this to be the nature of God, cannot think of him as not existing.

Thank you, good Lord, thank you, for it was by your gift that I first believed, and now by your illumination I understand; if I did not want to believe that you existed, still I should not be able not to understand it.

In the remaining chapters Anselm proceeds to demonstrate the more traditional Christian qualities of God: "just, true, blessed, and whatever it is better to be than not to be" (Ch. 5); just as much perceiving, all powerful, compassionate, and impassible as "alive, wise, good, blessed, eternal, and whatever it is better to be than not to be" (Ch. 11); life itself, wisdom itself, goodness itself, and so forth (Ch. 12); and unlimited by time and space and eternal (Ch. 13).[8]

Reprinted with permission of the publisher from *The Prayers and Meditations of Saint Anselm*, trans. Sister Benedicta Ward (New York: Penguin Classics, 1973), pp. 239–246. Copyright © Benedicta Ward, 1973.

CHAPTER SUMMARY

To exemplify the way of reasoned inquiry for Buddhism the excerpt from the *Milindapañha* presents a philosophical dialogue between an inquisitive and skeptical King Milinda and a calm and learned Buddhist philosopher. Their discussion takes up the "ultimate unreality" of what we ordinarily conceive the individual person to be, the transcendent nature of the ultimate state of enlightenment (*nirvāṇa/nibbāna*), and along the way the role of reasoning and wisdom in the pursuit of enlightenment. In addition to rationally plausible answers to fundamental questions, the reader is given a model of intellectual inquiry and argument that is itself a drawing near to *ultimate reality*⁰ as Buddhists conceive it.

As an illustration of the way of reasoned inquiry as found in the Christian tradition, Anselm's *Proslogion* is simultaneously an impassioned seeking of God and a philosophical meditation. It aims, through rational argumentation, to rouse the mind of the reader from meditating on an idea of God that faith has—"that being than which nothing greater can be conceived"—to a recognition of the infinite *reality*⁰ to which that idea points. Here rational inference fuses with intuitive insight and discursive argument culminates in mystical awareness. Here too a model is presented of a form of intellectual inquiry and argument that is itself a drawing near to *ultimate reality*⁰ as Christians conceive it.

STUDY QUESTIONS ON SIMILARITIES AND DIFFERENCES

On first reading, these excerpts from the *Milindapañha* and Anselm's *Proslogion* present two very different religious expressions, giving voice to what may seem to be unrelated, if not contradictory, religious beliefs. It is a challenge to find what features the two examples share in common. Spend some time comparing the accounts. Focus more on the process of thinking represented than on the specific thoughts, more on the inquiry and reasoning involved than on the explicit results. Keep in mind the danger of generalizing from these specific forms of *theology*ᵖ to all such forms in either tradition. Be mindful as well of how much may be involved implicitly in the actual practice of these specific forms of *theologizing*ᵖ that may be going unsaid in the excerpts. Consider the following questions.

1. What similarities do you find? (Consider, for example, how each appeals to reason and to the reader's interest in moving from intellectual puzzlement to understanding; how each cultivates the movement to a deeper intellectual understanding as itself a drawing near to the religious objective of at-one-ment with *ultimate reality*ᵖ; how *ultimate reality*ᵖ for each lies beyond ordinary, explicit modes of thought; how argumentation in each aims at provoking a shift in perspective and leap of intuitive insight to comprehend matters that transcend mundane frames of reference; etc.).

2. Assuming that both of these practices exemplify the same generic way of being religious in two distinct religious traditions, what if anything do the similarities identified in answer to the first question indicate that is essential to that way of being religious (which the framework identifies as the way of reasoned inquiry)?
   a. What do these two practices have in common regarding their respective means of approach to *ultimate reality*ᵖ?
   b. What characteristic existential problems are each concerned with and seeking to address? What do the accounts presume to be motivating their respective readers?
   c. Is there anything that indicates the characteristic way each interprets its broader tradition's scripture and symbol system in a manner distinct from other traditional ways of taking them? What sorts of features of *ultimate reality*ᵖ does each specifically highlight? That is, what kind of "face" does each envision *ultimate reality*ᵖ to have?
   d. What sorts of social structures (social organization, group activity, roles and responsibilities, etc.) do these excerpts each imply or presuppose for its way of being religious? (This question may be harder to answer in connection with these excerpts than with others.)
   e. What specific virtues in the practice of its form of religious life (i.e., the kind of religious intellectual inquiry it embodies) does each appear to commend, whether explicitly or implicitly, and what specific vices in that practice does each appear to condemn? (Be careful here to distinguish criticisms each may apparently offer of the religious practices of others from critical expectations set for its own followers.) That is, what ideal(s) of practice does each uphold? And what sorts of things would fall short of those ideals?

3. What differences do you find? (Consider, for example, the distinct conceptions of *ultimate reality*ᴾ in each; the readiness of the one to speak of *ultimate reality*ᴾ as a being and the unreadiness of the other to do so; the passionate desire for an intimate, personal rapport with *ultimate reality*ᴾ in the one and a relatively dispassionate, pragmatic interest in comprehending things for the sake of release from the treadmill of mundane life in the other; the acknowledgement in the one of divine grace in bestowing insight and understanding and the apparent absence of anything comparable in the other; etc.).

4. To what extent do there seem to be incompatibilities or contradictions between statements made in the two excerpts? Are these contradictions substantial or might they be apparent only?[9]

5. What among the differences identified in questions 3 and 4 seems to be due to what makes the one Buddhist (or specifically Theravada Buddhist) and the other Christian (or specifically Western Augustinian Christian)? (Again beware, here, of concluding that these practices represent all instances of the way of reasoned inquiry in their respective traditions.)

FOR FURTHER READING

Recommended articles in the *Encyclopedia of Religion*, edited by Mircea Eliade (New York: Macmillan, 1987), include *Wisdom; Truth; Reason; Knowledge and Ignorance; Buddhism, Schools of Buddhist Philosophy; Prajñā; Paramitās; Sunyam and Śūnyatā; Nirvāṇa; Saṃsāra; Mādhyamika; Yogācāra; Nāgārjuna; Dge-lugs-pa [Gelukpa]; Theology, Christian Theology; Scholasticism; Logos; Proofs for the Existence of God; Anselm; Thomas Aquinas; Augustine of Hippo.*

Herbert V. Guenther, *Tibetan Buddhism without Mystification* (Leiden, Netherlands: Brill, 1966). A general introduction to *Gelukpa* Tibetan philosophy.

David J. Kalupahana, *A History of Buddhist Philosophy: Continuities and Discontinuities* (Honolulu, HI: University of Hawaii Press, 1992). One of the better overviews of the history of Buddhist philosophy.

Guy Newland, *Compassion: A Tibetan Analysis* (London: Wisdom, 1984). Gives a good idea of what the give and take of Tibetan philosophical argumentation is like in practice.

Daniel Perdue, *Introductory Debate in Tibetan Buddhism* (Dharmshala, India: Library of Tibetan Works and Archives, 1976). A brief introduction to the tradition of Tibetan philosophical debate.

The Questions of King Milinda, trans. T. W. Rhys Davids, The Sacred Books of the East, Vols. 35, 36 (Delhi, India: Motilal Banarsidass, 1965; first published 1890–94). The complete work that has been excerpted above.

Frederick J. Streng, *Emptiness—A Study in Religious Meaning* (Nashville, TN: Abingdon Press, 1967). One of the best overall studies of the preeminent *Prajñā-pāramitā* "philosophical theologian," Nāgārjuna, in English—highly recommended.

Junjiro Takakusu, *Essentials of Buddhist Philosophy*, 2nd ed. (Honolulu, HI: University of Hawaii Press, 1949). Basic introduction to the essentials of different Buddhist philosophical schools.

John Hick and Arthur C. McGill, eds., *The Many-Faced Argument: Recent Studies on the Ontological Argument for the Existence of God* (New York: Macmillan, 1967). The essays collected here give a good idea of recent interpretations and criticisms of Anselm's argument for the existence of God.

Maurice De Wulf, *An Introduction to Scholastic Philosophy: Medieval and Modern* (New York: Dover, 1956). One of the better introductions to Scholastic philosophy, but does not give a very good idea of its living practice.

Etienne Gilson, *The Spirit of Medieval Philosophy* (Notre Dame, IN: University of Notre Dame Press, 1936). Still the best introduction to the heart of medieval Christian philosophy.

See Jean Leclerq, *The Love of Learning and the Desire for God: A Study of Monastic Culture* (New York: Fordham University Press, 1982). Perhaps the best introduction to medieval monastic theology. Very good on placing Anselm in context.

Armand A. Maurer, *Medieval Philosophy* (New York: Random House, 1962). One of the better histories of medieval European philosophy.

The Prayers and Meditations of Saint Anselm, trans. Benedicta Ward (New York: Penguin Books, 1973). A must in order to understand fully the thought of Anselm and to see it in its context of monastic spirituality.

Gregory Schufreider, *Confessions of a Rational Mystic: Anselm's Early Writings* (West Lafayette, IN: Perdue University Press, 1994). A comprehensive study of the place of rational argumentation within Anselm's mystical theology.

Benedicta Ward, "Anselm of Canterbury: A Monastic Scholar" Fairacres Publication 62 (Oxford, England: SLG Press, 1973/1990). [Reprinted in Benedicta Ward, *Signs and Wonders: Saints, Miracles and Prayers from the 4th Century to the 14th* (Brookfield, VT: Variorum/Ashgate, 1992), pp. 8–12.]. A good, brief overview of Anselm's thought.

NOTES

1. A reminder: words or phrases that are italicized and marked with a degree symbol are generic place-holders for a corresponding word or phrase from a specific tradition that articulates a specific conception uniquely suited to that tradition's conception of *ultimate reality°*. Strictly speaking, the word *theology* has little if any application in Buddhism. "*Theology°*" is used here and elsewhere to refer generically to the process and results of the way of reasoned inquiry into ultimate matters within any given religious tradition.

2. Bhikkhu Pesala, *The Debate of King Milinda: An Abridgement of the Milinda Panha* (Buddhist Traditions, vol. XIV; Dehli, India: Motilal Banarsidass, 1991), pp. 3–6, 19, and 83–86.

3. It was believed in ancient India that the great ocean did not retain the dead but cast up their corpses onto the shore.

4. Earlier in the *Milindapañha*, virtue is characterized as the supporting basis of all good qualities, as Theravada Buddhism accounts for them, namely, those that are conducive to Enlightenment.

5. See Jean Leclerq, *The Love of Learning and the Desire for God: A Study of Monastic Culture* (New York: Fordham University Press, 1982).

6. The first selection is from Benedicta Ward, "Anselm of Canterbury: a Monastic Scholar," Fairacres Publication 62 (Oxford, England: SLG Press, 1973/1990), reprinted in Benedicta Ward, *Signs and Wonders: Saints, Miracles and Prayers from the 4th Century to the 14th* (Brookfield, VT: Variorum/Ashgate, 1992), pp. 8–12. The second is from *The Prayers and Meditations of Saint Anselm*, trans. Benedicta Ward (New York: Penguin Books, 1973), pp. 239–246.

7. Ward is here quoting in her own translation Eadmer, *Vita Anselmi*, Vol. 1, xix. An English translation of the work is Eadmer, *Life of St. Anselm*, ed. and trans. by R. W. Southern (Oxford, 1972).

8. For a fine discussion of the entirety of the *Proslogion* in a manner consistent with the interpretation given here, see Anselm Stolz, "Anselm's Theology in the Proslogion," in *The Many-Faced Argument: Recent Studies on the Ontological Argument for the Existence of God*, ed. John Hick and Arthur C. McGill (New York: Macmillan, 1967), pp. 183–206.

9. Some recent attempts to rethink the nature of the existence of God coming out of the Buddhist-Christian dialogue—to rethink it in a manner true to Scripture but letting go of some cherished categories of traditional Christian theism deriving from ancient Greek philosophy—suggest that the apparent contradictions between Christian theology and Buddhist teachings may not be so radical as they first seem to be and that there may be a way to reconcile some of the differences. See Roger Corless and Paul F. Knitter, eds., *Buddhist Emptiness and Christian Trinity: Essays and Explorations* (New York: Paulist Press, 1990); Julia Ching, "Paradigms of the Self in Buddhism and Christianity," *Buddhist-Christian Studies* 4 (1984), pp. 31–50; and Donald W. Mitchell, *Spirituality and Emptiness: The Dynamics of Spiritual Life in Buddhism and Christianity* (New York: Paulist Press, 1991).

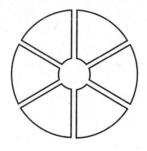

C H A P T E R   11

THE WAY OF RIGHT ACTION IN BUDDHISM AND CHRISTIANITY

A BUDDHIST EXAMPLE: THE SARVODAYA MOVEMENT IN SRI LANKA

Not long ago, the present Dalai Lama responded to the question, "What is a simple basic practice one should bear in mind if one finds it difficult to comprehend all the different levels of practice?" with the following answer: "I think in short that it's best, if you're able, to help others. If you're not able to do so, however, then at least do not harm others. This is the main practice."[1] Concern for appropriate action or virtuous conduct (*sīla/śīla*) has always been an important feature of Buddhism, whatever the subtradition, but it has tended to be regarded as an essential but penultimate focus of concern. This concern is manifest in several ways: adherence to the precepts (e.g., noninjury to sentient beings) and cultivation of the virtues (e.g., compassion) in one's personal conduct; communication of Buddhist teachings; charitable activities; efforts to promote public welfare; living an alternative, distinctively Buddhist form of community life (whether in monastic or quasi-monastic communities); and efforts to bring about social change in accordance with Buddhist teaching. Only rarely has the way of right action become the primary focus of a subtradition. But examples where it has become a primary focus in both Theravada and Mahayana can be found.

One illustrative example is the Sarvodaya movement in Sri Lanka in the last half of the twentieth century. It represents a relatively new but nevertheless very Buddhist kind of social activism that can be found in other places in Southeast Asia as well as other parts of the world. The following account by Ken Jones[2] describes this broader movement of Buddhist social activism as "a transcendental radicalism":

Transcendental Radicalism

In the first place, this radicalism is *transcendental* in that radical social change is necessarily and explicitly based on personal development within a spiritual context, that is, through mindfulness, meditation, and retreat, but also through trying to make a work of art of personal and group relations and following a [distinctively Buddhist] lifestyle [which Jones outlines in a previous chapter] . . . . Conventional political radicalism is *transcended* in that radical personal change is also included as an essential part of the process of fundamental social change. For most people and in the short term this development may in spiritual terms be quite modest: just becoming a little more human. But this is nonetheless significant, as is also the overarching spiritual perspective within which it takes place. This engaged spirituality is concerned with creating at the same time social conditions which will both relieve affliction and also support and foster personal growth.

In the second place, transcendental radicalism achieves social change through grass-roots initiatives of individuals and groups working in a spirit of community self-help and self-reliance. This reflects the tradition of self-reliance in Buddhist practice . . . . Emphasis is upon the development of networks of such groups and communities and the avoidance of hierarchical élites. Those who do the thinking also implement the decisions and those who implement the decisions also do the spade-work and take responsibility for it.

In the third place it follows that there is much emphasis on many different kinds of active learning, particularly from practical experience, and in a group, and through open dialogue, both for personal development and community and social development.

In the fourth place, transcendental radicalism is marked by its use of positive and active nonviolent strategies, which recognize the common humanity of the adversary and his dignity and autonomy. Change can only come through creative interaction (both inside and outside the movement) and the avoidance of negative forms of coercion even if they stop short of physical violence. . . . In particular, to appropriate the Buddhadharma to fortify one's own racial or national identity is grievously to pervert the Buddhadharma.

Fifthly, this is a conservative radicalism which seeks to foster all that is best in traditional culture and practice, and particularly the sense of community, regional and ethnic identity. Change has to be authentic and organic in character, from the roots, rather than imposed, mechanistic and manipulative. The old way of doing things, or some adaptation or evolution of it, may still be the best way. There is a particular concern to pioneer a Third Way of social and cultural development alternative to either Western capitalist-style "development" or communist-style socialism.

Sixthly, transcendental radicalism is pluralist, nonsectarian, fraternal and open-minded in its relations with other belief systems, whether secular or religious, which share the same broad human values and concerns.

Seventhly, this engaged spirituality thinks globally as well as acting locally, and is particularly concerned with communication and co-operation between people of the First and Third Worlds.

Grass-Roots Activism in Sri Lanka

Sarvodaya, which means "the awakening and welfare of all," refers to spiritually inspired, rural self-development movements in India and Sri Lanka. The Sarvodaya movement of post-colonial India attempted unsuccessfully to implement the Gandhian ideal of a network of autonomous village commonwealths, and Gandhi's heir, Jayaprakash Narayan followed his example of mass civil disobedience when the Congress government frustrated that ideal. By contrast the Sri Lanka movement evolved in the Asokan tradition[3] of a just relationship between village communities on the one hand and on the other a State which was perceived to be comparatively benevolent.

Sarvodaya began in Sri Lanka in 1958, when a young teacher, A. Y. Ariyaratne, encouraged his students to organize a fortnight "holiday work camp" in a destitute village. The students worked closely with the villagers and were concerned to learn what they themselves perceived as their needs and problems. Other schools and colleges followed this example, and a village self-help movement emerged, outside the official rural development programme. During the 1970s training centres for community co-ordinators and specialists were established with help from overseas aid agencies. These schemes included a programme for the systematic training and involvement of Buddhist monks, who traditionally are highly influential in village life. Over two and a half million people, living in 7000 of Sri Lanka's 23,000 village communities are now involved in Sarvodaya, aided by some 2000 monks. The Village Awakening Councils enjoy programme and budget autonomy, but receive much specialist support from area and regional centres backed by extensive training programmes. Projects include roads, irrigation works, preschool facilities, community kitchens, retail co-operatives and the promotion of village handicrafts (though impact on agriculture appears to have been disappointing). Joanna Macy describes the typical *shramadana* or voluntary co-operative work project as being "like a combination of road gang, town meeting, vaudeville show and revival service—and these many facets build people's trust and enjoyment of each other."[4]

Ariyaratne, now the movement's President, emphasizes that "The chief objective of Sarvodaya is personality awakening."[5] The root problem of poverty is seen as being a sense of personal and collective powerlessness. And "awakening" is to take place not in isolation but through social, economic and political interaction. Personal awakening is seen as being interdependent with the awakening of one's local community, and both play a part in the awakening of one's nation and the whole world.

The spiritual precondition for all-round social development is kept in the forefront through Sarvodaya's creative interpretation of traditional Buddhist teachings in forms which can be understood and experienced by people collectively and in social terms. Thus, the shared suffering of a community, the poverty, disease, exploitation, conflict and stagnation, is explored together by the members as is also the suffering experienced by each one of them. But, crucially, this suffering is shown to have its origins in individual egocentricity, distrust, greed and competitiveness, which demoralizes and divides the community and wastes its potential. In place of the corrupted traditional meaning of kamma [Pali for the Sanskrit *karma*] as "fate," Ariyaratne emphasizes the original Buddhist teaching. "It is one's own doing that reacts on one's own self, so it is possible to divert the course of our lives. . . . [(*Jones's interpolation*:) Once we understand that,] inactivity or lethargy suddenly transforms into activity leading to social and economic development."[6]

Similarly, each of the practices comprising the traditional Buddhist Eightfold Path is amplified socially. For example, Macy quotes a Sarvodaya trainer:

> *Right Mindfulness—that means stay open and alert to the needs of the village. . . . Look to see what is needed—latrines, water, road. . . . Try to enter the minds of the people, to listen behind their words. Practise mindfulness in the shramadana camp: is the food enough? are people getting wet? are the tools in order? is anyone being exploited?*[7]

The traditional Buddhist virtues and precepts provide guidelines for joint endeavor and a significant vocabulary in the open discussions which are the lifeblood of the movement. Thus *dana* had come to be identified with monastic almsgiving, but Sarvodaya extends it back to its original wider meaning of sharing time, skills, goods and energy with one's community and demonstrates the liberating power of sincere and spontaneous generosity to dissolve barriers between individuals and groups. Similarly, the meaning of the "Four Sublime Abodes" has been extended socially without, however, losing their original spirit. So, *metta* (lovingkindness) refers also to the active concern for others and refraining from any kind of coercion. *Karuna* (compassion) refers to active and selfless giving of energy in the service of others. *Mudita* (rejoicing in others' good fortune) refers to the feeling of well-being experienced when one has been able to make a tangible contribution to one's community. *Upekkha* (equanimity) refers to independence from the need to achieve results and obtain recognition. It is the Buddhist remedy against burn-out of campaigning energies. Macy quotes a District Co-ordinator: "*Upekkha* is dynamite. It is surprising the energy that is released when you stop being so attached. . . . You discover how much you can accomplish when nothing is expected in return."[8]

All these inspirational guidelines are presented in symbols, slogans, posters, murals, songs and stories, not as catechisms and commandments but as pointers and as tools of analysis. Above all, they are made fully meaningful through the practice of meditation, which is incorporated into Sarvodaya meetings and training sessions.

Sarvodaya aims at an economy of modest sufficiency, employing appropriate low and middle technology, with equitable distribution of wealth and concern for the quality of the environment. Local and national cultural identities and diversity are respected and nurtured, and it does in fact seem that the movement makes its strongest impact in the more traditional kinds of community.

The local knowledge and influence of the sangha [the monastic community] and the respect in which it is held at all levels of society enable the monks to make an extensive and significant contribution to Sarvodaya. Of the fifty-one members of the movement's executive committee no fewer than fifteen are monks. Macy writes that:

> The relationship between Sarvodaya and the Sangha is a symbiotic one, in that each benefits the other. As the monks serve as extension agents for the Movement's development program so do the Movement's ideology and expectations serve to revitalize their Order and their sense of vocation, restoring the wider social responsibilities they carried in precolonial days. This effect on the Sangha is not incidental or just a "spin-off," but an acknowledged goal of Sarvodaya.[9]

The Buddhist tradition of religious pluralism . . . is also present in Sarvodaya. Ariyaratne claims that "the Sarvodaya Movement, while originally inspired by the Buddhist tradition, is active throughout our multi-ethnic society, working with Hindu, Muslim and Christian communities and involving scores of thousands of Hindu, Muslim and Christian co-workers. Our message of awakening transcends any effort to categorize it as the teaching of a particular creed."[10]

As to Sarvodaya's relations with the State, Ariyaratne claims that "when some aspects of the established order conform with the righteous principles of the Movement, the Movement co-operates with those aspects. When they become unrighteous, in those areas the Movement does not co-operate and may even extend non-violent non-co-operation [though so far it has never done so—(Jones's interpolation)]. In between these two extremes there is a vast area . . . in which establishments like the government and the Sarvodaya Movement can co-operate."[11] In fact, since there is virtually a national consensus about the desirability of rural self-help schemes Sarvodaya has been able to operate over politically neutral ground. Whilst co-operating with relevant government policies and accommodating to the national and local power structure, the Sarvodaya Leadership's ambivalent and non-committal pragmatism has, arguably, so far enabled it to avoid compromising the movement's integrity.

Jones goes on from this point to describe in detail how since the 1970s Sarvodaya's growth in size and complexity and its relations with state economic policies have subjected it to new pressures that have raised controversial but by no means insurmountable questions about its character and future.

A CHRISTIAN EXAMPLE:
THE CATHOLIC WORKER MOVEMENT

The way of right action in Christianity has found expression in many forms over the history of Christianity—sometimes as a way unto itself but most often alongside other ways of being religious and frequently subordinate to them. Many subtraditions have given prominence to the way of right action but in diverse manners: some have focused attention primarily on private conduct, others on roles or ministries within the Christian community, some on evangelical or missionary work, others on intentionally living a different but distinctly Christian form of social life, some on charitable works on behalf of individuals or whole communities, others on efforts to bring about peace and reconciliation between individuals or social factions, some on efforts within the existing social system to promote social welfare and combat evil, and others on efforts to change unjust social and economic structures. Certain subtraditions have given it virtually no emphasis at all. However, it is probably impossible to find a Christian subtradition in which no one at any time felt that his or her rapport with God in Christ did not hinge upon some form of action or effort to make some kind of difference in the mundane world.

One example of a person who very definitely felt called to make a difference and in whom we can glimpse something of what a Christian expression of the way of right action might involve is Dorothy Day (1897–1980) and the Catholic Worker movement, which she cofounded with Peter Maurin in 1933. On the fiftieth anniversary of that founding, *Sojourners Magazine*, an ecumenical though largely Evangelical Protestant voice of Christian social activism that has in significant measure been inspired by the Catholic Worker movement, carried an article entitled "Thank God for the Catholic Worker," by Danny Collum.[12] Part of it reads as follows:

———————————————————————●———————————————————————

On May 1, 1933, in the depths of the great Depression, the first copies of the *Catholic Worker* were sold . . . at a May Day demonstration in Lower Manhattan's Union Square. The major themes of that first *Catholic Worker* were the plight of exploited and unemployed workers and the surprising news that Catholic Christianity had more to offer them than the incessant nay-saying to communism that dominated the church in the U.S. In the months and years that followed, the *Worker* continued to develop those themes with extensive coverage of hunger, evictions, and strikes, and with Peter Maurin's "Easy Essays," which presented a down-to-earth alternative social vision drawn from Scripture and the teachings of some of the popes and Catholic philosophers.

Even more remarkably, the paper's writers and editors put flesh on their ideas by starting soup kitchens and houses of hospitality, joining workers on the picket lines, and establishing a farm commune that they hoped would be a model of Maurin's agrarian society, where it would be easier for people to be good. The *Catholic Worker* paper soon became the Catholic Worker movement.

Later in the 1930s, the Catholic Worker movement's consistent preaching and practice of Christian non-violence became a controversial witness that in itself presented an alternative program for a world at war. The Worker's pacifism cost it a lot of the popularity gained when it mainly emphasized the poverty and injustice of the depression.

The problems began with the Spanish Civil War. The Catholic hierarchy was backing Franco's fascists, and the Catholic Worker's friends on the Left were sending off brigades to fight with the Republicans. The Catholic Worker backed neither side, insisting instead that Jesus' words to Peter, "Put away your sword," applied to both. As a result, many Catholic parishes that had been buying monthly bundles of the *Worker* cancelled their orders, and the paper's circulation plummeted. It of course dropped even further when the Worker maintained its advocacy of nonviolence and began encouraging and aiding conscientious objectors after the United States entered World War II. . . .

. The Catholic Worker began during a time of historic crisis, and its rapid growth was a sure sign that it was offering a message that was badly needed. In the face of the oppression, misery, and war caused by the collapse of industrial capitalism, the Catholic Worker posed a vision of a society organized around respect for the person. It talked about a society made up of voluntary, self-sustaining communities of sharing and mutual aid. It would be a society where no one would starve or go homeless, and where authority would not be synonymous with violence or coercion.

Much has been written about the influence of European syndicalism on Peter Maurin and about Dorothy Day's heritage in the American anarchist movement [before her conversion to the Roman Catholic Church], all of which is true enough. But the Catholic Worker vision was, and still is, first and foremost an attempt to imagine how we might live together in this world in closer accord with the gospel.

In addition to a rough blueprint for a new society, the Catholic Worker offered an answer to the revolutionary strategist's question, "What is to be done?" The Worker's "strategy" said simply: begin now to "build the new society in the shell of the old." This meant that you begin to change the world by changing yourself and the lives of those around you. And it meant that society cannot be transformed by threats or violence but only by the moral force of example. And above all it meant that living justly and peacefully could not be postponed until after "the revolution" or the Second Coming.

. . . Today we have the encouragement and inspiration of 50 years of the Catholic Worker to rely on, as well as the companionship of the very much alive-and-kicking Catholic Worker of the 1980s.

In the same 1983 issue of *Sojourners*, in a forum on civil disobedience, there appeared an article by Peggy Scherer,[13] then current editor of the *Catholic Worker* and worker in the New York City Catholic Worker house, from which the following excerpt is taken.

LIVING SYMBOLS

Any newspaper on any given day reminds us that violence abounds in the world. The arms race, repression in Central America, homeless people in our own country, all call to mind that violence appears in many forms. Yet the causes, as well as the results, are interrelated. How can we respond to it? How can we strike at the roots of this pervasive evil?

While there are many ways in which we might act, Gandhi, Martin Luther King, Jr., Dorothy Day, and others have taught me through their lives and their words that civil disobedience is an important and at times necessary way to confront power when that power protects injustice. They have also taught me that such a step can be effective in a profound sense, whether or not it "works" in the world's eyes, if it stems from and contributes to a genuine search for truth and justice.

Their witness teaches me that if we want a better world, we must act to build it. They teach, too, that the end is the result of the means. If we would build a society where justice and truth prevail, our efforts must be rooted in these qualities, not in those we reject.

The many manifestations of violence stem from the powerful judging who is to live, and under what circumstances. If we oppose what is violent, we must also reject the greed, deceit, injustice, and judgment on which it is based. Self-sacrifice, honesty, justice, and respect for all people, even if we disagree with them, even if we challenge their actions, must mark our efforts.

I think about these things because it is all too clear that the roots, if not the fruits, of violence are not only in the Pentagon and the Kremlin, but are also in all of us. Nuclear weapons and all the forms of violence that threaten and take life have not been developed in a vacuum. They exist to protect our way of life. They will not disappear unless we challenge and change the values and attitudes which justify them, as well as work to eliminate the weapons themselves.

In *Loves and Fishes*,[14] Dorothy Day writes:

> The greatest challenge of the day is: how to bring about a revolution of the heart, a revolution which has to start with each one of us? When we begin to take the lowest place, to wash the feet of others, to love our brothers and sisters with that burning love, that passion, which led to the cross, then we can truly say, "Now I have begun."

Many good things, some of them unexpected, can happen if we shape our lives, our homes, our work, as well as our demonstrations, to witness to our belief in a world where love is active and justice practiced. Such an example says more than any leaflet. A life of service and sharing is in itself a challenge to a greedy, materialistic society. Such a life offers a visible example of "what to do," an invitation.

Changing our lives can break down some of our own fears and prejudices. I have seen in myself that my hesitation to perform civil disobedience comes perhaps more from my fear of the unknown, my fear of breaking my routines, of appearing foolish or ineffective, than from hesitation about breaking a civil law that protects or promotes injustice. Through embracing a life where people are more important than things, my perspective has changed. Living at the Catholic Worker house in New York City, I come into daily contact with victims of rampant injustice. This shows me a human face of the injustice I oppose. My need to act comes from the heart; the urgency of the situation is no longer academic, and silence is more clearly a luxury. Civil disobedience and other efforts signify a continuation of my work rather than a break in my routines.

There is also a tempering effect in a life such as we live at the Catholic Worker. While our need becomes stronger to challenge and confront values and institutions, our daily life confronts us with our own weaknesses. Our life together has helped me see my own violent tendencies and self-righteousness, and has led me to be much more cautious about pointing a finger. Though our life is often rich and rewarding, revealing the possibilities of people of different backgrounds and points of view living in relative harmony, we are constantly reminded of the hard work and patience required for getting from where we are to where we want to be.

Reprinted with the permission of *Sojourners*, 2401 15th St. NW, Washington, DC 20009

In an earlier issue of *Sojourners Magazine* (January 1981) shortly after her death, the editor, Jim Wallis, published the following eulogy of Dorothy Day shortly after her death.[15]

AN EXPLOSION OF LOVE

I always thought I would go to her funeral. I met her only twice, but no one affected me like she did. I was on the road when I heard, and it was too late to get to the service.

The feeling of grief was overwhelming. She embodied everything I believe in. She, more than any other, made my faith seem real and possible to live. She took my most cherished visions and made them into realities. Now she was gone. It was like the end of an era.

Slowly the grief gave way to gratitude. We were richly blessed to have had her among us, if only for a while. She was an ordinary woman whose faith caused her to do extraordinary things. The gospel caught fire in this woman and caused an explosion of love. We will miss her like a part of ourselves.

Dorothy Day died on Saturday night, November 29, 1980. She was 83. Dorothy died in her room at Maryhouse, a place of hospitality she founded for homeless women on New York's Lower East Side.

It was in the Depression year of 1933 that she and Peter Maurin founded *The Catholic Worker*. They sold the first copies of the newspaper on May Day for a penny each. "Read *The Daily Worker*," shouted the communists selling their paper to the unemployed in Washington Square. "Read *The Catholic Worker* daily," answered back a little band of Catholics who said their faith had made them radicals.

For 47 years their paper has been the voice of a movement that has always concentrated on the basics of the gospel. Dorothy's grasp of her times was profound, but it was the simple things that captured her imagination and commitment—like the gospel being good news to the poor and the children of God living as peacemakers.

She always spoke of the "works of mercy" as the center of it all: feeding the hungry, housing the homeless, clothing the naked, comforting the lonely. For the cause of Christ, she literally spent her life on the side of the suffering and the afflicted, while relentlessly attacking the institutions and systems which lead to oppression and war.

In so doing she became an institution herself, and the Catholic Worker movement has served for almost half a century as the heart and conscience of the American Catholic Church and, for that matter, of American Christianity. Dorothy helped to found more than 40 houses of hospitality and about one dozen farms which became rare places that the poor could call home.

The poorest of the poor were Dorothy's constituency. Shunned by everyone else, they knew they could trust this woman. Streams of poor people from her Bowery neighborhood showed up at her funeral, mingling with the famous and powerful, but knowing that Dorothy belonged to them.

The voluntary poverty, service to the poor, and radical pacifism of the Catholic Worker kept the movement small, but influenced many over the years. For most of the volunteers, life at the Catholic Worker became a kind of school, an intense training ground in compassion that would shape the rest of their lives. The number of people touched by Dorothy is beyond counting.

This evangelical boy from the Midwest was one. I grew up being taught that the Bible should be taken literally. Dorothy Day is one of the few people I've ever met who actually did. She took the gospel at face value and based her life on it. Dorothy did what Jesus said to do. She was the most thoroughly evangelical Christian of our time, though the movement by that name never claimed her as its own.

Like any radicalism that endures, Dorothy's was rooted in very traditional soil. Her unswerving loyalty to the teachings and traditions of the church often caused consternation among her more progressive friends. But it was the strength of that very commitment to the gospel that made Dorothy such a radical. And it was this radical traditionalism that proved troublesome to the church she loved.

That same combination of conservative religion and radical politics is the energy behind Sojourners and became a point of strong solidarity between ourselves and the Catholic Worker movement. Probably the nicest thing anyone ever said about us was when some of our friends at the New York house of hospitality called Sojourners a "protestant Catholic Worker."

Much has been said about Dorothy Day and much more will be said. But perhaps the most important thing we can say is that she taught us what it means to be a Christian. She was a follower of Jesus Christ who fell in love with his kingdom and made it come alive in the most wretched circumstances of men and women. Dorothy believed that, in the end, "love is the measure." The following postscript is from her autobiography, *The Long Loneliness*:

We were just sitting there talking when Peter Maurin came in.

We were just sitting there talking when lines of people began to form, saying, "We need bread." We could not say, "go, be thou filled." If there were six small loaves and a few fishes [the reference here is to the story in the Gospels of Jesus' miraculous feeding of thousands from a few loaves and fishes], we had to divide them. There was always bread.

We were just sitting there talking and people moved in on us. Let those who can take it, take it. Some moved out and that made room for more. And somehow the walls expanded.

We were just sitting there talking and someone said, "Let's go live on a farm."

It was as casual as all that, I often think. It just came about. It just happened.

I found myself, a barren woman, the joyful mother of children. It is not easy always to be joyful, to keep in mind the duty of delight.

The most significant thing about The Catholic Worker is poverty, some say.

The most significant thing is community, others say. We are not alone any-more.

But the final word is love. At times it has been, in the words of Father Zossima [a character in Dostoyevski's novel, The Brothers Karamazov*], a harsh and dreadful thing, and our very faith in love has been tried by fire.*

We cannot love God unless we love each other, and to love we must know each other. We know Him in the breaking of bread [a reference to the Christian rite of Holy Communion], and we are not alone any more. Heaven is a banquet and life is a banquet, too, even with a crust, where there is com-panionship.

We have all known the long loneliness and we have learned that the only so-lution is love and that love comes with community.

It all happened while we sat there talking, and it is still going on.

The doctors said that she died of heart failure. But Dorothy's heart never failed us.

Reprinted with the permission of *Sojourners*, 2401 15th St. NW, Washington, DC 20009.

CHAPTER SUMMARY

As a Buddhist example of the way of right action, the Sarvodaya movement in Sri Lanka coordinates large numbers of lay and monastic Buddhists in communal self-help efforts to improve social and economic conditions of rural villages. Sarvodaya means "the awakening and welfare of all." Animating every phase of the movement is an awakening to Buddhist values creatively reinterpreted in a way that makes their relevance to lived social relationships more apparent and their meaning more readily implemented by all. Present suffering, for example, is not regarded primarily as a private concern of the individual and the fated product of choices in past lives as in much of conventional Buddhism; rather is it seen as a concern of the whole community. As such, suffering is regarded as something that locally coordinated effort can do something to alleviate. In other words, as Sarvodaya understands it, the *Dhamma* of the Buddha is concerned with bringing an end to suffering and has a unique orientation to how it should be done. Members of Sarvodaya are committed to implementing that vision in a social way.

Dorothy Day and the Catholic Worker movement that she and Peter Maurin founded are presented as a Christian example of the way of right action. In the heart of urban America the Catholic Worker movement attempts to articulate and embody a social vision grounded in the Christian Gospel that is radically alterna-tive to the dominant social order—a vision of a society organized around respect for each person. The Catholic Worker Movement envisions a society made up of voluntary, self-sustaining communities of sharing and mutual aid, where no one starves or goes homeless, where violence and coercion have no place, and where change comes from first changing oneself and then changing the lives of others by the moral force of example and nonviolent action. Not content merely to hold up this vision and call for changes in the existing order, from the beginning Catholic Workers have put flesh on their ideas through concrete acts of mercy to individual persons, starting soup kitchens, establishing some forty houses of hospitality, and organizing a dozen farm communes. Voluntary poverty, service to the poor, and radical pacifism—all in the service of Christ—have kept the movement small but simultaneously have given it a profoundly influential status as a voice of conscience for American Christianity.

Study Questions on Similarities and Differences

These two examples of religiously motivated social activism, the Sarvodaya Movement and the Catholic Worker Movement, possess a number of remarkable similarities as well as differences. Keeping in mind both the danger of generalizing from these specific forms of right action to all forms of right action in either tradition and how much may be involved in the actual practice of these specific forms that go unsaid in the two accounts just given, spend some time comparing the accounts. Consider the following questions.

1. Identify as many similarities as you can. How many of the basic characteristics of Buddhist "transcendental radicalism" described by Jones are also features of the Christian radicalism of the Catholic Worker Movement? How many features of the Catholic Worker Movement are also characteristics of Sarvodaya?

2. What do you suppose accounts for the depth of correspondence in basic principles, working strategies, and specific projects between Sarvodaya and the Catholic Worker movement? Assuming that both of these movements exemplify the same generic way of being religious in two distinct religious traditions, what if anything do the similarities identified in answer to the first question indicate that is essential to that way of being religious (which the framework identifies as right action)?

   a. What, if anything, do these two movements have in common regarding their respective means of approach to *ultimate reality*?

   b. What characteristic existential problems is each concerned with and seeking to address?

   c. Is there anything that indicates the characteristic way each interprets its broader tradition's scripture and symbol system as distinct from other

traditional ways of taking them? What sorts of features of *ultimate reality*
does each specifically highlight? That is, what kind of "face" does each
envision *ultimate reality* to have?

   d. What sorts of social structures (social organization, group activity, roles
   and responsibilities, etc.) does each have or recommend? What sorts of
   social structures does each criticize and endeavor to change?

   e. What specific virtues in the practice of its religious life does each appear
   to commend, whether explicitly or implicitly, and what specific vices in
   that practice does each appear to condemn? (Be careful here to distinguish criticisms each may apparently offer of the religious practices of
   others from critical expectations set for its own members.) That is, what
   ideal(s) of practice does each uphold? And what sorts of things would
   fall short of those ideals?

3. What differences can you find beyond the many profound similarities? Clearly,
   some differences are the direct reflection of different social and geographic
   contexts (e.g., one has been predominantly rural and the other predominantly urban).

4. What among the differences seem specifically due to different *theological*
   convictions of Buddhism (specifically Theravada Buddhism) and Christianity
   (specifically radical Roman Catholicism)?

5. What specific goals or objectives is each setting out to accomplish? What
   does their Buddhism or their Christianity respectively have to do with those
   specific goals? What does it have to do with their choices of means? What
   does it have to do with their motivation?

FOR FURTHER READING

Recommended articles in the *Encyclopedia of Religion*, edited by Mircea Eliade (New
   York: Macmillan, 1987) include *Morality and Religion; Merit (Buddhist Concepts,
   Christian Concepts); Community; Religious Communities; Politics and Religion; Love;
   Conscience; Martial Arts; Buddhist Ethics; Vinaya; Saṃgha; Karuṇā; Ahiṃsā, Karman;
   Christian Ethics; Christian Social Movements;* and *Day, Dorothy.*

Tson-khu-pa Blo-bzan-grags-pa, *Ethics of Tibet*, trans. Alex Wayman (Albany, NY: State
   University of New York Press, 1991). Tibetan Buddhist ethical teachings.
Fred Eppsteiner, ed., *The Path of Compassion: Writings of Socially Engaged Buddhism*,
   rev. ed. (Berkeley, CA: Parallax Press, 1988). Just what the title says.
Christopher Ives, *Zen Awakening and Society* (Honolulu, HI: University of Hawaii Press,
   1992). Implications of Zen Buddhism for ethical and social practice.
Ken Jones, *The Social Face of Buddhism: An Approach to Political and Social Activism*
   (London: Wisdom Publications, 1989). Perhaps the very best overview of social ac-
   tivism in Buddhism available.
Winston L. King, *In the Hope of Nibbana: An Essay on Theravada Buddhist Ethics* (LaSalle,
   IL: Open Court, 1964). A classic exposition of Theravada Buddhist Ethics.

Joanna R. Macy, *Dharma and Development: Religion as Resource in the Sarvodaya Self-help Movement*, rev. ed. (West Hartford, CT; Kumarian Press, 1985). The best treatment of Sarvodaya available.

Sulak Sivaraksa, *Seeds of Peace: A Buddhist Vision for Renewing Society* (Berkeley, CA: Parallax Press, 1992). One of the leading Buddhist spokespersons for social transformation in Southeast Asia today.

Arthur Paul Boers, *On Earth as in Heaven: Justice Rooted in Spirituality* (Scottsdale, PA: Herald Press, 1991). An attempt to articulate anew Mennonite Christian spirituality that is oriented to realizing social justice.

Robert Coles, *Dorothy Day: A Radical Devotion* (Reading, MA: A Merloyd Lawrence Book/Addison Wesley, 1987). An insightful introduction to Dorothy Day's own spirituality, by someone who knew her personally.

Dorothy Day, *Loaves and Fishes* (New York: Harper and Row, 1963). Dorothy Day's own account of the history and the vision of the Catholic Worker.

Deane William Ferm, ed., *Third World Liberation Theologies: A Primer* (Maryknoll, NY: Orbis Books, 1986). Just what the title says it is.

George F. Forell, ed., *Christian Social Teachings: A Reader in Christian Social Ethics from the Bible to the Present* (Minneapolis, MN: Augsburg, 1966). Gives a good historical overview of Christian social ethics.

Gerald Jonas, *On Doing Good: The Quaker Experiment* (New York: Charles Scribner's Sons, 1971). A good introduction to the social activism of another Radical Reformation tradition.

Bill Kellerman, ed., *A Keeper of the Word: Selected Writings of William Strengfellow* (Grand Rapids, MI: Eerdmans, 1994). Strengfellow is one of the quietly influential radical Protestant social activists of this century.

Malcolm Muggeridge, *Something Beautiful for God* (San Francisco: Harper and Row, 1971). A fine introduction to the work of Mother Teresa of Calcutta.

Mev Puleo, *The Struggle is One: Voices and Visions of Liberation* (Albany, NY: State University of New York Press, 1994). A reader in Brazilian liberation theology that conveys almost firsthand what the struggle is like among poor and rich, rural and urban.

Rosalie Riegel Troester, *Voices from the Catholic Worker* (Philadelphia, PA: Temple University Press, 1993). A compilation of interviews with some 208 individuals associated with the Catholic Worker.

NOTES

1. H. H. the fourteenth Dalai Lama, Tenzin Gyatso, "Love, Altruism, Vegetarianism, Anger and the Responsibilities of Teachers. Questions Answered by H. H. the Dalai Lami," *The Middle Way* 60:2 (August 1985), p. 69. Quoted by Ken Jones, *The Social Face of Buddhism: An Approach to Political and Social Activism* (London: Wisdom Publications, 1989), p. 154.
2. *Ibid.*, pp. 240–246.
3. See Chapter 7, p. 173.
4. Jones is here quoting Joanna R. Macy, *Dharma and Development: Religion as Resource in the Sarvodaya Self-help Movement*, rev. ed. (West Hartford, CT: Kumarian Press, 1985), p. 95.
5. *Ibid.*, p. 32.
6. *Ibid.*, p. 76.
7. *Ibid.*, p. 37.
8. *Ibid.*, p. 39.
9. *Ibid.*, p. 66.

10. *Ibid.*, p. 15.

11. Jones here quotes from Detlef Kantowsky, Sarvodaya: *The Other Development* (New Delhi, India: Vikas, 1980), p. 67.

12. Danny Collum, "Thank God for the Catholic Worker," *Sojourners Magazine* 12:5 (May 1983), p. 7.

13. Peggy Scherer, "Living Symbols," *Sojourners Magazine* 12:5 (May 1983), pp. 30–31.

14. Dorothy Day, *Loaves and Fishes* (New York: Harper and Row, 1963). This book sketches the history and the vision of the Catholic Worker. See also Robert Coles, *Dorothy Day: A Radical Devotion* (Reading, MA: A Merloyd Lawrence Book/Addison Wesley, 1987).

15. Jim Wallis, "An Explosion of Love," *Sojourners Magazine* 10:1 (January 1981), pp. 3–4.

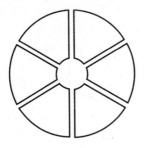

CHAPTER 12

THE WAY OF DEVOTION IN BUDDHISM AND CHRISTIANITY

A BUDDHIST EXAMPLE: SHINRAN AND PURE LAND DEVOTION

The way of devotion is well exemplified in Buddhism in the various expressions of what is called Pure Land Buddhism. Pure Land Buddhism, as discussed in Chapter 7, originally emerged as one of the Mahayana traditions in India, as evidenced by two extant Sanskrit texts and other references to the Pure Land of *Amitābha*. To what extent it found full or independent expression in India is now unknown. But it did find a full, enduring expression in East Asia. It focuses particular attention on three Mahayana scriptures, the longer and shorter Pure Land sutras and the Sutra of Contemplation on the Buddha *Amitāyus*. These scriptures present Gautama Buddha telling about the Buddha *Amitābha* ("Unlimited Light"), also called *Amitāyus* ("Unlimited Life"), the perfect embodiment of compassion for sentient beings in all worlds. *Amitābha* (called *Ami-to-fo* in Chinese and *Amida* in Japanese) is said to dwell in a pure Buddha-land, the Western paradise, *Sukhāvatī* ("happiness having"), which he has created by means of the infinite merit he has built up over countless aeons of time. In this Buddha-land, there are supposed to be no evil destinies, no rebirths—hence it transcends *saṃsāra* (the common human condition of suffering and rebirth) altogether. It is said to so purify those who enter it that all who find themselves there, regardless of their shortcomings in their previous life, are destined to attain Enlightenment without obstacles to be overcome. The question, then, becomes what does it take to be reborn there? According to the scripture, many eons ago, the Bodhisattva *Dharmākara* ("Treasury of Dharma;" *Hozo* in Japanese), who eventually became *Amitābha*, undertook some forty-eight vows, including one which said that whoever would call upon his name in sincere faith desiring to be reborn in his Pure Land would be reborn there. There is clear indication that initially Pure Land practice focused on an elaborate meditative visualization of the Pure Land. But the most popular form of Pure Land practice emerged in sixth century China under T'an-luan (476–542) and eventually to spread to all levels of Chinese society. It was to chant "*Na-mo A-mi-t'o Fo*" (Japanese: "*Namo Amida Butsu*"—meaning, "Hail, Amida Buddha!" or "Homage to Amida Buddha!"), calling upon the "Other power" of *Amitābha* to secure one's rebirth in his Pure Land.

In Japan, more than one Pure Land tradition developed. But the largest and most influential was founded by Shinran (1133–1212), called *Jodo-shin-shu* ("True Pure Land sect"). Shinran developed Pure Land doctrine in a distinctively new direction, in which absolute trust or faith in Amida's infinite compassion and grace alone, and not at all in one's own efforts, can hope to result in salvation. Initially, Shinran had undertaken rigorous monastic practice in the Tendai tradition, but after 20 years of effort he felt he had been unable to make significant progress toward enlightenment. In despair Shinran abandoned all such practices and came to discover that the salvation he had vainly sought through his own efforts was freely given through Dharmākara's "Primal Vow." In gratitude he devoted himself entirely to reliance upon the grace of Amida and tirelessly propagated his newfound faith among ordinary folk. Having abandoned the monastic life, Shinran took a wife and showed by example that the family could be the center of religious life. Though an aristocrat by birth, he joined in solidarity with the lower classes, sharing their way of life. His goodness and humility, compassion and sincerity, won him an undying reverence in the hearts of his followers. The first excerpt that follows is from his own works, translated and arranged by Gendo Nakai.[1]

---

1. The Divine Will

(1) Amida Nyorai[2] has two kinds of body; the one is His Spiritual and the other His Personal embodiment. The Spiritual Body is formless and, being one with Reality, is beyond description and thought. In order to make itself known to human beings, the Spiritual Body manifested itself in the form of a Bodhisattva named Hozo [the Japanese name for Dharmākara], who made forty-eight solemn Promises of various kinds to be fulfilled when He had reached Buddhahood. In one of these Promises, Hozo declared that His Light would be boundless and His Life infinite. These Promises were realized by Hozo the Bodhisattva; and He became the Buddha, whom Vasubandhu, i.e., Seshin in Japanese, praised as "the Tathāgata

of Boundless Light radiating unobstructedly in the Universe." The Personal Body of Amida Nyorai is also called the Body of Reward on account of its being the fulfillment of Divine Promises.

(2) Amida Nyorai declares Himself to be the Father and Mother of all human beings. Therefore we should believe that we are all of us His children.

(3) Suppose there are seven children in a family and one of them falls ill. Then the father and mother devote their whole minds to the patient's care, although they love all their children equally. So it is with Amida Nyorai. Although He loves all human beings without discrimination, He specially takes pity on the sin-stricken ones.

(4) There are two gifts which Amida Nyorai bestows: The one relates to our journey to the Land of Bliss, and the other concerns our return to this dense Forest of Birth and Death. The first is in order to enable us to enter Paradise and be reunited with Him, hence Amida Nyorai endows us with all the merits which He Himself has accumulated in order to attain Buddhahood. By the second gift He endows us with a marvelous power, so that we may aid Him in His own holy work by reincarnating ourselves in this world over and over again in order to save our fellow-beings from the suffering of Birth and Death. [This cycle is understood spiritually (i.e., figuratively) as well as literally, meaning that "entering Paradise" may happen in this life as one attains true faith (*shinjin*), from which one may spiritually re-enter this world carried by the infinite compassion of Amida for others.]

(5) One who learns of the Divine Will of Amida Nyorai cannot go through the experience without believing in it. The moment he believes and obeys with all his heart, he is filled by Amida with an abundance of precious grace. . . .

2. The Holy Name

(1) Gautama Buddha has arranged eighty-four thousand gates of diverse teachings by which to enable all human beings to accomplish the destruction of their ignorance and *karma* and the effects thereof. But not one of these gateways does surpass the power of Amida's Holy Name, that is Namo-amida-butsu ["Homage to Amida Buddha," the phrase which Pure Land Buddhists repeat to invoke his presence and acknowledge his lordship], which, once recited, completely snaps the chain of sin even as a sharp sword cuts with a single stroke.

(2) Amida, our Father, leads us unto Salvation by means of His Holy Name. So, when we hear it with our ears and repeat it with our lips, its boundless merits penetrate our spirit and become the seed of Buddhahood.

(3) On whosoever hears His Holy Name, believes and rejoices in it, Amida Nyorai bestows His own infinite merits. Then, since his destination is the Land of Bliss wherein he will be born, he will never swerve from his aim.

(4) Even though the whole world be ablaze, he who passes through it and hears the Holy Name will thereby be qualified to attain Buddhahood in the next life.

(5) Those who repeat Amida's Holy Name will receive in this earthly life the divine favour that is immeasurable. The sin which causes transmigration in the world of Birth and Death will be exterminated, and misfortune and untimely death avoided.

(6) Recite Amida's Holy Name with your trustful heart, for Kwannon and Daiseishi (Avalokiteshvara and Mahāsthānaprāpta Bodhisattvas) will, as the shadow follows the substance, always accompany you with a host of Bodhisattvas to protect you from evil spirits.

(7) Before his attainment of Buddhahood Amida Nyorai made a vow that He would receive into Paradise all those who should hear His Holy Name and believe in Him with their whole hearts. So, no matter whether they be poor or rich, ignorant or learned, virtuous or sinful, observing or transgressing the Law, those who are transformed by reciting His Holy Name will be changed from the lowest into the highest state of being, even as a stone is changed to gold.

(8) Whenever a person on the earth determines to recite Amida's Holy Name, there arises in the Happy Land of the West a new stem of lotus which will receive him on its blossom, when he, having never ceased to practise the Nembutsu [the invocation of Amida's name, "Namo-amida-butsu"], comes at last to the close of his days on earth.

3. Concerning Faith

(1) "Anuttra-samyaku-sambodhi"—the Unsurpassed Perfect Wisdom of Buddha— is attained through Faith [shinjin]. [Shinjin is not exactly equivalent to "faith" in English. In Jodo-shin-shu it connotes the displacement of self-centered power with the realization of Amida's Other Power in oneself.] Although there are a great many ways by which to attain it, they are all contained in the Faith in Amida Nyorai.

(2) By "Faith" is meant the whole-hearted acceptance of the Message which our ears have heard and the eyes of our soul have seen.

(3) He who hears the Vow of Amida to save all beings by virtue of His sole Power and doubts it not, is said to possess true Faith in Him.

(4) It is doubt and unbelief which cause one to return over and over again to the House of Birth and Death; but through Faith we enter into the peace of the Eternal City called Nirvāna. . . .

(6) To believe in Amida's Divine Will and practise the Nembutsu is hard for unbelievers, proud souls, and evil doers. It is the hardest of all things to do; and nothing is more difficult, indeed.

(7) There are three signs by which we can recognize a false faith: first of all, it is insincere and therefore wavering, one moment existing and the next disappearing; secondly, it is not whole-hearted, for it is undecided; thirdly, it does not last all through life, for other thoughts intervene to prevent its continuance. These three aspects hang together one upon another. As faith is not sincere it is undecided; and being undecided, it neither lasts long nor continues steadfast. Or, as faith is prevented from continuing, it is not whole-hearted; and as it is not whole-hearted, it now exists and then disappears. Contrary to these are the three proofs of true Faith [i.e., sincerity, whole-heartedness, and decisiveness], which justify the practice of the Nembutsu. . . .

(9) Two things are essential to Faith. The first is to be convinced of our own sinfulness; from the bondage of evil deeds we possess no means of emancipating ourselves. The second is, therefore, to throw our helpless souls wholly upon the Divine Power of Amida Nyorai in the firm belief that His forty-eight Vows were

for the express purpose of saving all beings who should put their trust in Him without the least doubt or fear. Such souls will be born surely into His Pure Land.

(10) Ask not, "How could Amida receive me into His Pure Land, seeing that I am so vile and sinful?" For it is a matter of fact that there is none of us but possesses a complete set of germs of worldly passions, sinful lusts, and evil deeds. But the compassionate power of Amida is so infinitely great that He can and will translate us into His pure Land if only we are willing to entrust ourselves wholly unto Him. Neither should you say, on the other hand: "I am good-hearted enough that I am sure to be born into the Pure Land." For that Pure Land can never be reached so long as we rely in the least upon our own power of merits. . . .

4. The Pure Land

(1) My brothers, I advise you one and all to turn to Amida Nyorai with your whole heart and set your faces towards His Pure Land of Bliss. When asked, "Where is your home?" you should answer that it is a seat which, beautifully adorned with jewels, arises out of a lotus pond in Paradise.

(2) Come! Let us start for the Pure Land. This evil world is not the place to remain in longer. In our past lives we have migrated through the six worlds [the realms of peaceful gods, men, wrathful gods, animals, hungry demons, and beings in hell, all subject to the cycle of suffering which is *saṃsāra*, Birth and Death], passing from one state of existence to another; and nowhere have we found happiness; but it has been only sorrow always. Therefore we ardently desire to enter the Eternal City of Nirvāna, when our present life closes.

(3) In the Pure Land which Amida Nyorai has founded in fulfillment of His Great Vows, there are no more stages or ranks to be gone through. For those who are born therein attain the full Enlightenment at a bound when their souls are received into that Pure Land. . . .

5. On the Right Attitude Toward Deities

(1) Those who believe in Amida Nyorai and practise the Nembutsu take refuge in the Buddha, in the Dharma, i.e., His Teaching, and in the Samgha, i.e., the priestly Order. They never follow any other religious teaching, nor worship *devas* or gods.[3] They neither look for good nor observe ill "luck" on certain days or at certain hours of the day.

(2) Set yourselves free from all wrong thoughts so that you may comprehend the right teaching of Gautama Buddha; you will then acquire ten kinds of merits. What are they? First of all, you will become a man of gentle spirit and of good heart; and second, believing in the Law of Karma, you will not commit any kind of crime or sin, even though you may be threatened with death. Thirdly, you will reverence the Three Treasures, namely, the Buddha, the Dharma and the Samgha; but you should never believe in other gods. Fourthly, with your heart and mind possessed by right thoughts, you will take no account of either good or bad fortune with regard to the year, the month, or the day. In the fifth place, you will not migrate through the infernal worlds; but (sixthly) you will become wise and good and be valued by people of intelligence. Seventhly, you will not cling to worldly

things, but will pursue the Holy Path. You will, in the eighth place, free yourselves from the prejudices both of affirmation and negation as regards the future life, and will believe that all existence depends upon the Law of Causality [i.e., the law of *karma*]. Ninthly, you will be in company with those who hold the right faith and observe right practices. [In these last three merits, you will be in conformity with traditional Buddhist teaching.] Tenthly, you will be born in Amida Nyorai's Pure Land of Bliss. . . .

Some Spiritual Maxims Preserved by the Disciples of Shinran Shonin

(2) I lack no good and fear no evil, because I believe in Amida's Divine Will, which is the highest good and cannot be obstructed by any evil. Nevertheless, most people think that without good deeds perfectly performed and without their deadly sins atoned for, we could not enter the Pure Land. They are not quite right. If we can cease to do evil and begin to practise good deeds whole-heartedly, with the desire to be born into the Pure Land, Amida Nyorai has nothing to do with us. How pitiful it is that whilst various crimes and sins are committed in spite of our efforts to the contrary, good deeds are always so difficult to perform! Amida Nyorai bestows the Highest Good upon those who give no thought to their own goodness or badness, but turn to him simply, trustfully and with obedient hearts.

(3) Some people ask, "If bad men are received into the Pure Land, how much more so good men?" But this thought is contrary to Amida's Divine Will and to the teaching of Gautama Buddha. It was not the saints but the common people whom Amida Nyorai sought to bless with His Highest Good. Therefore, if the common people failed to enter the Pure Land to be welcomed as His honoured guests, His Divine Will and Power would be in vain. Of the common people, again not good but bad men are the chief objects of His Saving Power. Therefore, it is correct to say, "good men are received into the Pure Land; how much more so bad men?"

(4) I have no "disciples," because I have nothing of my own to impart to anyone else. What I can tell people is simply about Amida Nyorai who bestows upon man the innumerable merits accumulated by Himself. So, those who receive my instruction are not my "disciples" but fellow-pilgrims who travel with me, my brothers in Amida's great family.

(5) The practice of the Nembutsu is the only way leading to the Pure Land— the Way obstructed by naught. Why? Because all the good spirits in heaven and on earth revere and at all times protect those who believe in Amida Nyorai, whilst every evil spirit flies away before them. And also because crimes and sins have no power to cause any evil effect upon them. . . .

Reprinted by permission of The Rev. Osanu Hayashidera from Rev. Gendo Nakai, *Shinran and His Religion of Pure Faith* (Kyoto: The Shinshu Research Institute, 1937), pp. 103–114, 116–117, 124–126.

One of the characteristic marks of traditions emphasizing the way of devotion is the celebration in shared stories, personal testimonies, of the religious experiences of its members, especially stories of conversion. Indeed, an emphasis on communal fellowship and mutual support between believers, where the individual with his or her personal vicissitudes is given a place and affirmed, is more characteristic of this way of being religious than any of the others. Jodo-shin-shu is quite typical in this respect. Several of the traditional still-told stories follow.[4]

Farmer Kuhei

Farmer Kuhei, who lived in the province of Iwami about two hundred years ago, is a good example of how personality may be changed through religious faith.

He was at first very ferocious of nature and would not get the worse of anyone or anything. But since he came to believe in Amida Nyorai, his disposition was changed gradually until he became a different person, gentle-hearted and sparing of violent language.

One day in summer, as Kuhei was going into the forest to cut firewood, he found by chance that somebody had dammed the irrigating water so that it would not run into his rice field. He suddenly returned to his house and hastened to worship Amida Nyorai in the altar, telling at the same time his family to do the same thing. They wondered why he had come home without wood and so hurriedly gone to worship Buddha. Kuhei told them what he saw in his rice-field and said: "If I were the man that I was before, I should have lost my temper and dammed the water into my own field at the cost of others. But now that a new life is born within myself, I have no ill feeling against him who turns the water only to his own purpose. I believe that I am now being repaid for my selfish deeds in the previous life. Isn't it due to the grace of Amida Nyorai that I blame myself instead of others?"

The story was soon abroad in the village. After that the neighbours thought better of it and let the water into Kuhei's field as well as their own.

A Devout Girl

O-shimo San was an eight-year-old daughter of Riyomon, a cotton cloth merchant in Kawachi Province. In her time, about a hundred and eighty years ago, there was no institution of compulsory public education. The children of well-to-do families learned to read and write at *terakoya*, private schools mostly conducted at Buddhist temples, which were the only places of education for common people. O-shimo San received a smattering education in a *terakoya* in her spare hours, though she had to take care of her baby brother. Strange to say, she would not amuse herself with play-things as other girls of her age did; but she preferred to go to the temple to worship the Buddha and listen to what the priest told about Amida's Divine Will.

One day O-shimo San surprised her teacher-priest by saying: "It is very precious that Amida Nyorai receives even sinful women into His Pure Land, when they surrender themselves to His almighty hand. But I am very sorry that I shall be an exception. Just listen to my story. Before I began to receive your instruction, I had once stolen a penny from a friend of mind to buy some sweets. Another time I had picked up a small piece of money offered to the Buddha at a temple, and bought something to eat. Because I was very much afraid of the punishment I should be sure to get in the future life, I offered for atonement two small pieces of money to the Buddha in your temple. But I am still afraid that my offences may not be fully atoned for and Amida Nyorai may turn his back on me. I shall be very happy if you will tell me what I may do in repentance of my sins, so that I may be received into Amida's Pure Land."

The teacher-priest was so deeply moved by the girl's confession that he could do for a time nothing but recite Amida's Holy Name in a low tone. After a while, he said to the little maid: "Fear not, my dear girl. It is doubtless that you will be born in Amida's Pure Land, because you are a good girl who believes in Him with your whole heart. Even the five hideous sins and the ten evil deeds[5] are as nothing under Amida's almighty power; and your offences of theft are lesser by far. Your destination was settled at the moment that your faith in Amida was assured. Care not about your past offences in the least; but be grateful for the immense grace of Amida."

Upon this, O-shimo San was released from the spiritual agony from which she had been suffering for long. She could not help but leap for the joy of it all.

One who has entrusted his soul to the Supreme One is often calm and self-possessed in face of an emergency. One day a strong earthquake occurred. Everybody in O-shimo San's family ran out of doors for their lives, with the exception of the little maid who without any fear of death, quietly remained on her knees reciting the Nembutsu before the Buddha's shrine in the house. When the family came in as the shock was over, they asked her why she had not run without. She replied: "If I have *karma* to lose my life by earthquake, I shall die even under the open sky. If my *karma* is otherwise, I shall be safe, although I stay in the house. Whether to live or to die, isn't it peaceful to stay with the Buddha?"

The Tender-Hearted Myoki

There once lived in a village called Tsurumi in Bungo Province a woman who was later known by her Buddhist name Myoki. As a housewife, she was faithful to her husband and dutiful to her parents-in-law. Their feudal lord had her publicly commended as a model wife, rewarding her with a prize. It was soon after this that a misfortune overtook her; she was bereaved of both her husband and her only son, one soon after the other. If she had been an ordinary woman, she would have been heart-broken and spent day after day in tears. A deep insight awakened on her mind. She realized the transient character of earthly human life and earnestly began to seek immortality. Giving up all family affairs, she went to temples to listen to the preaching of Shinran's religion, until finally she attained true faith in Amida Nyorai. It was from this time on that she converted herself into a nun, although she lived on with her parents-in-law as before, and assumed the new name Myoki given by her teacher-priest.

One day a man often given to pranks poured cold water on the nun to try her faith. Seeing her show no emotion, the man asked her why she was so calm and composed, to which she replied: "With whom should I be angry when I am caught in a shower!" As far as this story goes, this nun of the Island Empire is akin to the

Greek philosopher, Socrates, who, drenched wet with a bucketful of water poured on him by his angry wife, said: "When thunder rolls, a shower follows!" The latter constructed his character by disciplining himself by his own philosophical principle, whilst the former cultivated her tenderness and perseverance by always calling on Amida's Holy Name. It is because of His Divine Promise that those who live in His Light will become tender and gentle in disposition just as fruits color and ripen sweet in the light of the sun.

When Myoki was cooking rice one day, she burned her hand by putting it unknowingly into the kettle. Instead of complaining of the pains, she repeated the Nembutsu and thanked Buddha for His grace. A bystander laughed at her, saying: "How unendurable pains are given by Amida's grace!" Upon this she said with a smile: "How unfathomable Amida's grace is! If I were left alone under the power of *karma* I should have to suffer pains many hundreds of thousands times greater than the burns on my hand. But now that I believe in Amida and entrust my soul to His Divine Power, I am perfectly emancipated from the terrible retribution of *karma*. When I think of this, I cannot help thanking [Him] for His grace by calling on His Name."

Myoki was always healthy and never had trouble about her personal affairs, until she passed away at the age of ninety.

Reprinted by permission of the Rev. Osanu Hayashidera from Rev. Gendo Nakai, *Shinran and His Religion of Pure Faith* (Kyoto: The Shinshu Research Institute, 1937), pp. 167–170, 182–186, and 189–193.

A CHRISTIAN EXAMPLE: BILLY GRAHAM AND EVANGELICAL PIETY

There are many varieties of the way of devotion in Christianity, some more formal and less spontaneous than others, some taking a certain interpretation of certain biblical passages that leads them to different doctrinal views than others, some combining devotion with other ways in a manner differentiating them from other Protestant traditions. In current Protestantism, the most widespread grouping of traditions centrally emphasizing the way of devotion is known as Evangelical Protestantism. As such, it does not indicate a denomination, and many Protestant denominations have congregations that are more Evangelical than other congregations within the same denomination. What it does indicate is an emphasis on each person coming to develop and cultivate a personal, devotional relationship to Jesus Christ as Lord and Savior and on the imperative to evangelize—namely, to share the Gospel with others so that they too can come personally to experience salvation in Christ. An important third emphasis is on the vital importance of the Bible as Divine Revelation—above all, as revelation of the Gospel but also as a source of divine guidance for every aspect of life. This has led many to suppose that Evangelicals are Fundamentalists, but this is not so. Virtually all Protestant Fundamentalists are Evangelicals, but there are many, perhaps most Evangelicals, who are not Fundamentalists.

The excerpt chosen to represent the way of devotion in Christianity is by Billy Graham, internationally known Evangelical leader and revivalist of the twentieth century. His background is Baptist and Fundamentalist, and the early years of his ministry were much more conservative than he is today. Unlike Fundamentalism's concern to draw sharp, exclusive boundaries between "true Christians" and "false Christians," as Graham's ministry matured over the decades of the midcentury, he deliberately chose to identify with the broad mainstream of Evangelical Christianity and to enter into inclusive, ecumenical rapport with members of all of the mainstream denominations of Christianity. (This has resulted in the more extreme Fundamentalist groups repudiating Graham.) Probably no one widely recognized leader better represents that mainstream today than Graham. The excerpt is taken from the chapter, "Turning On," of his book, *The Jesus Generation*, published in 1971.[6] Although Graham has pointed out that some of the illustrations in *The Jesus Generation* are now dated, this excerpt contains a concise summary of basic evangelical convictions.

We get dirt off our bodies by turning on the water in the shower. We get the darkness out of a room by turning on the light. We get our automobiles to run by turning on the switch. The "hip" generation popularized the phrase "turning on" to describe the drug experience. Smoking pot, dropping acid, or shooting heroin, they turned on for a high and got into their trip.

To become a Christian, you must "turn on" to God by placing your full faith in Christ as Savior and confessing Him as Lord. And the wonderful thing about it is that it works.

I once conducted a crusade in a city that was having one crisis after another with its restless young people. One night I disguised myself and attended a rock festival in order to discover what attracted so many—thousands. Next day, I reported that I had been present and publicly invited the entire hippie set to attend our services. They responded by the hundreds, and when I invited them to receive Christ, scores came forward. Recently, one of them wrote to me.

"I came to the crusade because I thought you were a regular guy," he said. "To those of us who attended it was to be just another experience, something to relieve our boredom. But as you spoke, I began to hear another voice, and I knew what you were saying was 'truth.' When you asked us to come forward if we wanted to receive Christ, I rose almost spontaneously and walked down the aisle! Standing there, I felt more alive than I'd ever felt in my life. Everything I had searched for or longed for seemed to materialize in that one moment. I stayed on with my old friends a few more weeks, but presently I gravitated to those who had shared my spiritual experience. All of us began to pray regularly and to study the Bible. I am now attending seminary, studying for the ministry. I expect to spend the rest of my life spreading the thrilling news of God's love and forgiveness with all that will listen."

This young man had been "born again." He had been "turned on" spiritually. Jesus Christ works like that, channeling His revolutionary power into the lives of those who put their faith in Him. He talked frequently about drastic changes, but always they had to start in the heart. This is why He insisted on conversion and new birth. "Verily I say unto you, except ye be converted, and become as little children," He said, "ye shall not enter into the kingdom of heaven" (Matthew 18:3).

The shape of things to come has been apparent in our crusades for several years now, as a vast majority of our audiences included more and more young people, and as many thousands of them have marched across football stadiums and down the aisles of great indoor arenas to discover a new life. Their identity crisis is over! They have found what they were looking for by turning on to Jesus. . . .

Not long after my own conversion, I read a tract entitled "Four Things God Wants You to Know." Campus Crusade for Christ, which has played a major role in sparking the new "Jesus Revolution," has expanded these four items into a beautiful little booklet and given them away by the hundreds of thousands. Literally, it has helped countless young people to get "turned on" spiritually. [In a later book, Graham states clearly, "I do not believe . . . that there is a tidy little formula, or a recipe which has the Good Housekeeping seal of approval. However, I do believe these [kinds of summaries] have provided little handles which help people to understand how to receive Christ."[7]]

The first law is that God loves you and has a wonderful plan for your life. God loves you! Most young people have heard or perhaps memorized John 3:16, the most familiar verse in the Bible. In one modern version it reads: "For God loved the world so much that He gave His only Son so that everyone who believes in Him should not be lost, but should have eternal life."

Young people talk a lot about love. Most of their songs are about love. "All You Need is Love," "I Can't Live in a World Without Love," "The Glory of Love," "Man Without Love," "Love Can Make the Poorest Man a Millionaire" are recent examples.

"The supreme happiness of life," Victor Hugo said long ago, "is the conviction that we are loved." "Love is the first requirement for mental health," declared Sigmund Freud. The Bible teaches that "God is love" and that God loves you. To realize that is of paramount importance. Nothing else matters so much.

And loving you, God has a wonderful plan for your life. Who else could plan and guide your life so well? He, the Shepherd; you, one of His sheep. A young woman who came forward in one of our meetings told us how God had once seemed so far away; but now in Jesus Christ, He was always near at hand in every situation. "The will of Christ for me," she explained, "is wonderfully simple and simply wonderful."

The second spiritual law is that you must acknowledge you are a sinner—by nature and by practice. This sinful nature separates you from God and makes it impossible for you to experience either His love or His plan for your life. David, the great king of Israel, once wrote: "I was shaped in iniquity and in sin did my mother conceive me." Isaiah the prophet expressed the same idea, "All we like sheep have gone astray. We have turned everyone to his own way." Solomon, one of the wisest men who ever lived, explained that man's instinctive behavior when he excluded God, is invariably disastrous. "There is a way that seemeth right unto man, but the end thereof are the ways of death." Jesus made it clear that the easy, popular way is the wrong way, "Wide is the gate and broad is the way that leadeth to destruction and many (the majority) there be that go in thereat." But "straight is the gate and narrow is the way that leadeth into life and few there are that find it" (Matthew 7:13, 14). Paul argued to the Romans that the defilement of the human race was universal. "They have all gone out of the way" and "the way of peace they have not known . . . for all have sinned and come short of the glory of God." Not only does our sin make us come short of God's expectations, but it separates us from God. Isaiah taught, "Your sins have separated His face from you."

Youth senses this guilt, this alienation, this separation from God, and wonders what causes it. A reader wrote to "Dear Abby": "When a kid goes wrong, which factor is more responsible, his heredity or his environment?" Abby replied, "It's a toss-up." The Bible says exactly that! We are sinners both by heredity and environment; both by nature and by nurture; both by instinct and by practice. . . .

Because we *are* sinners, we often feel lonely, and unloved. A social scientist once polled the people of this country and discovered that at any time during the day about 135,000 Americans are saying "I'm sick and tired of everything!" In his first chapter, the prophet Isaiah described the sins of ancient Israel and noted the results: "The whole head is sick and the whole heart is faint." Look around! Listen to youth today. The Rolling Stones have made "I Can't Get No Satisfaction!" one of the most popular modern songs. The title speaks for itself. Sin brings no satisfaction. Inger Stevens won the Golden Globe Award as the best televised actress during the sixties and began the seventies by taking her own life. "Sometimes I get so lonely I could scream," she had said. That's alienation! The feeling is shared by the youth of every country in the world.

So why not quit beating around the bush! Why not call our problem by its real name, which is "sin." Sin is selfishness—it's a transgression of God's laws—it's coming short of God's moral requirements—and of these we are *all guilty*. Let's face it, admit it, and forsake it! That is called repentance. Jesus said, "Except ye repent, ye shall all likewise perish." That word repentance is used in the New Testament more than seventy times.

The third spiritual law is that Jesus Christ is God's only provision for man's sin. Only through Him can you know and experience God's love, forgiveness, salvation, and plan for you. "For at the very time when we were still sinners, then Christ died for the wicked," wrote Paul. John said, "In this was manifest the love of God toward us that the Father sent the Son to be the Saviour of the world." Jesus did not say that he was *a* way. He said: "I am *the* Way, *the* Truth, and *the* Life; no man comes to the Father but by me!"

Sometimes we miss the significance of the cross on which Jesus died, stumbling over its simplicity. Its uncomplicated meaning is that Jesus Christ has paid the price of our sins. By taking our place and our punishment, He gave us the gift of forgiveness, cleansing, and everlasting life.

All the religions of the world are simply men looking for God. But Christianity is not merely one more religion. In Christianity, God is searching *for* man—and revealing Himself *to* man. That is why God has placed in man's heart a restlessness and a frustration—until he finds God! God's search for man led to the cross where His only Son suffered and died—died for you. This sounds foolish to modern ears. And to the ancients as well. When Paul went to the pagan city of Corinth, he said: "The proclamation of the cross is foolishness unto them that perish." But then he added: "The foolishness of God is wiser than men and the weakness of God is stronger than men" (I Corinthians 1:25). In that ancient city, the cross of Christ was a stumbling block to the Jews, and to the Gentiles it was idiocy. Intellectual Corinthians preferred a system of philosophy predicated on the ability of man's mind to unravel the divine. They wanted something their minds could grasp. So Paul tells us that "the natural man receiveth not (cannot understand) the things of God" (1 Corinthians 2:14). Nor must you understand all God's mysteries in order to find Him and receive Him and know Him. A doctor writes a prescription which we cannot read for the treatment of a disease that we do not understand, and we gladly pay a sum which may seem unreasonable because we rely on his knowledge and have faith that he will make us well. Before the cross can have any meaning at all, the Spirit of God must open the mind. So long as we remain separated from God, the Scriptures teach, our minds are covered by a veil. To such a one—to an "outsider"—the cross must appear as a ridiculous symbol. To those of us who have experienced its transforming power, however, it represents the only cure for sin—the basic ill of humanity. The cross is the focal point of the life and ministry of Jesus Christ. His death upon it was no afterthought with God. When Christ took our places, our sin was laid on Him—and sin cannot be in two places at the same time. My sin was laid on Christ and, therefore, I have no sin charged to me. My sin is now Christ's burden. He has taken its load off me. He has become the sin bearer. Though I was indebted to God, Jesus paid off my debts. I will never suffer the shame of judgment or the terrors of hell, "As far as the east is from the west," said the psalmist, "so far hath he removed our transgressions from us" (Psalm 103: 12). . . .

Are you saying, "I don't understand any of this. It sounds ridiculous!" Listen! If a man were drowning and I threw him a life belt, would he say, "I'll not put this belt on until I know whether it's made of rubber or cork of if the material is strong enough to hold me"? No man in danger of drowning talks like that. No man who is ignorant of Christ is capable of comprehending the mystery of the cross as long as he is separated from God.

The Bible says that God was in Christ reconciling the world unto Himself. You are a part of that world. God wants you to be reconciled to Him—and He has provided a way in the person of Jesus.

The fourth spiritual law requires that you must openly accept Christ as your Savior and Lord. Only then can you know and experience God's love and plan for you.

Throughout one's youth, one struggles constantly to be "accepted." We want to be accepted by our parents, by our teachers, by our peers, and by our girl friend or boyfriend. To gain this acceptance, you will do almost anything. In the beginning of the letter written to the Ephesians, Paul exults in the fact that, as believers, God has "destined us—such is His will and pleasure—to be accepted as His sons through Jesus Christ." Think of it—sinners such as you and I *accepted* by God! No wonder John Newton, the slave trader, after his conversion wrote, "Amazing grace, that could save a wretch like me."

To "turn on" spiritually, you need only to open your heart to Jesus Christ and ask Him to come in. He says: "Here I stand knocking at the door; if anyone hears

My voice and opens the door, I will come in and sit down to supper with him and he with Me." How beautiful! How simple! How thrilling! . . .

We are supposed to do more than admire Jesus. We are to "put Him on." As Paul wrote to the Ephesians, "Put on the new nature . . . created after the likeness of God in true righteousness and holiness! The likeness to God that we had at the first, the likeness that we lost by sin, is created again in us when our lives are joined to Christ."

Paul the apostle often spoke of the Christian as being "in Christ."

That is a Christian person's true identity.

Having done this, now I know my past—it is sinful but forgiven—and where I come from; I came from God. I know what went wrong; I tried to play God instead of being satisfied to be a real man. I know my future; my destiny is Heaven. And I know the present; I live in the here and now having Jesus always within me, His Holy Spirit to guide, teach, and lead. . . .

Right now, thousands of young people are confronting the living Christ. You can too. Would you like to pray the short prayer we pray in our crusades with those who come forward to receive Christ?

Oh Lord, I am a sinner. I am sorry for my sins. I am willing to turn from my sins. I receive Jesus Christ as my Lord and Savior. I confess Him as Lord. I want to serve Him from this moment on in the fellowship of His Church. In Christ's name, Amen.

Reprinted by permission of the author from Billy Graham, *The Jesus Generation* (Grand Rapids, MI: Zondervan Publishing House, 1971), pp. 139–147, and 149.

You may have already noticed how Graham includes personal stories of the devotional religious experience of Christians in what he writes, which also reflects his preaching style. Sharing such personal testimonies is not unique to Graham, but is a pervasive feature of Evangelical Christian preaching and religious life generally. Other stories Graham cites include the following.[8]

One dark night, in the ancient city of Jerusalem, Jesus turned to one of the best-known intellectuals of his time and said, "I say to you, unless one is born again, he cannot see the kingdom of God" (John 3:3). In those words Jesus told us of both the necessity and the possibility of new birth—of spiritual transformation. Since that time untold millions throughout the ages have attested to the reality and the power of God in their lives through being born again. . . .

I think of the great Dutch Christian, Corrie ten Boom, who is now in her 80s. Her story of courage in the midst of Nazi persecution has inspired millions. She tells of an experience when she was only five years old when she said, "I want Jesus in my heart." She described how her mother took her little hand in hers and prayed with her. "It was so simple, and yet Jesus Christ says that we all must come as children, no matter what our age, social standing, or intellectual background." [Graham here is quoting from ten Boom's autobiography, *The Hiding Place*.]

Corrie ten Boom, at the age of five, had been born again.

I have had countless people tell me, in person and by letter, how they were born again and their lives were changed. A man from Milwaukee wrote, "Tonight my wife and I had come to the brink of ending our marriage. We felt we could no longer stay together under the conditions in which we were living. Both of us admitted that we thought we no longer loved each other. I no longer enjoyed her company nor appreciated my home life. We made bitter statements about each other. We could make no compromise, nor could we agree on how to improve our marriage even if we were to try.

"I believe it was God's will that I turned on the television and listened to your message about spiritual rebirth. As my wife watched with me, we began to search our hearts and felt a new life within us. I prayed that God would come into my heart and truly make me a new man and help me begin a new life. Our troubles seem rather slight now."

Both this man and his wife were born again. . . .

. . .[P]eople frantically pursue all sorts of promised cures for the renewal of their inner lives. Some people hunt for renewal at the psychiatrist's office. Others search for spiritual renewal in exotic oriental religions or processes of inward meditation. Still others seek for inner peace and renewal in drugs or alcohol. Whatever the path, however, they eventually come to a dead end. Why? Simply because man cannot renew himself. God created us. Only God can recreate us. Only God can give us the new birth we so desperately want and need.

Joel Quinones was a living example of a person whose mind was under attack. I met him in San Diego and heard his amazing story.

Joel was first thrown into prison at the age of eight for trying to kill a sadistic man who had beaten him and burned him with cigarettes. When Joel was released, he came out a bundle of hatred and from then on did everything he could to show his scorn to society. As a result Joel found himself in San Quentin at the age of nineteen and spent the next eleven years there. He was turned over to the prison psychiatrists, who examined him, gave him shock treatments, and finally diagnosed him as "criminally insane."

Joel was placed in with the incorrigibles. When they were fed, the food was placed on what appeared to be a large shovel with the handle long enough to push it under two separate security doors. "You don't even feed a tiger that way," Joel told us, "but that's the way they fed us."

After all those years in San Quentin, it was decided to get rid of the undesirable aliens, and Joel, along with a number of other Mexicans, was taken across the border and turned loose. He had a godly mother, a cook at a Bible school, who had been in the courtroom when Joel had been convicted for the first time. She had said to him then, "Joel, this isn't the end. Jesus has work for you to do."

When he was released in Mexico, his mother was there to greet him. Putting her arms around him, she said, "Joel, you need the Lord Jesus; you need to ask Him to forgive your sins, to give you a new heart and a new life."

Joel struggled with this, but before the Lord was finished with him he was a transformed person. He went to Bible school, married one of the graduates, and is today a prison chaplain in Mexico. He has won so many prisoners to Christ that he is busy trying to build a halfway house, a "City of Refuge" to which these prisoners can come for rehabilitation before returning to normal life.

Sin had affected Joel's mind, but the transforming power of Christ had given him new gifts.

Captain Mitsuo Fuchida was the Japanese naval air commander who led the bombing attack on Pearl Harbor. He relates that when the Japanese war prisoners were returning from America he was curious as to what kind of treatment they had received. An ex-prisoner he questioned told him what made it possible for those in the camp to forget their hate and hostility toward their captors. One young girl had been extremely kind and helpful and had shown such love and tenderness for them that their hearts were touched. They wondered why she was so good to them and were amazed when she told them it was because her parents had been killed by the Japanese army! She explained that her parents had been Christian missionaries in the Philippines at the beginning of the war but when the Japanese landed they were forced to flee to the mountains. They were later found by the Japanese, accused of being spies and put to death. But before they were killed they had asked for thirty minutes of time to pray, which was granted. The girl was convinced that her parents had spent that thirty minutes praying for forgiveness for their executioners, and because of this she was able to allow the Holy Spirit to remove the hate from her heart and replace it with love.

Captain Fuchida could not understand such love. Several months passed and one day in Tokyo he was given a leaflet as he left a railroad station. This told the story of Sergeant Jacob DeShazer who was captured by the Japanese, tortured, and held prisoner of war for forty months. While in prison camp he received Christ through reading the Bible. God's Word removed the bitter hatred for the Japanese from his heart and replaced it with such love that he was compelled to return to tell the Japanese people of this marvelous love of Christ.

Captain Fuchida bought a Bible and began to read. He faced the scene of the crucifixion of Christ and was struck by Jesus' words "Father forgive them; for they do not know what they are doing" (Luke 23:34). Jesus prayed for the very soldiers who were about to thrust the spear into His side. In his book *From Pearl Harbor to Golgotha* Captain Fuchida tells how he found the source of this miracle love that can forgive enemies, and how he could now understand the story of the American girl whose parents had been slain and the transformation in Jake DeShazer's life.

How to Be Born Again, Billy Graham, 1977, Word Publishing, Dallas, Texas. All rights reserved.

CHAPTER SUMMARY

Jodo-shin-shu as expounded by its founder, Shinran, is presented as a Buddhist example of the way of devotion. Jodo-shin-shu centers upon whole-hearted devotion to Amida Buddha, a devotion concretely expressed in the recitation, "*Namo-amida-butsu*," which invokes Amida's presence and acknowledges his lordship. The experience of faith (*shinjin*) in Amida's boundless compassion is said to involve a displacement of self-power with Amida's infinite power, where-by one assuredly is said to attain Rebirth and Enlightenment in Amida's Pure Land, be given abundant grace to meet the misfortunes and temptations of life, and be impassioned to embody Amida's compassion for others. For this faith to arise, it is necessary first to be convinced of one's helplessness to escape the predicament of human sin and second to throw oneself wholly upon the divine power of Amida, trusting in his promise to save. A sampling of stories is given that tell of persons who exemplify faith in Amida and the personal transforma-tion consequent to the arising of faith.

To exemplify the way of devotion in Christianity, an account by the Protestant Evangelist Billy Graham is given of what is involved in "finding God" and being "born again" as a Christian. Evangelical Christianity centers on whole-hearted de-votion to God for the gift of salvation in Jesus Christ, in whom redemption from the predicament of human sin is to be found. Reception of this gift in the experi-ence of Christian faith, according to Graham, involves four principles: (1) God loves each person and has a wonderful plan for that person's life; (2) the sinful nature that separates persons from God, God's love, and God's plan for their lives must be acknowledged and relinquished by them; (3) the redemption wrought by Jesus Christ's suffering and death on the cross is God's provision for sin, enabling reconciliation with God; and (4) openly placing faith in Christ as Savior and Lord opens the door to his revolutionary power to transform one's life, restore kinship with God, and renew God's plan for one's life in realizing his purposes in the world. Here too a sampling of stories is given that show what Christian faith and the life transformation consequent upon faith in Christ is all about.

STUDY QUESTIONS ON
SIMILARITIES AND DIFFERENCES

Between Evangelical Christianity as represented by the excerpts from Billy Graham's writings and Jodo-shin-shu as represented by the excerpts from Shinran's writings, the similarities are striking—so much so that one may be led to over-look the differences.[9] It should not prove difficult to identify the main features of each. In answer to the following questions, keep in mind both the danger of generalizing from these specific instances of the way of devotion to all forms of the way of devotion in either tradition and how much may be involved implicit-ly in the actual practice of these specific forms that may be going unsaid in the two accounts just given. Spend some time comparing the accounts.

1. Note as many similarities as you can. Seek to identify not just superficial similarities, but deep structural similarities. (For example, how is the respec-tive *ultimate reality* conceived? What in each account seems to be the key that releases the flood of divine grace? What kind of life changes allegedly

result from turning over one's life to the "other power of Amida," on the one hand, and "the love of God in Christ," on the other?)

2. Assuming that both of these movements exemplify the same generic way of being religious in two distinct religious traditions, what if anything do the similarities identified in answer to the first question indicate that is essential to that way of being religious (which the framework identifies as the way of devotion)?

   a. What, if anything, do these two accounts have in common regarding their respective means of approach to *ultimate reality*?

   b. What characteristic existential problems is each concerned with and seeking to address?

   c. Is there anything that indicates the characteristic way each interprets its broader tradition's scripture and symbol system as distinct from other traditional ways of taking them? What sorts of features of *ultimate reality* does each specifically highlight? That is, what kind of "face" does each envision *ultimate reality* to have?

   d. What sorts of social structures (social organization, group activity, roles and responsibilities, etc.) does each have?

   e. What specific virtues in the practice of its religious life does each appear to commend, whether explicitly or implicitly, and what specific vices in that practice does each appear to condemn? (Be careful here to distinguish criticisms each may apparently offer of the religious practices of others from critical expectations set for its own members.) That is, what ideal(s) of practice does each uphold? And what sorts of things would fall short of those ideals?

3. Finding so many deep structural similarities, it may seem difficult to identify differences. Try now to identify what dissimilarities there are between Jodo-shin-shu and Evangelical Christianity—not what is better or what is worse, but just what is different about each.

4. What among the differences identified in question 3 seem specifically due to different *theological* convictions of Buddhism (or specifically Jodo-shin-shu Buddhism) and Christianity (or Evangelical Protestantism of the sort that Graham represents)? For example, what differences in the two accounts directly reflect differences in their respective central stories—that is, differences between the story of Dharmakara becoming Amida Buddha and the story of the Son of God, Jesus, coming to die on the cross for the sins of the world—and doctrinal beliefs built upon those stories?

5. There is an apparent similarity between the use of the *Nembutsu* (calling upon Amida's name) among followers of Jodo-shin-shu and the use of the Jesus Prayer among Eastern Orthodox Christians as described in the excerpt on the way of mystical quest in Christianity in Chapter 9. Explore that apparent

similarity. Does it imply anything more than an apparent similarity? For example, could it perhaps indicate a fusion of the ways of mystical quest and devotion in each or at least some overlap in ways of being religious between them? What would justify such a conclusion? What would count against it?

FOR FURTHER READING

Recommended articles in the *Encyclopedia of Religion*, edited by Mircea Eliade (New York: Macmillan, 1987) include *Devotion; Popular Religion; Bhakti; Pure and Impure Lands; Mappō; Nien-fo; Jōdoshū; Jodo Shinshū; Shinran; Hōnen; Rennyo; Amitābha; Avalokitesvara; Faith; Pietism; Evangelical and Fundamental Christianity; Popular Christian Religiosity; Preaching;* and *Grace.*

Lloyd Arthur, *The Creed of Half Japan* (New York: E. P. Dutton, 1912). Though dated, still a good study of Jodo-shin-shu as it is found in this century.

John Blofeld, "The Path of Faith and Compassion," in his book, *Beyond the Gods: Taoist and Buddhist Mysticism* (London: Allen and Unwin, 1974), Ch. 4, pp. 69–88. This chapter nicely complements Unno's article below in a narrative exposition of the theology behind Chinese Pure Land practice.

Alfred Bloom, *Shinran's Gospel of Pure Grace*, Association for Asian Studies: Monographs and Papers 20 (Tucson, AZ: University of Arizona Press, 1965). Perhaps the best study in English of Shinran and his basic teachings.

Alfred Bloom, T*annisho: Resource for Modern Living* (Honolulu, HI: Buddhist Study Center, 1981). Captures well the vision of Shinran's teaching.

James C. Dobbins, *Jodo Shinshu: Shin Buddhism in Medieval Japan* (Bloomington, IN: Indiana University Press, 1989). A more historically specialized, but excellent study.

Yoshifumi Ueda and Dennis Hirota, *Shinran: An Introduction to His Thought, With Selections from the Shin Buddhism Translation Series* (Kyoto: Hongwanji International Center, 1989). An authoritative introduction to Shinran's teachings with a generous selection from the latest translations of several of his writings.

Taitetsu Unno, "The Nature of Religious Experience in Shin Buddhism," in *The Other Side of God: A Polarity in World Religions*, ed. Peter L. Berger (Garden City, NY: Anchor Books/Doubleday, 1981), pp. 252–271. This article beautifully analyzes the structure of Jodo-shin-shu religious experience and explains clearly how it is fully reconcilable with traditional Mahayana *Prajñā-pāramitā* teaching.

George C. Bedell, Leo Sandon, Jr., and Charles T. Wellborn, *Religion in America*, 2nd ed. (New York: Macmillan, 1982), Ch. 3: "Revivalism." A fine, brief overview of the mainstream tradition of Evangelical Revivalism in America.

Peter C. Erb, ed., *Pietists: Selected Writings* (New York: Paulist Press, 1983). A first-rate collection of writings exemplifying the theology and spirituality of the progenitors of Evangelical Protestantism, namely, the leaders of the European Pietist Movement.

Billy Graham, *How To Be Born Again* (Waco, TX: Word Books, 1977).

William G. McLoughlin, *Revivals, Awakenings, and Reform* (Chicago History of American Religion; Chicago, IL: University of Chicago Press, 1978). A more detailed focus on the nature and history of Evangelical Revivalism in America.

John Weborg, "Pietism: 'The Fire of God which flames in the heart of Germany,'" in *Protestant Spiritual Traditions*, ed. Frank C. Senn (New York: Paulist Press, 1986). A good, brief overview of the European movement that launched Evangelical Protestantism.

F. Ernest Stoeffler, *The Rise of Evangelical Pietism* (Studies in the History of Religions—Supplements to Numen, 9 (Leiden: Brill, 1965). One of the best historical treatments of the origins of Evangelical Protestantism.

Leonard I. Sweet, *The Evangelical Tradition in America* (Macon, GA: Mercer University Press, 1984). An excellent overview of the nature and history of Evangelical Protestantism in America.

Bernard A. Weisberger, *They Gathered at the River: The Story of the Great Revivalists and Their Impact upon Religion in America* (Boston, MA: Little, Brown, 1958). Just what the title says.

NOTES

1. Gendo Nakai, *Shinran and His Religion of Pure Faith* (Kyoto, Japan: The Shinshu Research Institute, 1937), pp. 103–114, 116–117, 124–126.

2. *Nyorai* is the Japanese equivalent of the Sanskrit word *tathāgata*—meaning, as stressed in Jodo-shin-shu, "one who has come from truth (*tathatā*)" or "manifestation of Absolute truth."

3. Buddhas and Bodhisattvas are supposed to be of a qualitatively different, extra-samsaric order than are gods (*devas*), who are understood to be subject to the cycle of *saṃsāra*.

4. *Ibid.*, pp. 167–170, 182–186, 190–193.

5. The five hideous sins are parricide, matricide, killing an *arhat* (one who has realized *nirvāna* by Theravada practice), causing schism in the *Saṃgha* (the Buddhist community, especially the monastic community), and shedding the blood of a Buddha. The ten evil deeds are (1) three deeds of the body, i.e., taking life, theft, and adultery; (2) four deeds of the mouth, i.e., lying, exaggeration, double-tongue, and abuse; and (3) three deeds of the mind, i.e., covetousness, anger, and ignorance.

6. Billy Graham, *The Jesus Generation* (Grand Rapids, MI: Zondervan, 1971), pp. 139–147, and 149.

7. Billy Graham, *How To Be Born Again* (Waco, TX: Word Books, 1977), p. 167.

8. *Ibid.*, pp. 8–9, 79–80, and 125–126.

9. The similarities are so striking that one is prompted to raise the question as to some historical influence. Others have raised it before, and so far no one has been able to come up with any significant historical connection. The philosophical assumption that there must be some such connection to account for the degree of similarity amounts to a denial that there can be a generic, more or less universal structure of a devotional way of being religious that can account for the similarity, a structure this book has been maintaining all along.

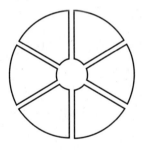

CHAPTER 13

THE WAY OF SHAMANIC MEDIATION IN BUDDHISM AND CHRISTIANITY

For Buddhists and Christians who identify with the modern worldview, shamanic phenomena in their respective traditions are viewed as archaic holdovers from an earlier credulous age, contaminations of "high religion" by animistic folk religion, and in no sense essential to true Buddhism or true Christianity. We shall not enter into this controversy here except to note that the evidence is fairly clear that shamanic phenomena have been a part of each tradition all along—at least on the fringes of institutionalized orthodoxy.

A full-blown shamanic tradition, however, has hardly ever emerged in either Buddhism or Christianity. This has to do with distinctive reasons each tradition has to be wary of shamanic practices. Buddhism's suspicion stems from two sources. On the one hand, it is stressed that the acquisition of supernatural powers poses a strong temptation to the very egoistic desires and aversions that it is Buddhism's goal to overcome. On the other hand, it is claimed that the exercise of supernatural powers is of no direct help in uprooting egoism in oneself or in others and may likely be counterproductive to that primary goal. Buddhism does not, however, cultivate disbelief in the existence of shamanic powers. As a matter of fact, it teaches that they are a natural byproduct of high levels of meditative attainment and their presence may be taken to indicate a specific level of attainment. Nor does Buddhism teach that these powers are evil. It does teach that they can be used for good and for evil, and there are many stories of the Buddha and Buddhists of high attainment exercising supernatural powers. Perhaps another reason for

Buddhism not developing its own shamanic traditions is its encounter with and tolerance of preexistent, indigenous shamanic traditions in the cultures to which it spread. These traditions served existential needs—needs that could be construed as egoistic or samsaric needs—other than those with which Buddhism was most concerned, which pertain to transcending *samsāra* altogether.

Christianity's suspicion stems from three sources. First of all, it stems from the conviction that there are spiritual powers at large in the world that are opposed to God and to the ultimate well-being of creation. Consequently, if one is to resort to supernatural resources at all, one should make absolutely sure that they are "of God" and not "of Satan." The power of the Holy Spirit apparently does not tolerate simultaneous resort to "other spiritual powers"—hence the biblical interdictions against resorting to occult practices (e.g., Leviticus 19:31, 20:6, and 27; Deuteronomy 18:9–22; and I Samuel 28). How one is to discern what is of God and what is of Satan is a matter of "spiritual discernment," and has been at times a matter of considerable controversy in Christian history. A second reason for Christianity's suspicion is similar to Buddhism's suspicion, namely, the temptation posed by the acquisition of supernatural power for egoistic motives and for the development of the sin of "spiritual pride." Indeed, the idea that resort to divine power for healing is contrary to a humble acceptance of the all-wise ordering of life by divine providence (a kind of Christian fatalism—for example, "God wouldn't allow me to suffer if he didn't intend it to happen.") seems to have been responsible for the virtual extinction of shamanic Christian healing within the early medieval church. A third reason is the intractability of shamanic power to the kind of order and control prized by the established clerical hierarchy.

Interestingly, both Buddhism and Christianity condemn sorcery, namely, the use of shamanic powers to implement egoistic, this-worldly motives, especially those that might harm and destroy.

Despite Buddhism's wariness toward shamanic practices, there seems to have emerged a full-fledged tradition of shamanic mediation (if not more than one) in connection with Vajrayana Buddhism in Tibet, China, and Japan. In Japan, one such tradition is known as *Shugendō* ("the way [*dō*] of mastering [*shu*] extraordinary religious power [*gen*]"). Outside of Vajrayana, whether a full-fledged tradition of Buddhist shamanic practice can be found or not, this author does not know well enough to say, although, as mentioned in Chapter 7, there are cases in Southeast Asia of apparently syncretic fusions of indigenous shamanic practices and Theravada Buddhist understandings. In Christianity, apart from the first few centuries of the Church, there does not seem to have existed a tradition of shamanic mediation as such—though there may be found numerous references at random to shamanic phenomena[1]—until the emergence of Pentecostalism and the Charismatic Movement in the twentieth century. The tradition of practice that has emerged in connection with these movements has been relatively slow and haphazard in formation, perhaps out of fear of domesticating what is taken to be the essentially intractable power and charisma of the Holy Spirit.

A Buddhist Example:
Healing and Exorcism
in Japanese Shugendō

The excerpts chosen to represent shamanic mediation in Buddhism tell primarily of two Japanese women in the *Shugendō* tradition of Buddhist mountain asceticism. Traditionally there are more men than women in Shugendō, but the role of women in shamanic practice in Japan, particularly in traditions other than Shugendō, has been very strong. In any case, these are women who serve as healers, exorcists, and oracles in rural Japan. They have acquired these powers (or, rather, they have become a mediator for these powers) and renew and maintain them (or maintain their role as effective mediator for them) through rigorous ascetic practices. These practices involve seclusion, fasting, dietary abstentions, cold-water showers (preferably under a waterfall), repeated recitation of words of magical power, ritual pilgrimage to sacred mountains (involving shamanic rituals of rebirth and possession), and demonstrations of their miraculous powers by feats such as fire walking (not just walking over burning coals but allegedly absorbing the heat from them so that other nonshamans can walk safely over them) and plunging their hands in boiling water. The following excerpts are by an English scholar of Japanese culture, Carmen Blacker, who has spent several years studying shamanic practices in Japan.[2]

They tell of Mrs. Hiroshima Ryūun, an ascetic renowned for her powers of healing and exorcism throughout the Kansai district of Japan in the first half of the twentieth century, and Mrs. Matsuyama, a healer and exorcist living near Kyoto in the mid-twentieth century. The context of the book from which the first excerpt is taken is a discussion by Professor Blacker of different types of ways in which ascetic shamans are initiated into their roles. Some are said to be forcibly chosen by a spiritual being, others voluntarily pursue the role. These two women illustrate both types.

———————————————————————————●———————————————————————————

Mrs Hiroshima Ryūun was a celebrated ascetic belonging to the category of peripatetic wanderers. During the war and the years immediately preceding it she traveled on foot throughout virtually the length and breadth of Japan. The shrine to her spirit kept in an upstairs room of the temple contained a map of the journeys she had accomplished, which could be seen at a glance to include not only the accredited pilgrim routes of Shikoku and central Japan, but also long, apparently haphazard journeys throughout much of the rest of the main island. Her dramatic cures through exorcism were particularly celebrated in the district of Nara and the Yamato plain.

This powerful woman *gyōja* ["ascetic," i.e., one who carries out ascetic practices designed to build up sacred power] was first called to the religious life by a vision of the archetypal ascetic En-no-Gyōja [an eighth century mountain ascetic, celebrated in many legends, and the model for all subsequent mountain ascetics in Japan]. Ringed staff in hand, he stood by her bedside and adjured her to take it upon herself to save those suffering from sickness in the world. Thereafter for three years, always under the direction of En-no-Gyōja, Mrs Hiroshima undertook a regime of austerities in which the local waterfall figured prominently. Often, her daughter assured me, she would stand under the waterfall in the middle of winter for the length of time it took her to recite a hundred Heart Sutras [a famous, somewhat enigmatic summary of *Prajñā -pāramitā* teaching, regarded as magically very powerful in Vajrayana Buddhism].

At the end of three years these strenuous efforts culminated in a terrific divine seizure. For a whole week, without a single pause for rest, she was in a continuous state of divine possession. She neither ate nor slept, and only salt water passed her lips while deity after deity from all over Japan came into her body and spoke through her mouth.

After this extraordinary experience she found herself in possession of powers of healing and of clairvoyant vision of the spiritual beings which caused sickness. She found also that En-no-Gyōja ceased to be her tutelary deity, his place being taken by a mysterious spirit called Magotarō Inari. When first possessed by this divinity, Mrs Hiroshima had no idea who he was. She had never heard his name in her life before. She found his shrine only after a long search, a small and unobtrusive place in the precincts of the Yakushiji temple near Nara. He was wont to appear in various forms, a fox or a small boy, but his real shape, only seldom manifested, was that of a snake. [Blacker explains how these archetypal forms recur throughout Japanese shamanism.] Thereafter, . . . it was entirely through the power of Magotarō Inari that Mrs Hiroshima was able to perform the dramatic cures which made her famous throughout the district. . . .

In . . . interior initiation [such as the case of Mrs. Hiroshima] . . . the ascetic is brought into contact with a superior guardian. It is he who forces him into his new life and confers on him the necessary powers.

The presence of such a supernatural figure is likewise necessary for those ascetics to whom the gift of a dream or possession is not vouchsafed, and whose decision to enter the religious life is therefore made of their own free will.

Such people usually begin from a state of despair or disgust with their ordinary human life. A succession of miseries and calamities reduce them to the condition known in Japanese as *happō-fusagari*, all eight directions blocked, or *yukizumari*, the feeling that you are up against a brick wall. The death of a husband or a child, a long and debilitating illness, hopeless alcoholism and its attendant financial ruin, miseries such as these are often cited as the *dōki* or motive which convinced them that their lives as hitherto lived were inadequate and meaningless and drove them to seek another kind of life in religion.

Mrs Matsuyama, a healer and exorcist living on the outskirts of Kyoto, told me in 1963 that at the age of twenty-two she had contracted what the doctors told her was an incurable sickness. Someone then told her that although medicine could not help her, the supernatural power of Fudō-Myōō [to be explained below] could. She must undertake under the tutelage of Fudō a regime of austerities on a mountain near Nara. To this place she accordingly repaired and threw herself, sick though she was, into a course of fasting and cold water exercises. At the end of the prescribed period she was not only cured, but had found an entirely new centre and direction to her life. She had accomplished a close bond with Fudō, who in the course of the austerities had conferred powers upon her, and who thereafter supervised her life down to the smallest detail.

Mrs Matsuyama's history may be taken as typical of the voluntary ascetic. If the gift is not given to them they may, with sufficient drive and will power, set out to find it for themselves.

Let us now examine more closely the kind of divinity who spontaneously appears as guardian to these people, and whose tutelage and overshadowing presence is so essential to their success.

Two broad categories of divinity seem to appear in this capacity.

First, there are Buddhist divinities of the classes known as Myōō, bright kings, and Gongen, figures which are theoretically supposed to be "temporary manifestations" of Buddhas or Bodhisattvas. The two characteristics which immediately strike the observer about both these classes of divinity are their ferocious raging visage and the halo of flames which surrounds them. Secondly, in the role of guardian there appears once more on the scene the figure of the supernatural snake.

Of the Buddhist angry, fiery deities the most frequent to appear in the role of guardian is Fudō-Myōō. Fudō is the central and paramount figure in the group of divinities known as the Godai Myōō or Five Great Bright Kings, who in esoteric Buddhism stand as emanations or modes of activity of the Buddha. Where the Buddha exists static and immovable, withdrawn from activity, the five Myōō act as his agents and messengers. Each presides over one of the five directions, the centre being the domain of Fudō.

Though never so horrendous in appearance as the Tibetan angry deities, the face of Fudō is nevertheless startling to those accustomed only to the gentle and compassionate iconography of the Buddha and Bodhisattva figures, and even more so to those such as the sixteenth-century Jesuits [missionaries to Japan] who associate fury with the diabolic order. He is usually found represented as blue, red or black. One eye glares downwards, the other squints divergently upwards. With one upper tooth grasping his lower lip and one lower tooth grasping his upper lip, his mouth is twisted into a peculiar snarl. His long hair hangs in a coil over his left shoulder. His right hand grasps a sword and his left a rope, and he stands not on a lotus or an animal mount as do many Buddhist divinities, but on an immovable rock, which rises sometimes from curling waves. Always he is ringed round with fire. . . .

This is the divinity whom the great majority of ascetics look upon as their guardian, who appears to them in dreams, who directs their austerities, who endues them with vitality and confers upon them their powers. In the doctrine of the Shugendō . . . he is regarded as the image of the perfect nature residing latently in every man and waiting to be released by the proper religious exercises. . . .

The second category of guardians is already familiar. They are deities who are either snakes in their "real form" or who appear frequently in a snake transformation.

The deity Ryūjin, a dragon in his own right, is frequently cited, especially by women ascetics, as the guardian presiding over their welfare, their source of power and upholding guide. So likewise are an extraordinary number of deities who choose to appear to the ascetic in snake form. . . . Mrs Hiroshima's guardian Magotarō Inari . . . turned out to have a "real form" which was a snake. . . .

Nor are these two classes of guardian, the furious fiery ones and the serpents, so dissociated from each other as might first appear. Fudō himself is frequently represented by his attribute, an erect sword, twined about by the dragon Kurikara. The sword stands upright on its thunderbolt hilt, its point inside the mouth of the dragon who has flung its coils round the shaft. Here is Fudō unmistakably linked with the serpent, and at the same time providing a bridge between the two categories of guardian deity.

[Later in the book, Blacker returns to these two women shamans to describe their healing practice.[3]]

Confronted by a sufferer complaining of aches, pains, hallucinations or compulsive actions which she suspects to be caused by some kind of possession, the exorcist's first task is to diagnose the trouble. He must discover first whether it is indeed caused by a spiritual agency rather than by indigestion or migraine or appendicitis, and second what kind of spiritual entity is responsible. For this task a good many ascetics rely on their power of *gantsū* or clairvoyant eyes. With this accomplishment the healer is able to see the inhabitants of the spiritual world, whether malignant or benign. Mrs Nakano, for example, a professional healer and ascetic from Skikoku who regularly appeared in full *yamabushi* costume[4] in Kyoto on August 1st to joint in the ritual ascent of Mt Ōmine, told me that for her diagnoses she relied chiefly on her power of clairvoyant vision. Armed with this faculty, she was able to see at once the cause of her patient's malady. The image of a dog, a snake, a resentful ancestor, or an incident from the past which had preyed on the patient's mind, would appear vividly before her eyes. Equally clearly, however, would appear the image of an inflamed appendix, should that be the true cause of the malady. She could also see what had become of people who had disappeared without trace, and during the war had had to respond to many calls from relatives of soldiers at the front to discover if, when and how these men had met their death. . . .

Another power which proves useful in the process of exorcism is *mimitsū*, clairaudient hearing. Mrs Nakano told me that her practice of austerities had given her clairaudient ears as well as clairvoyant eyes. She would hear a voice clearly speaking in her ear and explaining the cause of the patient's malady. . . .

Once diagnosed, the malignant possession must be overcome; either the cause of its misery and resentment must be removed or it must be brought to realise the error of its ways. Some living examples will best illustrate the methods customarily employed to this end.

Mrs Matsuyama, the professional ascetic healer living in Sagano whose course of austerities was described in a previous chapter, told me in the autumn of 1963 that for the final banishment of the fox or ghost she relied on the power of Fudō-Myōō himself working through her in a state of trance. [A "fox" is a characteristically Japanese, sub-human demonic form—said to be shaped more like a weasel than an actual fox—that causes mischief through possession, oppression, or poltergeist type manifestations. It was earlier described by Blacker.] She demonstrated her methods forthwith. Conducting me into the shrine room of her house, where in front of a large and glittering altar to Fudō was a *gomadan* or magic fire platform, she seated herself before it and began to recite in strong nasal tones the Middle Spell of Fudō:

> *Nōmaku samada basarada*
> *Senda makaroshana*
> *Sowataya untarata kamman.*

She then swung into the Heart Sutra, over and over again and constantly increasing in gabbling speed. Soon she began to make odd grunts and moans amidst the words of the sutra, followed by stertorous puffing sounds and one or two of the piercing magical yells called *kiai*, while her clasped hands shook violently up and down like a flail. Finally with frightful force she beat her stomach several times with her fists while bass roars burst from her mouth.

This violent seizure lasted about a minute. Then the chanting grew calmer and flatter, until suddenly, with a note on the gong, she was herself again, calm and businesslike.

That was Fudō who had taken possession of her, she announced. For her healing she would always invoke him into her body so that his power behind the words of the sutra would cause the evil spirit molesting the patient to capitulate. The sufferer would often fling herself frantically about the room, the fox inside her screaming that it was not afraid, that it was stronger than Fudō, sometimes even climbing up on to the roof in the effort to escape. But eventually it would capitulate and the patient would return to herself, dazed and astonished, and remembering nothing of what had occurred.

About a month after my first meeting with Mrs Matsuyama I was privileged to watch her methods in practice. Our mutual friend Miss Nakagawa sent me a message to say that a neighbour of hers, a Mrs Fukumoto, was suffering from fox possession and would be visiting Mrs Matsuyama the next day for treatment. I was to go early to Mrs Matsuyama's house, and be there in a casual way as though I were a pupil when the patient appeared.

Mrs Matsuyama was ready waiting when I arrived, in a white silk kimono. Shortly afterwards the patient herself appeared, a robust-looking woman in her fifties. At once she burst into a torrent of animated talk. She was greatly troubled by a voice constantly talking in her ear. Sometimes it gave her useful information, such as which road to take at an unfamiliar crossroads. But usually it was a tiresome nuisance, keeping her awake at night asking questions.

Mrs Matsuyama arranged two cushions in front of the glittering altar, for herself and her patient, and rosary in hand slipped quickly into her violent trance. Her loud and stern Heart Sutras soon gave way to a succession of bass roars and barks and stertorous puffs, while she pummeled her patient on the back, rubbed the rosary over her body and traced with her finger some characters on her back. Finally she gave three or four piercing *kiai* yells, pointing her hands at the patient in the mudra [magical hand gesture used in Vajrayana] called *hō-no-ken-in*, with two fingers outstretched like a sword.

Then with a shake she came to herself again and gravely addressed her patient.

"It is not a fox who is troubling you. It is your dead father. He died in the house of his concubine and hence has been unable to achieve rest. To get rid of the nuisance you must undertake the cold water austerity night and morning for twenty-one days." Mrs Fukumoto seemed appalled by this announcement and stammered that her husband would never allow it.

"In that case," Mrs Matsuyama replied, "you must do the next best thing, which is to get up at half-past midnight every night for three weeks and recite the Heart Sutra a hundred and eight times. Have a rosary of a hundred and eight beads in your hand and count the beads as you recite." It was not so quick a cure as the cold water, she added, but just as efficacious in the end.

Even this programme seemed daunting to Mrs Fukumoto, whose cheerful face looked dismayed as she asked whether it would really do her any good. Sternly Mrs Matsuyama assured her that it was the only way to get rid of the trouble. You must cast away all doubt, she said. Fudō has directed you to this course. Eat as little meat as possible and after three weeks come and see me again.

By these grave words Mrs Fukumoto seemed convinced, and took her departure looking much relieved.

Mrs Matsuyama's method of exorcism was thus to fall into a state of trance in which Fudō possessed her and used her voice to vanquish the fox or ghost. It is in fact rather an unusual one. The ascetic only rarely becomes entranced, even though in theory it is through the divine power of his guardian deity that he accomplishes his work. A more usual method is to overcome the foxes and ghosts by the power of the holy text which a previous course of austerities has activated. . . .

Finally let us look at a couple of the cases treated by Mrs Hiroshima Ryūun. . . . Some of the cures which she performed in the course of her travels were recorded by a pupil of hers in a manuscript book which in the summer of 1972 her daughter Mrs Hiroshima Umeko kindly allowed me to read. The manuscript is not dated, but internal evidence suggests that it was written shortly before the end of the war.

Among the many cures and exorcisms recorded in this interesting document, two examples will give some idea of Mrs Hiroshima's methods. Here is the story of the *muenbotoke* or wandering spirits.

Mrs Hiroshima, respectfully referred to throughout the book as 'sensei', master, was summoned to the house of a Mr Morimoto near Nara, whose baby was suffering from an obstinate swelling on the shoulder which the doctors were powerless to cure.

Sensei at once began to recite the Heart Sutra in front of the sick child. Soon there appeared to her clairvoyant eyes three spirits flashing like stars.

"Who are you?" she enquired.

"We are spirits belonging to this house," they replied. "We all died young and poor, with no descendants to care for us. We therefore made the Morimoto child sick in order to draw attention to our plight. Please tell the people here to recite requiem masses [presumably Buddhist requiem rites for the dead] for us, and then we will let the child get well and act as guardians to it into the bargain. We are buried in the ground to the south of this house."

When Mr Morimoto was told the tale, he remembered that some years before an uncle of his had been buried near the house, together with his two wives, who one after the other had died without children. Thus the family had died out, and no one had performed any of the necessary requiems for the dead spirits. It was quite natural, he realised, that they should call attention to themselves by making his baby ill. But as soon as the correct masses were said and offerings made, needless to say the child recovered at once.

A more unpleasant story is recorded under the title of "The New Ghost's Wish." Another family near Nara, also called Morimoto, was reduced to a desperate state of misery. The husband fell very ill with pneumonia, and despite the wife's devoted efforts to nurse him back to health and at the same time to earn enough to support the family, he was continually cursing her and upbraiding her for what he jealously imagined to be her unfaithfulness. At the end of 1942 he died. Soon afterwards his wife developed an appalling headache and had in her turn to take to her bed. Their kind go-between, realising that her sickness was outside the sphere of ordinary doctors, sent for Mrs Hiroshima.

Sensei entered the room to find the poor widow prostrated near the altar to her dead husband's spirit. At once she began the *hyakugan-shingyō* or Hundred Heart Sutras, which takes two-and-a-half hours to recite. At the end of this powerful service she was able to address the spirit.

"Who are you?" she demanded.

"The new ghost," it replied. "I have been waiting and waiting for you to come. Indeed, it was to get you to come here that I caused my wife to have this fearful headache. Magotarō [the name of Mrs Hiroshima's guardian deity], I died with great resentment in my heart and because of this I am wandering with nowhere to go. I died hating and loathing my wife because she was continually making me doubt her. If she marries again I cannot bear it."

When the poor woman was told of this speech, she admitted that her husband had been continually jealous, and that nothing she did ever pleased him.

"Promise me now," sensei said, "that you do not intend to marry again and will continue to honour your husband's spirit."

The woman promised. Sensei thereupon recited with ear-splitting force the nine magic syllables.

"*Rin-byō-tō-sha-kai-jin-retsu-zai-zen.*"

And at that instant the headache which had been tormenting the woman for so long vanished.

There are a good many more rather similar stories in this book, which describe how Mrs Hiroshima not only healed the sick of maladies which the doctors could not touch, but also brought to rest many spirits who for one reason or another were lost, resentful, wandering or miserable, unable to reach their proper salvation. Buried images of Jizō who wished to be dug up, ghosts of those who had died with worries or grudges in their hearts, more ghosts who died without descendants to give them their required nourishment—all these inhabitants of the other world had called attention to their plight by causing pain or sickness to some human being. Mrs Hiroshima as she passed through the village on one of her long journeys was called in to help, and through her treatment she healed the sick person and at the same time comforted the unhappy spirit.

Reprinted with permission of HarperCollins Publishers Limited from Carmen Blacker, *The Catalpa Bow: A Study of Shamanistic Practices in Japan* (London: Allen and Unwin Ltd., 1975), pp. 171–179, 235–240, and 242–244.

A CHRISTIAN EXAMPLE: HEALING AND EXORCISM IN A CHARISMATIC COMMUNITY

To illustrate the way of shamanic mediation in Christianity I have selected some excerpts from an excellent descriptive study by William Joseph Sneck of the Word of God community (abbreviated "WoG" below), an intentional community of Charismatic Roman Catholics in Ann Arbor, Michigan, founded in 1967. As Sneck explains, this group has evolved into the world headquarters of the Catholic Charismatic Renewal Movement. Sneck's study focuses on describing and understanding the "spiritual gifts" of prophecy, healing, and deliverance (exorcism). The first excerpt lists a series of propositions assembled by Sneck that in his judgment explain the main tenets of belief of Word of God members regarding spiritual gifts.[5]

(1)   God exists and is personal and active in His world, not remote and unconcerned.

(2)   Through Scriptural revelation especially, but also through the continuing revelation called prophecy, He calls a people to Himself to worship Him and serve each other.

(3)   God wants to initiate a personal relationship with this people and with each individual person.

(4)   Living in a community [in some degree, at least] is a necessary condition for this relationship; a community provides the locus of the relationship and of the reception and practice of various signs of God's favor, the spiritual gifts.

(5)   Praise is a most important human response to this relationship, and is often proclaimed "in tongues," ancient, extinct or foreign languages not studied or learned by the one offering praise [i.e., glossolalia, in which persons surrender themselves inwardly to the Holy Spirit to pray within them].

(6)   God speaks to the heart and mind of each person. Sometimes this "speech" takes the form of actual words heard interiorly. This interior prompting to utter prophecy, to heal (or not to heal!), to behave in some definable fashion is called the "Lord's leading," or a "sense from the Lord."

(7)   Through the exercise of the gift of "discernment," one learns by practice to distinguish between one's own thoughts and desires, the "Lord's leading," and

promptings of "the Evil One," or the devil/Satan/demons. (The demonic realm is just as real for charismatics as is the divine.)

(8)   The Lord's will is that men be whole and sound, physically and psychologically. Trust in Him has physiological and emotional correlates: healing the hurts of body and spirit should occur regularly and normally in a Christian community.

(9)   Often the "Lord's leading" takes the concrete form of a "Word of Wisdom," some concrete, practical and sound advice for a person or the community when a decision must be made.

(10)   A "Word of Knowledge" is another concretization of the "Lord's leading" wherein a counselor suddenly intuits a definite fact about his counselee's past life, often embarrassing and even forgotten by the latter, and employs his knowledge to further the process of inner healing.

(11)   "Expectant faith" is the best attitude for all to cultivate in anticipation of the Lord's dealing with His people to promote their personal growth, increase their numbers, and generally make the planet into a loving unity of brothers and sisters.

(12)   The history of cultures is best interpreted apocalyptically and eschatologically, that is, people, nations, and political systems not dedicated to the Lord are moving toward their own destruction, but the Second Coming of Jesus Christ will quite soon initiate a universal Kingdom of justice, love and peace.

Curiously, Sneck spends very little time discussing what to Charismatics is absolutely requisite to the receiving and implementation of spiritual gifts, namely, the experience of "Baptism in the Holy Spirit." According to Charismatics and Pentecostals, a person can become a Christian, receive the sacrament of Baptism, participate regularly in worship and the other sacraments—indeed, even experience being "born again" in surrendering devotionally to "the Lordship of Jesus Christ"—and still not have become connected with the supernatural power of the Spirit of God to live the Christian life as God fully intends. That connection they refer to as "Baptism in the Holy Spirit." In rare cases, they concede, it could take place without further steps. But normally for it to take place, a person must (a) seek it sincerely in prayer, (b) have others who have already received it lay hands upon her in prayer that she receive it, and (c) open herself to being "taken over" or "possessed" by the Holy Spirit (often but not always meaning entering a state of trance) and having its power released in her life to accomplish the work to which God calls her in the context of the Christian community. A typical way in which the "Baptism in the Spirit" is said to be manifest is glossolalia, or "speaking in tongues." But it is not the only way or necessarily the most favored way. There are other spiritual gifts, as the Apostle Paul writes in the First Letter to the Corinthians (12:4–11 [RSV]):

> Now there are varieties of gifts, but the same Spirit; and there are varieties of service, but the same Lord; and there are varieties of working, but it is the same God who inspires them all in everyone. To each is given the manifestation of the Spirit for the common good. To one is given through the Spirit the utterance of wisdom, and to another the utterance of knowledge according to the same Spirit, to another faith by the same Spirit, to another gifts of healing

by the one Spirit, to another the working of miracles, to another prophecy, to another the ability to distinguish between spirits, to another various kinds of tongues, to another the interpretation of tongues. All these are inspired by one and the same Spirit, who apportions to each one individually as he wills.

Sneck proceeds first to describe experiences of the gift of prophecy, which from the biblical list just given (in the understanding of members of the Word of God Community) includes not only "prophecy" per se but also "word of wisdom," "word of knowledge," "discernment" ("the ability to distinguish between spirits"), and "interpretation of tongues."[6] In portions of his study not reproduced here, Sneck discusses at length how members of the community go about discerning whether a putative prophecy is valid or genuine (i.e., "really from God") or not, and how the practice of the gift of prophecy has "matured" in the experience of the community.

The content of prophecies could be divided several ways: encouraging ("My People, I love you.") and exhortatory ("Repent. Change X in your life."); intended for the whole Community or for just a single individual; pragmatically concrete or poetically haunting. With eyes closed, the prophet speaks or sings in naturally flowing cadences, and in the first person as though in the name of the Deity. Often crucial phrases are repeated. Contrary to the popular understanding of the term, relatively few prophecies concern the future.

Abigail, self-described as cranky and crotchety, was told in prophecy, "The lion must be tamed slowly. I will diminish your snarl." She attributes her greater success in controlling her temper and her tongue to this and other similarly supportive prophecies.

Here is an example of a prophecy spoken to the entire community:

Remember the darkness that I have called you from and rejoice. Remember the bondage from which I have freed you, and rejoice. Remember how you were alone and spread far apart, and see how it is that I have brought you together and made you into a people, and rejoice. It is I who have brought you to birth, and it is I, myself, who have called each one of you by name. Yes, it is I, myself, who have promised to be your God and have made you into a people, and know that you have only begun to see what I would do among you.

Prophecies which do deal with the future often refer to coming political, economic and social cataclysms and warn the people to prepare especially through loyalty and obedience to their leaders. Prophecy has, to some extent, been brought under the control of the Community's leadership in that there is a "prophecy group" to which experienced prophets belong and who alone are entrusted with the task of prophecy at the large community gatherings—though all are encouraged to "yield to" the gift in smaller group settings, e.g., the households.

Sheila, a member of the prophecy group, provided the following definition of prophecy:

"Prophetic" for me is less, really less a prediction of the future—I haven't had any experience with that—as it is just really speaking the word of God's love, God's wisdom, God's plan for the body [of the community], for my life as an

individual, for our life as a family. It's operative in our family life. . . . I've been learning what it means to move more from a general sort of sense of what God wants to a more specific—speaking of God's love in general for us is always good; I think the Lord will always speak generally of His love for us. I guess by the word "prophetic" what I mean is getting a sense of how God sees things more clearly. The Lord wants to give us wisdom in different areas, whether a direction for the whole Community or a specific word of wisdom for somebody there at that meeting: God's Word, in a sharper way than just by reading Scripture, really penetrates through and speaks out.

In addition to defining prophecy, Sheila speaks concretely about her belief in and experience of the realities referred to . . . [as in the list given above] propositions one and three . . . : namely, that God's existence is not debated but a reality woven into daily family life; furthermore, that humans can and do enter into relationship with God; that God provides direction, encouragement, support, "wisdom," the various other gifts, etc. This experience of a relational awareness of and interaction with the Transcendent forms the fundamental basis of the religious experience of Community members. . . .

At the time of the study Sheila was a young mother of several children, a full-time homemaker. Yet she was very active in the Word of God community, an official member of the prophecy team. She initially joined the Catholic Renewal Movement in her college years and initially was quite skeptical about any and all of the gifts, but her experience led her to acceptance and eventual participation.[7]

Sheila . . . presents the case of a person who was given the gift of prophecy without having ever heard about it previously. At the time of the interview, she was a member both of the prophecy team and the official prophets, but seven years previously she had never heard of prophecy.

My first experience of prophecy happened soon after I first turned my life over to the Lord. I was praying after Mass in chapel. Besides personal hassles, I was worried over my mother's health. I felt very clearly something outside myself speaking very clearly about my mother's health. The Lord told me to stop thinking and kneel down and listen to Him. I was skeptical of people who claimed to hear the Lord. I remember thinking, "I must be thinking this up." My relationship with God was very distant then: I used to ask myself, "Is He real?" A friend came in then. It was like a large voice anyone could hear. It shook me up a lot. I got up and left—it frightened me. The friend asked, "Are you O.K.?" The priest asked me the same thing. Then I began to "prophesy," in the form, "God said this; I said that." Later that evening the priest felt I'd gotten the gift of prophecy. I was afraid of the gifts and didn't use it for two or three years till I came here.

After leaving college where this event had happened, Sheila had a similar experience as a young teacher. Again it was in a chapel but this time there was a physical "anointing," a feeling of God touching her on the shoulder, like a shock. Having arrived at Ann Arbor, she was encouraged by a coordinator [of the Community] to use the gift. She had had many doubts. She thought it was a "heavy thing," but now feels it is quite natural, and is as at ease with it as "in praying in tongues or reading Scripture." Use of the gift grew in conjunction with her spiritual life as she grew in her knowledge of the Lord's love for her and the body's [i.e., the Community's] love for her. She appreciates the encouragement she got especially in the 1972 meetings with the . . . [prophecy team, which made a serious practical study of the gift of prophecy]. "It was good to hear other people's apprehensions, doubts, victories."

At first, Sheila found it harder to control the physical reactions to feeling the urge to speak: these were not an anointing, but rapid heartbeat, foot-tapping and chest-heaving indicating fear about speaking. Her style of delivery evolved over time. She used to think there was only one right way to speak: solemnly. It was hard for her to understand that on some occasions God speaks in different ways. She had to learn how to "let the Lord use you so the Word comes across in the right way: by singing out softly and sweetly, or loudly and boldly." She was encouraged and found that various modes worked. When she felt very detached personally from the Word, she spoke calmly. When she was personally affected, it came across differently. She wants to make her prophecies shorter. Usually she has only a couple of words, occasionally just the sense. When younger in the gift, she would stumble a lot. Her fluency grew "partially through the response of the body, mostly from a sense from the Lord that 'That's right on to exactly what I wanted to say.'" Sometimes after speaking, she may have a sense that there is more to be proclaimed, and then others at the meeting will say it. During a prophecy, she feels the power of the Lord. Afterwards she might feel weak, or occasionally like wanting to dance. Sometimes she prophesies just to herself. "God's Word, when spoken precisely and simply, puts us in a wavelength of connection with the Lord." If it's a hard saying, she admits difficulty yielding to it as when having to pronounce repentance prophecies. More recently, she has felt a real connection between prophecy and the whole of her life: "I feel a direct sense from the Lord on how to proceed or *not* to proceed."

Sheila uses her gift in many contexts. The following brief vignette shows Sheila working with an individual.

> *Prophecy works really powerfully for individuals. I get a sense of how God really loves them. I still have trouble with authority figures and older people. At the women's retreat last Spring God spoke through me to a woman about her love, her holiness. She wept. The Lord said to me "You respect that woman just because she's lived that long and is precious to me."*

Interested in discovering just how the prophets' sense of "the Lord" differed from their own cognitive processes, I received the following simple reply from Sheila: "It feels better when the Lord does it. I feel more peace, clarity, precision, confidence. When I prophesy over somebody, there's a real confidence that now or twenty years from now there would be fruit."

Sneck next takes up the spiritual gift of healing.[8]

Members of WoG use this term for two different but related spiritual gifts:

(1) Healing of memories, by which is meant the removal of subjective pain surrounding memories of past events, plus the termination of reactive effects on others like bitterness to family members, inability to relate lovingly with one's parents, etc.

(2) Physical healings of all sorts of body ailments, major and minor. In discussing their healings, subjects often spoke about both types occurring together. . . .

Sneck explains that "at the time of the research, it was the consensus of those interviewed that WoG members were 'mature' in the gift of prophecy, but 'young,' that is, quite inexperienced, still needing more 'wisdom,' in the gift of healing."[9] Even so, numerous healings of both kinds are recounted, some from the perspective of the person healed and some from the standpoint of the person through whom the healing takes place. Some healings are immediate, some are gradual (sometimes involving repeated healing prayer), and some expected healings apparently do not take place. Sneck deals at length with how the Community deals with these experiences. They do not see themselves in competition with the medical community but work in conjunction with standard medical practice and consider healing resulting from medical practice as "from the Lord" as well.

The spiritual gift of healing is viewed by the Community as being given to the entire group, especially when gathered in prayer, and members do not regard the gift as limited only to a few. However, several have come to specialize, so to speak, by serving on healing teams, and the Community regards some as having a special gift—that is, a special effectiveness—for this work. Preparation for healing prayer will involve intensive prayer in expectant faith that some gift of healing be given by the Lord and that guidance be given to those in charge, occasional fasting (e.g., going from sundown to sundown with no food except liquids and juices), and seeking to eliminate from their lives anything that might be an obstacle to the healing power of God (e.g., an unrepented sin, lack of full confidence in God's interest in healing and power to heal, or not being fully surrendered to the Holy Spirit). They speak of the importance, though not inevitable requirement, of desire for healing and expectant faith for healing in the person who would be healed. Lois, a forty-year-old member of the community whose lifelong battle with cancer was won through prayer for physical healing, describes the usual procedure:[10]

. . . [After learning the condition for which the person seeks healing, t]he coordinators pray directly to the Lord. Then they rebuke the disability with or without a direct exorcism. Then they thank the Lord for what He's already doing. (In my case [i.e., Lois's case], the pain had already gone, of course. [Sometimes the persons receive assurance of healing, although they are still ill.]) Sometimes someone gets a relevant Scripture passage. There is praying in tongues or in silence, usually accompanied by laying of hands on the shoulders, hands, or head [and possibly upon the part of the body needing healing]. . . .

A twenty-two-year-old male university graduate, Hilary, who is one of the persons commissioned by the Community to pray with others for healing, describes a healing success:[11]

> *. . . I prayed with a brother who had a problem with tiredness. He would be sleepy all day, couldn't get into his work. I sensed an evil spirit bothering him. I had an understanding, insight, intuition that the cause was an evil spirit, a spirit of fatigue. I commanded it to leave. The brother shared about it at a gathering: it had happened for a long time. He wasn't bothered subsequent to prayer. The thing indeed was changed.*

Hilary's interaction with the spirit is dubbed "taking authority over" the evil spirit. Hilary, university educated, struggles to put into words his experiences with "spirits" while preserving his modern viewpoint and identity:

> *. . . We prayed twice with someone who had begun losing his sight. The first time I sensed something would really happen when we prayed. God was working in our prayer. We prayed a second time. It wasn't a case you could see something resulting immediately. My partner took authority over an evil spirit. I was thinking about it, but he did it. That was a factor. It's real vague, hard to sense what connection that might have with physical reality. I often sense that evil spirits are involved as a real factor. Sometimes I can name the spirit, often I can't. It might be a mean or angry spirit, a harassment weighing someone down. I internally get angry at it.*

In this case, the eye ailment was cured as mysteriously as it had come on. The physicians had prescribed mega-vitamins; the healers had used prayer and exorcism. The person got well and thanked both sets of professionals!

Geraldine, another member of the healing and prophecy teams, was a young wife who worked as a waitress and a nonresident head of a women's living situation.[12]

Although physical concomitants seem to occur regularly with prophecy, and the literature . . . indicates that healers too experience sensations, among the healers interviewed only Geraldine said she has felt such; in fact, Hilary has . . . mentioned *not* having these "charismatic signs and feelings." In Geraldine's own words:

> *. . . A month ago, a sister [i.e., a member of the community] came to be prayed with for her knee: she had had an accident. I didn't feel we even needed to pray: she seemed to have faith from her expression. I felt like the Lord was there and wanted to do something immediately. It was the only time I experienced something happen in my hands. They were hot as I put them on her leg. I was telling the Lord of His goodness. Then she stood up, started shaking her leg. Something was cracking. The pain was gone. She limped for a few days but the pain was gone. I don't feel that God doesn't heal because a person doesn't have enough faith, but the way a person looks at the Lord has a lot to do with when and how the Lord will heal.*

Elaine and Frank worked together on the healing team. At the time, they were university students. She was one of the official prophets of the community and he was also on the evangelism team that recruited members for the Community. Elaine describes their procedure.[13]

. . . *We meet after the Thursday gathering. We try to make them feel relaxed. From two to twelve people might come.* (There were usually more than twelve on the several occasions I [Sneck] had visited the healing prayer room. Perhaps Elaine means that she and Frank would see this many.) *There's a spirit of praise in the room. (After prayer together) we go around and ask what each wants healed. Sometimes we just ask the Lord for healing. Our approach is not to figure out a person's whole life and get everything worked out, but if we sense more is going on, for example anxiety, we suggest they talk to their head [i.e., their overseer] if they're in the Community. Sometimes we take authority over evil spirits. If they're not in the Community and we sense lots is going on, the best thing is to cast out evil spirits, ask the Lord what's best and give them words of encouragement.*

After praying with each awhile, we ask why they came and what they want praying over for, for example, eczema. Sometimes we feel, "that's it," and pray for it. Other times we ask more questions like "How long have you had it?" (When do you ask more questions?) *It's a combination of our own sense that we need to know more, and how much time we have.*

So much is out of our hands. There's no formula. The Lord gave us power to heal; He gave us instructions to lay hands on the sick. It's different for each person. We don't consciously seek the next step, but just trust the Holy Spirit to lead us. we ask them and they pray too. We ask how they experienced our prayer sometimes. Sometimes we have advice: "See your head."

If, say, there's a pain in their arm or they're not able to move it, we sometimes advise them to use it. We tell them to act in faith and do things never done with their arm before.

We end all together. The leader concludes with words about faith, about healing, etc.

Again in this narration, we hear about reliance upon the internal "sense from the Lord" about how best to proceed. There is also a balanced awareness that not all problems can be solved at once or even prayed for on a particular occasion. A distinction is made in the "prescription" given to Community and non-Community members. While Christians generally pray for the absent sick, the leader of the large prayer meeting always announces that only people with personal ailments should go to the healing room. Earlier in the Community's history, people could go for prayer by proxy, as it were, but this practice had been abandoned in favor of the presently described procedure.

Elaine's partner, Frank, adds his commentary. He, like Hilary, behaves forcefully and vigorously during healing prayer services though his soft-spoken conversational tone would not lead one to anticipate such intensity. He repeats a theme emphasized by Elaine: praise of God is an important element in a healing ritual. Notice too in his speech the frequent use of the words, "real" and "really." (Perhaps the attentive reader has caught on already to the somewhat idiosyncratically frequent usage of these words by WoG members.)

. . . I've been on the healing team since January. I missed about a month and a half because of a hundred and one special reasons. People have been coming with real serious kinds of illness to more minor things. When we pray with people in the healing prayer room, we experience really having a lot of faith and really believing that the Lord is really doing something to them and promised something or working some sort of healing. We encourage people not to get real worried and uptight and put pressure on themselves, but to look to the Lord. They should expect a healing from the Lord—maybe not this particular night, but maybe later on. Spiritually I felt real good about this.

. . . In this brief statement, he has already suggested a way to balance the need to help a healee relax while appealing for his faith-response. He puts the emphasis on the healer's expectancy while also working to draw it from the healee. Frank continues:

. . . I didn't see a lot of miraculous healings. I prayed over a guy who was bubbling over with praise of the Lord. I felt that at that time he really was healed. There was an improvement, greater freedom, lack of pain.

About a year and a half ago, Hilary prayed with a crippled brother whose foot straightened up and he could walk with a degree of freedom not experienced before. I prayed with him two or three times in the Fall and Winter. Each time he's made some improvement.

Both Frank and Elaine feel that healings should take place in an atmosphere characterized by praise as much as by expectancy. Yet Frank does not expect instantaneous healings in the way [some others do] . . . . We may wonder whether the delay in experience shapes the reduced expectation or vice-versa. Frank then spontaneously brought up the day of fasting [which the healing team had undertaken recently] . . . .

. . . Three weeks ago we fasted and had a day for the healing team, the first such. I felt the Lord encouraged us to take more authority. Since then there's been greater faith and more people are getting healed. I prayed over a brother with running ears. They stopped running while we were praying. While he was telling a friend later about the healing, he was feeling skeptical about the cure of the ear and it started to run again! He rebuked the Evil One, told him to stop, and it stopped running! From this he learned a spiritual lesson: we're to take authority over our own body in the name of the Lord.

By hearing many such vignettes as these repeated many times in public sharings and in private conversations, the WoG member's sense of the immanence of both divine and demonic activity is shored up, and finds echoes in the experience of each.

Deliverance prayer, or exorcism, has already been referred to in connection with healing prayer. If the Community's experience with the gift of healing is, in its members' own words, less "mature" than their experience with the gift of prophecy, their experience with the gift of deliverance is even less "mature." Sneck tells of some considerable disturbance, confusion, and uncertainty in the early months of their dealing with deliverance prayer—which, by the way, did not emerge until some time after the Community was founded. It was as if they were slowly learning by trial and error from the ground up how to utilize and how not to utilize the gift of deliverance, with little if any guidance from a living tradition of its practical use. Elaine describes dealing with a case of anxiety:[14]

> . . . I once knew a person was nervous. I knew anxiety would interfere with trust in the Lord. At other times there was no outward physical thing I could see. I wouldn't hear actual words that a person is anxious—it's more just a sense. I experience prophecy the same way, just a sense of what the situation really is. (Does the sense include what to do as well as the diagnosis?) From past experience, for example, with anxiety, I would pray for the person first. I would ask the Lord to relieve the anxiety. If I felt a spirit of anxiety, there's a different sense of what it is. (What's the difference between psychological anxiety and spirit-caused anxiety?) When I sense an evil spirit, I feel there's more seriousness, a darkness. It's not natural, not caused by circumstances in the world. It's an ugly spiritual force, against the Lord, evil. Sometimes I feel fear till I recall the Lord has the victory: then I feel anger. I come against it, banish it. I call on the name of the Lord. I pray that the person is in the Father's hand. In casting out the spirit, I address the spirit in the name of the Lord. (Afterwards, do you feel different?) There's an external difference in sensations, a physical calmness on them. They'll praise the Lord. I sense that the ugly, dark, evil thing is no longer present.

The final account is by Ursula, a single woman in her forties and the most practiced of those learned in inner healing.[15]

> . . . I met with X and Y weekly for a year. They did all the talking. I prayed at the beginning and at the end. Both were suicidal. I sensed a spirit of self-destruction. I felt the Lord wanted me to pray for deliverance. X broke down and cried a lot. He said he felt relieved. He hasn't talked about it with me since. Also Y: for a while he came everyday since he worked nights. He was so upset, so distressed, so disturbed. Before seeking him, I spent two hours in prayer. I had no training. We were members of the same household though. I didn't know what to do. I thought, "Take a long walk." We walked around campus. He was sent to another city. After ministering to him there, they said they couldn't minister to him any more. Then he came back here to live after trying yet another city. He came to me . . . where I live and said, "You're the most mature Christian around, an older person." I asked my head who said, "There's no one else." Y said, "I need the support of the Community."
>
> I remembered in prayer time the verse, "Christ stood before Pilate and didn't answer." He was very disturbed this one day. I didn't know if he would attack me. So I was quiet—though that's what the Lord wanted.

The Lord said, "There's a spirit in him trying to destroy him. It's named self-destruction."

He asked, "What's the matter with you?"

"I'm fighting a battle with the Lord."

"You better do what the Lord says."

"I don't want to."

"You better."

I addressed the Lord and then said, "In the name of Jesus I cast out the spirit of self-destruction."

After I prayed some time, he just changed, relaxed and was peaceful. As he was going out he was joyful. He said, "You really love me, don't you?" He couldn't believe it.

The Lord brought me to this situation. I thought, "I really ought to go and study counseling." But it's the Lord who's doing it for them. I see a great change in them. They're not strong and well yet. People were scared of Y; I never was. He was angry. Once he kicked a barrel and it went rolling down the street. I'm not called to pray for just anybody: a specific prayer for healing must come from God if He moves you. If a person asks, that's kind of a sign. With Jesus, people would ask, make the first approach.

Reprinted by permission of the author from William Sneck, *Charismatic Spiritual Gifts: A Phenomenological Analysis* (Washington, DC: University Press of America, 1981), pp. 130–131, 132–134, 158–161, 171–172, 184, 192–194, 198, 201, 202–205, 219, and 230–231.

●

Chapter Summary

The way of shamanic mediation as found in Buddhism is illustrated by an account of two women practitioners of Japanese Shugendō ("the way of mastering extraordinary religious power"), Mrs. Matsuyama and Mrs. Hiroshima Ryūun. Each carries on a professional practice of shamanic services for persons in need, including spiritual diagnosis of problems, healing, exorcism, necromancy, and so forth. Each experienced a dramatic course of events that led them to their role as shaman and both maintain regular ascetic practices to build up and maintain their shamanic powers (or, to say the same thing, to free themselves of obstructions for spiritual power to flow through them) for the meeting of human needs. The shamanic power they exercise is attributed in the one case to the active presence of *Fudō-Myōō* (an important supernatural deity in esoteric Buddhism, believed to be a manifestation of the cosmic Buddha) and in the other to *Magotarō Inari* (a supernatural deity of obscure theological connections). Both make use of shamanic rituals and recite magic formulas, notably including the Mahayana Buddhist Heart Sutra. Example accounts of their practice are given.

Shamanic mediation in Christianity is exhibited in an account of "spiritual gifts" in the Word of God Roman Catholic Charismatic community in Ann Arbor, Michigan. At the heart of the community's religious life is an experience its members identify as "Baptism in the Holy Spirit," by which they understand individuals to become supernaturally empowered by the Holy Spirit to live the Christian life, serve the needs of the Christian community, and cooperate with God in his redemptive activity in the world. Specific persons within the community (less as individuals than as members of the community) are believed to be especially gifted supernaturally with spiritual powers of prophecy, teaching, healing, exorcism, and so forth. Stories of the experience of these persons using their spiritual gifts are given. Certain ascetic practices such as fasting are apparently used to build up and maintain the ability freely to exercise these gifts. It is evident from the stories how understanding of spiritual gifts and proficiency in their practice in this specific community is evolving slowly, as there has apparently been no connection with an existing tradition from which to learn.

STUDY QUESTIONS ON
SIMILARITIES AND DIFFERENCES

Although differences between Buddhist Shugendō and Charismatic Christianity as described in these two accounts may seem apparent, significant similarities are present as well. Spend some time comparing the practices. Keep in mind the danger of generalizing from these specific instances of shamanic mediation to all forms of shamanic mediation in either tradition. Be mindful of how much may be involved implicitly in the actual practice of these specific forms that may be going unsaid in the two accounts just given. (For example, although trance is not discussed in the excerpt from Christianity, it occasionally is found in the material Sneck covers and it is pervasive in the experience of Pentecostal Christians. Also, in Blacker's account, Shugendō shamans frequently demonstrate their spirit power through engaging in superhuman feats such as firewalking. Although this is not found in Charismatic Christianity, in the older Pentecostal movement, from which it in part emerged, one can find some groups that practice handling poisonous snakes and drinking poisons to demonstrate the supernatural power of being "filled with the Holy Spirit." It is also worthwhile to note that Charismatic Christianity involves a fusion of the ways of shamanic mediation and devotion, with perhaps stronger emphasis placed on the latter than the former.) Answer the following questions.

1. First, note as many similarities as you can. Seek to identify not just superficial similarities, but deep structural similarities. (Consider, for example, the special "calling" to become a shaman or mediator of spiritual power; recognition of good and bad, lower and higher spiritual powers; kinds of shamanic services offered; offering such services out of compassion for others; resorting to ascetic spiritual disciplines to build up, or become a freer channel of, spiritual power; etc.).

2. Assuming that both of these movements exemplify the same generic way of being religious in two distinct religious traditions, what if anything do the similarities identified in answer to the first question indicate that is essential to that way of being religious (which the framework identifies as the way of shamanic mediation)?

   a. What, if anything, do these two accounts have in common regarding their respective means of approach to *ultimate reality*?

   b. What common existential problems is each concerned with and seeking to address—problems both in those persons who are being served by the shamanic practices and in those persons who are attracted to or called to the role of shaman?

   c. Is there anything that indicates the characteristic way each interprets its broader tradition's scripture and symbol system as distinct from other traditional ways of taking them? What sorts of features of *ultimate reality* does each specifically highlight? That is, what kind of "face" does each envision *ultimate reality* to have? (Note commonality here, despite the obvious differences.)

   d. What sorts of social structures (social organization, group activity, roles and responsibilities, etc.) are involved in each?

   e. What specific virtues in the practice of its religious life does each appear to commend, whether explicitly or implicitly, and what specific vices in that practice does each appear to condemn? (Be careful here to distinguish criticisms each may apparently offer of the religious practices of others from critical expectations set for its own members.) That is, what ideal(s) of practice does each uphold? And what sorts of things would fall short of those ideals?

3. Keeping in mind the similarities brought to light in answer to questions 1 and 2, try now to identify the dissimilarities between Shugendō and Charismatic Christianity. Avoid for the moment the questions having to do with what is better and what is worse, what is truly "of God" and what is not, and so forth, and attend simply to what is different about each.

4. To what extent is shamanic power concentrated in the individual shaman or spread out and shared with others? To what extent is that power regarded as a kind of "natural" supernatural force that is manipulable or acquirable through a given set of rigorous ascetic practices, or as having a mind of its own, which the shaman must discern and follow? How is the supernatural realm specifically conceived and what is the nature of the kinds of spiritual forces thought to be met with in that realm?

5. What is it like to experience the mediation of supernatural power in each? For example, how is the experience of exorcizing a demonic spirit similar and different in each? Also, compare the relationship between shaman and client in each.

6. What among the differences identified in questions 3, 4, and 5 seem specifically due to the differing *theological* convictions and symbol systems of Buddhism

(or specifically of Japanese Shugendō Buddhism) and Christianity (or specifically of Roman Catholic Charismatic Christianity)? (It may be that some differences may be specifically due to the strong presence of elements of the way of devotion in the latter and their virtually total absence in the former.)

FOR FURTHER READING

Recommended articles in the *Encyclopedia of Religion*, edited by Mircea Eliade (New York: Macmillan, 1987) include *Shamanism; Healing; Exorcism; Spirit Possession; Demons; Spells; Prophecy; Power; Miracles; Glossolalia; Visions; Shugendō, En no Gyōja; Mahāsiddhas; Pentecostal and Charismatic Christianity;* and *Cult of Saints.*

Carmen Blacker, *The Catalpa Bow: A Study of Shamanistic Practices in Japan* (London: Allen and Unwin, 1975). The entire book by Blacker, from which the excerpts above have been taken, is strongly recommended.

John Blofeld, *The Way of Power: A Practical Guide to the Tantric Mysticism of Tibet* (London: Allen and Unwin, 1970; reprint Boulder, CO: Prajna Press, 1982). An introduction to Tantric Buddhism with shamanic elements.

H. Byron Earhart, *A Religious Study of the Mount Haguro Sect of Shugendō: An Example of Japanese Mountain Religion* (Tokyo: Sophia University Press, 1970). The most thorough study available in English of the practices of a specific sect of Shugendo.

Ruth-Inge Heinze, *Trance and Healing in Southeast Asia Today* (Berkeley, CA: Independent Scholars of Asia, 1988). While not limited to Buddhism, this study of shamanism in Thailand, Malaysia, and Singapore presents several case studies of Buddhist shamans in Southeast Asia.

Melford E. Spiro, *Burmese Supernaturalism* (Englewood Cliffs, NJ: Prentice-Hall, 1967). Treats shamanic phenomena in a predominantly Theravada Buddhist context, but for the most part they are distinguished from Buddhism proper.

Rinbochay Khetsun Sangpo, *Tantric Practice in Nying-ma*, trans. Jeffrey Hopkins and Anne Klein (London: Rider, 1982). An in-depth exploration of one of the sects of Tibetan Buddhism that incorporates shamanic elements.

Stanley J. Tambiah, *Buddhism and the Spirit Cults in Northeast Thailand* (London: Cambridge University Press, 1970). Like Spiro, Tambiah treats shamanic phenomena in a predominantly Theravada Buddhist context.

Paul Wirtz, *Exorcism and Healing in Ceylon* (Leiden, Netherlands: E. J. Brill, 1954). Like Spiro and Tambiah, Wirtz treats shamanic phenomena in a predominantly Theravada Buddhist context.

Stevan L. Davies, *Jesus the Healer: Possession, Trance, and the Origins of Christianity* (New York: Continuum, 1995). An examination of Jesus as a spirit-possessed healer from the standpoint of contemporary anthropological studies of religious trance, possession, and healing practices.

Eleanor Dickinson and Barbara Benziger, *Revival!* (New York: Harper and Row, 1974). A somewhat impressionistic photographic introduction to small-town Southern Appalachian Pentecostal Christianity, accompanied primarily by lengthy quotation of participants. It includes coverage of the curious practices of snake handling and drinking of poison.

David E. Harrell, *All Things Are Possible: The Healing and Charismatic Revivals in Modern America* (Bloomington, IN: Indiana University Press, 1975). Excellent survey of post-World War II healing revivals and revivalists in America.

Francis MacNutt, *Healing* (Notre Dame, IN: Ave Maria Press, 1974). The most widely respected classic exposition of healing prayer—for physical healing, psychological healing, and exorcism—in the Charismatic movement.

Agnes Sanford, *The Healing Light*, rev. ed. (Plainfield, NJ: Logos International, 1972). One of the earliest important publications guiding the practice of healing prayer in the Charismatic movement, by an extraordinary Episcopalian laywoman who was something of a Christian shaman herself.

Gerhardus C. Oosthuizen, *The Healer Prophet in Afro-Christian Churches* (New York: E. J. Brill, 1992). An interesting introduction to the spontaneous rise of shamanic practices in independent South African Christian groups in response to the needs of the people and in competition with non-Christian shamanic practices.

William Joseph Sneck, *Charismatic Spiritual Gifts: A Phenomenological Analysis* (Washington, DC: University Press of America, 1981). The entire book by Sneck, from which the excerpts given above have been taken, is well worth studying. His first chapter contains a fine critical discussion of previous studies of charismatic prophecy, faith healing, and exorcism and of the Charismatic movement.

Vinson Synan, *The Holiness-Pentecostal Movement in the United States* (Grand Rapids, MI: Eerdmans, 1972). An excellent overview of the whole Pentecostal and Charismatic movements from their origins in the nineteenth-century Holiness movement.

Patricia Treece, *Nothing Short of a Miracle: The Healing Power of the Saints* (New York: Image Books/Doubleday, 1988). A longer historical view of the spiritual gift of healing in the Christian tradition, especially in the Roman Catholic tradition.

John Wimber with Kevin Springer, *Power Healing* (San Francisco, CA: Harper and Row, 1987). An informative introduction to the ministry of faith healing by the leader of one of the fastest growing denominations to emerge within the Charismatic Movement, the Vinyard Christian Fellowship. It is remarkable for its generous use of common sense and its readiness to learn from the hard-won lessons of his predecessors and avoid their mistakes.

NOTES

1. See, e.g., Patricia Treece, *Nothing Short of a Miracle: The Healing Power of the Saints* (New York: Image Books, 1988); and Patricia Treece, *The Sanctified Body* (New York: Doubleday, 1989).

2. Carmen Blacker, *The Catalpa Bow: A Study of Shamanistic Practices in Japan* (London: Allen and Unwin, 1975), pp. 171–179.

3. *Ibid.*, pp. 235–240 and 242–244.

4. A *yamabushi* ("one who lies in the mountains") is a member of the Shugendō order of mountain ascetics who look to En-no-Gyōja as their founder and patron saint, as it were. They wear a distinctive set of garments, striking in their color and symbolism.

5. William Joseph Sneck, *Charismatic Spiritual Gifts: A Phenomenological Analysis* (Washington, DC: University Press of America, 1981), pp. 130–131.

6. *Ibid.*, pp. 132–134. Sneck explains and illustrates these varying "prophetic-like" spiritual gifts on pp. 162–171.

7. *Ibid.*, pp. 158–161.

8. *Ibid.*, pp. 171–172.

9. *Ibid.*, p. 219.

10. *Ibid.*, p. 184.

11. *Ibid.*, pp. 198–199.

12. *Ibid.*, p. 201.

13. *Ibid.*, pp. 202–205.

14. *Ibid.*, pp. 230–231.

15. *Ibid.*, pp. 192–194.

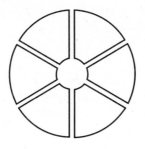

CHAPTER 14

THE WAY OF SACRED RITE IN BUDDHISM AND CHRISTIANITY

There are many types of rituals common to certain subtraditions of Buddhism and Christianity: veneration of images, symbols, and relics (involving bodily gestures, sometimes the use of incense); offering of food, material wealth, and so forth; penitential rites of confession; individual and corporate prayer; sung and/or chanted hymns of praise; reading and/or chanting of scripture; rites of blessing; annual cycle of holy days and holy seasons; pilgrimage; on rare occasions sacred drama; rites of initiation; rites of ordination; rites pertaining to death; and rites pertaining to the routines (daily and annual) of monastic life. Any and all of these are well worth comparative study and might well be chosen for illustration here.

Buddhists generally, but especially Theravada Buddhists, tend to play down the *sacramental* significance of their rituals and symbols—for example, denying that the Buddha is in any sense specially present in his images or relics, which are nonetheless elaborately venerated. Here, however, the principal concern is to deny what might be supposed to be the external efficacy of rituals to make progress toward enlightenment, as opposed to efforts that directly root out from within oneself the ego-centered causes of suffering. In this connection, trust in the power of rites and rituals is regarded as a fetter binding one to ego-centered striving in the round of *saṃsāra*, that is, as an obstacle to Enlightenment. In the way of sacred rite, however, sacramental rituals should not primarily be seen as means of accomplishing something external to the rites themselves or as leaving one's mundane ego unchallenged. Rather, their *sacramental* significance lies in affording direct participation in the archetypal aspects of *ultimate reality*[ᵖ]. Thus, an authentically Buddhist "sacramental ritual" would be a ritual expected to afford participation, in one respect or another, in the transcendence of *saṃsāra*—which necessarily would have to be (symbolically or sacramentally) a state of egolessness.

Some of the more interesting expressions of sacramental ritual in Buddhism are the ritual meditations of Vajrayana Buddhism. We do not to take them up here primarily because they are more directly fused with the way of mystical quest than any corresponding sacramental ritual within Christianity and because they are usually private rather than communal.

A different, very promising study, because so widespread in both Buddhism and Christianity, would be a comparison of initiation rituals—though even here the correspondence is not exact. These are, of course, not repeated rituals but are once-in-a-lifetime events for participants. The most widespread ritual of initiation in Christianity is Baptism. Depending on the subtradition, it is sometimes regarded as sacramental and sometimes not. Another important initiation ritual is Ordination to one of the priestly offices of the Church: deacon, priest, or bishop. Within the Roman Catholic tradition is the ritual of Profession, by which a person is initiated into a religious order in which vows are undertaken. A similar ritual initiation can be found in the Eastern Orthodox tradition and in the few instances of Protestant religious orders. For Buddhism, there is a rather elaborate ritual of initiation into monastic life. A layperson may become a Buddhist through undergoing a kind of scaled-down version of the same—the scale depending on the seriousness of the person's commitment—for example, from formally "taking refuge" in the Buddha, the Dharma, and the Sangha to undertaking intensified observance on the *uposatha* days of the Buddhist lunar month, undergoing ritual tonsure (shaving of the head), and temporarily assuming monastic life. In Theravada contexts, initiation into a probationary period of monastic life, *pravrajya* ("going forth"), and later full ordination, *upasampada* ("full attainment"), are significant events for the entire community, for laypersons and those already part of the monastic community, as well as for those undergoing the initiation. In sacramental Christian Baptism and and in Profession when entering a Christian religious order, there takes place a symbolic death and new birth, a symbolic identification with a major event in the central story of the Gospel, a bestowal of a new identity (often signified by means of a new name), and an adoption into a new family. Similarly in *pravrajya* and *upasampada* there takes place a symbolic death and new birth, a symbolic identification with a major event in the central story of Buddha, a bestowal of a new identity (with a new name), and an adoption into a new family. Differences come into play with respect to how the symbolic death and new birth are to be understood, the event in the central story with which the initiate identifies, the nature of the new identity, and the character of the new family or community into which the initiate enters.

Interesting and worthwhile as this comparison may be, we shall not attempt to explore it further here but instead, review examples of ritual communion: the

Buddhist Rinzai Zen Tea Ceremony of Japan and the Christian sacrament of Holy Communion as celebrated within the Eastern Orthodox Church. As in previous examples, here, too, much is implicit. Indeed, it is the essence of sacramental rituals that simple symbols signify whole constellations of meaning. Readers should beware taking them abstractly simply as presented here but should endeavor to imagine them placed fully within their respective traditional contexts of meaning and practice.

A BUDDHIST EXAMPLE:
RINZAI ZEN TEA CEREMONY

In the excerpt that immediately follows, a scholar of Japanese culture, Horst Hammitzsch, describes in detail one of his first experiences of ceremonial tea, *Cha-no-yu*.[1]

A marvelous autumn day, the sky high and clear, illuminating in their deep red the leaves of the dwarf maples. The yellow foliage of the gingko trees, which enclose the garden against a range of hills, still radiates back the warmth of the dying day. Leaving the house forecourt, which is enclosed by a whitewashed wall capped with blue-grey tiles, I follow a path laid with large, round, dark-hued pebbles. Then I step through a gate made of bamboo wickerwork into the garden. Here I come to a halt. Is this garden really a world made by human hands? It is an entrancing landscape such as one finds in the coastal valleys of the Japanese islands, a landscape that reflects all the characteristics of those valleys. The visitor fancies that he can detect in the distance the roar of the branches of ancient pines.

I follow the path, and it leads me to a simple hut with a shingle roof, nestling close against a grove of bamboo. Dark green moss spills from between its shingles. The place exudes an aura of secluded homeliness. I am the first guest to arrive at this *machiai*, or waiting lodge. Here I shall meet the other guests invited by my friend the Tea Master, in order to go on and experience the Tea Ceremony, *chanoyu*, together.

The waiting-lodge is open towards the garden. It contains a simple bamboo bench. On this lie a few cushions of woven straw, and next to it stands an incense-burner. I sit down and look out across the garden. Here and there are groups of stones with moss and dwarf bamboo growing luxuriantly between them. The star shaped blooms of clumps of wild asters twinkle white, lilac and dark red among the tree trunks. The crystal clear water of a tiny stream hurries gaily over coloured pebbles, a symbol of the impermanence of all earthly existence. The panicles of the pampas-grass bow to the gentle autumn wind. The foliage of the bushes has already been thinned by this year's fall, and behind it there is a glimpse of woodwork of artful simplicity, betraying the presence of a small bridge. A picture of quiet solitude, of secluded tranquillity—such is this garden.

Soon the other guests appear. They are four in all. An aged scholar of distinguished bearing, a well-known painter and his wife, and a merchant who has his fine taste to thank for his reputation as an art collector. We greet each other, bowing deeply from the waist. Few comments are exchanged. Merely the odd word of praise for the layout of the garden, for the beauty of the autumnal colours, for our host's exquisite taste. For the most part, however, we devote ourselves to the silent enjoyment of this hour of inner self-recollection, its solemnity deepened even further by the gentle rustling of the bamboo leaves in the breeze.

. . . [We guests are] left alone and without a guide to follow the narrow path that leads through the beauty of the garden to the silent, secluded waiting-lodge. And with every step into the depths of the garden, the everyday world, with its bustling haste, fades from the mind. One steps into a world that is free of everyday pressures, forgets the whys and ceases to enquire into the wherefores. The deeper the guest penetrates into the garden, this world of solemn tranquillity, the freer he becomes of everyday cares. The other guests, too, seem to have become changed people. The scholar, normally so reserved, is more communicative; the painter has lost his strong tendency to engage in aesthetic argument, the merchant his preoccupation with business deals. All of them have forgotten the everyday things that normally rule their lives from early morning until late at night. Casting them off, they have committed themselves unreservedly to this world of silence, of inner freedom.

After a short wait our host appears on the path that leads out of the grove of bamboos. With a serious solemn air he strides toward us. At a certain distance from us, he stops, bows low. That is his greeting. No word, no other gesture. Then he turns around and walks back along the path. Now he is ready to receive his guests—that is the meaning of this little ritual.

A moment of stillness follows. Then the *shōkyaku*, the principal guest, bows to the other guests and follows the host. In no particular order and at short intervals the others follow suit. I am the third guest to leave the waiting-lodge.

The path first leads for a short distance through the bamboo grove. Here the cicadas are shrilling their last song. Then the path slopes gently downhill. Clumps of sweet clover are displaying their pale pink blooms to right and left of the path. But this is no garden path in the European sense. The visitor is guided by a series of single stones, each set at a distance of a pace from its predecessor. *Tobiishi*, stepping-stones, they are called. Between the stones, rich green moss and thick shiba-grass luxuriate. Other paths cross our own. Occasional smaller stones, laid on the stepping-stones, show the walker which direction is closed to him. These small stones, called *tomeishi*, are inviolable barriers. Slowly I follow the windings of the path, hesitating here and there to admire the skillfully-contrived "natural" views of the garden landscape. There is no longer the slightest hint of their manmade nature. Via a bridge I cross the stream and then find myself standing before a large, flat stone. A basin has been hewn out of its surface, and fresh springwater trickles softly into it out of a bamboo pipe. A simple bamboo scoop lies beside the basin. A short distance away there rises a stone lantern, grey with age, its gently curving roof festooned with plaited hangings.

I take up the scoop, dip it into the water of the basin, fill it and take a sip of its contents to rinse out my mouth. The rest I let run over my hands. In this way I perform a symbolic purification. Now even the last dust clinging to me from that earthly world has been washed away. Clean and free, I can enter the world of tea and stillness.

Only a few more steps and there—I am brought to a sudden halt—what a symphony of art and nature, what an ensemble of perfect imperfection! There it is, the *chashitsu*, the tea-room. Expression of an indescribable taste; artistic and yet not artificial, consciously conceived and yet so pure in form and so natural in construction that it seems almost unbelievable to behold. Can the human creative spirit have produced such a work of nature? One might call the tea-room a mere hut, but for the fact that it displays this extraordinary refinement of taste. A deeply overhanging thatched roof, thick with moss. The guttering a length of split bamboo. The walls clad half in reed-wattles, half in daub. The entrance a low sliding-door covered with rice-paper of spotless white. In front of it, the stone threshold.

Bending low [after having removed my shoes], I slip into the tea room, walk slowly to the alcove—*tokonoma*—which lies diagonally opposite the door, sink to my knees before it and bow deeply to the floor. Then I contemplate the flower-arrangement that stands in the alcove. In a bamboo vase stands a branch bearing red berries against a background of autumnal foliage to which, like drops of dew, pearls of water are clinging. Next, after another slight bow, I stand up and take my place beside the guest who preceded me. The guests sit with their backs to the rice-papered sliding-doors that shut off the tea-room from the garden.

Not until the guests have all assembled does the host appear. Consequently I have time to examine the room. Four and a half *tatami*—mats of rice straw with a covering of rushes—cover the floor and at the same time establish the size of the tea-room as being some nine square metres in area. The flowers in the *tokonoma* provide the only decoration. In the centre of the room a piece of *tatami* has been left out. The space is occupied by the fire-pit with its dark wooden edging. Within it, a cone of fine ash has been brushed together to half conceal the glowing charcoal. A heavy iron kettle stands on a tripod over the fire, its colour bespeaking great antiquity. On a small stand I see an incense-burner and a small feather duster. Otherwise the room is without adornment. Unless, that is, one classes as adornment the exquisite graining of the woodwork that divides up the dark wall-surfaces, or the timber-clad ceiling.

As soon as we guests have begun to converse softly—a sign that we have concluded our contemplation of the tea-room—the host enters. He does so through a sliding-door that screens off the *mizuya*, the room which is used for preparing the Tea Ceremony. Kneeling down, he bows deeply to his guests. Then he disappears through the door again, returning at once with various utensils—a basket of charcoal, lifting-rings for raising the kettle from the fire, and so on. He also brings in a pan of fine ash. Then he settles down at the fire and heaps more ashes on top of the charcoal. He also sprinkles incense on the fire. During these manoeuvres we have all moved closer to the fire and have been watching attentively. Now, however, we resume our original places. The chief guest asks the Tea Master if he may examine the incense-holder more closely. The Tea Master duly brings the holder to where the guest is sitting and sets it thoughtfully down on his *fukusa*, a small piece of silken cloth. This cloth has an important role to play in supporting the tea utensils while they are being examined. The chief guest unfolds his own *fukusa*, a rich lilac in colour, and transfers the vessel onto his own cloth. Then he examines it thoroughly, and finally it is passed from guest to guest, until the last one hands it back gratefully to the host. The latter goes back into the *mizuya*, only to return and announce that the "simple meal" will now be served. One at a time he brings in five trays, one for each guest. The number of courses is less than the usual Japanese ceremonial meal, but for that reason the dishes are of choicer quality and most tastefully prepared. Even the cutlery displays exquisite taste. With a slight bow we receive the trays and take them with both hands from the host. The drink is hot *sake*, rice-wine. Finally, sweets are handed around. And so the tea meal, *kaiseki*, comes to an end. With a bow the host invites his guests to rest a lit-tle, and withdraws. Bowing once more before the *tokonoma*, we leave the tea-room in the same order as we entered it and make our way back to the waiting-lodge.

In the waiting-lodge a conversation strikes up, and the odd guest even lights up a cigarette or a little Japanese pipe. However, after a short interval, the sound of a gong reverberates from the tea-room—long, penetrating gong-beats, five in num-ber. Our conversation ceases on the first beat, and gives way to a reverent silence. One feels as though transported to a Zen temple in some secluded mountain-cleft. The atmosphere is solemn.

Once again the chief guest is the first to take the path back to the tea-room. We others follow in the same order as before. Between the stones and on the path it-self stand small bamboo lanterns, for dusk is now falling. At the water-basin each once again performs the purification ceremony and then re-enters the tea-room.

There, the flowers in the alcove have now given way to a hanging scroll. It bears a simple black-and-white drawing representing a broom made of bamboo shoots. On the fire in the fire-pit, the water in the kettle is gentle singing. On the *tatami* a *mizusashi* (a water jar) and the *cha'ire* (the tea caddy) are standing in their prescribed places. As soon as all the guests are present. the Tea Master ap-pears. He is carrying the tea-bowl with both hands. In the tea-bowl lies the *chasen*, the tea-whisk (a brush made of bamboo) and the *chakin*, a narrow, white linen cloth. Across the tea bowl lies the tea-scoop, *chashaku*. Going out again, he then brings back a water-vessel for used water, *koboshi*, the water dipper, *hishaku*, and the lid-stand, *futa'oki*, for the hot lid of the kettle. The tea-whisk, the white linen cloth and the water-dipper are new and sparkling clean. The rest of the tea uten-sils are clearly of great age and bear witness to a highly-developed artistic taste.

The Master sits down in the prescribed attitude, and the actual ceremony now begins. In a precisely predetermined series of gestures and movements, each indi-vidual part of the ceremony is performed in its correct sequence. The folding of the teacloth, the grasping of the water-dipper, the rinsing out of the tea-bowl with hot water, the movements of tea-whisking—all this is firmly established by tradi-tion and is carried out strictly according to the rules of the school in question.

While the host is attending to the initial preparations, the first guest takes one of the proferred sweet cakes and hands on the cake-stand to the next guest in the man-ner laid down. Then the host places the bowl of thick, green, whisked tea in front of the first guest. Mutual bows ensue, as well as a further bow on the part of the first guest to the one sitting next to him, as though to beg forgiveness for drinking before him. Only then does he take the tea-bowl, placing it on the palm of his left hand and supporting it with his right. He takes one sip, then a second and a third, each time gently swilling the bowl around. With a thin piece of white paper he then wipes clean the place on the rim from which he has drunk, and passes the bowl to the next guest, the prescribed bows once more being duly exchanged, And so on, in turn.

One praises the taste of the tea, its strength, its color, and generally speaks of such things as will fill the host with pleasure. All conversation in the tea-room takes place on a level far from everyday things. One speaks of painters, poets, Tea Masters and their achievements, of the tastes and opinions of various periods, of the exquisite tea utensils.

When the ceremony is at an end, the first guest asks if he may examine the utensils. And now there commences a detailed examination of the tea-bowl, the tea-caddy and the teaspoon. Questions and answers are exchanged between guests and host. We enquire about the origin and history of the tea utensils, the names of the craftsmen who made them, for every good piece has its own individual history. . . .

What impression did I take away with me from this first Tea Ceremony? . . . The effect of the Tea Ceremony was so strong as to engender a feeling of self-surrender, a feeling of oneness with all others, an extraordinary feeling of satisfaction with myself and with my surroundings. . . .

Hammitzsch begins to explain some of the meaning of the Tea Ceremony by reflecting on the lore that a person must assimilate to become a Tea Master.[2]

. . . There are innumerable rules to master before one can proceed to the performance of such a ceremony.[3] The rules are interlinked so closely, and in so organized a manner, that each always proceeds—must proceed—quite inevitably from the one before it. In fact the rules in their totality are so numerous, so comprehensive, that at first sight they seem to leave no room for the addition of any personal touch to either tea cult or Tea Ceremony. And yet such is not the case. . . .

The most basic principle underlying these rules is that everything must be in harmony with its surroundings; it must be simple, yet eschew the actual natural state itself; it must be honest—thus its true nature and construction must be recognizable and devoid of all pretense. And just as everything must be in harmony with its surroundings, so it must also stand in a harmonious relationship with the wider environment—with the seasons, for example. Winter imposes different constraints from summer on fireplace, temperature and similarly on the form of utensils. All these fine gradations and distinctions are extremely well-founded. Even the attitudes and movements of host and guests are subject to rules whose detailed rubric cannot be gone into here. The real question we shall be trying to answer is, where does the Tea Way lead? . . .

A Japanese will speak of *chadō*, of the Tea Way. There are many such Ways [*dō*] in Japan. There is a Way of Flowers, a Way of Painting, a Way of Poetry and numerous others. Each of the Japanese arts possesses its own Way. What inner significance, then, does the concept "Way" . . . hold? . . .

A Way comes from somewhere and leads to somewhere. Its goal is the grasping of eternal values, of Truth, *makoto*. In the process it acts as a strict guardian of tradition—which carries a valuation very different to that in Europe. Thus, in the Japanese view, it maintains an unbroken link between past, present and future. On this foundation is based the Master-pupil relationship that is so important for the development of the Japanese arts. It is seen as vital that the pupil should start by achieving a sure mastery of traditional ways.

In Japan, the learning of any one of the many arts is an almost wordless process. The Master supplies the model, the pupil copies it. This process is repeated again and again, month after month, year after year. For the Japanese learner this consti- tutes far less of a test of patience than it might seem to us. From childhood on, his method of upbringing has prepared him for it. The Master seeks nothing in the pupil, no gift, no genius. He simply trains the pupil fully to master the pure skills of the art in question. Once this mastery is attained, a day will eventually come when the pupil is able to represent perfectly what is there in his heart, precisely because the problem of formulation, of mere technical realization, no longer burdens him. Only when the heart has attained maturity does true spontaneity arise. Every art must, like every natural being, grow organically: it can never create by act of will.

. . . [T]he Tea Way . . . grants man a sense of liberation, a freedom that is si- multaneously a form of security. It translates him into a condition where earthly things are no longer of any significance. It is the strict rules and laws that have to be mastered by the celebrant, the firmly laid-down sequence governing the per- formance of individual actions, that provide the basis for this sense of freedom. This arises once the practitioner of the Tea Way has become free of them in his heart, in that he himself has *become* the law, and the law himself.

In connection with the ultimate grasping and experiencing of these basic teach- ings, we also have to bear in mind what the tea doctrine calls the secret transmis- sion, *hiden*, which was handed on by the Master of each school to his spiritual heir—that is to say, to the future transmitter of his teaching tradition. The true "se- cret doctrine" has nothing in common with the outer forms by means of which it is transmitted. These are merely teaching aids, in the Buddhist sense, to help the disciple experience the inner meaning that cannot be expressed in words. . . .

At the present time, we often find the purely aesthetic side of the Tea Way very much overdone. In the process the Way loses much of its authenticity. The core of *kei-wa-sei-jaku* [the central principles of the Way of Tea, to be briefly explained below[4]] is lost—that mutual willing-heartedness which resides in a total surren- der to the Whole, which exudes goodness and benevolence, and to which the aesthetic arrangements merely give external form. The essential point is not form, but the personality of the host and the goodwill that proceeds from his heart to- ward the guests. . . .

Implicit throughout the Tea Ceremony and its physical setting are princi- ples, values, and allusions that directly connect it with the Zen Buddhist tradition in which it remains rooted. The very architecture of the tea room analogically corresponds to the architecture of the Zen monastery, writes Okakura Kakuzo:[5]

The simplicity and purism of the tea-room resulted from emulation of the Zen monastery. A Zen monastery differs from those of other Buddhist sects inasmuch as it is meant only to be a dwelling place for the monks. Its chapel is not a place of worship or pilgrimage, but a college room where the students congregate for discussion and the practice of meditation. The room is bare except for a central alcove in which, behind the altar, is a statue of Bodhi Dharma, the founder of the sect or of Sakyamuni attended by Kashiapa and Ananda, the two earliest Zen patriarchs. On the altar, flowers and incense are offered up in memory of the great contributions which these sages made to Zen. We have already said that it was the ritual instituted by the Zen monks of successively drinking tea out of a bowl before the image of Bodhi Dharma, which laid the foundations of the tea-ceremony. We might add here that the altar of the Zen chapel was the prototype of the Tokonoma,—the place of honour in a Japanese room where paintings and flowers are placed for the edification of the guests.

All our great tea-masters were students of Zen and attempted to introduce the spirit of Zennism into the actualities of life. Thus the room, like the other equipment of the tea-ceremony, reflects many of the Zen doctrines. The size of the orthodox tea-room, which is four mats and a half, or ten feet square, is determined by a passage in the Sutra of Vikramadytia. In that interesting work, Vikramadytia welcomes the Saint Manjushiri and eighty-four thousand disciples of Buddha in a room of this size,—an allegory based on the theory of the non-existence of space to the truly enlightened. Again the roji, the garden path which leads from the machiai to the tea-room, signified the first stage of meditation,—the passage into self-illumination. . . .

Reprinted by permission of the publisher from Okakura Kakuzo, *The Book of Tea* (Rutland, VT: Charles E. Tuttle, 1956), pp. 58–60.

The religious significance of Tea Ceremony as embodying the essence of Zen Buddhism according to the Rinzai tradition is explored by Daisetz T. Suzuki:[6]

What is common to Zen and the art of tea is the constant attempt both make at simplification. The elimination of the unnecessary is achieved by Zen in its intuitive grasp of final reality; by the art of tea, in the way of living typified by serving tea in the tearoom. The art of tea is the aestheticism of primitive simplicity. Its ideal, to come closer to Nature, is realized by sheltering oneself under a thatched roof in a room which is hardly ten feet square but which must be artistically constructed and furnished. Zen also aims at stripping off all the artificial wrappings humanity has devised, supposedly for its own solemnization. Zen first of all combats the intellect [strictly speaking, the intellect as dominant, not the intellect as such]; for, in spite of its practical usefulness, the intellect goes against our effort to delve into the depths of being. . . . Zen—or, more broadly speaking, religion—is to cast off all one thinks he possesses, even life, and to get back to the ultimate state of being, the "Original Abode," one's own father or mother. This can be done by every one of us, for we are what we are because of it or him or her, and without it or him or her we are nothing. This is to be called the last stage of simplification, since things cannot be reduced to any simpler terms. The art of tea symbolizes simplification, first of all, by an inconspicuous, solitary, thatched hut erected, perhaps under an old pine tree, as if the hut were part of nature and not specially constructed by human hands. When form is thus once for all symbolized it allows itself to be artistically treated. It goes without saying that the principle of treatment is to be in perfect conformity with the original idea which prompted it, that is, the elimination of unnecessaries.

Tea was known in Japan even before the Kamakura era (1185–1338), but its first wider propagation is generally ascribed to Eisai (1141–1215), the Zen teacher, who brought tea seeds from China and had them cultivated in his friend's monastery grounds. It is said that his book on tea, together with some of the tea prepared from his plants, was presented to Minamoto Sanetomo (1192–1219), the Shōgun of the time, who happened to be ill. Eisai thus came to be known as the father of tea cultivation in Japan. He thought that tea had some medicinal qualities and was good for a variety of diseases. Apparently he did not teach how one conducts the tea ceremony, which he must have observed while at the Zen monasteries in China. The tea ceremony is a way of entertaining visitors to the monastery, or sometimes a way of entertaining its own occupants among themselves. The Zen monk who brought the ritual to Japan was Dai-ō the National Teacher (1236–1308), about half a century later than Eisai. After Dai-ō came several monks who became masters of the art, and finally Ikkyū (1394–1481), the noted abbot of Daitokuji, taught the technique to one of his disciples, Shukō (1422–1502), whose artistic genius developed it and succeeded in adapting it to Japanese taste. Shukō thus became the originator of the art of tea and taught it to Ashikaga Yoshimasa (1435–90), Shōgun of the time, who was a great patron of the arts. Later, Jō-ō (1504–55) and especially Rikyū further improved it and gave a finishing touch to what is now known as *cha-no-yu*, generally translated "tea ceremony" or "tea cult." The original tea ceremony as practiced at Zen monasteries is carried on independently of the art now in vogue among the general public. . . .

We can see now that the art of tea is most intimately connected with Zen not only in its practical development but principally in the observance of the spirit that runs through the ceremony itself. The spirit in terms of feeling consists of "harmony" (*wa*), "reverence" (*kei*), "purity" (*sei*), and "tranquillity" (*jaku*). These four elements are needed to bring the art to a successful end; they are all the essential constituents of a brotherly and orderly life, which is no other than the life of the Zen monastery. . . . While Zen teaching consists in grasping the spirit by transcending form, it unfailingly reminds us of the fact that the world in which we live is a world of particular forms and that the spirit expresses itself only by means of form. Zen is, therefore, at once antinomian and disciplinarian. . . .

Tranquillity, which is the last "principle" governing the art of tea, is the most pregnant one; where this is lacking, the art will lose its significance altogether. For each particular performance that goes to a successful conduct of the art is so contrived as to create the atmosphere of tranquillity all around. The massing of rocks, the trickling of water, the thatched hut, the old pine trees sheltering it, the moss-covered stone lantern, the sizzling of the kettle water, and the light softly filtering through the paper screens—all these are meant uniformly to create a meditative frame of mind. But in reality, the principle of tranquillity is something that emanates from one's inner consciousness as it is especially understood in the art of tea. This is where Zen Buddhism enters and turns the whole situation into an intimate relationship with the larger sphere of reality. The tearoom is a sense organ for the teaman to express himself. He makes everything in it vibrate with his subjectivity. The man and the room become one, and each speaks of the other. Those who walk into the room will at once realize it. Here is the art of tea. . . .

Tranquillity is *par excellence* Buddhistic. The character (*jaku* in Japanese, *chi* in Chinese) has a special connotation in Buddhism. Originally, and nowadays also, *jaku* means "to be quiet," or "to be lonely," but when it is used in the Buddhist and especially in the Zen sense, it acquires a deep spiritual significance. It points to a life transcending mere worldliness, or to a realm beyond birth and death, which men of penetrating spiritual insight alone are able to inhabit. The Buddhist stanza generally found affixed at the end of a Mahayana sutra reads:

> *All composite things are impermanent,*
> *They belong in the realm of birth and death;*
> *When birth and death is transcended,*
> *Absolute tranquillity is realized and blessed are we.*

Suzuki, Daisetz T., *Zen and Japanese Culture.* Copyright © 1959 by PUP. Reprinted by permission of Princeton University Press. Renewed 1987.

Horst Hammitzsch goes even further to explain the way in which the Tea Ceremony is itself not just an expression of Zen but a "way" (*dō*) of Zen, a practice of Zen that leads to Enlightenment. In doing so he translates from a revered classic on *Cha-no-yu, Zencharoku,* written by one of its great masters.[7]

The Tea Way . . . is a Way designed to bring man to the annihilation of the ego, to pave the way for the ultimate experience of enlightenment. And the well-known saying on the unity of Tea Way and Zen doctrine, *chazen-ichimi,* thus has every justification. We are informed specifically about this close association in a posthumous work by Sen Sōtan, which was handed down under the title *Chazen-dōitsumi,* but later appeared under another title. A pupil of the Tea Master Takuan of Edo had transcribed it, and in the year 1818 it appeared as *Zencharoku.*

The Zen Way as the heart of tea drinking

> The idea of making the Zen Way the heart of tea drinking originated with the Zen Master Ikkyu of the Purple Heather. For it so happened that Shukō of the Shōmyō temple in the southern capital of Nara became his spiritual pupil. He showed a special penchant for everything to do with tea and practised day after day. The Zen Master Ikkyū, observing this, came to the conclusion that the Tea Way accorded excellently with the essential points of the Buddha's teaching. Thus arose the Tea Way, which mirrors Zen ideas in the whisking of the tea, and causes us to reflect in our hearts on behalf of all living beings about the teaching of the Buddha. Thus there is no single aspect of the practice of the tea doctrine which deviates at all from the Way of Zen. . . .

> If, consequently, a person discovers within himself a serious inclination to Zen-tea, then given a willingness to practise, he has already fulfilled the main

prerequisite of our Way. Whisking tea is Zen practice in the truest sense, and a spiritual exercise leading to the clear understanding of our own deeper nature. When it comes to the essence of the doctrine, as Sākyamuni taught it for forty years, the heart is the sole valid means of bringing about the break-through of absolute enlightenment on behalf of all worlds and sentient beings. Apart from this there is no other possibility. Sākyamuni presented his teaching in various ways, using moralizing sermons, parables and speeches as his teaching aids. The tea doctrine likewise recognises as valid the use of teaching aids, in its case in the form of the procedure for preparing tea. It is this that now becomes the method of contemplation and the means of revealing the depths of the self. . . .

Anyone who scorns the spiritual exercise of Zen-tea, designed as it is to lead to the knowledge of the law of life, is like a blind man who destroys himself in despair, or like a person who beats himself with his own fists or belabours his own head. The followers of our school must fulfill this one, great, ethical duty with total reverence, as they practise that true tea drinking which has about it the taste of Zen.

The practice of the tea-doctrine

The essence of the Tea Way lies, not in selecting tea utensils according to their value, nor in discussing their form while the tea is being prepared, but only in entering the state of contemplation in which one spontaneously handles the utensils correctly, and in attaining the religious attitude of heart through which we may grasp the Buddha-nature within us. Now in this respect the religious practice of devoting oneself to the Tea Way as a means of seeking the basis of one's own being is without compare. Possessing a heart that is not shackled to outer things, and handling the tea utensils in this light, is the pur-pose of one's contemplation. Even if it is only a matter of the handling of the tea-scoop, let a person give his heart unreservedly to this tea-scoop and think of nothing else whatever; that is the correct way of going about it from begin-ning to end. Even when one lays the tea-scoop aside, let it be done with the same deep devotion of the heart as before. And not only does this apply to the tea-scoop—it is similarly valid for the handling of every utensil.

On the true meaning of the tea doctrine

The true meaning of the tea doctrine is equally the true meaning of Zen doctrine. Anyone who sets aside the true meaning of Zen doctrine will find no meaning in the tea doctrine. One who has no taste for Zen likewise has no taste for tea. On the other hand, the meaning of the tea doctrine as conceived of in profane circles is the mere cultivation of a kind of aestheticism. . . .

The quest of the Tea Way, then, is nothing less than the quest for . . . [an ulti-mate, that is to say, a religious] transformation—in the course of which one must allow nature to have its way, and which may not be consciously sought.

We follow these laws, and when we enter the tea-room we entrust ourselves to the spontaneous workings of nature, renounce our tiny knowledge and draw near to the absolute emptiness and silence: that is what we have to realize from beginning to end. Then, again, the distinguishing marks of Zen-tea are but few and there is no warrant for practising it as something secret or hidden. If, meanwhile, one is drawn to the various tea practices that have been mentioned, and wastes one's time hoping for Buddhahood, then one is not realizing the true Way—and when, in any case, would one then attain the mystery of transformation? But if one preserves the true form of Zen-tea and strives after it in religious devotion and practice, then one will enter automatically into the mystery of transformation.

A CHRISTIAN EXAMPLE:
ORTHODOX DIVINE LITURGY

In sacramental Christian traditions, the rite of Holy Communion is the central act of worship. It constitutes a center from which all other aspects of the Christian life are supposed to radiate and to which they are supposed to return. It is known by many names: the Divine Liturgy, the Mass, the Lord's Supper (a name less used in sacramental traditions), and the Eucharist (from the Greek *eucharistos*, meaning "thanksgiving," deriving from the Prayer of Thanksgiving which lies at its heart). The excerpt that immediately follows describes, in considerably simplified form, a typical celebration of the Divine Liturgy within the Eastern Orthodox Church:[8]

Nowhere does the power of liturgical worship to create a separate reality out of ordinary time and space, a reality in which the truths and deepest hopes of faith seem to become tangible, show itself more clearly than in the worship of the Eastern Orthodox church. The interior of the church building itself is truly like the household of God and a foretaste of heaven. It will probably be ornamented in the brightest of colors, gold to suggest the glory of eternity and red to hint at divine splendor. In the dome overhead may be painted Christ as Pantocrator, enthroned as ruler of the universe, surrounded by his saints and angels. To the front may be the infant King in the arms of his mother, a grave and wise woman who has become no less than a personification of divine wisdom.

All around the church are icons . . ., those characteristic Orthodox church objects of devotion which so well express its sense that heaven, eternity, is all around us all the time, imminently able to break through into the world of time. Icons are richly luminous paintings of Christ or a saint [or a biblical scene], done according to [the strict] . . . conventions [of Sacred Tradition] to represent the Holy One in his or her glorified, heavenly aspect, and opening the viewer into that transcendent reality. Orthodox people light candles and pray before the icons, and also kiss [them] . . . . Usually a church will have a prominent icon at the doorway [corresponding to the day or season of the liturgical calendar], for greeting upon entry, and others perhaps adorn the walls. The greatest assemblage, however, will be on the iconostasis, or icon screen, a splendid partition that separates the congregation from the altar. Like a visible face of heaven before earth, or a wall of glory shielding its deepest mysteries, the iconostasis is ablaze with saints in their holy magnificence. The iconostasis also contains [doors] . . . through which robed ministers process in and out during the service, like envoys from another world [the Kingdom of God, the World to Come], to read the Gospel or to present the Eucharistic elements of bread and wine. In the center is an opening [the Royal Doors], over which a curtain can be drawn at the most sacred moments, and through which the priest is visible standing at the altar. For, in the Eastern Christian tradition, that which is most holy is screened [but never opaquely and never closed off entirely], and allowed to abide in its transcendent mystery.

But if the church is a place of magnificence worthy of its divine proprietor, it is also a household, and there one who belongs can also feel at home. People of the Orthodox tradition treat their churches with a peculiar combination of reverent awe and informality that is not quite matched in Western Christianity. The devotion with which they kiss the icons and pray with the offering of the divine mysteries is unswerving, yet they also move about the church to light candles, or come and go during the long services with a freedom that suggests being at peace in the halls of an exalted but old and close friend. Evelyn Underhill says of the Orthodox liturgy: "The whole emphasis lies on the sacred wonder of that which is done; and the prevailing temper is that of a humble, contrite, and awe-struck delight. . . ."

The Sunday offering of the divine liturgy will begin in this characteristic atmosphere of reverential informality. Parishioners move quietly about the church, lighting candles and praying before various icons. At one side, a small choir sings a preparatory Matins service [—alternating with the fluid chanting of the priest and deacons, their hauntingly beautiful, non-instrumental singing of ancient hymns will suffuse most of the subsequent liturgy—] and the priest and his party of deacons and servers enter from the side almost inconspicuously. The first act is waving incense before all the icons [and the members of the congregation] which is itself an act of [venerating the image (= icon) of God in each] . . . . [Repeated censing at different points throughout the service completely fills the church with its fragrance.] After that, the priest proceeds to the altar to chant the opening words: "Blessed be the kingdom of the Father, and of the Son, and of the Holy Ghost, now, and for ever, and from all Ages to all Ages."[9] In the original Greek, "Ages" is "Aeons," and immediately this weekly offering is set in the midst of immense cosmic time where the eternity of the Trinity is manifest here and now.

And it is with the here and now that the next part of the service is concerned. The deacon begins with a long series of litany-like prayers, to which the choir responds "Lord, have mercy" at each, on behalf of such homely concerns as the city, the weather, those who travel, as well as divine protection of the faithful, and the commemoration of the saints. The role of the deacon is significant, as leader of the prayers and reader of the Gospel. While the priest represents the divine center of the mystery, the deacon is like an intermediary, catching up the petitions of the people and laying them at the altar, delivering to them the words of the promise of eternal life.

The petitions end in the ancient prayer called the *Trisagion*: "Holy God, Holy and Strong, Holy and Immortal . . ." repeated three times. (The number three echoes over and over again in the liturgy emphasizing the importance of the Trinitarian image.) Then a reader reads a lesson from one of the Epistles [i.e., one of the books of the New Testament other than the Gospels. And, after a solemn procession in which the lavishly ornamented book of the Gospels is carried out through the Royal Doors, the deacon intones a passage from the life of the Savior. The Gospels are much beloved by the Orthodox tradition, and have played a prominent role in Orthodox piety and mysticism, especially in Russia.

After the Gospel comes a spoken interpretation of the scriptural passages just read—that is, a sermon or homily expounding the meaning of the scripture and relating it to the lives of the people.

The Liturgy of the Eucharist proper begins at this point, the climax of the Liturgy, the celebration and sacramental presentation of the one great Eucharistic Feast. It begins with the deacon and priest joining with the people in prayer to God to cleanse and purify their souls and bodies from all defilement, that they might be made worthy of receiving the Holy Mysteries. Thereafter comes

. . . the celebrated Cherubic Hymn, usually sung to a particularly sweet and moving melody. It begins: "We who mystically represent the Cherubim, sing the Thrice-Holy hymn to the life-giving Trinity." As the liturgy advances and deepens, the assembled church has, as it were, passed into the heavenly places and shares in the adoration of the angels.

During this hymn the priest and deacon go to the preparation table, where lie the bread and wine that are to be consecrated. Preceded by acolytes carrying candles, the deacon carries the bread on a paten and the priest the chalice of wine, the paten and chalice covered with a small veil, out of the sanctuary by one of the side doors, process around the church, and then in the Great Entrance proceed through the Royal Doors to the altar, symbolizing both the entry of Jesus Christ into Jerusalem on Palm Sunday and his enthronement in the Heavenly Jerusalem, the Kingdom of God to come.

The offering is followed by more prayer and praises as this service like a river winds its way slowly and meanderingly; deep and contemplative, unchanging, drifting almost slower than the eye can detect, yet before its end it accumulates tremendous force. After the prayers, comes the symbolic kiss of peace [which expresses the reconciliation of each member with every other, saying, alternately, "Christ is in our midst! He is and will be!" Thereupon,] the deacon cries the words, "The doors! The doors!" Though no longer enforced, they recall the days in the early church . . . when from here on catechumens [(i.e., persons as yet unbaptised and under instruction), penitents (i.e., persons not in good standing), and unbelievers] were excluded [after first being dismissed] and the doors barred; what followed was the "[Liturgy] . . . of the Faithful" for fully initiated believers [in good standing] only.

The clergy and people next sum up their faith in a recital of the Nicene Creed, which expresses the principal tenets of the Christian faith. Then follows the *anaphora*, the elevation or lifting up, of the Gifts of bread and wine *and the clergy and people* into the very presence of the Holy Trinity—that there, by the working of the Holy Spirit, they may enter into of the Mysteries of Jesus Christ. It begins with

the exchange of verses beginning "Lift up your hearts"—the lines that mark the transition to the great Eucharistic prayer in the Orthodox, Roman Catholic, [Lutheran,] and Anglican liturgies alike. Then follows another feature common to all [four] . . . and to the ancient church, the short angelic hymn beginning, "Holy, Holy, Holy, Lord God of Hosts . . . " called the Sanctus.

The Eucharistic prayer in the Orthodox liturgy is typically long. It includes such basic features as the following: Christ's words of institution at the Last Supper are repeated . . . .

> [O]n the night in which He was given up, or rather gave Himself up for the life of the world, He took bread in his holy, most pure and blameless hands, and when He had given thanks and blessed and sanctified and broken it, He gave it to His holy disciples and apostles, saying: "Take! Eat! This is My body which is broken for you for the remission of sins." . . . And likewise, after supper, He took the cup saying: "Drink from it all of you! This is My blood of the New Testament, which is shed for you and for many, for the remission of sins!"[10]

[T]he Holy Spirit is invoked [to effect the sacramental change of bread and wine into the Body and Blood of Jesus Christ]; the Lord's Prayer is said; and the bread is broken, given out, and the priest and those of the faithful who desire and are prepared receive it in communion.

Communion in the Eastern Orthodox church is given on a spoon, on which both bread and wine are placed. Although there have been movements in the twentieth century to encourage more frequent communion, adults still frequently take communion only once or at most only a few times a year [out of a sense of its great holiness and their unworthiness]. To communicate [i.e., receive communion] properly, one must undergo a fairly serious preparation of prayer, confession, and fasting. . . . On the other hand, infants and small children are welcome to the sacrament and, being in a state of innocence and grace through their baptism and chrismation, need not submit themselves to arduous preparation. It is not uncommon to see a line of parents holding babies at communion time in the Orthodox liturgy, while they themselves do not partake.

After communion, thanksgivings are offered as the choir sings a short hymn whose words seem with particular power to sum up the meaning of the liturgy to the faithful as a mystery whose brightness opens into the supernal realities:

> We have seen the true Light.
> We have received the Heavenly Spirit.
> We have found the True Faith.
> Worshipping the Undivided Trinity,
> This is our salvation.

After the formal end of the service, an interesting custom is observed. The priest comes to the front of the congregation and a tray with a large pile of pieces of bread is placed or held beside him. The congregation files forward: each person greets the priest, kisses the cross he wears [or holds], and takes a piece of bread. This is not the bread of the Holy Communion as such; rather it reenacts the ancient church's *agape* or "love-feast" held after the Eucharist. But, in view of the infrequency of lay communions in the Orthodox church, it may to some extent [for them, if not officially,] take its place, and certainly the practice is in keeping with the intimate, homey atmosphere of informality, which is one important aspect of Eastern Orthodoxy.

Reprinted by permission of the publisher from James B. Wiggins and Robert S. Ellwood, *Christianity: A Cultural Perspective* (Englewood Cliffs, NJ: Prentice Hall, 1988, pp. 130–133.

The sacramental meaning of the Eucharist is explained rather well by a contemporary Anglican theologian, Kenneth Leech.[11]

. . . The Christian Eucharist or Mass depends upon the doctrine of Creation. It is because the created world is *sacramental* that we can have sacraments in the Christian Church. What does that mean? It means that God reveals himself and communicates himself through the created world, through matter. The divine glory is seen through the material creation. The seventeenth-century Anglican writer Thomas Traherne said:

> You never enjoy the world aright till the sea itself floweth in your veins, till you are clothed with the heavens and crowned with the stars, and perceive yourself to be the sole heir of the whole world, and more than so, because others are in it who are everyone sole heirs, as well as you.

. . . The specifically Christian sacraments are not freak interruptions of the natural order. All reality is sacramental. As the eastern Orthodox spiritual writers say, the world is a sacrament.

The poets and visionaries, Christian and non-Christian, have seen the world and natural things as sacramental. So Wordsworth spoke of flowers which suggested thoughts that lie too deep for tears; Tennyson spoke of the flower in the crannied wall as microcosm of God and man; Roden Noel of God's holy sacrament of Spring, and Kingsley of the wayside sacraments of our hedgerows. All sacraments, whether of nature or of grace, derive from the one great sacrament of Creation, for the universe is the form in which the beauty of God's mind manifests itself. The sacraments of sun, moon, sea and earth, bird and beast, are completed by the sacrament of man, the climax of the creative process, the image of God himself. The sacramental principle, the conveying of spirit through matter, runs through the entire universe. So Teilhard de Chardin, in his profoundly moving book *Hymn of the Universe* speaks of "the whole earth my altar."

It is within this created, sacramental, God-revealing world that the church is placed. The New Testament speaks of the church as the *pleroma* (fullness) of Christ. Christ is the great High Priest who, by offering his blood, has redeemed us, and the church shares in his priesthood. There in Christ is the perfect sacrament of God: he is the perfect Man who perfectly images God. So if Creation is the first fundamental sacrament, the second is the Incarnate Lord, and the third is the church, derived from Christ, the extension of the Incarnation, or, as Irenaeus calls the church, the Son of God. He writes:

> The church is the fountain of the living water that flows to us from the heart of Christ. Where the church is, there is the Spirit of God, and where the Spirit of God is, there is the church and all grace.

All our prayer takes place within the context of the church and of its *catholicity*. The word "catholic" tends nowadays to be used to mean "universal" as if it were a geographical or statistical notion. But it comes from the Greek *kath'holou* which denotes inner wholeness and fullness. The church is a symbol of the recreated world.

As the church is placed within the created universe, so the Eucharist, the Breaking of the Bread, the Mass, is placed within the church, and is the centre of its life and common prayer. The Christian Eucharist is the culminating point both of the action by which God sanctifies the world in Christ, and of the worship which the human family offers to God through Christ. From its earliest days the church has linked the Eucharist with creation. St Irenaeus speaks of it as "the first fruits of his own creation." Bread, "an element of creation," and wine, "which is of the same creation as ourselves," are offered "as the first fruits of his own gifts under the new covenant" (*Against Heresies*, 4.17).

. . . For the early Christians . . . this Eucharist was the focal point of all their life and prayer: and throughout the ages it has remained so. What do we do when we celebrate the Eucharist?

There are four actions, which follow from the actions of Jesus [at his last meal, the Last Supper, with his disciples]: he took, he blessed, he broke, and he gave. First, he took: the action which we now call the Offertory. Bread and wine are taken and offered, and with them we are offered. . . .

So at the Offertory of the Eucharist we offer bread and wine. In bread are contained the elements of earth, air, water, and fire, combined with the art and skill of the sower, reaper, and baker. The wine too is the fruit of the earth and of human work—the vine cut back in the winter so that it can burst forth into fruit, the symbol of sacrifice and joy, the wine of merriment. In offering these substances we offer not only the fruits of earth, for they are not wheat and grapes, but also the results of human work, and with them we offer our lives. As St Augustine said, "There are you on the paten, there are you in the chalice." . . .

Jesus took bread and wine, and so do we, offering with them the whole of human labour and human pleasure. We are offered—not just our "spiritual lives" but our total selves, our intellects, our sexuality, our physical defects, our psychological hang-ups, our spots, our warts, and our madness. What is not assumed cannot be healed. Blessed are you, Lord God of all creation. Through your goodness we have this person to offer, which the womb of woman has given, and human hands have influenced, shaped, and damaged. It will become the Body of Christ.

The second action of the Eucharist is the Great Thanksgiving, the Eucharistic Prayer, the "Canon of the Mass." Jesus blessed: and the central act of the Christian liturgy is the blessing invoked upon this bread and wine. The Eucharistic Prayer begins with an act of praise (the Preface) which reaches its climax in the hymn Holy, Holy, Holy, in which we join with the whole company of heaven. As St John Chrysostom says: "The angels surround the priest. The whole sanctuary and the space around the altar are filled with the heavenly powers to honour him who is present on the altar." And from the Sanctus we move to the prayer that the Holy Spirit may descend, the prayer which is known as the Epiclesis. . . .

It is the transforming power of the Holy Spirit which brings about the change, changing bread and wine into the Body and Blood of Christ, and changing human beings into his risen Body, sharers in his life.

By that power, Jesus Christ is said to be sacramentally present in such a way that Jesus' words, "This is My body . . . This is My blood . . . ," repeated in the Eucharistic Prayer, effectively actualize his claim to the offered bread and wine *and to the lives of those present* as extensions of his own life.

A recent Anglican-Roman Catholic document, the Agreed Statement on the Eucharist (1971), expressed it thus:

> In the eucharistic celebration we anticipate the joys of the age to come. By the transforming action of the Spirit of God, earthly bread and wine become the heavenly manna and the new wine, the eschatological banquet for the new man: elements of the first creation become pledges and first fruits of the new heaven and the new earth.

So bread and wine, and also human persons, are transformed, and in this action the Eucharist sums up and expresses the whole of Christian life and prayer. For in all life, the sanctifying power of the Spirit is fundamental. Unless the Spirit falls in flame, there is no life. All prayer, like all Eucharistic celebrations, is the work of the transforming Spirit. Our part is Offertory: God consecrates and transforms. So the Eucharistic Prayer is, in the words of the Roman Missal, a "prayer of thanksgiving and sanctification."

The Eucharistic Prayer is the centre of all Christian prayer, the centre of all liturgy, the centre of our common life together, and it is therefore extremely important that this Great Prayer, as it is sometimes called, should express as fully and completely as possible the beliefs and intentions of the church in this central act of its life. The Eucharist is the centre of the church's worship, and the Eucharistic Prayer is the centre of the Eucharist. In the Eucharist the sacrifice of Christ, his work of redemption, is made present and active. What is this sacrifice, and in what sense can we call the Eucharist a sacrifice?

The concept of sacrifice in modern day English is distorted somewhat from its original meaning. Commonly nowadays we think of sacrifice as involving a sorrowful forfeiture of something of value and of religious sacrifice in its highest form as involving a forfeiture of life—hence, a death. It becomes especially obvious that this is a rather distorted conception when we consider the generic phenomenon of sacrifice (from the Latin *sacra ficare*, "to make sacred") within the religions of the world. There it more typically is a symbolic, celebratory act of giving something which is of value and beauty—food, more often than not—to *the divine source of life*, appropriately (re-)acknowledging that source and its beneficence. It is a participation in a divine-human exchange in celebration of the relationship of human dependence upon divine beneficence.[12]

Returning now to the account given by Leech,

Sacrificial language has been applied to the Christian Eucharist from the second century onwards, for the sacrifice of Christ and the Eucharistic Memorial have always been seen as going together. They are not two separate sacrifices, nor is the latter a repetition of the former, as so many Protestant writers in the past have thought; they are the same sacrifice. The Eucharist is Christ, present and active now in the fullness of his redeeming work. And that fullness does not simply mean the Cross [i.e., Christ's death] but the whole work of God in Christ from his Incarnation through the Cross to his Resurrection, Ascension, and the pouring out of the Holy Spirit on the church. St John Chrysostom expressed it by saying: "we do not offer a different sacrifice like the high priest of old, but we ever offer the same. Or rather we offer the *anamnesis* [a recalling, a reliving that makes present] of the sacrifice."

The early Christian Fathers speak of the Eucharist as the new sacrifice of which the earlier sacrifices were simply types and shadows: the Eucharist however is the sacrifice of the last days. The sacrifice of Christ included not only his death but all that contributed to it, and culminates in his resurrection and ascension. The New Testament nowhere speaks of the "sacrifice of the cross" and does not equate sacrifice with death, for the essential priestly work of intercession continues in the heavens. "He holds his priesthood permanently because he continues for ever. Consequently he is able to save those who draw near to God through him, since he always lives to make intercession for them" (Heb. 7.24–5). . . .

The third action of the Eucharist is the breaking of the bread, the Fraction. . . . After blessing the bread, Jesus broke it. In the Didache or Teaching of the Twelve

Apostles, a document from the early church, this prayer is used over the broken bread:

> We give thanks to Thee, our Father, for the life and knowledge which thou didst make known to us through thy Son Jesus. To thee be the glory for ever and ever. As this broken bread was scattered upon the mountains, and being gathered together was made one, so may thy church be gathered together into thy Kingdom from the end of the earth.

So the breaking is associated with division and unifying, it is a sign of peace and fellowship. . . .

We can see the broken bread as a symbol of the Christian body, scattered throughout the world, and yet one. Yet there is another aspect of the breaking, for just as we are offered with the bread and wine at the offertory, so at the fraction, it is our lives which are to be broken and poured out in and for Christ. In all Christian life, there is the element of breaking. . . . Often the breaking point is seen as a breakdown, but breakdown can also be breakthrough. We break the bread in order to share it in unity: we are broken so that our lives can be shared with others in a deeper way.

And so we reach the climax of the Eucharist, the Communion, the sharing in the Body and Blood of Christ. Holy Communion is the climax not simply of the Eucharistic rite but of all Christian prayer. It is truly a communion in the Holy Spirit (2 Cor. 13.13). St Ephrem the Syrian said that Jesus

> called the loaf his living Body and filled it with himself and with the Spirit . . . Take it and eat it in faith, never doubting that it is my Body, and that whoever eats it in faith is eating fire and the Spirit. . . . Eat it, all of you, and eat the Spirit in it, for it is truly my Body.

The same writer wrote in one of his poems:

> In the Bread we eat the power that cannot be eaten;
> in the Wine we drink the Fire that cannot be drunk.

So in the Communion we become sharers in the Divine life, in the very communion of God. We receive the Body of Christ which we already are: so we eat what we are, and become what we are. And this communion with God is not simply a personal state of bliss, it is shared with the rest of the Body. It is truly and deeply mystical, the life hidden with Christ in God, and we are caught up into this hidden life as a family, as a common unity.

In the action of the Eucharist we can see the pattern of all spirituality: offering, blessing, breaking, and sharing. Our lives are offered to God within the redemptive offering of his Son. They are laid open to the sanctifying, consecrating power of the Spirit. They are broken and poured out in union with Christ for the life of the world. And they are, through Christ, brought into unity and communion in God with other lives which have been brought into Christ's Body. In this fourfold action we see the work of the Trinity, the creative, redemptive and sanctifying work of God in Christ through the Spirit. . . . The Eucharist is a sharing in, and continuation of, God's creation of the world. If Baptism is a microcosm of Christian life, so is the Eucharist. Together they symbolize and realize a life of cleansing and nourishing, both themes united in the Pauline symbol of the Body of Christ, the *soma Christou*. The Body which is plunged beneath the water is the Body which hung and suffered and rose, and it is the Body which we eat and are. So the Eucharistic action is the pattern of all Christian action: the offering of materials and human potential to be used only according to redeemed means and ends; the recognition that such offering and commitment to action involves brokenness of body and spirit; the movement towards a life and society which is marked not by competition and ego-centricity but by cooperation and self-transcendence.

CHAPTER SUMMARY

The example chosen to illustrate the way of sacred rite in Buddhism is *Cha-no-yu*, "Tea Ceremony," as found in the Rinzai Zen Buddhist tradition. Horst Hammitzsch narrates a vivid description of an actual Tea Ceremony, telling not only of the ceremonial actions but also of the specific artistry that has gone into creating the setting and mood of the ceremony via the traditional sacred arts of landscape and building architecture. Overt reference to Buddhist symbols and concepts is completely absent, yet the essence or spirit of Buddhism—especially Zen Buddhism—is pervasive in every aspect of the whole, as is brought out by the interpretive commentary following Hammitzsch's narrative. The timeless Buddhist themes of harmony, reverence, purity, and tranquillity are touchstones of the overall effect to be realized. So also, simplicity, stillness, silence, and empty space are essential features of the experience, sacramentally intimating the emptiness (*śūnyatā*)—the absence of "self-being"— that characterizes reality from an enlightened Mahayana perspective. At once rule-governed and beyond rules, artful and artless, evanescent and timeless, *Cha-no-yu* embodies the central paradox at the heart of Mahayana, that *nirvāṇa* is not other than *saṃsāra*. For one who is appropriately prepared, to participate in *Cha-no-yu* is sacramentally to be liberated from the defilements of *saṃsāra* and to enter, momentarily, into *nirvāṇa*—a *nirvāṇa* at one with *saṃsāra*. Moreover, the experience is not for oneself alone; it is essentially a shared, *communal* renewal of the sense of the enlightened, Buddha nature of each person and all other things. Nor is it for its own sake alone, for that renewed identity is then taken back into the everyday realm, and with it a renewed sensibility with which things may be perceived in what to Buddhism is their true nature.

The Christian example of the way of sacred rite given here is the Eastern Orthodox Divine Liturgy. First, a narrative of the ceremony is given, followed by an interpretive commentary on the Eucharist (another name of the Divine Liturgy) as understood in sacramental Christian traditions. Here too, mood and setting are essential complements to the elaborate ritual actions, presupposing such sacred arts as iconography and architecture. All elements conspire to convey a wondrous sense of whole-self participation in the Marriage Feast of Christ, the wedding of heaven and earth, creator and creation, eternity and time, God become a human being in Christ so that human beings might enter into the very life of God. The focal point of Eastern Orthodox Christian life, the Divine Liturgy, symbolizes the coincidence of two cosmic actions: that "by which God sanctifies the world in Christ" and "the worship that the human family offers to God through Christ." For one who is appropriately prepared, to participate in the Divine Liturgy is sacramentally to be caught up in the divine life of the Holy Trinity, for the moment to become one with Christ in the archetypal pattern of his one great sacrifice by which creator and creation are reconciled: offered, blessed, broken, and shared for the life of the world. Participants thereby renew their identity in common as members of the Body of Christ and refresh their sensibility for the everyday world as a world reconciled in Christ to God.

STUDY QUESTIONS ON SIMILARITIES AND DIFFERENCES

Similarities between the Zen Buddhist Tea Ceremony and the Eastern Orthodox Divine Liturgy are perhaps not as obvious as in the other examples, but they are there. Because they each have so much to do with what can be experienced in a sensory way, the sheer sensory differences may seem overwhelming. Spend some time comparing the accounts. Keep in mind the danger of generalizing from these specific forms of right action to all forms of right action in either tradition. Be mindful of how much may be involved implicitly in the actual practice of these specific forms that may be going unsaid in the two accounts just given. Answer the following questions.

1. Identify as many similarities as you can, looking beyond the surface to underlying similarities in function and purpose. (Consider, for example, how each involves the participant bodily with all of the senses; common or similar ritual gestures; the role of religious art and architecture; the significance of aesthetic beauty; the sense of mystery and the evocation of wonder; how each is a sacred communal meal; the extent to which each forges a sense of unity or bonding among participants; the extent to which each involves a divine-human exchange of gifts; etc.)

2. Assuming that both of these movements exemplify the same generic way of being religious in two distinct religious traditions, what if anything do the similarities identified in answer to the first question indicate that is essential to that way of being religious (which the framework identifies as sacred rite)?

    a. What, if anything, do these two movements have in common regarding their respective means of approach to *ultimate reality*?

    b. What characteristic existential problems is each concerned with and seeking to address?

    c. Is there anything that indicates the characteristic way each interprets its broader tradition's scripture and symbol system as distinct from other traditional ways of taking them? What sorts of features of the larger tradition's conception of *ultimate reality* does each specifically highlight? Is there a different kind of "face" that each envisions that *ultimate reality* to have relative to the "faces" envisioned in the examples of the other ways of being religious?

    d. What sorts of social structures (social organization, group activity, roles and responsibilities, etc.) does each have or recommend?

    e. What specific virtues in the practice of its religious life does each appear to commend, whether explicitly or implicitly, and what specific vices in that practice does each appear to condemn? (Be careful here to distinguish criticisms each may apparently offer of the religious practices of others from critical expectations set for its own members.) That is, what ideal(s) of practice does each uphold? And what sorts of things would fall short of those ideals?

3. What differences can you find beyond the many profound similarities? (Consider, for example, the explicit references to *theological realities* in the one and the virtual absence of explicit references in the other; the strong presence of nature and natural forms in the one and their minimal presence in the other; the different roles of silence and speaking in each; the relative intimacy of the one as compared with the large group involvement of the other; the different value placed on intuitive spontaneity and simplicity; the openness in principle to anyone's participation in the one and the exclusion to full participation of all but official members in the other; how the one traces its origin all the way back to the religion's founder while the other's origin is obscure and of more recent vintage; the way encouragement is given to expression of the individual creativity much more so in the one than the other; etc.)

4. What among the differences identified in question 3 seem specifically due to differences in the central sacred stories and *theological* convictions of Buddhism (or specifically Zen Buddhism) and Christianity (or specifically Eastern Orthodox Christianity)?

FOR FURTHER READING

Recommended articles in the *Encyclopedia of Religion*, edited by Mircea Eliade (New York: Macmillan, 1987) include *Worship and Cultic Life (Buddhist Cultic Life, Christian Worship)*; *Rites of Passage*; *Ritual*; *Priesthood*; *Ordination*; *Domestic Observances*; *Pilgrimage*

(*Buddhist Pilgrimage, Roman Catholic Pilgrimage, Eastern Christian Pilgrimage*); *The Sacred and the Profane*; *Architecture*; *Temple*; *Basilica*, *Cathedral*, *Church*; *Iconography* (*Buddhist Iconography*; *Christian Iconography*); *Images*; *Icons*; *Stupa Worship*; *Pūjā*; *Sacrifice*; *Liturgy*; *Sacrament*; *Eucharist*; *Baptism*; and *Christian Liturgical Year*.

Masaharu Anesaki, *Buddhist Art in Its Relation to Buddhist Ideals: With Special Reference to Buddhism in Japan* (Boston: Houghton Mifflin, 1915). Perhaps the best treatment of Buddhist aesthetics and Buddhist art generally.

Paul Varley and Kumakura Isao, eds., *Tea in Japan: Essays on the History of Chanoyu* (Honolulu, HI: University of Hawaii Press, 1989). A first-rate collection of essays on the history of different aspects of Tea Ceremony in Japan.

Horst Hammitzsch, *Zen in the Art of the Tea Ceremony* (New York: St. Martin's Press, 1980). Hammitzch's entire book is well worth reading.

Okakura Kakuzo, *The Book of Tea* (New York: Dodd, Mead, 1906; reprinted Rutland, VT: Charles E. Tuttle, 1956). By all accounts the best introduction in English to *Cha-no-yu*.

Jiyu Kennett, *Selling Water by the River: A Manual of [Soto] Zen Training* (New York: Vintage Books/Random House, 1972) [later published as *Zen is Eternal Life* (Emeryville, CA: Dharma Publications, 1976)]. Though focused on Soto Zen, this is a fine overview of the ritual structure of Zen monastic life.

Richard B. Pilgrim, *Buddhism and the Arts of Japan* (Chambersburg, PA: Anima Books, 1981). A fine overview of Buddhism's relationship to the traditional arts of Japan.

Daisetz T. Suzuki, *Zen and Japanese Culture*, Bollingen Series. 64 (Princeton University Press, 1959). A masterful survey of the influence of Zen upon Japanese culture, including three chapters on the tea ceremony.

Holmes Welch, *The Practice of Chinese Buddhism* (New York: Atheneum, 1968). Perhaps the best source of mainland Chinese Ch'an monastic life and its rituals before the Communist revolution.

Louis Bouyer, *Liturgy and Architecture* (Notre Dame, IN: University of Notre Dame Press, 1967). A useful resource for reflecting on the Christian counterpart of the integration of architecture and ritual in the tea ceremony.

Louis Bouyer, *Rite and Man: Natural Sacredness and Christian Liturgy* (Liturgical Studies VII; Notre Dame, IN: University of Notre Dame Press, 1963). Still a fine introduction to sacramental Christianity.

Nicholas Cabasilas, *The Life in Christ*, trans. Carmino J. de Catanzaro (Crestwood, NY: St. Vladimir's Seminary Press, 1974). A well-loved, classic commentary on the meaning of the Divine Liturgy in Orthodox Christianity.

Lucien Deiss, *The Mass*, trans. Lucien Deiss and Michael S. Driscoll (Collegeville, MN: The Liturgical Press, 1989). One of the better contemporary commentaries on the Roman Catholic Mass.

Kenneth Leech, *True Prayer: An Invitation to Christian Spirituality* (San Francisco, CA: Harper and Row, 1980), Ch. 4: "Prayer and Communion." The whole of Leech's account is well worth careful study.

Alexander Schmemann, *Introduction to Liturgical Theology* (Crestwood, NY: St. Vladimir's Seminary Press, 1966). One of the best overall introductions to Eastern Orthodox liturgical theology.

Max Thurian, *The Mystery of the Eucharist* (Grand Rapids, MI: Eerdmans, 1981). A good overview of different Christian conceptions of the meaning of the Eucharist, by a writer with a deep sacramental sensibility.

Archimandrite Vasilios, *Hymn of Entry*, trans. Elizabeth Briere (Crestwood, NY: St. Vladimir's Seminary Press, 1984). A wonderful introduction to the sacramental sensibility of Orthodox Christianity.

Mary Anthony Wagner, *The Sacred World of the Christian, Sensed in Faith* (Collegeville, MN: The Liturgical Press, 1993). A beautifully written overview of sacramental Christian life from a Roman Catholic perspective.

Benjamin D. Williams and Harold B. Anstall, *Orthodox Worship: A Living Continuity with the Synagogue, the Temple and the Early Church* (Minneapolis, MN: Light and Life, 1990). A good overview and explanation of the Divine Liturgy.

NOTES

1. Horst Hammitzsch, *Zen in the Art of the Tea Ceremony*, trans. Peter Lemesurier (New York: Arkana/Penguin, 1979), pp. 11–19.

2. *Ibid.*, pp 20–22, and 99–100.

3. Nancy Wilson Ross, in her edited collection, *The World of Zen: An East-West Anthology* (New York: Random House, 1960), p. 132, writes: "No less than one hundred rules for *cha-no-yu* were laid down in the sixteenth century. Many of these are concerned with the proper use of flowers, with how to scoop out tea, handle the hot water ladle, the charcoal, the caddies, the tea bowls—all to be done so as to create, with true Zen paradoxicality, a sense of artless naturalness. It is in the first few of these intricate rules, however, that we most clearly glimpse the Zen-inspired philosophy underlying the ritual.

"'If any one wishes to enter the Way of Tea he must be his own teacher. It is only by careful observation that one learns.

'He is a fool who gives his opinion without suitable experience.

'No pains must be spared in helping anyone anxious to learn.

'One who is ashamed to show ignorance will never be any good.

'To become expert one needs first love, second dexterity, and then perseverance.'"

4. For a fuller explanation, see Hammitzsch, *Zen in the Art of the Tea Ceremony, op. cit.,* pp. 66–75.

5. Okakura Kakuzo, "The Tea Room," in his *The Book of Tea* (Rutland, VT: Charles E. Tuttle, 1956), pp. 58–60.

6. Daisetz T. Suzuki, *Zen and Japanese Culture*, Bollingen Series 64 (Princeton, NJ: Princeton University Press, 1970), pp. 271–274, 305–306, and 308.

7. Hammitzsch, *Zen in the Art of the Tea Ceremony, op. cit.*, pp. 63–66 and 75–76.

8. James B. Wiggins and Robert S. Ellwood, *Christianity: A Cultural Perspective* (Englewood Cliffs, NJ: Prentice-Hall, 1988), pp. 130–133.

9. Here and in what follows Wiggins and Ellwood quote from *The Divine Liturgy of St. John Chrysostom* (London: Williams and Norgote, 1914).

10. Benjamin D. Williams and Harold B. Anstall, *Orthodox Worship: A Living Continuity with the Synagogue, the Temple and the Early Chruch* (Minneapolis, MN: Light and Life, 1990), p. 170.

11. Kenneth Leech, *True Prayer: An Invitation to Christian Spirituality* (San Francisco, CA: Harper and Row, 1980), pp. 94–96 and 102–110.

12. It should be said here that the generic concept of sacrifice is no doubt originally connected with the way of sacred rite. Its occurance within other ways of being religious in many religious traditions appears to maintain metaphoric allusion to that connection. Nevertheless, the concept itself appears to function within other ways of being religious, but amounting in practice to something characteristically different. Thus, for example, in the way of shamanic mediation, while ritual offering may be involved, the shaman or would-be shaman may offer herself in sacrifice to the source of supernatural spirit power to serve as a witness to its beneficent power and as a channel for the expression of that

power in the world. So also, the follower of the way of devotion might sacrifically conse-
crate himself wholly to the praise of "God." Or the follower of the way of right action
might sacrifically give herself wholly to being a prophetic witness against the corruption
of the present social order.

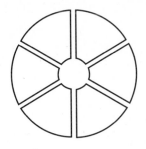

CHAPTER 15

CONCLUDING REFLECTIONS: COMPARING BUDDHISM AND CHRISTIANITY BY MEANS OF THE FRAMEWORK

The last eight chapters have applied the framework of ways of being religious in a comparative study of those ways in two major religious traditions, Buddhism and Christianity. One objective has been to further understanding of the relationships between the two religions, but the primary objectives have been to illustrate the power and promise of the framework in such an application and to show how the framework is meant to be applied. This final chapter offers several concluding reflections on the results of the application.

First, the correlation of examples from each of the two traditions in Chapters 9 through 14 is not meant to represent the only sort of correlation that might be carried out through use of the framework. As pointed out before, individual religious phenomena and specific subtraditions sometimes combine or fuse more than one way of being religious. Instances of fusions of the same two or more ways of being religious could fruitfully be compared. For example, the peculiar fusion of a kind of sacramental aesthetic simplicity found in some of the Zen-inspired traditional arts of Japan could fruitfully be juxtaposed with the spirit of Shaker craftsmanship or the sort of manual craftsmanship one finds in the Cistercian monastic tradition. A different fusion found in the Zen-inspired martial arts (which were also influenced by Taoism and Confucianism) could fruitfully be compared with the arts of chivalry and warfare found among medieval Christian religious-military subtraditions (and the ambivalence of members of other, more mainstream subtraditions of Buddhism and Christianity toward them).[1] Still another would be a correlation, say, of the combination of this-worldly asceticism, activist proselytizing, and identification of worldly prosperity with what is taken to be conformity to *ultimate reality* found in Japanese Sokka Gakkai Buddhism and a similar combination found in the Mormon tradition and in certain forms of American Evangelical Protestantism (and, here too, the ambivalence of members of other, more mainstream subtraditions of Buddhism and Christianity toward these practices). Reference to the ambivalence of other subtraditions to those last mentioned suggest possibilities of correlating, say, criticisms made of Buddhist variations on the ways of, say, mystical quest and right action by followers of the way of devotion in Buddhism (e.g., Jodo-shin-shu) with criticisms made of Christian variations on these same ways by followers of a way of devotion in Christianity (e.g., Evangelical Protestantism). The possibilities are almost limitless. The main point is to juxtapose instances of the same generic way or ways of carrying on religious life. Comparisons should not be limited to supposedly pure instances of any given way. It is worth recalling that some of the excerpts above are not of pure instances.

Second, application of the framework has brought out not only how diverse and complex both Buddhism and Christianity are, but also how they are diverse and complex in quite similar ways. Consequently, much of the initially overwhelming complexity (though likely not all of that complexity), apparent to an outsider, may begin to seem much more familiar and less overwhelming once one gets past its initial strangeness to glimpse the generic patterns. Thus, so far as one comes to understand that it is the way of right action that is primarily being pursued in the Catholic Worker Movement, one will not experience the frustration of trying to interpret it as addressing the concerns of the way of mystical quest or the way of reasoned inquiry. Similarly, so far as one understands that the way of shamanic mediation is primarily being pursued in Shugendō, one will not try to make sense of it as addressing concerns of the way of devotion or the way of sacred rite. Taken as whole traditions, all of the generic religious functions associated with the different ways (such as meeting the specific existential needs identified in Chapter 2) are served in Buddhism and Christianity, though not by all their subtraditions. (Of course, any given expression may serve still other functions.) The framework helps to identify and specify these functions and facilitates a kind of commonsense assessment (of the sort proposed in Chapter 5) of how well these functions are being served in given instances. Although Chapters 7 through 14 did not attempt to identify specific instances of degenerate and corrupt expressions of any given way in each religious tradition, it is not hard to imagine how there may be (or recognize that there are in fact) such expressions—indeed, of the specific practices cited in those chapters. Although the book cites and quotes examples from among the best expressions of these traditions, readers who know these traditions firsthand should have no trouble identifying less than ideal expressions of each.

Third, the juxtaposition of the sometimes strikingly similar examples in the last six chapters makes credible the possibility that there are valuable lessons to be learned from the collective experience of followers of a given way (or ways) in one tradition by followers of the same way (or ways) in a completely different religious tradition. The point is that Buddhist religious life is not simply a product of the unique, distinguishing traits of Buddhism, or Christian religious life simply the product of the unique, distinguishing traits of Christianity. It is in every case also partly a product of Buddhists and Christians wrestling with generic features of one or another way of being religious. And what a group of Buddhists in practical experience with a given way over time comes to learn works well or does not work well is often a very similar, if not identical, lesson a group of Christians had to learn in pursuing the same generic way, and vice versa. Such lessons could very well be shared between religions and solutions adapted from one tradition to the other without compromising what is essential to either tradition (such as a specific posture for women in meditation, a devotional attitude of gratitude for meeting the frustrations of everyday life, or a rational strategy for introducing by means of paradox a truth that must be grasped in an intuitive way). In this way the framework of ways of being religious facilitates a mutually enriching dialogue between religions.

Fourth, seeing praiseworthy examples of the several different ways of being religious from Buddhism and Christianity alongside each other—for example, the Sarvodaya and Catholic Worker movements, the Shugendō practitioners and the Word of God Charismatic community, Zen Tea Ceremony and the Eastern Orthodox Divine Liturgy—clearly illustrates how, in certain respects at least, all six of the ways belong to each religious tradition taken as a whole. Each way has an integral role to play in each tradition—or so it appears from a comparative frame of reference. The other ways do not suffice to serve the functions of that one way within the whole tradition. If one way is not present, functions specific to that way will not be served, or at least not effectively served. This is not to say that each way should be given equal voice or even that each way is somehow equivalent to other ways in significance and value to the whole of a religion. That would be a *theological* judgment that would appropriately be reached, if at all, only by knowledgeable insiders. My point is that each way has some claim, however limited a claim, to some place in the whole tradition—if only on the basis of the fact that praiseworthy instances of each way (praiseworthy on the basis of commonsense considerations) have historically emerged in each of Buddhism and Christianity that serve religious functions not served by other ways.

Fifth, given the rather extensive structural similarity of expressions of Buddhism and Christianity brought out by the framework of ways of being religious, what does all this imply about differences between instances of the same way in each of the two traditions and, more generally, about the differences between Buddhism and Christianity as whole traditions? Are they really just different paths to the same ultimate goal, different ways of meeting the same existential needs, as some have maintained? Could it be that Buddhism and Christianity are not ultimately contradictory but rather ultimately complementary in the sense that both are in some sense true and valid? These are difficult and complex questions to which there are no simple answers. If anything, the framework has helped to bring out how difficult and complex these questions are. Occasionally what has appeared on the surface to be a great difference, on closer and empathetic investigation, has turned out to be not such a difference after all. In other words, we have learned not to make sweeping judgments on the basis of apparent differences. We have found many profound similarities and commonalities, but not in all respects. The differences have not all dissolved—far from it. Significant differences remain, which have been made somewhat clearer by the use of the framework applied here. These differences need to be taken seriously. They are not simply summarized; however, they differ somewhat with each different way of being religious. For example, the apparently personal "face" of *ultimate reality*[P] in Jodo-shin-shu (i.e., Amida Nyorai) is different from the personal "face" of *ultimate reality*[P] in Evangelical Protestantism (Jesus Christ as Personal Lord and Savior), but that difference is not the same as the difference (however related it may be at a deeper level) between the "supernatural power" of Fudō-Myōō in Shugendō and the "supernatural power" of the Holy Spirit in the Word of God Charismatic community.

There is a serious danger in concentrating so much on generic features of religious life that the features distinctive to each tradition fail to be given their due. In other words, we must also learn not to make sweeping judgments on the basis of apparent similarities. Are Buddhism and Christianity just different paths (or sets of paths) to the same ultimate goal? It depends on what is meant by *ultimate goal*[P]. Generically conceived, both traditions set forth paths (or sets of paths) to at-onement with *ultimate reality*[P]. In that functional sense, they are clearly aiming at the same *functional* goal. And this functional goal can be further differentiated in terms of the same specific existential needs (discussed in Chapters 2 and 3) functionally served by instances of any one way of being religious in each of the two traditions. But what have we said when we have said that? Remember, the phrase, "*ultimate reality*[P]," is simply a place-holder, a variable; the phrase does not directly identify a substantive reality. It simply defers to the specific religious tradition to fill in the blank. Thus, although both Buddhism and Christianity pursue at-onement with *ultimate reality*[P], the *ultimate reality*[P] in either tradition is to all appearances something quite different. (It is not only not the same thing in each case, but many Buddhists would deny that *nirvāṇa*—or *śūnyatā, tatāgatha, tatathā, Dharma,* or *Dharmakāya,* for that matter—has the metaphysical status that God has for most Christians, and vice versa.) My point is that the *ultimate* nature of *ultimate reality*[P] cannot be determined in generic terms (i.e., on phenomenologically noncommittal grounds). It cannot be determined apart from an affirmation of religious faith. Any such determination is necessarily made at the level of specific *theological*[P] convictions at which particular people arrive in the context of particular tradi-tions and particular social and cultural circumstances. (This is not to say that someone could not attempt to develop a set of specific *theological* convictions within a generic vocabulary. Several have already tried to do so. But then, de-spite appearances, it would not be a phenomenologically based generalization over all religious traditions; it would still be simply one more set of *theological* convictions among others.)

More substantively, both Buddhism and Christianity consider egoism a vice. More than a vice, each conceives it (though not in identical ways) to be a condition opposed to at-onement with *ultimate reality*. Thus both traditions aim at the transcendence of egoism, and their different subtraditions seek to re-alize this goal in a variety of ways.[2] Are all ways within Buddhism equally ef-fective in reaching it? Are all equally effective within Christianity? It seems to be impossible to tell in the abstract and overall. And surely it depends to some ex-tent on the ability of any given way to serve in this capacity for a given person or personality type. Moreover, as indicated in Chapter 5, practice in each of the ways is capable of degenerating along the parameter between selflessness and egoism—which is to say, any given way by itself is not necessarily effective in combating egoism, let alone transcending it. Very much depends on how fully a person gives herself to the authentic practice of that way and to the process of transformation it is supposed to involve. Is Buddhism more effective on the whole than Christianity in transcending egoism, or vice versa? If it is difficult (if not impossible) to answer this question with regard to specific ways and subtra-ditions, it is even more difficult (and for all practical purposes impossible) to answer it with regard to whole traditions.

Buddhism and Christianity speak of the condition of the supposed transcen-dence of egoism in strikingly different ways. Buddhism speaks of the dissolution, even the extinction, of the grasping center of egoism, which Buddhists call the ego. What remains upon dissolution is said to be *nirvāṇa* (which itself is a nega-tive characterization, denoting a "blowing out" of the flame of egoistic desire) or "one's original Buddha-mind" (which is supposed to be not-other than the origi-nal Buddha-mind of any one else). Christianity largely speaks of transformation or transfiguration, of an "old man" and a "new man," of "life according to the flesh" which must die and "life according to the spirit" which is brought to new birth, and of not radical union but an intimate personal relationship of communion of the person with God in Christ in community with other persons. Can these al-leged transformations be said to be the same, or are they ultimately something different? It is not easy to say, and this author is not prepared to say so here.[3] In any case, the framework of ways of being religious is *not* designed to provide an answer to this question and, no matter how thoroughly it is applied to the study of Buddhism and Christianity, it is not, by itself, able to answer it. Such a frame-work does, however, go a long way toward sorting out much of precisely what has to be sorted out to come up with a responsible answer.

Worship of God (the Holy Trinity) in Christianity is surely not the same thing as worship of Buddha. The two foci of worship are different, and the respective central stories telling of each are significantly different. Making allowances for the different ways of being religious and pairing examples of worship within the same way of being religious within the respective traditions, the very *feel* of worship differs—though perhaps not as much as one might first suppose. For example, the Tea Ceremony *feels* different from the way the Divine Liturgy feels. So also does offering *pūjā* to the image of the Buddha feel different from offering gifts of bread and wine to Christ for him to transform them into his Body and his Blood. Nevertheless, much (certainly not all) involved in the worship of each is quite similar, if not the same. Depending on the subtradition of worship, some experiences of worship in Buddhism are closer in feeling to certain experiences of worship in Christianity than others. Much, as has already been mentioned, depends on matching the same or similar ways of being religious. There are no easy generalizations to be had. At their best, both the Tea Ceremony and the Divine Liturgy are profoundly sacramental: they are experienced by participants as rendering present to participants the *realities°* to which they allude. Even taking all of these things into consideration, one can still say that worship of the Buddha in Buddhism functions quite differently from the way worship of God (the Holy Trinity) does in Christianity. According to what many Buddhists say, the goal of Enlightenment is not itself expressed or realized in worship of the Buddha; worship here acknowledges the goal as embodied in the Buddha and honors the Buddha as teaching the way. Perhaps this is because most worship in Buddhism is nonsacramental or not fully sacramental in the full sense of sacred rite—though sometimes it is, as in the Tea Ceremony described in Chapter 14. In Christianity, the goal of at-onement with God is itself said to be expressed and realized (at least in a kind of foretaste or anticipation) in worship. The Christian tradition says that worship shall never end, that in Heaven worship will be full and complete in ways that are impossible in this life. In Buddhism, by contrast, worship of the Buddha is one of those things said to be like a raft that, once one crosses to the other shore, one leaves behind.

As a result of the kind of comparative study facilitated by the framework, is it possible for a devout person in one tradition to affirm without contradiction the validity (and truth) of the other tradition? Is it possible for one outside both traditions to affirm without contradiction the validity (and truth) of both? One might, of course, say yes to both questions, and many persons do. The crucial issue is whether they can do so without contradiction, and whether avoidance of contradiction does not empty the claim of significance. Much depends on what is meant by "affirming the validity (and truth)" of a tradition and what is meant by "a truly devout person in a tradition." On the one hand, it is certainly possible to find persons who seem to themselves and to all appearances "truly devout" yet who are abysmally ignorant of their own tradition—indeed, who may hold to views that, were they fully brought to light, flatly contradict orthodox expressions of the tradition to which they suppose they belong. Thorough knowledge of the tradition without illusions is needed to address the issue squarely. On the other hand, it is also possible to water down the meaning of the phrase *affirm the validity* of a tradition, so much that one who says it means nothing more than that one acknowledges that others believe and follow the tradition and that one chooses to accept and tolerate that fact. Belief alone, according to this view, makes a tradition valid regardless of its content and, as long as a person believes it, a tradition could not possibly be invalid or wrong for the person who believes it. The same, of course, would have to hold for one's affirmation of one's own tradition, thus emptying the term *validity* of objective significance altogether. The question would still remain, however, whether the objective contents of the two traditions, empathetically understood, were logically compatible. Is it possible to construe each tradition, without compromise to any crucial doctrine, in a manner that allows validity and truth to be recognized in the other tradition?

This main issue can be clarified and resolved only insofar as knowledgeable and devout representatives of a tradition are able to come together in honest dialogue in which they move past superficial appearances, misunderstandings, and idiosyncratic interpretations, but also beyond having to establish their own faith to be superior or presuming that there can be no fundamental disagreement. The objective would be for dialogue participants to enter empathetically in depth into each other's respective practice and experience to learn what of worth and meaning the other finds there, and to ponder what is thus found in light of their own tradition-forged sensibility for meaning and worth. Then and only then will we be in a position to reach clarity about, and resolution of, the issue. Happily, just such dialogues have recently been taking place between Buddhist *theologians°* and Christian *theologians°* and between Buddhist monastics and Christian monastics.[4]

Notice that such dialogues are precisely along the lines indicated by the framework of ways of being religious. The framework indicates still other fruitful dialogues that could take place, for example, between Buddhist social activists such as those in the Sarvodaya Movement and Christian social activists such as those in the Catholic Worker Movement, between Evangelical Christians and Pure Land Buddhists, between Buddhist shamanic healers and Charismatic Christian healers, and between Christian sacramental liturgists and their Buddhist counterparts. This author is not yet prepared to project a resolution of the issue, though enough has begun to emerge from these dialogues to indicate that some progress is being made. The framework of ways of being religious clearly indicates a way forward. It is a path well worth exploring—for Buddhists and Christians to be sure, but no less for believers of every tradition. It does not promise utopia. It does promise a measure of greater mutual understanding and respect, allowance for many of our differences, and the possibility of significant cooperation in addressing the pressing problems of the world we share in common. Surely that is sufficient reason to venture forward.

CHAPTER SUMMARY

This chapter offers some concluding reflections on the experience of comparing Buddhism and Christianity by means of the framework of ways of being religious in the preceding eight chapters. First, one should not limit one's imagination to the correlations made in Chapters 9 through 14; other correlations are suggested. Second, application of the framework has brought out how diverse and complex the traditions of Buddhism and Christianity are and how this diversity and complexity are similar in each tradition. Knowing the generic complexity in one tradition puts a student in a good position to recognize and comprehend it in another. Third, the similarities between expressions of Buddhism and Christianity highlighted by the framework in Chapters 9 through 14 give evidence of practical lessons and insights that can be shared in the dialogue between religious traditions, despite the theological differences between them. Fourth, recognition of praiseworthy historical examples of each way of being religious within Buddhism and Christianity, serving functions specific to that way, indicates that each way has at least some claim, however limited, to a place in filling out the whole of each tradition. Fifth and finally, given the deep structural similarities the framework has uncovered between expressions of Buddhism and Christianity, the significance of the differences that remain must not be overlooked. Although the framework itself makes no pronouncement on their significance, it facilitates in-depth exploration of the significance of these differences in depth through inter-religious dialogue.

STUDY QUESTIONS

1. Do a research project juxtaposing and then comparing and contrasting parallel phenomena from Buddhism and Christianity other than the phenomena juxtaposed in Chapters 9 through 14.

2. Reflect on what you have learned through studying Chapters 9 through 15. What are the chief understandings and principal insights that you have come to about Buddhism and Christianity and their relationship?

3. Has this comparative study given you a sense of the great diversity and complexity of the traditions? Has it helped to make that diversity and complexity more understandable?

4. Which of the understandings and insights identified in questions 2 and 3 seem to have been specifically due to (or aided by) use of the framework of ways of being religious to guide the comparative study? In what specific ways do you think it has helped in highlighting things that otherwise might be missed? Are there ways in which you think it has limited the study?

5. What other correlations between Buddhism and Christianity are suggested to you by the framework that you think would be worth study?

6. What sorts of practical lessons and insights embodied in any one of the traditional practices exemplified in Chapters 9 through 14 do you imagine might be useful to persons pursuing the same way of being religious in the other tradition? In other words, what things do you think would be fruitful points of common interest for dialogue between Buddhists and Christians?

7. Are you inclined to agree, or not to agree, with the idea that each of the ways exemplified in the practices presented in Chapters 9 through 14 are needed in some sense to fill out the whole of Buddhism on the one hand and Christianity on the other? What reasons would count for that idea? What reasons would count against it?

8. What are the most significant differences you have noted between Buddhism and Christianity, both in general and in relation to specific ways of being religious? Are those differences reconcilable? If you think so, what evidence supports your opinion? Or are they fundamentally irreconcilable? If you think so, what evidence supports your opinion? In respect to these questions, what do you think of the prospects of Buddhist-Christian dialogue?

9. Do a research project juxtaposing and then comparing and contrasting parallel phenomena from other religious traditions with phenomena from Buddhism or Christianity in the manner exemplified in Chapters 9 through 14.

FOR FURTHER READING

John H. Berthrong, *Interfaith Dialogue: An Annotated Bibliography* (Wofford Heights, CA: Multifaith Resources, 1993).
Society for Buddhist-Christian Studies Staff, *Resources for Buddhist-Christian Encounter: An Annotated Bibliography* (Wofford Heights, CA: Multifaith Resources, 1993).
Gerald D. Gort, Hendrik M. Vroom, Rein Fernhout, and Anton Wessels, eds., *On Sharing Religious Experience: Possibilities of Interfaith Mutuality*, Currents of Encounter, Vol. 4 (Amsterdam: Editions Rodopi/Grand Rapids, MI: Eerdmans, 1992).

Buddhist Christian Studies, a journal published annually since 1981 by the East-West Religions Project, University of Hawaii, 2530 Dole Street, Honolulu, HI 96822.
Bulletin of the North American Board for East-West Dialogue (focused on monastic inter-religious dialogue), published by the Abbey of Gethsemani, 3642 Monks Road, Trappsit, KY 40051-6102.
Society for Buddhist-Christian Studies Newsletter, published by the Society for Buddhist Christian Studies, Graduate Theological Union, 2400 Ridge Road, Berkeley, CA 94709.

Roger Corless and Paul F. Knitter, eds., *Buddhist Emptiness and Christian Trinity: Essays and Explorations* (New York: Paulist Press, 1990).
Gilbert G. Hardy, *Monastic Quest and Interreligious Dialogue* (New York: Peter Lang, 1990).
Patrick G. Henry and Donald K. Swearer, *For the Sake of the World: The Spirit of Buddhist and Christian Monasticism* (Minneapolis, MN: Fortress Press; Collegeville, MN: Liturgical Press, 1989).

Paul O. Ingram and Frederick J. Streng, eds., B*uddhist-Christian Dialogue: Mutual Renewal and Transformation* (Honolulu, HI: University of Hawaii Press, 1986).

Donald W. Mitchell, *Spirituality and Emptiness: The Dynamics of Spiritual Life in Buddhism and Christianity* (New York: Paulist Press, 1991).

Ninian Smart, *Buddhism and Christianity: Rivals and Allies* (Honolulu, HI: University of Hawaii Press, 1993).

Susan Walker, ed., *Speaking of Silence: Christians and Buddhists on the Contemplative Way* (New York: Paulist Press, 1987).

NOTES

1. See Winston L. King, *Zen and the Way of the Sword: Arming the Samurai Psyche* (New York: Oxford Unversity Press, 1993); and Marcus Bull, *Knightly Piety and the Lay Response to the First Crusade: The Limousin and Gascony c.970–c.1130* (New York: Oxford University Press, 1993).

2. It is not clear to me that transcendence of egoism is the ultimate goal in both traditions. It certainly appears to be so in certain formulations of Buddhism, whereas most knowledgeable Christians would consider it only part of the goal, a penultimate goal, or a by-product of attaining the goal of at-onement with God in Christ.

3. See Julia Ching, "Paradigms of the Self in Buddhism and Christianity," *Buddhist Christian Studies* 4 (1984), 31–50; and Winston L. King, "No-Self, No-Mind, and Emptiness Revisited," *Buddhist-Christian Dialogue: Mutual Renewal and Transformation*, eds. Paul O. Ingram and Frederick J. Streng (Honolulu: University of Hawaii Press, 1986), pp. 155–176.

4. See the recommended readings at the end of this chapter.

GLOSSARY OF TERMS

Words and phrases that are italicized and followed by a small circle are
meant to be variables standing in for concepts specific to religious traditions.

anamnesis A remembering or memorializing that makes present. Anamnesis is major feature of the way of sacred rite, whereby symbols no longer merely represent sacred archetypal forms but render them present. (p. 54)

archetype (or archetypal form) An original model or type after which other similar things are patterned. In religion, and specifically in the way of sacred rite, an archetype or archetypal form is an ideal divine model or pattern for some aspect of human life found in the *other world*° articulated in a tradition's system of symbols. (p. 53)

at-onement The state of being at-one with *ultimate reality*°. It encompasses in its range of meaning "reconciled with," "in right or appropriate relation with," "in rapport with," "in agreement with," "in harmony with," "in conformity to," and "in union with"—with the understanding that the precise characterization of this state of at-onement will differ from one tradition to another. (p. 25)

balance/imbalance of divergent forces One among three dimensions or parameters of variation in (commonsense) quality of practice within any of the ways of being religious. Actual religious practice inherently involves a living tension between a number of polarities in the lives of real persons: what is tangible and intangible, what is static and dynamic, what is old and fresh, what is active and receptive, what is temporal and eternal, what is ordered and spontaneous; what is formed and formless, letter and spirit, body and soul, extrinsic motivation and intrinsic motivation, this world and *the other world*°, ordinary reality and *ultimate reality*°—in short, a tension between *finitude* and *infinitude*. Excellence or virtue involves attaining balance between them and imbalance in regard to any tends to evil and is, accordingly, a vice to be avoided. (pp. 122–124)

canon The officially recognized and delimited collection of scriptural texts in a religion within a scribal or print (i.e., literate) culture; usually the principal locus of such a religion's primary system of symbols, containing its central sacred story (or stories), and itself constituting one of its primary symbols. Authenticity of practice and orthodoxy of belief within such a religion is normally gauged by demonstrable conformity to the scriptural canon. (p. 33)

catholic The inclusive quality of any religious tradition in its attitude to the full variety of ways of being religious (a specific usage relative to the framework of this book). In origin it refers to the quality of the Christian church as universal, comprehensive, and inclusive of all parts. Historically, it has come to differentiate those Christian traditions that assign special importance to the rulings of the Seven Ecumenical Councils (fourth through eighth century) as sources of doctrine, the sacraments as necessary means of grace, and the Apostolic Succession of bishops as authorized agents of Christ. (pp. 40, 108–109; see also 95)

common sense (religious)   Considerations of practical wisdom having to do with common aspects of being human involved in religious practice that are (in principle) mutually recognizable by thoughtful, reflective, and knowledgeable people of different religious traditions—i.e., generic practices, concerns, and values they share in common despite their many differences. Although they may not be common sense for all ways of being religious (though some considerations are), they constitute common sense among persons at home with any one way of being religious, though they be involved with that way in entirely different traditions. (pp. 41–42, 120–121)

competence/incompetence   One among three dimensions or parameters of variation in (commonsense) quality of practice within any of the ways of being religious. Along the parameter of competence/incompetence, vice is practice that fails to be competent—e.g., awkward, uncertain, fumbling, characterized by mistakes and improprieties, etc.—whereas virtue is competent, knowledgeable practice—e.g., confident, appropriate, characterized by minimal flaws and mastery of relevant details, etc. (p. 122)

devotion, way of   Cultivation of a personal relationship to *ultimate reality°* of whole-hearted adoration, devotional surrender to *its°* transforming grace, and trust in *its°* providential care, anticipating in return an influx of sustaining energy, hope, and a sense of affirming presence or at-onement. It typically involves a conversion experience and emotional purgation. (pp. 57–59)

empathetic objectivity   An objectivity appropriate to the study of human subjects and cultural phenomena such as religion. Specifically, it involves the effort to take into account and do full justice to the understanding and experience of the insider in developing a full or rounded understanding of the object of investigation. A disciplined empathy is thus an essential part of what is involved. (pp. 19–20)

empathy   An act of imaginatively stepping into another person's perspective and considering how things look from over there, *as if* one were an insider though one is not one in fact. Success in empathetic understanding would be a matter of having (temporarily, in an act of imagination) entered the perspective of the other person sufficiently well to be able to represent it credibly to others, especially and above all in a way that is recognizable and credible to those persons who themselves occupy that perspective. (pp. 18–20)

existential predicament/existential problem   A set of circumstances in human experience that in a specific way raises the problem of meaning. Each of the six ways of being religious corresponds to a different sort of existential predicament (= **problematic situation**). An existential predicament can also be articulated as an existential need, motivating involvement in the corresponding way of being religious. (p. 31)

finitude, vice of   When the animating spark of inspiration of a tradition is lost, and one is left with only outward form, the finite aspects of a religion. All the words, gestures, and actions may be right and correct, but somehow the spirit is absent. (p. 124)

heresy/heretical practice   Variations in teaching or practice that a tradition has established (for itself) to be unfaithful to its core system of authoritative symbols and/or to be beyond permissible boundaries. (p. 119)

hermeneutic   A specific orientation to the interpretation of some text or texts—in this case to the interpretation of the symbol system, and specifically the scripture(s), of a religious tradition. A hermeneutic generally is oriented according to certain questions it is intent on asking, to certain needs it seeks to have addressed. (pp. 36, 38)

infinitude, vice of   When the animating spark of inspiration is allowed to overwhelm one's respect for the finite, this-worldly, human aspects of oneself, one's practice, and one's community, with the result that one comes to deny, reject, or repress these things. One of its clearest signs is loss of a sense of humor. This is where one may find idolatry—where finite form (e.g., symbol, form of worship, method of meditation, moral rule, interpretation, judgment, type of experience) is invested with the esteem and passion that is due the infinite and the absolute is misidentified with the relative—and, in consequence, where one can probably find most of the evil done in the name of religion. (pp. 124–125)

mimesis   An imitation, reenactment, or embodiment. In the way of sacred rite, mimesis symbolically re-enacts or imitates the sacred archetypal forms in such a way that participants are ushered into their very presence. (p. 54)

moral prophet/moral sage/moral teacher   Religious leadership roles especially characteristic of the way of right action. When the ultimate moral order is understood to transcend and stand in judgment over the social order, the leader is more likely to assume the role of moral prophet (i.e., one who proclaims judgment upon the social order and leads the righteous out from under that order). But when it is understood to be immanent within the social order, despite the latter's failings, the leader tends to assume the role of moral sage (i.e., elder embodying practical wisdom). (p. 57)

mystic   A person who in pursuing the way of mystical quest has arrived at considerable attainment in that way (whether by her or his own efforts or by the grace of *ultimate reality*ᵖ). (p. 64)

mystical quest, way of   Employment of ascetic and meditative disciplines in a deliberate quest to interrupt, slow down, or otherwise break through and become free of, the obscuring limitations and distracting compulsions of ordinary life in order to attain a direct awareness of *ultimate reality*ᵖ, come to be wholly at-one with it, and have life and one's relations with all things become transparently grounded in it. (The way of mystical quest should not be confused with "mysticism" as the term is used at large or by other authors, though there is in most cases some overlap. "Mysticism" in common usage is in some respects much broader, is focused more on extraordinary experiences, and, except for individual authors, is not possessed of a single, clear definition.) (pp. 63–65)

objectivity   A striving to draw near to the object of investigation at the point where all relevant perspectives on it intersect, thus to comprehend it in its transcendence beyond any one perspective in a way that ideally commands the recognition of those who dwell within them and know them well. It is fundamentally a matter of doing justice to the object itself, the object in the round. (This meaning of objectivity is to be distinguished from that often associated with modern natural science, namely, a comprehensive methodology of distancing: of separating the investigating self from the object of investigation.) (pp. 17–18, 129)

other world °   See *world, other* °.

pastor/preacher/storyteller   Religious leadership role especially characteristic of the way of devotion. A pastor is one who nurtures, counsels, and guides the affections of devotees, especially in coping with the problems life offers. A preacher is one who inspires religious affections and who helps bring devotees to the point of purgation of those affections. A storyteller is one who through storytelling gives definition and context to religious affection. (p. 59)

phenomenology (of religion)   A discipline of study within the modern academic study of religion that seeks to bring about an empathetic understanding for persons outside a given religious tradition of what is understood and experienced by persons on the inside. (p. 19)

presentative symbol   A religious symbol that serves not only to represent some aspect of *ultimate reality*° but that in the appropriate circumstances serves for participants to render it present and enable direct participation in it. All presentative symbols are in the first place representative symbols, but the reverse is not true. See also **sacramental** ° **ritual/sacramental** ° **symbol**. (p. 36)

priest/priestess   A person who knows how appropriately to perform sacramental rituals and handle sacramental symbols and who is duly authorized to do so. A religious social role specifically characteristic of the way of sacred rite. (p. 54)

problem of meaning   The respect in which events in human experience from time to time in a variety of different ways pose a threat to the meaningfulness of life and disclose a felt disrelationship to *ultimate reality*°, a disrelationship to whatever is conceived to be the ultimate ground of meaning and purpose in life. The question is, how to cope with that threat and, in the face of it, attain to an affirmation of the meaning and worth of life despite it. There are at least six different ways that such a threat is posed, six aspects of the problem of meaning, corresponding to each of the six ways of being religious. (p. 27)

problematic situation   A set of circumstances in human experience that in a specific way raise the problem of meaning. Each of the six ways of being religious corresponds to a different type of problematic situation (= **existential predicament**). (p. 31)

qualitative variation in practice: Quality of practice refers to the merit or worth of a given expression of religious practice, how deserving it is of respect or disrespect. Any given way of being religious in any tradition can be taken up and practiced in qualitatively more excellent, more virtuous ways, in qualitatively degenerate, virtueless ways, and everything in between. Some criteria are unique to given traditions while others are of a generic, commonsense nature and tend to be specific to the six generic ways of being religious. (p. 119)

reasoned inquiry, way of   A rational, dialectical struggle to transcend conventional patterns of thinking in the effort to attain understanding of, and consciousness-transforming insight into, *the ultimate what, how, and why of things°*—i.e., to bring together and unite, so far as possible, mind with *the ultimate Mind°* and thereby acquire a portion of *divine wisdom°*. It typically involves systematic study of a tradition's scripture and previous attempts to articulate *what is ultimately the case°*. (pp. 65–68)

religion   A system of symbols (e.g., words and gestures, stories and practices, objects and places) that functions religiously, namely, an ongoing system of symbols that participants use to draw near to, and come into right or appropriate relationship with, what they deem to be ultimate reality. (pp. 22, 24)

religious function   A thing may be said to function religiously in the respect in which it serves for a participant as a means of drawing near to, and coming into right or appropriate relationship with, what she or he deems to be ultimate reality. (pp. 22, 24)

religious phenomenon   Whatever (e.g., a practice, a symbol, an object, a person, an encounter, an experience, a place, an intention, a doctrine, a story, etc.) serves for a person or group of persons in some way to refer to, or connect them with, what they take to be ultimately real. (pp. 21, 24)

right action, way of   Concerted effort to bring all of life, individual and communal, into conformity with *the way things are ultimately supposed to be°* (however understood)—i.e., to realize and fulfill *the sacred intendedness of life°*—that promises individual fulfillment, social justice, and the embodiment of *divine ideality°* in the midst of mundane, this-worldly life. (pp. 55–57)

rite (= ritual)   A prescribed sequence of words, gestures, and employment of special objects that symbolize, for participants, some kind of interaction with, or participation in, the *other world°* of a religious tradition. (p. 51)

sacramental ritual/*sacramental* symbol   A ritual or symbol that does not merely refer to a religious *reality°* (some feature of a religious tradition's *other world°*) or represent some participation in that *reality°*, but that for participants in appropriate circumstances itself renders that *reality°* present and constitutes participation in it. Where sacramental rituals and sacramental symbols are present, so is (in some measure) the way of sacred rite. Conventionally, "sacramental" means that which pertains to the Christian "sacraments" as understood and practiced within sacramental or liturgical Christian traditions. (p. 52)

sacred   The quality of a religious phenomenon of partaking directly of *ultimate reality°*, of being that in which, or by means of which, *ultimate reality°* is present, or of being that by means of which one becomes present to *ultimate reality°*. Though the concept is relevant to religious life generally, it is especially connected to the way of sacred rite. (p. 52)

sacred rite, way of   Participation in the *sacred archetypal patterns°* through which *ultimate reality°* is understood by participants to be manifest, by means of symbolic ritual enactments or presentations that enable participants repeatedly to enter their presence, attain at-onement for the moment with them, and thereby have established and renewed their sense of meaningful order, identity, and propriety. It is typically communal rather than individual. (pp. 51–55)

sage   One who possesses or embodies wisdom and understanding, especially practical wisdom. An ideal religious leadership role especially characteristic of the way of reasoned inquiry. Sometimes used in connection with the ways of mystical quest and right action. (p. 68)

sectarian tradition   A subtradition of a religion that rejects the rightness of the practice and/or beliefs of an earlier tradition or traditions from which it has differentiated itself in terms of a different conception of what constitutes fidelity to its sources; it draws the boundaries of permissible variation differently and usually more narrowly. (pp. 107, 119)

selflessness/egoism   One among three dimensions or parameters of variation in (commonsense) quality of practice within any of the ways of being religious. Along the parameter of selflessness/egoism, vice is practice that sets the immediate interests and concerns of the unreformed ego above those of other persons, other things, and the welfare of all, whereas virtue is transcendence of the preoccupations of the finite, egoistic self, enabling one to attend freely and uncompulsively to other persons and other things for their own sakes. (pp. 125–127)

shaman   A person (female or male) able to mediate between "supernatural" resources of power, vision, and guidance in what is believed to be an autonomous spirit world and the mundane world of ordinary life. A religious leadership role uniquely characteristic of the way of shamanic mediation. (p. 60)

shamanic mediation, way of   Entry into altered states of consciousness in which persons become mediators or channels for *the intervention of spiritual reality°*, in the expectation that *"supernatural" (trans-mundane)* *resources°* of imagination, power, and guidance will be released for solving or dealing with otherwise intractable problems of life. Expressed through phenomena such as "possession (trance)," "oracular utterance," "ecstatic vision," and/or "spirit journeying," this way seeks at-onement with *ultimate reality°* in what is taken to be *its°* readiness to bring about healing, well-being, and fulfillment for the world. (pp. 60–63)

spiritual master/spiritual director   A person who on the basis of years of personal experience, intimate observation of others, possible apprenticeship to other spiritual masters, and a measure of attainment on a specific path of mystical quest is in a position to provide guidance and direction appropriate to others on their own mystical quest. A religious social role specifically characteristic of the way of mystical quest. (p. 64)

storyteller   See **pastor/preacher/storyteller**.

symbol (religious)   One of the components of a religious tradition's **system of symbols** (see definition below). Religious symbols function religiously as part of a system of symbols, not on their own. Most such symbols have (at least potentially) multiple levels of meaning discernible to different hermeneutical orientations. (pp. 31–32).

syncretism   The merging of symbol systems from two or more religious traditions in a single religious expression or practice. It is to be distinguished from situations in which a hitherto dormant way of being religious emerges in a tradition as the result of cultural contact over time with a different religous tradition that emphasizes this specific way of being religious but within a completely different symbol system. (p. 104)

system of symbols   The complex of stories, scriptures (if the tradition is literate), rituals, symbolic forms, and particular vocabulary for referring to *ultimate reality°* that as an interconnected system constitute the core of a given religion. (pp. 31–32)

theologian°   A serious participant in the way of reasoned inquiry of a particular religious tradition who is not merely a student or apprentice but who has attained the stature of competence in the way and mastery of the classic texts of that tradition (a specific usage relative to the framework of this book). A religious social role specifically characteristic of the way of wisdom. Conventionally, a "theologian" is more narrowly associated with theistic religious traditions, i.e., traditions whose conception of *ultimate reality°* centers on a god or gods. (p. 68)

theological°   Pertaining generally to the beliefs concerning *ultimate reality°* of any given religious tradition and at times more narrowly to **theology°** (a specific usage relative to the framework of this book). Conventionally, "theological" more narrowly pertains to theistic religious beliefs, i.e., beliefs concerning *ultimate reality°* which centers on a god or gods. (p. 50)

theology°   The study of the nature of *ultimate reality°* and religious truth, or a specific interpretation of the nature of *ultimate reality°* and religious truth, within a given religious tradition (a specific usage relative to the framework of this book). Conventionally, "theology" is more narrowly associated with the study of *ultimate reality*° within theistic religious traditions, i.e., traditions whose conception of *ultimate reality*° centers on a god or gods. (p. 68)

threshold (of a system of symbols, of "another world to live in")   An entryway whereby one crosses the boundary from being outside the *other world*° of a tradition to being inside it. Though it may be symbolized by a physical threshold (as to a temple or shrine), it essentially refers to a shift of consciousness from *focally attending to* a tradition's symbols to *subsidiarily attending from* them to what they symbolize, which is to say *coming to dwell within* them. (p. 35)

threshold effect   A change in the appearance and experienced texture of religious symbols as one crosses the threshold of a tradition's system of symbols and enters the *other world*° to which it grants access, as one no longer looks at them from the outside but comes to dwell in them. On the outside, symbols are opaque and at best refer to matters within that other world. As one begins to cross the threshold, one begins to glimpse intimations of those matters more or less directly; the symbols become translucent. Insofar as one is able fully to cross the threshold, the symbols become transparent to their referents and serve to usher one into the very presence of them. (pp. 35–36)

***ultimate reality*°**   A variable standing for whatever the people of a given tradition take to be the ultimate ground of meaning and purpose in life—both how things are and how life ought to be lived. It stands for whatever is taken to make up the ultimate cosmic context of life that lies beyond the perspectives of ordinary human awareness and the mundane sphere of everyday life. (pp. 22–23)

vice   Variations of practice that do not contribute to, or are likely to interfere with, the distinctive religious satisfactions promised by a way of being religious, friendly relations between members of the immediate community involved, and the passing on intact of the practice (with the values to be realized through it) to subsequent generations. (pp. 121–127)

virtue   Variations of practice that contribute to and facilitate the distinctive religious satisfactions promised by a way of being religious, friendly relations between members of the immediate community involved, and the passing on intact of the practice (with the values to be realized through it) to subsequent generations. (pp. 121–127)

way of being religious   One generic manner and pattern among others of drawing near to and coming into right or appropriate relationship with what a religion takes to be ultimate reality. Each way is further characterized in terms of a mode of approach to *ultimate reality*°, an aspect of the problem of meaning to which it is addressed, a heremeneutical orientation, a pattern of social structures, and specific virtues and vices. (pp. 39–41)

world, other °   The imagined realm, the "other world to live in," to which one has access through the system of symbols constituting a religious tradition by dwelling in them (= attending from them subsidiarily). It is the realm wherein one encounters or at least makes connection with *ultimate reality* °. It is the "inside" that qualifies insiders as "insiders." (p. 35)

Index of Subjects and Names

Italic page references are to definitions.

Italicized terms or phrases followed by a degree symbol identify a generic role served (or fulfilled) by terms or phrases specific to the religious tradition to which they are applied; they function as variables substituting for a specific tradition's terms or phrases.

INDEX OF RELIGIOUS TRADITIONS

Christianity: Eastern Orthodox

Christianity: Oriental Orthodox

Christianity: Protestant